Organizational Behavior

McGraw-Hill SERIES IN MANAGEMENT

CONSULTING EDITORS
Fred Luthans and Keith Davis

Organizational Behavior

SEVENTH EDITION

FRED LUTHANS

George Holmes Distinguished Professor of Management
University of Nebraska

McGraw-Hill, Inc.

New York   St. Louis   San Francisco   Auckland   Bogotá   Caracas
Lisbon   London   Madrid   Mexico City   Milan   Montreal   New Delhi
San Juan   Singapore   Sydney   Tokyo   Toronto

Organizational Behavior

 This book is printed on recycled, acid-free paper containing 10% postconsumer waste.

2 3 4 5 6 7 8 9 0 DOW DOW 9 0 9 8 7 6 5

ISBN 0-07-039180-7

This book was set in Garamond Stemple by Better Graphics, Inc.
The editors were Lynn Richardson, Dan Alpert, and Peggy Rehberger;
the designer was Leon Bolognese;
the production supervisor was Kathryn Porzio.
R. R. Donnelley & Sons Company was printer and binder.

Library of Congress Cataloging-in-Publication Data

Luthans, Fred.
     Organizational behavior / Fred Luthans. — 7th ed.
       p.   cm. — (McGraw-Hill series in management)
     Includes bibliographical references and indexes.
     ISBN 0-07-039180-7
     1. Organizational behavior.   I. Title   II. Series.
HD58.7.L88   1995
658.4—dc20   94-14947

INTERNATIONAL EDITION

About the Author

FRED LUTHANS is the George Holmes Distinguished Professor of Management at the University of Nebraska at Lincoln. He received his B.A., M.B.A., and Ph.D. from the University of Iowa and did some postdoctoral work at Columbia University. While serving in the armed forces, he taught at the U.S. Military Academy at West Point. He has been at the University of Nebraska since 1967, his entire academic career, and won the distinguished teaching award in 1986. A prolific writer, he has published a number of major books and over one hundred articles in applied and academic journals. His book *Organizational Behavior Modification,* coauthored with Robert Kreitner, won the American Society of Personnel Administration award for the outstanding contribution to human resources management, and a more recent book titled *Real Managers* is the result of a four-year research study that observed managers in their natural settings. *International Management,* coauthored with Richard Hodgetts and also published by McGraw-Hill, is now in its second edition. His articles are widely reprinted and have brought him the American Society of Hospital Administration award. The consulting coeditor for the McGraw-Hill Management Series, Professor Luthans is also the editor for *Organizational Dynamics* and is on the editorial board of several journals. He has been very active in the Academy of Management over the years and was elected a Fellow in 1981. He is a former president of the Midwest Region. He was vice president, program chair of the National Academy meeting in Boston in 1984, and was president in 1986 for the celebration of the fiftieth anniversary of the Academy of Management and the Centennial of the academic field of management. Also active in the Decision Sciences Institute (DSI), he was elected a Fellow in 1987. Professor Luthans has a very extensive research program at the University of Nebraska. Most recently, his studies with Dianne Welsh on behavioral management (published in the February 1993 *Academy of Management Journal*) and managerial activities (published in the Fourth Quarter, 1993 issue of *Journal of International Business Studies*) are the first ever conducted in Russia. He has been a visiting scholar at a number of universities in the U.S. and has lectured at universities and conducted workshops for managers in many countries around the world. Most recently, he has been actively involved in a U.S. A.I.D. program conducted in Albania and Macedonia. In addition, he has been on the Executive Committee of the annual Pan Pacific Conference since its beginning in 1984. This international research and experience is reflected in his approach to the field of organizational behavior. He served on the Board of Directors of the Foundation of Administrative Research. In addition, he is an active consultant and trainer to both private- (such as Wal-Mart) and public-sector (such as the National Rural Electric Cooperative Association) organizations.

FOR
KAY, KRISTIN, BRETT, KYLE, AND PAIGE

Contents in Brief

Contents

Preface

As we approach the new millennium the saying that "the only certainty is change" is truer than ever before. The dizzying rate of change and the accompanying uncertainty has had and will continue to have a tremendous impact on our organizations and the way they are managed. Some of the popular buzzwords of the day such as globalization, information superhighway, total quality management, empowerment, reengineering, benchmarking, learning organizations, knowledge workers, and diversity are indicative of the challenges. Although technology has received the most attention, as the head of Chrysler recently noted, the only sustainable competitive advantage in today's environment is the people. How to effectively manage human resources has become the key challenge not only to compete, but to survive.

To genuinely like people and to want to work with them has become a basic prerequisite for effective management. Yet, however important and necessary it is to enjoy people, it is not sufficient. Managers must also understand and be able to apply innovative techniques to better manage their human resources. This is why the study and application of organizational behavior becomes so important in the years ahead. Like the previous editions, this latest version provides a strong conceptual framework for the study, understanding, and application of organizational behavior.

The previous edition recognized that we are now in a global economy and this international perspective is continued and expanded in this edition. Besides devoting an entire chapter to international organizational behavior, there are international examples in the text discussion, highlighted "International Application" boxes in many chapters throughout, and several end-of-chapter real cases from the international arena.

This edition also recognizes recent environmental developments with two new chapters: "Emerging Organizations: Information-Based, Total Quality, and Organizational Learning" and "Contemporary Challenges: Diversity and Ethics." These new perspectives are sustained with text examples and with highlighted "Total Quality Management (TQM) in Action" and "Managing Diversity in Action" application boxes that appear throughout the book.

Besides containing contemporary perspectives, the real strength of the book over the years has been its research base and its comprehensive, readable coverage of the important topics of the field of organizational behavior. This latest edition should enhance this reputation because it has been thoroughly revised and updated to include new research findings and the latest topics. Just as the actual practice side of management can no longer afford to slowly evolve, neither can the academic side of the field. With the world turned upside down for most organizations today, drastically new thinking, approaches, and techniques are needed both in the practice of management and in the way we study and apply the field of organizational behavior.

Conceptual Framework. The book contains twenty chapters in five major parts. Part 1 provides the foundation for the study and application of organizational behavior. The introductory chapter provides the perspective, historical background, methodology, and theoretical framework for the field of organizational behavior and a specific model for this text. This is followed by the two new chapters on the role of information technology, total quality, organizational learning, diversity, and ethics in the new paradigm facing today's organizations. After this foundation is laid, the subsequent parts of the text progress from a micro to a macro perspective and units of analysis.

The second part takes a very micro perspective with chapters on perception, personality and attitudes, two chapters on motivation (theoretical and applied), and learning (processes, reward systems, and behavioral management). The middle of the text, Part 3, is concerned with the dynamics of organizational behavior including chapters on group dynamics (with a new emphasis on teams), interactive conflict (with a new emphasis on negotiation skills), stress, power, and politics, and two chapters on leadership (background/processes and styles, activities, and a new emphasis on skills). Part 4 moves away from the micro-oriented concepts and applications and the mid-range dynamics of organizational behavior toward the macro end of the field. This macro part focuses on the processes and structure of organizational behavior with chapters on communication, decision making, organization theory and design, and organizational culture. Finally, Part 5 presents the horizons for organizational behavior with chapters on international organizational behavior and organizational change and development. These five parts and twenty chapters are fairly self-contained. Thus, a whole part, selected chapters, or even sections of chapters, could be dropped or studied in a different sequence without damaging the flow or content of the book.

New Topical Coverage. A number of new topics are added to this edition. These include topics such as the following:

- knowledge organizations
- nature of paradigm shifts
- information technology
- reengineering
- benchmarking
- empowerment
- organizational learning
- nature of diversity
- managing diversity
- impression management tactics
- "big five" personality traits
- three component commitment
- control theory
- agency theory
- realistic group conflict theory
- negotiation skills
- leadership skills
- communication technology
- radical humanism
- chaos theory
- network organization
- virtual organization
- horizontal organization
- cross cultural research
- transnational competencies

Pedagogical Features. As with the previous editions there are several strong pedagogical features. To reflect and reinforce the applications orientation of the text, two highlighted self-contained real-world application examples appear in each chapter. As mentioned earlier, some of these deal with international topics, total quality management, or ethics and diversity to maintain these important themes throughout the text. In addition to these applications boxes, the text also features experiential exercises and readings/cases. The end of each major part contains exercises (including several that are new to this edition) to get students involved in solving simulated problems or experiencing first-hand organizational behavior issues. Besides the usual end-of-chapter short discussion cases, there is also a "Real Case" at the end of each chapter. These cases are drawn from recent events (most are updated or new to this edition) and are intended to enhance the relevancy and application of the theories and research results presented in the chapter. The same is done for each of the five major parts. A brand new, longer, integrative real reading/case that is relevant to the preceding chapters is placed at the end of each part. These end-of-chapter and end-of-part real cases serve as both examples and discussion vehicles. It is suggested that students read them, especially the longer end-of-part cases, even if they are not discussed in class. The intent is that they can serve as outside readings as well as discussion cases.

This edition also contains learning objectives at the start of each chapter. These objectives should help students better focus and prepare for what follows in the chapter. Finally, the chapters have the usual end-of-chapter summaries and review and discussion questions.

Intended Audience. Despite the significant changes and additions, the purpose and the intended audience of the book remain the same. Like the earlier editions, this edition is aimed at those who wish to take a totally up-to-date, research-based approach to organizational behavior and human resources management. It does not assume the reader's prior knowledge of either management or the behavioral sciences. Thus, the book can be used effectively in the first or only course in four-year or two-year colleges. It is aimed primarily at the behavioral follow-up course to the more traditional introductory management course, or it can be used in the organizational behavior course in the M.B.A. program. I would like to acknowledge and thank my many colleagues in countries around the world who have used previous editions of the book and point out that the cultural and international perspective and coverage should continue to make this new edition very relevant and attractive. Finally, the book should be helpful to practicing managers who want to understand and more effectively manage their most important asset—their human resources.

Acknowledgments. Every author owes a great deal to others, and I am no exception. First and foremost, I would like to acknowledge the help on this as well as many other writing projects that I have received from Professor Richard M. Hodgetts of Florida International University. He has been an especially valued colleague and friend over the years. Next, I would like to acknowledge the interaction I have had with my colleagues John Schaubroeck, Steve Sommer, and Doug May in the organizational behavior area at the University of Nebraska. In particular, I would like to acknowledge the total support and standards of excellence provided by my department chairman, Sang M. Lee. Linda Rohn, Rhonda Lakey, Debbie Burns, and especially Cathy Jensen from the Management Department staff have been very helpful. Dean Gary Schwendiman has also been very supportive. In getting started in my academic career, I never want to forget the help, encouragement, and scholarly values I received from Professors Henry H. Albers and Max S. Wortman. Over the years, I have been very lucky to have been associated with excellent doctoral students. I would like to thank them all for teaching me as much as I have taught them. In particular, I would like to mention Professor Don Baack of Pittsburg State University, Elaine Davis of Saint Cloud State University, Tim Davis of Cleveland State University, Nancy Dodd of Montana State University, Marilyn Fox of Mankato State University, Avis L. Johnson of the University of Akron, Robert Kreitner of Arizona State University, Diane Lockwood of Seattle University, Mark Martinko of Florida State University, Harriette S. McCaul of North Dakota State University,

Nancy C. Morey of Western Illinois University, James L. Nimnicht of Central Washington University, Pam Perrewe of Florida State University, Stuart A. Rosenkrantz of the University of Central Florida-Daytona Beach, Carol Steinhaus of Indiana University-Purdue University at Fort Wayne, Linda Thomas of Bellevue College, Kenneth Thompson of DePaul University, Robert Waldersee of the University of New South Wales, Australia, Dianne H. B. Welsh of Eastern Washington University, Steve Williams of the National University of Singapore, and my current advanced doctoral students Deborah Buhro, Brooke Envick, Brenda Flannery, Paul Marsnik, Deryl Merritt, Rich Patrick, Doug Peterson, Laura Riolli, and Aleks Stajkovic as having had an especially important impact on my recent thinking about organizational behavior. I am also very grateful to those professors who used the previous editions of the book and gave me valuable feedback for making this revision. In particular, I would like to thank: Jeffrey A. Berman, Salem State College; Daniel N. Braunstein, Oakland University; Mark C. Butler, San Diego State University; Diane Dodd-McCue, University of Virginia; Joseph R. Foerst, Georgia State University; and Nell T. Hartley, Robert Morris College. I would also like to take this opportunity to publicly acknowledge the support, professional expertise, and dedication I have received from my McGraw-Hill editors over the years. In particular, I feel very fortunate to have worked with Senior Editor Lynn Richardson and Senior Associate Editor Dan Alpert in recent years. I would also like to thank Senior Editing Supervisor Peggy Rehberger and Production Supervisor Kathy Porzio. Finally, as always, I am deeply appreciative and dedicate *Organizational Behavior,* Seventh Edition, to my wife and now grown children, who have provided me with a loving, supportive climate needed to complete this and other projects over the years.

Fred Luthans

PART 1

The Foundation for Organizational Behavior

1 Introduction to Organizational Behavior

Learning Objectives

- **Provide** an overview of the major environmental challenges and the paradigm shift facing today's management.
- **Present** a new perspective, an organizational behavior perspective, for management.
- **Summarize** the Hawthorne studies as the starting point of modern organizational behavior.
- **Explain** the methodology that is used to accumulate knowledge and facilitate understanding of organizational behavior.
- **Relate** the various theoretical frameworks that serve as a foundation for a model of organizational behavior.

Effective management of today's organizations and the human resources that make them either go or not go is facing enormous challenges. Downsizing, diversity, the knowledge and information explosion, global competition, and total quality are not only some of the latest buzzwords, they are representative of the harsh reality facing managers now and in the future. There are many solutions being offered of how to deal with these complex challenges. Yet the simplest but most profound solution may be found in the words of Sam Walton, the founder of Wal-Mart and richest person in the world when he died. While having lunch with the author of this text, Sam was asked what was the answer to successful organizations and management. Sam quickly replied, "People are the key."

Understanding and the effective management of people are what this book is all about. Organizational behavior is involved with the study and application of the human side of management and organization.

This introductory chapter gives the perspective, background, methodology, and approach to the field. After a brief discussion of the current environmental challenges and the paradigm shift facing management, the historical background is touched upon. Particular attention is given to the famous Hawthorne studies, which are generally recognized to be the beginning of the systematic study and understanding of organizational behavior. Next, an overview of the methodology used in the scientific study of organizational behavior is given. The chapter concludes by defining exactly what is involved in organizational behavior and by providing a conceptual model for the rest of the text.

THE CHALLENGES FACING MANAGEMENT

Although the field of organizational behavior has been around for at least the past twenty to thirty years, as we move toward the year 2000, the new millennium, there are still significant human-oriented problems facing organizations. In the past decade, managers were preoccupied with restructuring their organizations to improve productivity and meet the competitive challenges in the international marketplace. Although the resulting "lean and mean" organizations offered some short-run benefits in terms of lowered costs and improved productivity, they won't be able to meet the challenges that lie ahead. In particular, the emerging new workplaces, sometimes called knowledge organizations, and the dramatically changing environment call for new understanding and new people-oriented solutions. The following discussion briefly summarizes these major challenges and the next two chapters go into them in more depth.

The New Workplace and Knowledge Organizations

Specific trends have emerged that will reshape the workplace. These include:

1. The traditional hierarchical organization will give way to a variety of organizational forms, the network of specialists foremost among these.
2. Technicians, or knowledge workers, will replace manufacturing operatives as the worker elite.
3. The vertical division of labor will be replaced by a horizontal division.
4. Work itself will be redefined: constant learning, more high-order thinking, less of a routine nine-to-five configuration.
5. The paradigm of doing business will shift from making a product to providing a service.[1]

These changes represent not an evolutionary, but a revolutionary, change in organizations and the way they are managed. As Peter Senge, the well-known architect of the "learning organization," has recently noted:

> We are in the midst of a worldwide, fundamental shift in management philosophy and practice. The traditional resource-based organization of the past is rapidly giving way to the emerging knowledge-based organization.[2]

Not only are the workplace and the basic nature and form of the organization dramatically changing, so is the surrounding environment that is driving these changes.

Environmental Changes: Globalization, Information Technology, Total Quality, and Diversity and Ethics

The starting place for recognizing the changing environment facing organizations and management is the global, one-world economy. The so-called Golden Triangle—the trade regions of North America (United States, Canada, and Mexico), the Pacific Rim (Japan and the now established "Four Tigers" of South Korea, Taiwan, Hong

Kong, and Singapore), and the European Union, or EU (Western and now Central and Eastern European countries)—will dominate this global economy in this decade.[3] However, the rest of the world, especially China and the export-driven countries of Southeast Asia, such as Thailand, Malaysia, Indonesia, and now even Vietnam, will also become major players in the global marketplace in the years ahead. This global competitiveness is certainly one of the biggest challenges facing the field of management going into the new millennium.

Another major environmental development is the second generation of the Information Age. The first generation was characterized by relatively straightforward automated data processing. This second generation has moved to automated decision making, more technology-based telecommunications, and the so-called information superhighway. Decision support and expert systems and E-mail, putting every member of the organization in direct communication with everyone else, even around the world through INTERNET, have become commonplace. Such an information explosion has tremendous implications for the field of management.

Still another major development that is of particular importance to the field of management is the "quality service revolution" that is occurring around the world. Quality of products and services has become the competitive edge in the world marketplace. Although price, brand loyalty, attractive design, and technical innovation are still important to consumers in developed countries, the quality of products has surged ahead in relative importance. Also, the delivery of quality in the exploding service sector has become critical.[4] The accompanying TQM in Action: Going for the Baldy discusses what is involved in applying for the prestigious Malcolm Baldrige National Quality Award.

There is accumulating evidence that the delivery of quality products and services to customers has a direct impact on the success of organizations. For example, the Profit Impact of Market Strategy (PIMS) study, conducted by the U.S.-based Strategic Planning Institute and based on comprehensive data from over 3000 firms over a fifteen-year period, found that those judged to have the best-quality products and services come out on top.[5] The key, of course, is to realize that the human resources of the firm, not advertising slogans nor statistical quality control, deliver quality goods and services.[6] The challenge for organizations across the world is to have their human resources deliver quality products and—especially—service to each other (internal customers) and to customers and clients.

A final major development that has had a significant environmental impact on organization and management is diversity and ethics. The emerging "rainbow coalition" of those of Asian, Pacific Island, African, Hispanic, and Native American descent not only has become significant, but cumulatively is projected to no longer be a minority in the U.S. population by the year 2050.[7] When women are included in this group, the coalition dominates the workplace.

The challenge for management is that this diverse work force contains those who have traditionally been discriminated against. Thus, diversity takes on ethical implications of how management can eliminate all forms of discrimination (age, sex, race, ethnic origin, religion, disability) and provide equal opportunity in all aspects of employment. Also stemming from the heightened sensitivity that results from the realization of a diverse work force is a focus on problems such as sexual harassment, the glass ceiling effect (women's not reaching top-level management positions), and work-family relationships.

The dramatic changes stemming from information technology, total quality, and diversity and ethics are given detailed attention in the next two chapters, and the

Going for the Baldy

In 1987 the U.S. government created the Malcolm Baldrige National Quality Award (MBNQA) to recognize companies that excelled in quality management. Since then hundreds of firms have applied for the "Baldy," and each year a handful are selected as winners. Examples range from such well-known firms as Motorola, Federal Express, Cadillac, and Xerox to lesser-known companies such as Marlow Industries, Solectron, and Zytec.

Each company uses its own approach in winning the award, but there are two things that all seem to have in common: (1) they are committed to changing their old ways of doing things in favor of approaches that require new behaviors and procedures, and (2) they are prepared to stay the course, refusing to believe that total quality is a fad that will soon fade. In operationalizing their approach to total quality and ensuring that everyone is committed, the firms blend the requirements for winning the Baldy with their own unique approach relevant to their situation. The major categories specified by the MBNQA are leadership, information and analysis, strategic quality planning, human resource utilization, quality assurance, quality results, and customer satisfaction. In addressing each of these categories, Baldrige winners determine the management strategies and techniques that are needed in each category. As a result, the company ends up focusing on such areas as encouraging visionary leadership, setting operational goals, establishing priorities, forming partnerships with outside suppliers and clients (outsourcing), empowering the personnel, reengineering processes, and creating cross-functional teams. By implementing such an approach, the firms are able to maximize their adherence to the MBNQA criteria.

By covering all bases, applicants overlook no area that the Baldrige examiners investigate. Total quality strategies and practices can be found everywhere, and any employee who is questioned by the examiners is able to relate what he or she is doing regarding implementation of the total quality effort. Those who have won the Baldrige are able to make quality an integral part of the way they do business and, simultaneously, develop world-class organizations that can compete anywhere with anybody.

international implications are covered in Chapter 19. The environmental challenges have become so important to the study, understanding, and effective application of organizational behavior that they must now be given specific attention along with the time-tested topics of attitudes, motivation, group dynamics, and leadership. These dramatic changes facing the field of organizational behavior can perhaps best be portrayed as a paradigm shift.

UNDERGOING A PARADIGM SHIFT

The term *paradigm* comes from the Greek *paradeigma*, which translates as "model, pattern, or example." First introduced over thirty years ago by the philosophy and science historian Thomas Kuhn,[8] the term "paradigm" is now used to mean a broad model, a framework, a way of thinking, or a scheme for understanding reality.[9] In the words of popular futurist Joel Barker, a paradigm simply establishes the rules (written or unwritten), defines the boundaries, and tells one how to behave within the boundaries to be successful.[10] The impact of internationalization, information technology, total quality, and diversity discussed earlier has led to a paradigm shift. In other words, for today's and tomorrow's organizations and management, there are new rules with different boundaries requiring new and different behavior inside the boundaries for organizations and management to be successful.

Those who study paradigm shifts, such as the shift that took place in the basic sciences from deterministic, mechanistic Cartesian-Newtonian to Einstein's relativity and quantum physics, note that "real controversy takes place, often involving substantial restructuring of the entire scientific community under conditions of great uncertainty."[11] Commonly called the "paradigm effect," a situation arises in which those in the existing paradigm may not even see the changes that are occurring, let alone reason and draw logical inferences and perceptions about the changes. This effect helps explain why there is considerable resistance to change and why it is very difficult to move from the old organization and management paradigm to the new.

U.S.-based organization and management were the very best under the old paradigm. Now that there is a new paradigm, there must be a shift. As noted by Hammer and Champy in their recent best-selling book *Reengineering the Corporation*:

> A set of principles laid down more than two centuries ago has shaped the structure, management, and performance of American businesses throughout the nineteenth and twentieth centuries. We say that the time has come to retire those principles and to adopt a new set. The alternative is for corporate America to close its doors and go out of business. The choice is that simple and that stark.[12]

The accompanying TQM in Action: Reengineering at GTE shows how one company has reengineered itself to meet the new paradigm challenges.

This text on organizational behavior has the goal to help today's and tomorrow's managers make the transition to the new paradigm. Some of the new paradigm characteristics include Chapter 2's coverage of second-generation information technology, total quality management (including empowerment, reengineering, and benchmarking), and learning organizations, and Chapter 3's description of and suggestions for managing diversity and ethics. The new paradigm sets the stage for the study, understanding, and application of the time-tested micro variables (Chapters 4–8), dynamics (Chapters 9–14), and macro variables (Chapters 15–18). However, before getting directly into the rest of the text, we must know why management needs a new perspective to help meet the environmental challenges and the shift to a new paradigm. We must gain an appreciation of the historical background, methodology, and theoretical frameworks that serve as the basis of this text's model for organizational behavior.

A NEW PERSPECTIVE FOR MANAGEMENT

How is management going to meet the environmental challenges and paradigm shift outlined above? Management is generally considered to have three major dimensions—technical, conceptual, and human. The technical dimension consists of the manager's expertise in computers or functional expertise in accounting or engineering or marketing. There seems little question that today's managers are competent in their functional specialization. They know the requirements of their jobs inside and out. This is a major reason why this country remains the most powerful in

**TQM
in Action**

Reengineering at GTE

Over the past five years the term "total quality management," or simply TQM, has been used to represent a wide array of changes being made by organizations determined to improve their overall productivity and profit. One of the major techniques of TQM that has now gained prominence is reengineering, which some experts have defined as "starting all over on a clean piece of paper." What this statement means is that instead of trying to make small, incremental changes in the way the work is done or in the steps of a process, the company will start from scratch and totally redesign the job or redo the process. How well is this reengineering technique paying off? The experience of GTE is a success story.

At the time GTE decided to try reengineering, the firm was earning 80 percent of its $20 billion annual revenue from telephone operations. Determined to maintain this business in the face of growing competition from other firms and alternate technologies, GTE decided to dramatically alter the way it delivered customer service, which involved a number of different processes and functions such as repair, billing, and general marketing. After talking to customers regarding the changes they would like to see, GTE decided to combine the various aspects of customer service into one job. So when someone called in needing a repair person and wanting to talk about a bill and also wanting to know about the various telephone services that the firm provided, he or she would talk to just one person and this individual would be knowledgeable in all these areas.

Now when someone calls GTE, he or she reaches a "front-end technician," who not only can take down all the information, but who also is tied into new software databases, which lets this one employee handle just about any customer request. How well has this reengineering effort worked out? So far GTE reports a 20 to 30 percent increase in productivity, and it has yet to fully implement this reengineered process throughout all its locales. When this happens, GTE is projected to be a premier leader in the industry for customer service.

---

the world. American managers have the functional know-how to get the job done. But few today would question that at least in the past, most practicing managers either ignored the conceptual and human dimensions of their jobs or made some overly simplistic assumptions.

Although there were certainly exceptions, most managers thought, and many still think, that their employees were basically lazy, that they were interested only in money, and that if you could make them happy, they would be productive. When such assumptions were accepted, the human problems facing management were relatively clear-cut and easy to solve. All management had to do was devise monetary incentive plans, ensure security, and provide good working conditions; morale would then be high, and maximum productivity would result. It was as simple as one, two, three. Human relations experts, industrial psychologists, and industrial engineers supported this approach, and personnel managers implemented it.

Unfortunately, this approach no longer works under the new environmental demands that the new paradigm managers are currently faced with. Although no real harm has been done, and some good actually resulted in the early stages of organizational development, it is now evident that such a simplistic approach falls far short of providing a meaningful solution to the complex challenges.

The major fault with the traditional approach is that it overlooks and oversimplifies far too many aspects of the problem. Human behavior at work is much more complicated and diverse than is suggested by the economic-security-working conditions approach. The new perspective assumes that employees are extremely complex and that there is a need for theoretical understanding backed by rigorous empirical research before applications can be made for managing people effectively. The transition has now been completed. The traditional human relations approach no longer has a dominant role in the behavioral approach to management. Few people would question that the organizational behavior approach, with its accompanying body of knowledge, dominates the behavioral approach to management now and will do so in the foreseeable future.

THE HISTORICAL BACKGROUND FOR MODERN ORGANIZATIONAL BEHAVIOR: THE HAWTHORNE STUDIES

The early management pioneers, such as Henry Ford, Alfred P. Sloan, Henri Fayol, and even the scientific managers such as Frederick W. Taylor, recognized the behavioral side of management. However, they did not emphasize the human dimension; they let it play only a minor role in comparison with the roles of hierarchical structure, specialization, and the management functions of planning and controlling. Although there were varied and complex reasons for the emergence of the importance of the behavioral approach to management, it is generally recognized that the Hawthorne studies mark the historical roots for the field of organizational behavior.

The Illumination Studies: A Serendipitous Discovery

In 1924, the studies started at the huge Hawthorne Works of the Western Electric Company outside of Chicago. The initial illumination studies attempted to examine the relationship between light intensity on the shop floor of manual work sites and employee productivity. A test group and a control group were used. The test group in an early phase showed no increase or decrease in output in proportion to the increase or decrease of illumination. The control group with unchanged illumination increased output by the same amount overall as the test group. Subsequent phases brought the level of light down to moonlight intensity; the workers could barely see what they were doing, but productivity increased. The results were baffling to the researchers. Obviously, some variables in the experiment were not being held constant or under control. Something besides the level of illumination was causing the change in productivity. This something, of course, was the complex human variable.

It is fortunate that the illumination experiments did not end up in the wastebasket. Those responsible for the Hawthorne studies had enough foresight and spirit to accept the challenge of looking beneath the surface of the apparent failure of the experiments. In a way, the results of the illumination experiments were a serendipitous discovery, which, in research, is an accidental discovery. The classic example is the breakthrough for penicillin which occurred when Sir Alexander Fleming accidentally discovered green mold on the side of a test tube. That the green mold was not washed down the drain and that the results of the illumination experiments were not thrown into the trash basket can be credited to the researchers' not being blinded by the unusual or seemingly worthless results of their experimentation. The serendipitous results of the illumination experiments provided the impetus for the further study of human behavior at work.

Subsequent Phases of the Hawthorne Studies

The illumination studies were followed by a study in the relay room where operators assembled switches. This phase of the study tried to test specific variables, such as length of workday, rest breaks, and method of payment. The results were basically the same as those of the illumination studies: each test period yielded higher productivity than the previous one. Even when the workers were subjected to the original conditions of the experiment, productivity increased. The conclusion was that the independent variables (rest pauses and so forth) were not by themselves causing the change in the dependent variable (output). As in the illumination experiments, something was still not being controlled.

Still another phase was the bank wiring room study. As in the preceding relay room experiments, the bank wirers were placed in a separate test room. The researchers were reluctant to segregate the bank wiring group because they recognized that this would alter the realistic factory environment they were attempting to simulate. However, for practical reasons, the research team decided to use a separate room. Unlike the relay room experiments, the bank wiring room study involved no experimental changes once the study had started. Instead, an observer and an interviewer gathered objective data for study. Of particular interest was the fact that the department's regular supervisors were used in the bank wiring room. Just as in the department out on the factory floor, their main function was to maintain order and control.

The results of the bank wiring room study were essentially opposite to those of the relay room experiments. In the bank wiring room there were not the continual increases in productivity that occurred in the relay room. Rather, output was actually restricted by the bank wirers. By scientific management analysis—for example, time and motion study—the industrial engineers had arrived at a standard of 7312 terminal connections per day. This represented 2½ equipments. The workers had a different brand of rationality. They decided that 2 equipments was a "proper" day's work. Thus, 2½ equipments represented the management norm for production, but 2 equipments was the informal group norm and the actual output. The researchers determined that the informal group norm of 2 equipments represented restriction of output rather than a lack of ability to produce at the company standard of 2½ equipments.

Of particular interest from a group dynamics standpoint were the social pressures used to gain compliance with the group norms. The incentive system dictated that the more an individual produced, the more money the individual would earn. Also, the best producers would be laid off last, and thus they could be more secure by producing more. Yet, in the face of this management rationale, almost all the workers restricted output. Social ostracism, ridicule, and name-calling were the major sanctions used by the group to enforce this restriction. In some instances, actual physical pressure in the form of a game called "binging" was applied. In the game, a worker would be hit as hard as possible, with the privilege of returning one "bing," or hit. Forcing rate-busters to play the game became an effective sanction. These group pressures had a tremendous impact on all the workers. Social ostracism was more effective in gaining compliance with the informal group norm than money and security were in attaining the scientifically derived management norm.

Implications of the Hawthorne Studies

Despite some obvious philosophical,[13] theoretical,[14] and methodological limitations by today's standards of research (which will be covered next), the Hawthorne studies did provide some interesting insights that contributed to a better understanding of human behavior in organizations.[15] For instance, one interesting aspect of the Hawthorne studies is the contrasting results obtained in the relay room and the bank wiring room. In the relay room, production continually increased throughout the test period, and the relay assemblers were very positive. The opposite was true in the bank wiring room; blatant restriction of output was practiced by disgruntled workers. Why the difference in these two phases of the studies?

One clue to the answer to this question may be traced to the results of a questionnaire administered to the subjects in the relay room. The original intent of the questions was to determine the health and habits of the workers. Their answers were generally inconclusive except that *all* the operators indicated they felt "better" in the test room. A follow-up questionnaire then asked about specific items in the test room situation. In discussions of the Hawthorne studies, the follow-up questionnaire results, in their entirety, usually are not mentioned. Most discussions cite the subjects' unanimous preference for working in the test room instead of the regular department. Often overlooked, however, are the workers' explanations for their choice. In order of preference, the workers gave the following reasons:

1. Small group
2. Type of supervision
3. Earnings
4. Novelty of the situation
5. Interest in the experiment
6. Attention received in the test room[16]

It is important to note that novelty, interest, and attention were relegated to the fourth, fifth, and sixth positions. These last three areas usually are associated with the famous Hawthorne effect. Many social scientists imply that the increases in the relay room productivity can be attributed solely to the fact that the participants in the study were given special attention and that they were enjoying a novel, interesting experience. This is labeled the *Hawthorne effect* and is, of course, a real problem with all human experimental subjects. But to say that all the results of the relay room experiments were due to such an effect on the subjects seems to ignore the important impact of the small group, the type of supervision, and earnings. All these variables (that is, experimental design, group dynamics, styles of leadership and supervision, and rewards), and much more, separate the old human relations movement and the modern approach to the field of organizational behavior. So do the refinement and fine-tuning of the research methodology used to accumulate meaningful knowledge about organizational behavior.

RESEARCH METHODOLOGY

The modern approach to organizational behavior depends upon a rigorous research methodology. The search for the truth of why people behave the way they do is a very delicate and complex process. In fact, the problems are so great that many scholars, chiefly from the physical and engineering sciences, argue that there can be no precise science of behavior. They maintain that humans cannot be treated like chemical or physical elements; they cannot be effectively controlled or manipulated. For example, the critics state that, under easily controllable conditions, 2 parts hydrogen to 1 part oxygen will always result in water and that no analogous situation exists in human behavior. Human variables such as motives, learning, perception, values, and even "hangovers" on the part of both subject and investigator confound the controls that are attempted. For these reasons, behavioral scientists in general and organizational behavior researchers in particular are often on the defensive and must be very careful to comply with accepted methods of science.

The Overall Scientific Perspective

Behavioral scientists in general and organizational behavior researchers in particular strive to attain the following hallmarks of any science:

1. The overall purposes are understanding/explanation, prediction, and control.
2. The definitions are precise and operational.
3. The measures are reliable and valid.
4. The methods are systematic.
5. The results are cumulative.

Figure 1.1 summarizes the relationship between the practical behavioral problems and unanswered questions facing today's managers, research methodology, and the existing body of knowledge. When a question arises or a problem evolves, the first place to turn for an answer is the existing body of knowledge. It is possible that the question can be answered immediately or the problem solved without going any further. Unfortunately, this usually is not true in the case of organizational behavior. One reason is that the amount of knowledge directly applicable to organizational behavior is relatively very small, primarily because of the newness of the field.

It must be remembered that behavioral science is relatively young and that organizational behavior is even younger—it is really a product of the 1970s. The Hawthorne studies go back over seventy years, but a behavioral science-based approach to the study and application of organizational behavior is very recent. The sobering fact is that many questions and problems in organizational behavior cannot be answered or solved directly by existing knowledge. Thus, a working knowledge of research methodology becomes especially important to future managers, both as

FIGURE 1.1
Simple relationships
between problems,
methodology, and
knowledge.

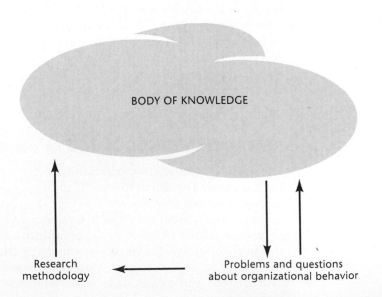

BODY OF KNOWLEDGE

Research
methodology

Problems and questions
about organizational behavior

knowledgeable and critical consumers of the rapidly expanding literature reporting the results of organizational behavior research and as sophisticated practitioners who are capable of applying appropriate research methods to solve difficult problems in the workplace.

Starting with Theory

It has often been said (usually by theoreticians) that there is nothing so practical as a good theory. Yet students of organizational behavior are usually "turned off" by all the theories that pervade the field. The reason for all the theories, of course, is the newness of the field and the fact that there are not yet many definitive answers. The purpose of any theory, including those found in organizational behavior, is to explain and predict the phenomena in question; theories allow the researcher to deduce logical propositions or hypotheses that can be tested by acceptable designs. Theories are ever changing on the basis of the research results. Thus, theory and research go hand in hand.

John Miner, in the introductory comments in his book *Theories of Organizational Behavior*, gives several criteria for how to "know a good theory when we see one":

1. It should contribute to the goals of science by aiding understanding, permitting prediction, and facilitating influence.
2. There should be clear boundaries of application so that the theory is not used in situations for which it was never intended.
3. It should direct research efforts toward important, high-priority problems and issues.
4. It should produce generalizable results beyond single research efforts.
5. It should be readily subject to further testing by using clearly defined variables and operational terms.
6. Not only should it be confirmed by research directly derived from it, but it should also be consistent within itself and with other known facts.
7. It should be stated in the simplest possible terms.[17]

The Use of Research Designs

The research design is at the very heart of scientific methodology; it can be used to answer practical questions or to test theoretical propositions/hypotheses. The three designs most often used in organizational behavior research today are the experimental, the case, and the survey designs. All three have played important roles in the development of meaningful knowledge. The experimental design is borrowed largely from psychology, where it is used extensively; the case and survey designs have traditionally played a bigger role in sociology. All three designs can be used effectively for researching organizational behavior.

A primary aim of any research design is to establish a cause-and-effect relationship. The experimental design offers the best possibility of accomplishing this goal. All other factors being equal, most organizational behavior researchers prefer this method of testing hypotheses. Simply defined, an experiment involves the manipulation of independent variables to measure their effect on, or the change in, dependent variables, while everything else is held constant or controlled. Usually, an experimental group and a control group are formed. The experimental group receives the input of the independent variables, and the control group does not. Any measured change in the dependent variable in the experimental group can be attributed to the independent variable, assuming that no change has occurred in any other variable and that no change has occurred in the control group. The controls employed are the key to the successful use of the experimental design. If all intervening variables are held constant or equal, the researcher can conclude with a high degree of confidence that the independent variable caused the change in the dependent variable.

The Validity of Studies

The value of any research study is dependent on its validity, that is, whether the study really demonstrates what it is supposed to demonstrate. In particular, a study must have both *internal validity* and *external validity* in order to make a meaningful contribution to the body of knowledge. A study has internal validity if there are no plausible explanations of the reported results other than those reported. The threats to internal validity include but are not limited to:

1. *History.* Uncontrolled intervening events that occur between the time the preexperiment measurement is taken and the time the postexperiment measurement is taken.
2. *Maturation.* Changes in the subject or subjects with the mere passing of time, irrespective of the experimental treatment.
3. *Testing.* The effect of previous testing on a subject's present performance.
4. *Instrumentation.* Changes in measures of subject performance due to changes in the instruments or observers over time.
5. *Regression.* Changes in performance due to subjects' going from extreme scores to more typical scores.
6. *Selection.* Changes due to the differences in the subjects rather than the treatment.
7. *Ambiguity about direction of causation.* Does A cause B, or does B cause A? This is a problem with correlational studies.
8. *Local history.* Changes due to the unique situation when the experimental group received the treatment.[18]

Laboratory studies usually control these threats to internal validity better than field studies do. But, as Daniel Ilgen has pointed out, this control afforded by the laboratory is purchased at the price of generalizability and relevance. "As a result, many behavioral scientists decry the use of any laboratory research and dismiss results obtained from such as irrelevant or, worse yet, misleading for the understanding of naturally occurring human behavior."[19]

But, in general, the threats can be minimized, even in field settings, by *pretests* (these allow the investigator to make sure that the experimental and control groups were performing at the same level before the experimental manipulations are made, and they give measurement over time); *control groups* (these permit comparison with experimental groups—they have everything the same except the experimental manipulation); and *random assignment* (this pretty well assures that the experimental and control groups will be the same, and it allows the correct use of inferential statistics to analyze the results). Thus, the threats to internal validity can be overcome with careful design of the study. This is not always true of external validity, which is concerned with the generalizability of the results obtained. In order for a study to have external validity, the results must be applicable to a wide range of people and situations.[20] Field studies tend to have better external validity than laboratory studies because at least the study takes place in a real setting.

In general, organizational behavior research can be improved by conducting studies longitudinally (over time) and attempting to design studies more from existing theory.[21] The best strategy is to use a number of different designs to answer the same question. The weaknesses of the various designs can offset one another and the problem of common method variance (the results are due to the design, rather than the variables under study) can be overcome.

Normally, the research would start with a laboratory study to isolate and manipulate the variable or variables in question. This would be followed by an attempt to verify the findings in a field setting. This progression from the laboratory to the field may lead to the soundest conclusions. However, free observation in the real setting should probably precede laboratory investigations of organizational behavior problems or questions. Multiple designs and multiple measures have the best chance for valid, meaningful research in organizational behavior.

DEFINING ORGANIZATIONAL BEHAVIOR

With a rich historical background such as the Hawthorne studies and an accepted scientific methodology as outlined above, the field of organizational behavior is beginning to develop and mature as an academic discipline. As with any other relatively new academic endeavor, however, there have been some rough spots and sidetracks in its development. Besides the healthy academic controversies over theoretical approach or research findings, perhaps the biggest problem that organizational behavior has had to face is an identity crisis. Exactly what is meant by organizational behavior? Is it an attempt to replace all management with behavioral science concepts and techniques? How, if at all, does it differ from good old applied or industrial psychology? Fortunately, these questions have now largely been answered to the satisfaction of most management academicians, behavioral scientists, and management practitioners.

Figure 1.2 shows in very general terms the relationships between and emphases of organizational behavior (OB) and the related disciplines of organization theory (OT), organization development (OD), and personnel/human resources (P/HR). As shown, OB tends to be more theoretically oriented and at the micro level of analysis. Specifically, OB draws from many theoretical frameworks of the behavioral sciences

FIGURE 1.2
The relationship of organizational behavior to other closely related disciplines.

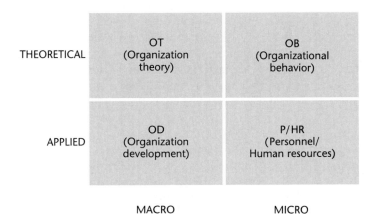

	THEORETICAL	OT (Organization theory)	OB (Organizational behavior)
APPLIED	OD (Organization development)	P/HR (Personnel/ Human resources)
	MACRO	MICRO

that are focused at understanding and explaining individual and group behavior in organizations. As with other sciences, OB accumulates knowledge and tests theories by accepted scientific methods of research. In summary, *organizational behavior* can be defined as the understanding, prediction, and management of human behavior in organizations.

Although Figure 1.2 is not intended to portray mutually exclusive domains for the related fields, because the lines are becoming increasingly blurred and there is not universal agreement of what belongs to what among academics or practitioners, most people in the field would generally agree with what is shown. Organization theory tends to be more macro-oriented than OB and is concerned primarily with organization structure and design. Yet, as in this text (Chapter 17 specifically and macro-oriented chapters such as 15, 16, and 18), OT topics are included in the study and application of OB. Organization development, on the other hand, tends to be both more macro and more applied than OB. But also like OT, as in this text (Chapter 20), OD topics are included in the study and application of OB. Finally, as shown, P/HR tends to have a more applied focus than OB. The personnel/human resources function is a part of practicing organizations as much as the marketing, finance, or production/operations functions are.

Personnel or human resource managers (the more modern term is the latter) are hired and found with this title in practicing organizations; organizational behaviorists are not. Yet, somewhat confusingly, those managers who apply and draw from the field of organizational behavior (whether they be marketing managers, finance managers, hospital administrators, operations managers, store managers, academic administrators, office managers, *or* personnel/human resource managers) are called "human resource managers." They are called human resource managers and have a human resource management role (in addition to their other technical, functional role), because they all manage people. Thus, all managers, regardless of their technical function, are human resource managers in this view because they deal with human behavior in organizations. All managers need to have an understanding and perspective of organizational behavior.

Organizational behavior represents the *behavioral* approach to management, not the whole of management. Other recognized approaches to management include the process, quantitative, systems, and contingency approaches. In other words, organizational behavior does not intend to portray the whole of management. The charge that old wine (applied or industrial psychology) has merely been poured into a new bottle (organizational behavior) has proved to be groundless. Although it is certainly true that the behavioral sciences make a significant contribution to both the theoretical and the research foundations of organizational behavior, it is equally true that applied or industrial psychology should not be equated with organizational behavior. For example, organization structure and management processes (decision making and communication) play an integral, direct role in organizational behavior, as in this text (Part 4), but have at most an indirect role in applied or industrial psychology. The same is true of many important dynamics and applications of organizational behavior. Although there will probably never be total agreement on the exact meaning or domain of organizational behavior—which is not necessarily bad, because it makes the field more exciting—there is little doubt that organizational behavior has come into its own as a field of study, research, and application.

This text on organizational behavior attempts to provide the specific, necessary background and skills to make the managers of today and tomorrow as effective with the conceptual and human dimensions of management as they have been in the past with its technical, functional dimensions.

THEORETICAL FRAMEWORKS

Although organizational behavior is extremely complex and includes many inputs, the cognitive, behavioristic, and social learning theoretical frameworks can be used to develop an overall model. After the theoretical frameworks are examined, the last section of the chapter presents an organizational behavior model that conceptually links and structures the rest of the text.

Cognitive Framework

The cognitive approach to human behavior has many sources of input. The micro-oriented chapters in the next part provide some of this background. For now, however, it can be said simply that the cognitive approach gives people much more "credit" than the other approaches. The cognitive approach emphasizes the positive and free-will aspects of human behavior and uses concepts such as expectancy, demand, and incentive. *Cognition*, which is the basic unit of the cognitive framework, is the act of knowing an item of information. Under this framework, cognitions precede behavior and constitute input into the person's thinking, perception, problem solving, and processing information. Concepts such as cognitive maps can be used as pictures or visual aids in comprehending a person's "understanding of particular, and selective, elements of the thoughts (rather than thinking) of an individual, group or organization."[22]

The classic work of Edward Tolman can be used to represent the cognitive theoretical approach. Although Tolman believed behavior to be the appropriate unit of analysis, he felt that behavior is purposive, that it is directed toward a goal. In his laboratory experiments, he found that animals learned to expect that certain events would follow one another. For example, animals learned to behave as if they expected food when a certain cue appeared. Thus, Tolman believed that learning consists of the *expectancy* that a particular event will lead to a particular consequence. This cognitive concept of expectancy implies that the organism is thinking about, or is conscious or aware of, the goal. Thus, Tolman and others espousing the cognitive approach felt that behavior is best explained by these cognitions.

Contemporary psychologists carefully point out that a cognitive concept such as expectancy does not reflect a guess about what is going on in the mind; it is a term that describes behavior. In other words, the cognitive and behavioristic theories are not as opposite as they appear on the surface and sometimes are made out to be—for example, Tolman considered himself a behaviorist. Yet, despite some conceptual similarities, there has been a controversy throughout the years in the behavioral sciences on the relative contributions of the cognitive versus the behavioristic framework. As often happens in other academic fields, debate has gone back and forth through the years.

Because of the recent advances from both theory development and research findings, there has been what some have termed a "cognitive explosion" in the field of psychology.[23] Applied to the field of organizational behavior, a cognitive approach has traditionally dominated through units of analysis such as perception (Chapter 4), personality and attitudes (Chapter 5), motivation (Chapter 6), and goal setting (Chapter 7). Very recently, there has been renewed interest in the role that cognitions can play in organizational behavior in terms of advancement in research on how managers make decisions and in the area of social cognition. The behavioral decision-making area is concerned with the cognitions involved in judgment and choice[24] and is given attention in Chapter 16. Social cognition involves the process of understanding or making sense of people's behavior[25] and is especially relevant to organizational behavior in terms of social perception (Chapter 4). In other words, both the traditional and newer approaches to cognitive theory and application play an important role in the theoretical framework of this text. However, before discussing the specific input that the cognitive approach can make to the study of organizational behavior, it is necessary to have an understanding of the behavioristic approach as well.

Behavioristic Framework

Chapter 8 discusses in detail the behavioristic theory in psychology. Its roots can be traced to the work of Ivan Pavlov and John B. Watson. These pioneering behaviorists stressed the importance of dealing with observable behaviors instead of the elusive mind that had preoccupied earlier psychologists. They used classical conditioning experiments to formulate the stimulus-response (S-R) explanation of human behavior. Both Pavlov and Watson felt that behavior could be best understood in terms of S-R. A stimulus elicits a response. They concentrated mainly on the impact of the stimulus and felt that learning occurred when the S-R connection was made.

Modern behaviorism marks its beginnings with the work of B. F. Skinner. Now deceased, Skinner is widely recognized for his contributions to psychology. He felt that the early behaviorists helped explain respondent behaviors (those behaviors elicited by stimuli) but not the more complex operant behaviors. In other words, the S-R approach helped explain physical reflexes; for example, when stuck by a pin (S), the person will flinch (R), or when tapped below the kneecap (S), the person will extend the lower leg (R). On the other hand, Skinner found through his operant conditioning experiments that the consequences of a response could better explain most behaviors than eliciting stimuli could. He emphasized the importance of the response-stimulus (R-S) relationship. The organism has to operate on the environment in order to receive the desirable consequence. The preceding stimulus does not cause the behavior in operant conditioning; it serves as a cue to emit the behavior. For Skinner, behavior is a function of its consequences.

Both classical and operant conditioning and the important role of reinforcing consequences are given detailed attention in Chapter 8. For now, however, it is important to understand that the behavioristic approach is environmentally based. It posits that cognitive processes such as thinking, expectancies, and perception may exist, but are not needed to predict and control or manage behavior. However, as in the case of the cognitive approach, which also includes behavioristic concepts, some behavioral scientists feel that there is room for cognitive variables in the behavioristic approach. In particular, a social learning approach has emerged in recent years that incorporates both cognitive and behavioristic concepts and principles.

Social Learning Framework

The cognitive approach has been accused of being mentalistic, and the behavioristic approach has been accused of being deterministic. Cognitive theorists argue that the S-R model, and to a lesser degree the R-S model, is much too mechanistic an explanation of human behavior. A strict S-R interpretation of behavior seems justifiably open to the criticism of being too mechanistic, but because of the scientific approach that has been meticulously employed by behaviorists, the operant model in particular has made a tremendous contribution to the study of human behavior. The same can be said of the cognitive approach. Much research has been done to verify its importance as an explanation of human behavior. Instead of polarization and unconstructive criticism between the two approaches, it now seems time to recognize that each can make an important contribution to the understanding, prediction, and control of human behavior. The social learning approach tries to integrate the contributions of both approaches.

It must be emphasized that the social learning approach is a behavioral approach. It recognizes that behavior is the appropriate unit of analysis. However, unlike a strict or radical behavioristic approach, the social learning approach suggests that people are self-aware and engage in purposeful behavior. Under a social learning approach, people are thought to learn about their environment, alter and construct their environment to make reinforcers available, and note the importance of rules and symbolic processes in learning.[26]

Although a number of psychologists are associated with social learning, the work of Albert Bandura is probably the most representative of this approach.[27] He takes the position that behavior can best be explained in terms of a continuous reciprocal interaction between cognitive, behavioral, and environmental determinants. The person and the environmental situation do not function as independent units but, in conjunction with the behavior itself, reciprocally interact to determine behavior. Bandura explains that "it is largely through their actions that people produce the environmental conditions that affect their behavior in a reciprocal fashion. The experiences generated by behavior also partly determine what a person becomes and can do, which, in turn, affects subsequent behavior."[28] The triangular model shown in Figure 1.3 takes this work of Bandura and translates it into relevant units of analysis and variables in organizational behavior.

The specifics of social learning, such as vicarious or modeling processes, the role of cognitive mediating processes, and the importance of self-efficacy are discussed in Chapter 8. But for now, it can be said that social learning, with its very comprehensive, interactive nature, serves as an appropriate theoretical framework for developing a model of organizational behavior.[29]

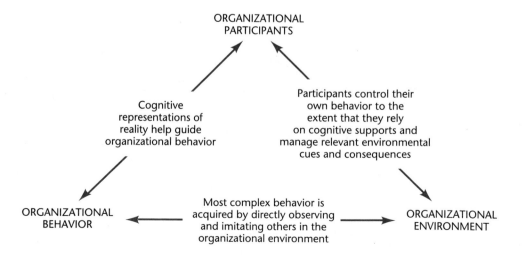

FIGURE 1.3
A social learning approach to organizational behavior.

ORGANIZATIONAL PARTICIPANTS

Cognitive representations of reality help guide organizational behavior

Participants control their own behavior to the extent that they rely on cognitive supports and manage relevant environmental cues and consequences

ORGANIZATIONAL BEHAVIOR

Most complex behavior is acquired by directly observing and imitating others in the organizational environment

ORGANIZATIONAL ENVIRONMENT

ORGANIZATIONAL BEHAVIOR MODEL

Organizational behavior has the advantage of being a relatively young and growing field of study. It can legitimately borrow, in an eclectic manner, the best from the various established frameworks for human behavior. Traditionally, most writers on organizational behavior have taken a humanistic, cognitive approach. For example, Douglas McGregor, who wrote the classic *Human Side of Enterprise* in 1960, took a humanistic approach, and well-known theorists such as Victor Vroom, Lyman Porter, and Edwin Locke depend mainly on cognitive concepts in their well-known writings on organizational behavior. In the last few years, the behavioristic model has begun to be used in theorizing and research on organizational behavior. In many ways, what the field of organizational behavior has been going through in recent years is a replay of the behavioristic-versus-cognitive controversy that has existed and, in many respects, still exists in psychology. Now, in organizational behavior, as in the more established behavioral sciences, the time seems to have come to recognize the contributions of both approaches and to begin to synthesize and integrate both into a comprehensive model for organizational behavior. The social learning approach provides a theoretical foundation for such an eclectic organizational behavior model.

The reason for presenting the cognitive and behavioristic theoretical frameworks was to better understand, not evaluate, the complex phenomena collectively called *human behavior*. Understanding human behavior in organizations is also a vital goal for a conceptual model for organizational behavior. In addition, however, because organizational behavior is not a basic behavioral science such as psychology or sociology, two other especially desirable goals besides understanding are prediction and control. The field of organizational behavior serves as the basis for modern human resources managers. Prediction and control of human resources are critical to the goals of the new approach to management that will help solve the problems and meet the environmental challenges and paradigm shift identified in the introductory comments of the chapter. Thus, the goals of a conceptual model for organizational behavior are to understand, predict, and manage human behavior in organizations.

The cognitive approach seems essential to the understanding of organizational behavior. The behavioristic approach can also lead to understanding, but perhaps even more important is the contribution it can make to prediction and control. For example, on the basis of Edward Thorndike's classic law of effect, the behavioristic approach would say that organizational behavior followed by a positive or reinforcing consequence will be strengthened and will increase in subsequent frequency and that organizational behavior followed by an unpleasant or punishing consequence will be weakened and will decrease in subsequent frequency. Thus, organizational behavior can be predicted and controlled on the basis of managing the contingent environment.

If the three goals of understanding, prediction, and control are to be met by a conceptual model for organizational behavior, both the cognitive and the behavioristic approaches become vitally important. Both the internal causal factors, which are cognitively oriented, and the external environmental factors, which are behavioristically oriented, become important. In other words, the social learning approach that incorporates both cognitive and behavioristic concepts is an appropriate conceptual model for organizational behavior that will help understand, predict, and control. Such a social learning–based organizational behavior model with corresponding chapter coverage is portrayed in Figure 1.4.

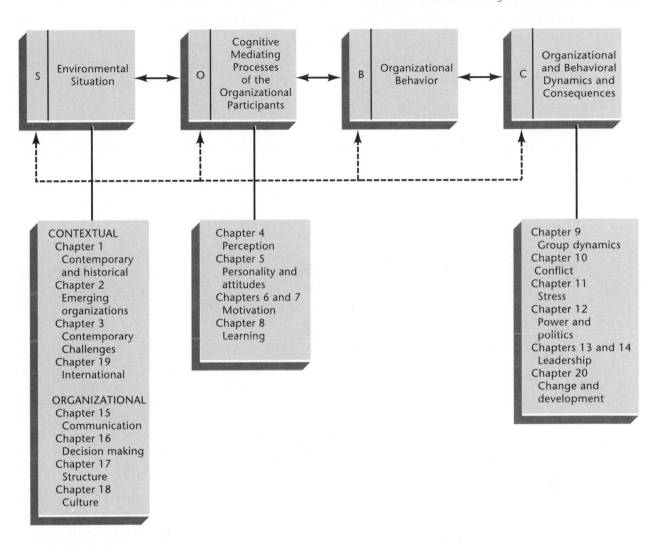

FIGURE 1.4

A conceptual model for the study of organizational behavior.

In a strictly social learning model, the letters in this model would stand for *s*timulus, *o*rganism, *b*ehavior, and *c*onsequence. The arrows recognize the interactive, reciprocal nature of the environmental (S and C), cognitive (O), and behavioral (B) variables. Figure 1.3 showed the social learning theoretical basis for these relationships. When adopted and extended into an organizational behavior model, the S represents the environmental *s*ituation, both contextual and organizational. The O becomes the cognitive understanding of *o*rganizational participants that mediates between the environmental situation and the resulting organizational behavior. The B is the organizational *b*ehavior. The C in this model represents the organizational and group dynamics and *c*onsequences that result from the previous interactions between the environmental, personal, and behavioral variables. As shown by the feedback interactions, the consequences also affect and are affected by the other variables.

Obviously, this S-O-B-C model gives only a bare-bones sketch of organizational behavior rather than a full-blown explanation. Nevertheless, it can serve as a conceptual framework and point of departure for how this text is organized. It helps explain why particular chapters are covered and how they relate to one another. As the chapters unfold, some of the fine points of this model should become clearer and some of the seemingly simplistic, unsupported statements will begin to make more sense. This model serves merely as the welcoming mat to the study of the exciting, but still developing, field of organizational behavior.

Summary

This chapter first gives a brief overview of the significant challenges currently facing management. Besides the new workplace and the knowledge organization, environmental changes such as internationalization, second-generation information technology, total quality to customers, and recognition and management of diversity and ethics have led to a paradigm shift. This shift is characterized by new rules, new boundaries, and importantly, new behaviors that are essential for organizations and managers to be successful or even survive. The new paradigm facing management requires a new perspective and an appreciation of the human, behavioral side of management. Thus, the field of organizational behavior becomes important now and in the future.

Organizational behavior is a relatively recent field of study and application. The beginnings are usually attributed to the famous Hawthorne studies, which had several phases (illumination, relay, bank wiring studies) and often overlooked implications for modern management. Whereas the Hawthorne studies are often criticized for methodological flaws, today's organizational behavior field is characterized by rigorous scientific methodology. Both theory development and research designs are given considerable attention. Specifically, the threats to internal validity are attempted to be eliminated or minimized through carefully designed experiments. Field studies are used over laboratory studies whenever possible in order to have more external (generalizable) validity.

Since organizational behavior is a relatively new field, it must be precisely defined: the understanding, prediction, and management of human behavior in organizations. It is also important to see how OB (micro, theoretical) relates to other closely related disciplines such as OT (macro, theoretical), OD (macro, applied), and P/HR (micro, applied). Finally, it is important to provide a theoretical foundation to develop a specific model which can be used as a conceptual framework for this text. The cognitive, behavioristic, and the emerging and more integrative social learning theories are used for such a foundation. The cognitive model gives the human being more "credit" and assumes that behavior is purposive and goal-oriented. Cognitive processes such as expectancy and perception help explain behavior. The behavioristic approach deals with observable behavior and the environmental contingencies of the behavior. Classical behaviorism explained behavior in terms of S-R, whereas more modern behaviorism gives increased emphasis to contingent consequences, or R-S. The social learning approach emphasizes that the person, the environment, and the behavior itself are in constant interaction with one another and reciprocally determine one another. This social learning approach incorporates both cognitive and behavioristic elements and is used as the theoretical foundation for the organizational behavior model. As noted, this S-O-B-C model is used as the conceptual framework to structure this text.

Questions for Discussion and Review

1. What are some of the major environmental challenges facing today's and tomorrow's organizations and management? Briefly describe these developments.
2. What is a paradigm? How will the paradigm shift affect management? What are the implications of this paradigm shift for organizational behavior?
3. Why do you feel the Hawthorne studies made such an important historical contribution to the study of organizational behavior?
4. Why are theory development and rigorous scientific methodology important to the field of organizational behavior? What role does validity play in the design of research studies?
5. How does organizational behavior relate to, or differ from, organizational development? Organization theory? Personnel and human resources management?
6. In your own words, identify and summarize the various theoretical frameworks for understanding organizational behavior. How does the social learning approach differ from the cognitive approach? How does the social learning approach differ from the behavioristic approach?
7. Explain the model for organizational behavior that is used in this text.

Footnote References and Supplemental Readings

1. Walter Kiechel, "How We Will Work in the Year 2000," *Fortune*, May 17, 1993, p. 39.
2. Peter M. Senge, "Transforming the Practice of Management," *Human Resource Development Quarterly*, Spring 1993, p. 5.
3. See Richard M. Hodgetts and Fred Luthans, *International Management*, 2d ed., McGraw-Hill, New York, 1994, Chap. 1 and 2.
4. George S. Easton, "The 1993 State of U.S. Total Quality Management," *California Management Review*, Spring 1993, pp. 32–54, and Myron Magnet, "Good News for the Service Economy," *Fortune*, May 3, 1993, pp. 46–52.
5. B. Uttal, "Companies That Serve You Best," *Fortune*, Dec. 7, 1987, pp. 98–116.
6. Fred Luthans, "Quality Is an HR Function," *Personnel*, May 1990, p. 72.
7. Brian Bremner and Joseph Weber, "A Spicier Stew in the Melting Pot," *Business Week*, Dec. 21, 1992, pp. 29–30.
8. Thomas S. Kuhn, *The Structure of Scientific Revolutions*, 2d ed., University of Chicago Press, Chicago, 1970. Kuhn discussed paradigms as far back as 1962.
9. Don Tapscott and Art Caston, *Paradigm Shift: The Promise of Information Technology*, McGraw-Hill, New York, 1993, p. xii.
10. Joel A. Barker, *Future Edge*, Morrow, New York, 1992, p. 32.
11. Norman Clark, "Similarities and Differences Between Scientific and Technological Paradigms," *Futures*, Feb. 1987, p. 28.
12. Michael Hammer and James Champy, *Reengineering the Corporation*, Harper Business, New York, 1993, p. 1.
13. For example, see Lyle Yorks and David Whitsett, "Hawthorne, Topeka, and the Issue of Science versus Advocacy in Organizational Behavior," *Academy of Management Review*, January 1985, pp. 21–30.
14. Gary W. Yunker, "An Explanation of Positive and Negative Hawthorne Effects: Evidence from the Relay Assembly Test Room and Bank Wiring Observation Room Studies," *Academy of Management Best Papers Proceedings*, 1993, pp. 179–183.
15. H. McIlvaine Parsons, "Hawthorne: An Early OBM Experiment," *Journal of Organizational Behavior Management*, vol. 12, no. 1, 1992, pp. 27–44.
16. C. E. Turner, "Test Room Studies in Employee Effectiveness," *American Journal of Public Health*, June 1933, p. 584.
17. John B. Miner, *Theories of Organizational Behavior*, Dryden Press, Hinsdale, Ill., 1980, pp. 7–9.
18. Thomas D. Cook and Donald T. Campbell, "The Design and Conduct of Quasi-Experiments and True Experiments in Field Settings," in M. D. Dunnette (ed.), *Handbook of Industrial and Organizational Psychology*, Rand McNally, Chicago, 1976,

pp. 224–246. Also see Terence R. Mitchell, "An Evaluation of the Validity of Correlational Research Conducted in Organizations," *Academy of Management Review*, April 1985, pp. 192–205.

19. Daniel R. Ilgen, "Laboratory Research: A Question of When, Not If," in Edwin A. Locke (ed.), *Generalizing from Laboratory to Field Settings*, Lexington Books, Lexington, Mass., 1986, p. 257.

20. For example, see Frank L. Schmidt, Kenneth Law, John E. Hunter, Hannah R. Rothstein, Kenneth Pearlman, and Michael McDaniel, "Refinements in Validity Generalization Methods: Implications for the Situational Specificity Hypothesis," *Journal of Applied Psychology*, February 1993, pp. 3–12.

21. Michael West, John Arnold, Martin Corbett, and Ben Fletcher, "Editorial: Advancing Understanding About Behavior at Work," *Journal of Occupational and Organizational Psychology*, March 1992, pp. 1–3.

22. Colin Eden, "On the Nature of Cognitive Maps," *Journal of Management Studies*, May 1992, p. 262. Also see C. Marlene Fiol and Anne Sigismund Huff, "Maps for Managers: Where Are We? Where Do We Go from Here?" *Journal of Management Studies*, May 1992, pp. 267–285.

23. Ronald E. Riggio, *Introduction to Industrial/Organizational Psychology*, Scott, Foresman/Little, Brown, Glenview, Ill., 1990, p. 16, and Andrew R. McGill, Michael D. Johnson, and Karen A. Bantel, "Cognitive Complexity and Conformity: The Effects on Performance in a Turbulent Environment," *Academy of Management Best Papers Proceedings*, 1993, pp. 379–383.

24. See R. J. Herrnstein, "Rational Choice Theory," *American Psychologist*, March 1990, pp. 356–367;

Robin M. Hogarth, *Judgment and Choice*, 2d ed., Wiley, New York, 1987; and Max H. Bazerman, *Judgment in Managerial Decision Making*, 2d ed., Wiley, New York, 1990.

25. See Stephen Worchel, Joel Cooper, and George Goethals, *Understanding Social Psychology*, 4th ed., Dorsey Press, Chicago, 1988, Chap. 2, and Robert S. Wyer, Jr., and Thomas K. Srull, *Memory and Cognition*, Erlbaum, Hillsdale, N.J., 1989.

26. Spencer A. Rathus, *Psychology*, 4th ed., Holt, Rinehart and Winston, Fort Worth, Tex., 1990, p. 410.

27. Albert Bandura, "Social Learning Theory," in J. T. Spence, R. C. Carson, and J. W. Thibaut (eds.), *Behavioral Approaches to Therapy*, General Learning Press, Morristown, N.J., 1976; Albert Bandura, *Social Learning Theory*, Prentice-Hall, Englewood Cliffs, N.J., 1977; Albert Bandura, "The Self System in Reciprocal Determinism," *American Psychologist*, April 1978, pp. 344–358; and Albert Bandura, *Social Foundations of Thought and Action: A Social-Cognitive Theory*, Prentice-Hall, Englewood Cliffs, N.J., 1986.

28. Bandura, *Social Learning Theory*, p. 9.

29. See Tim R. V. Davis and Fred Luthans, "A Social Learning Approach to Organizational Behavior," *Academy of Management Review*, April 1980, pp. 281–290; Robert Kreitner and Fred Luthans, "A Social Learning Approach to Behavior Management: Radical Behaviorists Mellowing Out," *Organizational Dynamics*, Autumn 1984, pp. 61–75; and Fred Luthans and Robert Kreitner, *Organizational Behavior Modification and Beyond*, Scott, Foresman, Glenview, Ill., 1985.

REAL CASE:
Going from
Fad to Fad

Many organizations today are becoming involved with reengineering jobs, flattening the structure, and empowering their people to make on-the-spot decisions. To facilitate these dramatic changes, most of these firms have set up expensive in-house training programs or have had special programs designed for them by the nation's leading business schools. However, despite these efforts, there is a gnawing "gut" feeling that continues to confront the management of these firms. Are all these latest training and development programs going to bring about the results they want, or is this just the latest round of fads that will soon be replaced by still other fads? Many managers and operating-level employees who have been with their company for a decade or more have seen these fads come and go. Management get all excited and implement the latest techniques and then, after a few years, abandon them and move on to something else.

Despite the justifiable cynicism, the top management of firms such as Motorola are betting that some of the latest developments, such as total quality, may indeed change, but the general thrust of these developments and what they stand for are here to stay. This is why Motorola now spends over $120 million annually on training and education. This is equivalent to 3.6 percent of its yearly payroll. Moreover, the company estimates that for every $1 it spends on training, it achieves $30 in productivity gains over the next three years. Since 1987 Motorola has cut costs by $3.3 billion by teaching people to simplify the processes they use and to reduce waste. As a result, between 1988 and 1992, sales per employee increased by more than 100 percent and profits went up 47 percent. One reason for this huge success story in difficult times is the practicality of the training. For example, not only does Motorola teach employees what empowerment is all about, it also allows them to learn on the job how to use empowerment effectively.

Despite success stories such as Motorola, there are still widespread fear and doubts that total quality management, reengineering, empowerment, flat structures, and all the other recently popular concepts will be out of vogue by the turn of the century. Fortunately, most firms are still pushing ahead on these new ideas and using them to help run the firm. They are doing so because there are some underlying themes and basic truths that appear to be important regardless of whether this is just a gimmick or a fad. Two that are singled out most often are employee empowerment and the tying of rewards to performance. There appears to be little doubt that the traditional ways of running organizations must be supplanted by new approaches. The question is which of the new methods are going to be most effective. While they are waiting around to see if there will be one best answer to this question, many firms are now using what is currently available. As one management professor recently put it, "Somebody's writing a book right now that will come up with a more popular phrase, and we'll all be doing that." In the interim, total quality–related concepts and techniques that can be directly applied will be popular and will remain so as long as they continue to make things happen and have a positive impact on performance. When they prove ineffective, they will be replaced by other concepts and techniques that will again change the paradigm.

1. How does training help organizations improve performance?
2. In what way does current training represent a change from the past?
3. Do you think that the commitment to training will increase or decrease in the years ahead? What types of concepts and techniques would you expect to be given more attention?

CASE:
How Is This Stuff
Going to Help Me?

Jane Arnold wants to be a manager. She enjoyed her accounting, finance, and marketing courses. Each of these provided her with some clear-cut answers. Now the professor in her organizational behavior course is telling her that there are really very few clear-cut answers when it comes to managing people. The professor has discussed some of the emerging environmental challenges and the historical background and says that behavioral science concepts play a big role in the course. Jane is very perplexed. She came to school to get answers on how to be an effective manager, but this course surely doesn't seem to be heading in that direction.

1. How would you relieve Jane's anxiety? How is a course in organizational behavior going to make her a better manager?
2. Why did the professor start off with a brief overview of emerging environmental challenges?
3. How does a course in organizational behavior differ from courses in fields such as accounting, finance, or marketing?

**CASE:
Too Nice
to People**

John has just graduated from the College of Business Administration at State University and has joined his family's small business, which employs twenty-five semiskilled workers. During the first week on the job, his dad called him in and said: "John, I've had a chance to observe you working with the men and women for the past two days and, although I hate to, I feel I must say something. You are just too nice to people. I know they taught you that human relations stuff at the university, but it just doesn't work here. I remember when we discussed the Hawthorne studies when I was in school and everybody at the university got all excited about them, but believe me, there is more to managing people than just being nice to them."

1. How would you react to your father's comments if you were John?
2. Do you think John's father understood and interpreted the Hawthorne studies correctly?
3. What phases of management do you think John's father has gone through in this family business? Do you think he understands the significance of recent trends in the environment and how the new paradigm will affect his business?
4. How would you explain to your father the new perspective that is needed and how the study of organizational behavior will help the business be successful in the new paradigm?

**CASE:
Conceptual Model:
Dream or Reality?**

Hank James has been section head for the accounting group at Yake Company for fourteen years. His boss, Mary Stein, feels that Hank is about ready to be moved up to the corporate finance staff, but it is company policy to send people like Hank to the University Executive Development Program before such a promotion is made. Hank has enrolled in the program; one of the first parts deals with organizational behavior. Hank felt that after fourteen years of managing people, this would be a snap. However, during the lecture on organizational behavior, the professor made some comments that really bothered Hank. The professor said:

> Most managers know their functional specialty but do a lousy job of managing their people. One of the problems is that just because managers have a lot of experience with people, they think they are experts. The fact is that behavioral scientists are just beginning to scratch the surface of understanding human behavior. In addition, to effectively manage people, we also have to somehow be able to better predict and control organizational behavior. Some models are just beginning to be developed that we hope will help the manager better understand, predict, and manage organizational behavior.

Hank is upset by the fact that his professor apparently discounts the value of experience in managing people, and he cannot see how a conceptual framework that some professor dreamed up can help him manage people better.

1. Do you think Hank is justified in his concerns after hearing the professor? What role can experience play in managing people?
2. What is the purpose of conceptual frameworks such as those presented in this chapter? How would you weigh the relative value of studying theories and research findings versus "school-of-hard-knocks" experience for the effective management of people?
3. Using the conceptual framework presented in the chapter, how would you explain to Hank that this could help him better manage people in his organization?

2

Emerging Organizations: Information-Based, Total Quality, and Organizational Learning

---

Learning Objectives

- **Examine** the impact that information technology has on emerging organizations.
- **Analyze** the total quality approach and specific popular techniques, such as reengineering and benchmarking.
- **Discuss** the role being played by empowerment in today's organizations.
- **Describe** the meaning, characteristics, and actual practices of newly emerging learning organizations.

Today's organizational environment is proving to be markedly different from that of the past. As pointed out in the opening chapter, global competition, information technology, the quality service revolution, and diversity and ethics are forcing management of all types of organizations to totally rethink their approach to both operations and human resources. As a result of this paradigm shift, new organizations are emerging that are more responsive to both their internal and external environments. These emerging organizations are characterized by state-of-the-art information technology, total quality management practices, and organizational learning. This chapter examines these new paradigm organizations.

THE ROLE OF INFORMATION TECHNOLOGY

Over the past ten years there have been dramatic changes in information technology.[1] These changes have ranged from new products such as cellular phones that allow managers to stay in touch with their field personnel no matter where they are, to computers that can handle inventory control and help employees communicate with each other via electronic mail, to compact disks that are able to store and retrieve billions of pieces of information.[2] This information technology has had a dramatic impact on overall organization structure and has been carried down to the redesign of individuals' jobs. Good examples are provided by electronic mail, electronic data interchanges, and neural networks, which are affecting both the organization's design and the way in which individual employees carry out their assigned tasks. The following sections examine these organizational changes.

The Flattening and Downsizing of Organizations

Information technology has led to the flattening and downsizing of today's organizations. For example, electronic mail (E-mail) allows everyone to communicate directly with everyone else, thus eliminating the need for levels of bureaucracy and a long chain of command. In other words, the organization becomes flatter. Additionally, since multiple copies of E-mail letters and memos can now be electronically transmitted in a matter of seconds to a large number of people, the need for "information switchers," "number crunchers," and "paper pushers" is eliminated. E-mail has prompted organizations to replace people with technology. In other words, the organization is able to downsize.

Downsizing (or "right sizing," a supposedly more humanistic term) is the process of reducing the number of people in the organization. In the 1980s, the greatest impact of downsizing was on operating-level employees; great numbers of auto, steel, and other manufacturing workers were permanently eliminated. In the 1990s, downsizing has been at the middle management levels, where information technology has eliminated many jobs that were traditionally staffed by middle managers. For example, at firms such as IBM, General Motors, and Xerox, many operating and middle management positions were eliminated. In the five-year period 1987–1992, companies with 500 or more employees recorded a net loss of 2.3 million jobs.[3] The result of this downsizing has been a flattening of the structure.

A Paperless Revolution

Besides the impact on organization structure, information technology has also had a dramatic effect on the way business is conducted in today's organizations. A good example is electronic data interchange. EDI (electronic data interchange) is a process by which customers, suppliers, and manufacturers can communicate directly on a computer-to-computer basis. This information technology has become a major force in creating what is now often called the "paperless revolution." Written sales and order forms are being eliminated, information is being entered directly into computers, and these machines are being programmed to interpret information and make decisions. As a result, EDI has eliminated some jobs, totally revamped other jobs, reduced operating time, empowered employees, and increased both productivity and profit. Here is an example of a company that has applied EDI to "go paperless":

> Two years ago, Connecticut Mutual Life Insurance Co. was drowning in a sea of paper. When one of its 1.2 million policyholders had a problem, someone at the Hartford Company often had to call for a file that was stored in a warehouse the size of a football field. Vans stuffed with paper shuttled between the office and warehouse every hour. Simple changes to a policy "could take weeks," says Senior Vice-President Jan L. Scites. Today, visitors to Connecticut Mutual might wonder whether it's still in the insurance business. Customer reps sit at IBM PCs, where they call up all the necessary forms and correspondence—converted into electronic forms—to answer most questions. The upshot: Response to queries is down from five days to a few hours, 20% fewer people are involved, and productivity is up more than 35%. Scites says: "That has given us an enormous competitive advantage."[4]

Many other organizations, such as Wal-Mart, General Electric, the Internal Revenue Service (IRS), and Sears, are also going paperless using EDI. At Wal-Mart all orders are placed electronically and computers help the firm manage inventory. When reorders are necessary, the machines automatically place these orders by sending electronic messages to supplier computers. General Electric uses a similar approach in dealing with its own suppliers and is currently halfway to its goal of handling 80 percent of all business transactions through direct EDI links. The IRS currently processes almost 2 billion pieces of paper annually and has launched an $8 billion program designed to make the agency "nearly paperless" by the end of this century. In 1992 the IRS electronically processed 11 million tax returns. The agency's objective for the year 2000: electronically process 100 million returns. At the same time the IRS intends to reduce return-processing time to two weeks from the current six weeks and to make old returns available instantly to taxpayers, a process which currently takes up to ten weeks. At Sears Roebuck's Discovery Card unit it used to take an average of six forms and fourteen days to sign up a new merchant. Now a portable computer is used to enter the information and a central mainframe helps a team of workers complete the approval cycle in just one day.[5]

Mimicking Brains

Another information technology breakthrough that is now beginning to change the way people do their jobs is neural networks, which are a combination of computer software and chips that are capable of mimicking brain functions.[6] These "brain" networks are currently regarded as one of the most important forms of emerging information technology, and they are going to have an impact on the way work is done now and in the coming years.

At the present time, neural networks are being used to supplement decision making in a wide variety of areas. For example, the Mellon Bank's Visa and Master-Card operation in Wilmington, Delaware, keeps daily track of 1.2 million accounts. One of the functions of this operation's computer is to scan customer purchases and look for spending patterns that may indicate stolen credit cards. Typical examples include large cash withdrawals or the purchase of expensive jewelry. With its previous computer program, the computer would spot 1000 potential defrauders each day. This number was so large that the bank's fraud investigators could not effectively follow up on all the potential leads. Now Mellon has put in a neural computer network, which is more sophisticated and better able to compare purchases with customer behaviors. As a result, the network now flags only 100 potential defrauders a day, a number that the investigators are able to handle effectively. Moreover, neural network systems are able to generate data without being told to do so because the system has been programmed to think like a human and take the initiative. When card thieves and counterfeiters recently began using a new ploy to test whether a card had been reported stolen, they began making $1 transactions. The neural network immediately picked up this purchase behavior and flagged the cards for the investigators. The bank estimates that the network paid for itself within six months.

These systems are being used for many other jobs as well. For example, Signet Bank of Glen Allen, Virginia, uses a neural network to process canceled checks and perform other optical character recognition chores. IBM France uses neural network software to provide early-warning failure in industrial machinery such as motors, cleaning tools, and pneumatic robots. The Fidelity Equity Fund employs a neural network to analyze and pick stock investments.

Today most neural nets take the form of mathematical simulations embedded in software that runs on ordinary microprocessors. The future will see the emergence of new network chips that will dramatically increase both the speed of operations and their work applications. In particular, these chips will be used to mimic operations and carry them out the way humans do. Here is what one observer recently had to say about the future of this information technology:

> Neural nets are still in their infancy, but some are already Wunderkinder. One example: a self-training robot that swings from bar to bar in the lab much as a monkey or a gibbon swings from branch to branch in the jungle. It can take as many as 200 tries for the robot to learn a new routine. As it learns, the robot often falls ignominiously, but once it masters the complex underhand and overhand moves through trial and error, it executes them with panache. The robot's developer, Toshio Fukuda of Nagoya University in Japan, says that one day such self-teaching robots might serve as workers on skyscraper construction sites, inside hazardous plants, and anywhere else that's dangerous.[7]

Neural networks will also allow computers to fly airplanes, run factories, hear, speak, and respond to commands. Like other forms of information technology, they will change the workplace in terms of both how people carry out their jobs and the ways in which they coordinate these tasks with other personnel. Information technology is also being closely linked to total quality efforts in today's and tomorrow's organizations.

TOTAL QUALITY MANAGEMENT

Total quality management, or simply TQM, is a widely publicized approach that focuses on trying to meet or exceed customer expectations. Through the years TQM has meant different things to different people and has been both "cussed" and discussed in the management literature and the actual practice of management. After the overall meaning of TQM is presented, the techniques especially relevant to organizational behavior (reengineering, benchmarking, and empowerment) are discussed.

What Is TQM?

Obviously, there are many definitions and connotations associated with TQM. Practically every management author, consultant, or practitioner has a different meaning for TQM.[8] One of the most comprehensive definitions is that TQM is an organizational strategy with accompanying techniques that deliver quality products and/or services to customers. In other words, from this perspective TQM is an organizational strategy, not just another technique. TQM is the way the organization is managed, not just something in addition to everything else. However, the definition does point out that there are TQM techniques that are employed to help *deliver* (the key word in TQM implementation) quality service to customers. To gain a depth of understanding of TQM, it would be helpful to examine each letter in the acronym for further refinement and expansion.

The "Total" Perspective of TQM. The "total" part of TQM differentiates the approach from the traditional inspection, quality control, or quality assurance approach. TQM is an overall organizational strategy that is formulated at the top management level and then is diffused throughout the entire organization. Everyone in the organization, from the general manager/CEO to the lowest-paid hourly workers and clerks, is involved in the TQM process.

The total part of TQM also encompasses not only the external end user and purchaser of the product or service, but also internal customers and outside suppliers and support personnel. This is how TQM differs from a traditional customer service orientation. Under TQM, not only the "Customer Is King" (as in Wal-Mart), but so are internal customers such as coworkers or other departments. Everyone who gives or passes on anything in the organization is a supplier, and anyone who receives anything from anyone in the organization is an internal customer. The same is true for external suppliers and support personnel such as those in maintenance; they are also a vital, integral part of the TQM approach. If suppliers and external support personnel do not deliver quality, then the organization cannot deliver quality to its customers.

In essence, TQM becomes the dominant culture of the organization. Some of the core values for everyone in the total quality organization might include the following:

1. Make it right for the customer at any cost.
2. Internal customers are as important as external customers.
3. Respond to every customer inquiry or complaint by the end of the day.
4. Answer the phone within two rings.
5. The customer is always right.
6. Not only meet customers' expectations, but delight the customers in the process.
7. Teamwork and cooperation are more important than individual action and gamesmanship.
8. Everyone is involved in the quality effort; no exceptions or bench sitting is allowed.
9. Respond to every employee suggestion for quality improvement within one week.
10. Never be satisfied with the level of quality; always strive for continuous improvement.

In order for TQM to become more than "just talk," the representative core values above cannot be just shallow, "gimmicky" slogans. All organizations have had quality slogans for years. But those slogans were just that; the organizations did not deliver on the quality promise. In fact, the slogans often raised the expectations of customers, and when the organizations did not deliver as promised, there were bigger problems than if there had been no slogan at all. In their well-known book *Service America*, Albrecht and Zemke conclude after considerable study that there is really no relationship between slogans and quality service.[9] The key is that there must be cultural values for quality, not just empty slogans. Cultural values must be accepted by the employees and drive their behavior to actually deliver quality to customers.

What Does "Quality" Stand for in TQM? When most people think of quality, they conjure up an image of defect-free products such as automobiles or electronic goods. In TQM, quality does mean no-defect products, but also much more. In fact, in terms of relative importance, TQM is more concerned with quality service than it is with quality products. This emphasis on service is a result of the growing importance in the postindustrial society of the service sector, which doesn't produce any products per se. However, even traditional goods-producing companies under a TQM approach become service companies, providing service to their customers.

Counting defects is an easy way to operationalize quality under the old product-oriented approach, but how is quality operationalized in the new service orientation? It has become widely recognized that under TQM, quality is operationally defined as meeting or exceeding customer expectations. Thus, quality is defined by the customer, not the organization or the manager or the quality control/assurance department. The service (or product) must meet or exceed what the customer wants or expects. These customer expectations are highly individualized by age, gender, personality, occupation, location, socioeconomic class, past experience with the organization, and many other variables. In other words, what is quality for one customer may not be quality for another customer. A challenge for TQM is to deliver quality to all customers.

What Is the "Management" Dimension in TQM? The "M" in TQM implies that this is a management approach, not just a narrow quality control or quality assurance function. Someone from the quality control function may head up and coordinate the TQM effort, but to get away from this more traditional, limited perspective, it would be more appropriate for someone from another department, someone who is respected and is a good communicator and "doer," to be the TQM project manager. This manager ideally should not only thoroughly understand and be able to train others in TQM, but also be a strong advocate and report directly to the general manager/CEO. However, it should be remembered, as discussed in the "total" section above, that everyone in the organization is involved in TQM, not just the project head. In other words, TQM is a very people-oriented approach and has many implications for the study and application of organizational behavior.

An example of how TQM relates to organizational behavior is provided by Figure 2.1, which details the criteria for winning the Baldrige, a total quality award that is given annually by the U.S. government to those applicant firms in small business, manufacturing, and services that have been judged to have the highest quality. While the Baldrige is only one of many awards that are given for quality, the criteria framework in the figure helps point out the important role that the human side plays in TQM. In particular, everyone in the organization must be involved in the process, there must be clear leadership provided by upper-level management, and all employees must feel a sense of ownership in order to obtain their commitment to the total quality management effort.[10] Three popular TQM techniques that are especially relevant to organizational behavior are reengineering, benchmarking, and empowerment.

Reengineering

According to Hammer and Champy in their best-selling book, *reengineering* is "the fundamental rethinking and radical redesign of business processes to achieve dramatic improvements in critical, contemporary measures of performance, such as cost, quality, service, and speed."[11] Many TQM approaches are designed to increase efficiency by streamlining current operations. Reengineering, however, involves a total redesign of operations by analyzing jobs and asking, How can this work be done most efficiently? Rather than modifying current work procedures, the reengineering process begins with a clean slate and plans the job from beginning to end.

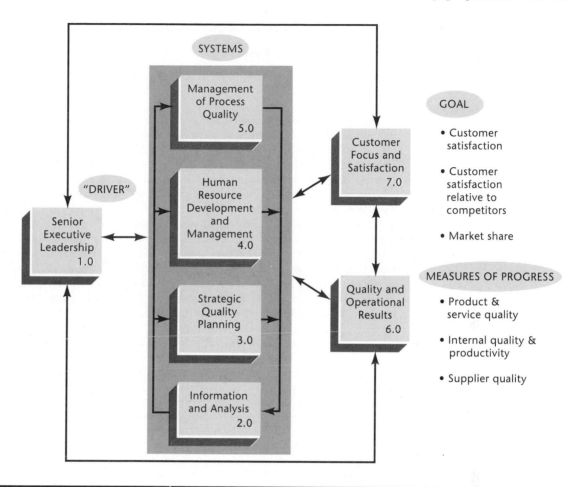

SYSTEMS

Management of Process Quality
5.0

GOAL

• Customer satisfaction

• Customer satisfaction relative to competitors

• Market share

"DRIVER"

Human Resource Development and Management
4.0

Customer Focus and Satisfaction
7.0

Senior Executive Leadership
1.0

Strategic Quality Planning
3.0

MEASURES OF PROGRESS

• Product & service quality

• Internal quality & productivity

• Supplier quality

Quality and Operational Results
6.0

Information and Analysis
2.0

FIGURE 2.1

Baldrige award criteria framework.

(*Source*: Information supplied by the U.S. Department of Commerce.)

Unsaddled with previous work procedures and rules, reengineering allows the organization to eliminate inefficiencies and increase productivity.

Although there are many different approaches, reengineering can be broken down into several steps. The goal of these steps is to improve efficiency and performance. Under the reengineered process, employees must become part of and must be trained in the new way of carrying out tasks. The first step of this process begins with top management's rethinking the basic mission of the organization and clearly deciding what business they are really in and what they want to be in. This step provides direction for the reengineering effort and ensures that the effort is not wasted on operations that will soon be discarded because they do not fit with the organization's mission. Second, top management will play an active role in leading the process, thus ensuring overall cooperation from the personnel. Third, management will create a sense of urgency among the personnel regarding the need for reengineering, thus ensuring their commitment and effort. Fourth, operations will be designed from the outside in by first finding out what the customer wants or needs and then creating the structure and teamwork for providing it. A final step will involve top-down and bottom-up initiatives, so that support for the reengineering process will extend the length and breadth of the organization.[12]

There are a number of examples of successful reengineering efforts. One was at Ford Motor's purchasing department, where 500 clerks spent the majority of their

TQM in Action

Reengineering for Profit

A number of firms have successfully applied reengineering to parts of their business and ended up with greater efficiency and profit. IBM Credit and Kodak are two examples.

IBM Credit is a wholly owned subsidiary of IBM and, if it were independent, would rank as one of the largest service companies in the country. Before undertaking a reengineering effort, IBM Credit's operations had many bureaucratic rules and procedures. When IBM salespeople called in a request for credit, they would reach one of fourteen people at the credit center, who would log the request. From here, there were a series of specialists who would each play a role in processing the credit request. Typically, it would take from six days to two weeks to get final approval. Upon analysis, IBM found that there was only ninety minutes of work involved in processing these requests. The rest of the time was spent moving the request through channels, where it would rest on the next person's desk. This credit process was reengineered by replacing the current group of specialists with a team of generalists, each of whom would see a credit request all the way through the system. As a result, the time needed to process requests was cut from six days to four hours, there was a slight reduction in the number of people working in the department, and there was an increase in the number of deals being handled by a multiple of 100.

In another example, Kodak has used reengineering to reduce the time needed to bring products to market. This began when the company's archrival, the Japanese firm Fuji, announced a new 35mm, single-use camera, which allows the customer to buy the unit loaded with film, use it once, and then return it to the manufacturer, who processes the film and breaks down the camera into parts for reuse. Kodak had no competitive offering, and its traditional product design process would have taken seventy weeks to produce a rival camera.

In the past Kodak had developed new products by using a combination of sequential development (one step at a time) and parallel development (people working on a number of steps in the process at the same time), but even this approach was slow. So Kodak reengineered its product development process through the innovative use of computer-aided design and computer-aided manufacturing. Teams of developmental people worked independently on their respective parts of the new camera, designing their input at computer workstations. Then each day the computer database would combine all the individual efforts into a coherent whole. Each morning design groups and individuals would inspect the database to see if any of the previous day's work created a problem for the overall design. If it did, the problem was resolved immediately. This redesigned work approach, called concurrent engineering, not only eliminated the common problems associated with independent work teams' having to coordinate their efforts, but, with the innovative use of technology, permitted manufacturing engineers to begin to design ten weeks into the development process. As a result, it took Kodak only thirty-eight weeks to develop a single-use camera, almost half the time it would have traditionally taken.

time handling accounts payable involving purchase orders, invoices, and other documents. In contrast, Mazda, the huge Japanese competitor that Ford looked into, had only five people in its purchasing department. Realizing that it would have to rethink the entire process by which accounts payable were handled, Ford undertook a reengineering effort. Today at Ford, purchasing supplies and materials is handled completely differently from the way it was in the past. Accounts payable personnel no longer match purchase orders with receiving documents because this step has been totally eliminated. Now when a purchase order is issued to a vendor, that buyer simultaneously enters the order into an on-line database. Then, when the goods are received at Ford, a person in receiving will check a computer terminal to ensure that the shipment corresponds to the purchase order in the database. If it does, the employee will enter this information into the database and the computer will automatically issue and send a check to the supplier. If it does not, the employee is empowered to refuse the shipment and the goods will be returned to the supplier.

Another example of reengineering is provided by Wal-Mart, which worked with Procter & Gamble (P&G) to reengineer the management of its Pampers diapers inventory system. Initially, Wal-Mart would warehouse the diapers at its distribution centers and fill store orders from these centers. When the distribution centers began to run low, Wal-Mart would then reorder from P&G. Realizing that P&G knew Wal-Mart's needs for the product, Wal-Mart reengineered the purchasing and warehouse functions and gave P&G authority to ship diapers directly to the stores. This new approach allowed P&G greater control over the production and shipment of the diapers and saved Wal-Mart the cost of ordering and centrally storing the diapers. As a result of the reengineering effort, both companies were able to save thousands of dollars annually. Other examples are provided in the accompanying TQM in Action: Reengineering for Profit.

Benchmarking

Besides the popular reengineering technique associated with TQM, other techniques, such as benchmarking, are also receiving attention. *Benchmarking* is the process of comparing work and service methods against the best practices and outcomes for the purpose of identifying changes that will result in higher-quality output. Benchmarking incorporates the use of human resources techniques such as goal setting to set targets that are pursued, identified, and then used as a basis for future action. The benchmarking process involves looking both inside and outside the organization for ways of improving the operation.

Benchmarking offers a number of benefits to organizations.[13] First, this technique helps organizations compare themselves against successful companies for the purpose of identifying improvement strategies. Second, benchmarking enables organizations to learn from others. Third, it helps create a need for change by showing the organization how procedures and work assignments should be altered and resources reallocated. There are a wide variety of examples in which benchmarking has helped organizations improve their total quality.

Some organizations use benchmarking at the very start of projects so that all planning and organizing efforts are conducted in light of state-of-the-art developments in the industry. This strategy typically begins with the formation of a team that defines the project's goals and carefully identifies the areas in which benchmarking will be used. In the case of new-product development, for example, IBM Rochester gathered a team of technical and marketing people to create a new minicomputer, the AS/400. During this process, the IBM Rochester group looked both in-house and at a variety of outside firms in order to gain insights into how to build the highest-quality minicomputer in the shortest amount of time. In-house they examined IBM Raleigh, which had a world-class defect prevention process, and IBM Manassas, which had outstanding hardware process documentation. The outside companies it benchmarked were (1) Xerox, from which it learned about the benchmarking process in general; (2) Motorola, which provided information on reducing quality defects; (3) 3M, which provided information that helped IBM Rochester's resource manufacturing planning capability; (4) Hewlett-Packard, which provided insights into the effective use of service representatives; and (5) Japanese firms, from which the company learned a great deal about just-in-time inventory.[14]

As a result of its benchmarking efforts, IBM Rochester was able to produce a minicomputer that exceeded all expectations. Within sixty days of the product launch, the company reached its annual sales projections for Europe, and at the end of eighteen months, the company had sold over 100,000 units, in a market that was growing at only 4 percent annually. By this time IBM Rochester had become a $14 billion business, the eighty-fifth largest global company in the world. As a result, the AS/400 was the most successful new computer introduction in IBM history.

Other organizations use benchmarking in carrying out their day-to-day activities. Common examples include developing benchmarking strategies to reduce manufacturing setup time, increase the number of customers served per hour, and cut delivery time. Benchmarking is also being used in training and development to create programs that are cost-effective and ensure that the personnel are performing their jobs as well as anyone else in the industry. This human resources focus is a new twist in benchmarking, but one that will be receiving increased attention during the years ahead. A good example is provided by Magnavox.[15]

All division managers at Magnavox were recently asked to provide annual training cost data to the corporate human resources (HR) department. The HR department quickly realized that there was no uniform thinking among the divisions regarding how to define training costs. Some divisions counted only direct costs, such as labor, materials, and outside consulting fees. Others included the wages of all participants and support personnel. The HR people then set about determining how to measure these costs uniformly and how to use this information to benchmark against other firms. In all, there were fourteen training measures or what they call metrics (see Table 2.1). In each case the company identified the specific metric, how it was to be calculated, and an example of how other firms were doing in this area.

As seen in Table 2.1, the company examined data for both the United States at large as well as from Baldrige winners in particular. The latter data were obtained from a survey questionnaire, a common method of benchmarking. As a result of this project, Magnavox is now able to track (1) the percent of payroll that is spent on training; (2) the percent of the work force that receives training; (3) the average percent of improvement in on-the-job performance as a result of training; (4) the amount of money that training saves the organization; and (5) the productivity and efficiency of its human resource development staff.

Empowerment

Empowerment is even more directly tied to the study and application of organizational behavior than is reengineering or benchmarking. *Empowerment* is the authority to make decisions within one's area of operations without having to get approval from anyone else. While this process is similar to that of delegated authority, there are two characteristics that make empowerment unique. One is that the personnel are encouraged to use their initiative and, as they say at Cummins Engine, "just do it."[16] The second is that employees are given not just authority but resources as well, so that they are able to make a decision and see that it is implemented. For example, if a customer calls and says that the cellular phone she ordered arrived this morning but it does not work, an empowered employee would be able to ship her a new one by overnight delivery and have the first unit picked up and returned to the firm. The

TABLE 2.1 Benchmarking Applied to Human Resource Development (HRD) Activities at Magnavox

Metric Name	Metric Type	How to Calculate	Example
Percent of payroll spent on training	Training Activity	Total training expenditures ÷ total payroll	U.S. average = 1.4 percent of payroll spent on training per year.
Training dollars spent per employee	Training Activity	Total training expenditures ÷ total employees served	Three Baldrige winners spent $1,100 per employee on training in 1990.
Average training hours per employee	Training Activity	Total number of training hours (hours × participants) ÷ total employees served	U.S. average for large firms (100 + employees) = 33 hours per employee in 1990.
Percent of employees trained per year	Training Activity	Total number of employees receiving training ÷ total employee population	Three Baldrige winners trained an average of 92.5 percent of their workforces in 1990.
HRD staff per 1,000 employees	Training Activity	Number of HRD staff ÷ total employee population × 1,000	Three Baldrige winners had an average of 4.1 HRD staff members per 1,000 employees.
Average percent of positive participant ratings per year	Training Results: Reactions	Total number of employees rating courses "good" or "effective" ÷ total number of employees who completed course surveys per year	Three Baldrige winners averaged 93 percent positive participant course ratings in 1990.
Average percent of satisfied HRD customers	Training Results: Reactions	Total number of customers rating HRD services "good" or "effective" ÷ total number of customers who completed customer-satisfaction surveys	Three Baldrige winners averaged 84 percent positive HRD customer-service ratings in 1990.
Average percent gain in learning per course	Training Results: Learning	Average percent of learning gain (difference between pre- and posttest) for each class, averaged over all classes tested	Three Baldrige winners averaged 70 percent learning gain in more than 50 technical classes in 1990.
Average percent of improvement in on-the-job performance after training, per course	Training Results: Behavior	Average job-performance gain (difference between pre- and post-training behavior) for each class, averaged over all classes measured	An electronics firm reported 49 percent improvement in management ratings after supervisor training in 1990.
Cost savings as a ratio of training expenses	Training Results: Bottom-Line	Total savings in scrap or waste ÷ dollars invested in training	A Baldrige winner reported saving $30 for every $1 spent on TQM training (for an ROI of 30:1).
Revenues per employee per year	Training Results: Bottom-Line	Total yearly revenues or sales ÷ total number of employees	Two Baldrige winners reported average revenues per employee of $94,000 in 1990.
Profits per employee per year	Training Results: Bottom-Line	Total yearly gross profits ÷ total number of employees	An electronics firm earned average profits per employee of $21,000 in 1990.
Training costs per student hour	Training Efficiency	Total costs of training ÷ total number of hours of training	Three Baldrige winners reported $27 in average training costs per hour of training in 1990.
Billable rate (time on task)	Training Efficiency	HRD staff time spent on billable or key tasks ÷ total HRD staff time	An electronics firm reported an HRD billable rate of .82 in 1991 (82 percent of staff time spent on billable tasks).

Source: Donald J. Ford, "Benchmarking HRD," *Training and Development Journal*, June 1993, p. 39. Copyright June 1993, the American Society for Training and Development. Reprinted with permission. All rights reserved.

person would be able to authorize payment for these services because the company will have given the individual a sum of money that can be used in any way the employee feels is necessary to ensure customer service. The TQM in Action: Just Doing It provides some specific examples of how Baldrige-winning companies apply this idea.

**TQM
in Action**

Just Doing It

Empowerment involves both giving employees the authority to make decisions and providing them with the financial resources to implement these decisions. For example, at the Ritz-Carlton hotel chain, employees are authorized to spend up to $2000 to handle a customer-related problem. This amount is usually more than sufficient for such common solutions as mailing a shirt to a guest who checked out and accidentally left a shirt or blouse in the room or bringing a guest with a cold a pot of herbal tea and some aspirin. At Zytec, a Minnesota-based designer and supplier of electronic equipment, employees can spend up to $1000 on customer service-related matters. When this sum of money is depleted, the personnel are given another $1000, and this continues indefinitely. So the funds are really continuous and are available to handle all customer-related needs.

At AT&T Universal Card Services, employees are put into teams that plan strategies for improving customer service. These teams identify "top 10" problems and then formulate strategies for dealing with them. When a particular customer service problem is solved, it is removed from the top 10 list and another is put in its place. In attacking these problems, team members are empowered to make those decisions that will reduce costs and increase customer delight (one of the company's primary objectives).

At Solectron, a small manufacturer of complex circuit boards and subsystems for computers and other electronic products, line workers are empowered to stop the production line any time they feel it is necessary. Meanwhile, customer service employees have full authority to return or replace products without getting approval from their boss; and manufacturing employees are trained to use statistical process control techniques and make whatever decisions they feel are justified based on their findings. Additionally, engineers and sales representatives are trained to interact effectively with customers and to make whatever decisions are needed to satisfy customer requirements.

At Motorola, empowered teams are given authority to carry out a wide array of functions, including creating production schedules and job assignments, setting up equipment and conducting routine maintenance, developing and managing budgets, and training new employees. In handling customer-related problems, the employees are provided funds that they can spend as they deem appropriate. In some cases, Motorola personnel are authorized to go as high as $5000 and these monies are replaced on a daily basis.

There are several basic conditions necessary for empowerment to become embedded in the organizational culture and become operational: participation, innovation, access to information, and accountability.[17]

Participation. Empowerment assumes that employees are willing to improve their daily work processes and relationships. On a positive note, a recent survey conducted by Brookings International reveals that 93 percent of American workers do feel personally responsible for organizational quality and performance. The problem for many organizations is that of reducing the bureaucratic red tape that prevents the employees from seizing the initiative. Additionally, many companies are now discovering that empowerment training can be extremely useful in teaching the employees how to participate more actively and make things happen.

A good example is provided by the chemical division of Georgia-Pacific, where a quality and environmental assurance supervisor and a plant operator who had both received empowerment training began sharing ideas for more effectively preparing test samples of a certain chemical. Once they finalized their ideas, they used their empowerment status to produce a demonstration video. After seeing the video, management asked the two employees to share the tape with quality assurance supervisors in other plants. In turn, the supervisor and operator encouraged these other employees to provide feedback on the video and to share their own ideas. As a result, a more efficient system of preparing test samples was developed company-wide.

Innovation. Empowerment encourages innovation because employees have the authority to try out new ideas and make decisions that result in new ways of doing things. In one major consumer goods company, two engineers used their empowered authority to design and test a new household product. After spending over $25,000 on the project, they realized that the product did not perform up to expectations. The design was faulty and performance was poor. The next day the president of the company sent for both of them. When they entered the executive office, they found they were guests of honor at a party. The president quickly explained that he appreciated all their efforts, and even though they were not successful, he was sure they would be in the future. By encouraging their innovative effort through empowerment, the president helped ensure that these two employees would continue to bring new ideas to the market.

Access to Information. When employees are given access to information, their willingness to cooperate and to use their empowerment is enhanced. At firms such as General Mills, self-managed work teams are given any information they need to do their jobs and improve their productivity. This includes information as far-ranging as profit and loss statements, manufacturing processes, and purchasing procedures. In addition, if employees want additional training, even if it is peripheral to their main jobs, it is provided to them. As a result of this accessibility, work teams are able to manage and control operations more effectively than under the old hierarchical rules and structure where access to information was provided on a need-to-know basis.

Accountability. Although employees are empowered to make decisions they believe will be most beneficial to the organization, they are also held accountable for results. However, this accountability is not intended to punish personnel or to generate immediate, short-term results. Instead, the intent is to ensure that the empowered employees are giving their best efforts, working toward agreed-upon goals, and behaving responsibly toward each other. If these behaviors are exhibited, then management continues to empower employees to proceed at their own pace and in their own way.

Putting Empowerment into Action

There are a number of ways that organizations go about implementing empowerment. One of the most common is to tie the technique to an action-driven approach. For example, Cummins Engine provides a five-day training program that combines empowerment with *kaizen* (a Japanese term that means "continuous improvement") and a series of what Cummins calls "just do it" principles. These principles or operational guidelines include: (a) discard conventional, fixed ideas about doing work; (b) think about how to do it, rather than why it cannot be done; (c) start by questioning current practices; (d) begin to make improvements immediately, even if only 50 percent of them can be completed; and (e) correct mistakes immediately.[18]

The first day of the Cummins empowerment training program begins with a discussion of what *kaizen* and "just do it" (JDIT) principles are all about. Participants learn about the need for teamwork and the use of group problem solving. The second day is spent applying these ideas to a work area where improvement is needed. Cross-functional JDIT teams of three to five people are sent to the work floor to observe, document, and evaluate work practices. The third day is used to implement the ideas that were identified and evaluated on the work floor. The next day is spent evaluating the improvements that have been initiated and making any final changes so that the new way of doing the work is more efficient than the previous way. The last day of the program is devoted to making a presentation on the results to an audience of managers, explaining the changes that were made and the results that were obtained.

Although empowerment implementation programs will vary, they are all based on a careful evaluation of the benefits and drawbacks of the process and the degree to which the organization is prepared to accept these ideas. Some enterprises, for example, have found that a high degree of empowerment works extremely well, while others have discovered that their organizations operate most efficiently with much less use of empowerment. To account for these differences, Bowen and Lawler have suggested that organizations first identify at which of four levels of empowerment they should operate: (1) very little involvement, as reflected by traditional production line firms; (2) moderate involvement, as reflected by organizations that employ suggestion programs and quality circles; (3) fairly substantial involvement, as reflected in organizations where jobs are designed so that employees can use a variety of skills and have a great deal of autonomy in carrying out their jobs; and (4) high involvement, as reflected by organizations in which the personnel throughout share information and work together to solve problems and complete tasks.[19] Table 2.2 illustrates how an analysis of these ideas can be evaluated and used to determine the degree of empowerment that is most effective for the organization.

TABLE 2.2 A Contingency Approach to Using Empowerment

Contingency Considerations	Little Empowerment	Score	Total Empowerment
Basic strategy	Low cost, high volume	1 2 3 4 5	Differentiated, personalized approach
Relationship to customer	Short-term	1 2 3 4 5	Long-term
Technology	Simple, routine	1 2 3 4 5	Complex, nonroutine
Environment	Stable, predictable	1 2 3 4 5	Dynamic, unpredictable
Type of personnel	Moderate to low growth needs, social skills, and interpersonal skills	1 2 3 4 5	High growth needs, social skills, and interpersonal skills

Scoring: Evaluate each contingency consideration on the 1-to-5 scale, and total the overall score.

Interpretation: A production-line approach is a good fit with situations that score in the 5–10 range; suggestion involvement is good for scores in the 11–15 range; job involvement with scores in the 16–20 range; and high involvement with scores in the 21–25 range.

Source: Adapted from David E. Bowen and Edward E. Lawler, "The Empowerment of Service Workers: What, Why, How, and When," *Sloan Management Review*, Spring 1992, pp. 36–39. Used with permission.

This type of contingency approach should be supplemented by a careful analysis of the benefits and drawbacks associated with empowerment. Some of the most commonly cited benefits include (1) more rapid response to customer needs; (2) reduction in the time needed to provide goods and services; (3) increased employee satisfaction with their jobs; (4) establishment of rapport between employees and customers; (5) generation of more and better employee ideas regarding how to improve the actual delivery of quality goods and services; and (6) greater retention of customer loyalty. Some of the most commonly cited drawbacks include (1) greater dollar investment in selecting personnel; (2) greater investment needed in training personnel; (3) higher labor costs; (4) slower or inconsistent service delivery due to the fact that some people must wait while others receive attention; (5) customer complaints that some people get a better deal from the company than do other customers; and (6) poor use of empowerment, such as overspending on service to ensure customer satisfaction. After evaluating the pros and cons of empowerment, organizations will then determine the degree to which they will employ the approach in their total quality efforts.

LEARNING ORGANIZATIONS

Advanced information technology and total quality have almost become the cost of entry into competition in the global economy. To become successful and gain a competitive advantage, organizations today and tomorrow must become learning organizations. The remainder of this chapter on emerging organizations defines what is meant by the learning organization and gives some specific examples of the learning organization in action.

What Is Meant by a Learning Organization?

The organization portrayed as a learning system is not new. In fact, at the turn of the century Frederick W. Taylor's learnings on scientific management were said to be transferable to workers to make the organization more efficient. However, the beginning of today's use of the term "learning organization" is usually attributed to the work of Chris Argyris and his colleagues, who made the distinction between first-order, or "single-loop," and second-order, or dentero or "double-loop," learning.[20] The differences between these two types of learning applied to organizations can be summarized as follows:

1. Single-loop learning involves improving the organization's capacity to achieve known objectives. It is associated with routine and behavioral learning. Under single-loop, the organization is learning without significant change in its basic assumptions.
2. Double-loop learning reevaluates the nature of the organization's objectives and the values and beliefs surrounding them. This type of learning involves changing the organization's culture. Importantly, double-loop consists of the organization's learning how to learn.[21]

More recently, Peter Senge and his colleagues have characterized the learning organization from a systems theory perspective and have made the important distinction between adaptive and generative learning.[22] The simpler adaptive learning is only the first stage of the learning organization, adapting to environmental changes.

In recent years, General Motors, IBM, and Sears have had many adaptive changes, but they experienced much difficulty under their basic assumptions, cultural values, and organization structure.[23] They did not go beyond mere adaptive learning. The more important generative learning was needed. Generative learning involves creativity and innovation, going beyond just adapting to change to being ahead of and anticipating change. The generative process leads to a total reframing of an organization's experiences and learning from that process.

Types of Learning Organizations

Table 2.3 differentiates four types of learning organizations. The "knowing organization" is the oldest model and the examples are some of the best-known companies. They are single-loop, or adaptive, and can be successful as long as their market remains relatively mature and static. In the words of McGill and Slocum, "knowing organizations can be successful so long as they don't *need* to learn. Real learning would require managers to give up control, predictability, and efficiency, and to open the organization up to an examination of its own experience."[24]

The "understanding" and "thinking" organizations summarized in Table 2.3 are sort of "mid-range" learning organizations. The true, double-loop, generative learning organization model on the far right is most distinctive by its approach to

TABLE 2.3 Types of Learning Organizations

	Knowing	Understanding	Thinking	Learning
Philosophy	Dedication to the one best way: • Predictable • Controlled • Efficient	Dedication to strong cultural values that guide strategy and action. Belief in the "ruling myth."	A view of business as a series of problems. If it's broke, fix it fast.	Examining, enhancing, and improving every business experience, including how we experience.
Management Practices	Maintain control through rules and regulations, "by the book."	Clarify, communicate, reinforce the company culture.	Identify and isolate problems, collect data, implement solutions.	Encourage experiments, facilitate examination, promote constructive dissent, model learning, acknowledge failures.
Employees	Follow the rules; don't ask why.	Use corporate values as guides to behavior.	Enthusiastically embrace and enact programmed solutions.	Gather and use information; constructively dissent.
Customers	Must believe the company knows best.	Believe company values ensure a positive experience.	Are considered a problem to be solved.	Are part of a teaching/learning relationship, with open, continuous dialogue.
Change	Incremental, must be a fine-tuning of "the best way."	Only within the "ruling myth."	Implemented through problem-solving programs, which are seen as panaceas.	Part of the continuous process of experience-examine-hypothesize-experiment-experience.
Real-World Organization Examples	The Walt Disney Company, UPS, Toys "R" Us, Blockbuster Video, Avis, McDonald's	Bank of America, Digital Equipment, IBM, Apple, Johnson & Johnson, Procter & Gamble, Sears, GM	Foley's Department Store	Home Depot, San Diego Zoo, Sony, 3M, Wal-Mart, Heinz, Southwest Airlines, Levi Strauss, Motorola, Honda

Source: Adapted from Michael E. McGill and John W. Slocum, Jr., "Unlearning the Organization," *Organizational Dynamics*, Autumn 1993, p. 85. Reprinted, by permission of the publisher, © 1993. American Management Association, New York. All rights reserved.

change. Whereas the others adapt to change within their existing cultural values and structure, in the double-loop, generative learning organization, change itself and learning from the change are part of the cultural values and structure. As McGill and Slocum note:

> The organization's entire approach to change is one of acceptance and normalcy. Change is an input that leads to learning. By viewing each change as a hypothesis to be proven and by examining the results of each experiment, the learning organization ensures that change enhances its experience, and thus promotes learning.[25]

Organizational Behavior in the Learning Organization

Taken to a more individual employee, organizational behavior level, the adaptive learning organization would be associated with employees' reacting to environmental changes with routine, standard responses that often result in only short-run solutions. In contrast, generative learning, with its emphasis on continuous experimentation and feedback, would directly affect the way personnel go about defining and solving problems. Employees in generative learning organizations are taught how to examine the effect of their decisions and to change their behaviors as needed. A good example is provided by the highly successful Taco Bell chain, which has dramatically changed the way the managers and employees carry out their jobs.

> The selection process now focuses on hiring store managers who hold positive attitudes toward responsibility, teamwork, customer service, and sharing. . . . The role of the supervisor also changed from providing direction and control for the store managers to coaching and support. Store managers now receive training and support in communication, performance management, team building, coaching, and empowerment, and they can draw upon this training to improve their human resource skills.[26]

Learning organizations are also characterized by human-oriented cultural values such as these: (1) everyone can be a source of useful ideas, so personnel should be given access to any information that can be of value to them; (2) the people closest to the problem usually have the best ideas regarding how to solve it, so empowerment should be promoted throughout the structure; (3) learning flows up and down the hierarchy, so managers as well as employees can benefit from it; (4) new ideas are important and should be encouraged and rewarded; and (5) mistakes should be viewed as learning opportunities.[27] The last point of learning from failures is an especially important cultural value for people in the learning organization.

Learning Organizations in Action

There are a number of ways that the learning organization can be operationalized into the actual practice of management.[28] For example, managers must be receptive to new ideas and overcome the desire to closely control operations. Many organizations tend to do things the way they have done them in the past. Learning organizations break this mold and teach their people to look at things differently. For example, while the Whirlpool Corporation was able to garner a large share of the U.S. market, economic analysis revealed that future market growth would be outside the United States. In order to teach its managers to change their thinking and begin focusing worldwide, the firm held a worldwide leadership conference in Europe and established cross-national/cross-functional teams to develop and implement specific plans of action. At British Petroleum openness is promoted through an upward appraisal system in which employees evaluate their managers in a wide range of areas. This technique helps the managers rethink their leadership styles and modify them to meet the changing demands of the workplace.

Another way to operationalize the learning process in organizations is to develop systemic thinking among managers. This involves the ability to see connections between issues, events, and data as a whole rather than a series of unconnected parts. Learning organizations teach their people to identify the source of conflict they may have with other personnel, units, and departments and to negotiate and make astute trade-offs both skillfully and quickly. Managers must also learn, especially how to encourage their people to redirect their energies toward the substance of disagreements rather than toward personality clashes or political infighting. For example, at Ford, GE, and Motorola, teams of interfunctional groups work on projects, thus removing the artificial barriers between functional areas and between line and staff.

Another practice of learning organizations is to develop creativity among the personnel. Creativity is the ability to formulate unique approaches to problem solving and decision making. In generative learning organizations, creativity is most widely acknowledged as a requisite skill and ability. Two critical dimensions of creativity, which promote and help unleash creativity, are personal flexibility and a willingness to take risks. As a result, many learning organizations now teach their people how to review their current work habits and change behaviors that limit their thinking. While typical organizations focus on new ways to use old thinking, learning organizations focus on getting employees to break their operating habits and think "outside the box." A good example is found in the contrast between the American and Japanese firms in the radio industry. American firms such as RCA and Emerson believed that radios would follow the natural growth curve, eventually reaching the maturity and then decline phases of the product life cycle. Because of this thinking, these firms diverted their profits from radios to other product lines. The Japanese, on the other hand, went "outside the box" of predictable thinking and looked at creative ways that the demand for radios could increase in the future.

> Japanese radio manufacturers, most notably Sony, saw different possibilities. Believing that they could create a new market, twisting the product cycle in a new direction, they aggressively and innovatively entered the arena. They studied when, where, and how people listened to radios. From their analyses, they created a product that focused on people's needs—the Sony Walkman.[29]

Creativity also includes the willingness to accept failure. Learning organizations see failure as feedback that contributes to future creativity, and managers encourage this behavior by providing a supportive environment. A cultural value or slogan such as "ready, fire, aim" depicts such an environment.

Still another practice is the development of a sense of personal efficacy, as characterized by an awareness of personal and organizational values and a proactive approach to problem solving. In learning organizations such as Harley-Davidson, the firm clearly spells out its sense of mission and values. Then the personnel are given the opportunity to identify and examine their own values. This helps employees better understand and work into the linkage between the two. In addition, the personnel are taught to evaluate the effects of their behavior on others, so as to maximize their own effectiveness. In the process, they also learn how to solve

TABLE 2.4 Traditional Versus Learning Organizations

Function	Traditional Organizations	Learning Organizations
Determination of overall direction	Vision is provided by top management.	There is a shared vision that can emerge from many places, but top management is responsible for ensuring that this vision exists and is nurtured.
Formulation and implementation of ideas	Top management decides what is to be done, and the rest of the organization acts on these ideas.	Formulation and implementation of ideas take place at all levels of the organization.
Nature of organizational thinking	Each person is responsible for his or her own job responsibilities, and the focus is on developing individual competence.	Personnel understand their own jobs as well as the way in which their own work interrelates and influences that of other personnel.
Conflict resolution	Conflicts are resolved through the use of power and hierarchical influence.	Conflicts are resolved through the use of collaborative learning and the integration of diverse viewpoints of personnel throughout the organization.
Leadership and motivation	The role of the leader is to establish the organization's vision, provide rewards and punishments as appropriate, and maintain overall control of employee activities.	The role of the leader is to build a shared vision, empower the personnel, inspire commitment, and encourage effective decision making throughout the enterprise through the use of empowerment and charismatic leadership.

Source: Adapted from Peter M. Senge, "Transforming the Practice of Management," *Human Resource Development Quarterly*, Spring 1993, p. 9.

problems before critical situations develop. This step-by-step approach helps employees analyze and evaluate situations with a view toward both addressing problems early and preventing their recurrence.

A final practice in learning organizations is to instill a sense of empathy and sensitivity. Personnel are taught to look at interpersonal relations over a long time dimension. When managers or departments have disagreements, this conflict can result in continual problems. Learning organizations teach their personnel to repair these relationships quickly through discussions of the sources of misunderstanding, refusal to assign individual blame, mutual problem solving, and the maintenance of confidence and trust in the other party. This proactive, empathetic approach ensures that the personnel work together in dealing with organizational problems.

Senge summarizes the differences between learning organizations and traditional organizations in Table 2.4. These differences help illustrate why learning organizations are gaining in importance and why an increasing number of enterprises are now working to develop a generative learning environment. They realize the benefits that can result. The use of information technology and total quality management is important to emerging organizations, but organizational learning takes this process a necessary step further to ensure not only that organizations can compete and be successful in the fast-changing, turbulent environment, but that they can even survive.

Summary

This chapter examines the impact that information technology, total quality management, and organizational learning have on emerging organizations. Information technology, such as electronic mail, electronic data interchanges, and neural networks, is not only helping enterprises perform work faster and more efficiently, but is also leading to downsizing, flat structures, a paperless revolution, and mimicking of the human brain in making decisions. These developments have created a whole new organizational environment for the study and application of organizational behavior.

Another important development has been total quality management. This is an overall philosophy of providing customers with the highest-quality goods and services, but also uses a number of currently popular techniques, such as reengineering, benchmarking, and empowerment. Reengineering is the radical redesign of business processes to achieve dramatic improvement in critical areas of performance. Benchmarking is the process of comparing a company's work and service methods against those of other departments or organizations for the purpose of identifying changes that will result in higher-quality output. Empowerment is the authority to make decisions within one's area of operations and to use the necessary resources to implement these actions under four basic conditions: participation, innovation, access to information, and accountability. Like information technology, the total quality movement in today's organizations has considerable implications for organizational behavior.

The last part of the chapter examines the most recent development, learning organizations. These emerging organizations are characterized by the use of double-loop, generative learning. They go beyond merely adapting to change; instead, they strive to anticipate and learn from change. Some of the common operational practices in learning organizations dealing with people are openness, systemic thinking, creativity, awareness of personal and organizational values, empathy, and sensitivity. Learning organizations constitute the future environment for the study and application of organizational behavior.

Questions for Discussion and Review

1. In what way is information technology playing a major role in today's and tomorrow's emerging organizations? Give examples.
2. How can reengineering help an organization increase the quality level of its goods and services? Give examples.
3. Why do organizations taking a total quality approach use benchmarking? What practical value does it have?
4. Many managers believe that empowerment is the key to a successful total quality organization. What is the reasoning behind this statement? Defend your answer.
5. What are four important conditions for empowerment? Which one do you think is most important? Why?
6. How does a learning organization differ from a traditional organization? What impact do these differences have on the way people are managed?

Footnote References and Supplemental Readings

1. See, for example, Mark Landler, "Media Mania," *Business Week*, July 12, 1993, pp. 109–119.
2. Mark Alpert, "CD-ROM: The Next PC Revolution," *Fortune*, June 29, 1992, pp. 68–73.
3. John A. Byrne, "Enterprise," *Business Week*, 1993 Special Issue, p. 12.
4. William C. Symonds, "Getting Rid of Paper Is Just the Beginning," *Business Week*, Dec. 21, 1992, p. 88.
5. Ibid., p. 89.
6. Gene Bylinsky, "Computers That Learn by Doing," *Fortune*, Sept. 6, 1993, p. 96.
7. Ibid., p. 102.

8. This discussion of TQM is drawn from the author's article: Fred Luthans, "Meeting the New Paradigm Challenges Through Total Quality Management," *Management Quarterly*, Spring 1993, pp. 2–13.

9. Karl Albrecht and Ron Zemke, *Service America*, Dow Jones–Irwin, Homewood, Ill., 1985, p. 48.

10. Rahul Jacob, "TQM: More Than a Dying Fad?" *Fortune*, Oct. 18, 1993, pp. 66–72.

11. Michael Hammer and James Champy, *Reengineering the Corporation: A Manifesto for Business Revolution*, HarperCollins, New York, 1993, p. 32.

12. For more on the strategy for reengineering, see Efraim Turban, "Business and Information Systems Re-Engineering," *Decision Line*, May 1993, p. 7.

13. Ellen F. Glanz and Lee K. Dailey, "Benchmarking," *Human Resource Management*, Spring/Summer 1992, p. 9.

14. Richard M. Hodgetts, *Blueprints for Continuous Improvement: Lessons from the Baldrige Winners*, American Management Association, New York, 1993, pp. 108–109.

15. Donald J. Ford, Benchmarking HRD," *Training and Development Journal*, June 1993, pp. 36–42.

16. David L. Taylor and Ruth Karin Ramsey, "Empowering Employees to 'Just Do It,' " *Training and Development Journal*, May 1991, p. 71.

17. John H. Dobbs, "The Empowerment Environment," *Training and Development Journal*, February 1993, pp. 55–57.

18. Taylor and Ramsey, op. cit., pp. 71–76.

19. David E. Bowen and Edward E. Lawler, "The Empowerment of Service Workers: What, Why, How, and When," *Sloan Management Review*, Spring 1992, pp. 36–39.

20. See Chris Argyris and Donald Schon, *Organizational Learning*, Addison-Wesley, Reading, Mass., 1978, and Chris Argyris, *Overcoming Organizational Defenses*, Allyn-Bacon, Needham Heights, Mass., 1990.

21. For the historical background on the learning organization and the distinctions between single-loop and double-loop learning, see Dave Ulrich, Mary Ann Von Glinow, and Todd Jick, "High-Impact Learning," *Organizational Dynamics*, Autumn 1993, p. 53.

22. See Peter M. Senge, *The Fifth Discipline: The Art and Practice of the Learning Organization*, Doubleday, New York, 1991, and Peter M. Senge, "The Leader's New Work: Building Learning Organizations," *Sloan Management Review*, Fall 1990, pp. 7–23.

23. See Carol J. Loomis, "Dinosaurs?" *Fortune*, May 3, 1993, pp. 36–42.

24. Michael E. McGill and John W. Slocum, Jr., "Unlearning the Organization," *Organizational Dynamics*, Autumn 1993, p. 70.

25. Ibid., p. 75.

26. Michael E. McGill, John W. Slocum, Jr., and David Lei, "Management Practices in Learning Organizations," *Organizational Dynamics*, Summer 1992, p. 9.

27. Tom Kramlinger, "Training's Role in a Learning Organization," *Training*, July 1992, p. 48.

28. McGill, Slocum, and Lei, op. cit., pp. 10–16.

29. Ibid., p. 13.

REAL CASE: Improving the Quality

Aware of the need to dramatically improve the quality of their goods and service, many organizations are now in the throes of introducing total quality management concepts and techniques. While there are a variety of steps that can be used in this process, three of the most important are data gathering, reengineering, and empowerment.

Data gathering focuses on answering the question, How well are we doing in providing goods and services to our customers? The most common data-gathering approaches are surveys, telephone interviews, and face-to-face meetings. AT&T Universal Card Services, for example, interviews 200 customers each month and conducts panel surveys of customers on a biannual basis. General Motors' Cadillac Division holds focus groups and product clinics and conducts surveys and more than 2.5 million interviews with customers each year. In the process, Cadillac gathers demographic (age, education, income) and psychographic (behavioral patterns and lifestyle) data to help determine the types of vehicles and vehicle attributes that will be in demand in the years ahead. Zytec visits its customers on a monthly basis and sponsors customer seminars during which buyers can discuss their problems and expectations from the company. These data are then used to help formulate the organization's annual plan.

Many companies use their data gathering as a basis for reengineering. This is particularly true when a firm learns that its current approaches are antiquated or inefficient. For example, Duke Power & Light in Charlotte, North Carolina, reengineered the reward process for their employees. Traditionally, this utility had separate wage and salary, benefit and recognition plans. The human resources department started the reward process over from scratch. The reengineering led to an interrelated single reward system that could be reshaped continually to support the business needs of the firm. This new reward system includes salary banding, variable compensation, hourly pay for performance, career development, individual and team incentive plans tied to performance, recognition awards for excellence, and flexible work and family benefits. This reengineered reward system is aimed at customer satisfaction, cost consciousness, innovation, risk taking, teamwork, employee involvement, information sharing, and ownership. A recent survey found that Duke's employees gave high marks for this reward system, and quality goals are being met.

Closely linked to reengineering is empowerment, which firms like Hampton Inns are now using to increase customer satisfaction and employee motivation. The company did this with a program called "100% Satisfaction Guarantee." To prepare its work force, management gave each employee a three-day training program, which included classroom-style teaching, open discussion, and role playing. Employees were taught to identify situations where they could improve the service being offered to the guests. For example, housekeepers were empowered to help guests who had misplaced their keys by opening the door for them with the master key. Dining room personnel were taught to provide fast service and deal with problems on the spot, for example, by ripping up the bill of a customer who complained about the quality of the food. Additionally, if at the end of the stay the guest is not 100 percent satisfied, the personnel are empowered to adjust the bill in a way that is acceptable to the guest. While many employees believed that this new policy would lead to people's taking advantage of Hampton Inns, this has not happened. Today the 100 percent guarantee is in effect at the firm's hotels all across the country. Employees support management's decision to implement the guarantee policy. Employees admit that this policy keeps them on their toes and challenges them to work more closely as a team. The whole culture in the motel revolves around keeping guests satisfied.

1. When a company decides to increase its total quality by gathering data from customers and acting on this information, how will this result in organizational behavior that is different from what it was before this approach was implemented?
2. What implications do TQM techniques such as reengineering have for organizational behavior?
3. Why does empowerment work so well at Hampton Inns? What changes in employees' values and behavior would be needed to ensure the continued success of the 100 percent satisfaction guarantee?

REAL CASE: Learning How to Learn

Many large companies, especially those that have been dominant in their field, are now finding themselves having to take steps toward becoming learning organizations. A good example is AT&T, which has made major changes since it was forced to divest itself of local operating companies in 1984. While the company has acquired the National Cash Register firm and McCaw Electronics over the last couple of years, this has not stopped the firm from redefining the way it does business and changing policies and procedures to improve efficiency. For example, in the past each division at AT&T used to operate semi-independently of the others. Now the executives of all major business groups meet several days each month to discuss their various operations and learn how to work together synergistically. This is a totally new way of doing things for the firm. Top management has also set up teams to explore and develop areas which they believe offer the greatest opportunity for the firm. Each team consists of representatives from all four business groups. The company's CEO recently explained the logic behind this new arrangement by noting, "The intent is to mix it up, get people talking, and figure out the businesses and structures that AT&T as a company will need."

IBM is also making strides toward becoming a learning organization. The company is now reorganizing and opening up lines of communication between all units. Lou Gerstner, the new CEO, has created an eleven-member executive panel, composed primarily of operating chiefs, and charged them with finding ways of better working together. He has also replaced the firm's three-member corporate executive council with a worldwide council of thirty-four executives. This team meets four to five times annually to compare practices, problems, and solutions, and to thrash out company-wide initiatives. The objective of these changes at IBM is to reduce the bureaucratic structure and force managers to learn new ways of doing things.

In addition to implementing structural changes, many firms are now rethinking the way they train their managers. To teach managers how to be more flexible and how to handle unique situations, firms such as General Electric, Motorola, Weyerhaeuser, and IBM are building their own in-house universities or closely monitoring the training efforts of those they bring in from the outside. For example, at Weyerhaeuser, the giant wood and paper company, an in-house Leadership Institute for Managers has been created. The firm has put 1240 of its managers through the program and reports that its wood products unit is more profitable than ever. At General Electric, in-house training is focused very heavily on action learning. Managers are divided into teams and taught how to gather information on business-related problems and present it to senior-level managers. Groups of GE executives are divided into teams and given free rein to go anywhere they want to gather the needed information. Some travel internationally during the thirty-day period they have for handling the assignment. Then, led by consultants, in-house trainers, and university professors, they organize, analyze, evaluate, and present their information. As a result of such programs, GE managers are learning how to rethink their old approaches to problem solving and to turn their enterprise into a learning organization that is able not only to cope with the ever-changing world of business, but also to anticipate and learn from change.

1. Why do firms such as AT&T and IBM need to be learning organizations?
2. How are the approaches used by AT&T and IBM similar? Identify and explain two similarities.
3. Why are learning organizations developing greater use of in-house training and management development programs?

3

Contemporary Challenges: Diversity and Ethics

Learning Objectives

- **Identify** what is meant by diversity and how it has emerged as an important challenge facing the field of management and organizational behavior.
- **Examine** diversity in today's organizations and the individual and organizational approaches to effectively manage diversity.
- **Discuss** the meaning of ethics and the major factors of ethical behavior.
- **Describe** some of the major areas of ethical concern, including sexual harassment, discrimination in pay and promotion, and the privacy issue.
- **Relate** some of the steps that can be taken to effectively address the major ethical concerns.

In the last few years, social issues have emerged that have had a dramatic effect on the study and application of management and organizational behavior. In the past, diversity was treated primarily as a legal issue; that is, it was against the law to discriminate against women, minorities, older employees, and those challenged by a disability. Now organizations are beginning to realize that diversity is not just something to deal with, but instead a reality to build upon to make a stronger, more competitive enterprise. The same is true regarding ethics. By paying closer attention to ethical behavior and the way in which it is rewarded and managed, organizations can become more effective. In other words, the contemporary challenges of diversity and ethics are no longer simply a "tack on" or afterthought in the study of organizational behavior, but play a central role in that discipline of study and application and therefore in framing the rest of this text.

This chapter first examines the nature of diversity, including the major reasons for its emergence and some of the age, gender, ethnicity, and education characteristics. Next, the focus turns to managing diversity. The multicultural organization and individual (learning and empathy) and organizational (testing, training, mentoring, and alternative work schedules) approaches are given specific attention. The last part is devoted to ethics. After a discussion of the overall nature of ethics and ethical behavior, attention turns to the important ethical problems surrounding sexual harassment, discrimination in pay and promotion, and rights to privacy.

THE NATURE OF DIVERSITY

Diversity in the realm of organizational behavior can be defined as the situation that exists when members of a group or organization differ from each other in terms of age, gender, ethnicity, and/or education. Over the past few years diversity has become a major challenge for many organizations because their work-force composition is changing. White male employees, who dominated so many organizations in the past, are now being supplemented, and in some cases replaced, by a very diverse group. Figure 3.1 shows that there are a number of reasons that help explain the emergence of such diversity.

Reasons for the Emergence of Diversity

The major reason for the emergence of diversity as an important challenge is changing demographics. Older workers, women, minorities, and those with more education are now entering the work force in record numbers. The statistics on these demographic developments are covered in the next section. However, for now it can be noted that the composition of tomorrow's work force will be much different from that of the past. Assuming talent and ability are equally distributed throughout the population and that everyone has an equal opportunity, this means that many of the new, diverse entrants into organizations should eventually enter the ranks of management. There should be diversity in every level of the organization. As is discussed later in this chapter, such an assumption may not be valid because diversity has not yet reached the upper levels of organizations.

Another pragmatic reason for diversity in today's organizations stems from legislation and lawsuits. The political and legal systems have compelled organizations

FIGURE 3.1
Major reasons for increasing diversity.

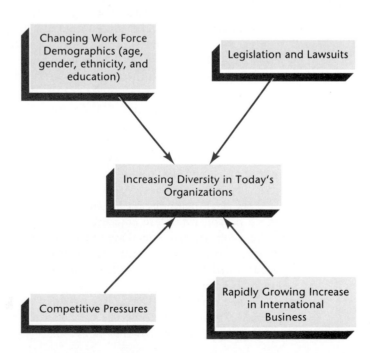

to hire more broadly and to provide equal opportunity for all employees. Although legislation going as far back as the Civil Rights Act of 1964 prohibited discrimination in employment, only recently have the full effects of that landmark law and other more recent legislation, such as the following, had an impact.

1. *Age Discrimination Act of 1978.* This law at first increased the mandatory retirement age from 65 to 70, and then was later amended to eliminate an upper age limit altogether.
2. *Pregnancy Discrimination Act of 1978.* This law gives full equal opportunity protection to pregnant employees.
3. *Americans with Disabilities Act of 1990.* This law prohibits discrimination against those essentially qualified individuals challenged by a disability and requires organizations to reasonably accommodate these individuals.
4. *Civil Rights Act of 1991.* This law refined the 1964 act and reinstated burden of proof to eliminate discrimination and ensure equal opportunity in employment to employers. It also allows punitive and compensatory damages through jury trials.
5. *Family and Medical Leave Act of 1993.* This law allows employees to take up to twelve weeks of unpaid leave for family or medical reasons each year.

These laws, along with lawsuits and the threat of lawsuits, have put teeth into the diversity challenge. Individuals and groups that have found themselves excluded from organizations or managerial positions can bring and have brought lawsuits in an effort to overcome discriminatory barriers and ensure themselves equal opportunity in employment.

Still another reason for the emergence of the diversity challenge is that organizations are beginning to realize that diversity can help them meet the competitive pressures they currently face. Firms that aggressively try to hire and promote women and minorities are going to end up with a more talented and capable work force than those which do not take such a proactive, affirmative action approach. Moreover, companies that gain a reputation for "celebrating diversity" are more likely to attract the best employees regardless of age, gender, or ethnicity. The most talented and qualified people will feel that their opportunities are better with these firms than with others. In other words, diversity can provide an organization with competitive advantage.

An example is Wal-Mart. This giant retailer gained its initial market position by offering good quality merchandise at discount prices. However, as Wal-Mart became larger (now the largest retailer, and some project it will be the largest company in the United States in a few years), management began realizing the need to address the diversity challenge. Today the firm has a growing number of women and minorities at all levels, including management positions, and is a major employer of older workers who are looking for part-time employment. Wal-Mart's ability to manage diversity has helped it develop a competitive advantage.

A final major reason for the emerging challenge of diversity is that more and more organizations are entering the international arena. A natural by-product of going international is increased diversity, in this case, cultural diversity. If domestic organizations have and promote diversity, then as they expand globally, they will be accustomed to working with people who have different cultures, customs, social norms, and mores.

The international arena is not a threatening place for diverse firms, a fact that is particularly important because of the major role that international operations and sales will play in the growth, and even survival, of companies in the global economy.

The percentage of overall revenues from international operations and sales is increasing dramatically. Trade developments, such as NAFTA (North American Free Trade Agreement), between the United States, Canada, and Mexico; the EU (European Union); and an increasingly unified Asia-Pacific Rim, are a sign of the times. The advantage of multinational companies that have and value cultural diversity becomes abundantly clear in this global, interconnected economy.

Specific Characteristics of Diversity

There are a number of specific, objective characteristics of diversity. The most widely recognized deal with age, gender, ethnicity, and education. A detailed description of these characteristics provides insights into the nature of diversity.

Age. The U.S. work force is getting progressively older, and this trend will continue well into the twenty-first century. The percent of employees under the age of thirty-five is declining, while the percent in the thirty-five to fifty-four age group is increasing. In fact, by the turn of the century about half the U.S. work force will be between thirty-five and fifty-four years old. This development is a result of a number of factors, including the baby-boom generation following World War II, which accounts for the increasing number of workers in their forties, and the declining birth rate among the post-baby-boom generation, which helps explain the decline in percentage of workers in their teens and twenties. A second contributing factor to an aging work force is the nation's improved health and medical care, which is helping people live longer, more productive lives. Still another factor is the removal of mandatory retirement rules, allowing people who are capable of doing their jobs to continue working well into their sixties and beyond.

The changing age composition of the work force is forcing organizations to make a number of adjustments. One is learning how to deal effectively with older workers. In the past this was not a problem because older workers were forced to retire. Now with no mandatory retirement age, older employees have recourse when they are let go. As a result, the number of age discrimination complaints has increased dramatically. The Equal Employment Opportunity Commission, the federal agency that investigates discrimination in the workplace, reported almost 20,000 complaints in the 1993 fiscal year. This number was a third more than in 1989. As Chapter 2 points out, in order to reduce costs and increase productivity, many firms are downsizing. The high-priced veterans are let go and are replaced by information technology or low-priced, newly educated or trained employees. The key here is that organizations cannot discriminate on the basis of age. Organizations must begin to listen to their older employees, determine how their needs are different from those of younger workers, and learn to draw from the expertise and experience that older employees can offer.

On the other side of the coin, organizations must also learn how to deal with younger employees, who have values markedly different from those of their older counterparts. The days of total loyalty and commitment to the company in exchange for guaranteed employment are a thing of the past. Young employees do not have such loyalty values, and organizations in recent years have made it clear that there is no such thing as lifetime employment. Even firms such as IBM and AT&T, long known for their unwillingness to let people go, have been cutting back their work forces at all levels in an effort to become more efficient and maintain their competitiveness. This era of downsizing has affected both older and younger employees.

Gender. Besides age composition, there are also changes occurring in gender composition. Women have been entering the work force in record numbers over the last four decades. By 1975 they accounted for approximately 40 percent of the total and by 1990 constituted approximately 47 percent. The estimates are that by the turn of the century women will make up almost half of the work force. This diversity development can and should dramatically change the policies and day-to-day practices of organizations.

Even though laws spelling out equal pay and opportunity for women have been on the books for over thirty years, companies are still finding out that they must carefully examine their compensation and promotion policies and practices. For example, one of the major issues remaining is the so-called *glass ceiling effect*, a term used in reference to women's being prevented from receiving promotions into top management positions. This ceiling is often subtle and is uncovered only by looking at promotion statistics and seeing that women are greatly underrepresented in the executive suite. For example, if a firm has 10,000 employees of whom 5000 are women, and there are 150 senior-level managers of whom only one is a woman, there is good reason to believe that a glass ceiling exists. No matter how far up the organization a woman advances, there still seems to be this ceiling, not always visible, like glass, that halts her progress.

The same goes for pay. The latest statistics show that women are still being paid far less than men. Some analyses try to explain away this disparity by noting that many women do not have the same time on the job as men, so their salaries are lower. Another commonly cited reason is that many women want to spend time at home with their children, so they are willing to accept slower career progression and lower salaries. These types of reasons fall short of explaining the large disparities that still exist between men and women in the workplace. To meet the challenge of true equal pay and opportunity in employment, firms must continue to examine and change their policies and practices to eliminate gender bias and discrimination.

Ethnicity. The term *ethnicity* refers to the ethnic composition of a group or organization. Census statistics indicate that between 1995 and 2050 not only will the U.S. population increase from 263 to 392 million, but as the pie charts in Figure 3.2 show, the racial mix will change dramatically. Hispanics are projected to pass African Americans as the nation's largest minority in the early part of the twenty-first century. These changes in the racial mix of the overall population are reflected in the work force.

In 1988, whites made up approximately 80 percent of the work force, but by the year 2000, this will decline to less than three-fourths, and by 2050, to about half. African Americans, who constituted approximately 12 percent of the work force in 1988, will increase to around 14 percent by the turn of the century, while the Hispanic percentage will rise from 7 percent in 1988 to 10 percent by 2000, and Asians, who made up 1 percent of the work force in 1988, will double their percentage by the turn of the century.[1] During this twelve-year period minorities will account for one-third of the new entrants into the work force.[2] These changing racial patterns point to greater work-force diversity. The challenge for management will be to deal with these ethnicity changes, as with the changes regarding gender, in terms of policies and practices concerning pay and promotions. Like women, minorities on the average are paid less and are less well represented in the upper management ranks.

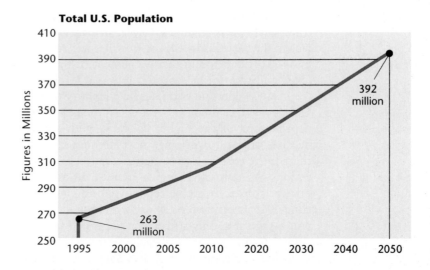

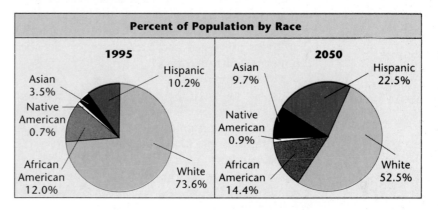

FIGURE 3.2
Overall population
growth and racial
composition.
(*Source*: U.S. Census
Bureau report released
September 1993.)

Education. The educational level of the U.S. work force has been rising. The proportion of eighteen- to twenty-four-year-olds enrolled in college, which hovered around 30 percent in the 1980s, jumped sharply to 41 percent in 1991, the last year from which Census Bureau data are available.[3] Paradoxically, however, while new entrants and existing employees have on average more education, the other end of the spectrum, those with little or no education or basic knowledge, is also increasing. For instance, some analysts have noted that while the top third of the nation's young people are the best educated in the world, the bottom third are at Third World standards. A survey by the Educational Testing Service of 3600 young people (ages twenty-one to twenty-five) found that less than a third were able to determine the tip and the correct change for a two-item restaurant bill, and less than a quarter could interpret a complicated business schedule.[4] Young people are not the only ones who lack basic educational skills. It is estimated that there are over 25 million adult Americans who are functionally illiterate.

In the workplace, illiteracy and employees' lack of basic knowledge can be devastating for organizations trying to move ahead. For example, a manufacturing company with 4200 employees in seventeen plants nationwide moved to implement a total quality program. However, management soon learned that their employees lacked the basic knowledge to do what was required. They then administered a test of basic skills and found that 30 percent of the employees read below the fifth-grade level, and two-thirds scored below that level on basic math skills.[5]

These data and examples help identify one of the major challenges that will face U.S. firms over the next decade. On the one hand, there is the challenge to meet the expectations of the highly educated with shrinking opportunities for promotion because of the downsizing and flattening of organizations, and on the other hand, there is the challenge of bringing employees up to speed in knowledge-based organizations. As technology increases and the skills required to remain competitive in the quality-conscious, global economy continue to rise, companies will have to train and educate their employees. Those with high school educations will find that these skills will carry them only so far and additional training and education are needed. Even engineers and other high-tech personnel will need to continually upgrade their knowledge. Businesses will also find that job redesign (covered in Chapter 7) and reengineering (covered in Chapter 2) will be necessary in order to streamline the work, and the employees must be able to adjust to these expanding knowledge requirements. This challenge is why firms such as Motorola now require their employees to have at least forty hours of education and training annually, and this amount is being increased.[6]

Other Characteristics of Diversity. In addition to age, gender, ethnicity, and education, there are a number of other characteristics that describe diversity in the work force. For example, for most employees English is the primary language used in communicating, but increasingly, workers in south Texas, southern California, south Florida, and New York City, Spanish is the primary language. In dealing with these Hispanic employees, firms must exhibit care and accommodation to ensure effective communication. Also, those challenged with a disability are another group that is receiving increased attention. The Americans with Disabilities Act and changing work-force norms are helping companies focus on equal employment opportunities for these people. Other groups that are contributing to the growing diversity of the workplace include single parents, dual-career couples, and gays and lesbians. Each group presents different challenges to management, but those who recognize and promote diversity are finding that there are competitive advantages to meeting these challenges.

MANAGING DIVERSITY

There are a number of approaches and specific steps that can be taken to effectively manage diversity. To begin with, there must be a truly multicultural organization developed. After this step is accomplished, then both individual- and organizational-level strategies and techniques can be employed to further manage diversity.

Developing the Multicultural Organization

The foundation and point of departure for effectively managing diversity is the development of a truly multicultural organization. A multicultural organization has been described as one which:

1. Reflects the contributions and interests of diverse cultural and social groups in its mission, operations, and product or service
2. Acts on a commitment to eradicate social oppression in all forms within the organization
3. Includes the members of diverse cultural and social groups as full participants, especially in decisions that shape the organization
4. Follows through on broader external social responsibilities, including support of other institutional efforts to eliminate all forms of social oppression[7]

Several stages have been identified in leading up to such a multicultural organization:[8]

1. *Exclusionary organization.* This type of organization is the farthest from a multicultural organization. It is devoted to maintaining the dominance of one group over all others on factors such as age, education, gender, or race. This organization is characterized by exclusionary hiring practices and other forms of discrimination. Even though such organizations are directly violating laws, they unfortunately still exist.
2. *Club organization.* This organization is characterized by the maintenance of privileges by those who traditionally have held power. These organizations may technically get around the laws by hiring and promoting women and minorities, but only those who are deemed to have the "right" credentials and perspectives.
3. *Compliance organization.* This type of organization is committed to removing some of the discriminatory practices that are inherent in the exclusionary and club organizations. For example, women and minorities are hired and promoted to give the impression of openness and fair play. However, the strategy is more of meeting the letter of the laws, not the spirit. For example, only tokenism is carried out; the basic exclusionary or club culture of the organization remains entrenched.
4. *Affirmative action organization.* This type of organization is committed to proactively eliminating discriminatory policies and practices and the inherent biases created by the exclusionary and club cultures. The affirmative action organization goes beyond the letter of the laws and proactively supports the growth and development of women, minorities, older employees, those challenged with a disability, and other groups and individuals that have previously been denied equal access and opportunity. At the same time, however, the norms and practices of the dominant group continue to guide the affirmative action organization's view of the world.
5. *Redefining organization.* This newly emerging organization is characterized by an examination of all activities for the purpose of evaluating their impact on all employees' opportunity to both participate in and contribute to their own and the firm's growth and success. Redefining the organization goes beyond being just proactively antiracist and antisexist. This approach questions the core cultural values of the organization as manifested in the mission, structure, technology, psychosocial dynamics, and products and services. The redefining organization not only deals with but recognizes the value of a diverse work force; it engages in visionary planning and problem solving to tap the strength of the diversity. This approach involves both developing and implementing policies and practices that distribute power among all diverse groups in the organizations.
6. *Multicultural organization.* The true multicultural organization is characterized by core cultural values and an ongoing commitment to eliminate social oppression throughout the organization. All members of diverse cultural and social groups

are involved in the decisions that shape the mission, structure, technology, psychosocial dynamics, and products and services of the organization. The true multicultural organization as defined is the stated ideal of an increasing number of organizations, although most are still in transition to this sixth stage. If carefully studied and objectively analyzed, most of today's organizations would still be best described by one of the other forms discussed above.

Moving toward and building a truly multicultural organization is perhaps most important, but there are also some individual- and organizational-level steps and techniques that can be used to effectively manage diversity.

Individual Approaches to Managing Diversity

Individual approaches to managing diversity typically take two interdependent paths: learning and empathy. The first is based on acquiring real or simulated experience; the second is based on the ability to understand feelings and emotions.

Learning. Many managers are often unprepared to deal with diversity; because of their inexperience they are unsure of how to respond. To better prepare themselves, managers must work hard to learn and experience as much as they can about developing appropriate behavior. At the heart of this learning process is communication. Managers must openly communicate one-on-one with young and old employees, women, minorities, and those challenged with disability in order to determine how best to understand and interact with them. In this way managers can learn more about a diverse group's personal values and how the individuals like to be treated.

Managers can also begin to develop a personal style that works well with each member of a diverse group. For example, to their amazement, many managers have learned that people who are challenged with a disability do not want special treatment. They want to be treated like everyone else, asking only for equal opportunities in employment. Many managers are unaware of their biased treatment of these employees. For example, after a review of the research literature in this area, the following conclusion was drawn:

> It should be noted that several of these studies have found that the physically challenged workers were more intelligent, motivated, better qualified, and had higher educational levels than their nonphysically challenged counterparts. While these findings may help account for the superior performance of those physically challenged, they may also reflect hidden biases whereby a physically challenged person must be overqualified for a specific job. In addition, they may reflect hesitancy to promote physically challenged individuals: the physically challenged may stay in entry-level jobs whereas similarly qualified nonphysically challenged individuals would be rapidly promoted.[9]

In this learning process, managers can also encourage diverse employees to give them candid feedback regarding how they are being treated. In this way, when the manager does something that an employee does not feel is proper, the manager quickly learns this and can adjust his or her behavior. This form of feedback is particularly important in helping organizations gain insights to effectively manage diversity.

Empathy. Closely linked to the individual learning strategy is empathy, the ability to put oneself in another's place and see things from that person's point of view.

Empathy is particularly important in managing diversity because members of diverse groups often feel that only they can truly understand the challenges or problems they are facing. For example, many women believe that they are discriminated against or harassed at work because of their gender and, despite surface efforts to discourage these problems, discrimination and a "chilly climate" for women have become institutionalized through male-dominated management. In this view, discrimination and harassment have in essence become the way things are done. These feelings have sometimes resulted in sex bias or sexual harassment suits against organizations, and in recent years, the courts have favorably ruled on these charges. (For example, as is discussed later, a 1993 Supreme Court decision has made it easier to prove sexual harassment.)

Empathy is an important way to deal with these more subtle problems because it helps the manager understand the diverse employee's point of view. For example, many women in business offices say that they are willing to get coffee for their male counterparts or bosses if they are on their way to the coffee room, but, importantly, they feel that they should be given similar treatment and have coffee brought to them on the same basis. Similarly, many managers try very hard to promote minorities into management positions and to give them work-related experiences that can help their careers. At the same time, however, these managers need to empathize with the fact that some minority members may be ambivalent or have mixed emotions about being promoted. They may like to advance in terms of pay and prestige, but at the same time they are concerned about receiving special treatment, failing, or not living up to everyone's expectations. By learning how to empathize with these feelings and by offering encouragement, guidance, and after-the-fact backup support, the manager can play an important individual role in more effectively managing diversity.

Organizational Approaches to Managing Diversity

Organizational approaches to managing diversity include a variety of techniques. Some of the most common involve testing, training, mentoring, and the use of alternative work schedules designed to help personnel effectively balance their work and family life. The following sections examine each of these techniques.

Testing. A problem that organizations have encountered with the use of tests for selection and evaluation is that they are commonly culturally biased. As a result, women, minorities, or even those who are functionally illiterate may be able to do the job for which they are being tested, but their test scores indicate that they should be rejected as candidates. Most tests traditionally used in selection and evaluation are not suited nor valid for a diverse work force. As a result, in recent years a great deal of attention has been focused on developing tests that are indeed valid for selecting and evaluating diverse employees.

One way to make tests more valid for diverse employees is to use job-specific tests rather than general aptitude or knowledge tests. For example, a company hiring word processing personnel may give applicants a timed test designed to measure their speed and accuracy. The applicant's age, gender, or ethnic background are not screening criteria. This approach differs sharply from using traditional tests that commonly measure general knowledge or intelligence (as defined by the test). People from different cultures (foreign or domestic) often did poorly on the traditional tests because they were culturally biased toward individuals who had been raised in a white, middle-class neighborhood. Older applicants and those who were functionally illiterate may also do poorly on such culturally biased tests. Job-specific tests help prevent diversity bias by focusing on the work to be done.

Besides being culturally unbiased, tests used in effectively managing diversity should be able to identify whether the applicant has the necessary skills for doing the job. The word processing example above is a good illustration because it measures the specific skills, not the subjective personal characteristics, required for the work. In some cases carefully conducted interviews or role playing can be used because this is the only effective way of identifying whether the person has the necessary skills. For example, a person applying for a customer service job would need to understand the relevant language of customers and be able to communicate well. The customer service job would also require someone who listens carefully, maintains his or her composure, and is able to solve problems quickly and efficiently. Carefully constructed and conducted interviews could be useful in helping identify whether the applicant speaks well, can communicate ideas, and has the necessary personal style for dealing effectively with customers. Role-playing exercises could be useful in helping identify the applicant's ability to focus on problems and solve them to the satisfaction of the customer. Also, the applicant could be given a case or exercise in a group setting to assess interpersonal skills. The point is that multiple measures and multiple trained raters would yield the most valid assessment of needed complex skills.

If pencil-and-paper tests are used, then to help ensure that they are not biased, scientific norming should be used. This is a process that assures the tests are equivalent across cultures. As a result, all test questions have the same meaning regardless of the person's cultural background. The accompanying Managing Diversity in Action: Nonbiased Testing describes some of the approaches that are currently being used in some specific companies to ensure that their testing is not culturally biased.

Training. There are two ways in which training can play a key role in managing diversity. One way is by offering training to diverse groups. Members from a diverse group can be trained for an entry-level skill or how to more effectively do their existing or future job. The other approach is to provide training to managers and other employees who work with diverse employees. In recent years a number of approaches have been used in providing such diversity training.

Most diversity training programs get the participants directly involved. An example is provided by Florida International University's Center for Management Development (CMD). This center provides diversity training to employers in south Florida, a geographic area where Latinos and African Americans constitute a significant percentage of the population. One of CMD's programs involves putting trainees into groups based on ethnic origin. Then each group is asked to describe the others and to listen to the way its own group is described. The purpose of this exercise is to gain insights into the way one ethnic group is perceived by another ethnic group. Each group is also asked to describe the difficulties it has in working with other ethnic groups and to identify the reasons for these problems. At the end of the training, both managers and employees relate that they have a better understanding of their personal biases and the ways in which they can improve their interaction with members of the other groups.

Another widely used approach is diversity board games, which require the participants to answer questions related to areas such as gender, race, cultural differences, age issues, sexual orientation, and disabilities. On the basis of the

Managing Diversity in Action

Nonbiased Testing

As the U.S. working population becomes more diverse and an increasing number of young and old people from both genders and all races seek employment, business firms are trying to develop new strategies for the valid use of testing. For example, Kraft General Foods screens all its entry-level applicants with tests that focus only on work-related skills. Kraft's reasoning is that it is more efficient to find out at the start what people can and cannot do and then, if the person is hired, use training programs to correct any deficiencies. Because of the work-related skills focus, the company avoids diversity-related problems. At the same time, the firm is not hesitant to use pencil-and-paper testing because this helps identify problems that might not otherwise be caught. For example, a functionally illiterate person can do extremely well in an interview and give no hint of any problem. However, the person cannot hide this shortcoming during a pencil-and-paper test.

Procter & Gamble hires only at the entry level and uses testing in combination with other selection tools. Part of the process consists of pencil-and-paper cognitive testing, but all of it is directed toward finding out if the person possesses the key skills for doing the job. The firm's approach is so successful that in recent years it has been able to attract 20 percent of its recruits from the minority ranks and has managed to keep most of them.

Other firms are no less vigorous in their efforts to overcome cultural bias in testing, which often includes being frank and open about the demands of the job. For example, before deciding a woman cannot do a job that involves heavy lifting, some industrial firms are now pointing out the physical demands of the job and then asking the woman applicant if she feels qualified to do the work. If she answers affirmatively, then she is given the same physically demanding test as all other applicants. Another example is companies who have foreign applicants for door-to-door sales positions. These individuals are typically asked, "Do you feel that your mastery of English and local cultural selling patterns is sufficient for you to do this job?" If the applicants believe they are, then the company will proceed with the screening process.

In each case, business firms are wrestling with a problem that has previously been overlooked and, now in diverse organizations, demands careful attention. By concentrating on ensuring the validity of its tests, these organizations are finding that they can overcome the built-in bias that was so common in the past.

---

response, the game players are able to advance on the board or are forced to back up.[10] For example, in helping participants gain an understanding of the legal issues involved in employment practices, one game asks the players this question:

> Two white workers and one African-American worker were charged with theft of company property. The white employees were discharged, but the African-American employee was retained because of concerns about racial-discrimination lawsuits. The employer's action was:
> a. Illegal. The law prohibits racial discrimination.
> b. Legal. The law protects only minorities.
> c. Legal. This case involved theft.

The answer is "a" and participants who answer correctly are allowed to advance on the board or are given some form of reward such as a token that counts toward a higher score. The objective of these types of games is in a nonthreatening manner to acquaint the players with legal rules and restrictions regarding how to manage members of diverse groups.

Other training games help participants focus on cultural issues such as how to interact with personnel from other cultures. Here is an example:

In Hispanic families, which one of the following values is probably most important?
a. Achievement
b. Money
c. Being on time
d. Respect for elders

The correct answer is "d." As participants play the game, they gain an understanding of the values and beliefs of other cultures and learn how better to interact with a diverse work force.

In many cases these diversity-related games are used as supplements to other forms of training. For example, they are often employed as icebreakers to get diversity training sessions started or to maintain participant interest during a long program.

Mentoring. A *mentor* is a trusted counselor, coach, or advisor who provides advice and assistance. In recent years, many organizations have begun assigning mentors to women and minorities. The purpose of the mentor program is to help support members of a diverse group in their jobs, socialize them in the cultural values of the organization, and pragmatically help their chances for development and advancement.[11] There are a number of specific benefits that mentors can provide to those they assist, including the following:

1. Provide instruction in specific skills and knowledge critical to successful job performance
2. Help in understanding the unwritten rules of the organization and how to avoid saying or doing the wrong things
3. Answer questions and provide important insights
4. Offer emotional support
5. Serve as a role model
6. Create an environment in which mistakes can be made without losing self-confidence[12]

A number of organizations now require their managers to serve as mentors. Examples include Bell Laboratories, NCR, Hughes Aircraft, Johnson & Johnson, and Merrill Lynch. The formal process for establishing the mentoring program typically involves several steps. First, top management support is secured for the program. Then mentors and their protégés are carefully chosen. The mentor, who provides the advice and guidance, is paired with an individual who is very likely to profit from the experience. Third, both mentors and protégés are given an orientation. The mentors are taught how to conduct themselves, and the protégés are given guidance on the types of questions and issues that they should raise with their mentor so that they can gain the greatest value from the experience. Fourth, throughout the mentoring period, which typically lasts one year or less, mentor and protégé individually and together meet with the support staff of the program to see how well things are going. Fifth, and finally, at the end of the mentoring cycle, overall impressions and recommendations are solicited from both mentors and protégés regarding how the process can be improved in the future. This information is then used in helping the next round of mentors do a more effective job.

Alternative Work Schedules. Increasingly, there are families in which both the mother and father have jobs. This dual-career family has given rise to the need for alternative work schedules, which allow the parents flexibility in balancing their home and work demands. Three of the most common alternative work schedule arrangements are flextime, the compressed workweek, and job sharing.

Flextime allows employees greater autonomy by permitting them to choose their daily starting and ending times within a given time period called a bandwidth, as shown in Figure 3.3. For example, consider the case of two parents who are both employed at a company which has a bandwidth of 7 A.M. to 7 P.M. Everyone working for the firm must put in his or her eight hours during this time period. For example, the father may go to work at 7 A.M. and work until 3 P.M., at which time he leaves and picks up the children from school. The mother, meanwhile, drops the children at school at 8:45 A.M. and works from 9:30 A.M. to 5:30 P.M. Thus both parents are able to adjust their work and home schedules to fit within the bandwidth. The other characteristic of flextime is the core period, which is the time during which everyone must be at work. This period is typically the one with the heaviest workload, when the organization needs everyone there to meet work demands. If the core period in this case is 10 A.M. to 3 P.M. (see Figure 3.3), the two working parents will have no trouble wrapping their home-related responsibilities around this work requirement. Many companies, as seen in the Managing Diversity in Action: Balancing Work and Family Responsibilities, are using this concept and similar ones to help their employees meet both organizational and personal demands.

Another alternative work arrangement is the compressed workweek. This arrangement, which has been widely used in Europe,[13] compresses the workweek into fewer days. For example, while the typical workweek is forty hours spread over five days, a compressed workweek would be four ten-hour days. For those working a thirty-five-hour week, the time could be compressed into three days of approximately twelve hours each. These arrangements give employees more time with their families, although their full impact on productivity, profitability, and employee satisfaction must still be determined.

Job sharing is the splitting of a full-time position between two people, each of whom works part-time. This arrangement is more common in professional positions in banking, insurance, and teaching. A husband and wife, or any two people, could share the job fifty-fifty or in any other combination. For example, parents who want to return to work on a part-time basis only have found job sharing to be an attractive employment alternative.

FIGURE 3.3
A flextime framework.

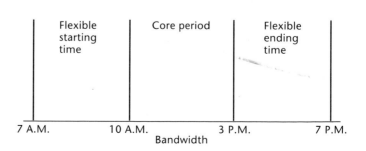

| Flexible starting time | Core period | Flexible ending time |

7 A.M.   10 A.M.   3 P.M.   7 P.M.
Bandwidth

**Managing
Diversity
in Action**

Balancing Work and Family Responsibilities

A growing number of firms are finding that when it comes to work and family responsibilities, it does not have to be an either-or decision. Employees want to meet their commitments to the company, but they also desire the necessary organizational flexibility that allows them to meet their personal responsibilities. Moreover, recent research reveals that firms that are able to provide this flexibility have higher morale and productivity than those that do not. For example, studies at Johnson & Johnson have found that absenteeism among employees who use flexible time and family-leave policies was approximately 50 percent less than that of the work force at large. The investigators also found that 58 percent of the employees who were surveyed reported that flextime and family-leave policies were very important in their decision to stay with the firm. The American Telephone & Telegraph company found that the average cost of giving new parents up to one year of unpaid parental leave was 32 percent of the person's annual salary, in contrast to 150 percent of the salary that was needed to replace the person. Moreover, the company found that 60 percent of new parents were back on the job within three months and all but 10 percent returned to work within six months.

Smaller firms are also finding that these flexible arrangements pay off. At Fel-Pro Inc., a Skokie, Illinois, auto parts manufacturer, investigators found a strong link between those who used flexible benefits and their productivity. Employees who took advantage of the company's family-responsive policies were also more likely to be highly involved in team problem solving and were twice as likely to submit suggestions for improving processes and products.

These companies, and many others like them, have also changed their attitude regarding how to manage people effectively. In the past they focused on fairness, which meant treating all employees the same. Today they focus on equitableness, which means replacing uniformity with flexibility. For example, the Continental Corporation, a large New York-based insurer with more than 12,000 employees, has done away with the practice of tracking employee absences and using the results in performance reviews. The company concluded that there was too much rigidity and structure in the way people were being managed. Greater flexibility and freedom was needed—and the changes in policy are having a positive effect. Since making these changes, the firm has reported a 15 percent increase in productivity and a 50 percent reduction in turnover. Quite clearly, the balancing of work and personal responsibilities is proving profitable to both employees and companies.

In the future other alternative work schedules are also likely to gain in popularity. Telecommuting, which entails receiving and sending work between home and the office, is an example that is currently being used to supplement the typical work arrangement. For instance, employees may come into the office on Monday and Tuesday, work out of their homes on Wednesday and Thursday via telecommuting, and come in again on Friday. By varying the on-site assignments of the personnel, companies are able to reduce the number of people who are in the building at any one time, thus cutting down on the amount of floor space and parking spots they need to rent. The future of telecommuting and other emerging alternative work arrangements is still unclear, but one thing is certain: The work patterns of the future will be quite different because the work and family responsibilities of the employees will demand new configurations and greater flexibility.

ETHICS AND ETHICAL BEHAVIOR IN ORGANIZATIONS

Ethics involves moral issues and choices and deals with right and wrong behavior. Only recently has ethics been included in the study of organizational behavior. It is now realized that not only individuals and groups, but also a number of relevant factors from the cultural, organizational, and external environment determine ethical behavior. Cultural influences on ethical behavior are reflected by the impact of family, friends, neighbors, education, religion, and the media. Organizational influences come from ethical codes, role models, policies and practices, and reward and punishment systems. The external forces having an impact on ethical behavior include political, legal, and economic developments. These factors often work interdependently in shaping ethical behavior of individuals and groups in organizations. For example, minimum wage jobs may lock people into an economic existence that prevents them from bettering their lives.[14] Is it ethical to pay people only a minimum wage? Or consider the fact that many obese workers report that they are discriminated against in the workplace.[15] Is it ethical to treat these workers differently, given that there is very limited legal protection afforded to them and so they have no recourse?

These questions help illustrate the problems and controversy in determining what is ethical behavior. Moreover, while many people would argue that they are highly ethical in their own personal dealings, empirical research has found that such people are often viewed as unlikable by their peers in the organization.[16] Simply put, there is peer pressure on many people to be less ethical. Additionally, what one person or group finds unethical may be viewed differently by another individual or group. For example, a study investigated attitudes toward unauthorized copying of microcomputer software among both business executives and business faculty members. It was found that the faculty members did not view this to be as big an ethical problem as did the executives.[17]

These examples all help illustrate the elusiveness and contingent nature of determining guidelines for ethical behavior. Besides the obvious ethical concerns relating to the use of bribes, price fixing, or other illegal activities, it is now recognized that ethics is important in the study of organizational behavior because of the impact on the way employees are treated and how they perform their jobs. In other words, ethics can affect the well-being of employees and their performance. In particular, the current ethical problems dealing with organizational participants concerning sexual harassment, discrimination in pay and promotion, and the right to privacy are especially relevant to the study of organizational behavior.

Sexual Harassment

Sexual harassment in the workplace can be defined as unwelcome sexual advances, requests for sexual favors, or other verbal or physical conduct of a sexual nature. This harassment has been prohibited as far back as the 1964 Civil Rights Act (as amended). Specifically, the guidelines to date provide that the above-mentioned activities constitute illegal sexual harassment when (1) submission to such conduct is made either explicitly or implicitly a term or condition of an individual's employment; (2) submission to or rejection of such conduct by an individual is used as the basis for employment decisions affecting such individual; or (3) such conduct has the purpose or effect of unreasonably interfering with an individual's work performance or creating a work environment that is intimidating, hostile, or offensive.[18]

Recent data reveal that almost three-fourths of working women report that they have been harassed at some point in their career.[19] A few of these instances have resulted in lawsuits.[20] One of the most recent was *Harris v. Forklift Systems, Inc.* (1993) in which the plaintiff charged her boss with repeatedly embarrassing her with sexual remarks. The Supreme Court ruled in Harris's favor, making it easier for employees to prove illegal sexual harassment. In particular, the Court lowered the burden of prove on plaintiffs, holding that it is unnecessary for those making charges to prove that sexual harassment severely damaged them psychologically or seriously impaired their work performance. Thus, this decision reaffirms and strengthens the rights of employees to a work environment that is free of sexual harassment.[21]

There are a number of steps that organizations are taking to ensure that their personnel do not engage in sexual harassment and, if they do, are dealt with properly.[22] In particular, these initiatives include carefully complying with current legal requirements as well as taking steps such as the following:

1. Taking the initiative to implement a meaningful program that addresses personal biases and values that foster harassment of individuals based on sex
2. Securing commitment from top management, since without it all efforts are doomed from the start
3. Developing and implementing a program that strives to change behaviors, not just attitudes, in the short run
4. Using the resources of an employee assistance program to develop a company policy regarding sexual harassment and making sure that the program has the ability to address claims of sexual harassment before the first one ever occurs[23]

To the extent that organizations follow these types of guidelines and focus on changing their cultures so as to address the ethical challenge of sexual harassment, the problem can be largely prevented. However, since it is an ongoing challenge, organizations are finding that they must be continually alert to any sexual harassment so that they can begin taking immediate action to correct the situation.

Pay and Promotion Discrimination

As discussed earlier under characteristics of diversity, there remains an ethical problem concerning equality of pay and promotion opportunities for both women and minorities. For example, recent statistics indicate that while it has been over thirty years since the passage of the Equal Pay Act, there has been only a small improvement in the median annual wages between men and women.[24] In 1963 women earned 60 cents for every dollar earned by men. Twenty-eight years later they earned 70 cents. At this rate it will take until the year 2175 to completely close the gap. Moreover, in the case of African-American and Hispanic women, earnings are 62 and 54 percent, respectively, of those earned by white males. Another interesting fact about these wage differentials is that part of the reason the gap has closed somewhat is because men's wages have fallen in recent years.

Wage differentials vary by industry, but in almost every case women are paid less. For example, Bureau of Labor studies report that in 1992 median wages for female financial managers was only 62 percent that of their male counterparts. In the case of doctors and lawyers, the percentages were 72 and 78 percent, respectively, while for engineers, architects, and surveyors, the percentage was 86 percent, and for secretaries, stenographers, and typists, it was 92 percent.

There is considerable evidence that women and minorities are denied access to the upper management ranks. This helps explain why average salaries for women are often significantly lower than those for men in the same company. Additionally, some companies offer lucrative incentives to keep their top people from leaving the firm. Since women are not part of this group, they are systematically denied these incentives.[25]

One of the most commonly cited reasons for the lack of promotion is the glass ceiling effect cited earlier under the diversity discussion. The U.S. Department of Labor has even recognized the glass ceiling as "artificial barriers based on attitudinal or organizational bias that prevent qualified [women] from advancing upward in their organization into [senior] management level positions."[26] Despite efforts to explain and deal with the problem, it continues to exist. The explanation that women have not yet had enough experience to reach the top of organizations no longer can be used. Although significant numbers of women have entered managerial positions for a sufficient number of years, women still are noticeably absent from the top levels of today's organizations. Also, some of the academic explanations of why women are not reaching the top are being questioned. For example, some experts have argued that women have lower self- and organization-referent attitudes, and this is what holds them back. Noting that such conclusions have been based on laboratory studies of school-age children, a researcher on women in management counters this argument as follows:

> In fact, there is absolutely no reliable, empirical evidence based on truly comparable samples of men and women who are actually employed in work organizations that women's self- and organization-referent attitudes are systematically lower than men's. Indeed, my associates and I have demonstrated consistently that when the effects of organizational level or position are controlled, women's self- and organization-referent attitudes are usually more positive than men's. We believe strongly that the experiences women should have in the workplace . . . can counteract all or nearly all of the societal factors that have caused girls and women to manifest less positive attitudes in nonwork research settings.[27]

Other reasons for explaining the glass ceiling are also now being rejected as erroneous. For example, the popular media have helped promote the belief that female managers choose family over career and this is why they are underrepresented in the upper ranks of management. However, there is accumulating evidence that the primary reason women leave their organizations is the lack of career advancement opportunities.[28] Another reason for the glass ceiling is the charge that women do not manifest the same leadership skills as men. Yet studies, such as AT&T's, have found no differences between male and female managers on their overall levels of leadership skills per se. In fact, what was found in this study was that women are better performers than men in many of the foundation skills required for effective leadership and management performance. Specifically, women were found to be superior to their male counterparts in interpersonal skills, perception of social cues, work involvement, behavior flexibility, personal impact, and freedom from prejudice against racial, ethnic, and other social groups.[29]

Not only has recent research brought into question some of the traditional explanations for the glass ceiling, it is also becoming clear that the widely recommended ways for dealing with the glass ceiling simply do not work. For example, an affirmative action approach, which is perhaps the most commonly employed strategy for dealing with discrimination of women and minorities in the workplace, has had only very marginal success in breaking the glass ceiling. A number of reasons can be cited for this result, including a lukewarm management commitment to the effort and the widely held belief that women promoted on the basis of affirmative action efforts would never have gotten there on their own ability. Another action strategy, gender training, often results in short-term results, at best, and sometimes only seems to magnify the differences between men and women. The same could be said for the seeding strategy of directly placing women into senior-level positions. This bypasses the glass ceiling, but the problem is that the seeding strategy typically involves putting women into upper-level staff rather than line jobs, where their authority and ability to use their talents are much more limited. They are viewed almost as interns, rather than full-fledged managers. This type of staff position is a dead-end job.

The glass ceiling issue is not going to be solved overnight, but there are strategies and programs that firms must attempt to implement. To begin with, there must be a realization that the reasons for sex segregation patterns in organizations are neither simple nor attributable just to women. Organizations must design and implement programs that systematically attack discrimination and segregation at multiple levels of the structure. Sound research is needed to draw valid conclusions concerning the best approach to eliminate pay and promotion discrimination, and not rely on hunches, opinions, and general intuition.

Employee Privacy Issues

In addition to sexual harassment and discrimination in pay and promotion, another major ethical issue involves privacy in the workplace. In recent years, a number of developments have occurred which directly influence employees' right to privacy. One such development is computer technology that now makes it ever easier for employers to learn information about their employees. Another is mandatory drug testing, a policy that has been instituted by many organizations. A third is efforts of organizations to control the lifestyles of their employees.

Besides computer data banks that keep all types of personal information, another way that computer technology is having an impact on employee privacy is by allowing others to tap into one's communications. For example, an increasing number of employees use electronic mail (E-mail) and have a special identification code that supposedly ensures them privacy. Unfortunately, these codes can and do get out and the messages in the person's E-mail file can be read. In a recent case, still in litigation, two U.S. Nissan trainers had their E-mail messages reviewed by their supervisor, who found nasty comments made about himself. He rebuked the two trainers who, in turn, sued the company for violation of their privacy. They charged that they had a reasonable expectation of privacy when using E-mail. Nor does technological snooping end here. A recent survey by *Macworld*, a magazine for computer users, found that supervisors in 21 percent of the 301 companies responding had examined employees' computer files, E-mail, or telephone voice mail in order to help measure worker performance or investigate company thefts.[30]

Another important privacy issue involves drug testing. An ethical question is whether such testing violates an employee's right to privacy. An increasing number of firms do not feel that it does. They are requiring such testing for new employees, and many also make it a condition of employment that all workers be periodically tested. The American Management Association recently reported that of the 630 member companies who responded to a survey, 85 percent conduct drug testing, which is up sharply from the 52 percent who required such testing at the beginning of the decade. In addition, the federal government requires that all contractors who do more than $20,000 worth of government business conduct random tests on a cross section of the workers. Other organizations, such as Motorola, test all employees every three years, no matter how long they have been with the firm.[31]

A relatively new threat to privacy comes in the form of companies' dictating the personal lifestyles of their employees. For example, can a company dismiss two employees who begin dating each other because it has a policy that forbids workers' fraternizing with each other? Can the firm refuse to hire smokers and enforce a no-smoking policy in the workplace? Can the company insist that employees not race motorcycles or bungee jump? These are all examples of personal lifestyle choices that have gotten employees into trouble with their employers in recent years. In some cases the employers can enforce such policies because the workers are not legally protected.[32] For example, a growing number of firms now refuse to hire smokers and point to the additional costs in medical claims and sick days that result from smoking. Similarly, some hospitals now offer their employees financial incentives if they have good lifestyle habits (no smoking, drinking in moderation, keeping weight within prescribed limits). The justification for these programs is based on lower health care and insurance costs and greater work productivity. On the other hand, there are many people who oppose these lifestyle-related regulations on ethical grounds, feeling that the organization is attempting to dictate and control people's lives.

Privacy issues are likely to be an increasing ethical concern in the years ahead. To more effectively manage the privacy issue, organizations could take steps such as the following:

1. Tell the employees up front what types of limits the firm is going to put on their behavior.
2. Explain the reasons for these decisions.
3. Continually monitor the program to ensure that the information that is being collected or the decisions that are being made have the best interests of the individual employee and the overall organization in mind.

If employees are told up front, so that they can understand what is happening and why, then they are less likely to feel that the firm is snooping or trying to invade their privacy. They are more likely to understand that an intrusion in their lives is minimal and designed to be helpful to all concerned.

Summary

Two of the major challenges facing modern organizations are diversity and ethics. Diversity exists when members of a group or organization differ from each other in terms of age, gender, ethnicity, and/or education. There are a number of reasons for the rise of diversity in organizations, including the increasing number of women, minorities, and older employees in the work force, and legislative rulings that now require organizations to ensure equal opportunity to women, minorities, older employees, and those challenged by a disability. There are individual and organizational approaches to managing diversity. Approaches at the individual level include learning and empathy; at the organizational level, testing, training, mentoring, and the use of alternative work schedules can be implemented.

Ethics is involved with moral issues and choices and deals with right and wrong behavior. A number of cultural (family, friends, neighbors, education, religion, and the media), organizational (ethical codes, role models, policies and practices, and reward and punishment systems), and external forces (political, legal, and economic developments) help determine ethical behavior. These influences, acting interdependently, serve to help identify and shape ethical behavior in today's organizations. Some of the major ethical issues especially relevant to the study of organizational behavior include sexual harassment, discrimination in pay and promotion, and the rights of privacy. Each of these ethical issues represents a challenge to today's organizations and must be given recognition and attention and be carefully managed.

Questions for Discussion and Review

1. What is meant by diversity, and what are the major reasons that have made it a challenge for today's organizations?
2. What are some of the major characteristics of diversity?
3. How can diversity be managed? Offer suggestions at both the individual and organizational levels.
4. What is meant by ethics, and what types of factors influence ethical behavior?
5. Many organizations are determined to eliminate sexual harassment. What are some steps that can be taken?
6. There are a number of misconceptions that people have about the glass ceiling. What are some of these? Also, what can organizations do to help break the glass ceiling?
7. Because privacy issues are likely to become increasingly important in the years ahead, what can organizations do to effectively deal with this ethical challenge?

Footnote References and Supplemental Readings

1. *Occupational Outlook Handbook*, U.S. Bureau of Labor Statistics, Washington, D.C., 1990–1991, pp. 8–12.
2. Howard N. Fullerton, Jr., "New Labor Force Projections, Spanning 1988–2000," *Monthly Labor Review*, November 1989, pp. 3–12. Also see Brian Bremner and Joseph Weber, "A Spicier Stew in the Melting Pot," *Business Week*, Dec. 21, 1992, pp. 29–30.
3. Aaron Bernstein, "The Young and the Jobless," *Business Week*, Aug. 16, 1993, p. 107.
4. For more on this topic, see Lynn R. Offermann and Marilyn K. Gowing, "Organizations of the Future: Changes and Challenges," *American Psychologist*, February 1990, pp. 95–108.
5. Patrick J. O'Connor, "Getting Down to Basics," *Training and Development*, July 1993, pp. 62–63.
6. Richard M. Hodgetts, *Continuous Improvement: Lessons from the Baldrige Winners*, American Management Association, New York, 1993, p. 89.
7. Bailey W. Jackson, Frank LaFasto, Henry G. Schultz,

and Don Kelly, "Diversity," *Human Resource Management*, Spring/Summer 1992, p. 22.
8. Ibid., pp. 22–24.
9. Sara M. Freedman and Robert T. Keller, "The Handicapped in the Workforce," *Academy of Management Review*, July 1981, p. 453.
10. Dawn Gunsch, "Games Augment Diversity Training," *Personnel Journal*, June 1993, pp. 76–83.
11. See Belle Rose Ragins and John L. Cotton, "Gender and Willingness to Mentor in Organizations," *Journal of Management*, Spring 1993, pp. 97–111.
12. Richard M. Hodgetts and K. Galen Kroeck, *Personnel and Human Resource Management*, Dryden Press, Fort Worth, Tex., 1992, p. 403.
13. Terence Roth, "Europe Ponders the Shorter Work Week," *The Wall Street Journal*, Nov. 12, 1993, p. A10.
14. Tony Horwitz, "Minimum Wage Jobs Give Many Americans Only a Miserable Life," *The Wall Street Journal*, Nov. 12, 1993, pp. A1, 4.

15. Wade Lambert, "Obese Workers Win On-the-Job Protection Against Bias," *The Wall Street Journal*, Nov. 12, 1993, pp. B1, 7.

16. Linda Klebe Trevino and Bart Victor, "Peer Reporting of Unethical Behavior: A Social Context Perspective," *Academy of Management Journal*, March 1992, pp. 38–64.

17. G. Stephen Taylor and J. P. Shim, "A Comparative Examination of Attitudes Toward Software Piracy Among Business Professors and Executives," *Human Relations*, April 1993, pp. 419–433.

18. "Guidelines on Discrimination on the Basis of Sex," *Equal Employment Opportunity*, Washington, D.C., Nov. 10, 1980, p. 2.

19. Brigid Moynahan, "Creating Harassment-Free Work Zones," *Training and Development Journal*, May 1993, p. 67.

20. For some examples of court decisions, see David E. Terpstra and Douglas D. Baker, "Outcomes of Federal Court Decisions on Sexual Harassment," *Academy of Management Journal*, March 1992, pp. 181–190.

21. For more on this topic, see Robert K. Robinson, Billie M. Allen, Geralyn McClure Franklin, and David L. Duhon, "Sexual Harassment in the Workplace: A Review of the Legal Rights and Responsibilities of All Parties," *Public Personnel Management*, Spring 1993, pp. 123–136.

22. See, for example, John M. D. Kremer and Jenny Marks, "Sexual Harassment: The Response of Management and Trade Unions," *Journal of Occupational and Organizational Psychology*, March 1992, pp. 5–15.

23. Virginia M. Gibson, "Beyond Legal Compliance: What's Next?" *Personnel*, July 1993, p. 17.

24. Joan E. Rigdon, "Three Decades After the Equal Pay Act, Women's Wages Remain Far from Parity," *The Wall Street Journal*, June 9, 1993, pp. B1, 3.

25. Julie Amparano Lopez, "Firms Use Contracts and Cash to Prevent Talent Raids by Departing Executives," *The Wall Street Journal*, July 9, 1993, pp. B1–2.

26. "A Report on the Glass Ceiling Initiative," *Office of Information and Public Affairs*, U.S. Department of Labor, Washington, D.C., 1991, p. 1.

27. Robert A. Snyder, "The Glass Ceiling for Women: Things That Don't Cause It and Things That Won't Break It," *Human Resource Development Quarterly*, Spring 1993, p. 99.

28. C. Trost, "Women Managers Quit, Not for Family, but to Advance Their Corporate Climb," *The Wall Street Journal*, May 2, 1990, pp. B1–2, and H. M. Rosin and K. Korabik, "Marital and Family Correlates of Women Managers' Attribution from Organizations," *Journal of Vocational Behavior*, vol. 37, 1990, pp. 104–120.

29. Ann Howard and Douglas Bray, *Managerial Lives in Transition*, Guilford Press, New York, 1988.

30. Lee Smith, "Whose Office Is This Anyhow?" *Fortune*, Aug. 9, 1993, p. 93.

31. Lee Smith, "What the Boss Knows About You," *Fortune*, Aug. 9, 1993, pp. 90–91.

32. Lee Smith, "Can Smoking or Bungee Jumping Get You Canned?" *Fortune*, Aug. 9, 1993, p. 92.

**REAL CASE:
Not Treating
Everyone
the Same**

As recently as the 1980s, managers in some of the most productive organizations in the country used to pride themselves on treating all their employees equally. This typically meant holding the line on rules and regulations so that everyone conformed to the same set of guidelines. Moreover, when people were evaluated, they were typically assessed on the basis of their performance at the workplace. In recent years there has been a dramatic change in management's thinking. Instead of treating everyone the same, some organizations are now trying to meet the specific needs of employees. What is done for one individual employee may not be done for another. Additionally, instead of evaluating all employees on how well they work at the workplace, attention is being focused on how much "value added" people contribute regardless of how many hours they are physically at the workplace. This new philosophy is also spilling over into the way alternative work arrangements are being handled.

An example is Aetna Life & Casualty, where workers are given the option of reducing their workweek or compressing the time into fewer days. Under this arrangement, a parent who wants to spend more time at home with the children can opt to cut working hours from forty down to thirty per week or put in four ten-hour days and have a long weekend with the kids. In either case, these personal decisions do not negatively affect the employee's opportunities for promotion. Why is the company so willing to accommodate the personal desires of the workers? One of the main reasons is that Aetna was losing hundreds of talented people every year and felt that the cost to the company was too great. Something had to be done to keep these people on the payroll. As a result, today approximately 2000 of Aetna's 44,000 employees work part-time, share a job, work at home, or are on a compressed workweek arrangement. The company estimates that it saves approximately $1 million annually by not having to train new workers. Moreover, the company reported that in one recent year 88 percent of those employees who took family leave returned to work. An added benefit of this program is the fact that Aetna's reputation as a good place to work has been strengthened. The Families and Work Institute recently named Aetna one of the top four "family-friendly" companies.

Duke Power & Light is another good example of how companies are changing their approach to managing employees. Realizing that child care is a growing need among many employees, since in most households both parents now work, the company joined forces with other employers to build a child-care center. The firm has also changed its work schedule assignments. In the past, many employees reported that they hated working swing shifts: days one week, evenings the next, and then nights. So the firm created twenty-two work schedules and now lets employees bid on them annually, based on seniority. Some of these shifts are the traditional five-day week of eight-hour days. Others, however, are compressed workweek alternatives, including four ten-hour days and three twelve-hour days. At the same time, the company has been turning more authority over to the personnel and has driven up its employee-to-manager ratio from 12 to 1 to 20 to 1. As a result, the company now has an attrition rate that is over three times lower than the industry average and most of this attrition is a result of people's transferring to other jobs in the utility. As one manager put it, "We needed to recognize that people have lives." On the basis of results, it is obvious that the new arrangement is a win-win situation for both the workers and the firm.

1. How is the new management philosophy described in this case different from that of the old, traditional philosophy? Identify and describe the differences.
2. In what way are alternative work schedules proving helpful to managing diversity?
3. Do you think these new programs are likely to continue or will they taper off? Why?

**REAL CASE:
Putting
Harassment
in Its Place**

Sexual harassment in the workplace has occurred over the years, but only in recent years has it received widespread attention. For example, in 1987 there were over 5000 sexual harassment complaints filed with the Equal Employment Opportunity Commission; in five years this number had doubled to over 10,000. Another development is provided by a recent Supreme Court ruling in *Harris v. Forklift Systems, Inc.* in which the plaintiff charged that she was continually harassed by her boss's sexual remarks. Reaffirming the legal standards it established in the mid-1980s, the Court has now gone further and held that it is no longer necessary to prove that one has suffered serious psychological damage. As one of the justices, writing for the majority of the Court, put it, "It suffices to prove that a reasonable person subjected to the discriminatory conduct would find, as the plaintiff did, that the harassment so altered working conditions as to 'make it more difficult to do the job.'" This new ruling has many companies so concerned with their approach to sexual harassment that they are rethinking their strategies and procedures for handling complaints.

For openers, today's organizations are more carefully spelling out their policy on sexual harassment and ensuring that everyone is fully aware of what this policy means. Experts on the subject report that while most firms have a policy on sexual harassment, as many as 90 percent of the people in the firm do not know what it is. As a result, programs are now being offered to correct this deficiency, and they appear to be having the desired effect. After one was offered at Aetna, a participant remarked: "The guys in the class were absolutely not resistant to it, not at all. In fact, it's a relief to have someone spell out exactly what sexual harassment is. The men in my session were all saying, 'It's about time.'"

Another development is the creation of special training programs designed to help participants both identify and deal with sexual harassment. Hundreds of major companies now report that they are planning to increase the amount of training given to their managers and employees. Included in this group are DuPont, Federal Express, General Mills, Levi Strauss, Merck, and Syntex. As part of the process, most organizations are also formulating a strategy for both developing and implementing the training. Steps such as the following are suggested:

1. Employees are surveyed to find out the extent of sexual harassment that takes place in their work environment.
2. A strongly worded sexual harassment policy is written and circulated through the company, giving specific examples of prohibited behavior and describing possible disciplinary actions that will be taken against proven harassers.
3. A reporting procedure is created for reporting violations of the policy and for protecting the rights of both the complainants and those accused of harassment.
4. A system for ensuring prompt and fair investigations is put into effect.
5. Strong managerial support is garnered for both developing and implementing sexual harassment training, including having senior-level managers convey their commitment to all employees.
6. Programs are created not only for educating the employees about harassment issues but also for helping eliminate unacceptable behavior.

There are two major reasons companies are determined to stamp out sexual harassment. One is that they want to create a positive, equitable, and productive work climate. The other is that they want to reduce their legal costs. There is evidence that 90 percent of the Fortune 500 companies have dealt with sexual harassment complaints and the average company spends over $6.5 million annually dealing with this problem. Moreover, each complaint that is investigated and found to be valid, whether or not it gets to court, costs the firm an average of $200,000. Quite clearly, it is in the best interests of the firm to end harassment in the workplace.

1. Why is it important that employees understand their company's sexual harassment policy?
2. How useful are training programs in dealing with sexual harassment? Explain.
3. In addition to training, what other steps are useful in combating sexual harassment in the workplace?

INTEGRATIVE CONTEMPORARY CASE/READING FOR PART 1

Welcome to the Revolution

Let us not use the word cheaply. Revolution, says Webster's, is "a sudden, radical, or complete change . . . a basic reorientation." To anyone in the world of business, that sounds about right. We all sense that the changes surrounding us are not mere trends but the workings of large, unruly forces: the globalization of markets; the spread of information technology and computer networks; the dismantling of hierarchy, the structure that has essentially organized work since the mid-19th century. Growing up around these is a new, information-age economy, whose fundamental sources of wealth are knowledge and communication rather than natural resources and physical labor.

Each of these transformations is a no-fooling business revolution. Yet all are happening *at the same time*—and fast. They cause one another and affect one another. As they feed on one another, they nourish a feeling that business and society are in the midst of a revolution comparable in scale and consequence to the Industrial Revolution. Asks George Bennett, chairman of the Symmetrix consulting firm: "If 2% of the population can grow all the food we eat, what if another 2% can manufacture all the refrigerators and other things we need?"

Good question. The parking lot of General Electric's appliance factory in Louisville, Kentucky, was built in 1953 to hold 25,000 cars. Today's work force is 10,000. In 1985, 406,000 people worked for IBM, which made profits of $6.6 billion. A third of the people, and all of the profits, are gone now. Automaker Volkswagen says it needs just two-thirds of its present work force. Procter & Gamble, with sales rising, is dismissing 12% of its employees. Manufacturing is not alone in downsizing: Cigna Reinsurance, an arm of the Philadelphia giant, has trimmed its work force 25% since 1990.

Change means opportunity as well as danger, in the same way that the Industrial Revolution, while it wrought havoc in the countryside and in the swelling town, brought undreamed-of prosperity. No one can say for certain what new ways of working and prospering this revolution will create; in a revolution the only surety is surprise.

The transition may be difficult. As Neal Soss, chief economist for C.S. First Boston, puts it: "Adjustment is the dismal part of the dismal science." And, as Robespierre might have observed on his way to the guillotine, this time it's personal—for the inescapable tumult involves your company and your career. The paragraphs and stories that follow explain the causes and consequences of this era of radical change—and introduce some business leaders who are meeting the challenges it poses.

General Electric Lighting is an ancient business begun in 1878. It is headquartered in Cleveland on a leafy campus of brick Georgian buildings separated by placid lawns. Like sin into Eden, the world burst through the gates in 1983, when traditional rival Westinghouse sold its lamp operations to Philips Electronics of Holland. To John Opie, GE Lighting's chief, the memory is so vivid that he describes it in the present tense: "Suddenly we have bigger, stronger competition. They're coming to our market, but we're not in theirs. So we're on the defensive."

Source: Thomas A. Stewart, "Welcome to the Revolution," *Fortune,* December 13, 1993, pp. 66–68, 70, 72, 76, 78.

Not long: GE's 1990 acquisition of Hungarian lighting company Tungsram was the first big move by a Western company in Eastern Europe. Now, after buying Thorn EMI in Britain in 1991, GE has 18% of Europe's lighting market and is moving into Asia via a joint venture with Hitachi. As recently as 1988, GE Lighting got less than 20% of its sales from outside the U.S. This year, Opie says, more than 40% of sales will come from abroad; by 1996, more than half will. In a few short years, Opie's world changed utterly.

What happened at GE Lighting illustrates the surprises and paradoxes of globalization. Surprise: Globalization isn't old hat. Global competition has accelerated sharply in just the past few years. The market value of U.S. direct investment abroad rose 35%, to $776 billion, from 1987 to 1992, while the value of foreign direct investment in America more than doubled, to $692 billion.

You ain't seen nothin' yet. The extraordinary rise in overseas telephone traffic may best gauge how much more often people in different nations feel they have something urgent to say to one another—a good deal of it coordinating business activity. First Boston's Neal Soss points out that in the past five years or so the commercial world has been swelled by the former Soviet empire, China, India, Indonesia, and much of Latin America—billions of people stepping out from behind political and economic walls. This is the most dramatic change in the geography of capitalism in history.

Paradox: Though it's hard to imagine a more macroeconomic subject, globalization is intensely parochial. Globalization's strongest effects are on companies. Says Anant Sundaram, professor at Dartmouth's Tuck School of business: "Statistics at the macro level grossly underestimate globalization's presence and impact." For example, Chrysler got just 7% of sales from outside the U.S. and Canada in 1992, but in the 1980s global competition nearly killed it.

Investment numbers also reveal too little, for they do not count minority ownership or alliances—or the impact of competition originating abroad. Notes Frederick Kovac, vice president for planning at Goodyear, whose products can be found on all seven continents and the moon: "The major strategic decisions of our biggest competitors are made in France and Japan." Sales by overseas subsidiaries of American corporations are about three times greater than the value of all U.S. exports. Thus a lot of commerce that looks domestic to an economist—such as the Stouffer's frozen dinner you bought last week—looks international to a chief financial officer, in this case Nestlé's.

This makes for a profound change, Mr. CFO, in your job. Some observers argue that it is time you forget about the business cycle, or at least pay a lot less mind to it. Says Gail Fosler, chief economist of the Conference Board: "It's every industry on its own. When I talk to companies, it's very difficult to describe a business environment that's true for everybody." For example, she argues, as FORTUNE's economists also hold, that capital spending "is no longer driven by business cycle considerations but by global competition." If the world is your oyster, an oyster is your whole world.

Horace "Woody" Brock, president of Strategic Economic Decisions, an advisory firm in California, agrees. He says a nation's economy should be viewed as a portfolio of businesses whose fates are less and less linked: "What happens in the U.S. copper industry may be caused by shocks in Africa, and will have no effect on Silicon Valley. Silicon Valley may drive events in Japan's electronics industry, but these in turn will be uncorrelated with the auto industry in either Japan or Detroit." Look at Seattle, Brock says, where two great technology companies, Boeing and Microsoft, operate side-by-side, one sagging, one booming—"utterly out of sync."

For a nation, the net effect should be more stability, with long odds against all sectors booming or busting together. For individual businesses, however, it's a different story. Says Brock: "If your competitor in Germany does something, you react *immediately*—you don't wait for interest rates or recovery or anything else."

Fortunately, the revolution in information technology is creating tools that permit just such agility.

Robert Immerman is the founder of InterDesign, a private company in Solon, Ohio, with annual sales above $10 million. InterDesign sells plastic clocks, refrigerator magnets, soap dishes, and the like. Wal-Mart, Kmart, and Target are customers, as are hundreds of houseware stores.

There's not a high-tech item among its products, but computers have changed the business. In the past 12 years, InterDesign's employment has tripled, total space has quintupled, and sales have octupled, but its megabytes of computer memory have gone up 30-fold. Seven years ago Immerman dug deep and found $10,000 to buy a used disk drive that had 288 megabytes of storage—capacity that costs about $350 today. Says Immerman: "In the Seventies we went to the Post Office to pick up our orders. In the early Eighties we put in an 800 number. Late Eighties, we got a fax machine. In 1991, pressured first by Target, we added electronic data interchange."

Now, just two years later, more than half of InterDesign's orders arrive via modem straight into company computers. Errors in order entry and shipping have all but disappeared. Immerman says: "We had 50 weeks perfect with a big chain. Then one week we missed part of the order for one item on a long list—and they're on the phone wondering what's wrong." Staffers who used to man phones taking orders now track sales by product, color, customer, region—valuable information that Immerman once couldn't afford to collect.

InterDesign's story is typical. In Alcoa's Davenport, Iowa, factory, which rolls aluminum foil, sheet, and plate, a computer stands at every work post to control machinery or communicate data about schedules and production. Practically every package deliverer, bank teller, retail clerk, telephone operator, and bill collector in America works with a computer. Microchips have invaded automobiles and clothes dryers. Three out of ten American homes have a PC.

The revolution begins when these computers hook up to one another. Already two out of five computers in the U.S. are part of a network—mostly intracompany nets, but more and more are crossing company lines, just as InterDesign's electronic data interchange does. Data traffic over phone wires is growing 30% a year, says Danielle Danese, a telecommunications analyst at Salomon Brothers. Traffic on the global Internet doubles every year.

The potential for information sharing is almost unimaginable. On the wall of every classroom, dorm room, and office at Case Western Reserve University is a box containing a phone jack, coaxial cable, and four fiber-optic lines. Through that box a student could suck down the entire contents of the Library of Congress in less than a minute, if the library were on-line and she had room to store it.

For years CEOs and economists lamented that billions invested in information technology had returned little to productivity. That dirge is done. Says William Wheeler, a consultant at Coopers & Lybrand: "For the first time the computer is an enabler of productivity improvement rather than a cause of lack of productivity."

Instantaneous, cross-functional communication about orders and scheduling enabled M.A. Hanna, the $1.3-billion-in-annual-sales polymer maker, to speed production, reduce inventory, and cut waste so much that the company needs a third less working capital to get a dollar of sales than it did four years ago. CEO Martin D. Walker notes that this gain came entirely within the four walls of the company; he estimates that an equal gain in working capital turnover is waiting to be found by networking with suppliers and customers.

Efficiency is a first-order effect of new technology: That's how you justify the capital expenditure. The second-order effects are more interesting, because unpredicted. One disorienting result of the spread of computer nets has been the transformation of sales, marketing, and distribution. To see the change, says Fred Wiersema, a consultant at CSC Index in Cambridge, Massachusetts, dig a ten-year-old marketing plan out of the file and compare it with a new one: "The distribution channel is a mess. Customers have much more power. There's fragmentation in media and advertising. The activities of the sales force are completely different."

The next trend, says William Bluestein, director of computing strategy research for Forrester Research, a Massachusetts firm: "Companies that empower their customers." Soon, pursuing cost savings, suppliers and customers will be able to rummage around in each other's computers, entering orders directly, checking stock and shipping status. One vehicle manufacturer can already go into Goodyear's system. Says strategist Kovac: "There will be a day in the not-distant future when customers will get data on the tests of a new tire as soon as our engineers do. They'll see everything—warts and all."

From there it's a short step before customers start comparing notes—maybe on your network. Says Bluestein: "If I were Ralph Nader, I'd set up a consumer chat line so someone who was thinking of buying a Saturn could ask people who have one how they like it. If GM were smart, they'd do it themselves."

Like globalization, information technology vastly extends a company's reach—but has the paradoxical effect of rewarding intimacy. Computers enormously increase the amount of information a company can have about its market—but deliver premium returns less to careful planning than to quick responses to changing circumstances.

Both phenomena have powerful implications for the way work is organized.

In 1958 *Harvard Business Review* published an article called "Management in the 1980s" by Harold J. Leavitt and Thomas L. Whisler, professors at the Carnegie Institute of Technology and the University of Chicago. It predicted that the computer would do to middle management what the Black Death did to 14th-century Europeans. So it has: If you're middle management and still have a job, don't enter your boss's office alone. Says GE Lighting's John Opie: "There are just two people between me and a salesman—information technology replaced the rest."

Leavitt and Whisler, knowing only mainframes, foresaw an Orwellian workplace in which the surviving middle managers were tightly controlled from on high, little different from the proles they bossed. In a world of expensive, centralized computing, it might have happened that way. But distributed computing redistributes power. Says Goodyear's Kovac: "It used to be, if you wanted information, you had to go up, over, and down through the organization. Now you just tap in. Everybody can know as much about the company as the chairman of the board. That's what broke down the hierarchy. It's not why we bought computers, but it's what they did."

The management revolution has many fathers, some more venerable than the computer; self-managed teams and total quality management have intellectual roots reaching back half a century. Why, then, does it seem as if the mores and structures of management are undergoing *discontinuous* change? Is this really new? Or are we deluding ourselves, the way each generation of teenagers thinks it discovered sex?

The evidence suggests a basic shift in the organization of work. Look first at the ubiquity of change. No longer is the management revolution confined to the same dozen trendsetting companies, the GEs, Motorolas, and Xeroxes. Says Stephen Gage, president of the Cleveland Advanced Manufacturing Program, a federally subsidized organization that helps small business apply new technology: "I doubt if there's a company around here that isn't experimenting with something having to do with dismantling Taylorism."

Equally striking, leading companies now envision an endlessly changing organizational design. Kovac says: "The key term is 'reconfigurable.' We want an organization that's reconfigurable on an annual, monthly, weekly, daily, even hourly basis. Immutable systems are dinosaurs." To make this sort of agility possible, leaders are honing such techniques as rapid product development, flexible production systems, and team-based incentives.

At bottom, the management revolution triumphs because the underlying economics of communication and control have changed, and those changes favor small, flexible organizations, not big ones. The argument, developed by microeconomists influenced by Berkeley's Oliver Williamson (and here oversimplified), goes like this:

A transaction can be accomplished in one of two basic ways: You can go out and buy something from someone else, or you can produce it yourself. (Yes, there are hybrid forms, but remember that we're oversimplifying.) Call the first system a market and the second a hierarchy. Vertically integrated businesses, in which transactions take place between divisions, each with its own organizational ziggurat, are hierarchies. Each system has its advantages. Markets generally deliver the lowest price, because of competition. But hierarchies usually have lower coordinating costs—such as for salesmen, advertising, or debt collection. Depending on how those costs and benefits line up, a given industry will tend to be more or less vertically integrated, feature larger or smaller companies, and display a bureaucratic or entrepreneurial management style.

Now buy a computer. The costs change. In particular, hierarchies begin to lose their comparative advantage in coordinating costs. Invoicing is automated, decimating armies of clerks. Electronic order-entry cuts selling costs. Says Thomas W. Malone, professor at the Sloan School of Management at MIT: "Coordinating activities are information-intensive, and computers make coordinating better and cheaper." The result, Malone argues, is to increase the range of transactions in which markets are more desirable. Result: More companies decide to buy what they once produced in-house.

The nice thing about this argument is that it checks out. Big companies are breaking up; outsourcing is on the rise. According to Roy Smith, vice president of Microelectronics & Computer Technology Corp., three out of ten large U.S. industrial companies outsource more than half their manufacturing.

Businesses are more tightly focused: Conference Board figures show that between 1979 and 1991 the number of three-digit standard industrial classifications (SIC codes) in which an average U.S. manufacturer does business dropped from 4.35 to 2.12. Companies are also smaller: Census data show that the number of employees at the average U.S. workplace is 8% lower than it was in 1980. Combining those figures with data on spending for information technology, MIT's Malone and several colleagues found the shrinkage is greatest in industries where IT spending is highest.

Smaller payrolls are not simply the result of automation, for gross shipments and value-added also decline. The strong implication: In an information-age business, small is beautiful.

Of the four horsemen of revolutionary change, the hardest to grasp is the invention of an information-age economy. How can a whole economy be based on intangible knowledge and communication? Yet intellectual capital—knowledge that can be captured and deployed to create advantage over competitors—is as vital a business concern as capital of the familiar monetary sort. Intellectual labor, too, is where the action is, a fact demonstrated by the widening gap between the pay of college-educated workers and those less schooled.

Though knowledge assets and outputs are intangible, they are no less real for being so. It is possible to track the "intellectual content" of the economy. In 1991, business investment in computers and telecommunications equipment—tools of the new economy that create, sort, store, and ship knowledge—for the first time exceeded capital spending for industrial, construction, and other "old economy" equipment. The figures, while impressive, understate investment in knowledge machines because they do not show the growing intellectual ability of industrial gear. For example, more than half of machine-tool spending in the U.S. is for equipment with built-in computer numerical controls that, often, can be connected to networks. Says Jodie Glore, vice president of the automation group at industrial-controls powerhouse Allen-Bradley: "The electromechanical boxes we used to sell had a macho feel. You could *tell* that they cost a lot. Now it's, 'You see this disk . . . ?'"

The new economy will transform the old and reduce its relative importance, but will not kill it. The Industrial Revolution did not end agriculture, because we still have to eat, and the Information Revolution will not end industry, because we still need cans to hold beer. Microsoft Chairman Bill Gates, up to now the preeminent capitalist of the knowledge age, spends his money on a big house and fancy cars, tangible stuff indeed.

The first effect of intellectual capital and knowledge work is to alter the economics of familiar goods and services—a process well under way. For example, in the now misnamed "industrialized" world, the amount of energy needed to produce a given amount of GDP has fallen 2% a year, compounded, for more than 20 years. Factory labor is less physically demanding: Gone the heroic workman, a WPA mural in living flesh, ruddy in the glow of the blast furnace; now she's likely to be a middle-aged mom, sitting in front of a screen, who attends night school to study statistical process control. Many auto repairs will soon be made not by a grease monkey with a wrench but by a technician who fixes an engine knock by reprogramming a microchip.

As the usefulness of information, information technology, and information work grows, businesses find more ways to substitute them for expensive investments in physical assets, such as factories, warehouses, and inventories. By using high-speed data communications networks to track production, stock, and orders, GE Lighting has closed 26 of 34 U.S. warehouses since 1987 and replaced 25 customer service centers with one new, high-tech center. In effect, those buildings and stockpiles—physical assets—have been replaced by networks and databases—intellectual assets.

Similarly, the cost of establishing a retail bank branch has shrunk: You can find one inside the door of the supermarket, next to the Coke machine. Especially in the Christmas shopping season, each day's mail brings you a stack of department stores.

For the right products, catalogue retailers will migrate to computer or television networks. Rent in cyberspace is even cheaper than catalogue space, and much lower than rent at the mall.

The shift to the information economy, like globalization, computerization, and the management revolution, appears first as a way of doing old jobs more cheaply. For those on efficiency's receiving end, it is a threat. But the drive for efficiency has also paid to string 12 million miles of optical fiber in the U.S., and, long before any couch potato has ordered up video-on-demand, efficiency will pay for a lot more construction of the electronic superhighway, the infrastructure of the information economy.

That endeavor, says Paul Saffo, an analyst at the Institute for the Future in Menlo Park, California, "is a full-employment act for entrepreneurs." Compared with trade in traditional goods and services, commerce in knowledge is startup heaven. Entry barriers are low. Distribution and marketing of information need little capital; they don't even require access to a printing press anymore. Many products and services can be distributed electronically.

The second-order effect of change, opportunity, is the unpredictable one. Gottlieb Daimler, Ransom Olds, and their pals thought they had invented an improvement on the horse. They did not know that the automobile would fill the countryside with suburbs—which, in turn, created thousands of jobs building houses, making lawnmowers, and delivering pizza. The knowledge economy is still so young that we have few hints of its second-order effects, in the view of Richard Collin, who studies the subject as director of Neurope Lab, a think tank in Archamps, France, near Geneva. Says Collin: "Today we are thinking in terms of using knowledge to improve productivity in our old businesses—how to do the same with less. Tomorrow we will think of competition—how to do more in new businesses."

It makes sense that the core business of the knowledge economy will be . . . knowledge. Information, like electricity, does nothing unless it is harnessed in useful devices, like appliances. All kinds of appliance makers—writers of software, creators of databases—are beginning to fill the information-age business directory.

The most valuable devices will be those that help business and people cope with change. Says consultant Fred Wiersema: "Management today has to think like a fighter pilot. When things move so fast, you can't always make the right decision—so you have to learn to adjust, to correct more quickly." The same imperative holds for individuals. Says Kovac: "Today the job is You Inc. When I came to Goodyear in 1958, my chances of promotion were one in eight. For a young person today, they are one in 30, and it's going to one in 50. But I think my children and grandchildren will have more opportunities than I did. They'll just be different."

1. Do you agree that the changes organizations are currently facing are indeed best described as a revolution? What are the major changes? Which one do you think has had and will have the greatest impact? Why?
2. Some questions raised in the article are: "Why, then, does it seem as if the mores and structures of management are undergoing *discontinuous* change? Is this really new? Or are we deluding ourselves, the way each generation of teenagers thinks it discovered sex?" Answer these questions.
3. What do all these environmental changes have to do with the study and application of organizational behavior?

EXPERIENTIAL EXERCISES FOR PART 1

EXERCISE: Synthesis of Student and Instructor Needs*

Goals:
1. To "break the ice" in using experiential exercises
2. To initiate open communication between the students and the instructor regarding mutual learning goals and needs
3. To stimulate the students to clarify their learning goals and instructional needs and to commit themselves to these
4. To serve as the first exercise in the "experiential" approach to management education

Implementation:
1. The class is divided into groups of four to six students each.
2. Each group openly discusses what members would like from the course and drafts a set of learning objectives and instructional aims. The group also makes up a list of learning/course objectives which they feel the instructor wants to pursue. (About twenty minutes.)
3. After each group has "caucused," a group spokesperson is appointed to meet with the instructor in an open dialogue in front of the class about course objectives.
4. The instructor meets with each group representative at the front of the classroom to initiate an open dialogue about the semester of learning. (About thirty minutes.) Several activities are carried out:
   a. Open discussion of the learning objectives of both the students and the instructor
   b. Recognition of the constraints faced by each party in accommodating these goals
   c. Identification of areas of goal agreement and disagreement, and feasible compromises
   d. Drafting a set of guidelines for cooperation between the parties, designed to better bring about mutual goal attainment

EXERCISE: Work-Related Organizational Behavior: Implications for the Course*

Goals:
1. To identify course topic areas from the participant's own work experience
2. To introduce experiential learning

Implementation:

Task 1: Each class member does the following:

1. Describes an experience in a past work situation that illustrates something about organizational behavior. (Some students have had only part-time work experience or summer jobs, but even the humblest job is relevant here.)

---

* *Source:* "Synthesis of Student and Instructor Needs" was suggested by Professor Philip Van Auken and is used with his permission; "Work-Related Organizational Behavior: Implications for the Course" is from "Getting Acquainted Triads," in J. William Pfeiffer and John E. Jones (eds.), *A Handbook of Structured Experiences,* vol. 1, University Associates, San Diego, Calif., 1969, and "Defining Organizational Behavior," in James B. Lau, *Behavior in Organizations,* Irwin, Homewood, Ill., 1975.

2. Explains what it illustrates about organizational behavior. (Time: five minutes for individuals to think about and jot down notes covering these two points.)

Task 2: The class forms into triads and each triad does the following:

1. Member A tells his or her experience to member B. Member B listens carefully, paraphrases the story back to A, and tells what it illustrates about organizational behavior. Member B must do this to A's satisfaction that B has understood fully what A was trying to communicate. Member C is the observer and remains silent during the process.
2. Member B tells his or her story to C, and A is the observer.
3. Member C tells his or her story to A, and B is the observer. (Each member has about five minutes to tell his or her story and have it paraphrased back by the listener. The instructor will call out the time at the end of each five-minute interval for equal apportionment of "airtime" among participants. Total time: fifteen minutes.)

Task 3: Each triad selects one of its members to relate his or her incident to the class. The instructor briefly analyzes for the class how the related story fits in with some topic to be studied in the course, such as perception, motivation, communication, conflict, or leadership. The topic areas are listed in the table of contents of this book.

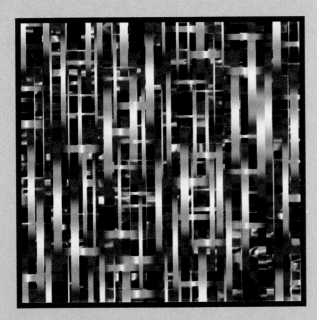

PART 2

A Micro Perspective of Organizational Behavior

4

The Perception Process and Impression Management

Learning Objectives

- **Define** the overall nature of perception, explaining how it differs from sensation.
- **Discuss** perceptual selectivity, including the external attention factors and internal set factors.
- **Explain** perceptual organization, including figure-ground, grouping, constancy, context, and defense principles.
- **Identify** the dimensions of social perception, including attribution, stereotyping, and halo.
- **Examine** the processes and strategies of impression management.

This chapter focuses on the important cognitive process of perception and how it can be applied through impression management. As indicated in Chapter 1, cognitions are basically bits of information, and the cognitive processes involve the ways in which people process that information. In other words, the cognitive processes suggest that, like computers, humans are information processors. However, today's complex computers are very simple information-processing units when compared with *human information processing*.

People's individual differences and uniqueness are largely the result of the cognitive processes. Although there are a number of cognitive processes (imagination, perception, and even thinking), it is generally recognized that the perceptual process is a very important one that takes place between the situation and the behavior and is most relevant to the study of organizational behavior. For example, the observation that a department head and a subordinate may react quite differently to the same top management directive can be better understood and explained by the perceptual process. Also, recent research indicates that things such as age perceptions can affect promotion and performance. One such study found that a merger largely failed because one company's forty-year-old executives and the other company's sixty-five-year-old executives differed over which group was better able to make decisions.[1] It was a matter of differing age perceptions.

In this text, perception is presented as an important cognitive process in understanding organizational behavior. The environment (both antecedent and consequent), plus other psychological processes, such as learning and motivation, and the whole of personality, is also important. However, although much of the material on perception is basic knowledge in the behavioral sciences, it has been largely overlooked or not translated for use by those in the organizational behavior field. All the topics covered in this chapter are concerned with understanding organizational behavior, and they have many direct applications to organization and management practice. In particular, the concluding section of this chapter shows how the perceptual process can be applied to people's attempt to control or manage how others perceive them. Commonly called impression management, this application of the perceptual process can be an important strategy not only in getting selected for a position in an organization but also in becoming successful in life or in an organization.

The first major section presents a theoretical discussion of the general nature and significance of the perceptual process. The relationship between sensation and perception is clarified, and some of the important perceptual subprocesses are discussed. The second section covers the various aspects of perceptual selectivity. Both external factors (intensity, size, contrast, repetition, motion, and novelty and familiarity) and internal ones (motivation, personality, and learning) are included. The third section is concerned with perceptual organization. The principles of figure-ground, grouping, constancy, and context are given primary emphasis. The next section focuses on social perception—the phenomena of attribution, stereotypes, and the halo effect. Finally, attention is given to impression management, which has direct implications for organizational behavior.

THE NATURE AND IMPORTANCE OF PERCEPTION

The key to understanding perception is to recognize that it is a unique *interpretation* of the situation, not an exact recording of it. In short, perception is a very complex cognitive process that yields a unique picture of the world, a picture that may be quite different from reality.

Recognition of the difference between the perceptual world and the real world is vital to the understanding of organizational behavior. A specific example would be the universal assumption made by managers that subordinates always want promotions, when, in fact, many subordinates really feel psychologically *forced* to accept a promotion. Managers seldom attempt to find out, and sometimes subordinates themselves do not know, whether the promotion should be offered. In other words, the perceptual world of the manager is quite different from the perceptual world of the subordinate, and both may be very different from reality. If this is the case, what can be done about it from a management standpoint? The best answer seems to be that a better understanding of the concepts involved should be developed. Direct applications and techniques should logically follow complete understanding. The place to start is to clearly understand the difference between sensation and perception and have a working knowledge of the major cognitive subprocesses of perception.

Sensation Versus Perception

There is usually a great deal of misunderstanding about the relationship between sensation and perception. Behavioral scientists generally agree that people's "reality" (the world around them) depends on their senses. However, the raw sensory input is not enough. They must also process these sensory data and make sense out of them in order to understand the world around them. Thus, the starting point in the study of perception should clarify the relationship between perception and sensation.

The physical senses are considered to be vision, hearing, touch, smell, and taste. There are many other so-called sixth senses. However, none of these sixth senses such as intuition are fully accepted by psychologists. The five senses are constantly bombarded by numerous stimuli that are both outside and inside the body. Examples of outside stimuli include light waves, sound waves, mechanical energy of pressure, and chemical energy from objects that one can smell and taste. Inside stimuli include energy generated by muscles, food passing through the digestive system, and glands secreting behavior-influencing hormones. These examples indicate that sensation deals chiefly with very elementary behavior that is determined largely by physiological functioning. In this way, the human being uses the senses to experience color, brightness, shape, loudness, pitch, heat, odor, and taste.

Perception is more complex and much broader than sensation. The perceptual process can be defined as a complicated interaction of selection, organization, and interpretation. Although perception depends largely upon the senses for raw data, the cognitive process may filter, modify, or completely change these data. A simple illustration may be seen by looking at one side of a stationary object such as a statue or a tree. By slowly turning the eyes to the other side of the object, the person probably *senses* that the object is moving. Yet the person *perceives* the object as stationary. The perceptual process overcomes the sensual process and the person "sees" the object as stationary. In other words, the perceptual process adds to, and subtracts from, the "real" sensory world. The following are some organizational examples that point out the difference between sensation and perception:

1. The purchasing agent buys a part that she thinks is best, not the part that the engineer says is the best.
2. A subordinate's answer to a question is based on what he heard the boss say, not on what the boss actually said.
3. The same worker may be viewed by one supervisor as a very good worker and by another supervisor as a very poor worker.
4. The same widget may be viewed by the inspector to be of high quality and by a customer to be of low quality.

The accompanying Application Example: Help from the Public Sector shows that people even have misperceptions of organizations and entire institutions in society.

Subprocesses of Perception

The existence of several subprocesses gives evidence of the complexity and the interactive nature of perception. Figure 4.1 shows how these subprocesses relate to one another. The first important subprocess is the *stimulus* or *situation* that is present. Perception begins when a person is confronted with a stimulus or a situation. This confrontation may be with the immediate sensual stimulation or with the total physical and sociocultural environment. An example is the employee who is confronted with his or her supervisor or with the total formal organizational environment. Either one or both may initiate the employee's perceptual process. In other words, this represents the stimulus situation interacting with the person.

In addition to the situation-person interaction there are the internal cognitive processes of *registration*, *interpretation*, and *feedback*. During the registration phenomenon, the physiological (sensory and neural) mechanisms are affected; the physiological ability to hear and see will affect perception. Interpretation is the most significant cognitive aspect of perception. The other psychological processes will affect the interpretation of a situation. For example, in an organization, employees' interpretations of a situation are largely dependent upon their learning and motivation and their personality. An example would be the kinesthetic feedback (sensory impressions from muscles) that helps manufacturing workers perceive the speed of

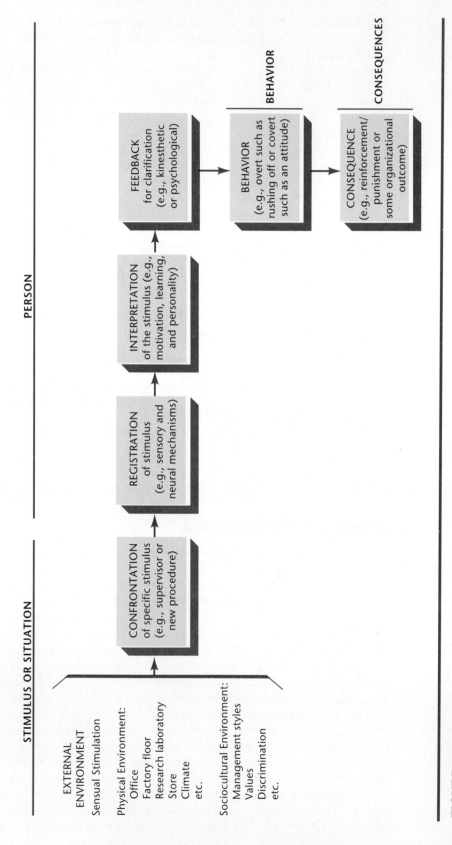

FIGURE 4.1 The subprocesses of perception.

Help from the Public Sector

Most people have perceptions of organizations that are often incorrect. For example, a widespread belief is that Chrysler is the smallest of the big three American automakers because it has the highest costs and is the least innovative. In reality, in recent years Chrysler's costs per car have been significantly lower than at least General Motors', and the firm has become a new-car innovator. For example, it took Chrysler only thirty-one months from drawing board to showroom to develop the innovative Neon, at a relatively very low cost of $1.3 billion. Similarly, many people believe that state and local agencies are terribly inefficient and often waste millions of taxpayer dollars. However, a close look at what many of them are doing reveals that they are not only efficient, but are performing important low-cost social services for their respective communities.

An example of the latter is the South Carolina state government, which works very hard to attract outside businesses so that South Carolinians can be gainfully employed. Although the state spends millions of dollars for worker training and development, it is beginning to be cost-effective. Companies looking to set up new operations are attracted to South Carolina's pool of highly talented workers. In the case of BMW, which recently chose South Carolina as its U.S.-based location, the state guaranteed that there would be five qualified candidates for each job opening in the plant. Other states are learning this lesson and are getting into job training.

At the local level, community colleges are beginning to carve out a niche for themselves by retraining workers for growing industries. Since community colleges are able to provide training less expensively than companies can do themselves, more and more companies are calling on community colleges for assistance. For example, Hewlett-Packard, Motorola, and Johnson & Johnson all have entered into agreements with community colleges for help in meeting their corporate training needs. Quite obviously, the perception of the general public is not accurate in understanding the important role that state and local agencies and educational institutions are playing, not only in social services to the disadvantaged, but also in job training and in their regional and local economies.

materials moving by them in the production process. An example of psychological feedback that may influence an employee's perception is the supervisor's raised eyebrow or a change in voice inflection. The behavioral termination of perception is the reaction or behavior, either overt or covert, which is necessary if perception is to be considered a behavioral event and thus an important part of organizational behavior. As a result of perception, an employee may move rapidly or slowly (overt behavior) or make a self-evaluation (covert behavior).

As shown in Figure 4.1, all these perceptual subprocesses are compatible with the social learning conceptual framework presented in Chapter 1. The stimulus or environmental situation is the first part; registration, interpretation, and feedback occur within the complex person; then there is the resulting behavior; and the consequences of this behavior make up the final part. The subprocesses of registration, interpretation, and feedback are internal cognitive processes that are unobservable, but the situation, behavior, and consequences indicate that perception is indeed related to behavior. Recent summaries of research using the meta-analysis technique have found empirical support for the relationship between cognitive variables such as perception and behaviors.[2] Besides the subprocesses shown in the model, perceptual dimensions such as selectivity and organization, which are discussed next, help further clarify the cognitive aspects of perception.

PERCEPTUAL SELECTIVITY

Numerous stimuli are constantly confronting everyone. The noise of the air conditioner or furnace, the sound of other people talking and moving, and outside noises from cars, planes, or street repair work are a few of the stimuli affecting the senses—plus the impact of the total environmental situation. Sometimes the stimuli are below the person's conscious threshold, a process called subliminal perception.

With all this stimulation impinging upon people, how and why do they select out only a very few stimuli at a given time? Part of the answer can be found in the principles of perceptual selectivity.

External Attention Factors

Various external and internal attention factors affect perceptual selectivity. The external factors consist of outside environmental influences such as intensity, size, contrast, repetition, motion, and novelty and familiarity.

Intensity. The intensity principle of attention states that the more intense the external stimulus, the more likely it is to be perceived. A loud noise, strong odor, or bright light will be noticed more than a soft sound, weak odor, or dim light. Advertisers use intensity to gain the consumer's attention. Examples include bright packaging and television commercials that are slightly louder than the regular program. Supervisors may yell at their subordinates to gain attention. This last example also shows that other, more complex psychological variables may overcome the simple external variable. By speaking loudly, the supervisor may actually be turning the subordinates off instead of gaining their attention. These types of complications enter into all aspects of the perceptual process. As with the other psychological concepts, a given perceptual principle cannot stand alone in explaining complex human behavior. The intensity principle is only one small factor in the perceptual process, which is only a part of the cognitive processes, which are only a part of what goes into human behavior. Yet, for convenience of presentation and for the development of basic understanding, these small parts can be effectively isolated for study and analysis.

Size. Closely related to intensity is the principle of size. It says that the larger the object, the more likely it will be perceived. The largest machine "sticks out" when personnel view a factory floor. The maintenance engineering staff may pay more attention to a big machine than to a smaller one, even though the smaller one costs as much and is as important to the operation. A 6-foot 5-inch, 250-pound supervisor may receive more attention from his subordinates than a 5-foot 10-inch, 160-pound supervisor. In advertising, a full-page spread is more attention-getting than a few lines in the classified section.

Contrast. The contrast principle states that external stimuli which stand out against the background or which are not what people are expecting will receive their attention. Figure 4.2 demonstrates this perceptual principle. The black circle on the right appears much larger than the one on the left because of the contrast with the background circles. Both black circles are exactly the same size. In a similar manner, plant safety signs which have black lettering on a yellow background or white lettering on a red background are attention-getting; and when the 6-foot 5-inch, 250-

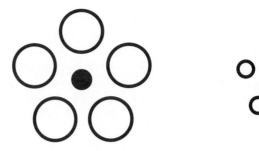

FIGURE 4.2
The contrast principle of perception: Which black circle is larger?

pound supervisor mentioned above is placed next to a 5-foot 2-inch, 120-pound supervisor, the smaller one will probably receive as much notice as the bigger one. A worker with many years of experience hardly notices the deafening noise on the factory floor of a typical manufacturing operation. However, if one or more of the machines should come suddenly to a halt, the person would immediately notice the difference in noise level.

The contrast principle can be demonstrated by the experience of some companies with training disadvantaged, unskilled workers. In designing these training programs, some firms have found that they have more success when they conduct the initial sessions in the disadvantaged person's own environment. The familiar location relieves some of the tension and creates a more favorable learning atmosphere. However, at some point the disadvantaged person must make the transition to the organizational environment. A regular, quiet classroom in the organization does not seem to be enough. One company learned that when the entire training of the disadvantaged trainees was conducted in a clean, quiet factory classroom, their subsequent performance was very poor. Fortunately, the company did not jump to the conclusion that the workers were "no good" or untrainable. Instead, through rational behavior analysis, the company discovered that the poor performance was due to the extremely loud noises that occurred on the assembly line. The workers were not accustomed to the noise because their training had taken place under nice, clean, quiet conditions. When the workers were placed on the noisy factory floor, the contrasting din drew all their attention and adversely affected their performance. To solve this problem, the company conducted the training sessions right next to the noisy factory floor. By the end of the training sessions, the workers were used to the noise, and they performed very well when subsequently placed on the job.

Repetition. The repetition principle states that a repeated external stimulus is more attention-getting than a single one. Thus, a worker will generally "hear" better when directions for a dull task are given more than once. This principle partially explains why supervisors have to give directions over and over again for even the simplest of tasks. Workers' attention for a boring task may be waning and the only way they hear directions for the task is when the supervisors repeat themselves several times. Advertisers trying to create a unique image for a product which is undifferentiated from its competitors—such as aspirin, soap, and deodorant—rely heavily on repetitious advertising.

Motion. The motion principle says that people will pay more attention to moving objects in their field of vision than they will to stationary objects. Workers will notice materials moving by them on a conveyor belt, but they may fail to give proper attention to the maintenance needs of the stationary machine next to them. In addition, the assembly line workers may devote their attention to the line of slowly moving materials they are working on and fail to notice the relatively nice working conditions (pastel-colored walls, music, and air-conditioning). Advertisers capitalize on this principle by creating signs which incorporate moving parts. Las Vegas at night is an example of advertisement in motion.

Novelty and Familiarity. The novelty and familiarity principle states that either a novel or a familiar external situation can serve as an attention getter. New objects or events in a familiar setting or familiar objects or events in a new setting will draw the attention of the perceiver. Job rotation is an example of this principle. Changing workers' jobs from time to time will tend to increase the attention they give to the task. Switching from columns of numbers to color graphics may not motivate the managerial staff, but it will increase their attention until they become accustomed to the new method of presenting weekly performance data. The same is true for the previously mentioned disadvantaged people newly trained for their first job assignments. The work environment is a completely novel experience for them. If supervisors use familiar street jargon in communicating with the employees, they may receive more attention from them. However, once again, this approach could backfire unless properly handled. The same is true in a foreign context. The accompanying International Application Example: Sometimes It Doesn't Translate shows some of the blunders U.S. advertising language has made in foreign countries.

Internal Set Factors

The concept of *set* is an important cognition in selectivity. It can be thought of as an internal form of attention-getting and is based largely on the individual's complex psychological makeup. People will select out stimuli or situations from the environment that appeal to, and are compatible with, their learning, motivation, and personality. Although these aspects are given specific attention in subsequent chapters, a very brief discussion here will help in the understanding of perception.

Learning and Perception. Although interrelated with motivation and personality, learning may play the single biggest role in developing perceptual set. Read the sentence in the triangle below:

TURN
OFF THE
THE ENGINE

It may take several seconds to realize there is something wrong. Because of familiarity with the sentence from prior learning, the person is perceptually set to read "Turn off the engine." This illustration shows that learning affects set by creating an *expectancy* to perceive in a certain manner. As pointed out in Chapter 1, such expectancies are a vital element in the cognitive explanations of behavior. This view states simply that people see and hear what they expect to see and hear. This can be further demonstrated by pronouncing the following words very slowly:

> ### Sometimes It Doesn't Translate
>
> Although marketing people in the United States have produced some outstanding advertisements, it is not always possible to take these same ads and use them in other countries. Why not? Because the perceptions are not the same. Here are some classic examples:
>
> 1. "Schweppes Tonic Water" was initially translated to the Italian as "il water." However, the copywriters quickly corrected their mistake and changed the translation to "Schweppes Tonica." In Italian, "il water" means water in the bathroom commode.
> 2. When Pepsi-Cola ran an ad slogan of "Come Alive with Pepsi," it did very well in the United States. However, the company had to change its slogan in some foreign countries because it did not translate correctly. In German the translation of "come alive" is "come out of the grave." In Asia the phrase is translated "bring your ancestors back from the grave."
> 3. When General Mills attempted to capture the British market with its breakfast cereal, it ran a picture of a freckled, red-haired, crew-cut grinning kid saying, "See kids, it's great!" The company failed to realize that the typical British family, not so child-centered as the U.S. family, would not be able to identify with the kid on the carton. Result: Sales were dismally low.
> 4. General Motors initially had trouble selling its Chevrolet Nova in Puerto Rico. It failed to realize that while the name "Nova" in English means "star," in Spanish the word sounds like "no va," which means "it doesn't go."
> 5. Rolls-Royce attempted to market one of its models in Germany under the name "Silver Mist." It soon discovered that the word "mist" in German means "excrement."

M-A-C-T-A-V-I-S-H

M-A-C-D-O-N-A-L-D

M-A-C-B-E-T-H

M-A-C-H-I-N-E-R-Y

If the last word was pronounced "Mac-Hinery" instead of "machinery," the reader was caught in a verbal response set.

There are many other illustrations that are commonly used to demonstrate the impact of learning on the development of perceptual set. Figure 4.3 is found in many introductory psychology textbooks. What is perceived in this picture? If one sees an apparently young woman, the perceiver is in agreement with about 60 percent of the people who see the picture for the first time. On the other hand, if an old woman is seen, the viewer is in agreement with about 40 percent of first viewers. Obviously, two completely distinct women can be perceived in Figure 4.3. Which woman is seen depends on how the person is set to perceive. How did you come out?

How Figure 4.3 is perceived can be radically influenced by a simple learned experience. When first shown a clear, unambiguous picture of a young woman (Figure 4.4) and then shown Figure 4.3, the person will almost always report seeing the young woman in Figure 4.3. If the clear picture of the old woman is seen first (Figure 4.4), the viewer will subsequently report seeing the old woman in Figure 4.3.

In addition to the young woman–old woman example, a wide variety of commonly used illusions effectively demonstrate the impact of learned set on percep-

FIGURE 4.3
Ambiguous picture of a young woman and an old woman.
(*Source:* Edwin G. Boring, "A New Ambiguous Figure," *American Journal of Psychology*, July 1930, p. 444. Also see Robert Leeper, "A Study of a Neglected Portion of the Field of Learning—The Development of Sensory Organization," *Journal of Genetic Psychology*, March 1935, p. 62. Originally drawn by cartoonist W. E. Hill and published in *Puck*, Nov. 6, 1915.)

tion. An illusion may be thought of as a form of perception that badly distorts reality. Figures 4.5 and 4.6 show some of the most frequently used forms of perceptual illusion. The two three-pronged objects in Figure 4.5 are drawn contrary to common perceptions of such objects. In Figure 4.6*a*, the length of the nose (from the tip to the X) is exactly equal to the vertical length of the face. In Figure 4.6*b*, the height of the hat is exactly equal to the width of the brim. Both shapes in Figure 4.6*c* are exactly the same size, and in Figure 4.6*d*, the lines *AX*, *CX*, *CB*, and *XD* are of equal length.

Figure 4.7 brings out the role that learned set plays in perception even more strongly than Figure 4.6. The three men in Figure 4.7 are drawn exactly equal in height. Yet they are perceived to be of different heights because the viewer has

FIGURE 4.4
Clear picture of the young and old woman.
(*Source:* Robert Leeper, "A Study of a Neglected Portion of the Field of Learning—The Development of Sensory Organization," *Journal of Genetic Psychology*, March 1935, p. 62.)

Old Woman

Young Woman

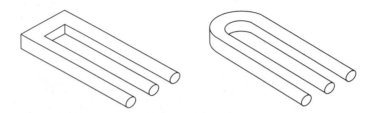

FIGURE 4.5
Common illusions.

learned that the cues found in the picture normally imply depth and distance. A lot of what a person "sees" in the world is a result of past experience and learning. Even though the past experience may not be relevant to the present situation, it is nevertheless used by the perceiver.

Perceptual Set in the Workplace. Perceptual set has many direct implications for organizational behavior. In organizational life, some employees have learned to perceive the world around them in the same way. For example, the single sentence "I cannot recommend this young man too highly" was reproduced and distributed to several managers in the same organization. Although this statement is ambiguous and unclear, without exception all the managers interpreted this to be a positive recommendation.[3] They had all learned to perceive this statement the same way—positive and favorable.

FIGURE 4.6
Common perceptual illusions.
(*Source:* These illusions are found in almost all introductory psychology textbooks.)

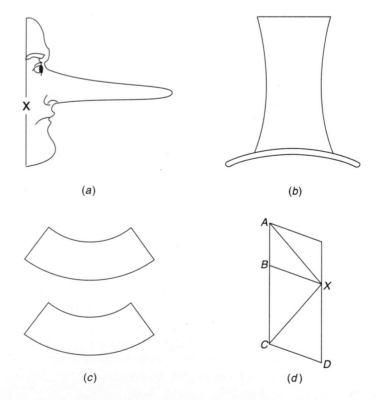

FIGURE 4.7
The role that learning
plays in perception.

In most cases, however, learning leads to extreme individual differences. For example, the young woman–old woman illustration demonstrates that the same stimulus may be perceived two completely different ways (young or old) because of the way the individual is set to perceive. Numerous instances of this situation occur in a modern organization. Participants may perceive the same stimulus or situation in entirely different ways. A specific organizational example might be a poor output record in the production department of a manufacturing plant. The engineer perceives the solution to this problem as one of improved machine design. The personnel manager perceives the solution as one of more training and better wage incentives. The department head perceives the solution to be more effective organizing, planning, and controlling. On the other hand, the workers may perceive the low output with pleasure because it is a way of "getting back" at their supervisor, whom they dislike. For the purpose of this discussion, it is not important who is right or wrong in this example; rather, the point is that all the relevant personnel perceive the *same* situation in completely *different* ways.

Another common example is the differences in perception that occur between the union and management. Some industrial relations researchers believe that perceptual differences are a major explanation for industrial disputes. The same "facts" in a dispute are perceived quite differently by union members and by management. For example, union members may perceive that they are underpaid, whereas management perceive that these workers are overpaid for the amount of work they do. In reality, pay may have nothing to do with the ensuing dispute. Maybe it is a matter of the workers' not having control over their own jobs and not getting any recognition, and they are reacting by perceiving that they are underpaid.

Motivation and Perception. Besides the learned aspects of perceptual set, motivation also has a vital impact on perceptual selectivity. The primary motives of sex and hunger could be used to demonstrate the role that motivation plays in perception.

In traditional American culture, the sex drive has been largely suppressed, with the result being an unfulfilled need for sex. Accordingly, any mention of sex or a visual stimulus dealing with sex is very attention-getting to the average American. The picture of a scantily clad or naked male or female is readily perceived. On the other hand, as nudity becomes increasingly commonplace in magazines, motion pictures, live entertainment, and fashions, the human anatomy slowly begins to lose its appeal as an attention getter. Analogously, however, if there is a great need for food in the culture, the mention, sight, or smell of food is given a great deal of attention.

The secondary motives also play an important role in developing perceptual set. A person who has a relatively high need for power, affiliation, or achievement will be more attentive to the relevant situational variables. An example is the worker who has a strong need for affiliation. When such a worker walks into the lunchroom, the table where several coworkers are sitting tends to be perceived, and the empty table or the one where a single person is sitting tends to get no attention. Although very simple, the lunchroom example points out that perception may have an important impact on motivation, and vice versa. This demonstrates once again the interrelatedness of these concepts.

Personality and Perception. Closely related to learning and motivation is the personality of the perceiving person, which affects what is attended to in the confronting situation. For example, senior-level executives often complain that the new young "hot shots" have trouble making the "tough" personnel decisions concerning terminating or reassigning people and paying attention to details and paperwork. The young managers, in turn, complain about the "old guard" resisting change and using rules and paperwork as ends in themselves. The senior- and junior-level executives' personalities largely explain these perceptions. The same could be said for the glass ceiling problem facing women in the workplace. As brought out in the last chapter, women still are not reaching the top levels of organizations. At least part of this problem can be attributed to perceptual barriers such as the established managerial hierarchy's not being able to "see" (perceive) that qualified women should be promoted into top-level positions.

Besides the gender gap, there is also a generation gap that may contribute to differing perceptions. An example can be found in the perceptions of modern movies. Older people tend either to be disgusted by or to not understand some of the popular movies of recent years. Those in the thirty-five to forty-five age group tend to perceive these movies as "naughty but neat." Young, college-age people tend to perceive them as "where it's at." They tend to get neither uptight nor titillated. Of course, there are individual differences in all age categories, and the above example tends to stereotype (a topic discussed later in the chapter) people by age. Yet it does show how personalities, values, and even age may affect the way people perceive the world around them.

PERCEPTUAL ORGANIZATION

The discussion of perceptual selectivity was concerned with the external and internal variables that gain an individual's attention. This section focuses on what takes place in the perceptual process once the information from the situation is received. This aspect of perception is commonly referred to *as perceptual organization*. An individual seldom perceives patches of color or light or sound. Instead, the person will perceive organized patterns of stimuli and identifiable whole objects. For example, when a college student is shown a basketball, the student does not normally perceive it as the color brown or as grain-leather in texture or as the odor of leather. Rather, the student perceives a basketball which has, in addition to the characteristics named, a potential for giving the perceiver fun and excitement as either a participant or a spectator. In other words, the person's perceptual process organizes the incoming information into a meaningful whole.

Figure-Ground

Figure-ground is usually considered to be the most basic form of perceptual organization. The figure-ground principle means simply that perceived objects stand out as separable from their general background. It can be effectively demonstrated as one is reading this paragraph. In terms of light-wave stimuli, the reader is receiving patches of irregularly shaped blacks and whites. Yet the reader does not perceive it this way. The reader perceives black shapes—letters, words, and sentences—printed against a white background. To say it another way, the reader perceptually organizes incoming stimuli into recognizable figures (words) that are seen against a ground (white page).

Another interesting figure-ground illustration is shown in Figure 4.8. At first glance, one probably perceives a jumble of black, irregular shapes against a white background. Only when the white letters are perceptually organized against a black background will the words FLY and TIE literally jump out with clarity. This illustration shows that perceptual selectivity will influence perceptual organization. The viewer is set to perceive black on white because of the black words (figures) throughout the book. However, in Figure 4.8 the reverse is true. White is the figure and black is the ground.

FIGURE 4.8
Illustrations of figure-ground.

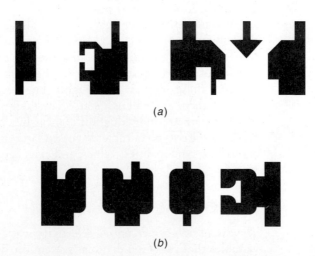

(a)

(b)

Perceptual Grouping

The grouping principle of perceptual organization states that there is a tendency to group several stimuli together into a recognizable pattern. This principle is very basic and seems to be largely inborn. There are certain underlying uniformities in grouping. When simple constellations of stimuli are presented to people, they will tend to group them together by closure, continuity, proximity, or similarity.

Closure. The closure principle of grouping is closely related to the gestalt school of psychology. A basic gestalt principle is that a person will sometimes perceive a whole when one does not actually exist. The person's perceptual process will close the gaps which are unfilled from sensory input. In the formal organization, participants may either see a whole where none exists or not be able to put the pieces together into a whole that does exist. An example of the first case is the department head who perceived complete agreement among the members of her department on a given project when, in fact, there was opposition from several members. The department head in this situation closed the existing gaps and perceived complete agreement when, in fact, it did not exist. An example of the other side of the coin is the adage of not being able to see the forest (whole) because of the trees (parts). High degrees of specialization have often resulted in functionally oriented managers' losing sight of the whole organization's objectives. Specialists may get so caught up in their own little area of interest and responsibility that they may lose sight of the overall goal. They cannot close their part together with the other parts to perceive the whole. It is because of this problem that some new paradigm organizations have promoted interfunctional structures by emphasizing horizontal rather than traditional vertical, hierarchical structural arrangements. Chapter 17 on organization theory and design goes into detail on some of these new organizational designs.

Continuity. Continuity is closely related to closure. Some psychologists do not even bother to make a distinction between the two grouping principles. However, there is a slight difference. Closure supplies *missing* stimuli, whereas the continuity principle says that a person will tend to perceive *continuous* lines or patterns. This type of continuity may lead to inflexible, or noncreative, thinking on the part of organizational participants. Only the obvious, continuous patterns or relationships will be perceived. For example, a new design for some productive process or product may be limited to obvious flows or continuous lines. New, innovative ideas or designs may not be perceived. Continuity can greatly influence the systems design of an organizational structure.

Proximity. The principle of proximity, or nearness, states that a group of stimuli that are close together will be perceived as a whole pattern of parts belonging together. For example, several employees in an organization may be identified as a single group because of physical proximity. Several workers who work on a particular machine may be perceived as a single whole. If the output is low and the supervisor reports a number of grievances from the group, management may perceive all the workers on the machine as one troublemaking group when, in fact, some of the workers are loyal, dedicated employees. Yet, the fact remains that often department or work groups are perceived as a single entity because of physical proximity. As teams become more and more common in today's organizations, this principle of proximity will help identify them as a single entity. This perception may help solidify the team and promote teamwork. Chapter 9 on group dynamics and teams examines such processes in detail.

Similarity. The principle of similarity states that the greater the similarity of the stimuli, the greater the tendency to perceive them as a common group. Similarity is conceptually related to proximity but in most cases is stronger than proximity. In an organization, all employees who wear white collars may be perceived as a common group, when, in reality, each worker is a unique individual. Similarity also applies to minorities and women. There is a tendency to perceive minority and women employees as a single group, the famous "they." This of course can lead to stereotyping problems, which are discussed in a later section.

Perceptual Constancy

Constancy is one of the more sophisticated forms of perceptual organization. It gives a person a sense of stability in a changing world. This principle permits the individual to have some constancy in a tremendously variable and highly complex world. Learning plays a much bigger role in the constancy phenomenon than in figure-ground or grouping phenomena.

The size, shape, color, brightness, and location of an object are fairly constant regardless of the information received by the senses. It should be pointed out that perceptual constancy results from *patterns* of cues. These patterns are for the most part learned, but each situation is different and there are interactions between the inborn and learned tendencies within the entire perceptual process.

If constancy were not at work, the world would be very chaotic and disorganized for the individual. An organizational example would be the worker who must select a piece of material or a tool of the correct size from a wide variety of materials and tools at varying distances from a workstation. Without perceptual constancy, the sizes, shapes, and colors of objects would change as the worker moved about and would make the job almost impossible.

Perceptual Context

The highest, most sophisticated form of perceptual organization is context. It gives meaning and value to simple stimuli, objects, events, situations, and other persons in the environment. The principle of context can be simply demonstrated by doodles such as the one shown in Figure 4.9 (explanation is given in footnote reference 4). The visual stimuli by themselves are meaningless. Only when the doodle is placed in a verbal context does it take on meaning and value to the perceiver.

The organizational culture and structure provide the primary context in which workers and managers do their perceiving. Thus, a verbal order, a memo, a new policy, a suggestion, a raised eyebrow, or a pat on the back takes on special meaning and value when placed in the context of the work organization. The preceding three chapters on the environmental challenges, Chapters 17 and 18 on organization structure and culture, and Chapter 19 on the international arena examine the major context in which organizational participants perceive.

FIGURE 4.9
Doodles illustrate the role that context plays in perception.

Perceptual Defense

Closely related to context is perceptual defense. A person may build a defense (a block or a refusal to recognize) against stimuli or situational events in the context that are personally or culturally unacceptable or threatening. Accordingly, perceptual defense may play an influential role in understanding union-management or supervisor-subordinate relationships.

Although there is some conflicting evidence, most studies verify the existence of a perceptual defense mechanism. Two examples are classic studies which found barriers to perceiving personality-threatening words[5] and identification thresholds for critical, emotionally toned words.[6] In another study more directly relevant to organizational behavior, the researchers describe how people may react with a perceptual defense that is activated in them when they are confronted with a fact that is inconsistent with a preconceived notion.[7] In this study, college students were presented with the word "intelligent" as a characteristic of a factory worker. This was counter to their perception of factory workers, and they built defenses in the following ways:

1. *Denial.* A few of the subjects denied the existence of intelligence in factory workers.
2. *Modification and distortion.* This was one of the most frequent forms of defense. The pattern was to explain away the perceptual conflict by joining intelligence with some other characteristic, for example, "He is intelligent, but doesn't possess the initiative to rise above his group."
3. *Change in perception.* Many of the students changed their perception of the worker because of the intelligence characteristic. The change, however, was usually very subtle; for example, "He cracks jokes" became "He's witty."
4. *Recognition, but refusal to change.* Very few subjects explicitly recognized the conflict between their perception of the worker and the characteristic of intelligence that was confronting them. For example, one subject stated, "the traits seem to be conflicting . . . most factory workers I have heard about aren't too intelligent."[8]

The general conclusion to be drawn from this classic study is that people may learn to avoid perceiving certain conflicting, threatening, or unacceptable aspects of the context.

These and other relevant experiments have been summarized into three general explanations of perceptual defense:

1. Emotionally disturbing information has a higher threshold for recognition (that is, we do not perceive it readily) than neutral or nondisturbing information. This is why a chain of events may be seen differently by those who are not personally involved and by those who are involved; thus, warning signs of trouble are often not seen by those who will be most affected by the trouble.
2. Disturbing information and stimuli are likely to bring about substitute perceptions which are distorted to prevent recognition of the disturbing elements. In this way a manager can perceive that workers are happy, when actually they are disgruntled. Then when a grievance committee is formed or a strike takes place, the manager cannot perceive that these "happy" workers are participating willingly and concludes that it is because they have fallen victim to some agitator and that things in the shop are still basically fine.

3. Emotionally arousing information actually does arouse emotion, even though the emotion is distorted and directed elsewhere. Kicking the cat, snarling at the kids, cutting someone off for trying to pass you on the right while driving home, and browbeating an underling all offer a sense of relief and are good substitutes for perceiving that people "upstairs" think you are an idiot.[9]

Such findings as the above help explain why some people, especially supervisors and workers in an organization, have a "blind spot." They do not "see" or they consistently misinterpret certain events or situations.

SOCIAL PERCEPTION

Although context and perceptual defense are closely related to social perception, this section gives recognition to social perception per se. The social aspects of perception are given detailed coverage because they play such an important role in organizational behavior. Social perception is directly concerned with how one individual perceives other individuals: how we get to know others.

Characteristics of Perceiver and Perceived

A summary of research findings on some specific characteristics of the perceiver and the perceived reveals a profile of the perceiver as follows:

1. Knowing oneself makes it easier to see others accurately.
2. One's own characteristics affect the characteristics one is likely to see in others.
3. People who accept themselves are more likely to be able to see favorable aspects of other people.
4. Accuracy in perceiving others is not a single skill.[10]

These four characteristics greatly influence how a person perceives others in the environmental situation.

There are also certain characteristics of the person being perceived which influence social perception. Research has shown that:

1. The status of the person perceived will greatly influence others' perception of the person.
2. The person being perceived is usually placed into categories to simplify the viewer's perceptual activities. Two common categories are status and role.
3. The visible traits of the person perceived will greatly influence others' perception of the person.[11]

These characteristics of the perceiver and the perceived suggest the extreme complexity of social perception. Organizational participants must realize that their perceptions of another person are greatly influenced by their own characteristics and the characteristics of the other person. For example, if a manager has high self-esteem and the other person is pleasant and comes from the home office, then the manager will likely perceive this other person in a positive, favorable manner. On the other hand, if the manager has low self-esteem and the other person is an arrogant salesperson, the manager will likely perceive this other person in a negative, unfavorable manner. Such attributions that people make of others play a vital role in their social perceptions and resulting behavior.

Participants in formal organizations are constantly perceiving one another. Managers are perceiving workers, workers are perceiving managers, line personnel are perceiving staff personnel, staff personnel are perceiving the line personnel, managers are perceiving subordinates, subordinates are perceiving managers, and on and on. There are numerous complex factors which enter into such social perception, but the primary factors are found in psychological processes such as the attributions people make and the problems associated with stereotyping and the halo effect.

Attribution

Attribution refers simply to how people explain the cause of another's or their own behavior. It is the process by which people draw conclusions about the factors that influence, or make sense of, one another's behavior.[12] Applied to social perception, there are two general types of attributions that people make: *dispositional attributions*, which ascribe a person's behavior to internal factors such as personality traits, motivation, or ability, and *situational attributions*, which attribute a person's behavior to external factors such as equipment or social influence from others.[13] In recent years, attribution theories have been playing an increasingly important role in work motivation, performance appraisal, and leadership,[14] but also are recognized to influence perceptions.

Attributions have been found to strongly affect evaluations of others' performance, to determine the manner in which supervisors behave toward subordinates, and to influence personal satisfaction with one's work.[15] These attribution theories of motivation are covered in Chapter 6. Applied to social perception, attribution is the search for causes (attributes) in making interpretations of other persons or of oneself. For example, what the manager perceives as the cause of a subordinate's behavior will affect the manager's perception of, and resulting behavior toward, the subordinate. If the subordinate's outstanding performance is attributed to situational factors such as a new machine or an engineering procedure, the perception and resulting treatment will be different from the perception and resulting treatment if the performance is attributed to dispositional factors such as ability and drive. The same is true of attributions made of one's own behavior.[16] Perceptions and thus behaviors will vary depending on whether internal dispositional attributions or external, situational attributions are made. In other words, the type of causal attributions one makes greatly affects perception, and, as the later discussions of motivation and leadership indicate, there is growing evidence that the attributional process and the form it takes seem to greatly affect the resulting organizational behavior and performance.[17]

Stereotyping

In addition to attribution, there are two other important areas of social perception that are especially relevant to the understanding of organizational behavior. These are the common errors or problems that creep into social perception called *stereotyping* and the *halo effect*.

The term *stereotype* refers to the tendency to perceive another person (hence social perception) as belonging to a *single* class or category. From attribution theory, a stereotype also involves general agreement on the attributed traits and the existence of a discrepancy between attributed traits and actual traits.

The word "stereotype" is derived from the typographer's word for a printing plate made from previously composed type. In 1922, Walter Lippmann applied the word to perception. Since then, stereotyping has become a frequently used term to describe perceptual errors. In particular, it is employed in analyzing prejudice. Not commonly acknowledged is the fact that stereotyping may attribute favorable or unfavorable traits to the person being perceived. Most often a person is put into a stereotype because the perceiver knows only the overall category to which the person belongs. However, because each individual is unique, the real traits of the person will generally be quite different from those the stereotype would suggest.

Stereotyping greatly influences social perception in today's organizations. Common stereotyped groups include managers, supervisors, union members, minorities, women, white- and blue-collar workers, and all the various functional and staff specialists, for example, accountants, salespeople, computer programmers, and engineers. There is a consensus about the traits possessed by the members of these categories. Yet in reality there is often a discrepancy between the agreed-upon traits of each category and the actual traits of the members. In other words, not all engineers carry calculators and are coldly rational, nor are all personnel managers do-gooders who are trying to keep workers happy. On the contrary, there are individual differences and a great deal of variability among members of these groups. In spite of this, other organization members commonly make blanket perceptions and behave accordingly. For example, in one classic research study it was found that individuals will both perceive and be perceived according to whether they are identified with a union or a management group. "Thus, 74 percent of the subjects in the managerial group chose the word 'honest' as a description of Mr. A, *when he was identified as a manager*. The same managerial subjects, however, chose the word 'honest' to describe Mr. A only 50 percent of the time when he was identified as a representative of the union."[18] There are numerous other research studies[19] and common, everyday examples which point out the stereotyping that occurs in organizational life.

The Halo Effect

The *halo effect* in social perception is very similar to stereotyping. Whereas in stereotyping the person is perceived according to a single category, under the halo effect the person is perceived on the basis of one trait. Halo is often discussed in performance appraisal when a rater makes an error in judging a person's total personality and/or performance on the basis of a single trait such as intelligence, appearance, dependability, or cooperativeness. Whatever the single trait is, it may override all other traits in forming the perception of the person. For example, a person's physical appearance or dress may override all other characteristics in making a selection decision or in appraising the person's performance.

The halo *error* problem has been given considerable attention in research on performance appraisal. For example, a comprehensive review of the performance appraisal literature found that halo effect was the dependent variable in over a third of the studies and was found to be a major problem affecting appraisal accuracy.[20] The current thinking on halo can be summarized from the extensive research literature as follows:

1. It is a common rater error.
2. It has both true and illusory components.
3. It has led to inflated correlations among rating dimensions and is due to the influence of a general evaluation and specific judgments.
4. It has negative consequences and should be avoided or removed.[21]

Many research studies offer refinements of the above. For example, one classic research study noted three conditions under which the halo effect is most marked: (1) when the traits to be perceived are unclear in behavioral expressions, (2) when the traits are not frequently encountered by the perceiver, and (3) when the traits have moral implications.[22] Other studies have pointed out how the halo effect can influence perception. For example, one study found that when two persons were described as having identical personalities except for one trait—the character qualities in one list included the trait *warm*, and in the other list, the trait *cold*—two completely different perceptions resulted.[23] In other words, one trait blinded the perceiver to all other traits in the perceptual process. Another study also documented the impact of the halo effect on employee perceptions in a company that was in receivership (undergoing bankruptcy). Although the company paid relatively high wages and provided excellent working conditions and at least average supervision, the employees did not perceive these favorable factors. The insecurity produced an inverse halo effect so that insecurity dominated over the pay and positive conditions of the job.[24] The results of this study make the point that "when there's one important 'rotten' attitude, it can spoil the 'barrel' of attitudes."[25]

Like all the other aspects of the psychological process of perception discussed in this chapter, the halo effect has important implications for the study and eventual understanding of organizational behavior. Unfortunately, even though halo effect is one of the longest recognized and most pervasive problems associated with applications such as performance appraisal in the field of organizational behavior, the recent critical analysis of the considerable research concludes that we still do not know much about the effects of halo error[26] and attempts at solving the problem have not yet been very successful.[27] In other words, overcoming perceptual problems such as stereotyping and the halo effect remain important challenges for effective human resources management.

IMPRESSION MANAGEMENT

Whereas social perception is concerned with how one individual perceives other individuals, *impression management* (sometimes called "self-presentation") is the process by which people attempt to manage or control the perceptions others form of them. There is often a tendency for people to try to present themselves in such a way as to impress others in a socially desirable way. Thus, impression management has considerable implications for areas such as the validity of performance appraisals (is the evaluator being manipulated into giving a positive rating?) and a pragmatic, political tool for one to climb the ladder of success in organizations.

The Process of Impression Management

As with other cognitive processes, impression management has many possible conceptual dimensions[28] and has been researched in relation to aggression, attitude change, attributions, and social facilitation, among other things.[29] Most recently, however, two separate components of impression management have been identified—impression motivation and impression construction.[30] Especially in an employment situation, subordinates may be motivated to control how their boss perceives them. The degree of this motivation to impression-manage will depend on such factors as the relevance the impressions have to the individual's goals, the value of these goals, and the discrepancy between the image one would like others to hold and the image one believes others already hold.[31]

Impression construction, the other major process, is concerned with the specific type of impression people want to make and how they go about doing it.

Although some theorists limit the type of impression only to personal characteristics, others include such other things as attitudes, physical states, interests, or values. Using this broader approach, five factors have been identified as being especially relevant to the kinds of impressions people try to construct: the self-concept, desired and undesired identity images, role constraints, target's values, and current social image.[32] Although there is considerable research on how these five factors influence the type of impression that people try to make, there is still little known of how they select the way to manage others' perceptions of them. For example, do they directly tell their boss things such as "I'm really competitive and want to get ahead" or do they make indirect statements such as "I really like racquetball; it is really competitive."

Employee Impression Management Strategies

There are two basic strategies of impression management that employees can use. If employees are trying to minimize responsibility for some negative event or to stay out of trouble, they may employ a demotion-preventative strategy. On the other hand, if they are seeking to maximize responsibility for a positive outcome or to look better than they really are, then they can use a promotion-enhancing strategy.[33] The demotion-preventative strategy is characterized by the following:

1. *Accounts.* These are employees' attempts to excuse or justify their actions. Example excuses are not feeling well or not getting something done on time because of another higher-priority assignment.
2. *Apologies.* When there is no logical way out, the employee may apologize to the boss for some negative event. Such an apology not only gives the impression that the individual is sorry but also indicates that it will not happen again. The employee is big enough to face up to a problem and solve it.
3. *Disassociation.* When employees are indirectly associated with something that went wrong (for example, they are a member of a committee or work team that made a bad decision), they may secretly tell their boss that they fought for the right thing but were overruled. Employees using this approach try to remove themselves both from the group and from responsibility for the problem.[34]

The promotion-enhancing strategies involve the following:

1. *Entitlements.* Under this approach, employees feel that they have not been given credit for a positive outcome. They make sure that it is known through formal channels. Or they may informally note to key people that they are pleased their suggestions or efforts worked out so well.
2. *Enhancements.* Here, employees may have received credit, but they point out that they really did more and had a bigger impact than originally thought. For example, their effort or idea not only served a customer well or met a difficult deadline, but can be used in the future to greatly increase profits.
3. *Obstacle disclosures.* In this strategy, employees identify either personal (health or family) or organization (lack of resources or cooperation) obstacles they had to overcome to accomplish an outcome. They are trying to create the perception that because they obtained the positive outcome despite the big obstacles, they really deserve a lot of credit.
4. *Association.* Here, the employee makes sure to be seen with the right people at the right times. This creates the perception that the employee is well connected and is associated with successful projects.[35]

The above strategies help construct impressions or perceptions. The motivation on the part of employees may or may not be a deliberate attempt to enhance themselves in terms of political power, promotions, and monetary rewards. Managers should be aware of deliberate manipulation of perceptions when making evaluations of their people. By the same token, such impression management could be used to get ahead in an organization or keep good relations with customers.

Here are some guidelines that have been offered for organizational members that will help them recognize various impression management tactics and the motives behind them:

1. One should be on the lookout for high-probability impression management strategies. For example, recruiters should be careful to separate pure self-promotion and legitimate claims of competence, and those in positions of power or status should be aware of subordinates' efforts to ingratiate them ("buttering up the boss" and "apple-polishing").
2. There should be an attempt to minimize personal, situational, and organizational features that foster undesirable impression management. For example, organizations in which task performance is ambiguous and/or resources are scarce tend to generate relatively high levels of ingratiation.
3. One should look for ulterior motives and avoid being overly influenced by impression management. For example, a manager who is able to distinguish between pure self-promotion and true competence is less likely to be biased by an invalid claim when appraising a staff member's performance.[36]

In total, there is no question that deliberately employing an impression management strategy or even something as simple as dressing for success can have an impact on both an individual's and even an organization's outcomes.[37] For example, Figure 4.10 uses the conspicuousness (the extent to which the dress of an organiza-

FIGURE 4.10
Comparing organizations on the basis of dress.
(*Source:* Anat Rafaeli and Michael G. Pratt, "Tailored Meanings: On the Meaning and Impact of Organizational Dress," *Academy of Management Review*, January 1993, p. 39. Used with permission.)

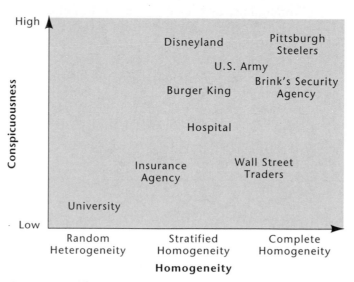

This figure is offered for illustrative purposes. Systematic observations are necessary to compare the exact locations of these various examples.

tional member stands out from the dress of nonmembers) and homogeneity (similarity) of dress to compare organizations.

In conclusion, probably the best advice is that offered by William Gardner at the end of his analysis of impression management. He states: "When selecting an image, never try to be something you're not. People will see through the facade. In sum, make every effort to put your best foot forward—but never at the cost of your identity or integrity!"[38]

Summary

Perception is an important mediating cognitive process. Through this complex process, persons make interpretations of the stimulus or situation they are faced with. Both selectivity and organization go into perceptual interpretations. Externally, selectivity is affected by intensity, size, contrast, repetition, motion, and novelty and familiarity. Internally, perceptual selectivity is influenced by the individual's motivation, learning, and personality. After the stimulus situation is filtered by the selective process, the incoming information is organized into a meaningful whole. Figure-ground is the most basic form of perceptual organization. Another basic form is the grouping of constellations of incoming stimuli by closure, continuity, proximity, and similarity. The constancy, context, and defensive aspects of perceptual organization are more complex. The social context in particular plays an important role in understanding human behavior in organizations. Of particular importance to social perception are the attributions people make (how people explain the cause of another's or their own behavior) and the two major problems of stereotyping (the tendency to perceive another person as belonging to a single class or category) and the halo effect or error (the tendency to perceive a person on the basis of one trait).

The last part of the chapter deals with controlling and constructing perceptions through impression management. Only recently recognized by the field of organizational behavior, impression management, or self-presentation, is the process by which people attempt to manage or control the perceptions others form of them. If employees are trying to minimize responsibility for some negative event or stay out of trouble, they may employ a demotion-preventative strategy characterized by accounts, apologies, and/or disassociation. If they are seeking to maximize responsibility for a positive outcome or trying to look better than they really are, then they can use a promotion-enhancing strategy characterized by entitlements, enhancements, obstacle disclosures, and/or associations. Organization members should be aware of how impression management is being used on them and of impression management strategies that they can use. Although there is nothing wrong with looking as good as one can, one must always be true to oneself.

Questions for Discussion and Review

1. Do you agree with the opening observation that people are human information processors? Why?
2. How does sensation differ from perception?
3. Give some examples of the external factors that affect perceptual selectivity.
4. Explain how perceptual constancy works.
5. What does stereotyping mean? Why is it considered to be a perceptual problem?

6. What is meant by the halo effect? Summarize the current thinking on halo error.
7. What is meant by impression management? What is meant by impression motivation and impression construction?
8. What are some of the major strategies employees can use in impression management?

Footnote References and Supplemental Readings

1. *The Wall Street Journal*, Dec. 2, 1986, p. 1.
2. Min-Sun Kim and John E. Hunter, "Attitude-Behavior Relations: A Meta-Analysis of Attitudinal Relevance and Topic," *Journal of Communication*, Winter 1993, pp. 101–142, and Min-Sun Kim and John E. Hunter, "Relationships Among Attitudes, Behavioral Intentions, and Behavior," *Communication Research*, June 1993, pp. 331–364.
3. John Swanda, *Organizational Behavior*, Alfred, Sherman Oaks, Calif., 1979, p. 91.
4. An explanation to the doodle in Figure 4.9 is the start of a "rat race."
5. Jerome S. Bruner and Leo Postman, "Emotional Selectivity in Perception and Reaction," *Journal of Personality*, September 1947, pp. 69–77.
6. Elliott McGinnies, "Emotionality and Perceptual Defense," *Psychological Review*, September 1949, pp. 244–251.
7. Mason Haire and Willa Freeman Grunes, "Perceptual Defenses: Processes Protecting an Organized Perception of Another Personality," *Human Relations*, November 1950, pp. 403–412.
8. Ibid., pp. 407–411.
9. David J. Lawless, *Organizational Behavior*, Prentice-Hall, Englewood Cliffs, N.J., 1979, p. 85.
10. Sheldon S. Zalkind and Timothy W. Costello, "Perception: Some Recent Research and Implications for Administration," *Administrative Science Quarterly*, September 1962, pp. 227–229.
11. Ibid., p. 230.
12. Donald L. McCabe and Jane E. Dutton, "Making Sense of the Environment: The Role of Perceived Effectiveness," *Human Relations*, May 1993, pp. 623–643.
13. Spencer A. Rathus, *Psychology*, 4th ed., Holt, Rinehart and Winston, Fort Worth, Tex., 1990, pp. 613–614.
14. For summaries of this literature, see James C. McElroy, "A Typology of Attribution Leadership Research," *Academy of Management Review*, July 1982, pp. 413–417; James C. McElroy and Charles B. Shrader, "Attribution Theories of Leadership and Network Analysis," *Journal of Management*, vol. 12, no. 3, 1986, pp. 351–362; and Christy L. DeVader, Allan G. Bateson, and Robert G. Lord, "Attribution Theory: A Meta-Analysis of Attributional Hypotheses," in Edwin A. Locke (ed.), *Generalizing from Laboratory to Field Settings*, Lexington (Heath), Lexington, Mass., 1986, pp. 63–81.
15. See Robert A. Baron, *Behavior in Organizations*, Allyn and Bacon, Boston, 1986, pp. 131–132, 190, and Joseph F. Porac, Gail Nottenburg, and James Eggert, "On Extending Weiner's Attributional Model to Organizational Contexts," *Journal of Applied Psychology*, February 1981, pp. 124–126.
16. Paul E. Levy, "Self-Appraisal and Attributions: A Test of a Model," *Journal of Management*, Spring 1993, pp. 51–62.
17. For example, see Gary Blau, "Testing the Relationship of Locus of Control to Different Performance Dimensions," *Journal of Occupational and Organizational Psychology*, June 1993, pp. 125–138.
18. Mason Haire, "Role-Perception in Labor-Management Relations: An Experimental Approach," *Industrial and Labor Relations Review*, January 1955, p. 208.
19. For example, see Linda A. Jackson, Linda A. Sullivan, and Carole N. Hodge, "Stereotype Effects on Attributions, Predictions, and Evaluations: No Two Social Judgments Are Quite Alike," *Journal of Personality and Social Psychology*, July 1993, pp. 69–84.
20. H. John Bernardin and Peter Villanova, "Performance Appraisal," in Locke, op. cit., pp. 45, 53.
21. Kevin R. Murphy, Robert A. Jako, and Rebecca L. Anhalt, "Nature and Consequences of Halo Error: A Critical Analysis," *Journal of Applied Psychology*, April 1993, p. 218.
22. Jerome S. Bruner and Renato Tagiuri, "The Perception of People," in Gardner Lindzey (ed.), *Handbook of Social Psychology*, Addison-Wesley, Reading, Mass., 1954, p. 641.
23. S. E. Asch, "Forming Impressions of Personalities," *Journal of Abnormal and Social Psychology*, July 1946, pp. 258–290.
24. Byron A. Grove and Willard A. Kerr, "Specific Evidence on Origin of Halo Effect in Measurement of Employee Morale," *Journal of Social Psychology*, August 1951, pp. 165–170.

25. Timothy W. Costello and Sheldon S. Zalkind, *Psychology in Administration*, Prentice-Hall, Englewood Cliffs, N.J., 1963, p. 35.

26. Murphy, Jako, and Anhalt, op. cit., pp. 218–225.

27. Rick Jacobs and Steve W. J. Kozlowski, "A Closer Look at Halo Error in Performance Ratings," *Academy of Management Journal*, March 1985, pp. 201–212.

28. For example, see Kimberly D. Elsbach and Robert Sutton, "Acquiring Organizational Legitimacy Through Illegitimate Actions: A Marriage of Institutional and Impression Management Theories," *Academy of Management Journal*, October 1992, pp. 699–738, and Kenneth J. Dunegan, "Framing, Cognitive Modes, and Image Theory: Toward an Understanding of a Glass Half Full," *Journal of Applied Psychology*, June 1993, pp. 491–503.

29. For example, see R. F. Baumeister, "A Self-Presentational View of Social Phenomena," *Psychological Bulletin*, vol. 91, 1982, pp. 3–26; R. F. Baumeister (ed.), *Public Self and Private Self*, Springer-Verlag, New York, 1986; and B. R. Schlenker, *Impression Management: The Self-Concept, Social Identity, and Interpersonal Relations*, Brooks/Cole, Monterey, Calif., 1980.

30. Mark R. Leary and Robin M. Lowalski, "Impression Management: A Literature Review and Two-Component Model," *Psychologccal Bulletin*, vol. 107, no. 1, 1990, pp. 34–47.

31. Ibid., pp. 38–39.

32. Ibid., pp. 40–42.

33. Robert A. Giacalone, "Image Control: The Strategies of Impression Management," *Personnel*, May 1989, pp. 52–55.

34. Ibid., p. 54.

35. Ibid., pp. 54–55.

36. These guidelines are adapted from William L. Gardner, "Lessons in Organizational Dramaturgy: The Art of Impression Management," *Organizational Dynamics*, Summer 1992, pp. 43–44.

37. See Anat Rafaeli and Michael G. Pratt, "Tailored Meanings: On the Meaning and Impact of Organizational Dress," *Academy of Management Review*, January 1993, pp. 32–55.

38. Gardner, op. cit., p. 45.

REAL CASE: Is Patriotism for Sale?

There currently is a debate raging in the United States regarding the role of lobbyists in Washington. The reason for this debate is that many people perceive lobbyists as using "inside" information that they have acquired through their experience working for organizations such as the Office of the U.S. Trade Representative or the International Trade Commission. Since 1973, one-third of all former top officials from the Trade Representative office now work as lobbyists for the Japanese. Some observers of the Washington scene feel that by using this experience, these lobbyists have been able to influence Congress and the administration into giving Japanese businesses special treatment. For example, a few years ago Japanese automakers shipped light trucks to the United States but claimed that they were cars and thus the "cars" were not subject to import duty. Working through its Washington lobbyists, the automakers were able to get the Customs Department to allow the vehicles to be reclassified and thus avoided $500 million in duties. Then the lobbyists went to work to get the vehicles reclassified as light trucks so that they would not have to have all of the auto emission equipment required in cars.

Commenting on the manipulation of the American political and economic system by Japanese lobbyists, many business people are very upset. Lee Iacocca has remarked: "If an American CIA agent quit one day and went to work for a foreign intelligence service the next, we'd call it treason. But when American trade officials . . . defect in droves to the Japanese, we don't even bat an eye."

The major problem in dealing with this issue is that the lobbyists are doing nothing that is illegal. As long as government officials refrain from lobbying for one year after they leave their jobs, they are free to trade on their knowledge and influence in Washington circles. There are efforts currently under way to extend this time period from the current one year to five years, thus greatly reducing the likelihood that people will take government jobs as a sabbatical during which they will gather experience and information to be used in their new job, lobbying. This has led one analyst to raise the issue: What are the demands of patriotism in a world where global economic rivalry has replaced the cold war? Many observers believe that Americans are too quick to sell their services to the highest bidder. There must be changes in the way business is being done. A report on the topic recently concluded:

> Americans who work to advance the causes of foreign governments or corporations have an obligation to be wary that their activities do not harm the national interest. A global economy is no excuse for continuing to tolerate a laissez-faire ethical climate in which all of Washington is available to the highest bidder.

1. What is Lee Iacocca's perception of Japanese lobbyists? Why?
2. Why would lobbyists disagree with the point of view espoused by this case?
3. Do you think the government should exercise more control over lobbyists for foreign companies or countries? What does your answer relate about your perception?

**CASE:
Space Utilization**

Sherman Adder, assistant plant manager for Frame Manufacturing Company, is chairperson of the ad hoc committee for space utilization. The committee is made up of the various department heads in the company. The plant manager of Frame has given Sherman the responsibility for seeing whether the various office, operations, and warehouse facilities of the company are being optimally utilized. The company is beset by rising costs and the need for more space. However, before okaying an expensive addition to the plant, the plant manager wants to be sure that the currently available space is being utilized properly.

Sherman opened up the first committee meeting by reiterating the charge of the committee. Then Sherman asked the members if they had any initial observations to make. The first to speak was the office manager. He stated: "Well, I know we are using every possible inch of room that we have available to us. But when I walk out into the plant, I see a lot of open spaces. We have people piled on top of one another, but out in the plant there seems to be plenty of room." The production manager quickly replied: "We do not have a lot of space. You office people have the luxury facilities. My supervisors don't even have room for a desk and a file cabinet. I have repeatedly told the plant manager we need more space. After all, our operation determines whether this plant succeeds or fails, not you people in the front office pushing paper around." Sherman interrupted at this point and said: "Obviously, we have different interpretations of the space utilization around here. Before further discussion I think it would be best if we have some objective facts to work with. I am going to ask the industrial engineer to provide us with some statistics on plant and office layouts before our next meeting. Today's meeting is adjourned."

1. What perceptual principles are evident in this case?
2. What concept was brought out when the production manager labeled the office personnel a bunch of "paper pushers"? Can you give other organizational examples of this concept?
3. Do you think that Sherman's approach to getting "objective facts" from statistics on plant and office layout will affect the perceptions of the office and production managers? How does such information affect perception in general?

**CASE:
Same Accident,
Different
Perceptions**

According to the police report, on July 9 at 1:27 P.M., bus number 3763 was involved in a minor noninjury accident. Upon arriving at the scene of the accident, police were unable to locate the driver of the bus. Since the bus was barely drivable, the passengers were transferred to a backup bus, and the damaged bus was returned to the city bus garage for repair.

The newly hired general manager, Aaron Moore, has been going over the police report and two additional reports. One of the additional reports was submitted by Jennifer Tye, the transportation director for the City Transit Authority (CTA), and the other came directly from the driver in the accident, Michael Meyer. According to Tye, although Mike has been an above-average driver for almost eight years, his performance has taken a drastic nosedive during the past fifteen months. Always one to join the other drivers for an after-work drink or two, Mike recently has been suspected of drinking on the job. Furthermore, according to Tye's report, Mike was seen having a beer in a tavern located less than two blocks from the CTA terminal at around 3 P.M. on the day of the accident. Tye's report concludes by citing two sections of the CTA Transportation Agreement. Section 18a specifically forbids the drinking of alcoholic beverages by any CTA employee while on duty. Section 26f prohibits drivers from leaving their buses unattended for any reason. Violation of either of the two sections results in automatic dismissal of the employee involved. Tye recommends immediate dismissal.

According to the driver, Michael Meyer, however, the facts are quite different. Mike claims that in attempting to miss a bicycle rider he swerved and struck a tree, causing minor damage to the bus. Mike had been talking with the dispatcher when he was forced to drop his phone receiver in order to miss the bicycle. Since the receiver broke open on impact, Mike was forced to walk four blocks to the nearest phone to report the accident. As soon as he reported the accident to the company, Mike also called the union to tell them about it. Mike reports that when he returned to the scene of the accident, his bus was gone. Uncertain of what to do and a little frightened, he decided to return to the CTA terminal. Since it was over a 5-mile walk and because his shift had already ended at 3 P.M., Mike stopped in for a quick beer just before getting back to the terminal.

1. Why are the two reports submitted by Jennifer and Mike so different? Did Jennifer and Mike have different perceptions of the same incident?
2. What additional information would you need if you were in Aaron Moore's position? How can he clarify his own perception of the incident?
3. Given the information presented above, how would you recommend resolving this problem?
4. Can transportation director Jennifer Tye use impression management? What strategy would she use if her recommendation is accepted? If her recommendation is overruled?

5 Personality and Attitudes

Learning Objectives

- **Define** the overall meaning of personality.
- **Discuss** personality development and socialization.
- **Describe** the meaning of attitudes and the emotional, informational, and behavioral components.
- **Explain** how attitudes are formed, the functions they perform, and how they are changed.
- **Examine** the major sources and outcomes of job satisfaction and organizational commitment.

This chapter discusses the cognitive, micro variables of personality and attitudes. These two constructs are very popular ways to describe and analyze organizational behavior. Yet, like the other cognitive processes, personality and attitudes are quite complex. The aim of this chapter is to facilitate a better understanding of such complexities of today's employees. Such an analysis of personality and attitudes is vital to the study of organizational behavior.

The first section of the chapter defines and clarifies the concept of personality. The next section is devoted to personality development (including the relevant theories of Levinson, Hall, and Argyris) and the socialization process. The remaining sections of the chapter then focus on attitudes, starting with their nature and dimensions. This discussion is followed by a detailed analysis of the two most relevant attitudes to organizational behavior, job satisfaction and organizational commitment.

THE MEANING OF PERSONALITY

Through the years there has not been universal agreement on the exact meaning of personality. Much of the controversy can be attributed to the fact that people in general and behavioral sciences define "personality" from different perspectives. Most people tend to equate personality with social success (being good or popular, or having "a lot of personality") and to describe personality by a single dominate characteristic (strong, weak, or polite). When it is realized that more than 4000 words can be used to describe personality this way, the definitional problem becomes staggering. Psychologists, on the other hand, take a different perspective. For example, the descriptive-adjective approach commonly used by most people plays only a small part. However, scholars cannot agree on a definition of personality because they operate from different theoretical bases. As long as there is disagreement on the theory of personality, there will be disagreement on its definition.

The word "personality" has an interesting derivation. It can be traced to the Latin words *per sona*, which are translated as "to speak through." The Latin term was used to denote the masks worn by actors in ancient Greece and Rome. This Latin meaning is particularly relevant to the contemporary analysis of personality. Common usage of the word emphasizes the role which the person (actor) displays to the public. The academic definitions are concerned more directly with the person (actor) than with the role played. Probably the most meaningful approach would be to include both the person and the role.

In addition, some personality theorists emphasize the need to recognize the person-situation *interaction*, that is, the social learning aspects of personality. Such a social learning interpretation may be the most comprehensive and meaningful to the overall study of organizational behavior. Thus, a comprehensive discussion of personality should include the uniqueness of each situation (rather than the commonality assumed by the more traditional approaches to personality), and any measure of personality must attempt to assess the person-situation interaction.

In summary, in this text *personality* will mean how people affect others and how they understand and view themselves, as well as their pattern of inner and outer measurable traits, and the person-situation interaction. How people affect others depends primarily upon their external appearance (height, weight, facial features, color, and other physical aspects) and traits. In terms of external appearance, a very tall worker will have an impact on other people different from that of a very short worker. Obviously, all the ramifications of perception enter into these physical aspects of personality.

Of more importance to organizational behavior are the personality traits. In particular, five personality traits (the so-called big five) have recently emerged from research as being especially related to job performance. Characteristics of these traits can be summarized briefly as follows:

1. *Extraversion.* Sociable, talkative, and assertive
2. *Agreeableness.* Good-natured, cooperative, and trusting
3. *Conscientiousness.* Responsible, dependable, persistent, and achievement-oriented
4. *Emotional stability.* Viewed from a negative standpoint: tense, insecure, and nervous
5. *Openness to experience.* Imaginative, artistically sensitive, and intellectual[1]

Although some of these constructs, such as conscientiousness, hold up better than others, and although they depend on the type and nature of the job being performed, the identification of these "big five" traits that relate to performance indicates the important role that personality plays in organizational behavior.

Besides physical appearance and personality traits, the aspects of personality dealing with the self-concept (both self-esteem and self-efficacy) and the person-situation interaction also play important roles.

The Self-Concept: Self-Esteem and Self-Efficacy

People's attempts to understand themselves are called the *self-concept* in personality theory. The self is a unique product of many interacting parts and may be thought of as the personality viewed from within. This self is particularly relevant to the concepts of self-esteem and self-efficacy in the field of organizational behavior.

People's *self-esteem* has to do with their self-perceived competence and self-image.[2] There is considerable research on the role that self-esteem may play in organizational behavior and its outcomes. As with other constructs in the field, there are both mixed and even inconclusive results on the impact of self-esteem,[3] but both early[4] and the most recent studies indicate that self-esteem plays at least an important moderating role in areas such as emotional and behavioral responses[5] and stress[6] of organizational members. As was recently noted, "Both research and everyday experience confirm that employees with high self-esteem feel unique, competent, secure, empowered, and connected to the people around them."[7]

Self-efficacy is concerned with self-perceptions of how well a person can cope with situations as they arise.[8] Those with high self-efficacy feel capable and confident of performing well in a situation. Only recently given attention in the field of organizational behavior, self-efficacy is conceptually close to self-esteem. Miner points out the differences by noting that self-esteem tends to be a generalized trait (it will be present in any situation), while self-efficacy tends to be situation specific.[9] Self-efficacy has been shown to have an empirical relationship with organizational performance and other dynamics of organizational behavior. For example, a recent review of this literature found that self-efficacy is associated with life insurance sales, faculty research productivity, ability to cope with difficult career-related tasks, career choice, learning and achievement, and adaptability to new technology.[10] There is also growing evidence that training employees can lead to their enhanced self-efficacy.[11]

Since self-efficacy is so situationally based, it is closely associated with social learning and is given more attention in Chapter 8. The remaining dimension of personality, the person-situation interaction, is covered next.

Person-Situation Interaction

The dimensions of personality traits and the self-concept add to the understanding of the human personality. The person-situation interaction dimension of personality provides further understanding. Each situation, of course, is different. The differences may seem to be very small on the surface, but when filtered by the person's cognitive mediating processes, they can lead to quite large, subjective differences and diverse behavioral outcomes. Thus, this last dimension suggests that people are not static, acting the same in all situations, but instead are ever changing and flexible. For example, employees can change depending on the particular situation they are in interaction with. Even everyday work experience can change people. The sections in this chapter dealing with the socialization process are especially relevant to this important person-situation interaction.

In summary, the personality is a very diverse and complex cognitive process. It incorporates almost everything covered in this text, and more. As defined above, personality is the whole person and is concerned with external appearance and traits, self, and situational interactions. Probably the best statement on personality was made many years ago by Kluckhohn and Murray, who said that, to some extent, a person's personality is like all other people's, like some other people's, and like no other people's.[12]

THE DEVELOPMENT OF PERSONALITY AND SOCIALIZATION

Study of, and research on, the development of personality has traditionally been an important area for understanding human behavior. Modern developmental psychology does not get into the argument of heredity versus environment or of maturation (changes that result from heredity and physical development) versus learning. The human being consists of both physiological *and* psychological interacting parts. Therefore, heredity, environment, maturation, and learning *all* contribute to the human personality.

The study of personality has attempted to identify specific physiological and psychological stages that occur in the development of the human personality. This "stage" approach has been theoretical in nature. There are many well-known stage theories of personality development. However, as with most aspects of personality, there is little agreement about the exact stages. In fact, a growing number of today's psychologists contend that there are *no* identifiable stages. Their argument is that personality development consists of a continuous process, and the sequence is based solely upon the learning opportunities available. The opposing view supports stages in personality development. Particularly relevant to the understanding of organizational behavior are the theories provided by Levinson, Hall, and Argyris.

Adult Life Stages

The work of Daniel Levinson on adult life stages has received attention. At first, he believed that "the life structure evolves through a relatively orderly sequence throughout the adult years,"[13] and, unlike other stage theories that were event-oriented (for example, marriage, parenthood, or retirement), his was age-based. In particular, he believed there was little variability (a maximum of two or three years) in four identifiable stable periods:

1. Entering the adult world (ages twenty-two to twenty-eight)
2. Settling down (ages thirty-three to forty)
3. Entering middle adulthood (ages forty-five to fifty)
4. Culmination of middle adulthood (ages fifty-five to sixty)

He identified four transitional periods:

1. Age-thirty transition (ages twenty-eight to thirty-three)
2. Mid-life transition (ages forty to forty-five)
3. Age-fifty transition (ages fifty to fifty-five)
4. Late adult transition (ages sixty to sixty-five)

Like historically significant stage theories of personality such as those by Sigmund Freud and Erik Erikson, Levinson's theory of adult life stages had a lot of intuitive and popular appeal, but, as is also the case with previous stage theories, the research is quite mixed. For example, one study utilizing longitudinal data found no support for Levinson's hypothesis that there should be greater variability in work attitudes during transitional as compared with stable developmental periods or that the greatest variability occurs during the mid-life transition.[14] In other words, there may be such large individual differences among people that stage theories such as Levinson's don't really hold up. As a result, Levinson has reformulated his stages into what he now calls "eras" (early adult, mid-life, and late adult) and includes a transition-in period, a period of stability, and a transition-out period.[15] In contrast to his earlier work discussed above, in which mobility or stability characterized whole stages of development, this new approach examines the interplay of mobility and stability within each life stage.[16]

Hall has synthesized Levinson's theory and other adult stage theories (in particular the work of Erikson and Super) into an overall model for career stages. Figure 5.1 shows that there are four major career stages. During the first stage there is considerable *exploration*. The young employee is searching for an identity and undergoes considerable self-examination and role tryouts. This stage usually results in taking a number of different jobs and is, in general, a very unstable and relatively unproductive period in the person's career. In the second stage, *establishment*, the employee begins to settle down and indicates a need for intimacy. This is usually a growing, productive period in the employee's career. The third stage of *maintenance* occurs when the person levels off into a highly productive plateau and has a need for generativity (the concern to leave something to the next generation). This need often leads the person to assume a paternalistic or perhaps a mentor role with younger subordinates. As shown in Figure 5.1, the person may either have a growth spurt or become stagnant and decline during this third career stage. The final stage, *decline*, is self-explanatory. The person indicates a need for integrity (that is, the person needs to feel satisfied with his or her life choices and overall career). With the recent changes in mandatory retirement laws (there is no longer an upper age limit for mandatory retirement), better medical treatment, and the expectations of society concerning "gray power," this last stage may undergo drastic changes in the years ahead.

There is recent evidence that the heretofore assumed direct, linear relationship between age and job satisfaction may not be true.[17] As Figure 5.2 shows, toward the

FIGURE 5.1
Douglas T. Hall's career stage model.

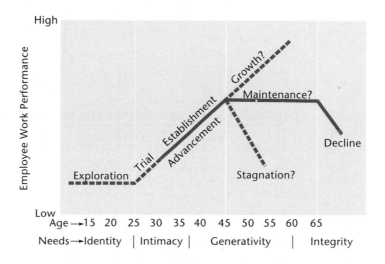

FIGURE 5.2
The relationship between age and job satisfaction.
(*Source*: Adapted from Fred Luthans and Linda T. Thomas, "The Relationship between Age and Job Satisfaction," *Personnel Review*, vol. 18, no. 1, 1989, p. 25.)

end of employees' careers, there may be a downturn in their satisfaction. This decline would agree with the career stage model, shown in Figure 5.1, but may be happening at an earlier age. The decline may be the result of unmet expectations and the downsizing and "merger mania" that have left long-term employees feeling unwanted and with no sense of loyalty or belonging.

Immaturity to Maturity

In a departure from the strict stage approach, well-known organizational behavior theorist Chris Argyris has identified specific dimensions of the human personality as it develops. Argyris proposes that the human personality, rather than going through precise stages, progresses along a continuum from immaturity as an infant to maturity as an adult. However, at any age, people can have their degree of development plotted according to the seven dimensions shown in Table 5.1.

Argyris carefully points out that this model does not imply that all persons reach or strive for all dimensions on the mature end of the continuum. He further explains:

1. The seven dimensions represent only one aspect of the total personality. Much also depends upon the individual's perception, self-concept, and adaptation and adjustment.
2. The seven dimensions continually change in degree from the infant to the adult end of the continuum.

TABLE 5.1 The Argyris Immaturity-Maturity Continuum

Immaturity Characteristics	Maturity Characteristics
Passivity	Activity
Dependence	Independence
Few ways of behaving	Diverse behavior
Shallow interests	Deep interests
Short time perspective	Long time perspective
Subordinate position	Superordinate position
Lack of self-awareness	Self-awareness and control

3. The model, being only a construct, cannot predict specific behavior. However, it does provide a method of describing and measuring the growth of any individual in the culture.

4. The seven dimensions are based upon latent characteristics of the personality, which may be quite different from the observable behavior.[18]

In contrast to the classic stage theories of Freud and Erikson, Argyris's immaturity-maturity model of personality is specifically directed to the study and analysis of organizational behavior. Argyris assumes that the personalities of organizational employees can be generally described by the mature end of the continuum. This being the case, in order to obtain full expression of employees' personalities, the formal organization should allow for activity rather than passivity, independence rather than dependence, long rather than short time perspective, occupation of a position higher than that of peers, and expression of deep, important abilities.[19] Argyris argues that too often the exact opposite occurs. The mature organizational participant becomes frustrated and anxious and is in conflict with the modern formal organization. In other words, Argyris sees a *basic incongruity* between the needs of the mature personality and the nature of the formal organization.

This incongruity premise is an important cornerstone for the entire conceptualization of person-organization structure interaction, which is discussed in relation to the organizational behavior model used in this text. The fit between individual personality characteristics and organizational requirements is also frequently used today to explain job performance and work-related attitudes,[20] as is discussed in the last part of this chapter and in the analysis of frustration and conflict in Chapter 10 and of stress in Chapter 11.

The Socialization Process

Besides the developmental aspects of personality, there is increasing recognition given to the role of other relevant persons, groups, and especially, organizations, which greatly influence an individual's personality. This continuous impact from the social environment is commonly called the *socialization process*. It is especially relevant to organizational behavior because the process is not confined to early childhood; rather, it takes place throughout one's life. In particular, evidence is accumulating that socialization may be one of the best explanations for why employees behave the way they do in today's organizations. For example, Edgar Schein notes: "It is high time that some of our managerial knowledge and skill be focused on those forces in the organization environment which derive from the fact that organizations are social systems which do socialize their new members. If we do not learn to analyze and control the forces of organizational socialization, we are abdicating one of our primary managerial responsibilities."[21] A recent study found that the socialization tactics that organizations employ (providing information to newcomers, guiding new recruits through common learning experiences, and so forth) do have the intended impact. It was found that different patterns of socialization lead to different forms of newcomer adjustment to organizations.[22]

Socialization starts with the initial contact between a mother and her new infant. After infancy, other members of the immediate family (father, brothers, and sisters), close relatives and family friends, and then the social group (peers, school friends, and members of the work group) play influential roles. Of particular interest is Schein's idea that the organization itself also contributes to socialization.[23] He points out that the process includes only the learning of those values, norms, and behavior patterns which, from the organization's and the work group's points of view, are necessary for any new organization member to learn.

The following are widely accepted characteristics of organizational socialization of employees:

1. Change of attitudes, values, and behaviors
2. Continuity of socialization over time
3. Adjustment to new jobs, work groups, and organizational practices
4. Mutual influence between new recruits and their managers
5. Criticality of the early socialization period[24]

Accordingly, organization members must learn things like not to drive a Ford if they are working for Chevrolet, not to criticize the company in public, and not to wear the wrong kind of clothes or be seen in the wrong kind of place.[25] They must understand "who holds power and who does not, which informal networks of communication are reliable and which are unreliable, and what political maneuvers they are likely to encounter in their department or unit. In short, if they wish to survive and prosper in their new work home, they must soon come to 'know the ropes.' "[26] The same is true for expatriates in oversees assignments. They must be socialized into the correct conduct in dealing with the local culture. The accompanying International Application Example: Gift Giving in Western Europe provides some guidelines for correct behavior in that part of the world.

Studies have indicated that socialization is important not only to new organization members but also in the manager-subordinate relationship and when people

Gift Giving in Western Europe

Culture is important in understanding the socialization not only of Americans but of those living in other countries as well. Western Europe is a good example. The United States does considerable business there, so it is very helpful for American expatriates to know how to act in this corner of the globe. For example, when you are doing business with Europeans, when is it acceptable to give a gift and how should it be done? The following are some useful guidelines for gift giving in Western Europe:

1. Do not give a business gift at the first meeting. This is considered bad manners.
2. If you are going to send flowers to your dinner hostess, send them ahead rather than handing them to her upon your arrival. This gives her time to arrange and place them as she wants. It also prevents any embarrassment among the other guests who may show up at the same time you do and be empty-handed.
3. When sending flowers, be sure of your choice. In France, chrysanthemums are associated with mourning. In France and Germany, red roses are a gift only between lovers.
4. Good chocolates and liqueurs are excellent house gifts. If the occasion demands something more elaborate, small porcelain and silver gifts such as candlesticks or table lighters are good choices.
5. Never give perfume or men's cologne as a gift. This is considered too personal for a business gift to or from either sex.
6. Do not enclose your business card with the gift. This is considered crass. Instead, write a note on a blank card.

switch jobs (for example, when they move from a line to a staff position) or are promoted.[27] Van Maanen also suggests specific socialization strategies, such as formal or informal, individual or collective, sequential or nonsequential, and fixed or variable.[28] For example, a company may use a sequential socialization strategy to groom people for top management positions by first rotating them through a series of relevant functional specialties. Another organization, say, a government agency, may take someone with political power from the rank and file and make that person the head of the agency. This nonsequential strategy will result in different personal (that is, the personality will be affected) and organizational outcomes.

Specific techniques of socializing new employees would include the use of mentors or role models, orientation and training programs, reward systems, and career planning.[29] Specific steps that can lead to successful organizational socialization would include the following:

1. Provide a challenging first job.
2. Provide relevant training.
3. Provide timely and consistent feedback.
4. Select a good first supervisor to be in charge of socialization.
5. Design a relaxed orientation program.
6. Place new recruits in work groups with high morale.[30]

Such deliberate socialization strategies have tremendous potential impact on human resources management and organizational effectiveness.

THE NATURE AND DIMENSIONS OF ATTITUDES

Both personality and attitudes are complex cognitive processes. The difference is that personality usually is thought of as the whole person, while attitudes may make up the personality.

The term "attitude" frequently is used in describing people and explaining their behavior. For example: "He has a poor attitude." "I like her attitude." "Our workers turn out poor quality products because they have poor attitudes." More precisely, an *attitude* can be defined as a persistent tendency to feel and behave in a particular way toward some object. For example, George does not like working the night shift. He has a negative attitude toward his work assignment.

Attitudes can be characterized three ways. First, they tend to persist unless something is done to change them. For example, if George is transferred to the day shift, his attitude may become positive. Second, attitudes can fall anywhere along a continuum from very favorable to very unfavorable. At the present time, George's attitude may be moderately unfavorable. If he is transferred to the day shift, his attitude may change to highly favorable. Third, attitudes are directed toward some object about which a person has feelings (sometimes called "affect") and beliefs. In George's case this is the work shift. The following sections discuss the various dimensions of attitudes, including the basic components, antecedents, and functions, and, finally, how attitudes can be changed.

Components of Attitudes

Attitudes can be broken down into three basic components: emotional, informational, and behavioral. The emotional component involves the person's feelings, or affect—positive, neutral, or negative—about an object. Thus, emotion is given the greatest attention in the organizational behavior literature in relation to job satisfaction.[31] In addition, the expression of emotions—either positive, like a customer service representative; negative, like a bill collector or police officer; or neutral, like an academic administrator or public servant—is also important to work behavior.

The informational component consists of the beliefs and information the individual has about the object. It makes no difference whether or not this information is empirically real or correct. A supervisor may believe that two weeks of training is necessary before a worker can operate a particular piece of equipment. In reality, the average worker may be able to operate the machine successfully after only four days of training. Yet the information the supervisor is using (that two weeks is necessary) is the key to his attitude about training.

The behavioral component consists of a person's tendencies to behave in a particular way toward an object. For example, the supervisor in the above paragraph may assign two weeks of machine training to all his new people.

It is important to remember that of the three components of attitudes, only the behavioral component can be directly observed. One cannot see another person's feelings (the emotional component) or beliefs (the informational component). These two components can only be inferred. For example, when the supervisor assigns a new employee to two weeks of training on the equipment, it is only inferred that (1) the supervisor has strong feelings about the length of training required and (2) the individual believes that this length of training is necessary. Yet, understanding the antecedents of work-related attitudes is important in the study of organizational behavior.

Antecedents of Work-Related Attitudes

Traditionally, the situational determinants of attitudes received the most attention. In particular, Salancik and Pfeffer noted that the social context provided information to the employees to form their feelings, or affect (their job-related attitudes).[32] More recently, personality traits or dispositions have been receiving increasing attention as antecedents of work-related attitudes.[33] In particular, the dispositions of positive affectivity (PA) and negative affectivity (NA) have been found to be important antecedents to attitudes about one's job. As explained by George,[34] NA reflects a personality disposition to experience negative emotional states; those with high NA tend to feel nervous, tense, anxious, worried, upset, and distressed. Accordingly, those with high NA are more likely to experience negative affective states—they are more likely to have a negative attitude toward themselves, others, and the world around them. Those with high PA have the opposite disposition and tend to have an overall sense of well-being, see themselves as pleasurably and effectively engaged, and tend to experience positive attitudes. Such PA and NA states are important in understanding job satisfaction[35] and work stress.[36]

Functions of Attitudes

An understanding of the functions of attitudes is important to the study of organizational behavior for a number of reasons. One is that attitudes help predict work behavior.[37] For example, if an attitude survey shows that workers are upset by a change in the work rules and the next week absenteeism begins to increase sharply, management may conclude that a negative attitude toward work rules led to an increase in worker absenteeism. Another reason why an understanding of attitudes is important is that attitudes help people adapt to their work environment. Katz has noted that attitudes serve four important functions in this process.[38]

The Adjustment Function. Attitudes often help people adjust to their work environment. When employees are well treated by the boss, they are likely to develop a positive attitude toward supervision and the organization. When employees are berated and given minimal salary increases, they are likely to develop a negative attitude toward supervision and the organization. These attitudes help employees adjust to their environment and are a basis for future behaviors. For example, if employees who are well treated are asked about supervision or the organization, they are likely to say good things. Just the reverse would probably be true for those berated and given minimal salary increases.

The Ego-Defensive Function. Besides helping employees adjust, attitudes also help them defend their self-images. For example, an older manager whose decisions are continually challenged by a younger subordinate manager may feel that the latter is brash, cocky, immature, and inexperienced. In truth, the younger subordinate may be right in challenging the decisions. The older manager may not be a very effective leader and may constantly make poor decisions. On the other hand, the older manager is not going to admit this, but will try to protect his ego by putting the blame on the other party. As a result, the older manager will have a negative attitude toward the younger one. The same is undoubtedly true for the younger manager, who will feel that the boss is not doing a good job. This attitude helps the younger person protect her ego. If the subordinate were to change this perception and believe that the boss was doing a good job, she would also have to stop criticizing the boss. Quite obviously, this is something that the younger person does not want to do. So the attitude serves to justify the action and to defend the ego.

The Value-Expressive Function. Attitudes provide people with a basis for expressing their values. For example, a manager who believes strongly in the work ethic will tend to voice attitudes toward specific individuals or work practices as a means of reflecting this value. A supervisor who wants a subordinate to work harder might put it this way: "You've got to work harder. That's been the tradition of the company since it was founded. It helped get us where we are today, and everyone is expected to subscribe to this ethic." A company president who believes strongly in the need to support the United Way campaign might tell the top management: "Everyone in this firm from top to bottom ought to support United Way. It's a wonderful organization and it does a great deal of good for our community. I don't know where we'd be without it." In both these cases, attitudes serve as a basis for expressing one's central values.

The Knowledge Function. Attitudes help supply standards and frames of reference that allow people to organize and explain the world around them. For example, a union organizer may have a negative attitude toward management. This attitude may not be based in fact, but it does help the individual relate to management. As a result, everything that management say is regarded by the union organizer as nothing more than a pack of lies, a deliberate distortion of the truth, or an attempt to manipulate the workers. Regardless of how accurate a person's view of reality is, attitudes toward people, events, and objects help the individual make sense out of what is going on.

Changing Attitudes

Employee attitudes can be changed, and sometimes it is in the best interests of management to try to do so. For example, if employees believe that their employer does not take care of them, management would like to change this attitude. Sometimes attitude change is difficult to accomplish because of certain barriers. After these barriers are identified, some ways of overcoming them and effectively changing attitudes are examined.

Barriers to Changing Attitudes. There are two basic barriers that can prevent people from changing their attitude. One is called prior commitments, which occurs when people feel a commitment to a particular course of action and are unwilling to change. There is even theory and research support for *escalation of commitment*, the tendency for decision makers to persist with failing courses of action.[39]

The following scenario presents an example of escalation of commitment: The president of the company graduated from an Ivy League school and was personally instrumental in hiring the new head of the marketing department, who had graduated from the same school. Unfortunately, things are not working out well. The marketing manager is not very good. However, because the president played such a major role in hiring this manager, the chief executive is unwilling to admit the mistake. Using the ego-defensive function of attitudes, the president distorts all negative information received about the marketing manager and continues to believe that everything is going well and the right selection decision was made.

A second barrier is a result of insufficient information. Sometimes people do not see any reason to change their attitude. The boss may not like a subordinate's negative attitude, but the latter may be quite pleased with his or her own behavior. Unless the boss can show the individual why a negative attitude is detrimental to career progress or salary raises or some other desirable personal objective, the subordinate may continue to have a negative attitude. This is particularly true when the attitude is a result of poor treatment by management. The worker will use the negative attitude to serve an adjustment function: "I can't respect a manager who treats me the way this one does."

Providing New Information. Fortunately, there are ways in which the barriers can be overcome and attitudes can be changed. One of these is by providing new information. Sometimes this information will change a person's beliefs and, in the process, his or her attitudes. In one classic study it was found that union workers had an antimanagement attitude. However, when some of the workers were promoted into the management ranks, their attitudes changed.[40] They became aware of what the company was doing to help the workers, and, over time, this new information resulted in a change in their beliefs about management and in their attitude toward both the company and the union. They became more procompany and less prounion.

Use of Fear. A second way of changing attitudes is through the use of fear. Some researchers have found that fear can cause some people to change their attitudes. However, the degree of fear seems to be important to the final outcome. For example, if low levels of fear arousal are used, people often ignore them. The warnings are not strong enough to warrant attention. If moderate levels of fear arousal are used, people often become aware of the situation and will change their attitudes. However, if high degrees of fear arousal are used, people often reject the message because it is too threatening and thus not believable. They essentially dig in their heels and refuse to be persuaded. A good example is provided in the case of anti-cigarette smoking commercials. The Department of Health and Human Services found that when it ran ads using patients who were dying of cancer, the message was so threatening to smokers that they shut it out; they refused to listen. As a result, the commercials did not have the desired impact. Health officials found that commercials using only moderate fear arousal were the most effective ones.

Resolving Discrepancies. Another way in which attitudes can be changed is by resolving discrepancies between attitudes and behavior. For example, research shows that when job applicants have more than one offer of employment and are forced to choose, they often feel that their final choice may have been a mistake. However, this mild conflict, or dissonance, does not usually last very long. The theory of cognitive dissonance says that people will try to actively reduce the dissonance by attitude and behavior change.[41] Thus, when people take new jobs and begin working, they also start to have negative feelings toward the firms that were not chosen and positive ones toward the company that was chosen. The result may be that the new employees conclude they did indeed make the right choice.

Influence of Friends or Peers. Still another way in which attitude changes can come about is through persuasion from friends or peers. For example, if Joe Smith has been padding his expense account and finds out that his friends in sales have not, he is likely to change his own attitude. This assumes that Joe likes his coworkers and they have some persuasive control over him. On the other hand, if Joe believes that the other salespeople are all lazy and would pad their accounts if they only knew how, he is unlikely to change his attitude toward doing so.

Additionally, it is important to remember that when a particular matter is of personal interest to people, they are likely to reject extreme discrepancies between their current behavior and that of others. For example, if the other salespeople tell Joe that they never pad their expenses while he is padding his by several thousand dollars annually, Joe is unlikely to let them influence him. There are too many benefits to be achieved if he just keeps on doing what he has been doing. This is why unethical behavior is so difficult to combat.

The Coopting Approach. A final way in which attitude changes often take place is by coopting, which means taking people who are dissatisfied with a situation and getting them involved in improving things. For example, Nancy Jones feels that more needs to be done in improving employee benefits. As a result, the company appoints Nancy as a member of the employee benefits committee. By giving her the opportunity to participate in employee benefits decision making, the company increases the chances that Nancy's attitude will change. Once she begins realizing how these benefits are determined and how long and hard the committee works to ensure that the personnel are given the best benefits possible, she is likely to change her attitude.

JOB SATISFACTION

Specific employee attitudes relating to job satisfaction and organizational commitment are of major interest to the field of organizational behavior and the practice of human resource management. Whereas the discussion of attitudes so far has direct implications, the discussion of job satisfaction focuses on employees' attitudes toward their job and the discussion of organizational commitment focuses on their attitudes toward the overall organization. The more widely recognized job satisfaction is first discussed. The more recently recognized attitude of organizational commitment follows.

What Is Meant by Job Satisfaction?

Locke gives a comprehensive definition of job satisfaction as "a pleasurable or positive emotional state resulting from the appraisal of one's job or job experience."[42] Job satisfaction is a result of employees' perception of how well their job provides those things which are viewed as important. It is generally recognized in the organizational behavior field that job satisfaction is the most important and frequently studied attitude.[43]

There are three important dimensions to job satisfaction. First, job satisfaction is an emotional response to a job situation. As such, it cannot be seen; it can only be inferred. Second, job satisfaction is often determined by how well outcomes meet or exceed expectations. For example, if organizational participants feel that they are working much harder than others in the department but are receiving fewer rewards, they will probably have a negative attitude toward the work, the boss, and/or coworkers. They will be dissatisfied. On the other hand, if they feel they are being treated very well and are being paid equitably, they are likely to have a positive attitude toward the job. They will be job-satisfied. Third, job satisfaction represents several related attitudes. Smith, Kendall, and Hulin have suggested that there are five job dimensions that represent the most important characteristics of a job about which people have affective responses. These are:

1. *The work itself.* The extent to which the job provides the individual with interesting tasks, opportunities for learning, and the chance to accept responsibility
2. *Pay.* The amount of financial remuneration that is received and the degree to which this is viewed as equitable vis-à-vis that of others in the organization
3. *Promotion opportunities.* The chances for advancement in the hierarchy
4. *Supervision.* The abilities of the supervisor to provide technical assistance and behavioral support
5. *Coworkers.* The degree to which fellow workers are technically proficient and socially supportive[44]

Influences on Job Satisfaction

There are a number of factors that influence job satisfaction.[45] For example, one recent study even found that if college students' majors coincided with their jobs, this relationship predicted subsequent job satisfaction.[46] However, the main influences can be summarized along the dimensions identified above.

The Work Itself. The content of the work itself is a major source of satisfaction. For example, research related to the job characteristics approach to job design, covered in Chapter 7, shows that feedback from the job itself and autonomy are two of the major job-related motivational factors. Some of the most important ingredients of a satisfying job uncovered by surveys include interesting and challenging work, work that is not boring, and a job that provides status.[47]

Pay. Wages and salaries are recognized to be a significant, but complex, multidimensional factor in job satisfaction.[48] Money not only helps people attain their basic needs but is instrumental in providing upper-level need satisfaction. Employees often see pay as a reflection of how management view their contribution to the organization. Fringe benefits are also important, but they are not as influential. One reason undoubtedly is that most employees do not even know how much they are receiving in benefits. Moreover, most tend to undervalue these benefits because they cannot see their practical value.[49] However, recent research indicates if employees are allowed some flexibility in choosing the type of benefits they prefer within a total package, called a flexible benefits plan, there is a significant increase in both benefit satisfaction and overall job satisfaction.[50]

Promotions. Promotional opportunities seem to have a varying effect on job satisfaction. This is because promotions take a number of different forms and have a variety of accompanying rewards. For example, individuals who are promoted on the basis of seniority often experience job satisfaction but not as much as those who are promoted on the basis of performance. Additionally, a promotion with a 10 percent salary raise is typically not as satisfying as one with a 20 percent salary raise. These differences help explain why executive promotions may be more satisfying than promotions that occur at the lower levels of organizations.

Supervision. Supervision is another moderately important source of job satisfaction. Chapter 14 discusses the impact of leadership skills. For now, however, it can be said that there seem to be two dimensions of supervisory style that affect job satisfaction. One is employee-centeredness, which is measured by the degree to which a supervisor takes a personal interest in the employee's welfare. It commonly is manifested in ways such as checking to see how well the subordinate is doing, providing advice and assistance to the individual, and communicating with the worker on a personal as well as an official level. American employees generally complain that their supervisors don't do a very good job on these dimensions. For example, a large survey found that less than half of the respondents felt their bosses provided them regular feedback or tried to solve their problems.[51]

The other dimension is participation or influence, as illustrated by managers who allow their people to participate in decisions that affect their own jobs. In most cases, this approach leads to higher job satisfaction. For example, comprehensive meta-analysis concluded that participation does have a positive effect on job satisfaction. A participative climate created by the supervisor has a more substantial effect on workers' satisfaction than does participation in a specific decision.[52]

Work Group. The nature of the work group will have an effect on job satisfaction. Friendly, cooperative coworkers are a modest source of job satisfaction to individual employees. The work group serves as a source of support, comfort, advice, and assistance to the individual worker. A "good" work group makes the job more enjoyable. However, this factor is not essential to job satisfaction. On the other hand, if the reverse conditions exist—the people are difficult to get along with—this factor may have a negative effect on job satisfaction.

Working Conditions. Working conditions are another factor that have a modest effect on job satisfaction. If the working conditions are good (clean, attractive

Managing Diversity in Action

Flexibility Is the Key

An increasing number of firms are recognizing that a key element of managing the diverse work force is flexibility. They are developing programs that allow the personnel to make adjustments in their work schedules and thus better meet the demands that are being placed on them. For example, a recent large survey found that unpaid childbirth leave beyond the normal disability period has become widely available for women (85 percent). Also, flextime is widespread (77 percent), as is unpaid family leave to care for sick family members (75 percent). Interestingly, more than half of the companies reported equal lengths of unpaid parenting leave for men and women.

In some cases, new parents want to bring their preschool children to work. Firms such as Corning, Inc., offer child care services. Some firms allow two or three persons to share one job. Then, when the parent or parents are ready to return to work full-time, there is a position waiting. Others, like the Continental Corporation, offer such job sharing and also the opportunity to stay at home some days and work via telecommunication.

In each of these examples the company has been able to more effectively manage its increasingly diverse work force. Some firms have even recently appointed a full-time work/family coordinator. At the same time, each firm has reported that these programs have helped increase the involved employees' productivity and the firm's profit. Thus, by addressing the special needs of their diverse work force, the firms are finding that they can develop programs that are both personally and financially rewarding for all involved.

surroundings, for instance), the personnel will find it easier to carry out their jobs. If the working conditions are poor (hot, noisy surroundings, for example), personnel will find it more difficult to get things done. In other words, the effect of working conditions on job satisfaction is similar to that of the work group. If things are good, there will not be a job satisfaction problem; if things are poor, there will be.

Most people do not give working conditions a great deal of thought unless they are extremely bad. Additionally, when there are complaints about working conditions, these sometimes are really nothing more than manifestations of other problems. For example, a manager may complain that his office has not been properly cleaned by the night crew, but his anger is actually a result of a meeting he had with the boss earlier in the day in which he was given a poor performance evaluation. However, in recent years, because of the increased diversity of the work force, working conditions have taken on new importance. For example, for some organizations, conditions have expanded to include programs to give employees more flexibility in their work schedules, as shown in the accompanying Managing Diversity in Action: Flexibility Is the Key.

Outcomes of Job Satisfaction

To society as a whole as well as from an individual employee's standpoint, job satisfaction in and of itself is a desirable outcome. However, from a pragmatic managerial and organizational effectiveness perspective, it is important to know how, if at all, satisfaction relates to outcome variables. For instance, if job satisfaction is high, will the employees perform better and the organization be more effective? If job satisfaction is low, will there be performance problems and ineffectiveness? This question has been asked by both researchers and practitioners through the years. There are no simple answers.[53] In examining the outcomes of job satisfaction, it is important to break down the analysis into a series of specific subtopics. The following sections examine the most important of these.

Satisfaction and Productivity. Are satisfied workers more productive than their less satisfied counterparts? This "satisfaction-performance controversy" has raged over the years. Although most people assume a positive relationship, the preponderance of research evidence indicates that there is no strong linkage between satisfaction and productivity. For example, a comprehensive meta-analysis of the research literature found only a .17 average correlation between job satisfaction and productivity.[54] Satisfied workers will not necessarily be the highest producers. There are many possible mediating variables, the most important of which seems to be rewards. If people receive rewards they feel are equitable, they will be satisfied and this is likely to result in greater performance effort.[55] Also, recent research evidence indicates that satisfaction may not necessarily lead to individual performance improvement, but does lead to organizational-level improvement.[56] Finally, there is still considerable debate whether satisfaction leads to performance or performance leads to satisfaction. The next chapter examines in detail these and other possible dimensions of the relationship.

Satisfaction and Turnover. Does high employee job satisfaction result in low turnover? Unlike that between satisfaction and productivity, research has uncovered a moderate relationship between satisfaction and turnover.[57] High job satisfaction will not, in and of itself, keep turnover low, but it does seem to help. On the other hand, if there is considerable job dissatisfaction, there is likely to be high turnover. One group of researchers found that for women eighteen to twenty-five, satisfaction was an excellent predictor of whether or not they changed jobs. On the other hand, as job tenure (length of time on the job) increased, there was less likelihood of their leaving.[58] Tenure has also been found to lessen the effects of dissatisfaction among male employees.[59]

There are other factors, such as commitment to the organization (covered in the next major section), that play a role in this relationship between satisfaction and turnover. Some people cannot see themselves working anywhere else, so they remain regardless of how dissatisfied they feel. Another factor is the general economy. When things in the economy are going well and there is little unemployment, typically there will be an increase in turnover because people will begin looking for better opportunities with other organizations. Even if they are satisfied, many people are willing to leave if the opportunities elsewhere promise to be better. On the other hand, if jobs are tough to get, dissatisfied employees will stay where they are. On an overall basis, however, it is accurate to say that job satisfaction is important in employee turnover. Although absolutely no turnover is not necessarily beneficial to the organization, a low turnover rate is usually desirable because of training costs and the drawbacks of inexperience.

Satisfaction and Absenteeism. Research has pretty well demonstrated an inverse relationship between satisfaction and absenteeism.[60] When satisfaction is high, absenteeism tends to be low; when satisfaction is low, absenteeism tends to be high. However, as with the other relationships with satisfaction, there are moderating variables such as the degree to which people feel that their jobs are important. For example, research among state government employees has found that those who believed that their work was important had lower absenteeism than did those who did not feel this way. Additionally, it is important to remember that while high job satisfaction will not necessarily result in low absenteeism, low job satisfaction is likely to bring about high absenteeism.[61]

Other Effects of Job Satisfaction. In addition to those noted above, there are a number of other effects brought about by high job satisfaction. Research reports that highly satisfied employees tend to have better mental and physical health, learn new job-related tasks more quickly, have fewer on-the-job accidents, and file fewer grievances. On the positive side, it has also recently been found that satisfied employees are more likely to exhibit prosocial "citizenship" behaviors and activities, such as helping coworkers, helping customers, and being more cooperative.[62]

From an overall standpoint, then, most organizational behavior researchers as well as practicing managers would argue that job satisfaction is important to an organization. Some critics have argued, however, that this is pure conjecture because there is so much we do not know about the positive effects of satisfaction. On the other hand, when job satisfaction is low, there seem to be negative effects on the organization that have been documented. So if only from the standpoint of viewing job satisfaction as a minimum requirement or point of departure, it is of value to the organization's overall health and effectiveness and is deserving of study and application in the field of organizational behavior.

ORGANIZATIONAL COMMITMENT

The job satisfaction attitude has received the most attention over the years. Recently, the more global organizational commitment attitude has emerged out of the research literature as being important to understanding and predicting organizational behavior. Although a strong relationship between satisfaction and commitment has been found,[63] recent research gives some support that commitment causes satisfaction.[64] However, most studies treat satisfaction and commitment differently and, especially in light of the "downsizing syndrome" of modern organizations, commitment deserves special attention.

The Meaning of Organizational Commitment

As with other topics in organizational behavior, a wide variety of definitions and measures of organizational commitment exist. As an attitude, organizational commitment is most often defined as (1) a strong desire to remain a member of a particular organization; (2) a willingness to exert high levels of effort on behalf of the organization; and (3) a definite belief in, and acceptance of, the values and goals of the organization.[65] In other words, this is an attitude about employees' loyalty to their organization and is an ongoing process through which organizational participants express their concern for the organization and its continued success and well-being.[66] Using this definition, it is commonly measured by the Organizational Commitment Questionnaire shown in Figure 5.3.

The organizational commitment attitude is determined by a number of personal (age, tenure in the organization, and dispositions such as positive or negative affectivity, or internal or external control attributions) and organizational (the job design and the leadership style of one's supervisor) variables.[67] Even nonorganiza-

Listed below are a series of statements that represent possible feelings that individuals might have about the company or organization for which they work. With respect to your own feelings about the particular organization for which you are now working (company name) please indicate the degree of your agreement or disagreement with each statement by checking one of the seven alternatives below each statement.*

---

1. I am willing to put in a great deal of effort beyond what is normally expected in order to help this organization be successful.
2. I talk up this organization to my friends as a great organization to work for.
3. I feel very little loyalty to this organization. (R)
4. I would accept almost any type of job assignment in order to keep working for this organization.
5. I find that my values and the organization's values are very similar.
6. I am proud to tell others that I am a part of this organization.
7. I could just as well be working for a different organization as long as the type of work was similar. (R)
8. This organization really inspires the very best in me in the way of job performance.
9. It would take very little change in my present circumstances to cause me to leave this organization. (R)
10. I am extremely glad that I chose this organization to work for over others I was considering at the time I joined.
11. There's not too much to be gained by sticking with this organization indefinitely. (R)
12. Often, I find it difficult to agree with this organization's policies on important matters relating to its employees. (R)
13. I really care about the fate of this organization.
14. For me this is the best of all possible organizations for which to work.
15. Deciding to work for this organization was a definite mistake on my part. (R)

---

*Responses to each item are measured on a 7-point scale with scale point anchors labeled: (1) strongly disagree; (2) moderately disagree; (3) slightly disagree; (4) neither disagree nor agree; (5) slightly agree; (6) moderately agree; (7) strongly agree. An "R" denotes a negatively phrased and reverse scored item.

FIGURE 5.3
Organizational Commitment Questionnaire (OCQ).
(*Source*: R. T. Mowday, R. M. Steers, and L. W. Porter, "The Measure of Organizational Commitment," *Journal of Vocational Behavior*, vol. 14, 1979, p. 288. Used with permission.)

---

tional factors, such as the availability of alternatives after making the initial choice to join an organization, will affect subsequent commitment.[68]

Because of this multidimensional nature of organizational commitment, there is growing support for a three-component model proposed by Meyer and Allen.[69] The three dimensions are as follows:

1. *Affective commitment* involves the employee's emotional attachment to, identification with, and involvement in the organization.
2. *Continuance commitment* involves commitment based on the costs that the employee associates with leaving the organization.
3. *Normative commitment* involves the employee's feelings of obligation to stay with the organization.

There is considerable research support for this three-component conceptualization of organizational commitment.[70]

The Outcomes of Organizational Commitment

As is the case with job satisfaction, there are mixed outcomes of organizational commitment. Both early[71] and recent research summaries[72] support a positive relationship between organizational commitment and desirable outcomes such as performance, turnover, and absenteeism. There is also evidence that employee commitment relates to other desirable outcomes, such as the perception of a warm, supportive organizational climate.[73] Yet, as with satisfaction, there are some studies that do not show strong or any relationships between commitment and outcome variables, and there may be problems defining and interpreting commitment.[74] On balance, however, most researchers would agree that the organizational commitment attitude as defined here is a somewhat better predictor of outcome variables than is job satisfaction.[75]

Summary

Personality and attitudes represent important micro, cognitively oriented variables in the study of organizational behavior. Personality represents the "whole person" concept. It includes perception, learning, motivation, and more. According to this definition, people's external appearance and traits, their inner awareness of self, and the person-situation interaction make up their personalities. Levinson's and Hall's stage theories of personality development have made significant contributions to areas such as career development, but Argyris's seven-dimension continuum of immaturity-maturity, leading to his basic incongruency hypothesis between mature employees and the requirements of formal organizations, makes a significant contribution to the overall conceptualization of organizational behavior, and contributes to the model used in this text. The socialization process of personality development is also very relevant to the understanding and application of organizational behavior.

Whereas personality deals with the whole person, an attitude is a persistent tendency to feel and behave in a particular way toward some object. Like personality, attitudes are a complex cognitive process, which have three basic characteristics: they persist unless changed in some way; they range along a continuum; and they are directed toward an object about which a person has feelings, or affect, and beliefs. Attitudes also have three components: emotional, informational, and behavioral. Both situational and personality traits or dispositions such as positive affectivity (PA) and negative affectivity (NA) are important antecedents to attitudes about one's job.

Attitudes often help employees adapt to their work environment. There are four functions that attitudes have in this process: (1) they help people adjust to their environment; (2) they help people defend their self-image; (3) they provide people with a basis for expressing their values; and (4) they help supply standards and frames of reference that allow people to organize and explain the world around them.

It is sometimes difficult to change attitudes. One reason is prior commitments. A second is insufficient information on the part of the person having an attitude to be changed. Research shows that some of the ways of bringing about attitude changes are providing new information, use of fear, resolving discrepancies between behavior and attitude, persuasion from friends or peers, and coopting.

Job satisfaction is a pleasurable or positive emotional state resulting from the appraisal of one's job or job experience. A number of factors influence job satisfaction. Some of the major ones are the work itself, pay, promotions, supervision, the work group, and working conditions. There are a number of outcomes of job satisfaction. For example, although the relationship with productivity is not clear, low job satisfaction tends to lead to both turnover and absenteeism, while high job satisfaction often results in fewer on-the-job accidents and work grievances and less time needed to learn new job-related tasks. Most recently, satisfied workers have been found to exhibit prosocial "citizenship" behaviors and activities.

Closely related to job satisfaction is the organizational commitment attitude. It involves the employees' loyalty to the organization and is determined by a number of personal, organizational, and nonorganizational variables. Recently, commitment has been conceived as having three components: affective (emotional attachment), continuance (costs of leaving), and normative (obligation to stay). Like job satisfaction, the organizational commitment attitude has mixed results but in general, is thought to have a somewhat stronger relationship with organizational outcomes such as performance, absenteeism, and turnover.

Questions for Discussion and Review

1. Critically analyze the statement that "the various psychological processes can be thought of as pieces of a jigsaw puzzle, and personality as the completed puzzle picture."
2. What is the comprehensive definition of "personality"? Give brief examples of each of the major elements, giving special emphasis to the so-called big five personality traits.
3. How does personality relate to organizational behavior?
4. In your own words, what is an attitude? What are three characteristics and three components of attitudes?
5. Attitudes serve four important functions for individuals. What are these four functions?
6. What types of barriers prevent people from changing their attitudes? How can attitudes be changed?
7. What is meant by the term "job satisfaction"? How does it relate to attitudes?
8. What are some of the major factors that influence job satisfaction?
9. What are some of the important outcomes of job satisfaction?
10. What is organizational commitment? What three components have recently emerged to help better explain the complexities of commitment? Why may an understanding of organizational commitment be especially important in the years ahead?

Footnote References and Supplemental Readings

1. Murray R. Barrick and Michael K. Mount, "Autonomy as a Moderator of the Relationships Between the Big Five Personality Dimensions and Job Performance," *Journal of Applied Psychology*, February 1993, p. 111.
2. Abraham K. Korman, *The Psychology of Motivation*, Prentice-Hall, Englewood Cliffs, N.J., 1974, p. 227.
3. See S. E. Jackson and R. S. Schuler, "A Meta-Analysis and Conceptual Critique of Research on Role Ambiguity and Role Conflict in Work Settings," *Organizational Behavior and Human Decision Processes*, vol. 36, 1985, pp. 16–78.
4. K. W. Mossholder, A. G. Bedeian, and A. A. Armenakis, "Role Perceptions, Satisfaction, and Performance: Moderating Effects of Self-Esteem and Organizational Level," *Organizational Behavior and Human Performance*, vol. 28, 1981, pp. 224–234, and K. W. Mossholder, A. G. Bedeian, and A. A. Armenakis, "Group Process–Work Outcome Relationships: A Note on the Moderating Impact of Self-Esteem," *Academy of Management Journal*, vol. 25, 1982, pp. 575–585.
5. Jon L. Pierce, Donald G. Gardner, Randall B. Dunham, and Larry L. Cummings, "Moderation by Organization-Based Self-Esteem of Role Condition-Employee Response Relationships," *Academy of Management Journal*, April 1993, pp. 271–288.
6. Daniel C. Ganster and John Schaubroeck, "Work Stress and Employee Health," *Journal of Management*, vol. 17, 1991, pp. 235–271, and Daniel C. Ganster and John Schaubroeck, "Role Stress and Worker Health: An Extension of the Plasticity Hypothesis of

Self-Esteem," *Journal of Social Behavior and Personality*, vol. 6, 1991, pp. 349–360.

7. Roy J. Blitzer, Colleen Petersen, and Linda Rogers, "How to Build Self-Esteem," *Training and Development*, February 1993, p. 59.

8. Albert Bandura, "Self-Efficacy Mechanism in Human Agency," *American Psychologist*, vol. 37, 1982, pp. 122–147.

9. John B. Miner, *Organizational Behavior*, Random House, New York, 1988, p. 84.

10. Marilyn E. Gist and Terence R. Mitchell, "Self-Efficacy: A Theoretical Analysis of Its Determinants and Malleability," *Academy of Management Review*, April 1992, p. 183.

11. Dov Eden and Arie Aviram, "Self-Efficacy Training to Speed Reemployment: Helping People to Help Themselves," *Journal of Applied Psychology*, June 1993, pp. 352–360, and Jane George-Falvy, Terence R. Mitchell, Denise Daniels, and Heidi Hopper, "Effects of Training on Self-Efficacy, Expectations, and Task Performance During Skill Acquisition," *Academy of Management Best Papers Proceedings*, 1993, pp. 106–110.

12. Clyde Kluckhohn and H. A. Murray, "Personality Formation: The Determinants," in C. Kluckhohn and H. A. Murray (eds.), *Personality*, Knopf, New York, 1948, p. 35.

13. Daniel J. Levinson, *The Seasons of a Man's Life*, Knopf, New York, 1978, p. 49.

14. Richard E. Kopelman and Michael Glass, "Test of Daniel Levinson's Theory of Adult Male Life States," *National Academy of Management Proceedings*, 1979, pp. 79–83.

15. D. J. Levinson, "A Conception of Adult Development," *American Psychologist*, vol. 41, 1986, pp. 3–13.

16. Daniel C. Feldman, "Careers in Organizations: Recent Trends and Future Directions," *Journal of Management*, vol. 15, 1989, p. 142.

17. Fred Luthans and Linda T. Thomas, "The Relationship Between Age and Job Satisfaction," *Personnel Review*, vol. 18, no. 1, 1989, pp. 23–26.

18. Chris Argyris, *Personality and Organization*, Harper, New York, 1957, pp. 51–53.

19. Ibid., p. 53.

20. For example, see Charles A. O'Reilly, David F. Caldwell, and Richard Mirable, "A Profile Comparison Approach to Person-Job Fit: More Than a Mirage," *Academy of Management Best Papers Proceedings*, 1992, pp. 237–241.

21. Edgar H. Schein, "Organizational Socialization and the Profession of Management," in David Kolb, Irwin Rubin, and James McIntyre (eds.), *Organizational Psychology: A Book of Readings*, Prentice-Hall, Englewood Cliffs, N.J., 1971, pp. 14–15.

22. Gareth R. Jones, "Socialization Tactics, Self-Efficiency, and Newcomers' Adjustments to Organizations," *Academy of Management Journal*, June 1986, pp. 262–279. Also see Cheri Ostroff and Steve W. J. Kozlowski, "Organizational Socialization as a Learning Process: The Flow of Information Acquisition," *Personnel Psychology*, Winter 1992, pp. 849–874.

23. Schein, op. cit., p. 3.

24. Daniel C. Feldman and Hugh J. Arnold, *Managing Individual and Group Behavior in Organizations*, McGraw-Hill, New York, 1983, pp. 79–80.

25. Schein, op. cit., p. 3.

26. Robert A. Baron, *Behavior in Organizations*, 2d ed., Allyn and Bacon, Boston, 1986, p. 65.

27. John Gabarro, "Socialization at the Top: How CEOs and Subordinates Evolve Interpersonal Contracts," *Organizational Dynamics*, Winter 1979, pp. 3–23.

28. John Van Maanen, "People Processing: Strategies of Organizational Socialization," *Organizational Dynamics*, Summer 1978, pp. 19–36.

29. Gregory B. Northcraft and Margaret A. Neale, *Organizational Behavior*, Dryden, Chicago, 1990, p. 475.

30. Feldman and Arnold, op. cit., pp. 83–86.

31. Anat Rafaeli and Robert I. Sutton, "Expression of Emotion as Part of the Work Role," *Academy of Management Review*, January 1987, p. 23.

32. Gerald Salancik and Jeffrey Pfeffer, "A Social Information Processing Approach to Job Attitudes and Task Design," *Administrative Science Quarterly*, June 1978, pp. 224–253.

33. For example, see Barry Staw and Jerry Ross, "Stability in the Midst of Change: A Dispositional Approach to Job Attitudes," *Journal of Applied Psychology*, vol. 70, 1985, pp. 469–480.

34. Jennifer M. George, "Personality, Affect, and Behavior in Groups," *Journal of Applied Psychology*, vol. 75, no. 2, 1990, p. 108.

35. For example, see Timothy A. Judge, "Does Affective Disposition Moderate the Relationships Between Job Satisfaction and Voluntary Turnover?" *Journal of Applied Psychology*, June 1993, pp. 395–401, and Augustine O. Agho, James L. Price, and Charles W. Mueller, "Discriminant Validity of Measures of Job Satisfaction, Positive Affectivity and Negative Affectivity," *Journal of Occupational and Organizational Psychology*, September 1992, pp. 185–196.

36. A. P. Brief, M. J. Burke, J. M. George, B. Robinson, and J. Webster, "Should Negative Affectivity Remain an Unmeasured Variable in the Study of Job Stress?" *Journal of Applied Psychology*, vol. 73, 1988, pp. 193–198.

37. See Min-Sun Kim and John E. Hunter, "Relationships Among Attitudes, Behavior Intentions, and Behav-

ior," *Communication Research*, June 1993, pp. 331–364, and Min-Sun Kim and John E. Hunter, "Attitude-Behavior Relations: A Meta-Analysis of Attitudinal Relevance and Topic," *Journal of Communication*, Winter 1993, pp. 101–142.

38. D. Katz, "The Functional Approach to the Study of Attitudes," *Journal of Opinion Quarterly*, Summer 1960, pp. 163–204.

39. Joel Brockner, "The Escalation of Commitment to a Failing Course of Action: Toward Theoretical Progress," *Academy of Management Review*, January 1992, pp. 39–61.

40. S. Lieberman, "The Effect of Changes in Roles on the Attitudes of Role Occupants," *Human Relations*, November 1956, pp. 385–402.

41. Leon Festinger, *A Theory of Cognitive Dissonance*, Stanford University, Stanford, Calif., 1957.

42. E. A. Locke, "The Nature and Cause of Job Satisfaction," in M. D. Dunnette (ed.), *Handbook of Industrial and Organizational Psychology*, Rand McNally, Chicago, 1976, p. 1300.

43. Terence R. Mitchell and James R. Larson, Jr., *People in Organizations*, 3d ed., McGraw-Hill, New York, 1987, p. 146.

44. P. C. Smith, L. M. Kendall, and C. L. Hulin, *The Measure of Satisfaction in Work and Retirement*, Rand McNally, Chicago, 1969.

45. Vernon A. Quarstein, R. Bruce McAfee, and Myron Glassman, "The Situational Occurrences Theory of Job Satisfaction," *Human Relations*, August 1993, pp. 859–873.

46. Mary Ann M. Fricko and Terry A. Beehr, "A Longitudinal Investigation of Interest Congruence and Gender Concentration as Predictors of Job Satisfaction," *Personnel Psychology*, September 1992, pp. 99–118.

47. Jane Ciabattari, "The Biggest Mistake Top Managers Make," *Working Woman*, October 1986, p. 48.

48. See Timothy A. Judge, "Validity of the Dimensions of the Pay Satisfaction Questionnaire: Evidence of Differential Prediction," *Personnel Psychology*, Summer 1993, pp. 331–355.

49. Brenda Major and Ellen Konar, "An Investigation of Sex Differences in Pay Expectations and Their Possible Causes," *Academy of Management Journal*, December 1984, pp. 777–792.

50. Alison E. Barber, Randall B. Dunham, and Roger A. Formisano, "The Impact of Flexible Benefits on Employee Satisfaction: A Field Study," *Personnel Psychology*, September 1992, pp. 55–76.

51. "Labor Letter," *The Wall Street Journal*, Dec. 22, 1987, p. 1.

52. Katharine I. Miller and Peter R. Monge, "Participation, Satisfaction, and Productivity: A Meta-Analytic

Review," *Academy of Management Journal*, December 1986, p. 748.

53. For example, see Barry M. Staw and Sigal G. Barsade, "Affect and Managerial Performance: A Test of the Sadder-but-Wiser vs. Happier-and-Smarter Hypotheses," *Administrative Science Quarterly*, June 1993, pp. 304–331.

54. M. T. Iffaldano and P. M. Muchinsky, "Job Satisfaction and Job Performance: A Meta-Analysis," *Psychological Bulletin*, vol. 97, 1985, pp. 251–273.

55. P. M. Podsakoff and L. J. Williams, "The Relationship Between Job Performance and Job Satisfaction," in E. A. Locke (ed.), *Generalizing from Laboratory to Field Settings*, Lexington Books, Lexington, Mass., 1986.

56. Cheri Ostroff, "The Relationship Between Satisfaction, Attitudes, and Performance: An Organizational Level Analysis," *Journal of Applied Psychology*, December 1992, pp. 963–974.

57. For an example of a recent study that verifies the relationship between satisfaction and turnover, see Thomas W. Lee and Richard T. Mowday, "Voluntarily Leaving an Organization: An Empirical Investigation of Steers and Mowday's Model of Turnover," *Academy of Management Journal*, December 1987, pp. 721–743. Also see Robert P. Tett and John P. Meyer, "Job Satisfaction, Organizational Commitment, Turnover Intention, and Turnover: Path Analyses Based on Meta-Analytic Findings," *Personnel Psychology*, Summer 1993, pp. 259–294.

58. Sookom Kim, Roger Roderick, and John Shea, *Dual Careers: A Longitudinal Study of the Labor Market Experience of Women*, vol. 2, U.S. Government Printing Office, Washington, D.C., 1973, pp. 55–56.

59. Herbert Parnes, Gilbert Nestel, and Paul Andrisani, *The Pre-Retirement Years: A Longitudinal Study of the Labor Market Experience of Men*, vol. 3, U.S. Government Printing Office, Washington, D.C., 1973, p. 37.

60. K. Dow Scott and G. Stephen Taylor, "An Examination of Conflicting Findings on the Relationship Between Job Satisfaction and Absenteeism: A Meta-Analysis," *Academy of Management Journal*, September 1985, pp. 599–612.

61. C. W. Clegg, "Psychology of Employee Lateness, Absenteeism, and Turnover: A Methodological Critique and an Empirical Study," *Journal of Applied Psychology*, February 1983, pp. 88–101.

62. D. W. Organ, *Organizational Citizenship Behavior: The Good Soldier Syndrome*, Lexington Books, Lexington, Mass., 1987. For a recent study, see Robert H. Moorman, "The Influence of Cognitive and Affective-Based Job Satisfaction Measures on the Relationship Between Satisfaction and Organizational

Citizenship Behavior," *Human Relations*, vol. 46, 1993, p. 759.

63. Edwin A. Locke and Gary P. Latham, *A Theory of Goal Setting and Task Performance*, Prentice-Hall, Englewood Cliffs, N.J., 1990, pp. 249–250.

64. Robert J. Vandenberg and Charles E. Lance, "Examining the Causal Order of Job Satisfaction and Organizational Commitment," *Journal of Management*, March 1992, pp. 153–167.

65. R. T. Mowday, L. W. Porter, and R. M. Steers, *Employee-Organization Linkages*, Academic Press, New York, 1982.

66. Northcraft and Neale, op. cit., p. 465.

67. For example, see Fred Luthans, Donald Baack, and Lew Taylor, "Organizational Commitment: Analysis of Antecedents," *Human Relations*, vol. 40, no. 4, 1987, pp. 219–236.

68. Northcraft and Neale, op. cit., p. 472.

69. J. P. Meyer and N. J. Allen, "A Three-Component Conceptualization of Organizational Commitment," *Human Resource Management Review*, vol. 1, 1991, pp. 61–89.

70. For some recent tests of the Meyer and Allen model, see Rich D. Hackett, Peter Bycio, and Peter Hausdoft, "Further Assessments of a Three-Component Model of Organizational Commitment," *Academy of Management Best Papers Proceedings*, 1992, pp. 212–216, and Mark John Somers, "A Test of the Relationship Between Affective and Continuance Commitment Using Non-Recursive Models," *Journal of Occupational and Organizational Psychology*, June 1993, pp. 185–192.

71. R. T. Mowday, R. M. Steers, and L. W. Porter, "The Measurement of Organizational Commitment," *Journal of Vocational Behavior*, vol. 14, 1979, pp. 224–247.

72. J. E. Mathieu and D. M. Zajac, "A Review and Meta-Analysis of the Antecedents, Correlates, and Consequences of Organizational Commitment," *Psychological Bulletin*, vol. 108, 1990, pp. 171–199, and T. A. De Cotiis and T. P. Summers, "A Path Analysis of a Model of the Antecedents and Consequences of Organizational Commitment," *Human Relations*, vol. 40, 1987, pp. 445–470.

73. Fred Luthans, La Vonne K. Wahl, and Carol S. Steinhaus, "The Importance of Social Support for Employee Commitment," *Organizational Development Journal*, Winter 1992, pp. 1–10.

74. Donna M. Randall, Donald B. Fedor, and Clinton O. Longenecker, "The Behavioral Expression of Organizational Commitment," *Journal of Vocational Behavior*, vol. 36, 1990, pp. 210–224, and A. E. Reichers, "A Review and Reconceptualization of Organizational Commitment," *Academy of Management Review*, July 1985, pp. 465–476.

75. Lynn McMarlane Shore, George C. Thornton, and Lucy A. Newton, "Job Satisfaction and Organizational Commitment as Predictors of Behavioral Intentions and Employee Behavior," *Academy of Management Proceedings*, 1989, pp. 229–333, and Locke and Latham, op. cit., p. 250.

**REAL CASE:
Looking for an
Equal Chance**

There are many myths that exist about women in the workplace. For example, a common argument is that women are paid less than men because they really want to stay home with children rather than work. Yet, in sheer numbers, almost half of all mothers are currently working, and they certainly all expect to receive equitable pay. Another myth is that while things may be bad for women at the lower, operating levels of the organization, the upper-level female executives do quite well. Once again, the facts say otherwise. There are very few women at the top levels of corporate America, and they are paid less than their male counterparts. What follows is the profile of those few who have made it to the top of their respective companies:

- Many successful women are married, but not all have a family. Nearly half of the women on the 1990 *Fortune* list of highly paid executives were childless. Those who do have children find that the demands of the job require them to carefully structure their home life so that everything runs smoothly. For example, Phyllis Swersky, executive vice president of AlCorp, has a live-in nanny, a live-in housekeeper, and a supportive husband, who all help manage house affairs and look after the three young children, ages four to eight. Notes Swersky, "I don't take care of the house. I don't cook. I don't do laundry. I don't market. I don't take my children to malls and museums. And I don't have close friends."

- Some women find that marriage and work cannot both be accommodated, so they remain single. Claudia Goldin, the first tenured economics professor at Harvard, falls into this category. Commenting on her choice, she says, "I'm at the top of my profession now, and it took a tremendous amount of concentration and focus in a brief period of time. If I were married and had kids, I wouldn't have had the energy."
- These women work extremely long hours. For example, Maria Monet, chief financial officer for the Ogden Corporation, reports that she works eleven-hour days and then works out for one and a half hours at a nearby health club. Swersky reports that she leaves home at 8 A.M. and does not return before 7 P.M.
- All of the women have chosen to work for companies where their expectations and those of the employer are compatible. Kathryn Braun, senior vice president of Western Digital, has pointed out that in her industry there is no old-boy network, so there is less resistance to promoting women into senior-level positions.
- Women who want to get to the top have to take the same route as men: aim for line positions, not staff jobs like personnel and public relations. They also need to take risks and show that they can succeed. As Mary Rudie Barneby of the Dreyfus Corporation puts it: "You have to prove you're a leader. You have to show you're willing to steal second base."
- Despite the admitted gains in wages and salaries in recent years, women still make only about 70 percent as much as their male counterparts, and their average pay has dipped (along with that of males) in recent years. This wage gap is relatively greater among older women than younger women, and is more pronounced for those women without college degrees.

1. How might Argyris's immaturity-maturity theory help explain why many women are not being promoted into top-level management positions?
2. In what way can culture be a barrier to the upward mobility of women in business?
3. How did the brief sketch of the women in this case help illustrate how they blended their abilities with the culture of the company?
4. Do you think these women are satisfied and committed? Are women employees in general satisfied and committed? Do you think a lack of satisfaction and commitment affects their performance? How can their satisfaction and commitment be improved?

CASE:
Ken Leaves the
Company

Firms are laying people off. Consumer confidence is plunging. Given the uncertain economic climate, why would anyone give up a steady job?

It may seem odd, but good people—valuable employees—do it every day. Usually, they leave for better positions elsewhere. Take Ken, an experienced underwriter in a Northeastern insurance company, who scribbled the following remarks on his exit interview questionnaire:

> This job isn't right for me. I like to have more input on decisions that affect me— more of a chance to show what I can do. I don't get enough feedback to tell if I'm doing a good job or not, and the company keeps people in the dark about where it's headed. Basically, I feel like an interchangeable part most of the time.

In answer to the question about whether the company could have done anything to keep him, Ken replied simply, "Probably not."

Why do so many promising employees leave their jobs? And why do so many others stay on but perform at minimal levels for lack of better alternatives? One of the main reasons—Ken's reason—can be all but invisible, because it's so common in so many organizations: a system-wide failure to build and maintain employee self-esteem.

Corporations should be concerned about the self-esteem of employees like Ken. By investing in it, they may actually help reduce turnover, protect training investments, increase productivity, improve quality, and reap the benefits of innovative thinking and teamwork.

Human resource professionals and managers can contribute to corporate success by encouraging employees' empowerment, security, identity, "connectedness," and competence. How? By recognizing the essential components of self-esteem and by understanding what enhances and diminishes those components in people.

Ken doubts that his company will ever change, but other organizations are taking positive steps to focus on and enhance employee self-esteem. As a result, they're reducing turnover, improving quality, increasing productivity, and protecting their training investments.

1. Do you think that Ken's self-esteem had anything to do with his leaving the firm?
2. What do you think Ken's satisfaction and commitment were to the job and firm he is leaving? How does this relate to the research on the determinants and outcomes of satisfaction and commitment?
3. What lesson can this company learn from the case of Ken? What can and should it now do?

CASE:
Doing His Share

When Ralph Morgan joined the Beacher Corporation, he started out as an assembler on the line. Ralph remained in this position for five years. During this time there were two major strikes. The first lasted five weeks; the second went on for eighteen weeks. As a member of the union, Ralph was out of work during both of these periods, and in each case the strike fund ran out of money before a labor agreement was reached.

Last year Ralph was asked if he would like to apply for a supervisory job. The position paid $2500 more than he was making, and the chance for promotion up the line made it an attractive offer. Ralph accepted.

During the orientation period, Ralph found himself getting angry at the management representative. This guy seemed to believe that the union was too powerful and management personnel had to hold the line against any further loss of authority. Ralph did not say anything, but he felt the speaker was very ill informed and biased. Two developments have occurred over the last six months, however, that have led Ralph to change his attitude toward union-management relations at the company.

One was a run-in he had with a shop steward who accused Ralph of deliberately harassing one of the workers. Ralph could not believe his ears. "Harassing a worker? Get serious. All I did was tell him to get back to work," he explained to the steward. Nevertheless, a grievance was filed and withdrawn only after Ralph apologized to the individual whom he supposedly harassed. The other incident was a result of disciplinary action. One of the workers in his unit came late for the third day in a row and, as required by the labor contract, Ralph sent him home without pay. The union protested, claiming that the worker had really been late only twice. When Ralph went to the personnel office to get the worker's clock-in sheets, the one for the first day of tardiness was missing. The clerks in that office, who were union members, claimed that they did not know where it was.

In both of these cases, Ralph felt the union went out of its way to embarrass him. Earlier this week the manager from the orientation session called Ralph. "I've been thinking about bringing line supervisors into the orientation meetings to discuss the union's attitude toward management. Having been on the other side, would you be interested in giving them your opinion of what they should be prepared for and how they should respond?'' Ralph said he would be delighted. ''I think it's important to get these guys ready to take on the union and I'd like to do my share,'' he explained.

1. What was Ralph's attitude toward the union when he first became a supervisor? What barriers were there that initially prevented him from changing his attitude regarding the union?
2. Why did Ralph's attitude change? What factors accounted for this?
3. Are workers who are recruited for supervisory positions likely to go through the same attitude changes as Ralph?

6

Motivation: Needs, Content, and Processes

Learning Objectives

- **Define** motivation.
- **Identify** the primary, general, and secondary needs.
- **Discuss** the major content theories or work motivation.
- **Explain** the major process theories of work motivation.
- **Present** the contemporary equity and attribution theories of work motivation.

Motivation is a basic psychological process. Few would deny that it is the most important focus in the micro approach to organizational behavior. Many people equate the causes of behavior with motivation. Chapter 1 and the two preceding chapters emphasize that the causes of behavior are much broader and more complex than can be explained by motivation alone. However, motivation should never be underrated. Along with perception, personality, attitudes, and learning, it is presented here as a very important process in understanding behavior. Nevertheless, it must be remembered that motivation should not be thought of as the only explanation of behavior. It interacts with and acts in conjunction with other mediating processes and the environment. It must also be remembered that, like the other cognitive processes, motivation cannot be seen. All that can be seen is behavior. Motivation is a hypothetical construct that is used to help explain behavior; it should not be equated with behavior. In fact, while recognizing the "central role of motivation," many of today's organizational behavior theorists "think it is important for the field to reemphasize behavior."[1]

This chapter presents motivation as a basic psychological process. The more applied aspects of motivation are covered in the next chapter, on job design and goal setting. The first section of this chapter clarifies the meaning of motivation by defining the relationship between its various parts. The need-drive-incentive cycle is defined and analyzed. The next section is devoted to an overview of the various types of needs, or motives: primary, general, and secondary. The motives within the general and secondary categories are given major attention, and a summary of supporting research findings on these motives is included. The final sections of the chapter present the content and process theories of work motivation and give particular attention to contemporary equity and attribution theories.

FIGURE 6.1
The basic motivation
process.

NEEDS ──────────────▶ DRIVES ──────────────▶ INCENTIVES

THE MEANING OF MOTIVATION

Today, virtually all people—practitioners and scholars—have their own definition of motivation. Usually one or more of the following words are included in the definition: "desires," "wants," "wishes," "aims," "goals," "needs," "drives," "motives," and "incentives." Technically, the term "motivation" can be traced to the Latin word *movere*, which means "to move." This meaning is evident in the following comprehensive definition: *Motivation* is a process that starts with a physiological or psychological deficiency or need that activates behavior or a drive that is aimed at a goal or incentive. Thus, the key to understanding the process of motivation lies in the meaning of, and relationship between, needs, drives, and incentives.

Figure 6.1 graphically depicts the motivation process. Needs set up drives aimed at incentives; this is what the basic process of motivation is all about. In a systems sense, motivation consists of these three interacting and interdependent elements:

1. *Needs.* Needs are created whenever there is a physiological or psychological imbalance. For example, a need exists when cells in the body are deprived of food and water or when the personality is deprived of other people who serve as friends or companions. Although psychological needs may be based on a deficiency, sometimes they are not. For example, an individual with a strong need to get ahead may have a history of consistent success.
2. *Drives.* With a few exceptions,[2] drives, or motives (the two terms are often used interchangeably), are set up to alleviate needs. A physiological drive can be simply defined as a deficiency with direction. Physiological and psychological drives are action-oriented and provide an energizing thrust toward reaching an incentive. They are at the very heart of the motivational process. The examples of the needs for food and water are translated into the hunger and thirst drives, and the need for friends becomes a drive for affiliation.
3. *Incentives.* At the end of the motivation cycle is the incentive, defined as anything that will alleviate a need and reduce a drive. Thus, attaining an incentive will tend to restore physiological or psychological balance and will reduce or cut off the drive. Eating food, drinking water, and obtaining friends will tend to restore the balance and reduce the corresponding drives. Food, water, and friends are the incentives in these examples.

PRIMARY MOTIVES

Psychologists do not totally agree on how to classify the various human motives, but they would acknowledge that some motives are unlearned and physiologically based. Such motives are variously called *physiological, biological, unlearned,* or *primary.* The last term is used here because it is more comprehensive than the others. The use of the term "primary" does not imply that this group of motives always takes precedence over the general and secondary motives. Although the precedence of primary motives is implied is some motivation theories, there are many situations in which general and secondary motives predominate over primary motives. Common examples are celibacy among priests and fasting for a religious, social, or political cause. In both cases, learned secondary motives are stronger than unlearned primary motives.

Two criteria must be met in order for a motive to be included in the *primary* classification: It must be *unlearned*, and it must be *physiologically based*. Thus defined, the most commonly recognized primary motives include hunger, thirst, sleep, avoidance of pain, sex, and maternal concern. Because people have the same basic physiological makeup, they will all have essentially the same primary needs. This is not true of the learned secondary needs.

GENERAL MOTIVES

A separate classification for general motives is not always given. Yet such a category seems necessary because there are a number of motives which lie in the gray area between the primary and secondary classifications. To be included in the general category, a motive must be unlearned but not physiologically based. While the primary needs seek to reduce the tension or stimulation, these general needs induce the person to increase the amount of stimulation. Thus, these needs are sometimes called "stimulus motives."[3] Although not all psychologists would agree, the motives of curiosity, manipulation, activity, and affection seem best to meet the criteria for this classification. An understanding of these general motives is important to the study of human behavior—especially in organizations. General motives are more relevant to organizational behavior than are primary motives.

The Curiosity, Manipulation, and Activity Motives

Early psychologists noted that the animals used in their experiments seemed to have an unlearned drive to explore, to manipulate objects, or just to be active. This was especially true of monkeys that were placed in an unfamiliar or novel situation. These observations and speculations about the existence of curiosity, manipulation, and activity motives in monkeys were later substantiated through experimentation. In this case, psychologists feel completely confident in generalizing the results of animal experiments to humans. It is generally recognized that human curiosity, manipulation, and activity drives are quite intense; anyone who has reared or been around small children will quickly support this generalization.

Although these drives often get the small child into trouble, curiosity, manipulation, and activity, when carried forward to adulthood, can be very beneficial. If these motives were stifled or inhibited, the total society might become very stagnant. The same is true on an organizational level. If employees are not allowed to express their curiosity, manipulation, and activity motives, they may not be motivated. For example, sticking an employee behind a machine or a desk for eight hours a day may stifle these general motives.

The Affection Motive

Love or affection is a very complex form of general drive. Part of the complexity stems from the fact that in many ways love resembles the primary drives and in other ways it is similar to the secondary drives. In particular, the affection motive is closely associated with the primary sex motive on the one hand, and with the secondary affiliation motive on the other. For this reason, affection is sometimes placed in all three categories of motives, and some psychologists do not even recognize it as a separate motive.

Affection merits specific attention because of its growing importance to the modern world. There seems to be a great deal of truth to the adages, "Love makes the world go round" and "Love conquers all." In a world where we suffer from interpersonal, intraindividual, and national conflict, and where quality of life and human rights are becoming increasingly important to modern society, the affection motive takes on added importance in the study of human behavior.

SECONDARY MOTIVES

Whereas the general drives seem relatively more important than the primary ones to the study of human behavior in organizations, the secondary drives are unquestionably the most important. As a human society develops economically and becomes more complex, the primary drives, and to a lesser degree the general drives, give way to the learned secondary drives in motivating behavior. With some glaring exceptions that have yet to be eradicated, the motives of hunger and thirst are not dominant among people living in the economically developed world. This situation is obviously subject to change; for example, the "population bomb" or the "greenhouse effect" may alter certain human needs. But for now, the learned secondary motives dominate.

Secondary motives are closely tied to the learning concepts that are discussed in Chapter 8. In particular, the learning principle of reinforcement is conceptually and practically related to motivation. The relationship is obvious when reinforcement is divided into primary and secondary categories and is portrayed as incentives. Some discussions, however, regard reinforcement as simply a consequence serving to increase the *motivation* to perform the behavior again,[4] and they are treated separately in this text. Once again, however, it should be emphasized that although the various behavioral concepts can be separated for study and analysis, in reality, concepts like reinforcement and motivation do not operate as separate entities in producing human behavior. The interactive effects are always present.

A motive must be learned in order to be included in the *secondary* classification. Numerous important human motives meet this criterion. Some of the more important ones are power, achievement, and affiliation, or, as they are commonly referred to today, *n Pow*, *n Ach*, and *n Aff*. In addition, especially in reference to organizational behavior, security and status are important secondary motives. Table 6.1 gives examples of each of these important secondary needs.

The Power Motive

The power motive is discussed first because it has been formally recognized and studied for a relatively long time. The leading advocate of the power motive was the pioneering behavioral scientist Alfred Adler. Adler officially broke his close ties with Sigmund Freud and proposed an opposing theoretical position. Whereas Freud stressed the impact of the past and of sexual, unconscious motivation, Adler substituted the future and a person's overwhelming drive for superiority or power.

TABLE 6.1 Examples of Key Secondary Needs

Need for Achievement
- Doing better than competitors
- Attaining or surpassing a difficult goal
- Solving a complex problem
- Carrying out a challenging assignment successfully
- Developing a better way to do something

Need for Power
- Influencing people to change their attitudes or behavior
- Controlling people and activities
- Being in a position of authority over others
- Gaining control over information and resources
- Defeating an opponent or enemy

Need for Affiliation
- Being liked by many people
- Being accepted as part of a group or team
- Working with people who are friendly and cooperative
- Maintaining harmonious relationships and avoiding conflicts
- Participating in pleasant social activities

Need for Security
- Having a secure job
- Being protected against loss of income or economic disaster
- Having protection against illness and disability
- Being protected against physical harm or hazardous conditions
- Avoiding tasks or decisions with a risk of failure and blame

Need for Status
- Having the right car and wearing the right clothes
- Working for the right company in the right job
- Having a degree from the right university
- Living in the right neighborhood and belonging to the country club
- Having executive privileges

Source: Adapted from Gary Yukl, *Skills for Managers and Leaders*, Prentice-Hall, Englewood Cliffs, N.J., 1990, p. 41. The examples of need for status were not covered by Yukl.

To explain the power need—the need to manipulate others or the drive for superiority over others—Adler developed the concepts of *inferiority complex* and *compensation*. He felt that every small child experiences a sense of inferiority. When this feeling of inferiority is combined with what he sensed as an innate (inborn) need for superiority, the two rule all behavior. The person's lifestyle is characterized by striving to compensate for feelings of inferiority, which are combined with the innate drive for power.

Although modern psychologists do not generally accept the tenet that the power drive is inborn and so dominant, in recent years it has prompted renewed interest. The quest for power is readily observable in modern American society. The politician is probably the best example, and political scandals make a fascinating study of the striving for, and use of, power in government and politics. However, in addition to politicians, anyone in a responsible position in business, government, unions, education, or the military may also exhibit a considerable need for power. The power motive has significant implications for organizational leadership and for the informal, political aspects of organizations. Chapter 12 examines in detail the dynamics of power. It has emerged as one of the most important dynamics in the study of organizational behavior.

The Achievement Motive

Whereas the power motive has been recognized and discussed for a long time, only very recently has there been any research activity. The opposite is true of the achievement motive. Although it does not have as long a history as the other motives, more is known about achievement than about any other motive because of the tremendous amount of research that has been devoted to it.[5] The Thematic Apperception Test (TAT) has proved to be a very effective tool in researching achievement. The TAT can effectively identify and measure the achievement motive. The test works in the following manner: One picture in the TAT shows a young man plowing a field; the sun is about to sink in the west. The person taking the test is supposed to tell a story about what he or she sees in the picture. The story will project the person's major motives. For example, the test taker may say that the man in the picture is sorry the sun is going down because he still has more land to plow and he wants to get the crops planted before it rains. Such a response indicates high achievement. A low achiever might say that the man is happy the sun is finally going down so that he can go into the house, relax, and have a cool drink. The research approach to achievement has become so effective that it is often cited by psychologists as a prototype of how knowledge and understanding can be gained in the behavioral sciences.

David C. McClelland, a Harvard psychologist, is most closely associated with study of the achievement motive, and, as Chapter 12 indicates, he is now doing considerable research on power as well. McClelland thoroughly investigated and wrote about all aspects of *n Ach* (achievement). Out of this extensive research has emerged a clear profile of the characteristics of the high achiever. Very simply, the achievement motive can be expressed as a desire to perform in terms of a standard of excellence or to be successful in competitive situations. The specific characteristics of a high achiever are summarized in the following sections.

Moderate Risk Taking. Taking moderate risks is probably the single most descriptive characteristic of the person possessing high *n Ach*. On the surface it would seem that a high achiever would take high risks. However, once again research gives an answer different from the commonsense one. The ring-toss game can be used to demonstrate risk-taking behavior. It has been shown that when ring tossers are told that they may stand anywhere they want to when they toss the rings at the peg, low and high achievers behave quite differently. Low achievers tend either to stand very close and just drop the rings over the peg or to stand very far away and wildly throw the rings at the peg. In contrast, high achievers almost always carefully calculate the exact distance from the peg that will challenge their own abilities. People with high *n Ach* will not stand too close because it would be no test of their ability simply to drop the rings over the peg. By the same token, they will not stand ridiculously far away because luck and not skill would then determine whether the rings landed on the peg. In other words, low achievers take either a high or low risk, and high achievers take a moderate risk. This seems to hold true both for the simple children's game and for important adult decisions and activities.

Need for Immediate Feedback. Closely connected to high achievers' taking moderate risks is their desire for immediate feedback. People with high *n Ach* prefer activities which provide immediate and precise feedback information on how they are progressing toward a goal. Some hobbies and vocations offer such feedback, and others do not. High achievers generally prefer hobbies such as woodworking or mechanics, which provide prompt, exact feedback, and they shy away from the coin-collecting type of hobby, which takes years to develop. Likewise, high achievers tend to gravitate toward, or at least to be more satisfied in, jobs or careers, such as sales or certain managerial positions, in which they are frequently evaluated by specific performance criteria. On the other end of the scale, high *n Ach* persons are generally not to be found, or tend to be frustrated, in research and development or teaching vocations, where feedback on performance is very imprecise, vague, and long-range.

Satisfaction with Accomplishments. High achievers find accomplishing a task intrinsically satisfying in and of itself; they do not expect or necessarily want the accompanying material rewards. A good illustration of this characteristic involves

Application Example

High Achievers in Action

One of the best examples of high achievers are entrepreneurs who start and manage their own businesses. While many of these owner-managers do not stay in business more than five years, a large percentage are very successful and manage to keep their enterprises afloat for an indefinite period. How do successful entrepreneurs operate? By sidestepping the potential pitfalls and problems before they even open the doors of their new venture. Prior to starting, they take steps to ensure that the enterprise is able to survive the first two years—the most critical period for most small business ventures. Some of the strategic steps they take include the following:

1. *Draw up a five-year plan.* This assures entrepreneurs that they will have goals to aim for during the first sixty months of operation. The plan often has both annual and quarterly forecasts.
2. *Raise more money than is needed.* One of the biggest problems is running out of capital. To ensure that this does not happen, successful entrepreneurs allow for a margin of error by starting out with more money than they estimate will be needed. Then, if sales are not generated as quickly as forecasted, the new company has enough capital to tide it over.
3. *Test the market.* Successful entrepreneurs look over their market and ensure that there is sufficient demand for their goods or services. If the demand is weak, they look for different geographic locales. If the demand is strong, they look for specific target markets they can further exploit.
4. *Don't take no for an answer.* If the bank turns down an application for a loan, successful entrepreneurs find out why. If there is something wrong with their financial plan, they fix it. If their projected costs of operations are too high, they figure out ways of reducing them. They then return to the bank and get the loan—or find another financial institution that is willing to give them the loan.

---

money, but not for the usual reasons of wanting money for its own sake or for the material benefits that it can buy. Rather, high *n Ach* people look at money as a form of feedback or measurement of how they are doing. Given the choice between a simple task with a good payoff for accomplishment, and a more difficult task with a lesser payoff, other things being equal, high achievers generally choose the latter.

Preoccupation with the Task. Once high achievers select a goal, they tend to be totally preoccupied with the task until it is successfully completed. They cannot stand to leave a job half finished and are not satisfied with themselves until they have given their maximum effort. This type of dedicated commitment is often reflected in their outward personalities, which frequently have a negative effect on those who come into contact with them. High achievers often strike others as being unfriendly and as "loners." They may be very quiet and may seldom brag about their accomplishments. They tend to be very realistic about their abilities and do not allow other people to get in the way of their goal accomplishments. Obviously, with this type of approach, high achievers do not always get along well with other people. Typically, high achievers make excellent salespersons but seldom good sales managers.

The accompanying Application Example: High Achievers in Action gives the strategies entrepreneurs use to start new businesses. Almost all such entrepreneurs have a relatively high need for achievement.

The Affiliation Motive

Affiliation plays a very complex but vital role in human behavior. Sometimes affiliation is equated with social motives and/or group dynamics. As presented here, the affiliation motive is neither as broad as is implied by the definition of social motives nor as comprehensive or complex as is implied by the definition of group dynamics. The study of affiliation is further complicated by the fact that some behavioral scientists believe that it is an unlearned motive. Going as far back as the Hawthorne studies, the importance of the affiliation motive in the behavior of organizational participants has been very clear. Employees, especially rank-and-file employees, have a very intense need to belong to, and be accepted by, the group. This affiliation motive is an important part of group dynamics, which is the subject of Chapter 9.

The Security Motive

Security is a very intense motive in a fast-paced, highly technological society such as is found in modern America. The typical American can be insecure in a number of areas of everyday living—for example, being liable for payments on a car or house, keeping a lover's or a spouse's affections, staying in school, getting into graduate school, or obtaining and/or keeping a good job. Job insecurity, in particular, has a great effect on organizational behavior. For example, the Chapter 5 discussion of organizational commitment indicates that, because of the downsizing mania of the last several years, most employees at all levels are feeling very insecure about their jobs. On the surface, security appears to be much simpler than other secondary motives, for it is based largely on fear and is avoidance-oriented. Very briefly, it can be said that people have a learned security motive to protect themselves from the contingencies of life and actively try to avoid situations which would prevent them from satisfying their primary, general, and secondary motives.

   In reality, security is much more complex than it appears on the surface. There is the simple, conscious security motive described above, but there also seems to be another type of security motive that is much more complicated and difficult to identify. This latter form of security is largely unconscious but may greatly influence the behavior of many people. The simple, conscious security motive is typically taken care of by insurance programs, personal savings plans, and other fringe benefits at the place of employment. An innovative company such as the Washington, D.C.-based insurance company Consumers United Group never lays off its employees and has a minimum annual salary of $18,000 designed to give a family a secure, decent living.[6] On the other hand, the more complex, unconscious security motive is not so easily fulfilled but may have a greater and more intense impact on human behavior. Although much attention has been given to the simple security motive, much more understanding is needed concerning the role of the unconscious, complex security motive.

The Status Motive

Along with security, the status or prestige motive is especially relevant to a dynamic society. The modern affluent person is often pictured as a status seeker. Such a person is accused of being more concerned with the material symbols of status—the right clothes, the right car, the right address, and a swimming pool or the latest computer software—than with the more basic, human-oriented values in life. Although the symbols of status are considered a unique by-product of modern society, the fact is that status has been in existence since there have been two or more persons on the earth.

Status can be simply defined as the *relative* ranking that a person holds in a group, organization, or society. Under this definition, any time two or more persons are together, a status hierarchy will evolve, even if both have equal status. The symbols of status attempt to represent only the relative ranking of the person in the status hierarchy. The definition also corrects the common misconception that "status" means "high status." Everyone has status, but it may be high or low, depending on how the relative positions are ranked.

How are status positions determined? Why is one person ranked higher or lower than another? In the final analysis, status determination depends upon the prevailing cultural values and societal roles. Status-determining factors generally have quite different meanings, depending on the values of the particular culture. An example of the impact of cultural values on status is the personal qualities of people. In some cultures, the older people are, the higher their status. However, in other cultures, once a person reaches a certain age, the status goes downhill. It must be remembered that such cultural values are highly volatile and change with the times and circumstances. There are also many subcultures in a given society which may have values different from the prevailing values of society at large and correspondingly different statuses.

WORK–MOTIVATION APPROACHES

So far, motivation has been presented as a basic psychological process consisting of primary, general, and secondary motives, and drives such as the *n Pow, n Aff*, and *n Ach* motives. In order to understand organizational behavior, these basic motives must be recognized and studied. However, these serve as only background and foundation for the more directly relevant work-motivation approaches.

Figure 6.2 graphically summarizes the various theoretical streams for work motivation. In particular, the figure shows four major approaches. The content theories go as far back as the turn of the century, when pioneering scientific managers such as Frederick W. Taylor, Frank Gilbreth, and Henry L. Gantt proposed sophisticated wage incentive models to motivate workers. Next came the human relations movement, and then the content theories of Maslow, Herzberg, and Alderfer. Following the content movement were the process theories. Based mainly on the cognitive concept of expectancy, the process theories are most closely associated with the work of Victor Vroom and Lyman Porter and Ed Lawler. More recently, equity and, especially, attribution theories have received the most attention in work motivation.

Figure 6.2 purposely shows that at present there is a lack of integration or synthesis of the various theories. In addition to the need for integration, a comprehensive assessment of the status of work-motivation theory also noted the need for contingency models and group/social processes.[7] At present the group of content and process theories have become established explanations for work motivation, and there is continued research interest in equity and attribution theories, but no agreed upon overall theory exists. The rest of the chapter gives an overview of the various theories of work motivation.

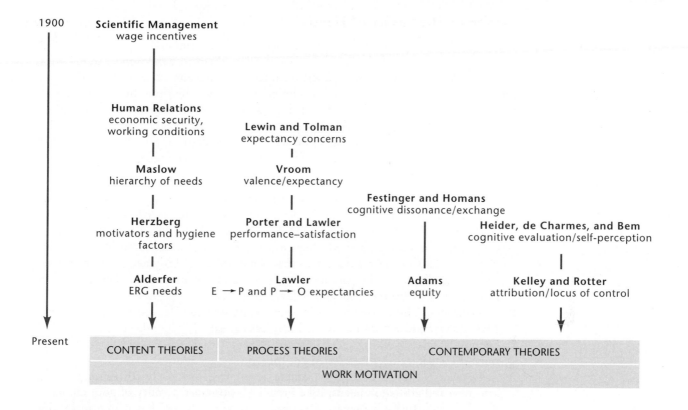

FIGURE 6.2
The theoretical development of work motivation.

THE CONTENT THEORIES OF WORK MOTIVATION

The content theories of work motivation attempt to determine what it is that motivates people at work. The content theorists are concerned with identifying the needs/drives that people have and how these needs/drives are prioritized. They are concerned with the types of incentives or goals that people strive to attain in order to be satisfied and perform well. The content theories are referred to as "static" because they incorporate only one or a few points in time and are either past- or present-time-oriented. Therefore, they do not necessarily predict work motivation or behavior, but are still important to understanding what motivates people at work.[8]

At first, money was felt to be the only incentive (scientific management), and then a little later it was felt that incentives include working conditions, security, and perhaps a democratic style of supervision (human relations). More recently, the content of motivation has been deemed to be the so-called "higher-level" needs or motives, such as esteem and self-actualization (Maslow); responsibility, recognition, achievement, and advancement (Herzberg); and growth and personal development (Alderfer). A thorough study of the major content theories contributes to understanding and leads to some of the application techniques of motivation covered in the next chapter.

Maslow's Hierarchy of Needs

Although the first part of the chapter discusses the most important primary, general, and secondary needs of humans, it does not relate them to a theoretical framework. Abraham Maslow, in a classic paper, outlined the elements of an overall theory of motivation.[9] Drawing chiefly on his clinical experience, he thought that a person's motivational needs could be arranged in a hierarchical manner. In essence, he believed that once a given level of need is satisfied, it no longer serves to motivate. The next higher level of need has to be activated in order to motivate the individual.

Maslow identified five levels in his need hierarchy (see Figure 6.3). They are, in brief, the following:

1. *Physiological needs.* The most basic level in the hierarchy, the physiological needs, generally corresponds to the unlearned primary needs discussed earlier. The needs of hunger, thirst, sleep, and sex are some examples. According to the theory, once these basic needs are satisfied, they no longer motivate. For example, a starving person will strive to obtain a carrot that is within reach. However, after eating his or her fill of carrots, the person will not strive to obtain another one and will be motivated only by the next higher level of needs.

2. *Safety needs.* This second level of needs is roughly equivalent to the security need. Maslow stressed emotional as well as physical safety. The whole organism may become a safety-seeking mechanism. Yet, as is true of the physiological needs, once these safety needs are satisfied, they no longer motivate.

3. *Love needs.* This third, or intermediate, level of needs loosely corresponds to the affection and affiliation needs. Like Freud, Maslow seems guilty of poor choice of wording to identify his levels. His use of the word "love" has many misleading connotations, such as sex, which is actually a physiological need. Perhaps a more appropriate word describing this level would be "belongingness" or "social."

4. *Esteem needs.* The esteem level represents the higher needs of humans. The needs for power, achievement, and status can be considered part of this level. Maslow carefully pointed out that the esteem level contains both self-esteem and esteem from others.

5. *Needs for self-actualization.* This level represents the culmination of all the lower, intermediate, and higher needs of humans. People who have become self-actualized are self-fulfilled and have realized all their potential. Self-actualization

FIGURE 6.3
Maslow's hierarchy of needs.

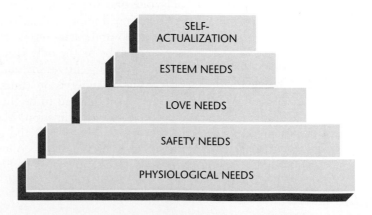

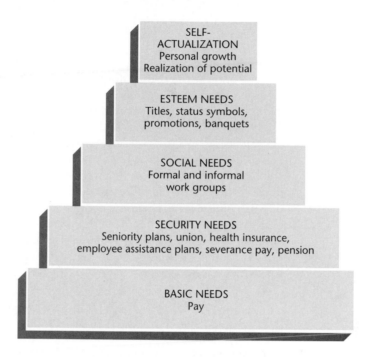

FIGURE 6.4
A hierarchy of work
motivation.

is closely related to the self-concept discussed in Chapter 5. In effect, self-actualization is the person's motivation to transform perception of self into reality.

Maslow did not intend that his need hierarchy be directly applied to work motivation. In fact, he did not delve into the motivating aspects of humans in organizations until about twenty years after he originally proposed his theory. Despite this lack of intent on Maslow's part, others, such as Douglas McGregor, in his widely read book *The Human Side of Enterprise*, popularized the Maslow theory in management literature. The need hierarchy has had a tremendous impact on the modern management approach to motivation.

In a very rough manner, Maslow's need hierarchy theory can be converted into the content model of work motivation shown in Figure 6.4. If Maslow's estimates are applied to an organization example, the lower-level needs of personnel would be generally satisfied (85 percent of the basic needs and 70 percent of the security needs), but only 50 percent of the social needs, 40 percent of the esteem needs, and a mere 10 percent of the self-actualization needs would be met.

On the surface, the content model shown in Figure 6.4 and the estimated percentages given by Maslow seem logical and applicable to the motivation of employees in today's organizations. Maslow's need hierarchy has often been uncritically accepted by writers of management textbooks and by practitioners. Unfortunately, the limited research that has been conducted lends little empirical support to the theory. About a decade after publishing his original paper, Maslow did attempt to clarify his position by saying that gratifying the self-actualizing need of growth-motivated individuals can actually increase rather than decrease this need. He also hedged on some of his other original ideas, for example, that higher needs may emerge after lower needs that have been unfulfilled or suppressed for a long period are satisfied. He stressed that human behavior is multidetermined and multimotivated.

Most research findings indicate that Maslow's is not the final answer in work motivation. Yet the theory does make a significant contribution in terms of making management aware of the diverse needs of employees at work. As one recent comprehensive analysis concluded, "indeed, the general ideas behind Maslow's theory seem to be supported, such as the distinction between deficiency needs and growth needs."[10] However, the number and names of the levels are not so important, nor, as the studies show, is the hierarchical concept. What is important is the fact that employees in the workplace have diverse motives, some of which are "high-level." In other words, such needs as esteem and self-actualization are important to the content of work motivation. The exact nature of these needs and how they relate to motivation are not clear. To try to overcome some of the problems of the Maslow hierarchy, Alderfer has more recently proposed the ERG theory, which contains three well-known groups of needs. The ERG theory is covered after the discussion of Herzberg's two-factor theory.

Herzberg's Two-Factor Theory of Motivation

Herzberg extended the work of Maslow and developed a specific content theory of work motivation. He conducted a widely reported motivational study on about 200 accountants and engineers employed by firms in and around Pittsburgh, Pennsylvania. He used the critical incident method of obtaining data for analysis. The professional subjects in the study were essentially asked two questions: (1) When did you feel particularly good about your job—what turned you on; and (2) when did you feel exceptionally bad about your job—what turned you off?

Responses obtained from this critical incident method were interesting and fairly consistent. Reported good feelings were generally associated with job experiences and job content. An example was the accounting supervisor who felt good about being given the job of installing new computer equipment. He took pride in his work and was gratified to know that the new equipment made a big difference in the overall functioning of his department. Reported bad feelings, on the other hand, were generally associated with the surrounding or peripheral aspects of the job—the job context. An example of these feelings was related by an engineer whose first job was to keep tabulation sheets and manage the office when the boss was gone. It turned out that his boss was always too busy to train him and became annoyed when he tried to ask questions. The engineer said that he was frustrated in this job context and that he felt like a flunky in a dead-end job. Tabulating these reported good and bad feelings, Herzberg concluded that job satisfiers are related to job content and that job dissatisfiers are allied to job context. Herzberg labeled the satisfiers *motivators*, and he called the dissatisfiers *hygiene factors*. The term "hygiene" refers (as it does in the health field) to factors that are preventive; in Herzberg's theory the hygiene factors are those that prevent dissatisfaction. Taken together, the motivators and the hygiene factors have become known as Herzberg's *two-factor theory of motivation*.

Relation to Maslow's Need Hierarchy. Herzberg's theory is closely related to Maslow's need hierarchy. The hygiene factors are preventive and environmental in nature (see Table 6.2), and they are roughly equivalent to Maslow's lower-level needs (see Figure 6.5). These hygiene factors prevent dissatisfaction, but they do not lead to satisfaction. In effect, they bring motivation up to a theoretical zero level and are a

TABLE 6.2 Herzberg's Two-Factor Theory

Hygiene Factors	Motivators
Company policy and administration	Achievement
Supervision, technical	Recognition
Salary	Work itself
Interpersonal relations, supervisor	Responsibility
Working conditions	Advancement

necessary "floor" to prevent dissatisfaction, and they serve as a takeoff point for motivation. By themselves, the hygiene factors do not motivate. Only the motivators motivate employees on the job. They are roughly equivalent to Maslow's higher-level needs. According to Herzberg's theory, an individual must have a job with a challenging content in order to be truly motivated.

Contribution to Work Motivation. Herzberg's two-factor theory casts a new light on the content of work motivation. Up to this point, management had generally concentrated on the hygiene factors. When faced with a morale problem, the typical solution was higher pay, more fringe benefits, and better working conditions. However, as has been pointed out, this simplistic solution did not really work. Management are often perplexed because they are paying high wages and salaries, have an excellent fringe-benefit package, and provide great working conditions, but their employees are still not motivated. Herzberg's theory offers an explanation for this problem. By concentrating only on the hygiene factors, management are not motivating their personnel.

There are probably very few workers or managers who do not feel that they deserved the raise they received. On the other hand, there are many dissatisfied workers and managers who feel they did not get a large-enough raise. This simple observation points out that the hygiene factors seem to be important in preventing dissatisfaction but do not lead to satisfaction. Herzberg would be the first to say that the hygiene factors are absolutely necessary to maintain the human resources of an organization. However, as in the Maslow sense, once "the belly is full" of hygiene factors, which is the case in most modern organizations, dangling any more in front of employees will not motivate them. According to Herzberg's theory, only a challenging job which has the opportunities for achievement, recognition, responsibility, advancement, and growth will motivate personnel.

Critical Analysis of Herzberg's Theory. Although Herzberg's two-factor theory remains a very popular textbook explanation of work motivation and makes sense to practitioners, it also is true that from an academic perspective the theory oversimplifies the complexities of work motivation. When researchers deviate from the critical incident methodology used by Herzberg, they do not get the two factors. There seem to be job factors that lead to both satisfaction and dissatisfaction. These findings indicate that a strict interpretation of the two-factor theory is not warranted.

In spite of the obvious limitations, few would question that Herzberg has contributed substantially to the study of work motivation. He extended Maslow's need hierarchy concept and made it more applicable to work motivation. Herzberg also drew attention to the importance of job content factors in work motivation, which previously had been badly neglected and often totally overlooked. The job design technique of job enrichment is also one of Herzberg's contributions. Job enrichment is covered in detail in the next chapter. Overall, Herzberg added much to the better understanding of job content factors and satisfaction, but, like his predecessors, he fell short of a comprehensive theory of work motivation. His model describes only some of the content of work motivation; it does not adequately describe the complex motivation process of organizational participants.

Alderfer's ERG Theory

An extension of the Herzberg and, especially, the Maslow content theories of work motivation comes from the work of Clayton Alderfer. He formulated a need category model that was more in line with the existing empirical evidence. Like Maslow and Herzberg, he does feel that there is value in categorizing needs and that there is a basic distinction between lower-order needs and higher-order needs.

Alderfer identified three groups of core needs: existence, relatedness, and growth (hence ERG theory). The *existence needs* are concerned with survival (physiological well-being). The *relatedness needs* stress the importance of interpersonal, social relationships. The *growth needs* are concerned with the individual's intrinsic desire for personal development. Figure 6.5 shows how these groups of needs are related to the Maslow and Herzberg categories. Obviously, they are very close, but the ERG needs do not have strict lines of demarcation.

Alderfer is suggesting more of a continuum of needs than hierarchical levels or two factors of prepotency needs. Unlike Maslow and Herzberg, he does not contend that a lower-level need has to be fulfilled before a higher-lever need is motivating or that deprivation is the only way to activate a need. For example, under ERG theory the person's background or cultural environment may dictate that the relatedness

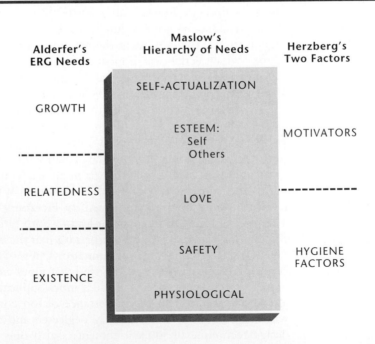

FIGURE 6.5
The relationship between Alderfer's ERG needs, Maslow's five-level hierarchy, and Herzberg's two-factor theory.

needs will take precedence over unfulfilled existence needs and that the more the growth needs are satisfied, the more they will increase in intensity.

There has not been a great deal of research on ERG theory. Although there is some evidence to counter the theory's predictive value, most contemporary analyses of work motivation tend to support Alderfer's theory over Maslow's and Herzberg's. Overall, ERG theory seems to take some of the strong points of earlier content theories but is less restrictive and limiting. The fact remains, however, that the content theories in general lack explanatory power over the complexities of work motivation and, with the possible exception of the implications for job design of Herzberg's work, do not readily translate to the actual practice of human resources management.

THE PROCESS THEORIES OF WORK MOTIVATION

The content models attempt to identify what motivates people at work (for example, self-actualization, responsibility, and growth); they try to specify correlates of motivated behavior. The process theories, on the other hand, are more concerned with the cognitive antecedents that go into motivation or effort and, more important, with the way they relate to one another. As Figure 6.2 shows, the expectancy notion from cognitive theory makes a significant contribution to the understanding of the complex processes involved in work motivation. After the process theories are examined, equity and attribution theories are presented and analyzed as modern cognitive models of work motivation.

Vroom's Expectancy Theory of Motivation

The expectancy theory of work motivation has its roots in the cognitive concepts of pioneering psychologists Kurt Lewin and Edward Tolman, as shown in Figure 6.2, and in the choice behavior and utility concepts from classical economic theory. However, the first to formulate an expectancy theory directly aimed at work motivation was Victor Vroom. Contrary to most critics, Vroom proposed his expectancy theory as an alternative to content models, which he felt were inadequate explanations of the complex process of work motivation. At least in academic circles, his theory has become a popular explanation for work motivation and continues to generate considerable research.[11]

Figure 6.6 briefly summarizes the Vroom model. As shown, the model is built around the concepts of valence, instrumentality, and expectancy, and is commonly called the *VIE theory.*

Meaning of the Variables. By *valence,* Vroom means the strength of an individual's preference for a particular outcome. Other terms that might be used include *value, incentive, attitude,* and *expected utility.* In order for the valence to be positive, the person must prefer attaining the outcome to not attaining it. A valence of zero occurs when the individual is indifferent toward the outcome; the valence is negative when the individual prefers not attaining the outcome to attaining it. Another major input into the valence is the *instrumentality* of the first-level outcome in obtaining a desired second-level outcome. For example, the person would be motivated toward superior performance because of the desire to be promoted. The superior performance (first-

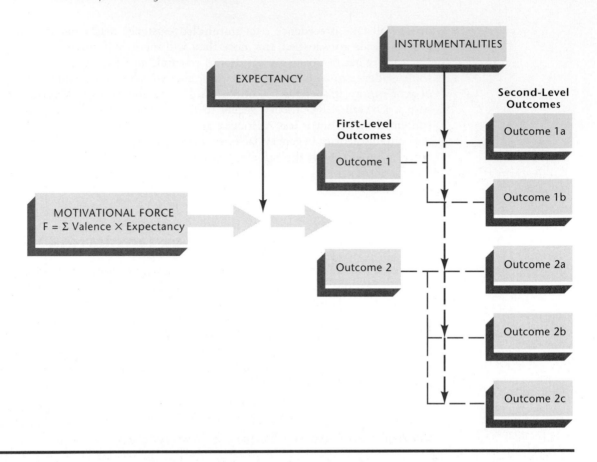

FIGURE 6.6

The Vroom expectancy, or VIE, theory of work motivation.

level outcome) is seen as being instrumental in obtaining a promotion (second-level outcome).

Another major variable in the Vroom motivational process is *expectancy*. Although psychological theorists all agree that expectancies are mental, or cognitive, states, there is little agreement about the nature of these states.[12] Although at first glance the expectancy concept may seem to be the same as the instrumentality input into valence, it is actually quite different. Expectancy relates efforts to first-level outcomes (see Figure 6.6), while instrumentality relates first-level outcomes and second-level outcomes. In other words, expectancy in Vroom's theory is the probability (ranging from 0 to 1) that a particular action or effort will lead to a particular *first-level* outcome. *Instrumentality* refers to the degree to which a first-level outcome will lead to a desired *second-level* outcome. In summary, the strength of the motivation to perform a certain act will depend on the algebraic sum of the products of the valences for the outcomes (which include instrumentality) times the expectancies.

Implications of the Vroom Model for Organizational Behavior. Vroom's theory departs from the content theories in that it depicts a process of cognitive variables that reflects individual differences in work motivation. It does not attempt to describe what the content is or what the individual differences are. Everyone has a unique combination of valences, instrumentalities, and expectancies. Thus, the

Vroom theory indicates only the conceptual determinants of motivation and how they are related. It does not provide specific suggestions on what motivates organizational members, as the Maslow, Herzberg, and Alderfer models do.

Although the Vroom model does not directly contribute much to the techniques of motivating personnel in an organization, it is of value in understanding organizational behavior. It can clarify the relationship between individual and organizational goals. For example, suppose workers are given a certain standard for production. By measuring the workers' output, management can determine how important their various personal goals (second-level outcomes such as money, security, and recognition) are; the instrumentality of the organizational goal (the first-level outcomes, such as the production standard) for the attainment of the personal goals; and the workers' expectancies that their effort and ability will accomplish the organizational goal. If output is below standard, it may be that the workers do not place a high value on the second-level outcomes; or they may not see that the first-level outcome is instrumental in obtaining the second-level outcomes; or they may think that their efforts will not accomplish the first-level outcome. Vroom feels that any one, or a combination, of these possibilities will result in a low level of motivation to perform. The model is designed to help management understand and analyze workers' motivation and identify some of the relevant variables; it does not provide specific solutions to motivational problems. Besides having an application problem, the model also assumes, as earlier economic theory did, that people are rational and logically calculating. Such an assumption may be too idealistic.

Importance of the Vroom Model. Probably the major reason Vroom's model has emerged as an important modern theory of work motivation and has generated so much research is that it does not take a simplistic approach. The content theories oversimplify human motivation. Yet the content theories remain extremely popular with practicing managers because the concepts are easy to understand and to apply to their own situations. On the other hand, the VIE theory recognizes the complexities of work motivation, but it is relatively difficult to understand and apply. Thus, from a theoretical standpoint, the VIE model seems to help managers appreciate the complexities of motivation, but it does not give them much practical help in solving their motivational problems.

In some ways Vroom's expectancy model is like marginal analysis in economics. Business people do not actually calculate the point where marginal cost equals marginal revenue, but it is still a useful concept for a theory of the firm. The expectancy model attempts only to mirror the complex motivational process; it does not attempt to describe how motivational decisions are actually made or to solve actual motivational problems facing a manager.

The Porter-Lawler Model

Comments in Chapter 5 on job satisfaction refer to the controversy over the relationship between satisfaction and performance that has existed since the human relations movement. The content theories implicitly assume that satisfaction leads to improved performance and that dissatisfaction detracts from performance. The Herzberg model is really a theory of job satisfaction, but still it does not deal with the relationship between satisfaction and performance. The Vroom model also largely avoids the relationship between satisfaction and performance. Although satisfactions make an input into Vroom's concept of valence and although the outcomes have

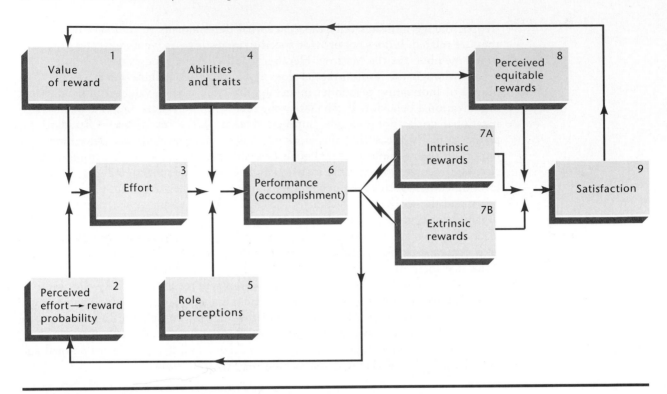

FIGURE 6.7
The Porter-Lawler
motivation model.

performance implications, it was not until Porter and Lawler refined and extended Vroom's model (for example, the relationships are expressed diagrammatically rather than mathematically, there are more variables, and the cognitive process of perception plays a central role) that the relationship between satisfaction and performance was dealt with directly by a motivation model.

Porter and Lawler start with the premise that motivation (effort or force) does not equal satisfaction or performance. Motivation, satisfaction, and performance are all separate variables and relate in ways different from what was traditionally assumed. Figure 6.7 depicts the multivariable model used to explain the complex relationship that exists between motivation, performance, and satisfaction. As shown in the model, boxes 1, 2, and 3 are basically the same as the Vroom equation. It is important, however, that Porter and Lawler point out that effort (force or motivation) does not lead directly to performance. It is mediated by abilities and traits and by role perceptions. More important in the Porter-Lawler model is what happens after the performance. The rewards that follow and how these are perceived will determine satisfaction. In other words, the Porter-Lawler model suggests—and this is a significant turn of events from traditional thinking—that performance leads to satisfaction.

The model has had a fair degree of research support over the years. For example, a recent field study found that effort level and direction of effort are important in explaining individual performance in an organization.[13] Also, a comprehensive review of research verifies the importance of rewards in the relationship between performance and satisfaction. Specifically, it was concluded that performance and satisfaction will be more strongly related when rewards are made contingent upon performance than when they are not.[14]

Implications for Practice. Although the Porter-Lawler model is more applications-oriented than the Vroom model, it is still quite complex and has proved to be a difficult way to bridge the gap to actual management practice. To Porter and Lawler's credit, they have been very conscious of putting their theory and research into practice. They recommend that practicing managers go beyond traditional attitude measurement and attempt to measure variables such as the values of possible rewards, the perceptions of effort-reward probabilities, and role perceptions. These variables, of course, can help managers better understand what goes into employee effort and performance. Giving attention to the consequences of performance, Porter and Lawler also recommend that organizations critically reevaluate their current reward policies. They stress that management should make a concentrated effort to measure how closely levels of satisfaction are related to levels of performance. These types of recommendations have been verified by research. However, both recent studies[15] and comprehensive analyses[16] continue to point out the complex impact that the cognitive process has in relation to rewards and other outcomes in organizations.

Contributions to Work Motivation. The Porter and Lawler model has definitely made a significant contribution to the better understanding of work motivation and the relationship between performance and satisfaction, but, to date, it has not had much impact on the actual practice of human resources management. Yet the expectancy models provide certain guidelines that can be followed by human resources management. For example, on the front end (the relationship between motivation and performance), it has been suggested that the following barriers must be overcome:

1. Doubts about ability, skill, or knowledge
2. The physical or practical possibility of the job
3. The interdependence of the job with other people or activities
4. Ambiguity surrounding the job requirements[17]

In addition, on the back end (the relationship between performance and satisfaction), guidelines such as the following have been suggested:

1. Determine what rewards each employee values.
2. Define desired performance.
3. Make desired performance attainable.
4. Link valued rewards to performance.[18]

The last point above is getting recognition in the management compensation plans of many big companies, as indicated by the accompanying TQM in Action: Linking Managers' Rewards with Unit Performance.

CONTEMPORARY THEORIES OF WORK MOTIVATION

Although it is recognized that work-motivation theories are generally categorized into content and process approaches, equity and attribution theories have emerged in recent years and command most of the research attention. An understanding of these two theoretical developments is now necessary to the study of work motivation in organizational behavior.

TQM in Action

Linking Managers' Rewards with Unit Performance

Linking rewards to performance has received attention in top management, as well as in low-level employee ranks. Traditionally, top management bonuses and profit sharing have been tied into overall company performance. However, with the increased diversity and autonomy of large companies, a manager in one division may be performing very well while the overall company profits are down. This high-performing manager may not be rewarded. Now, companies such as Westinghouse (with twenty-three units ranging from broadcasting to nuclear power) have moved to link rewards to unit, rather than overall company, performance results. As the head of compensation for Westinghouse noted, "we can't have one [incentive] formula that applies to everyone because each business is different. Some are in tough growth markets, and others are in stable, cash-cow markets." Thus, companies such as Westinghouse are dropping their bonus and stock-option incentives based on overall corporate profits and instead tying rewards more to unit profit centers.

This is proving to be particularly effective among those firms that, like Westinghouse, have adopted total quality management programs, and in many cases it does not result in mere financial rewards. For example, at Marlow Industries there is a hall of fame where the pictures of those who have made contributions to the quality program are displayed. At the Ritz-Carlton employees are recognized for doing a good job through a thank-you card that is sent to them by those who wish to express their appreciation. But, of course, there are still financial awards for outstanding performance, as in the case of Solectron which, like many other Baldrige quality award winners, gives both individual team bonuses and profit sharing as a way of saying thanks. In each case, however, the reward is closely linked to unit quality performance.

Equity Theory of Work Motivation

Equity theory has been around just as long as the expectancy theories of work motivation. However, only recently has equity received widespread attention in the organizational behavior field. As Figure 6.2 indicates, its roots can be traced back to cognitive dissonance theory and exchange theory. As a theory of work motivation, credit for equity theory is usually given to social psychologist J. Stacy Adams. Simply put, the theory argues that a major input into job performance and satisfaction is the degree of equity (or inequity) that people perceive in their work situation. In other words, it is another cognitively based motivation theory, and Adams depicts how this motivation occurs.

Inequity occurs when a person perceives that the ratio of his or her outcomes to inputs and the ratio of a relevant other's outcomes to inputs are unequal. Schematically, this is represented as follows:

$$\frac{\text{Person's outcomes}}{\text{Person's inputs}} < \frac{\text{other's outcomes}}{\text{other's inputs}}$$

$$\frac{\text{Person's outcomes}}{\text{Person's inputs}} > \frac{\text{other's outcomes}}{\text{other's inputs}}$$

Equity occurs when

$$\frac{\text{Person's outcomes}}{\text{Person's inputs}} = \frac{\text{other's outcomes}}{\text{other's inputs}}$$

Both the inputs and the outputs of person and other are based upon the person's perceptions. Age, sex, education, social status, organizational position, qualifications, and how hard the person works are examples of perceived input variables. Outcomes consist primarily of rewards such as pay, status, promotion, and intrinsic interest in the job. In essence, the ratio is based upon the person's *perception* of what the person is giving (inputs) and receiving (outcomes) versus the ratio of what the relevant other is giving and receiving. This cognition may or may not be the same as someone else's observation of the ratios or the same as the actual situation.

If the person's perceived ratio is not equal to the other's, he or she will strive to restore the ratio to equity. This "striving" to restore equity is used as the explanation of work motivation. The strength of this motivation is in direct proportion to the perceived inequity that exists. Adams suggests that such motivation may be expressed in several forms. To restore equity, the person may alter the inputs or outcomes, cognitively distort the inputs or outcomes, leave the field, act on the other, or change the other.

It is important to note that inequity does not come about only when the person feels cheated. For example, Adams has studied the impact that perceived overpayment has on equity. His findings suggest that workers prefer equitable payment to overpayment. Workers on a piece-rate incentive system who feel overpaid will reduce their productivity in order to restore equity. More likely, however, is the case of people who feel underpaid (outcome) or overworked (input) in relation to others in the workplace. In the latter case, there would be motivation to restore equity in a way that may be dysfunctional from an organizational standpoint. For example, the owner of an appliance store in Oakland, California, allowed his employees to set their own wages. Interestingly, none of the employees took an increase in pay, and one serviceman actually settled on lower pay because he did not want to work as hard as the others.[19]

To date, research that has specifically tested the validity of Adams's equity theory has been fairly supportive. A comprehensive review found considerable laboratory research support for the "equity norm" (persons review the inputs and outcomes of themselves and others, and if inequity is perceived, they strive to restore equity) but only limited support from more relevant field studies.[20] One line of field research on equity theory uses baseball players. The first study of players who played out their option year, and thus felt they were inequitably paid, performed as the theory would predict.[21] Their performance decreased in three of four categories (not batting average) during the option year, and when they were signed to a new contract, the performance was restored. However, a second study using the same type of sample, only larger, found the opposite of what equity theory would predict.[22] Mainly, performance improved during the option year. The reason, of course, was that the players wanted to look especially good, even though they felt they were inequitably paid, in order to be in a stronger bargaining position for a new contract. In other words, there are no easy answers nor is there 100 percent predictive power when applying a cognitive process theory such as equity.

Despite such inconsistencies, recent studies using more sophisticated statistical techniques to estimate pay equity in ball players[23] and sharper focus on subsequent performance and other outcomes are more in line with equity theory predictions. For example, one study found a significant relationship between losing final-offer salary arbitration and postarbitration performance decline. The ball players who were losers of the arbitration were also significantly more likely to change teams and leave major league baseball.[24] In another recent study using baseball and basketball players, it was found that the underrewarded players behaved less cooperatively.[25] This type of equity theory development and research goes beyond expectancy theory as a cognitive explanation of work motivation and serves as a point of departure for attribution theory and locus of control explanations.

Attribution Theory

Chapter 4, on perception, discusses the important role of attributions in the cognitive processes of individuals. Recently, the attributions that people make have emerged as important explanations of work motivation. Unlike the other motivation theories, attribution theory is more a theory of the relationship between personal perception and interpersonal behavior than a theory of individual motivation. There are an increasing variety of attribution theories. A recent analysis of these theories, however, concludes that all of them share the following common assumptions:

1. We seek to make sense of our world.
2. We often attribute people's actions either to internal or external causes.
3. We do so in fairly logical ways.[26]

Well-known theorist Harold Kelley stresses that attribution theory is concerned mainly with the cognitive processes by which an individual interprets behavior as being caused by (or attributed to) certain parts of the relevant environment. It is concerned with the "why" questions of motivation and behavior. Since most causes, attributes, and "whys" are not directly observable, the theory says that people must depend upon cognitions, particularly perception. The attribution theorist assumes that humans are rational and are motivated to identify and understand the causal structure of their relevant environment. It is this search for attributes that characterizes attribution theory.

Although attribution theory has its roots in all the pioneering cognitive theorists' work (for example, that of Lewin and Festinger), in de Charmes's ideas on cognitive evaluation, and in Bem's notion of "self-perception," the theory's initiator is generally recognized to be Fritz Heider. Heider believed that both internal forces (personal attributes such as ability, effort, and fatigue) and external forces (environmental attributes such as rules and the weather) combine additively to determine behavior. He stressed that it is the *perceived*, not the actual, determinants that are important to behavior. People will behave differently if they perceive internal attributes than they will if they perceive external attributes. It is this concept of differential ascriptions that has very important implications for work motivation.

Locus of Control Attributions. Using *locus of control*, work behavior may be explained by whether employees perceive their outcomes as controlled internally or externally. Employees who perceive internal control feel that they personally can influence their outcomes through their own ability, skills, or effort. Employees who perceive external control feel that their outcomes are beyond their own control; they feel that external forces control their outcomes. What is important is that this perceived locus of control may have a differential impact on their performance and satisfaction. For example, studies by Rotter and his colleagues suggest that skill versus chance environments differentially affect behavior.[27] In addition, a number of studies have been conducted in recent years to test the attribution theory–locus of control model in work settings. One study found that internally controlled employees are generally more satisfied with their jobs, are more likely to be in managerial positions, and are more satisfied with a participatory management style than employees who perceive external control.[28] Other studies have found that internally controlled managers are better performers,[29] are more considerate of subordinates,[30] tend not to burn out,[31] and follow a more strategic style of executive action.[32] In addition, the attribution process has been shown to play a role in coalition formation in the political process of organizations. In particular, coalition members made stronger internal attributions, such as ability and desire, and non-members made stronger external attributions, such as luck.[33]

The implication of these studies is that internally controlled managers are better than externally controlled managers. However, such generalizations are not yet warranted because there is some contradictory evidence. For example, one study concluded that the ideal manager may have an external orientation because the results indicated that externally controlled managers were perceived as initiating more structure and consideration than internally controlled managers.[34] In addition to the implications for managerial behavior and performance, attribution theory has been shown to have relevance in explaining goal-setting behavior,[35] leadership behavior,[36] and poor employee performance.[37] A review article concludes that locus of control is related to the performance and satisfaction of organization members and may moderate the relationship between motivation and incentives.[38]

In addition, attributions are related to *organizational symbolism*, which in effect says that in order to understand organizations, one must recognize their symbolic nature.[39] Much of organization is based on attributions rather than physical or observed realities under this view.[40] For example, research has found that symbols are a salient source of information used by people in forming their impressions of psychological climate.[41]

Other Attributions. Attribution theory seems to hold a great deal of promise for the better understanding of organizational behavior. However, for the future, other dimensions besides the internal and external locus of control will have to be accounted for and studied. One social psychologist, for example, suggests that a stability (fixed or variable) dimension must also be recognized.[42] Experienced employees will probably have a stable internal attribution about their abilities, but an unstable internal attribution concerning effort. By the same token, these employees may have a stable external attribution about task difficulty but an unstable external attribution about luck.

Besides the stability dimension, Kelley suggests that dimensions such as consensus (do others act this way in a situation?), consistency (does this person act this way in this situation at other times?), and distinctiveness (does this person act differently in other situations?) will affect the type of attributions that are made.[43] Figure 6.8 shows how this type of information affects the attributes that are made in evaluating employee behavior. To keep these dimensions straight, it can be remembered that consensus relates to other *people*, distinctiveness relates to other *tasks*, and consistency relates to *time*.[44] As shown in Figure 6.8, if there is high consensus, consistency, and distinctiveness, then attribution to external or situational/environmental causes will probably be made. The external attribution may be that the task is too difficult or that outside pressures from home or coworkers are hindering performance. However, if there is low consensus, high consistency, and low distinctiveness, then attributions to internal or personal causes for the behavior will probably be made. The supervisor making an internal attribution may conclude that the subordinate just doesn't have the ability or is not giving the necessary effort

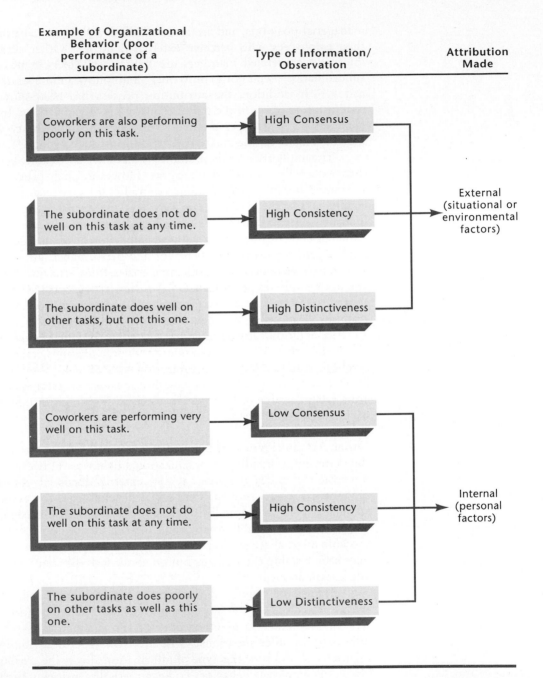

FIGURE 6.8
Kelley's model
of attribution.

or motivation to perform well. There is some research evidence from field settings to directly support predictions from the Kelley model.[45]

In addition to Kelley, other well-known motivation theorists, such as Bernard Weiner, use attribution theory to help explain achievement motivation and to predict subsequent changes in performance and how people feel about themselves.[46] Some research findings from Weiner's work include the following:

1. Bad-luck attributions (external) take the sting out of a negative outcome, but good-luck attributions (external) reduce the joy associated with success.

2. When individuals attribute their success to internal rather than external factors, they have higher expectations for future success, report a greater desire for achievement, and set higher performance goals.[47]

Attribution Errors. Recently, social psychologists have given attention to two potent biases when people make attributions. The first is called the *fundamental attribution error*. Research has found that people tend to ignore powerful situational forces when explaining others' behavior.[48] People tend to attribute *others'* behavior to personal factors (for example, intelligence, ability, motivation, attitudes, or personality), even when it is very clear that the situation or circumstances caused the person to behave the way he or she did.

Another attribution bias that has emerged from the research is that people tend to present themselves favorably. This *self-serving bias* has been found in study after study; people readily accept credit when told they have succeeded (attributing the success to their ability and effort), yet often attribute failure to such external, situational factors as bad luck or the problem's inherent "impossibility."[49] For example, in explaining their victories, athletes commonly credit themselves, but are more likely to attribute losses to something else—bad breaks, poor officiating, or the other team's superior effort.[50]

When something goes wrong in the workplace, there is a tendency for the boss to blame the inability or poor attitude of the subordinates, but the situation is blamed as far as he or she is concerned. The reverse is true of the subordinates. They blame the situation for their difficulties, but make a personal attribution in terms of their boss. By the same token, if something goes well, the boss makes personal attributions for him- or herself and situational attributions for subordinates, and the subordinates make personal attributions for themselves but situational attributions for the boss. In other words, it is typical to have conflicting attributional biases between managers and subordinates in organizations. As a way of creating more productive relationships, researchers suggest that efforts must be made to reduce divergent perceptions and perspectives between the parties through increased interpersonal interaction, open communication channels and workshops, and team-building sessions devoted to reducing attributional errors.[51]

The Role of Self-Efficacy in Attributions. Closely related to the attribution errors is the recently popular concept of self-efficacy (discussed in Chapters 5 and 11). Taking off from the self-serving bias, self-efficacy (how effective people think they, themselves, are) will affect the attributions people make. If individuals have high self-efficacy, they will tend to make positive internal attributions about their successes and attribute setbacks as situational or as a fluke, or to think, "I need a new approach."[52] By the same token, attributions also affect a person's self-efficacy. If people make internal attributions for their successful performance, this will enhance their self-efficacy beliefs.[53]

These various dimensions of attribution theory recognize the complexity of human behavior, and this realization must be part of a theory that attempts to *explain* and *understand* organizational behavior. As has recently been pointed out, attribution theory should not be restrictive. Theoretical, information processing, and situational factors all affect the attribution models of organizational behavior.[54] Despite this complexity, and unlike some of its predecessors in the cognitive approaches to motivation discussed earlier, attribution theory does seem to have more potential for application and relevance, instead of being a purely academic exercise in theory building.

Other Emerging Theories

In addition to the micro-oriented expectancy, equity, and attribution motivation theories coming out of cognitive psychology, there are other, more broad-based theories beginning to emerge in organizational behavior. Representatives of these recent theories are control theory and agency theory.

One version of *control theory*, like the other theories discussed so far, is essentially a cognitive phenomenon relating to the degree that individuals perceive they are in control of their own lives, or are in control of their jobs. Recent studies have shown that those who believe they have such personal control tolerate unpleasant events and experience less stress on the job than those who do not perceive such control.[55] There is also some evidence that perceived control will affect job satisfaction and absenteeism.[56] Another version of control theory, which also has implications for organizational behavior, relates to the more traditional management function of control. Traditional guidelines for effective management have included controlling both the inputs and outputs of organizations, but recent research has also analyzed strategically controlling human resources as well.[57]

Similar to control theory's being taken from the traditional management literature, agency theory comes from the financial economics literature. An agency relationship involves one or more individuals (the principal) engaging another person or persons (the agent) to perform some service on their behalf.[58] The key to *agency theory* is the assumption that the interests of principals and agents diverge or may be in conflict with one another. The implications for organizational behavior involve how the principals (owners, board members, or top management) can limit divergence from their interests or objectives by establishing appropriate rewards or incentives for the agent (subordinate, middle management, or operating employees) for appropriate outcomes. There is beginning research evidence supporting an agency theory interpretation of areas in organizational behavior such as pay for performance.[59]

Summary

Motivation is probably more closely associated with the micro perspective of organizational behavior than is any other topic. A comprehensive understanding of motivation includes the need-drive-incentive sequence, or cycle. The basic process involves needs, which set drives in motion to accomplish incentives (anything which alleviates a need and reduces a drive). The drives, or motives, may be classified into *primary, general,* and *secondary* categories. The primary motives are unlearned and physiologically based. Common primary motives are hunger, thirst, sleep, avoidance of pain, sex, and maternal concern. The general, or stimulus, motives are also unlearned but are not physiologically based. Curiosity, manipulation, activity, and affection are examples of general motives. Secondary motives are learned and are most relevant to the study of organizational behavior. The needs for power, achievement, affiliation, security, and status are major motivating forces in the behavior of organizational participants.

When the theories of motivation are specifically focused on work motivation, there are several popular approaches. The Maslow, Herzberg, and Alderfer models attempt to identify specific content factors in the individual (in the case of Maslow and Alderfer) or in the job environment (in the case of Herzberg) that motivate employees. Although such a content approach has surface logic, is easy to understand, and can be readily translated into practice, the research evidence points out some definite limitations. There is very little research support for these models' theoretical basis and predictability. The trade-off for simplicity sacrifices true understanding of the complexity of work motivation. On the positive side, however, the content models have given emphasis to important content factors that were largely ignored by the human relationists. In addition, the Alderfer model allows more flexibility, and the Herzberg model is useful as an explanation for job satisfaction and as a point of departure for job design, which is covered in the next chapter.

The process theories provide a much sounder theoretical explanation of work motivation. The expectancy model of Vroom and the extensions and refinements provided by Porter and Lawler help explain the important cognitive variables and how they relate to one another in the complex process of work motivation. The Porter-Lawler model also gives specific attention to the important relationship between performance and satisfaction. Porter and Lawler propose that performance leads to satisfaction, instead of the human relations assumption of the reverse. A growing research literature is somewhat supportive of these expectancy models, but conceptual and methodological problems remain. Unlike the content models, these expectancy models are relatively complex and difficult to translate into actual practice, and consequently, they have generally failed to meet the goals of prediction and control of organizational behavior.

More recently, in academic circles, equity theory and, especially, attribution theory have received increased attention. Both theories—equity theory, which is based upon perceived input-outcome ratios, and attribution theory, which ascribes internal, external, and other causes to behavior—lend increased understanding to the complex cognitive process of work motivation but have the same limitation as the expectancy models for prediction and control in the practice of human resources management. Attribution theory can make potentially important contributions to the cognitive development of work-motivation theory and may be able to overcome some of the application limitations of the expectancy and equity theories of work motivation and bring us closer to the goals of prediction and control. Finally, control and agency theories, coming from other disciplines, are briefly mentioned as representative of other approaches receiving recent attention in organizational behavior.

Questions for Discussion and Review

1. Briefly define the three classifications of needs, or motives. What are some examples of each?
2. What are the characteristics of high achievers?
3. How is status defined? What are some determinants of status?
4. What implications does the security motive have for modern human resources management?
5. In your own words, briefly explain Maslow's theory of motivation. Relate it to work motivation and Alderfer's ERG model.
6. What is the major criticism of Herzberg's two-factor theory of motivation? Do you think it has made a contribution to the better understanding of motivation in the workplace? Defend your answer.
7. In Vroom's model, what are valence, expectancy, and force? How do these variables relate to one another and to work motivation? Give realistic examples.
8. In your own words, briefly explain the Porter-Lawler model of motivation. How do performance and satisfaction relate to each other?

9. Briefly give an example of an inequity that a manager of a small business might experience. How would the manager strive to attain equity in the situation you describe?
10. What is attribution theory? How can analysis of locus of control be applied to workers and managers?
11. What two important attribution errors or biases have surfaced? Give an example of each.
12. Briefly describe control theory and agency theory. What implications can these two theories have for work motivation?

Footnote References and Supplemental Readings

1. Martin G. Evans, "Organizational Behavior: The Central Role of Motivation," *Journal of Management*, vol. 12, no. 2, 1986, p. 203.
2. The most frequently cited exception is the need for oxygen. A deficiency of oxygen in the body does not automatically set up a corresponding drive. This is a fear of high-altitude pilots. Unless their gauges show an oxygen leak or the increased intake of carbon dioxide sets up a drive, they may die of oxygen deficiency without a drive's ever being set up to correct the situation. The same is true of the relatively frequent deaths of teenagers parked in "lovers' lanes." Carbon monoxide leaks into the parked automobile, and they die from oxygen deficiency without its ever setting up a drive (to open the car door).
3. Spencer A. Rathus, *Psychology*, 4th ed., Holt, Rinehart and Winston, Fort Worth, Tex., 1990, p. 312.
4. Ronald E. Riggio, *Introduction to Industrial/Organizational Psychology*, Scott Foresman/Little, Brown, Glenview, Ill., 1990, p. 175.
5. For examples of recent research on the achievement motive, see N. T. Feather, "Authoritarianism and Attitudes Toward High Achieverism," *Journal of Personality and Social Psychology*, July 1993, pp. 152–164, and Daniel Turban and Thomas L. Keon, "Organizational Attractiveness: An Interactionist Perspective," *Journal of Applied Psychology*, April 1993, pp. 184–193.
6. "Labor Letter," *The Wall Street Journal*, Mar. 31, 1987, p. 1.
7. Terence R. Mitchell, "Motivation: New Directions for Theory, Research, and Practice," *Academy of Management Review*, January 1982, p. 86.
8. James L. Bowditch and Anthony F. Buono, *A Primer on Organizational Behavior*, 3d ed., Wiley, New York, 1994, p. 72.
9. A. H. Maslow, "A Theory of Human Motivation," *Psychological Review*, July 1943, pp. 370–396.
10. Robert A. Baron, *Behavior in Organizations*, 2d ed., Allyn and Bacon, Boston, 1986, p. 78.
11. Some examples of recent research using Vroom's concepts include Mark E. Tubbs, Donna M. Boehne, and James G. Dahl, "Expectancy, Valence, and Motivational Force Functions in Goal-Setting Research: An Empirical Test," *Journal of Applied Psychology*, June 1993, pp. 361–373; N. T. Feather, "Expectancy-Value Theory and Unemployment Effects," *Journal of Occupational and Organizational Psychology*, December 1992, pp. 315–330; and Anthony J. Mento, Howard J. Klein, and Edwin A. Locke, "Relationship of Goal Level to Valence and Instrumentality," *Journal of Applied Psychology*, August 1992, pp. 395–405.
12. Anthony Dickinson, "Expectancy Theory in Animal Conditioning," in Stephen B. Klein and Robert R. Mowrer (eds.), *Contemporary Learning Theories*, Erlbaum, Hillsdale, N.J., 1989, p. 280.
13. Gary Blau, "Operationalizing Direction and Level of Effort and Testing Their Relationships to Individual Job Performance," *Organizational Behavior and Human Decision Processes*, June 1993, pp. 152–170.
14. Philip M. Podsakoff and Larry Williams, "The Relationship Between Job Performance and Job Satisfaction," in Edwin Locke (ed.), *Generalizing from Laboratory to Field Settings*, Lexington Books, Lexington, Mass., 1986, p. 244. Also see Edwin A. Locke and Gary P. Latham, *A Theory of Goal Setting and Task Performance*, Prentice-Hall, Englewood Cliffs, N.J., 1990, pp. 265–267, and E. Brian Peach and Daniel A. Wren, "Pay for Performance from Antiquity to the 1950's," *Journal of Organizational Behavior Management*, vol. 12, 1992, pp. 5–26.
15. Erik P. Thompson, Shelly Chaiken, and J. Douglas Hazlewood, "Need for Cognition and Desire for Control as Moderators of Extrinsic Reward Effects: A Person × Situation Approach to the Study of Intrinsic Motivation," *Journal of Personality and Social Psychology*, June 1993, pp. 987–999.
16. James N. Baron and Karen S. Cook, "Process and Outcome: Perspectives on the Distribution of Rewards in Organizations," *Administrative Science Quarterly*, vol. 37, 1992, pp. 191–197.
17. James M. McFillen and Philip M. Podsakoff, "A

Coordinated Approach to Motivation Can Increase Productivity," *Personnel Administrator*, July 1983, p. 46.

18. Robert A. Baron, *Behavior in Organizations*, Allyn and Bacon, Boston, 1983, p. 137.

19. Robert E. Callahan, C. Patrick Fleenor, and Harry R. Knudson, *Understanding Organizational Behavior*, Merrill, Columbus, Ohio, 1986, pp. 108–109.

20. Michael R. Carrell and John E. Dittrich, "Equity Theory: The Recent Literature, Methodological Considerations, and New Directions," *Academy of Management Review*, April 1978, pp. 202–210.

21. Robert G. Lord and Jeffrey A. Hohenfeld, "Longitudinal Field Assessment of Equity Effects on the Performance of Major League Baseball Players," *Journal of Applied Psychology*, February 1979, pp. 19–26.

22. Dennis Duchon and Arthur G. Jago, "Equity and Performance of Major League Baseball Players: An Extension of Lord and Hohenfeld," *Journal of Applied Psychology*, December 1981, pp. 728–732.

23. Larry W. Howard and Janis L. Miller, "Fair Pay for Fair Play: Estimating Pay Equity in Professional Baseball with Data Envelopment Analysis," *Academy of Management Journal*, August 1993, pp. 882–894.

24. Robert D. Bretz, Jr., and Steven L. Thomas, "Perceived Equity, Motivation, and Final-Offer Arbitration in Major League Baseball," *Journal of Applied Psychology*, June 1993, pp. 280–287.

25. Joseph W. Harder, "Play for Pay: Effect of Inequity in a Pay-for-Performance Context," *Administrative Science Quarterly*, June 1992, pp. 321–335.

26. David G. Myers, *Social Psychology*, 2d ed., McGraw-Hill, New York, 1990, p. 71.

27. Julian B. Rotter, Shephard Liverant, and Douglas P. Crowne, "The Growth and Extinction of Expectancies in Chance-Controlled and Skilled Tasks," *The Journal of Psychology*, July 1961, pp. 161–177.

28. Terence R. Mitchell, Charles M. Smyser, and Stan E. Weed, "Locus of Control: Supervision and Work Satisfaction," *Academy of Management Journal*, September 1975, pp. 623–631.

29. The higher performance of internally controlled managers was verified by the use of student subjects in a study by Carl R. Anderson and Craig Eric Schneier, "Locus of Control, Leader Behavior and Leader Performance Among Management Students," *Academy of Management Journal*, December 1978, pp. 690–698. For a more recent study, see Gary Blau, "Testing the Relationships of Locus of Control to Different Performance Dimensions," *Journal of Occupational and Organizational Psychology*, June 1993, pp. 125–138.

30. Margaret W. Pryer and M. K. Distenfano, "Perceptions of Leadership, Job Satisfaction, and Internal-External Control Across Three Nursing Levels,"

Nursing Research, November–December 1971, pp. 534–537.

31. Eli Glogow, "Research Note: Burnout and Locus of Control," *Public Personnel Management*, Spring 1986, p. 79.

32. Danny Miller, Manfred F. R. Kets DeVries, and Jean-Marie Toulouse, "Top Executive Locus of Control and Its Relationship to Strategy-Making, Structure, and Environment," *Academy of Management Journal*, June 1982, pp. 237–253.

33. John A. Pearce and Angelo S. DeNisi, "Attribution Theory and Strategic Decision Making: An Application to Coalition Formation," *Academy of Management Journal*, March 1983, pp. 119–128.

34. Douglas E. Durand and Walter R. Nord, "Perceived Leader Behavior as a Function of Personality Characteristics of Supervisors and Subordinates," *Academy of Management Journal*, September 1976, pp. 427–428.

35. Dennis L. Dossett and Carl I. Greenberg, "Goal Setting and Performance Evaluation: An Attributional Analysis," *Academy of Management Journal*, December 1981, pp. 767–779.

36. Bobby J. Calder, "An Attribution Theory of Leadership," in Barry Staw and Gerald Salancik (eds.), *New Directions in Organizational Behavior*, St. Clare Press, Chicago, 1977, pp. 179–204; James C. McElroy, "A Typology of Attribution Leadership Research," *Academy of Management Review*, July 1982, pp. 413–417; Gregory Dobbins, "Effects of Gender on Leaders' Responses to Poor Performers: An Attributional Interpretation," *Academy of Management Journal*, September 1985, pp. 587–598; and James C. McElroy and Charles B. Shrader, "Attribution Theories of Leadership and Network Analysis," *Journal of Management*, vol. 12, no. 3, 1986, pp. 351–362.

37. Terence R. Mitchell and Robert E. Wood, "Supervisors' Responses to Subordinate Poor Performance: A Test of an Attribution Model," *Organizational Behavior and Human Performance*, February 1980, pp. 123–138.

38. Paul E. Spector, "Behavior in Organizations as a Function of Employees' Locus of Control," *Psychological Bulletin*, May 1982, pp. 482–497. Also see Leslie Kren, "The Moderating Effects of Locus of Control on Performance Incentives and Participation," *Human Relations*, September 1992, p. 991.

39. Peter J. Frost, "Special Issue on Organizational Symbolism," *Journal of Management*, vol. 11, no. 2, 1985, pp. 5–9.

40. Farzad Moussavi and Dorla A. Evans, "Emergence of Organizational Attributions: The Role of a Shared Cognitive Schema," *Journal of Management*, Spring 1993, pp. 79–95.

41. Suzyn Ornstein, "Organizational Symbols: A Study

of Their Meanings and Influences on Perceived Psychological Climate," *Organizational Behavior and Human Decision Processes*, October 1986, pp. 207–229.

42. Bernard Weiner, *Theories of Motivation*, Rand McNally, Chicago, 1972, Chap. 5.

43. Harold H. Kelley, "The Process of Causal Attribution," *American Psychologist*, February 1973, pp. 107–128.

44. Robert Kreitner and Angelo Kinicki, *Organizational Behavior*, 2d ed., Irwin, Homewood, Ill., 1992, p. 148.

45. Mitchell and Wood, op. cit., pp. 123–138.

46. Bernard Weiner, "An Attribution Theory of Achievement Motivation and Emotion," *Psychological Review*, October 1985, pp. 548–573.

47. See Kreitner and Kinicki, op. cit., p. 150, for a summary of this research.

48. Myers, op. cit., pp. 74–77.

49. Ibid., p. 82.

50. B. Mullen and C. A. Riordan, "Self-Serving Attributions for Performance in Naturalistic Settings," *Journal of Applied Social Psychology*, vol. 18, 1988, pp. 3–22.

51. Bowditch and Buono, op. cit., p. 90.

52. Myers, op. cit., p. 95.

53. Raymond A. Katzell and Donna E. Thompson, "Work Motivation," *American Psychologist*, February 1990, pp. 145–146.

54. Robert G. Lord and Jonathan E. Smith, "Theoretical, Information Processing, and Situational Factors Affecting Attribution Theory Models of Organizational Behavior," *Academy of Management Review*, January 1983, pp. 50–60.

55. See "Control in the Workplace and Its Health-Related Aspects," in S. L. Sauter, J. J. Hurrell, and C. L. Cooper (eds.), *Job Control and Worker Health*, Wiley, Chichester, England, 1989, pp. 129–159; D. C. Ganster and M. R. Fusilier, "Control in the Workplace," in C. L. Cooper and I. T. Robertson (eds.), *International Review of Industrial and Organizational Psychology*, Wiley, Chichester, England, 1989, pp. 235–280; and Marilyn L. Fox, Deborah J. Dwyer, and Daniel C. Ganster, "Effects of Stressful Job Demands and Control on Physiological and Attitudinal Outcomes in a Hospital Setting," *Academy of Management Journal*, April 1993, pp. 289–318.

56. D. J. Dwyer and D. C. Ganster, "The Effects of Job Demands and Control on Employee Attendance and Satisfaction," *Journal of Organizational Behavior*, vol. 12, 1991, pp. 595–608.

57. For example, see Scott A. Snell, "Control Theory in Strategic Human Resource Management: The Mediating Effect of Administrative Information," *Academy of Management Journal*, June 1992, pp. 292–327.

58. For some of the original development of agency theory, see M. C. Jensen and W. H. Meckling, "Theory of the Firm, Managerial Behavior, Agency Costs, and Ownership Structure," *Journal of Financial Economics*, vol. 3, 1976, pp. 305–360. For recent applications of agency theory to the management literature, see Charles W. L. Hill and Thomas M. Jones, "Stakeholder-Agency Theory," *Journal of Management Studies*, March 1992, pp. 131–154.

59. See H. L. Tosi and L. R. Gomez-Mejia, "The Decoupling of CEO Pay and Performance: An Agency Theory Perspective," *Administrative Science Quarterly*, vol. 34, 1989, pp. 169–189, and Luis R. Gomez-Mejia and David B. Balkin, "Determinants of Faculty Pay: An Agency Theory Perspective," *Academy of Management Journal*, December 1992, pp. 921–955.

REAL CASE: Keeping Them Motivated

Over the last couple of years there has been a marked change in the way some firms are attempting to motivate their personnel. While such factors as interesting work and the opportunity to use their abilities still rank high on the list of what management are trying to provide their people, there is growing interest in linking pay to performance. Employees who thrive on challenge are responding to the pay-for-performance approach, and there are an increasing number of firms that are moving in this direction.

A good example of a pay-for-performance firm is the highly successful Charlotte-based steel producer, Nucor. This innovative company pays its plant managers about 25 percent less base salary than those in competitive firms. However, if Nucor managers perform up to expectations, they can earn as much as 100 percent of their salary in annual bonus. So a relatively low-salaried plant manager can still do quite well through incentive pay if he or she performs well.

AT&T is another firm that has begun adopting a pay-for-performance approach. When the firm had a monopoly in the telephone business, it paid very high salaries.

However, when it became deregulated, the company began holding down base salaries and moving more toward bonus pay. Today, many of AT&T's managers make less than their counterparts who work for competitors MCI and Sprint. However, when the annual bonus is added into the compensation package, the high-performing AT&T managers come out ahead. Today, 80,000 middle managers and 30,000 researchers, scientists, and other technical people are covered by such an approach. All are linked to an "economic value added" (EVA) plan, which is based on net operating profits after deductions for capital uses, inventory, and accounts receivable. Managers who meet their targets can expect bonuses equal to 15 to 20 percent of their annual salary.

Scott Paper uses an approach similar to AT&T's with 70 percent of managers' bonuses dependent on their business unit's EVA and the other 30 percent on the success of the individual or a small team of people with whom the person works. If a unit achieves its EVA, the bonus will run around 20 percent of annual pay. If the unit exceeds its goal by 50 percent, the bonus percentage will jump to almost 50 percent of annual pay. So there is a major incentive for the Scott Paper managers to reach and surpass EVA targets.

In pursuing such incentive goals, most firms give their people a great deal of operating freedom. At Yoplait Yogurt, for example, teams set their own targets and determine how to reach them. Recently, the Yoplait group set a target of increasing operating earnings by 100 percent. Their success resulted in bonuses to the managers of between $30,000 and $50,000. The team was able to accomplish its goal by introducing new products such as brightly packaged Trix yogurt for kids, while simultaneously cutting costs by using low-cost contract manufacturers.

This new trend in pay for performance is attracting more and more entrepreneurially oriented people who want the opportunity to do things their own way and be rewarded for their performance. A by-product of such incentive plans is that the organization is also sharply increasing its annual earnings.

1. What particular needs does money satisfy? Incorporate Maslow's need hierarchy into your answer.
2. Is the need for recognition and challenge more important than that for money?
3. How could equity theory be used to help explain the best way to motivate a successful manager? Give an example.

CASE: Star Salesperson

While growing up, Jerry Slate was always rewarded by his parents for showing independence. When he started school, he was successful both inside and outside the classroom. He was always striving to be things like traffic patroller and lunchroom monitor in grade school. Yet his mother worried about him because he never got along well with other children his own age. When confronted with this, Jerry would reply: "Well, I don't need them. Besides, they can't do things as well as I can. I don't have time to help them; I'm too busy improving myself." Jerry went on to do very well in both high school and college. He was always at or near the top of his class academically and was a very good long-distance runner for the track teams in high school and college. In college he shied away from joining a fraternity and lived in an apartment by himself. Upon graduation he went to work for a large insurance company and soon became one of the top salespersons. Jerry is very proud of the fact that he was one of the top five salespersons in six of the eight years he has been with the company.

At the home office of the insurance company, the executive committee in charge of making major personnel appointments was discussing the upcoming vacancy of the sales manager's job for the Midwestern region. The human resources manager gave the following report: "As you know, the Midwestern region is lagging far behind our other regions as far as sales go. We need a highly motivated person to take that situation over and turn it around. After an extensive screening process, I am recommending that Jerry Slate be offered this position. As you know, Jerry has an outstanding record with the company and is highly motivated. I think he is the person for the job."

1. Do you agree with the human resources manager? Why or why not?
2. Considering Jerry's background, what motives discussed in the chapter would appear to be very intense in Jerry? What motives would appear to be very low? Give specific evidence from the case for each motive.
3. What type of motivation is desirable for people in sales positions? What type of motivation is desirable for people in managerial positions?

CASE:
What Do They Want?

Pat Riverer is vice president of manufacturing and operations of a medium-size pharmaceutical firm in the Midwest. Pat has a Ph.D. in chemistry but has not been directly involved in research and new-product development for twenty years. From the "school of hard knocks" when it comes to managing operations, Pat runs a "tight ship." The company does not have a turnover problem, but it is obvious to Pat and other key management personnel that the hourly people are only putting in their eight hours a day. They are not working anywhere near their full potential. Pat is very upset with the situation because, with rising costs, the only way that the company can continue to prosper is to increase the productivity of its hourly people.

Pat called the human resources manager, Carmen Lopez, and laid it on the line: "What is it with our people, anyway? Your wage surveys show that we pay near the top in this region, our conditions are tremendous, and our fringes choke a horse. Yet these people still are not motivated. What in the world do they want?" Carmen replied: "I have told you and the president time after time that money, conditions, and benefits are not enough. Employees also need other things to motivate them. Also, I have been conducting some random confidential interviews with some of our hourly people, and they tell me that they are very discouraged because, no matter how hard they work, they get the same pay and opportunities for advancement as their coworkers who are just scraping by." Pat then replied: "Okay, you are the motivation expert; what do we do about it? We *have* to increase their performance."

1. Explain the "motivation problem" in this organization in terms of the content models of Maslow, Alderfer, and Herzberg. What are the "other things" that the human resources manager is referring to in speaking of things besides money, conditions, and fringe benefits that are needed to motivate employees?
2. Explain the motivation of the employees in this company in terms of one or more of the process models. On the basis of the responses during the confidential interviews, what would you guess are some of the expectancies, valences, inequities, and attributions of the employees in this company? How about Pat? Do you think this manager is internally or externally controlled?
3. How would you respond to Pat's last question and statement if you were the human resources manager in this company?

CASE:
Tom, Dick, and Harry

You are in charge of a small department and have three subordinates—Tom, Dick, and Harry. The key to the success of your department is to keep these employees as motivated as possible. Here is a brief summary profile on each of these subordinates.

Tom is the type of employee who is hard to figure out. His absenteeism record is much higher than average. He greatly enjoys his family (a wife and three small children) and thinks they should be central to his life. The best way to describe Tom is to say that he is kind of a throwback to the hippie generation and believes deeply in the values of that culture. As a result, the things that the company can offer him really inspire him very little. He feels that the job is simply a means of financing his family's basic needs and little else. Overall, Tom does an adequate job and is very conscientious, but all attempts to get him to do more have failed. He has charm and is friendly, but he is just not "gung-ho" for the company. He is pretty much allowed to "do his own thing" as long as he meets the minimal standards of performance.

Dick is in many respects opposite from Tom. Like Tom, he is a likable guy, but unlike Tom, Dick responds well to the company's rules and compensation schemes and has a high degree of personal loyalty to the company. The problem with Dick is that he will not do very much independently. He does well with what is assigned to him, but he is not very creative or even dependable when he is on his own. He also is a relatively shy person who is not very assertive when dealing with people outside the department. This hurts his performance to some degree because he cannot immediately sell himself or the department to other departments in the company or to top management.

Harry, on the other hand, is a very assertive person. He will work for money and would readily change jobs for more money. He really works hard for the company but expects the company also to work for him. In his present job, he feels no qualms about working a sixty-hour week, if the money is there. Even though he has a family and is supporting his elderly father, he once quit a job cold when his employer didn't give him a raise on the premise that he was already making too much. He is quite a driver. A manager at his last place of employment indicated that, while Harry did do an excellent job for the company, his personality was so strong that they were glad to get rid of him. His former boss noted that Harry just seemed to be pushing all the time. If it wasn't for more money, it was for better fringe benefits; he never seemed satisfied.

1. Can you explain Tom's, Dick's, and Harry's motivations by one or more of the work-motivation models discussed in this chapter?
2. Using Alderfer's ERG theory, what group of core needs seems to dominate each of these three subordinates?
3. Using the attribution theory approach, what type of locus of control do you feel guides each of these three employees in his present job?

7 Motivating Performance Through Job Design and Goal Setting

Learning Objectives

- **Discuss** the background of job design as an applied area of work motivation.
- **Define** the job enrichment and job characteristics approaches to job design.
- **Present** the quality of work life (QWL) and sociotechnical approaches to job design.
- **Explain** goal-setting theory and guidelines from research.
- **Describe** the application of goal setting to overall systems performance.

The preceding chapter is devoted to the basic motivational process and the various theoretical approaches to work motivation. In this chapter the more applied areas of motivating performance are examined: job design and goal setting. In recent years, relatively more research has been generated in these two areas than elsewhere in the field of organizational behavior. It is becoming increasingly clear that appropriately designing jobs can have a positive impact on both employee satisfaction and quality of performance. The same is true of goal setting, which has been held up as a prototypical model for how theory should or can lead to application. The purpose of this chapter is to give some of the background, review the related research, and spell out some of the specific applications for these important areas of the field of organizational behavior.

JOB DESIGN

Job design has emerged as an important application area for work motivation and the study of organizational behavior. In particular, job design is based on an extensive and still growing theoretical base, it has had considerable research attention in recent years, and it is being widely applied to the actual practice of management.

Initially, the field of organizational behavior paid attention only to job enrichment approaches to job design. Now, with *quality of work life* (QWL) becoming a major societal issue in this country and throughout the world, job design has taken a broader perspective. Figure 7.1 summarizes the various dimensions and approaches to job design, starting with the historically significant job engineering. Job enrichment still dominates the job design literature on organizational behavior, but from

174

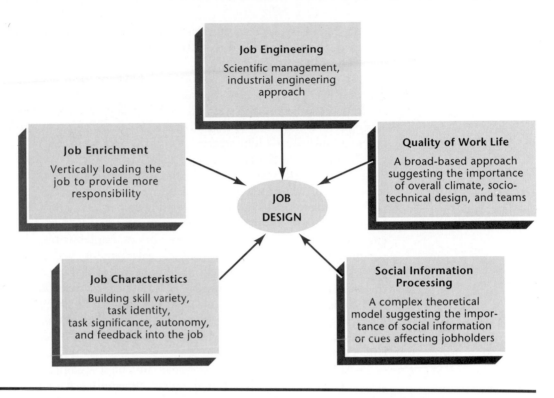

FIGURE 7.1
Various approaches to
job design.

the perspective of job characteristics rather than from Herzberg's motivators. The social information processing approach recognizes some of the theoretical complexity in job design, and the QWL approach recognizes the overall importance of the climate or culture and the role of more specific sociotechnical and team techniques in job design.

Background on Job Design

Job design concerns and approaches are usually considered to have begun with the scientific management movement at the turn of the century. Pioneering scientific managers such as Frederick W. Taylor and Frank Gilbreth systematically examined jobs with techniques such as time and motion analysis. Their goal was to maximize human efficiency in jobs. Taylor suggested that task design might be the most prominent single element in scientific management.

The scientific management approach evolved into what is now generally called *job engineering.* This industrial engineering approach is concerned with product, process, and tool design; plant layout; standard operating procedures; work measurement and standards; worker methods; and human-machine interactions. It has been the dominant form of job design analysis since the turn of the century; it went hand in hand with automation in the previous generation, and it has been closely associated with cybernation (automatic feedback control mechanisms) and sophisticated computer applications involving artificial intelligence (AI) and expert systems. These computer systems have had a positive impact by reducing task and work-flow uncertainty.[1] At first blue-collar production jobs, but then white-collar jobs as well, became highly specialized (the employee did one or a very few tasks) and standardized (the employee did the task the same way every time).

The often cited example of the employee on the assembly line putting a nut on a bolt as the product moves by on the conveyor belt became quite common in manufacturing plants across the country. The same types of specialized jobs became common in banks, offices, hospitals, schools, and every other kind of organizational setting. The consensus was that these highly specialized, standardized jobs were very efficient and led to a high degree of control over workers. Up to recent times, few people questioned the engineering approach to job design. Top management could readily determine and see immediate cost savings from job engineering. But side effects on quality, absenteeism, and turnover were generally ignored.

Starting in the 1950s, some practicing managers around the country, such as the founder of IBM, Thomas Watson, became concerned about the impact of job engineering approaches to work and began implementing job enlargement and rotation programs. Essentially, the job enlargement programs horizontally loaded the job (expanded the number of operations performed by the worker, that is, made the job less specialized), and the job rotation programs reduced boredom by switching people around to various jobs. Then, starting in the late 1960s, there began to be increasing concern with employee dissatisfaction and declining productivity. These problems were felt to be largely the result of so-called blue-collar blues and white-collar woes.

Although boredom at work may still be a significant problem,[2] in the last several years, attention has shifted to new, demanding challenges facing employees in jobs. For example, because of the downsizing of organizations in the 1980s and the increase of advanced technology, jobs have suddenly become much more demanding and employees must think in different ways to adapt to unpredictable changes.[3] For example, in manufacturing, assembly line methods are being replaced by flexible, "customized" production. This new manufacturing approach requires workers to deal with an ever increasing line of products. Similar job changes have occurred in the white-collar service industry. For example, bank tellers must not only demonstrate facility with computers but also be marketers—rather than just number crunchers and clerks.[4]

For both academicians and practitioners, job design takes on special importance in today's human resource management. It is essential to design jobs so that stress (covered in Chapter 11) can be reduced, motivation can be enhanced, and satisfaction of employees (covered in Chapter 5) and their performance can be so improved that organizations can effectively compete in the global marketplace.

Job Enrichment

Job enrichment represents an extension of the earlier, more simplified job rotation and job enlargement techniques of job design. Since it is a direct outgrowth of Herzberg's two-factor theory of motivation, the assumption is that in order to motivate personnel, the job must be designed to provide opportunities for achievement, recognition, responsibility, advancement, and growth. The technique entails "enriching" the job so that these factors are included. In particular, *job enrichment* is concerned with designing jobs that include a greater variety of work content; require a higher level of knowledge and skill; give workers more autonomy and responsibility in terms of planning, directing, and controlling their own performance; and provide the opportunity for personal growth and a meaningful work experience. As

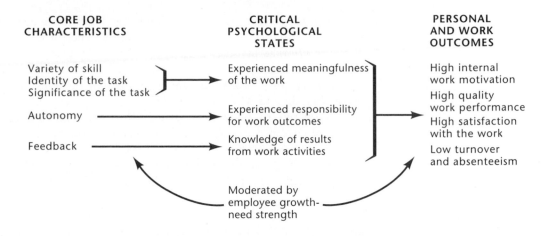

FIGURE 7.2
The Hackman-Oldham job characteristics model of work motivation.

opposed to job enlargement, which horizontally loads the job, job enrichment *vertically* loads the job; there are not necessarily more tasks to perform, but more responsibility and accountability. For example, instead of having workers do a mundane, specialized task, then passing off to another worker doing another minute part of the task, and eventually having an inspector at the end, under job enrichment, the worker would be given a complete module of work to do (job enlargement) and, importantly, inspect his or her own work (responsibility), and put an identifying tag on it (accountability).

As with the other application techniques discussed in this text, job enrichment is not a panacea for all job design problems facing modern management. After noting that there are documented cases where this approach to job design did not work, Miner concluded that the biggest problem is that traditional job enrichment has little to say about when and why the failures can be expected to occur.[5] Yet job enrichment is still a viable approach, and recent research provides continuing evidence that it has mostly beneficial results (more employee satisfaction and customer service, less employee overload, and fewer employee errors).[6] However, management must still use job enrichment selectively and give proper recognition to the complex human and situational variables. The newer job characteristics models of job enrichment are beginning to do this.

The Job Characteristics Approach to Task Design

To meet some of the limitations of the Herzberg approach to job enrichment (which he prefers to call *orthodox job enrichment,* or OJE), a group of researchers began to concentrate on the relationship between certain job characteristics, or the job scope, and employee motivation. J. Richard Hackman and Greg Oldham developed the most widely recognized model of job characteristics,[7] shown in Figure 7.2. This model recognized that certain job characteristics contribute to certain psychological states and that the strength of employees' need for growth has an important moderating effect. The core job characteristics can be summarized briefly as follows:

1. *Skill variety* refers to the extent to which the job requires the employee to draw from a number of different skills and abilities.

2. *Task identity* refers to whether the job has an identifiable beginning and end. How complete a module of work does the employee perform?
3. *Task significance* involves the importance of the task. It involves both internal significance—how important is the task to the organization?—and external significance—how proud are employees to tell relatives, friends, and neighbors what they do and where they work?
4. *Autonomy* refers to job independence. How much freedom do employees have to, for example, schedule their own work, make decisions, or determine the means to accomplish objectives?
5. *Feedback* refers to objective information about progress and performance and can come from the job itself or from supervisors or an information system.

The critical psychological states can be summarized as follows:

1. *Meaningfulness.* This cognitive state is the degree to which employees experience work as making a valued contribution, as being important and worthwhile.
2. *Responsibility.* This state is concerned with the extent to which employees experience a sense of being personally responsible or accountable for the work being done.
3. *Knowledge of results.* Coming directly from the feedback, this psychological state involves the degree to which employees understand how they are performing in the job.

In essence, the model says that certain job characteristics lead to critical psychological states. That is, skill variety, task identity, and task significance lead to experienced meaningfulness; autonomy leads to the feeling of responsibility; and feedback leads to knowledge of results. The more these three psychological states are present, the more employees will feel good about themselves when they perform well. Hackman states: "The model postulates that internal rewards are obtained by an individual when he *learns* (knowledge of results) that he *personally* (experienced responsibility) has performed well on a task that he *cares* about (experienced meaningfulness)."[8] Hackman then points out that these internal rewards are reinforcing to employees, causing them to perform well. If they don't perform well, they will try harder in order to get the internal rewards that good performance brings. He concludes: "The net result is a self-perpetuating cycle of positive work motivation powered by self-generated rewards. This cycle is predicted to continue until one or more of the three psychological states is no longer present, or until the individual no longer values the internal rewards that derive from good performance."[9]

An example of an enriched job, according to the Hackman-Oldham characteristics model, would be that of a surgeon. Surgeons must draw on a wide variety of skills and abilities; usually surgeons can readily identify the task because they handle patients from beginning to end (that is, they play a role in the diagnosis, perform the operation, and are responsible for postoperative care and follow-up); the job has life-and-death significance; there is a great deal of autonomy, since surgeons have the final word on all decisions concerning patients; and there is clear, direct feedback during the operation itself (real-time monitoring of the vital signs and the "scalpel"-"scalpel" type of feedback communication) and, of course, the patient's recovery and subsequent health determine the success of the operation. Under this explanation, these job characteristics determine the surgeon's considerable motivation, not the needs developed while growing up nor his or her valences, instrumentalities, and expectancies.

At the other extreme would be traditional blue-collar and white-collar jobs. All five job dimensions would be relatively low or nonexistent in the eyes of many such job holders and thus can help explain the motivation problem with these low-level jobs. In other words, the job design, not just the person holding the job, helps explain the motivation to perform under this approach.

Diagnosing and Measuring Task Scope

There are several ways that the Hackman-Oldham model can be used to diagnose the degree of task scope that a job possesses. For instance, a manager could simply assess a particular job by clinically analyzing it according to the five core dimensions, as was done in the example of the surgeon's job discussed above. Others have suggested a specific checklist, which would include such items as the use of inspectors or checkers, labor pools, or narrow spans of control, to help pinpoint deficiencies in the core dimensions.[10] More systematically, Hackman and Oldham have developed a questionnaire, the Job Diagnostic Survey (JDS), to analyze jobs. The questions on this survey yield a quantitative score that can be used to calculate an overall measure of job enrichment, or what is increasingly called *job scope*—to differentiate it from Herzberg-type job enrichment. The formula for this motivating potential score (MPS) is the following:

$$MPS = \left[\frac{\text{skill variety} + \text{task identity} + \text{task significance}}{3} \right] \times \text{autonomy} \times \text{feedback}$$

Notice that the job characteristics of skill variety, task identity, and task significance are combined and divided by 3, while the characteristics of autonomy and feedback stand alone. Also, since skill variety, task identity, and task significance are additive, any one or even two of these characteristics could be completely missing and the person could still experience meaningfulness, but if either autonomy or feedback were missing, the job would offer no motivating potential (MPS = 0) because of the multiplicative relationships.

The JDS is a widely used instrument to measure task characteristics or task scope, but the research on the impact that the motivating potential of a job has on job satisfaction and performance is not that clear. Most of the support for the model comes from Hackman and his colleagues, who claim that people on enriched jobs (according to their characteristics as measured by the JDS) are definitely more motivated and satisfied and, although the evidence is not as strong, may have better attendance and performance effectiveness records.[11] In a recent study, and one of the very few that has looked at the long-term impact, some fairly encouraging results were found. Using about a thousand tellers from thirty-eight banks of a large holding company, the following results were obtained from the job redesign intervention:

1. Perceptions of changed job characteristics increased quickly and held at that level for an extended period. Thus, employees perceive meaningful changes that have been introduced into their jobs and tend to recognize those changes over time.
2. Satisfaction and commitment attitudes increased quickly, but then diminished back to their initial levels.
3. Performance did not increase initially, but did increase significantly over the longer time period. The implication here is that managers and researchers need to be more patient in their evaluation of work redesign interventions.[12]

In addition to this large longitudinal study, a meta-analysis of about 200 studies of the job characteristics model found general support for its structure and for its effects on motivation and satisfaction and performance outcomes.[13] However, recent studies that try to theoretically refine and extend the job characteristics model have mixed results on both the prescribed moderators/critical psychological states[14] (see Figure 7.2) and outcomes.[15] The model also did not hold cross-culturally when it failed to increase the performance of a group of Russian factory workers.[16] Despite these nonsupporting results, the job characteristics model on balance still has considerable positive research evidence, and along with goal setting (covered in the last half of this chapter), remains one of the best application techniques for motivating human resources for performance improvement.

Guidelines for Redesigning Jobs

Specific guidelines such as those found in Figure 7.3 are offered to redesign jobs. Such easily implementable guidelines make the job design area popular and practical for more effective human resource management. An example would be the application in a large department store.[17] In a training session format, the sales employees' jobs were redesigned in the following manner:

1. *Skill variety.* The salespeople were asked to try to think of and use
   a. Different selling approaches
   b. New merchandise displays
   c. Better ways of recording sales and keeping records
2. *Task identity.* The salespeople were asked to
   a. Keep a personal record of daily sales volume in dollars

FIGURE 7.3
Specific guidelines for redesigning jobs for the more effective practice of human resources management.

Core Job Characteristics	Guidelines for Practice
SKILL VARIETY	Provide cross-training / Expand duties requiring more skills
TASK IDENTITY	Give projects / Form work modules
TASK SIGNIFICANCE	Communicate importance of the job / Enhance image of the organization
AUTONOMY	Empower to make decisions / Give more responsibility and accountability
FEEDBACK	Implement information systems / Supervisors give objective, immediate information

    b. Keep a record of number of sales/customers

    c. Mark off an individual display area that they consider their own and keep it complete and orderly

3. *Task significance.* The salespeople were reminded that

    a. Selling a product was the basic overall objective of the store

    b. The appearance of the display area was important to selling

    c. They are "the store" to customers; they were told that courtesy and pleasantness help build the store's reputation and set the stage for future sales

4. *Autonomy.* The salespeople were

    a. Encouraged to develop and use their own unique approach and sales pitch

    b. Allowed freedom to select their own break and lunch times

    c. Encouraged to make suggestions for changes in all phases of the policy and operations

5. *Feedback from the job itself.* Salespeople were

    a. Encouraged to keep personal records of their own sales volume

    b. Encouraged to keep a sales/customer ratio

    c. Reminded that establishing a good rapport with customers is also a success; they were told that if the potential customer leaves with a good feeling about the store and its employees, the salesperson has been successful

6. *Feedback from agents.* Salespeople were encouraged to

    a. Observe and help each other with techniques of selling

    b. Seek out information from their boss and relevant departments on all phases of their jobs

    c. Invite customer reactions and thoughts concerning merchandise, service, and so forth

Both the salespeople's functional (conversing with customers, showing merchandise, handling returns, and so forth) and dysfunctional (socializing with coworkers or visitors, idly standing around, being gone for no legitimate reason) performance behaviors moved in the desired directions and a subanalysis also indicated they were more satisfied. A control group of salespeople, with everything else the same except they did not have their jobs redesigned, showed no change in their performance behaviors. Thus, there is some evidence that the job characteristics approach can be practically applied with desirable performance and satisfaction results. Such well-known companies as 3M, AT&T, Xerox, and Motorola are among those that have actually implemented job design changes in accordance with the job characteristics model.[18]

A Social Information Processing Approach

A social information processing approach (SIPA) to work motivation in general[19] and task design in particular[20] has emerged in recent years. As Salancik and Pfeffer explain it, the basic premise of SIPA is that "individuals, as adaptive organisms, adapt attitudes, behaviors, and beliefs to their social context and to the reality of their own past and present behavior and situation."[21] Thus, according to SIPA, there are three major causes of a jobholder's perceptions, attitudes, and actual behavior:

1. The jobholder's cognitive evaluation of the real task environment

2. The jobholder's past actions, including reinforcement history and learning

3. The information that the immediate social context provides

Salancik and Pfeffer give the third point above the most weight. They suggest that social information or social cues are much more dominant in how jobholders view their tasks than the real task environment or past actions are.

The SIPA model of job design is quite complex. As explained by Moorhead and Griffin, it suggests that through a variety of processes, commitment (discussed in Chapter 5), rationalization (self-interpretation of behavior), and information saliency (or importance) are defined. These processes include the following:

1. *Choice.* The freedom to choose different behaviors
2. *Revocability.* The ability to change behaviors
3. *Publicness.* The degree of visibility to others
4. *Explicitness.* The ability to be clear and obvious
5. *Social norms and expectations.* The knowledge of what others expect from someone
6. *External priming.* The receiving of cues from others[22]

These attributional processes combine with social information (from others and the organizational environment) to form and influence the jobholder's perceptions, attitudes, and behaviors.

The SIPA model of job design has generated considerable research over the last several years.[23] As with the job characteristics approach, results have been mixed.[24] Some studies do support the notion that social cues, such as negative versus positive coworker comments, may be more important to the way employees perceive their tasks than characteristics such as whether the job is enriched or unenriched. In other words, as in other areas of organizational behavior, the importance of the social environment is becoming recognized in the job design area. However, most recently, research suggests that an integrated approach to job design that includes both objective job characteristics and social information may be the most effective.[25]

QUALITY OF WORK LIFE AND SOCIOTECHNICAL DESIGN

So far, the discussion of job design has revolved mainly around job characteristics, job enrichment, and social information processing. The concern for quality of work life (QWL) and the accompanying sociotechnical approach to job design take a more macro perspective.

Unlike the job enrichment and social information processing approaches, QWL is not based on a particular theory, nor does it advocate a particular technique for application. Instead, QWL is more concerned with the overall climate of work. One analysis of QWL described it as "(1) a concern about the impact of work on people as well as on organizational effectiveness, and (2) the idea of participation in organizational problem solving and decision making."[26] Recent research evidence indicates that when employees have such a participatory, problem-solving approach to QWL, they are both more committed to their organization and, if union members, to their union.[27]

The overriding purpose of QWL is to change the climate at work so that the human-technological-organizational interface leads to a better quality of work life. Although how this is actually accomplished and exactly what is meant by a better *quality* of work life are still unclear, there are a number of analyses and applications of the closely associated sociotechnical approach to job design.

Unlike the more general concept of QWL, the sociotechnical approach to job design (which is sometimes even equated with QWL) has a systems theoretical base. In particular, the sociotechnical approach to job design is concerned with the interface and harmony between personal, social, and technological functioning.[28] In application, this translates into the redesign of technological work processes and the formation of autonomous, self-regulating work groups or teams. A few widely publicized projects have used this approach.

The Volvo Project

The sociotechnical approach to job design has an international flavor, and although the Swedish automaker Saab pioneered the use of autonomous work groups to work on automobile subassembly, the more widely publicized example is that of a Volvo automobile plant in Sweden. When Pehr Gyllenhammar took over as the head of Volvo, Sweden's largest employer, he was convinced that the very serious turnover and absenteeism problems were symptomatic of the values of the employees. Hand in hand with the emerging values of society as a whole, the Volvo employees were demanding more meaningful work—better pay and security, but also participation in the decision-making process and self-regulation. But the technological work process for making automobiles (that is, the assembly lines) did not allow such values to be expressed, and the results were turnover, absenteeism, and low-quality performance.

Under Gyllenhammar's leadership, which took a sociotechnical approach, technological changes were made to reflect more of a natural module of work rather than a continuous work flow, and autonomous work groups were formed. These groups consisted of five to twelve workers who elected their own supervisors and scheduled, assigned, and inspected their own work. Group rather than individual piece rates were used, and all group members made the same amount, except the elected supervisor.

This sociotechnical approach (changing the technological process and using autonomous, self-regulating work groups) was at first applied on a piecemeal basis around the company. Then the new Kalmar assembly plant was completely redesigned along the lines of a sociotechnical approach. On the technological side, the conventional continuous assembly line was changed so that the work remains stationary. A special carrier was developed to transport the car to the various work groups. On the social side, about twenty-five groups made up of about twenty members each perform work on the various modules of an automobile (electrical system, instrumentation, steering and controls, interior, and so forth). These work teams organize any way they want, and they contract with management to deliver a certain number of products per day, for example, brake systems installed or interiors finished. The workers have almost complete control over their own work, scheduling the pace of work and break times. Also important, these teams inspect their own work, and feedback is given to each group via a TV screen at the workstation.

In line with more general quality of work life objectives, a more humane work climate was designed for this Volvo plant. The plant layout is set up to be very light and airy and have a low noise level. There are carpeted "coffee corners," where the groups take their breaks, and there are well-equipped changing rooms.

After this approach to job design was installed at Volvo, turnover and absenteeism were reduced, and quality of work life was reportedly improved. To date, however, no systematic analysis has demonstrated that casual inferences can be made. However, the Volvo top management feel that their new approach to job design has been successful. The latest update from those at the scene is that there have been "false starts, errors, outright failures and, periodically, brilliant breakthroughs."[29] Objectively, the fact is that Kalmar, where QWL is used, has the lowest assembly costs of all Volvo plants.

The General Foods Pet Food Plant

Although the Volvo project is the most famous historically, a few companies in the United States also tried a sociotechnical approach to job design. Probably the most widely reported example was that of the General Foods plant in Topeka, Kansas, which produces Gaines pet food. Similar to the Kalmar Volvo plant, this Topeka plant was technologically designed to be compatible with autonomous work groups. The groups were set up in basically the same way as those at the Volvo plant. They had shared responsibility and worked for a coach rather than a supervisor. Status symbols such as parking privileges were abolished.

Initially, the reports on this General Foods project were very favorable. The employees themselves expressed very positive attitudes toward this new approach to work, and management reported that after implementing the project, 35 percent fewer employees were needed to run the plant, quality rejects dipped 92 percent below the industry norm, annual savings of $600,000 resulted from the reduction of variable manufacturing costs, and turnover dropped below the company average.[30] However, more recent reports do not paint such a rosy picture.[31] Some former employees at the Topeka plant indicate that the approach has steadily eroded. Apparently, some managers at the plant are openly hostile to the project because it has undermined their power, authority, and decision-making flexibility. The project became a media event, and some of the results need tempering.

Modern Approaches to QWL: Self-Managed Teams

Both the Volvo project and the Topeka General Foods plant are historically important, but more recently QWL has evolved into and has become closely associated with autonomous, or self-managed, teams. Just a few years ago, self-managed teams were being used only in a very few innovative companies such as Procter and Gamble, Digital Equipment, and TRW. However, now, because of the influence of the Japanese and the need to become more competitive in the new paradigm discussed in Chapter 1, more and more companies are turning to this approach to QWL. There are many success stories from well-known companies such as General Mills, Federal Express, and 3M on how their teams and an empowerment strategy have greatly contributed to cost savings and improved productivity.[32] The accompanying TQM in Action: Power to the People provides real-world examples of firms that employ an empowerment strategy to create a higher quality of work life for their employees.

However, along with the successes are some new problems. One such problem is increased stress and conflict. Here are how these problems are explained at Corning Glass, with about 3000 teams in operation:

> "People problems are the issue," says Sherri Hadrich, a 29-year-old kiln operator. For instance, some teams have felt pulled down by one lazy member. "If there's conflict," she says, "we're expected to resolve it," instead of turning to a supervisor. "If someone isn't feeling well or pulling their weight, we can't let it go on or it'll just be a bigger problem," she adds, noting how it's difficult to confront a coworker. (A new training course focuses on how to get along with teammates.)[33]

**TQM
in Action**

Power to the People

One of the lessons that American management has learned in the total quality movement is that downsizing is not enough. Anyone can come into a company and reduce the number of workers, come up with a lean structure, and reduce short-run costs. However, getting the employees to do the work over the long run, and do it well, is sometimes another story. Quite often, those who remain after downsizing are concerned that they too will be let go. As a result, they do not try very hard. Instead of getting improved quality, the firm ends up with less. For a few companies, a new rule is being followed: Eliminate work, not the workers. This means cutting out wasteful procedures and revising operating methods while giving the workers more authority to handle those matters that directly affect productivity. A good example is found in the case of Kodak.

For six years, Kodak had tried to cut costs, but this approach had been both difficult and slow. Then the company introduced a supplemental method. It began by empowering its operating personnel and making them responsible for more of what happened in the factory. For example, at its precision components manufacturing division, assembly workers who make x-ray cassettes and spools, canisters, and cartons for Kodak film now arrange their own hours, keep track of their productivity, and fix their machines. People who used to run punch presses for eight hours a day now coach fellow team members in how to use statistical process controls. These empowered workers also meet with suppliers, interview prospective recruits, and help manage just-in-time inventory. Result: The Kodak team has been able to cut production time for x-ray cassettes by nearly 67 percent with an operation more efficient than ever. By giving the personnel control over their operations and allowing them to do things their own way, Kodak is managing to create a more profitable company.

Empowerment has also proved useful to many other firms that are using TQM. For example, Coors uses empowerment to improve both new-product development as well as customer service. The Ritz-Carlton hotel chain employs it in helping employees address customer problems. AT&T Universal Card uses it to both reduce costs and improve customer service. Motorola goes even further, insisting that its quality teams all accept empowered positions and the responsibility that goes with this authority. The empowerment strategy not only has improved the quality delivered to these firms' customers but also has been able to drive down their costs and increase their profitability.

Besides the popular press testimonials of the successes and failures of self-managed teams and QWL in general, there is a need for more systematic evaluations before any broad conclusions can be drawn. Chapter 9 on group dynamics and teams makes such an analysis. There are many other approaches to QWL besides self-managed teams, and these are given attention in subsequent chapters. For now, however, the other major motivation application technique of goal setting is given attention.

GOAL SETTING

Goal setting is often given as an example of how the field of organizational behavior should progress from a sound theoretical foundation to sophisticated research to the actual application of more effective management practice. There has been considerable theoretical development of goal setting, coming mainly from the cognitively based work of Edwin Locke and his colleagues. To test the theory, there has been considerable research in both laboratory and field settings on the various facets of goal setting. Finally, and important to an applied field such as organizational behavior, goal setting has become an effective tool for the practice of human resources management and an overall performance system approach.

Theoretical Background of Goal Setting

A 1968 paper by Locke is usually considered to be the seminal work on a theory of goal setting.[34] He gives considerable credit to Ryan[35] for stimulating his thinking on the role that intention plays in human behavior, and he also suggests that goal-setting theory really goes back to scientific management at the turn of the century. He credits its first exponent, Frederick W. Taylor, with being the "father of employee motivation theory,"[36] and he says that Taylor's use "of tasks was a forerunner of modern day goal setting."[37]

Although Locke argues that expectancy theories of work motivation originally ignored goal setting and were nothing more than "cognitive hedonism,"[38] his theoretical formulation for goal setting is very similar. He basically accepts the purposefulness of behavior, which comes out of Tolman's cognitive theorizing (see Chapter 1), and the importance of values, or valence, and consequences. Thus, as in the expectancy theories of work motivation (see Chapter 6), *values and value judgments,* which he defines as the things the individual acts upon to gain and/or to keep, are important cognitive determinants of behavior. He then goes on to say that emotions or desires are the way the person experiences these values. In addition to values, *intentions* or *goals* play an important role as cognitive determinants of behavior. It is here, of course, where Locke's theory of goal setting goes beyond expectancy theories of work motivation. He feels that people strive to attain goals in order to satisfy their emotions and desires. Goals provide a directional nature to people's behavior and guide their thoughts and actions to one outcome rather than another. The individual then responds and performs according to these intentions or goals, even if the goals are not attained. Consequences, feedback, or reinforcement are the result of these responses.

Figure 7.4 summarizes the goal-setting theory. Reviews of the literature generally provide considerable support for the theory.[39] A survey of scholars in the field of organizational behavior was conducted to rate fifteen major work-motivation theories on the criteria of scientific validity and practical usefulness. Goal-setting theory was ranked first in validity and second in practical usefulness.[40]

As previously noted, except for the concept of intentions or goals, Locke's theory is very similar to the other process theories (most notably the expectancy theories). In particular, recent refinements of goal theory involving difficulty[41] and overall goal-setting research[42] use the concepts of expectancy, valence, and instrumentality, as defined in Chapter 6. Also, attribution theory, as discussed in Chapter 6, has been applied to goal setting.[43] Although the expectancy theories are frequently

FIGURE 7.4
Locke's goal-setting theory of work motivation.

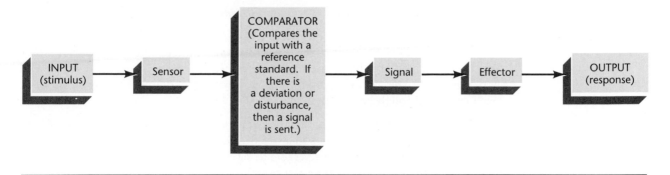

FIGURE 7.5
Control theory.

used as a theoretical foundation for goal setting, Locke carefully points out that goal setting is not the only, or necessarily the most important, concept of work motivation. He notes that the concepts of need and value are the more fundamental concepts of work motivation and are, along with the person's knowledge and premises, what determine goals.

Unlike many other theorists, Locke is continually refining and developing his theory. Recently he has given attention to the role that commitment plays in the theory. He recognized from the beginning that if there is no commitment to goals, goal setting will not work. However, to clarify some of the confusion surrounding its use, Locke and his colleagues define commitment as "one's attachment to or determination to reach a goal, regardless of the goal's origin" and developed a cognitive model to explain the process.[44] Recently it has been suggested that commitment is a moderator of the goal-performance relationship[45] and a meta-analysis found that goal commitment significantly affects goal achievement.[46]

Locke is an ardent supporter of the cognitive interpretation of behavior and is an outspoken critic of other theories, for he says that goal setting is really the underlying explanation for the other theories—whether that be Vroom's VIE theory, Maslow's or Herzberg's motivation theories, or—especially—operant-based behaviorism.[47] He is also critical of more recent *control theory*,[48] and feels that it—like earlier theories—can be interpreted in terms of goal theory.

Control theory is briefly mentioned at the end of Chapter 6 as a recent motivation theory and is depicted in Figure 7.5. Locke and Latham translate this form of control theory into goal theory as follows: "The input is feedback from previous performance, the reference signal is the goal, the comparator is the individual's conscious judgment, and the effector or response is his or her subsequent action which works to reduce the discrepancy between the goal and performance."[49] This, of course, is logical, but by the same token, control theory or the other theories could also be used to explain goal-setting theory.

Although Locke is critical of operant-based behaviorism as being too mechanistic, he is supportive of Bandura's expanded social learning theory (explained in Chapters 1 and 8) and more recent social cognitive theory[50] (how people come to understand what others are like and explain others' behavior) as being compatible with goal-setting theory. In particular, he feels that social cognitive theory not only includes goal setting but adds the important dimensions of role modeling, with significant effects on goal choice and goal commitment and self-efficacy (covered in Chapters 4, 6, and 11)—which affects goal choice, goal commitment, and response to feedback.[51]

Research on the Impact of Goal Setting

Locke's theory has generated considerable research. In particular, a series of laboratory studies by Locke and his colleagues and a series of field studies by Gary Latham and his colleagues have been carried out to test the linkage between goal setting and performance.[52] The following provides some practical guidelines for how to improve performance through goal setting:

1. *Specific goals* are better than vague or general goals such as "do your best." In other words, giving a salesperson a specific quota or a worker an exact number of units to produce should be preferable to setting a goal such as "try as hard as you can" or "try to do better than last year."
2. *Difficult, challenging goals* are better than relatively easy, mundane goals. However, these goals must be reachable and not so hard to attain that they would be frustrating.
3. *"Owned" and accepted goals* arrived at through participation seem preferable to assigned goals. Although the research is not as clear here as in the first two guidelines,[53] there is evidence that people who set their goals through a participative process, and who thus own their own goals, will perform better than those who are told what their goals are going to be. As the accompanying Application Example: Making Personal Goal Setting Pay Off demonstrates, personal goals can lead individuals to career success.
4. *Objective, timely feedback about progress toward goals* is preferable to no feedback. Although researchers are still trying to understand the exact effect of feedback[54] (discussed further in Chapter 8), it is probably fair to say that feedback is a necessary but not sufficient condition for successful application of goal setting.

To give some idea of the tremendous backup for these "core findings," Locke and Latham recently concluded the following:

> Goal-setting theory is based on the results of some 393 findings on the goal difficulty and difficulty versus do best aspects of the theory alone. The success rate or partial success rate of these studies, regardless of study quality, is over 90 percent. The core findings of the theory are based on data from close to forty thousand subjects in eight countries; eighty-eight different tasks; numerous types of performance measures; laboratory and field settings; experimental and correlational designs; time spans ranging from one minute to three years; studies of assigned, self-set, and participatively set goals; and data from the group and organizational as well as individual level of analysis.[55]

Although the practical guidelines from goal-setting theory and research are as sound as any in the entire field of organizational behavior, it must be remembered that, as with any complex phenomenon, there still appear to be many important moderating variables in the relationship between goal setting and performance, and there are some contradictory findings.[56] For example, a study by Latham and Saari found that a supportive management style had an important moderating effect and that, contrary to the results of previous studies, specific goals did not lead to better performance than a generalized goal such as "do your best."[57] However, another study did find a highly significant relationship between goal level and performance.[58] Another recent analysis indicated there are also some unexplored areas, such as the distinction between quantity and quality goals,[59] and task complexity,[60] that limit the application of goal setting.

There are also some practical limitations in goal setting. For example, setting difficult goals increases the level of risk managers and employees are willing to take,

**Application
Example**

Making Personal Goal Setting Pay Off

Entrepreneurs have long been the focal point of interest by researchers seeking to explain why some people are successful in business and others are not. However, one does not have to be an entrepreneur to be a success in life. Success can often be achieved by simply identifying and pursuing carefully chosen personal goals. These goals not only help people perform better, but can also be an important means of improving career opportunities and getting top dollar. For example, some goals that seem to have particular value to those interested in building a reputation as an expert in their career include the following:

1. *Get something published in your area of expertise.* Examples are writing an article or, even better, a book. Publications help one's expertise and are a good credential to have. The best publisher to use is one that currently markets to those in related career fields. Hence, the publication is likely to be read by relevant others, and the author's reputation will spread. Another good outlet is the local newspaper, which often publishes business-related articles. Many papers have a business section that caters specifically to those interested in picking up the latest information and tips.
2. *Be a lecturer or panelist.* This is another good way to get publicity, and there are many opportunities. Three common ones are guest teaching at a local university, being a luncheon speaker at a local club or professional group, and serving as a panelist for a job seminar at a local college.
3. *Get media coverage.* Work to get on radio or TV programs. Quite often local programmers are looking for people to interview or to discuss some recent topic of interest. If you can become known as a local expert in some area that is continually in the news, such as productivity problems or how to manage people more effectively, you will be asked back time and again.
4. *Use professional associations.* The best way to become known as an expert in your area is by receiving recognition from your peers in professional associations. By joining these associations and becoming active first at the local- and then national-level meetings, you ensure that others in your field get to know who you are and what you stand for. As a result, your visibility in the marketplace increases and so do your chances of being tapped for more important, higher-paying jobs either in your company or with the competition.

---

and this increase may be counterproductive.[61] Also, a recent study found that goals inhibited subjects from helping others who were requesting assistance, which has implications for teamwork.[62] Other studies have found that difficult goals may lead to stress, put a perpetual ceiling on performance, cause the employees to ignore nongoal areas, and encourage short-range thinking, dishonesty, or cheating.[63] However, Locke and Latham do provide specific guidelines of how these potential pitfalls can be overcome by better communication, rewards, and setting examples.[64] On balance, there has been impressive support for the positive impact of setting specific, difficult goals that are accepted and of providing feedback on progress toward goals.

The Application of Goal Setting to Organizational System Performance

A logical extension of goal setting is the traditionally used management-by-objectives, or MBO, approach to planning, control, personnel appraisal, and overall system performance. This approach has been around for over thirty years and thus

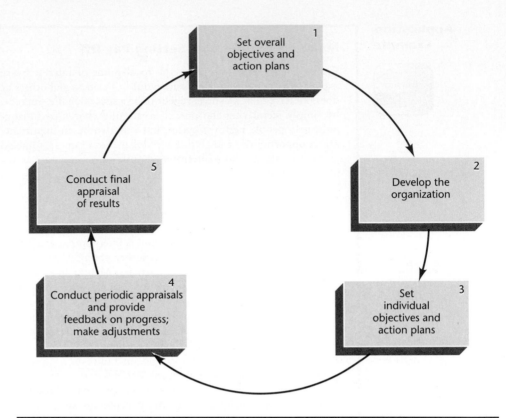

FIGURE 7.6
The application of goal setting to system performance.

preceded the theory and research on goal setting per se. Management by objectives is usually attributed to Peter Drucker, who coined the term and suggested that a systematic approach to setting of objectives and appraising by results would lead to improved organizational performance and employee satisfaction. Today, the term "MBO" may no longer be used. Instead, MBO has evolved into an overall systems performance approach using goal setting and appraisal by results. For example, Locke and Latham recently noted that "MBO can be viewed as goal setting applied to the macro or organizational level."[65]

The application of goal setting and appraisal by results of overall organizational systems generally follows the series of systematic steps outlined in Figure 7.6. As shown, once the overall objectives have been set and the organization is developed to the point of accommodating the performance system, individual objectives are set. These individual objectives are determined by each manager-subordinate pair, starting at the top and going down as far as the system is to be implemented. The scenario for this process would be something like the following: The boss would contact each of his or her subordinates and say:

> As you know, we have completed our system performance improvement orientation and development program, and it is now time to set individual objectives. I would like you to develop by next Tuesday a proposed set of objectives for your area of responsibility. Remember that your set of objectives should be in line with the organization's overall objectives, which you have a copy of, and should be able to contribute to the objectives that you interact with, namely, my objectives, the other units' objectives on your same level, and your subordinates' objectives. Your

objectives should be stated in quantifiable, measurable terms and should have a target date. I will also have some suggestions that I think should be given top priority for your area of responsibility. We will sit down and have an open give-and-take session until we reach a *mutually* agreeable set of objectives for your area of responsibility.

In line with the goal-setting research, these objectives should be specific, difficult, and accepted. Like the overall objectives, this set of individual objectives should also be accompanied by action plans developed to spell out how the objectives are to be accomplished.

Although the goal-setting dimension is most closely associated with this approach to system performance, as shown in Figure 7.6, feedback and appraisal by results also play an important role. Individuals will be given feedback and will be appraised on the basis of how they perform in accordance with the objectives that are set. This feedback and appraisal process takes place on both a periodic (at least every quarter in most systems) and an annual basis. The appraisal sessions attempt to be diagnostic rather than purely evaluative. This means simply that the subordinate's manager assesses the reasons why objectives were either attained or not attained, rather than giving punishments or rewards for failure or success in meeting objectives.

Periodic reviews are conducted in order to provide feedback and evaluate progress toward the attainment of objectives. They give the opportunity to make the necessary changes in objectives. Every organization is operating in such a dynamic environment that objectives set at the beginning of the period (usually the fiscal year) may be rendered obsolete in a few months because of changing conditions. Priorities and conditions are constantly changing; these must be monitored in the periodic review sessions, and the needed changes must be made. Constant revision of the individual objectives and, to a lesser degree, of the overall objectives makes a living system that is adaptable to change. At the annual review session, an overall diagnosis and evaluation is made according to results attained, and the system starts over again.

The research results on MBO-type performance systems have been mixed.[66] The most recent comprehensive analyses conclude that these overall goal-setting systems have a slightly positive effect on employee satisfaction, but a much larger, but still modest, effect on performance.[67]

Summary

This chapter deals with two of the most important application areas that have emerged in the field of organizational behavior and human resources management. The first part examines job design. Although the concern for designing jobs goes back to the scientific management movement at the turn of the century, the recent concern for the quality of work life (QWL) has led to renewed interest in, and research on, job design. The older job engineering and job enlargement and rotation approaches have given way to a job enrichment approach. Based primarily on the work of Herzberg, job enrichment has been popular (at least in the literature) but may be overly simplistic.

The more recent approach to job design tries to determine the important job characteristics that relate to psychological or motivational states that in turn relate to employee satisfaction and performance. Characteristics such as skill variety, task identity, task significance, autonomy, and feedback do seem to be related to employee satisfaction and quality of work. But the way employees perceive these characteristics and the importance of moderating variables such as growth-need strength are being shown to have an important impact on the relationship between job scope and job satisfaction and employee performance. Alternative models such as the social information processing approach (SIPA) have also emerged to account for social effects. Also, increased attention is being given to the impact of more macro-oriented variables such as organization structure and technology. More in line with this macro perspective and incorporating QWL concerns is the sociotechnical approach to job design. Sociotechnical projects at Volvo in Sweden and at General Foods and other companies in this country have important historical significance. Most recently, self-managed teams are having a surge of interest as companies try to use Japanese-style management approaches to meet their competitive problems. These traditional (Volvo and General Foods) and modern applications of self-managed teams have reportedly been very successful. Yet, as is true of the other techniques discussed in this text, more systematic research is needed for the future.

The last part of the chapter deals with the applications-oriented areas of goal setting in general and an MBO-type performance system approach in particular. Basing his approach on a cognitive perspective, Locke has developed a goal-setting theory of motivation. This theory emphasizes the important relationship between goals and performance. Laboratory and field studies have generally verified this relationship. In particular, the most effective performance seems to result when specific, difficult goals are accepted and when feedback on progress and results is provided. An extension and systematic application of the goal-setting approach is MBO, which has evolved into a total performance system approach with a positive, but modest, impact on satisfaction and performance.

Questions for Discussion and Review

1. Compare and contrast the engineering versus the enrichment approach to job design.
2. What are the core job characteristics in the Hackman-Oldham model? How do you calculate the motivating potential of a job? How would a professor's job and a janitor's job measure up on these characteristics? Be specific in your answer.
3. Describe the sociotechnical project at Volvo. Would you rather work there or at the typical automobile plant in this country? Why?
4. Considering that former employees at the General Foods plant indicate there may be some problems with sociotechnical design, what do you think the future holds for this type of approach? Do you think QWL will and should be legislated? Why?
5. In your own words, describe the theory behind goal setting. What has the research generally found in testing this theory?
6. Summarize the five basic steps of an overall performance systems approach using goal setting. What have been the research findings on this approach?

Footnote References and Supplemental Readings

1. Don Hellriegel, John W. Slocum, Jr., and Richard W. Woodman, *Organizational Behavior*, 5th ed., West, St. Paul, Minn., 1989, p. 334.

2. See Cynthia D. Fisher, "Boredom at Work: A Neglected Concept," *Human Relations*, March 1993, p. 395

3. For example, see Ronald Henkoff, "Companies That Train Best," *Fortune,* Mar. 22, 1993, pp. 62–75.

4. Alecia Swasy and Carol Hymowitz, "The Workplace Revolution," *The Wall Street Journal,* Feb. 9, 1990, p. R6.

5. John B. Miner, *Organizational Behavior,* Random House, New York, 1988, p. 201.

6. Michael A. Campion and Carol L. McClelland, "Follow-Up and Extension of the Interdisciplinary Costs and Benefits of Enlarged Jobs," *Journal of Applied Psychology,* June 1993, pp. 339–351.

7. J. Richard Hackman and Greg R. Oldham, "Motivation Through the Design of Work: Test of a Theory," *Organizational Behavior and Human Performance,* vol. 16, 1976, pp. 250–279.

8. J. Richard Hackman, "Work Design," in J. Richard Hackman and J. Lloyd Suttle (eds.), *Improving Life at Work,* Goodyear, Santa Monica, Calif., 1977, p. 129.

9. Ibid., p. 130.

10. David Whitsett, "Where Are Your Enriched Jobs?" *Harvard Business Review,* January–February 1975, pp. 74–80.

11. J. Richard Hackman, Greg R. Oldham, Robert Janson, and Kenneth Purdy, "A New Strategy for Job Enrichment," *California Management Review,* Summer 1975, pp. 55–71.

12. Ricky W. Griffin, "Work Redesign Effects on Employee Attitudes and Behaviors: A Long-Term Field Experiment," *Academy of Management Best Papers Proceedings,* 1989, pp. 216–217.

13. Y. Fried and G. R. Ferris, "The Validity of the Job Characteristics Model: A Review and Meta-Analysis," *Personnel Psychology,* vol. 40, 1987, pp. 287–322.

14. For example, see Gary Johns, Jia Lin Xie, and Yongqing Fang, "Mediating and Moderating Effects in Job Design," *Journal of Management,* vol. 18, 1992, pp. 657–676; Robert Tiegs, Lois E. Tetrick, and Yitzhak Fried, "Growth Need Strength and Context Satisfactions as Moderators of the Relations of the Job Characteristics Model," *Journal of Management,* vol. 18, 1992, pp. 575–593; and Joseph E. Champoux, "A Multivariate Analysis of Curvilinear Relationships Among Job Scope, Work Context Satisfactions, and Affective Outcomes," *Human Relations,* January 1992, p. 87.

15. John Kelly, "Does Job Re-Design Theory Explain Job Re-Design Outcomes?" *Human Relations,* August 1992, pp. 753–774.

16. Dianne H. B. Welsh, Fred Luthans, and Steven M. Sommer, "Managing Russian Factory Workers: The Impact of U.S.-Based Behavioral and Participative Techniques," *Academy of Management Journal,* February 1993, pp. 58–79.

17. Fred Luthans, Barbara Kemmerer, Robert Paul, and Lew Taylor, "The Impact of a Job Redesign Intervention on Salespersons' Observed Performance Behaviors," *Group and Organization Studies,* March 1987, pp. 55–72.

18. Gregory Moorhead and Ricky W. Griffin, *Organizational Behavior,* 2d ed., Houghton Mifflin, Boston, 1989, p. 238

19. Terence R. Mitchell, "Motivation: New Directions for Theory, Research and Practice," *Academy of Management Review,* January 1982, p. 80.

20. Gerald Salancik and Jeffrey Pfeffer, "A Social Information Processing Approach to Job Attitudes and Task Design," *Administrative Science Quarterly,* June 1978, pp. 224–253.

21. Ibid., p. 226.

22. Moorhead and Griffin, op. cit., p. 245. For those wishing a more technical discussion, see Robert S. Wyer, Jr., and Thomas K. Srull, *Memory and Cognition in Its Social Context,* Erlbaum, Hillsdale, N.J., 1989, Chap. 2, "A General Model of Social Information Processing," pp. 13–32.

23. See Gary J. Blau and Ralph Katerberg, "Toward Enhancing Research with the Social Information Processing Approach to Job Design," *Academy of Management Review,* October 1982, pp. 543–550; William H. Glick, G. Douglas Jenkins, and Nina Gupta, "Method Versus Substance: How Strong Are Underlying Relationships Between Job Characteristics and Attitudinal Outcomes?" *Academy of Management Journal,* September 1986, pp. 441–464; and Joe G. Thomas, "Sources of Social Information," *Human Relations,* vol. 39, no. 9, 1986, pp. 855–870.

24. Joe Thomas and Ricky W. Griffin, "The Social Information Processing Model of Task Design: A Review of the Literature," *Academy of Management Review,* October 1983, pp. 672–682.

25. Ricky W. Griffin, Thomas S. Bateman, Sandy J. Wayne, and Thomas C. Head, "Objective and Social Factors as Determinants of Task Perceptions and Responses: An Integrated Perspective and Empirical Investigation," *Academy of Management Journal,* September 1987, pp. 501–523, and Donald J. Campbell, "Task Complexity: A Review and Analysis," *Academy of Management Review,* January 1988, pp. 40–52.

26. David A. Nadler and Edward E. Lawler III, "Quality of Work Life: Perspectives and Directions," *Organizational Dynamics,* Winter 1983, p. 26.

27. Mitchell W. Fields and James W. Thacker, "Influence of Quality of Work Life on Company and Union Commitment," *Academy of Management Journal,* June 1992, pp. 439–450.

28. Raymond A. Katzell and Donna E. Thompson,

"Work Motivation: Theory and Practice," *American Psychologist,* February 1990, p. 145.

29. Berth Jönsson and Alden G. Lank, "Volvo: A Report on the Workshop on Production Technology and Quality of Working Life," *Human Resources Management,* Winter 1985, p. 463.

30. Richard E. Walton, "How to Counter Alienation in the Plant," *Harvard Business Review,* November-December 1972, p. 77.

31. "Stonewalling Plant Democracy," *Business Week,* Mar. 28, 1977, pp. 78–81, and Lyle Yorks and David Whitsett, "Hawthorne, Topeka, and the Issue of Science Versus Advocacy in Organizational Behavior," *Academy of Management Review,* January 1985, pp. 24–26.

32. Brian Dumaine, "Who Needs a Boss?" *Fortune,* May 7, 1990, pp. 52–53.

33. Swasy and Hymowitz, op. cit., p. R8.

34. Edwin A. Locke, "Toward a Theory of Task Motivation and Incentives," *Organizational Behavior and Human Performance,* May 1968, pp. 157–189.

35. T. A. Ryan and P. C. Smith, *Principles of Industrial Psychology,* Ronald, New York, 1954, and T. A. Ryan, *International Behavior,* Ronald, New York, 1970.

36. Edwin A. Locke, "The Ubiquity of the Technique of Goal Setting in Theories and Approaches to Employee Motivation," *Academy of Management Review,* July 1978, p. 600.

37. Edwin A. Locke, "The Ideas of Frederick W. Taylor: An Evaluation," *Academy of Management Review,* January 1982, p. 16.

38. Edwin A. Locke, "Personnel Attitudes and Motivation," *Annual Review of Psychology,* vol. 26, 1975, pp. 457–480, 596–598.

39. A. J. Mento, R. P. Steele, and R. J. Karren, "A Meta-Analytic Study of the Effects of Goal Setting on Task Performance: 1966–1984," *Organizational Behavior and Human Decision Processes,* vol. 39, 1987, pp. 52–83.

40. C. Lee and P. C. Earley, "Comparative Peer Evaluations of Organizational Behavior Theories," College of Business Administration, Northeastern University, Boston, 1988. This study is reported in Edwin A. Locke and Gary P. Latham, *A Theory of Goal Setting and Task Performance,* Prentice-Hall, Englewood Cliffs, N.J., 1990, p. 46.

41. Anthony J. Mento, Howard J. Klein, and Edwin A. Locke, "Relationship of Goal Level to Valence and Instrumentality," *Journal of Applied Psychology,* August 1992, pp. 395–405, and K. Dow Scott and Anthony M. Townsend, "A Test of Eden's Expectancy/Goal Difficulty Model Among Sales Representatives," *Academy of Management Best Papers Proceedings,* 1992, pp. 242–246.

42. Mark E. Tubbs, Donna M. Boehne, and James G. Dahl, "Expectancy, Valence, and Motivational Force Functions in Goal-Setting Research: An Empirical Test," *Journal of Applied Psychology,* June 1993, pp. 361–373.

43. Locke, "Personnel Attitudes and Motivation," pp. 457–480, 597–598.

44. Edwin A. Locke, Gary P. Latham, and Miriam Erez, "The Determinants of Goal Commitment," *Academy of Management Review,* January 1988, p. 24.

45. Mark E. Tubbs, "Commitment as a Moderator of the Goal-Performance Relation: A Case for Clearer Construct Definition," *Journal of Applied Psychology,* February 1993, pp. 86–97.

46. J. C. Wofford, Vicki L. Goodwin, and Steven Premack, "Meta-Analysis of the Antecedents of Personal Goal Level and of the Antecedents and Consequences of Goal Commitment," *Journal of Management,* September 1992, pp. 595–615.

47. See Edwin A. Locke, "The Myths of Behavior Mod in Organizations," *Academy of Management Review,* October 1977, pp. 543–553, and Edwin A. Locke, "Resolved: Attitudes and Cognitive Processes Are Necessary Elements in Motivational Models," in Barbara Karmel (ed.), *Point and Counterpoint in Organizational Behavior,* Dryden Press, Hinsdale, Ill., 1980, pp. 19–42.

48. See M. A. Campion and R. G. Lord, "A Control System Conceptualization of the Goal-Setting and Changing Process," *Organizational Behavior and Human Performance,* vol. 30, 1982, pp. 265–287; R. G. Lord and P. J. Hanges, "A Control System Model of Organizational Motivation: Theoretical Development and Applied Implications," *Behavioral Science,* vol. 32, pp. 161–178; and M. E. Hyland, "Motivational Control Theory: An Integrative Framework," *Journal of Personality and Social Psychology,* vol. 55, 1988, pp. 642–651.

49. Edwin A. Locke and Gary P. Latham, *A Theory of Goal Setting and Task Performance,* Prentice-Hall, Englewood Cliffs, N.J., 1990, p. 19.

50. Albert Bandura, *Social Foundations of Thought and Action,* Prentice-Hall, Englewood Cliffs, N.J., 1986.

51. Locke and Latham, *A Theory of Goal Setting,* pp. 23–24.

52. Locke, "Toward a Theory of Task Motivation and Incentives," summarizes the laboratory studies; Gary P. Latham and Gary A. Yukl, "A Review of the Research on the Application of Goal Setting in Organizations," *Academy of Management Journal,* December 1975, pp. 824–845, summarize the field studies. Comprehensive summaries of this research can be found in Edwin A. Locke, Karylle A. Shaw, Lise M. Saari, and Gary P. Latham, "Goal Setting and

Task Performance: 1969–1980," *Psychological Bulletin*, July 1981, pp. 125–152; Gary P. Latham and Thomas W. Lee, "Goal Setting," in Edwin A. Locke (ed.), *Generalizing from Laboratory to Field Settings*, Lexington Books, Lexington, Mass., 1986, pp. 101–117; and Mark E. Tubbs, "Goal Setting: A Meta-Analytic Examination of the Empirical Evidence," *Journal of Applied Psychology*, vol. 71, no. 3, 1986, pp. 474–483.

53. For example, see Gary P. Latham and Gary A. Yukl, "The Effects of Assigned and Participative Goal Setting on Performance and Job Satisfaction," *Journal of Applied Psychology*, April 1976, pp. 166–171, and Katherine I. Miller and Peter Monge, "Participation, Satisfaction, and Productivity: A Meta-Analytic Review," *Academy of Management Journal*, December 1986, pp. 727–753.

54. For example, see Poppy Lauretta McLeod, Jeffrey K. Liker, and Sharon A. Lobel, "Process Feedback in Task Groups: An Application of Goal Setting," *Journal of Applied Behavioral Science*, March 1992, pp. 15–41.

55. Locke and Latham, *A Theory of Goal Setting*, p. 62.

56. See Richard D. Arvey, H. Dudley Dewhirst, and Edward M. Brown, "A Longitudinal Study of the Impact of Changes in Goal Setting on Employee Satisfaction," *Personnel Psychology*, Autumn 1978, pp. 595–608, and John R. Hollenbeck and Arthur P. Brief, "The Effects of Individual Differences and Goal Origin on Goal Setting and Performance," *Organizational Behavior and Human Decision Processes*, vol. 40, 1987, pp. 392–414.

57. Gary P. Latham and Lise M. Saari, "Importance of Supportive Relationships in Goal Setting," *Journal of Applied Psychology*, April 1979, pp. 151–156.

58. Howard Garland, "Goal Level and Task Performance: A Compelling Replication of Some Compelling Results," *Journal of Applied Psychology*, April 1982, pp. 245–248.

59. James T. Austin and Philip Bobko, "Goal Setting Theory: Unexplored Areas and Future Research Needs," *Journal of Occupational Psychology*, vol. 58, no. 4., 1985, pp. 289–308.

60. Donald J. Campbell, "Task Complexity: A Review and Analysis," *Academy of Management Review*, January 1988, pp. 40–52.

61. E. A. Locke and G. P. Latham, *Goal Setting: A Motivational Technique That Really Works*, Prentice-Hall, Englewood Cliffs, N.J., 1984, pp. 171–172.

62. Patrick M. Wright, Jennifer M. George, S. Regena Farnsworth, and Gary C. McMahan, "Productivity and Extra-Role Behavior: The Effects of Goals and Incentives on Spontaneous Helping," *Journal of Applied Psychology*, June 1993, pp. 374–381.

63. Locke and Latham, *Goal Setting: A Motivational Technique*, pp. 171–172.

64. Ibid.

65. Locke and Latham, *A Theory of Goal Setting and Task Performance*, p. 15.

66. For example, see J. M. Ivancevich, "Changes in Performance in a Management by Objectives Program," *Administrative Science Quarterly*, vol. 19, 1974, pp. 563–574; Jan P. Muczyk, "A Controlled Field Experiment Measuring the Impact of MBO on Performance Data," *Journal of Management Studies*, October 1978, pp. 318–329; and Kenneth R. Thompson, Fred Luthans, and Will Terpening, "The Effects of MBO on Performance and Satisfaction in a Public Sector Organization," *Journal of Management*, Spring 1981, pp. 53–69.

67. Locke and Latham, *A Theory of Goal Setting and Task Performance*, p. 244. Also see Raymond A. Katzell and Donna E. Thompson, "Work Motivation: Theory and Practice," *American Psychologist*, February 1990, pp. 149–150.

REAL CASE:
Made by Hand

A recognized competitive advantage for car makers is quality. Each year, quality improves and those who were ahead one year often find themselves falling behind the next. It is a never-ending struggle in which some car firms are able to win the annual battle, but all realize that the war continues and must be waged again and again.

In this industry of "dog eat dog," there is one firm that seems to maintain consistent quality, year after year: Rolls-Royce. The firm claims that approximately 60 percent of all models built since its founding in 1904 are roadworthy. No one disputes the claim. At the same time, the company has not had to engage in a never-ending race to couple advanced technology to the auto line. If anything, Rolls has resisted the introduction of high tech and still has managed to turn out one of the world's highest-quality cars. (Some would say, *the* highest-quality cars.) One sheet-metal worker who solders six radiator shells a week has noted: "Every so often, someone comes up with the bright idea of bringing in welding machines. But we always come back to hand-molding." And this is not the only area in which handcrafting occurs. Most of the car is made by hand, and in those cases where technology is employed, machine tools are often fifty or more years old. However, this does not stop Rolls from turning out approximately 3200 high-quality automobiles each year. Employing a laborious assembly process, the firm manages to keep its 80,000 parts flowing in sync with the personnel. As a result, the right parts are always at hand and the work is done correctly the first time.

Handcrafting at Rolls-Royce takes a variety of forms. For example, the body shell of each Rolls is cleaned and treated for four days before paint is applied. Some of the hydraulic components are assembled in oil to prevent contamination by dirt. At the same time, the firm is careful to keep the car up to date in terms of technological innovation, yet it refuses to hurry the process. For example, Rolls added antiskid brakes five years after most of the other luxury makers did so, because it wanted to refine the system and ensure that the car would not lose its ultrasensitive brake pedal. The latest cars also contain such major innovations as a microprocessor-controlled suspension system, which took the firm four years to develop. Rolls also encourages feedback from the customer regarding ways to improve the car. Thanks to such suggestions the company has developed wood-veneer covers that slide over sun visors when not in use. In the planning stage are additions of slots to steady glasses in the picnic tables that drop from the rear of the front seats.

So while Rolls-Royce is certainly not a giant auto manufacturer, the company knows that it can continue to maintain its market niche through careful handcrafting and high quality. This combination of old-time quality and the careful introduction of advanced technology appears likely to keep the Rolls reputation intact.

1. Does the company use job enrichment in its auto production? Explain.
2. Does Rolls' approach to building cars incorporate any of the critical psychological states in the job characteristics model?
3. Will Rolls need to change its process and incorporate sociotechnological developments? Explain.

CASE:
The Rubber
Chicken Award

Kelly Sellers is really fed up with his department's performance. He knows that his people have a very boring job, and the way the technological process is set up leaves little latitude for what he has learned about vertically loading the job through job enrichment. Yet he is convinced that there must be some way to make it more interesting to do a dull job. "At least I want to find out for my people and improve their performance," he thinks.

The employees in Kelly's department are involved in the assembly of small hair dryer motors. There are twenty-five to thirty steps in the assembly process, depending upon the motor that is being assembled. The process is very simple, and currently each worker completes only one or two steps of the operation. Each employee has his or her own assigned workstation and stays at that particular place for the entire day. Kelly has decided to try a couple of things to improve performance. First, he has decided to organize the department into work groups. The members of each group would be able to move the workstations around as they desired. He has decided to allow each group to divide the tasks up as they see fit. Next, Kelly has decided to post each group's performance on a daily basis and to reward the group with the highest performance by giving them a "rubber chicken" award that they can display at their workbenches. The production manager, after checking with engineering, has reluctantly agreed to Kelly's proposal on a trial basis.

1. Do you think Kelly's approach to job redesign will work? Rate the core job dimensions from the Hackman-Oldham model of Kelly's employees before and after he redesigned their jobs. What could he do to improve these dimensions even more?
2. How do you explain the fact that Kelly feels he is restricted by the technological process but has still redesigned the work? Is this an example of sociotechnical job redesign?
3. What will happen if this experiment does not work out and the production manager forces Kelly to return to the former task design?

**CASE:
Specific Goals for
Human Service**

Jackie Jordan is the regional manager of a state human services agency that provides job training and rehabilitation programs for deaf persons. Her duties include supervising counselors as well as developing special programs. One of the difficulties that Jackie has had was with a project supervisor, Kathleen O'Shean. Kathleen is the coordinator of a three-year federal grant for a special project for the deaf. Kathleen has direct responsibility for the funds and the goals of the project. The federal agency that made the grant made continuance of the three-year grant conditional upon some "demonstrated progress" toward fulfilling the purpose of the grant. Jackie's problem with Kathleen was directly related to this proviso. She repeatedly requested that Kathleen develop some concrete goals for the grant project. Jackie wanted these goals written in a specific, observable, and measurable fashion. Kathleen continually gave Jackie very vague, nonmeasurable platitudes. Jackie, in turn, kept requesting greater clarification, but Kathleen's response was that the work that was being done was meaningful enough and took all her time. To take away from the work itself by writing these specific goals would only defeat the purpose of the grant. Jackie finally gave up and didn't push the issue further. One year later the grant was not renewed by the federal government because the program lacked "demonstrated progress."

1. Do you think Jackie was right in requesting more specific goals from Kathleen? Why or why not?
2. Do you think the federal government would have been satisfied with the goal-setting approach that Jackie was pushing as a way to demonstrate progress?
3. Would you have handled the situation differently if you were Jackie? How?

8 Learning: Processes, Reward Systems, and Behavioral Management

---

Learning Objectives

- **Define** the theoretical processes of learning: behavioristic, cognitive, and social.
- **Discuss** the principle of reinforcement, with special attention given to the law of effect, positive and negative reinforcers, and punishment.
- **Analyze** organizational reward systems, emphasizing both monetary and non-financial rewards.
- **Present** the steps and results of behavioral management.

Although learning has not been as popular a construct in organizational behavior as motivation or attitudes, both scholars and practitioners would agree on its importance to both the understanding and effective development and management of human resources. In fact, practically all organizational behavior is either directly or indirectly affected by learning. For example, a worker's skill, a manager's attitude, a staff assistant's motivation, or an accountant's mode of dress are all learned. With the application of learning processes and principles, employees' behavior can be managed to improve their performance.

The purpose of this chapter is to provide an overview of the learning process and principles that serve as a foundation and point of departure for presenting organizational reward systems and the behavioral management approach. The first section summarizes the theories of learning: behavioristic, cognitive, and social. Next, the principles of reinforcement and punishment are given attention. Following the discussion of reinforcement is the presentation of both monetary and nonmonetary organizational reward systems. The last part of the chapter is devoted to behavioral management. Both the steps of organizational behavior modification, or O.B. Mod., and the results of its application are given attention.

THE THEORETICAL PROCESSES OF LEARNING

The most basic purpose of any theory is to better explain the phenomenon in question. When theories become perfected, they have universal application and should enable prediction and control. Thus, a perfected theory of learning would have to be able to explain all aspects of learning (how, when, and why), have universal application (for example, to children, college students, managers, and workers), and predict and control learning situations. To date, no such theory of learning exists. Although there is general agreement on some principles of learning, there is still disagreement on the theory behind them. This does not mean that no attempts have been made to develop a theory of learning. In fact, the opposite is true. The most widely recognized theoretical approaches incorporate the behavioristic and cognitive approaches and the newly emerging social learning theory. An understanding of these three learning theories is important to the study of organizational behavior.

Behavioristic Theories

The most traditional and researched theory comes out of the behaviorist school of thought in psychology. Most of the principles of learning, organizational reward systems, and the behavioral management approach discussed in this chapter are based on behavioristic theories, or behaviorism.

The classical behaviorists, such as the Russian pioneering behaviorist Ivan Pavlov and the American John B. Watson, attributed learning to the association or connection between stimulus and response (S-R). The operant behaviorists, in particular the well-known American psychologist B. F. Skinner, give more attention to the role that consequences play in learning, or the response-stimulus (R-S) connection. The emphasis on the connection (S-R or R-S) has led some to label these the *connectionist theories* of learning. The *S-R* deals with classical, or respondent, conditioning, and the *R-S* deals with instrumental, or operant, conditioning. An understanding of these conditioning processes is vital to the study of learning and serves as a point of departure for understanding and modifying organizational behavior.

Classical Conditioning. Pavlov's classical conditioning experiment using dogs as subjects is undoubtedly the single most famous study ever conducted in the behavioral sciences. A simple surgical procedure permitted Pavlov to measure accurately the amount of saliva secreted by a dog. When he presented meat powder (unconditioned stimulus) to the dog in the experiment, Pavlov noticed a great deal of salivation (unconditioned response). On the other hand, when he merely rang a bell (neutral stimulus), the dog had no salivation. The next step taken by Pavlov was to accompany the meat with the ringing of the bell. After doing this several times, Pavlov rang the bell without presenting the meat. This time, the dog salivated to the bell alone. The dog had become classically conditioned to salivate (conditioned response) to the sound of the bell (conditioned stimulus). Thus, *classical conditioning* can be defined as a process in which a formerly neutral stimulus, when paired with an unconditioned stimulus, becomes a conditioned stimulus that elicits a conditioned response; the S-R connection is learned. The Pavlov experiment was a major breakthrough and has had a lasting impact on the understanding of learning.

Despite the theoretical possibility of the widespread applicability of classical conditioning, most modern theorists agree that it represents only a very small part of total human learning. Skinner in particular felt that classical conditioning explains only respondent (reflexive) behaviors. These are the involuntary responses that are elicited by a stimulus. Skinner felt that the more complex, but common, human behaviors cannot be explained by classical conditioning alone. He felt that most human behavior affects, or operates on, the environment. The latter type of behavior is learned through operant conditioning.

Operant Conditioning. *Operant conditioning* is concerned primarily with learning that occurs as a consequence of behavior, or R-S. It is not concerned with the eliciting causes of behavior, as classical, or respondent, conditioning is. The specific differences between classical and operant conditioning may be summarized as follows:

1. In classical conditioning, a change in the stimulus (unconditioned stimulus to conditioned stimulus) will elicit a particular response. In operant conditioning, one particular response out of many possible ones occurs in a given stimulus situation. The stimulus situation serves as a cue in operant conditioning. It does not elicit the response, but serves as a cue for a person to emit the response. The critical aspect of operant conditioning is what happens as a consequence of the response. The strength and frequency of classically conditioned behaviors are determined mainly by the frequency of the eliciting stimulus (the environmental event that precedes the behavior). The strength and frequency of operantly conditioned behaviors are determined mainly by the consequences (the environmental event that follows the behavior).

2. During the classical conditioning process, the unconditioned stimulus, serving as a reward, is presented every time. In operant conditioning, the reward is presented only if the organism gives the correct response. The organism must operate on the environment in order to receive a reward. The response is instrumental in obtaining the reward. Table 8.1 gives some examples of classical (S-R) and operant (R-S) conditioning.

Operant conditioning has a much greater impact on human learning than classical conditioning. Operant conditioning also explains, at least in a very simple sense, much of organizational behavior. For example, it might be said that employees work eight hours a day, five days a week, in order to feed, clothe, and shelter themselves and their families. Working (conditioned response) is instrumental only in obtaining the food, clothing, and shelter. Some significant insights can be gained directly from this kind of analysis. The consequences of organizational behavior can change the environmental situation and largely affect subsequent employee behaviors. Managers can analyze the consequences of organizational behavior to help

TABLE 8.1 Examples of Classical and Operant Conditioning

	Classical Conditioning	
	(S) Stimulus ⟶	(R) Response
The individual:	is stuck by a pin	flinches
	is tapped below the kneecap	flexes lower leg
	is shocked by an electric current	jumps/screams
	is surprised by a loud sound	jumps/screams

	Operant Conditioning	
	(R) Response ⟶	(S) Stimulus
The individual:	works	is paid
	talks to others	meets more people
	enters a restaurant	obtains food
	enters a library	finds a book
	works hard	receives praise and a promotion

accomplish the goals of prediction and control. Some organizational behavior researchers are indeed using the operant framework to analyze the effectiveness of managers at work.[1] In addition, this theory serves as the foundation for behavioral management, which is presented at the end of the chapter.

Cognitive Theories

Edward Tolman is widely recognized as a pioneering cognitive theorist. He felt that *cognitive learning* consists of a relationship between cognitive environmental cues and expectation. He developed and tested this theory through controlled experimentation. He was one of the first to use the now famous white rat in psychological experiments. He found that a rat could learn to run through an intricate maze, with purpose and direction, toward a goal (food). Tolman observed that at each choice point in the maze, expectations were established. In other words, the rat learned to expect that certain cognitive cues associated with the choice point might eventually lead to food. If the rat actually received the food, the association between the cue and the expectancy was strengthened, and learning occurred. In contrast to the S-R and R-S learning in the classical and operant approaches, Tolman's approach could be depicted as *S-S* (stimulus-stimulus), or learning the association between the cue and the expectancy.

Besides being the forerunner of modern social learning theory, Tolman's S-S cognitive theory also had a great impact on the early human relations movement. Industrial training programs in the 1940s and 1950s drew heavily on Tolman's ideas. Programs were designed to strengthen the relationship between cognitive cues (supervisory, organizational, and job procedures) and worker expectations (incentive payments for good performance). The theory was that the worker would learn to be more productive by building an association between taking orders or following directions and expectancies of monetary reward for this effort.

Today, the cognitive sciences focus more on the structures and processes of human competence (for example, the role of memory and information processing) rather than on the acquisition and transition processes that have dominated learning theory explanations.[2] In organizational behavior, the cognitive approach has been applied mainly to motivation theories. Expectations, attributions and locus of control, and goal setting (which are in the forefront of modern work motivation) are all cognitive concepts and represent the purposefulness of organizational behavior. Many researchers are currently concerned about the relationship or connection between cognitions and organizational behavior.[3]

Social Learning Theory

Social learning theory combines and integrates both behaviorist and cognitive concepts and emphasizes the interactive, reciprocal nature of cognitive, behavioral, and environmental determinants. It is important to recognize that social learning theory is a behavioral theory and draws heavily from the principles of classical and operant conditioning. But equally important is the fact that social learning theory goes beyond classical and operant theory by recognizing that there is more to learning than direct learning via antecedent stimuli and contingent consequences. Social learning theory posits that learning can also take place via vicarious, or modeling, and self-control processes. Thus, social learning theory agrees with classical and operant conditioning processes, but says they are too limiting and adds modeling and self-control processes and cognitive personality dimensions such as self-efficacy.

Modeling Processes. The vicarious, or modeling, processes essentially involve observational learning. "Modeling in accordance with social learning theory can account for certain behavior acquisition phenomena that cannot be easily fitted into either operant or respondent conditioning."[4]

Many years ago, Miller and Dollard suggested that learning need not result from discrete stimulus-response or response-consequence connections. Instead, learning can take place through imitating others. Albert Bandura is most closely associated with the modern view of modeling as an explanation of learning. He states:

> Although behavior can be shaped into new patterns to some extent by rewarding and punishing consequences, learning would be exceedingly laborious and hazardous if it proceeded solely on this basis. . . . [It] is difficult to imagine a socialization process in which the language, mores, vocational activities, familial customs and educational, religious and political practices of a culture are taught to each new member by selective reinforcement of fortuitous behavior, without benefit of models who exemplify the cultural patterns in their own behavior. Most of the behaviors that people display are learned either deliberately or inadvertently, through the influence of example.[5]

Bandura has done considerable research that demonstrates that people can learn from others.[6] This learning takes place in two steps. First, the person observes how others act and then acquires a mental picture of the act and its consequences (rewards and punishers). Second, the person acts out the acquired image, and if the consequences are positive, he or she will tend to do it again. If the consequences are negative, the person will tend not to do it again. This, of course, is where there is a tie-in with operant theory. But because there is cognitive, symbolic representation of the modeled activities instead of discrete response-consequence connections in the acquisition of new behavior, modeling goes beyond the operant explanation. In particular, Bandura concludes that *modeling* involves interrelated subprocesses such as attention, retention, and motoric reproduction, as well as reinforcement. Others emphasize that a primary basis of vicarious learning is a cognitively held "script" on the part of the observer of a model.[7] This *script* is a procedural knowledge or cognitive structure or framework for understanding and doing behaviors.

Self-efficacy. Drawing from social learning theory, self-efficacy has recently become an important construct in organizational behavior. Bandura has defined *self-efficacy* as the self-perceptions of how well a person can cope with situations as they arise.[8] In particular, people who think they can perform well on a task (high self-efficacy) do better than those who think they will fail (low self-efficacy).[9] Importantly for the field of organizational behavior, a stream of research studies has established a fairly clear relationship between self-efficacy and work-related performance[10] and the tendency to remain calm in a stressful situation.[11] In other words, there is evidence that those employees with high self-efficacy tend to persevere and end up doing a good job without suffering stress or burnout.

PRINCIPLES OF LEARNING: REINFORCEMENT AND PUNISHMENT

Reinforcement and punishment play a central role in the learning process. Most learning experts agree that reinforcement is more important than punishment and is the single most important principle of learning. Yet there is much controversy over its theoretical explanation. The first theoretical treatment given to reinforcement in learning and the framework that still dominates today is Thorndike's classic law of effect.

Law of Effect

In Thorndike's own words, the *law of effect* is simply stated thus: "Of several responses made to the same situation, those which are accompanied or closely followed by satisfaction (reinforcement) . . . will be more likely to recur; those which are accompanied or closely followed by discomfort (punishment) . . . will be less likely to occur."[12] From a strictly empirical standpoint, most behavioral scientists, even those with a cognitive orientation, generally accept the validity of this law. It has been demonstrated time after time in highly controlled learning experiments and is directly observable in everyday learning experiences. Desirable, or reinforcing, consequences will increase the strength of a response and increase its probability of being repeated in the future. Undesirable, or punishing, consequences will decrease the strength of a response and decrease its probability of being repeated in the future.

Although there is wide acceptance of the law of effect, there are occasions when a person's cognitive rationalizations may neutralize it. For example, people with inaccurate self-efficacy beliefs may not be affected by the consequences of their actions. In the workplace, this is a real problem for managers. Those with inaccurate self-efficacy beliefs who experience performance failures time after time will not learn from their mistakes nor respond to the manager on how to correct the problem. They have high self-efficacy (they believe that their behaviors are appropriate to successfully accomplish the task) and they are wrong.[13] In addition to this type of cognitive processing that may neutralize the law of effect, there is some disagreement when it is carried a step further and used as an overall theory or an absolute requirement for learning.

Despite the theoretical controversy, few would argue against the importance of reinforcement to the learning process. Theoretical attempts besides the law of effect have generally failed to explain reinforcement fully. However, as with the failure to develop a generally accepted overall theory of learning, the lack of an accepted theory of reinforcement does not detract from its extreme importance.

Definition of Reinforcement

An often cited circular definition of reinforcement says that it is anything the person finds rewarding. This definition is of little value because the words "reinforcing" and "rewarding" are used interchangeably, but neither one is operationally defined. A more operational definition can be arrived at by reverting to the law of effect. Under this law, *reinforcement* can be defined as anything that both increases the strength of response and tends to induce repetitions of the behavior that preceded the reinforcement.

A *reward*, on the other hand, is simply something that the person who presents it deems to be desirable. A reward is given by the person who thinks it is desirable. Reinforcement is functionally defined. Something is reinforcing only if it strengthens the response preceding it and induces repetitions of the response. For example, a manager may ostensibly reward an employee who found an error in a report by publicly praising the employee. Yet, upon examination it is found that the employee is embarrassed and harassed by coworkers, and error-finding behavior decreases in the future. In this example, the "reward" is not reinforcing. Even though there is this technical difference between a reward and a reinforcer, the terms are often used interchangeably.

A better understanding of reinforcers requires, besides clearing up differences between reinforcers and rewards, making the distinctions between positive and negative reinforcers.

Positive and Negative Reinforcers

There is much confusion surrounding the terms "positive reinforcement," "negative reinforcement," and "punishment." First of all, it must be understood that reinforcement, positive or negative, strengthens the response and increases the probability of repetition. But the positive and negative reinforcers accomplish this impact on behavior in completely different ways. *Positive reinforcement* strengthens and increases behavior by the presentation of a desirable consequence. *Negative reinforcement* strengthens and increases behavior by the termination or withdrawal of an undesirable consequence. Figure 8.1 briefly summarizes the differences between positive and negative reinforcement and punishment. Giving praise to an employee for the successful completion of a task could be an example of positive reinforcement (if this does in fact strengthen and subsequently increase this task behavior). On the other hand, a worker is negatively reinforced for getting busy when the supervisor walks through the area. Getting busy terminates being "chewed out" by the supervisor.

Negative reinforcement is more complex than positive reinforcement, but it should not be equated with punishment. In fact, they have opposite effects on behavior. Negative reinforcement strengthens and increases behavior, while punishment weakens and decreases behavior. However, both are considered to be forms of negative control of behavior. Negative reinforcement is really a form of social blackmail, because the person will behave in a certain way in order not to be punished. A clearer understanding of punishment will help clarify how it differs from negative reinforcement.

FIGURE 8.1
Summary of the operational definitions of positive and negative reinforcement and punishment.

Consequence of Contingent	Reward (something desirable)	Noxious stimuli (something aversive and undesirable)
Application	POSITIVE REINFORCEMENT (Behavior increases)	PUNISHMENT (Behavior decreases)
Withdrawal	PUNISHMENT (Behavior decreases)	NEGATIVE REINFORCEMENT (Behavior increases)

The Meaning and Use of Punishment

Punishment is one of the most used but least understood and badly administered aspects of learning. Whether in rearing children or dealing with subordinates in a complex organization, parents and supervisors or managers often revert to punishment instead of positive reinforcement in order to modify or control behavior. Punishment is commonly thought to be the reverse of reinforcement but equally effective in altering behavior. However, this simple analogy with reinforcement may not be warranted. The reason is that punishment is a very complex phenomenon and must be carefully defined and used.

Punishment is anything that weakens behavior and tends to decrease its subsequent frequency. Punishment usually consists of the application of an undesirable or noxious consequence, but as shown in Figure 8.1, it can also be defined as the withdrawal of a desirable consequence.[14] Thus, taking away certain organizational privileges from a manager who has a poor performance record could be thought of as punishment.

Regardless of the distinction between punishment as the application of an undesirable consequence and as the withdrawal of a desirable consequence, in order for punishment to occur, there must be a weakening of, and a decrease in, the behavior which preceded it. Just because a supervisor gives a tongue-lashing to a subordinate and thinks this is a punishment, it is not necessarily the case unless the behavior that preceded the tongue-lashing weakens and decreases. In many situations when supervisors think they are punishing employees, they are in fact reinforcing them because they are giving attention, and attention tends to be very reinforcing. This explains the common complaint that supervisors often make: "I call Joe in, give him heck for goofing up, and he goes right back out and goofs up again." What is happening is that the supervisor thinks Joe is being punished, when operationally, what is obviously happening is that the supervisor is reinforcing Joe's undesirable behavior by giving him attention and recognition.

Opinions on administering punishment range all the way from the one extreme of dire warnings never to use it to the other extreme that it is the only effective way to modify behavior. As yet, research has not been able to support either view completely. However, there is little doubt that the use of punishment tends to cause many undesirable side effects. Neither children nor adults like to be punished. The punished behavior tends to be only temporarily suppressed rather than permanently changed, and the punished person tends to get anxious or uptight and resentful of the punisher. Thus, the use of punishment as a strategy to control behavior is a lose-lose approach. Unless the punishment is severe, the behavior will reappear very quickly, but the more severe the punishment, the bigger the side effects such as hate and revenge.

To minimize the problems with using punishment, persons administering it must always provide an acceptable alternative to the behavior that is being punished. If they do not, the undesirable behavior will tend to reappear and will cause fear and anxiety in the person being punished. The punishment must always be administered as close in time to the undesirable behavior as possible. Calling subordinates into the office to give them a reprimand for breaking a rule the week before is not effective. All the reprimand tends to do at this time is to punish them for getting caught. The punishment has little effect on the rule-breaking behavior. When punishment is administered, it should be remembered that there is also an effect on the relevant others who are observing the punishment.[15]

A rule of thumb for human resource managers should be: Always attempt to reinforce instead of punish in order to change behavior. Furthermore, the use of a reinforcement strategy is usually more effective in accelerating desirable behaviors than the use of punishment is for decelerating undesirable behaviors because no bad side effects accompany reinforcement. As one comprehensive analysis of punishment concluded: "In order to succeed, [punishment] must be used in an orderly, rational manner—not, as is too often the case, as a handy outlet for a manager's anger or frustration. If used with skill, and concern for human dignity, it can be useful."[16] Perhaps the best practical advice is the old red-hot-stove rule of discipline—like the stove, punishment should give advance warning, and be immediate, consistent, and impersonal. In addition, most modern approaches stress that punishment should be situationally applied (a crew of nineteen-year-old high school dropouts should be treated differently from a $100,000-per-year professional) and progressive.[17] The progressive discipline may start off with a clarifying verbal discussion, then move to a written contract signed by the person being disciplined, and finally move to time off with or without pay and end in termination.

ORGANIZATIONAL REWARD SYSTEMS

Since positive consequences (rewards and reinforcers) are so important to employee behavior, reward systems become critical to employee performance and organizational success. The organization may have the latest technology, well-thought-out strategic plans, detailed job descriptions, and comprehensive training programs, but unless the people are rewarded for their performance-related behaviors, the "up-front" variables (technology, plans, and so on) or the rules that govern their behavior[18] have little impact. In other words, going back to Skinner's original conception, the antecedent cues (technology, plans, and the like) have power to control or provide rules for behavior only if there are reinforcing consequences. Thus, organizational reward systems become the key, often overlooked, factor in bringing about improved performance and success.

When anyone mentions organizational reward systems, money comes quickly to mind. Monetary reward systems do play a dominate role. However, as organizations in recent years have become leaner and more efficient, monetary rewards have become very limited and increasingly are just not available. More and more interest is now being given to nonfinancial rewards. The following sections examine both monetary and nonfinancial rewards that can be used to manage employee behavior for performance improvement.

Monetary Rewards

Despite the tendency in recent years to downgrade the importance of money as an organizational reward, there is ample evidence that money can be positively reinforcing for most people. The downgrading of money is partly the result of the popular motivation theories such as Maslow's hierarchy of needs, plus the publicity given to surveys that consistently place wages and salaries near the middle of the list of employment factors that are important to workers and managers.

There are also recent studies indicating that a salary increase, no matter how large (for example, CEOs of big U.S. corporations pulled down a record $3,842,247 in average total pay last year[19]), merely intensifies the belief that they deserve more.[20]

**Application
Example**

Monetary Reward Systems in Action

Although money plays an obvious and dominant role in today's organizational reward systems, it is often downplayed and degraded. Yet, even though employees at all levels may respond in a research study or an organizational survey that money is not very important to them, there is considerable subjective and objective evidence that people greatly value and will work very hard for money. Some facts to support this include: (1) Three-fourths of women with children are working in addition to maintaining their household obligations; (2) two-thirds of families have two or more people holding jobs in order to meet living expenses. In addition, there are numerous example of companies that have applied monetary rewards to improve employee performance. Here is a sampling of such successful applications:

1. *Taco Bell.* The 1600 restaurant managers in this successful division of PepsiCo are evaluated and given bonuses based on targeted profit, customer service, and total revenues. On average, the managers receive a bonus worth almost a third of their base pay, and doubling the base pay is not uncommon. Since this monetary reward system has been in effect, food costs as a percentage of sales have decreased, customer service scores have been the best the company has ever had, and there have been record profits.

2. *Lincoln Electric.* This widely publicized Cleveland-based welding equipment and motors manufacturer has used monetary reward systems for almost 100 years. Through the use of piece-work pay, shared profits, and year-end bonuses, the 2700 employees last year received monetary rewards averaging between $18,000 and $22,000, which represented about three-fourths of their salaries. The company largely attributes its productivity rate of double to triple that of the competition and its stable prices over the years to this monetary reward system. [For more details on this unique company see the end-of-part case/reading.]

3. *Rolling Hills Hospital.* This Pennsylvania health care facility demonstrates that the successful application of monetary rewards is not restricted to the business world. Teams of nurses in this hospital compete for monetary rewards. During the first eighteen months this program was in place, management determined that quality of patient care improved and costs were reduced and, more specifically, the nurses' sick leave was reduced by 5400 hours and tardiness was reduced by 2245 hours.

Although the above represent the success stories, few would question that money is still very important to people. These representative examples show that organizations can use money as an effective reward for improved employee performance.

The idea here is that once the money covers the basic needs, people use it to get ahead, which is always just out of reach. Although money was probably over-emphasized in classical management theory and motivation techniques, the pendulum now seems to have swung too far in the opposite direction. Money remains a very important but admittedly complex potential reinforcer. The Application Example: Monetary Reward Systems in Action provides some specific examples.

In terms of Maslow's well-known hierarchy of needs, money is often equated only with the most basic requirements of employees. It is viewed in the material sense of buying food, clothing, and shelter. Yet, money has a symbolic as well as an economic, material meaning. It can provide power and status and can be a means to measure achievement. In the latter sense, money can be used as an effective positive reinforcement intervention strategy to improve performance.

Compensation Techniques. The standard *base-pay* technique provides for minimum compensation for a particular job and is a type of continuous reinforcement schedule. Pay by the hour for workers and the base salary for managers are examples. The technique does not reward above-average performance or penalize below-average performance, and it is administered on a continuous basis controlled largely by the job rather than by the person performing the job. A *variable-pay* technique, however, is an intermittent type of reinforcement schedule and attempts to reward according to individual or group differences. Thus, it is more human- than job-controlled. Seniority variable-pay plans recognize age and length-of-service differentials, and merit pay and individual- or group-incentive plans attempt to reward contingently on the basis of performance.[21]

Managers have been rewarded by incentive pay and bonus plans based on performance for years.[22] For example, at USX, cash bonuses may run up to 85 percent of an executive's base salary. There is considerable evidence that this approach is becoming more popular.[23] Also, work groups and whole departments are receiving monetary rewards. For example, Du Pont's Fibers Division has moved to a variable pay program providing bonuses when performance objectives are exceeded.[24] Besides managers and groups, lower-level employees are also now being rewarded by monetary incentives. For example, at the food products company Borden, some 28,000 workers at 180 different plants can get bonuses ranging from $250 to $800 each, depending on specific behaviors relating to attendance, safety, quality, and quantity.[25] At the other extreme are scientists and engineers in high-tech firms who make such significant contributions as inventing a new product or developing a new software program, but who cannot be adequately rewarded by the typical merit pay plan. The majority of high-tech firms now have pay plans in place to reward such innovations and thus help retain their best people. For example, IBM has a Corporate Award (IBM recently awarded $150,000 each to two of its scientists who won Nobel Prizes) and Outstanding Innovation Awards (these are given for important inventions or scientific discoveries and range from $2500 to $25,000).[26]

Incentive plans involve piece rates, bonuses, or profit sharing. A third technique, supplementary pay, has nothing to do with the job or performance per se. The extensive fringe-benefit package received by employees in most modern organizations is an example. These supplements can be very costly to organizations. The U.S. Chamber of Commerce reported that employee benefits on average represented one-third of payroll costs and about $10,000 per employee.[27]

Analyses of Monetary Rewards. Analyses of the role of money are usually couched in cognitive terms.[28] However, from these cognitive explanations it is very clear that the real key in assessing the use of monetary reward systems is not necessarily whether it satisfies inner needs but rather how it is administered. In order for money to be effective in the organizational reward system, it must be as objective and fair as possible[29] and be administered contingently on the employee's exhibiting critical performance behaviors. Some of the new monetary incentive systems in industry are beginning to recognize this. For example, Borden used to peg monetary incentives to return on equity. However, as one senior executive at the firm pointed out, this technical (a behaviorist would say noncontingent) financial target was "too difficult for the hourly employee to understand."[30] Now, Borden has successfully moved to the more contingent pay for specific performance behaviors.

Unfortunately, about the only reinforcing function that pay often has in organizations is to reinforce employees for walking up to the pay window or for opening an envelope every two weeks or every month. With the exception of such companies as Borden and other very specific, piece-rate incentive systems and commissions paid to salespersons, pay is generally not contingent on the performance of critical behaviors.[31] One experimental study clearly demonstrated that money contingently administered can have a positive effect on employee behavior. A contingently administered monetary bonus plan significantly improved the punctuality of workers in a Mexican division of a large U.S. corporation.[32] It should be pointed out, however, that the mere fact that money was valued by the Mexican workers in this study does not mean that it would have the same impact on all workers. For example, in a study of managers in the Social Security Administration, merit pay seemingly had no effect on organizational performance[33] and some compensation experts argue that merit pay only makes employees unhappy because they view it as an unfair way to reward for past performance instead of being geared to improved future performance.[34]

In a society with an inflationary economy and nonmaterialistic social values, money may be less likely to be a potential reinforcer for critical job behaviors. However, money certainly cannot be automatically dismissed as a positive reinforcer. There should be an objective assessment to determine whether in fact money is an effective positive reinforcer for the critical behavior in question. Because of the complexity of money as a reinforcer, nonfinancial incentives are now receiving increased attention in organizational reward systems.

Nonfinancial Rewards

Table 8.2 summarizes some of the major categories of nonfinancial rewards. Notice that even though these are considered nonfinancial, they may still cost the organization. This is true of the consumables, manipulatables, visual and auditory rewards, and certainly the tokens. For example, Riverside Methodist Hospital in Columbus, Ohio, runs a highly successful convenience center for its employees (a manipulatable nonfinancial reward). This unique benefit saves employees considerable time and trouble by offering a one-stop source for a variety of services ranging from dry cleaning to food shopping. Although this is rated as the most desired and least expensive benefit at this hospital, it is still estimated to cost about $8 per employee.[35] On the other hand, the social and job design categories cost nothing, and they may be even more powerful than the monetary and cost-based nonfinancial rewards. The same is true for feedback, which is not listed in the table, but which has become an importantly recognized dimension of the nonfinancial reward system of today's organization.

Social Rewards.   Recognition, attention, and praise tend to be very powerful social rewards for most people. In addition, few people become satiated or filled up with social rewards. However, similar to monetary rewards, social rewards should be administered on a contingent basis to have a positive effect on employee performance. For example, a pat on the back or verbal praise that is insincere or randomly given (as under the old human relations approach) may have no effect or even a punishing, "boomerang" effect. But genuine social rewards, contingently adminis-

TABLE 8.2 Categories of Nonfinancial Rewards

Consumables	Manipulatables	Visual and Auditory Rewards	Tokens	Social Rewards	Job Design
Coffee-break treats	Desk accessories	Office with a window	Early time off with pay	Friendly greetings	Jobs with more responsibility
Free lunches	Wall plaques	Piped-in music	Stocks	Informal recognition	Job rotation
Food baskets	Company car	Redecoration of work environment	Stock options	Formal acknowledgment of achievement	Special assignments
Easter hams	Watches		Movie passes		Cross-training
Christmas turkeys	Trophies	Company literature	Trading stamps	Solicitation of suggestions	Knowledge training
Dinners for the family on the company	Commendations	Private office	Paid-up insurance policies	Solicitation of advice	Authority to schedule own work
	Rings/tie pins	Popular speakers or lecturers	Dinner and theater tickets	Compliment on work progress	Flexible hours
Company picnics	Appliances and furniture for the home	Book club discussions	Vacation trips	Recognition in house organ	Flexible breaks
After-work wine and cheese parties	Home shop tools		Coupons redeemable at local stores	Pat on the back	Job sharing
	Garden tools			Smile	Participation in decisions
	Clothing			Verbal or nonverbal recognition or praise	Participation in teams
	Club privileges				
	Use of company recreation facilities				
	Use of company convenience center				
	Use of company facilities for personal projects				

Source: Adapted from Fred Luthans and Robert Kreitner, *Organizational Behavior Modification and Beyond*, Scott, Foresman, Glenview, Ill., 1985, p. 127, and used with permission.

tered for performance of the target behavior, can be a very effective positive reinforcer for most employees. The added benefit of such a strategy, in contrast to the use of monetary rewards, is that the cost of social rewards to the organization is absolutely nothing.

Feedback as a Reward. There is little question that despite the tremendous amount of data being generated by computerized information systems in modern organizations, individuals still receive very little, if any, feedback about their performance. People generally have an intense desire to know how they are doing, especially if they have some degree of achievement motivation. Even though feedback has been found to be complex in research studies, it is generally accepted that feedback enhances individual performance.[36] A recent comprehensive review (thirty laboratory and forty-two field experiments) concluded that objective feedback had a positive effect.[37] In general, feedback should be as *p*ositive, *i*mmediate, *g*raphic, and *s*pecific—thus, the acronym PIGS—as possible to be effective.[38]

Despite the recognized importance, there is still disagreement among scholars as to whether feedback per se is automatically reinforcing or simplistic.[39] For example, after reviewing the existing research literature on feedback, one researcher concluded that its impact is contingent upon factors such as the nature of the feedback information, the process of using feedback, individual differences among the recipients of the feedback, and the nature of the task.[40] One study, for instance, found that self-generated feedback with goal setting had a much more powerful effect on technical or engineering employees than externally generated feedback with goal setting.[41] Also, another study found subjects rated specific feedback more positively than they rated nonspecific feedback, and preferred feedback that suggested an external cause of poor performance to feedback that suggested an internal cause.[42] And the source of the feedback seems important as well.[43] Not only are the amount and the frequency of feedback generated by a source important, but also the consistency and usefulness of the information generated, as a study found. Individuals viewed feedback from formal organizations least positively, from coworkers next, then from supervisors and tasks, with the best being self-generated feedback.[44] Also, recent studies have found that choice of reward interacting with feedback had a positive impact on task performance in a laboratory exercise,[45] but workers in highly routine jobs in fast-food restaurants who received positive feedback did not improve their performance.[46]

Despite these qualifications and contingencies, a general guideline regarding feedback about performance is that it can be an effective component of the organizational reward system. For example, a supervisor faced with the problem of workers' taking unscheduled breaks successfully used feedback to reinforce them for staying on the job. Specifically, the supervisor calculated the exact cost for each worker in the unit (in terms of lost group piece-rate pay) every time any one of them took an unscheduled break. This information regarding the relatively significant amount of lost pay when any one of them took an unscheduled break was fed back to the employees of the unit. After this feedback, staying on the job increased in frequency, and taking unscheduled breaks dramatically decreased. The feedback pointed out the contingency that staying on the job meant more money. At least in this case, money proved to be a more reinforcing consequence than the competing contingencies of enjoying social rewards with friends in the rest room and withdrawing from the boring job. The feedback in this case clarified the monetary contingency. Such analysis of contingencies is a basic part of behavioral management.

BEHAVIORAL MANAGEMENT

Behavioral management applies the principles of behavioristic learning theory, especially operant conditioning and reinforcement. The environmental contingencies of employee behavior, antecedents, and, particularly, consequences, and their impact on performance effectiveness is the focus of attention. The term *organizational behavior modification*, or simply, O.B. Mod., has been developed and used by Luthans and Kreitner to represent a behavioral approach to the management of human resources for performance improvement.[47] The steps of applying O.B. Mod. are summarized in Figure 8.2.

Step 1: Identification of Performance Behaviors

In this first step the critical behaviors that make a significant impact on performance (making or selling widgets or providing a service to clients or customers) are identified. In every organization, regardless of type or level, numerous behaviors are occurring all the time. Some of these behaviors have a significant impact on performance, and some do not. The goal of the first step of O.B. Mod. is to identify the critical behaviors—the 5 to 10 percent of the behaviors that may account for up to 70 or 80 percent of the performance in the area in question.

The process of identifying critical behaviors can be carried out in a couple of ways. One approach is to have the person closest to the job in question—the

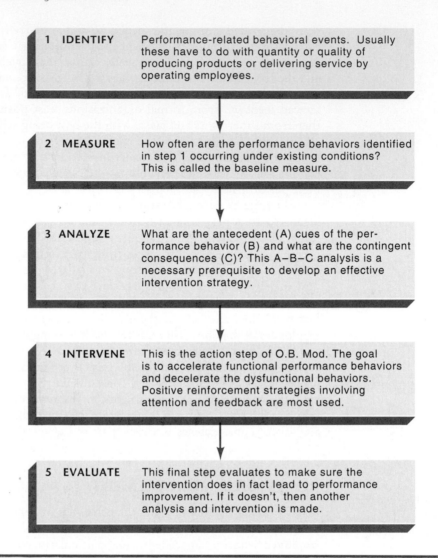

FIGURE 8.2
Luthans and Kreitner's
Steps of O.B. Mod.

immediate supervisor or the actual jobholder—determine the critical behaviors. This goes hand in hand with using O.B. Mod. as a problem-solving approach for the individual manager. Its advantages are that the person who knows the job best can most accurately identify the critical behaviors, and, because that person is participating, he or she may be more committed to carrying the O.B. Mod. process to its successful completion.

Another approach to identifying critical behaviors would be to conduct a systematic *behavioral audit*. The audit would use internal staff specialists and/or outside consultants. The audit would systematically analyze each job in question, in the manner that jobs are analyzed using job analysis techniques commonly employed in personnel administration. The advantages of the personal approach (where the jobholder and/or the immediate supervisor makes a vital input into the audit) can be realized by the audit. In addition, the advantages of staff expertise and consistency can be gained.

Regardless of the method used, there are certain guidelines that can be helpful in identifying critical behaviors. First, only direct performance behaviors are included. An employee's "bad attitude" and someone's "goofing off" all the time are unacceptable. Only direct performance behaviors such as absenteeism or attendance, tardiness or promptness, or complaints or constructive comments are identified. Specifically, doing or not doing a particular task or procedure that leads to quantity and/or quality outcomes plays the major role in O.B. Mod. Something like goofing off is not acceptable because it is not operationally measurable. It could be broken down into measurable behaviors such as not being at the workstation, being tardy when returning from breaks, spending time at the water cooler, disrupting co-workers, and even socializing with coworkers. However, for a behavior to be identified as a critical behavior appropriate for O.B. Mod., there must be a positive answer to the question (1) can it be measured? and (2) does it have a significant impact on a performance outcome?

Most organizations do not have problems with their technology or the ability or training of their people, but they have many behaviorally related performance problems. Functional behaviors (those that contribute to performance goals) need to be strengthened and accelerated in frequency, and dysfunctional behaviors (those that detract from, or are detrimental to, performance goals) need to be weakened and decelerated in frequency. As in the initial step of any problem-solving process, these behaviors must be properly identified, or the subsequent steps of O.B. Mod. become meaningless for attaining the overall goal of performance improvement.

Step 2: Measurement of the Behavior

After the performance behaviors have been identified in step 1, they are measured. A *baseline measure* is obtained by determining (either by observing and counting or by extracting from existing records) the number of times that the identified behavior is occurring under present conditions. Often this baseline frequency is in and of itself very revealing. Sometimes it is discovered that the behavior identified in step 1 is occurring much less or much more frequently than anticipated. The baseline measure may indicate that the problem is much smaller or much bigger than was thought to be the case. In some instances, the baseline measure may cause the "problem" to be dropped because its low (or high) frequency is now deemed not to need change. For example, attendance may have been identified in step 1 as a critical behavior that needed to be improved. The supervisor reports that the people "never seem to be here." The baseline measure, however, reveals that on average there is 96 percent attendance, which is deemed to be acceptable. In this example, the baseline measure rules out attendance as being a problem. The reverse, of course, could also have occurred. Attendance may have been a much bigger problem than anticipated.

The purpose of the baseline measure is to provide objective frequency data on the critical behavior. A baseline frequency count is an operational definition of the strength of the behavior under existing conditions. Such precise measurement is the hallmark of any scientific endeavor, and it separates O.B. Mod. from more subjective human resource management approaches, such as participation. Although the baseline is established before the intervention to see what happens to the behavior as a result of the intervention, it is important to realize that measures are taken after the intervention as well. Busy managers may feel that they do not have time to record behavioral frequencies objectively, but, at least initially, they should record them in order to use the O.B. Mod. approach effectively.

Step 3: Functional Analysis of the Behavior

Once the performance behavior has been identified and a baseline measure has been obtained, a functional analysis is performed. A *functional analysis* identifies both the antecedents (A) and consequences (C) of the target behavior (B), or simply stated, an A-B-C analysis is performed. As discussed under behavioristic learning theory and operant conditioning, both the antecedent and the consequent environments are vital to the understanding, prediction, and control of human behavior in organizations. In Table 8.3 a simple operant-based A-B-C functional analysis is shown. Remember that in an operant approach, cognitive mediating processes do not play a role. Such an omission may detract from the comprehensive understanding of organizational behavior and the analysis of modeling and self-control processes, but for pragmatic application, an A-B-C functional analysis is sufficient.[48] In the A-B-C functional analysis, A is the antecedent cue, B is the performance behavior identified in step 1, and C is the contingent consequence. Table 8.3 identifies some of the A's, B's, and C's for attendance and absenteeism. A review of absenteeism found work unit size, worker responsibility, and organizational scheduling three potential antecedent influences that could be used to improve employee attendance, and feedback, rewards, and punishers as effective attendance control procedures.[49]

TABLE 8.3 An Example of Functional Analysis

Functional Analysis of Attendance Behaviors

A ⟶ Antecedent Cues	B ⟶ Behaviors	C ⟶ Consequences
Awareness of any consequence	Going to bed on time	Reward programs
Advertising	Setting the alarm	Contingent time off
Meetings	Waking up	Gifts and prizes
Memorandums	Getting dressed	Preferred jobs
Orientation	Getting children off	Social
Bulletin board	to school	Attention
Observation of any consequence	Leaving home	Recognition
Social status and pressure	Getting a baby-sitter	Praise
Temporal cues	Driving to work	Feedback
Special events	Reporting to work	Data on attendance
Weather		

Functional Analysis of Absenteeism Behaviors

A ⟶ Antecedent Cues	B ⟶ Behaviors	C ⟶ Consequences
Illness/accident	Getting up late	Discipline programs
Hangover	Sleeping in	Verbal reprimands
Lack of transportation	Staying home	Written reprimands
Traffic	Drinking	Pay docks
No day-care facilities	Fishing/hunting	Layoffs
Family problems	Working at home	Dismissals
Company policies	Visiting	Social consequences from
Group personal norms	Caring for sick child	coworkers
Seniority/age		Escape from and avoid-
Awareness/observation of any		ance of working
consequence		Nothing

Source: Fred Luthans and Mark Martinko, "An Organizational Behavior Modification Analysis of Absenteeism," *Human Resources Management*, Fall 1976, p. 15. Used with permission.

**Application
Example**

Functional Analysis in Action

In an actual case of an O.B. Mod. application, a production supervisor in a large manufacturing firm identified unscheduled breaks as a critical behavior affecting the performance of his department. It seemed that workers were frequently wandering off the job, and when they were not tending their machines, time—and irrecoverable production—was lost. When a baseline measure of this critical behavior was obtained, the supervisor was proved to be right. The data indicated that unscheduled breaks (defined as leaving the job for reasons other than to take a scheduled break or to obtain materials) were occurring in the department on a relatively frequent basis. The functional analysis was performed to determine the antecedent(s) and consequence(s) of the unscheduled-break behavior.

It was found that the clock served as the antecedent cue for the critical behavior. The workers in this department started work at 8 A.M., they had their first scheduled break at 10 A.M., and they had lunch at noon. They started again at 1 P.M., had a break at 3 P.M., and quit at 5 P.M. The functional analysis revealed that almost precisely at 9 A.M., 11 A.M., 2 P.M., and 4 P.M., the workers were leaving their jobs and going to the rest room. In other words, the clock served as a cue for them to take an unscheduled break midway between starting time and the first scheduled break, between the first scheduled break and lunch, between lunch and the scheduled afternoon break, and between the afternoon break and quitting time. The clock did not cause the behavior; it served only as a cue to emit the behavior. On the other hand, the behavior was under stimulus control of the clock because the clock dictated when the behavior would occur. The consequence, however, was what was maintaining the behavior. The critical behavior was a function of its consequences. The functional analysis revealed that the consequence of the unscheduled-break behavior was escaping from a dull, boring task (that is, the unscheduled-break behavior was being negatively reinforced) and/or meeting with coworkers and friends to socialize and have a cigarette (that is, the unscheduled-break behavior was being positively reinforced). Through such a functional analysis, the antecedents and consequences are identified so that an effective intervention strategy can be developed.

This functional analysis step of O.B. Mod. brings out the problem-solving nature of the approach. Both the antecedent cues that emit the behavior, and sometimes control it, and the consequences that are currently maintaining the behavior must be identified and understood before an effective intervention strategy can be developed. The accompanying Application Example: Functional Analysis in Action gives the functional analysis of a production supervisor's problem of his workers' taking unscheduled breaks.

The functional analysis pinpoints one of the most significant practical problems of using an O.B. Mod. approach to change critical performance behaviors. Only the contingent consequences have an impact on subsequent behavior. The functional analysis often reveals that there are many competing contingencies for every organizational behavior. For example, a supervisor may be administering what he or she believes to be contingent punishment for an undesirable behavior. In many cases, the persons who are supposedly being punished will allow their coworkers' rewards to be the contingent consequence, and their undesirable behavior will increase in subsequent frequency. In other words, the supervisor's punishment is not contingent; it has no impact on the subordinates' subsequent behavior. The functional analysis must make sure that the contingent consequences are identified, and the analyst must not be deluded by the consequences that on the surface appear to be affecting the critical behavior.

Step 4: Development of an Intervention Strategy

The first three steps in an O.B. Mod. approach are preliminary to the action step, the intervention. The goal of the intervention is to strengthen and accelerate functional performance behaviors and/or weaken and decelerate dysfunctional behaviors. There are several strategies that can be used, but the main ones are positive reinforcement and punishment–positive reinforcement.

A Positive Reinforcement Strategy. Positive, not negative, reinforcement is recommended as an effective intervention strategy for O.B. Mod. The reason is that positive reinforcement represents a form of *positive control of behavior*, while negative reinforcement represents a form of *negative control of behavior*. Traditionally, and to a large extent still today, organizations depend on negative control. People come to work in order not to be fired, and they look busy when the supervisor walks by in order not to be punished. Under positive control, the person behaves in a certain way in order to receive the desired consequence. Under positive control, people come to work in order to be recognized for making a contribution to their department's goal of perfect attendance, or they keep busy whether the supervisor is around or not in order to receive incentive pay or because they get self-reinforcement from doing a good job. Positive control through a positive reinforcement intervention strategy is much more effective and longer lasting than negative control. It creates a much healthier and more productive organizational climate.

A positive reinforcer used as an O.B. Mod. intervention strategy could be anything, as long as it increases the performance behavior. Most often money is thought of as the logical, or sometimes the only, positive reinforcer available to managers using this approach. However, as the discussion of monetary reward systems points out, money is potentially a very powerful reinforcer, but it often turns out to be ineffective because it is not contingently administered as a consequence of the behavior being managed. Besides money, positive reinforcers that are also very powerful, readily available to all behavioral managers, and cost nothing are the social reinforcers (attention and recognition) and performance feedback. These reinforcers (money, attention, recognition, and feedback) can be and, as is demonstrated in the last section, have been effectively used as an effective O.B. Mod. strategy to improve employee performance.

A Punishment–Positive Reinforcement Strategy. There is little debate that a positive reinforcement strategy is the most effective intervention for O.B. Mod. Yet realistically it is recognized that in some cases the use of punishment to weaken and decelerate undesirable behaviors cannot be avoided. This would be true in the case of something like unsafe behaviors that need to be immediately decreased. However, as was pointed out earlier, so many negative side effects accompany the use of punishment that it should be avoided if at all possible. Punished behavior tends to be only temporarily suppressed; for example, if a supervisor reprimands a subordinate for some dysfunctional behavior, the behavior will decrease in the presence of the supervisor but will surface again when the supervisor is absent. In addition, a punished person becomes very anxious and uptight; reliance on punishment may have a disastrous impact on employee satisfaction and create unnecessary stress.

Perhaps the biggest problem with the use of punishment, however, is that it is very difficult for a supervisor to switch roles from punisher to positive reinforcer. Some supervisors and managers rely on punishment so much in dealing with their subordinates that it is almost impossible for them to administer positive reinforcement effectively. This is a bad situation for the management of human resources because the use of positive reinforcement is a much more effective way of changing employee behavior. If punishment is deemed necessary, the desirable alternative behavior (for example, safe behavior) should be positively reinforced at the first opportunity. Use of this combination strategy will cause the alternative desirable behavior to begin to replace the undesirable behavior in the person's behavioral repertoire. Punishment should never be used alone as an O.B. Mod. intervention. If punishment is absolutely necessary, it should always be used in combination with positive reinforcement.

Step 5: Evaluation to Ensure Performance Improvement

A glaring weakness of most human resource management programs is the absence of any systematic, built-in evaluation.[50] A comprehensive analysis of the evaluation of human resources programs concluded that the typical approach is "to review a program with one or two vice presidents at the corporate office, various managers in the field, and perhaps a group of prospective trainees. It continues to be used until someone in a position of authority decides that the program has outlived its usefulness. All of this is done on the basis of opinion and judgment."[51] Such haphazard evaluations have resulted in the termination of some effective programs and the perpetuation of some ineffective ones. In either case, there are severe credibility problems, and today all programs dealing with people, whether they are government social service programs or human resource management programs, are under the pressure of accountability. Human resource managers no longer have the luxury of just trying something new and different and hoping they can improve performance. Today there is pressure for everything that is tried to be proved to have value. As in the case of the validity of selection and appraisal techniques, which are currently under scrutiny, systematic evaluations of human resource management techniques should have been done all along.

O.B. Mod. attempts to meet the credibility and accountability problems head-on by including evaluation as an actual part of the process. In this last step of the approach, the need for four levels of evaluation (reaction, learning, behavioral change, and performance improvement) is stressed. The reaction level refers simply to whether the people using the approach and those having it used on them like it. If O.B. Mod. is well received and there is a positive reaction to it, there is a better chance of its being used effectively. In addition, reaction evaluations are helpful because (1) positive reactions help ensure organizational support, (2) they can provide information for planning future programs, (3) favorable reactions can enhance the other levels of evaluation (learning, behavioral change, and performance improvement), and (4) they can provide useful comparative data between units and across time.[52]

The second level of evaluation is learning, which is especially important when first implementing an O.B. Mod. approach. Do the people using the approach understand the theoretical background and underlying assumptions and the meaning of, and reasons for, the steps in the model? If they do not, the model will again tend to be used ineffectively. The third level is aimed at behavioral change. Are behaviors actually being changed? The charting of behaviors gives objective data for this level of evaluation. The fourth and final level, performance improvement, is the most important. The major purpose of O.B. Mod. is not just to receive a favorable reaction, learn the concepts, and change behaviors. These dimensions are important mainly because they contribute to the overriding purpose, which is to improve performance. "Hard" measures (for example, data on quantity and quality, turnover, absenteeism, customer complaints, employee grievances, length of patient stay, number of clients served, and rate of return on investment) and scientific methodology are used whenever possible to evaluate systematically the impact of O.B. Mod. on performance.

Application of Behavioral Management

There is a body of research that has evaluated the effectiveness of behavioral management when applied in manufacturing as well as in nonmanufacturing service-oriented organizations. In addition to the direct application of O.B. Mod. as described above, considerable basic research has been conducted on operant and social learning variables in experimental psychology. For many years and in very recent times, a number of studies have assessed the application of the behavioral management approach to improving employee performance in a number of different areas. The *Handbook of Organizational Behavior Management* summarizes these findings as follows:[53]

1. *Employee productivity.* Most applications by far have focused on performance output. The considerable number of research studies clearly indicate that employee productivity or task completion is positively affected by behavioral management techniques. After reviewing a number of field studies, it was concluded that the improvement of either quantity or quality of employee output cuts across virtually all organizational settings and all intervention techniques.[54]
2. *Absenteeism and tardiness.* This is probably the second biggest area of application. Studies that have examined this area have used some combination of rewards (for example, small monetary bonuses or lottery incentive systems) for attendance or promptness and/or punishers for absenteeism or tardiness. One extensive search of this literature found very positive results.[55] The six most sound methodological studies reported an 18 to 50 percent reduction in the absence rate and a 90 percent reduction in the frequency of tardiness. One study found a positive, causal impact that an O.B. Mod. program had on the attendance of employees in a bank.[56]
3. *Safety and accident prevention.* Most organizations, especially manufacturing firms and others in which dangerous equipment is used, are very concerned about safety. However, since accidents occur at such a relatively low frequency, most studies have focused on reducing identifiable safety hazards or increasing safe behaviors (for example, wearing earplugs, which went from 35 to 95 percent compliance according to one study;[57] wearing hard hats; and keeping the safety guard in place on dangerous equipment). A review of the research indicates the considerable success that behavioral management techniques have had in these areas.[58] Some actual company examples are Boston Gas, where employees without accidents are eligible for lottery drawings; Virginia Power, where employees can win from $50 to $1000 for safe work habits; Southern New England Telecommunications, which gives gift coupons to employees without accidents; and Turner Corporation, a New York–based engineering and construction firm,

where employees can earn company stock if they meet safety goals. All these companies report improved accident rates through the use of a behavioral management approach.[59]

4. *Sales performance.* Sales managers and trainers have traditionally relied on internal motivation techniques to get their salespeople to improve their performance. For example, one behavioral management consultant tells about a company that gave its sales personnel a typical high-powered, multimedia training program, which supposedly taught them effective selling skills. However, when the enthusiastic trainees finished the program and actually tried the things presented to them in the program, they received little, if any, feedback or reinforcement. Within a few weeks the enthusiasm began to wane, and, most important, actual sales performance began to decline.[60] In other words, even though these salespeople had probably acquired effective selling skills during their training, the environment did not support (reward) the use of these skills. A behavioral management approach, in which important selling behaviors such as customer approach, suggestive statements, and closing statements are identified, measured, analyzed, intervened in, and evaluated, would be an alternative to the motivation-skill-teaching approach. A comprehensive review of the behavioral approach to sales in restaurants, retail stores, wholesale establishments, and telephone operations found considerable success.[61] When a combination of antecedent and consequence intervention strategies were used, dramatic improvements were shown in areas such as wine and dessert sales, average customer transactions, customer assistance, sales forecasting, sales-call frequency, sales of telephone services, and airline reservations. A recent study of fast-food restaurants also found that antecedent prompts ("Can I get you some fries with that?") significantly increased consumer purchases.[62] The successful application of O.B. Mod. to the selling, absent-from-the-workstation, and idle-time behaviors of clerks in a large retail store was also found.[63]

Although the above results are not exhaustive and do not always reflect the exact O.B. Mod. model outlined in this chapter, they are representative of the growing application of the behavioral management approach. In addition, comprehensive reviews generally support the above findings.[64]

The specific O.B. Mod. model described earlier has also been directly tested and has been found to have positive performance results in both manufacturing[65] and service organizations (retail and hospital).[66] Very recently the O.B. Mod. approach has "gone international" and has been shown to have a positive impact on the performance behaviors and output of Russian factory workers[67] and retail clerks.[68] The implications of these findings are that behavioral management systematically applied through steps such as the O.B. Mod. model can help meet the performance improvement challenges facing today's organizations in the highly competitive global economy.

Summary

Learning is a major psychological process, but it has not been as popular in the study of organizational behavior as constructs such as attitudes or motivation. Also, it has not been generally recognized that there are different types of learning and different theoretical explanations of learning (behavioristic, cognitive, and social). Despite the controversy surrounding learning theory, there are many accepted principles of learning that are derived largely from experimentation and the analysis of operant conditioning. Reinforcement is probably the single most important concept in the learning process and is probably most relevant to the study of organizational behavior. On the basis of the classic law of effect, reinforcement can be operationally defined as anything that increases the strength of a response and that tends to induce repetitions of the behavior that preceded the reinforcement. Reinforcers may be positive (the application of a desirable consequence) or negative (termination or withdrawal of an undesirable consequence), but both have the impact of strengthening the behavior and increasing its frequency. Punishment, on the other hand, decreases the strength and frequency of the behavior.

The major direct application of learning theories and principles is through organizational reward systems and behavioral management. Monetary rewards are most closely associated with organizational rewards, but unless contingently administered, may be depended upon too much and may not have the desired impact on employee performance. More systematic attention must be given to nonfinancial rewards, especially social rewards and feedback. Behavioral management can be applied through O.B. Mod. steps: identify the performance-related behavior; measure it to determine the baseline frequency; functionally analyze both the antecedents and the consequences of the behavior (A-B-C); intervene through a positive reinforcement strategy to accelerate the critical performance behaviors; and evaluate to make sure the intervention is, in fact, increasing performance. The behavioral management approach in general and O.B. Mod. in particular have been demonstrated to have a significant positive impact on employee performance in both manufacturing and nonmanufacturing, service-oriented organizations.

Questions for Discussion and Review

1. Do you agree with the statement that learning is involved in almost everything that everyone does? Explain.
2. What are the major dimensions of behavioristic, cognitive, and social learning theories?
3. What is the difference between classical and operant conditioning?
4. What is the difference between positive and negative reinforcement? What is the difference between negative reinforcement and punishment? Provide some examples.
5. What role does and should money play in the organizational reward system? What could be done to make it more effective?
6. What are some examples of nonfinancial rewards? How can these be used to improve employee performance?
7. What are the five steps of O.B. Mod.? Briefly summarize the critical dimensions of each step that will help improve employee performance.
8. In what areas has behavioral management been successfully applied?

Footnote References and Supplemental Readings

1. For example, see Judith L. Komaki, "Toward Effective Supervision: An Operant Analysis and Comparison of Managers at Work," *Journal of Applied Psychology*, vol. 71, no. 2, 1986, pp. 270–279; Fred Luthans and Robert Kreitner, *Organizational Behavior Modification*, Scott, Foresman, Glenview, Ill., 1975; Fred Luthans and Robert Kreitner, *Organizational Behavior Modification and Beyond*, Scott,

Foresman, Glenview, Ill., 1985; and W. E. Scott, Jr., and P. M. Podsakoff, *Behavioral Principles in the Practice of Management*, John Wiley, New York, 1985.

2. Robert Glaser, "The Reemergence of Learning Theory Within Instructional Research," *American Psychologist*, January 1990, p. 29.

3. For example, see Dennis A. Gioia and Henry P. Sims, Jr., "Cognition-Behavior Connections: Attribution and Verbal Behavior in Leader-Subordinate Interactions," *Organizational Behavior and Human Decision Processes*, vol. 37, 1986, pp. 197–229.

4. Thomas C. Mawhinney, "Learning," in Dennis W. Organ and Thomas Bateman, *Organizational Behavior*, 3d ed., Business Publications, Plano, Tex., 1986, pp. 90–91.

5. Albert Bandura, "Social Learning Theory," in J. T. Spence, R. C. Carson, and J. W. Thibaut (eds.), *Behavioral Approaches to Therapy*, General Learning, Morristown, N.J., 1976, p. 5.

6. For a summary of this research, see Albert Bandura, *Social Foundations of Thought and Action: A Social-Cognitive View*, Prentice-Hall, Englewood Cliffs, N.J., 1986.

7. Dennis A. Gioia and Charles C. Manz, "Linking Cognition and Behavior: A Script Processing Interpretation of Vicarious Learning," *Academy of Management Review*, July 1985, pp. 527–539.

8. Albert Bandura, "Self-Efficacy Mechanism in Human Agency," *American Psychologist*, vol. 37, 1982, pp. 122–147.

9. Marilyn E. Gist and Terence R. Mitchell, "Self-Efficacy: A Theoretical Analysis of Its Determinants and Malleability," *Academy of Management Review*, April 1992, pp. 183–211.

10. For a summary of this research, see Gist and Mitchell, loc. cit., and Edwin A. Locke and Gary P. Latham, *A Theory of Goal Setting and Task Performance*, Prentice-Hall, Englewood Cliffs, N.J., 1990, pp. 70–75.

11. A. Bandura, C. B. Taylor, S. C. Williams, I. N. Medford, and J. D. Barchas, "Catecholamine Secretion as a Function of Perceived Coping Self-Efficacy," *Journal of Consulting and Clinical Psychology*, vol. 53, 1985, pp. 406–414.

12. Edward L. Thorndike, *Animal Intelligence*, Macmillan, New York, 1911, p. 244.

13. Gregory B. Northcraft and Margaret A. Neale, *Organizational Behavior*, Dryden, Chicago, 1990, p. 162.

14. For example, see Ronald E. Riggio, *Introduction to Industrial/Organizational Psychology*, Scott, Foresman/Little, Brown, Glenview, Ill., 1990, p. 175.

15. Linda Klebe Trevino, "The Social Effects of Punishment in Organizations: A Justice Perspective," *Academy of Management Review*, October 1992, pp. 647–676.

16. Robert A. Baron, *Behavior in Organizations*, Allyn and Bacon, Boston, 1986, p. 51.

17. Walter Kiechel, "How to Discipline in the Modern Age," *Fortune*, May 7, 1990, pp. 179–180.

18. Judy L. Agnew and William K. Redmon, "Contingency Specifying Stimuli: The Role of 'Rules' in Organizational Behavior Management," *Journal of Organizational Behavior Management*, vol. 12, no. 2, 1992, pp. 67–76, and Richard W. Mallott, "A Theory of Rule-Governed Behavior," *Journal of Organizational Behavior Management*, vol. 12, no. 2, 1992, pp. 45–65.

19. John A. Byrne and Chuck Hawkins, "Executive Pay: The Party Ain't Over Yet," *Business Week*, Apr. 26, 1993, pp. 56–57.

20. "Labor Letter," *The Wall Street Journal*, Jan. 20, 1987, p. 1.

21. For a recent comprehensive review, see Gary P. Latham and Vandra L. Huber, "Schedules of Reinforcement: Lessons from the Past and Issues for the Future," *Journal of Organizational Behavior Management*, vol. 12, no. 1, 1992, pp. 125–149.

22. E. Brian Peach and Daniel A. Wren, "Pay for Performance from Antiquity to the 1950s," *Journal of Organizational Behavior Management*, vol. 12, no. 1, 1992, pp. 5–26.

23. Sally Solo, "Stop Whining and Get Back to Work," *Fortune*, Mar. 12, 1990, p. 50.

24. Robert P. McNutt, "Achievement Pays Off at DuPont," *Personnel*, June 1990, pp. 5–10.

25. "All Pulling Together, to Get the Carrot," *The Wall Street Journal*, Apr. 30, 1990, p. B1.

26. Luis R. Gomez-Mejia, David B. Balkin, and George T. Milkovich, "Rethinking Rewards for Technical Employees," *Organizational Dynamics*, Spring 1990, p. 67.

27. *Nation's Business*, March 1990, p. 12.

28. Sylvie St. Onge, "Variables Influencing Pay-for-Performance Perception in a Merit Pay Environment," *Academy of Management Best Papers Proceedings*, 1993, pp. 121–125.

29. Bob Filipczak, "Why No One Likes Your Incentive Program," *Training*, August 1993, pp. 19–25.

30. "All Pulling Together," loc. cit.

31. See Raymond A. Katzell and Donna E. Thompson, "Work Motivation," *American Psychologist*, Feb. 1990, pp. 148–149.

32. Jaime A. Hermann, Ana I. deMontes, Benjamin Domingues, Francisco deMontes, and B. L. Hopkins, "Effects of Bonuses for Punctuality on the Tardiness of Industrial Workers," *Journal of Applied Behavioral Analysis*, Winter 1973, pp. 563–570.

33. Jone L. Pearce, William B. Stevenson, and James L. Perry, "Managerial Compensation Based on Organizational Performance: A Time Series Analysis of the Effects of Merit Pay," *Academy of Management Journal*, June 1985, pp. 261–278.

34. Donald Brookes, "Merit Pay: Does It Help or Hinder Productivity?" *HR Focus*, January 1993, p. 13.

35. Karen Matthes, "Giving Employees the Benefit of Time," *HR Focus*, August 1993, p. 3.

36. D. M. Prue and J. A. Fairbank, "Performance Feedback in Organizational Behavior Management: A Review," *Journal of Organizational Behavior Management*, Spring 1981, pp. 1–16.

37. Richard E. Kopelman, "Objective Feedback," in Edwin A. Locke (ed.), *Generalizing from Laboratory to Field Settings*, Lexington Books, Lexington, Mass., 1986, pp. 119–145.

38. Fred Luthans, Richard M. Hodgetts, and Stuart A. Rosenkrantz, *Real Managers*, Ballinger, Cambridge, Mass., 1988, pp. 141–142.

39. Daniel R. Ilgen, Cynthia D. Fisher, and M. Susan Taylor, "Consequences of Individual Feedback on Behavior in Organizations," *Journal of Applied Psychology*, August 1979, pp. 349–371, and Edwin A. Locke and Gary P. Latham, *A Theory of Goal Setting and Task Performance*, Prentice-Hall, Englewood Cliffs, N.J., 1990, pp. 185–189.

40. David A. Nadler, "The Effects of Feedback on Task Group Behavior: A Review of the Experimental Research," *Organizational Behavior and Human Performance*, June 1979, pp. 309–338.

41. John M. Ivancevich and J. Timothy McMahon, "The Effects of Goal Setting, External Feedback, and Self-Generated Feedback on Outcome Variables: A Field Experiment," *Academy of Management Journal*, June 1982, pp. 291–308.

42. Robert C. Linden and Terence R. Mitchell, "Reactions to Feedback: The Role of Attributions," *Academy of Management Journal*, June 1985, pp. 291–308.

43. Kenneth M. Nowack, "360-Degree Feedback: The Whole Story," *Training and Development*, January 1993, pp. 69–72.

44. David M. Herold, Robert C. Linden, and Marya L. Leatherwood, "Using Mutliple Attributes to Assess Sources of Performance Feedback," *Academy of Management Journal*, December 1987, pp. 826–835.

45. Steve Williams and Fred Luthans, "The Impact of Choice of Rewards and Feedback on Task Performance," *Journal of Organizational Behavior*, vol. 13, 1992, pp. 653–666.

46. Robert Waldersee and Fred Luthans, "The Impact of Positive and Corrective Feedback on Customer Service Performance," *Journal of Organizational Behavior*, vol. 14, 1993, pp. 83–95.

47. Fred Luthans and Robert Kreitner, *Organizational Behavior Modification and Beyond*, Scott, Foresman, Glenview, Ill., 1985.

48. See Fred Luthans, "Resolved: Functional Analysis Is the Best Technique for Diagnostic Evaluation of Organizational Behavior," in Barbara Karmel (ed.), *Point and Counterpoint in Organizational Behavior*, Dryden, Hinsdale, Ill., 1980, pp. 48–60.

49. V. Mark Daniel, "Employee Absenteeism: A Selective Review of Antecedents and Consequences," *Journal of Organizational Behavior Management*, Spring/Summer 1985, p. 157.

50. See Ellen Ernst Kossek, "Why Many HR Programs Fail," *Personnel*, May 1990, p. 52.

51. Kenneth N. Wexley and Gary P. Latham, *Developing and Training Human Resources*, Scott, Foresman, Glenview, Ill., 1981, p. 78.

52. Ibid., pp. 81–84.

53. See Lee W. Frederiksen (ed.), *Handbook of Organizational Behavior Management*, Interscience-Wiley, New York, 1982, pp. 12–14; these findings are summarized in Fred Luthans and Robert Kreitner, *Organizational Behavior Modification and Beyond*, Scott, Foresman, Glenview, Ill., 1985, Chap. 8.

54. Frederiksen, op. cit., p. 14.

55. R. W. Kempen, "Absenteeism and Tardiness," in Frederiksen, op. cit., p. 372.

56. Fred Luthans and Terry L. Maris, "Evaluating Personnel Programs Through the Reversal Technique," *Personnel Journal*, October 1979, pp. 696–697.

57. Dov Zohar and Nahum Fussfeld, "A System Approach to Organizational Behavior Modification: Theoretical Considerations and Empirical Evidence," *International Review of Applied Psychology*, October 1981, pp. 491–505.

58. Beth Sulzer-Azaroff, "Behavioral Approaches to Occupational Health and Safety," in Frederiksen, op. cit., pp. 505–538. Also see Robert A. Reber, Jerry A. Wallin, and David L. Duhon, "Preventing Occupational Injuries Through Performance Management," *Public Personnel Management*, Summer 1993, pp. 301–312.

59. "Labor Letter," loc. cit.

60. Thomas K. Connellan, *How to Improve Human Performance*, Harper & Row, New York, 1978, pp. 170–174.

61. Robert Mirman, "Performance Management in Sales Organizations," in Frederiksen, op. cit., pp. 427–475.

62. Mark J. Martinko, J. Dennis White, and Barbara Hassell, "An Operant Analysis of Prompting in a Sales Environment," *Journal of Organizational Behavior Management*, vol. 10, no. 1, 1989, pp. 93–107.

63. Fred Luthans, Robert Paul, and Douglas Baker, "An Experimental Analysis of the Impact of Contingent

Reinforcement on Salespersons' Performance Behaviors," *Journal of Applied Psychology*, June 1981, pp. 314–323, and Fred Luthans, Robert Paul, and Lew Taylor, "The Impact of Contingent Reinforcement on Retail Salespersons' Performance Behaviors: A Replicated Field Experiment," *Journal of Organizational Behavior Management*, Spring/Summer 1985, pp. 25–35.

64. See Kirk O'Hara, C. Merle Johnson, and Terry A. Beehr, "Organizational Behavior Management in the Private Sector: A Review of Empirical Research and Recommendations for Further Investigation," *Academy of Management Review*, October 1985, pp. 848–864; Gerald A. Merwin, John A. Thompson, and Eleanor E. Sanford, "A Methodology and Content Review of Organizational Behavior Management in the Private Sector 1978–1986," *Journal of Organizational Behavior Management*, vol. 10, no. 1, 1989, pp. 39–57; and Frank Andrasik, "Organizational Behavior Modification in Business Settings: A Methodological and Content Review," *Journal of Organizational Behavior Management*, vol. 10, no. 1, 1989, pp. 59–77.

65. Robert Ottemann and Fred Luthans, "An Experimental Analysis of the Effectiveness of an Organizational Behavior Modification Program in Industry," *Academy of Management Proceedings*, 1975, pp. 140–142; Fred Luthans and Jason Schweizer,

"How Behavior Modification Techniques Can Improve Total Organizational Performance," *Management Review*, September 1979, pp. 43–50; and Fred Luthans, Walter S. Maciag, and Stuart A. Rosenkrantz, "O.B. Mod.: Meeting the Productivity Challenge with Human Resource Management," *Personnel*, March–April 1983, pp. 28–36.

66. Luthans, Paul, and Baker, loc. cit.; Luthans, Paul, and Taylor, loc. cit.; and Charles A. Snyder and Fred Luthans, "Using O.B. Mod. to Increase Hospital Productivity," *Personnel Administrator*, August 1982, pp. 67–73.

67. Dianne H. B. Welsh, Fred Luthans, and Steven M. Sommer, "Managing Russian Factory Workers: The Impact of U.S.-Based Behavioral and Participative Techniques," *Academy of Management Journal*, February 1993, pp. 58–79, and Dianne H. B. Welsh, Fred Luthans, and Steven M. Sommer, "Organizational Behavior Modification Goes to Russia: Replicating an Experimental Analysis Across Cultures and Tasks," *Journal of Organizational Behavior Management*, vol. 13, no. 2, 1993, pp. 15–35.

68. Dianne H. B. Welsh, Steven M. Sommer, and Nancy Birch, "Changing Performance Among Russian Retail Workers: Effectively Transferring American Management Techniques," *Journal of Organizational Change Management*, vol. 6, no. 2, 1993, pp. 34–50.

REAL CASE: Thanks for the Favor

Ethics is a major concern for many companies, and because of some of the activities of companies over the last decade, this concern is a welcome change. A good example is provided in the case of Michael Milken, the junk bond king who was sentenced to jail in late 1990 after pleading guilty to violating federal securities laws. One of the crimes that he was not charged with, but which was presented to the judge by the prosecution in an effort to supply a guilty conviction, related to the Wickes Company, a California retailer. The heart of the story rests with the 10 percent convertible preferred issue on which Wickes was paying $15 million in annual dividends. The president of Wickes realized that if he could get this preferred issue converted into common stock, the company would save the $15 million in dividends. However, the stock price was too low and none of the holders of the preferred issue were willing to convert to common stock. There were only two ways to get rid of this $15 million annual burden. One was to wait another two years, at which time the stock, by previous agreement, could be converted at the option of the company. The other was if the stock closed above $6 a share for twenty trading days out of any consecutive thirty. The company decided that this latter course was the best one to pursue. Working with Michael Milken's brokerage, Drexel Burnham, Wickes made an offer to buy the National Gypsum Company. Its own stock then rose above $6 a share, because investors felt that—with National Gypsum—Wickes would be a more valuable holding. The stock closed above $6 a share for nineteen of twenty-eight trading days. However, on the twenty-ninth day it fell below $6. The company had only one more day to get the price above $6.

Milken's company was legally forbidden from trading in Wickes stock, since it was helping with the National Gypsum takeover and was now regarded as an insider in the deal. However, this did not prevent Milken from urging his people to find clients to buy Wickes. At the same time, he had one of his associates call Ivan Boesky, another convicted inside trader who had done a great deal of business with Drexel, and ask him "as a favor" to buy the stock. Within twenty minutes of the close of the stock exchange, Milken's people were able to get 1.6 million shares purchased. However, this was only enough to stabilize the price at $6. They then called the broker on the trading floor of the New York Stock Exchange and learned that, in order to get the price to $6⅛ by the close, they would have to buy another 300,000 shares. This was done immediately and the stock closed at $6⅛. Five days later, Wickes exercised its option and called in the preferred stock and replaced it with common stock. In the process, the company saved itself $15 million in dividends for the next two years. Those who helped push the stock over $6 then began disposing of their holdings. Within three weeks, they were out of the stock. The total cost to those who helped out was about $500,000 including brokerage fees. In turn, Wickes saved a total of $30 million. Drexel, which over a three-and-a-half-year period earned $118 million in investment banking fees from Wickes, was able to keep its client happy.

1. Was money a reinforcer in this case?
2. Later investigation uncovered that Boesky's firm lost about $400,000 for doing this favor for Milken. Why then was it willing to help Milken?
3. When the judge sentenced Milken to ten years in prison, the harshest sentence ever given to anyone for violating federal security laws, how was she using learning theory to send a message?

**CASE:
Contrasting Styles**

Henry Adams has been a production supervisor for eight years. He came up through the ranks and is known as a tough but hardworking supervisor. Jane Wake has been a production supervisor for about the same length of time and also came up through the ranks. Jane is known as a nice, hardworking boss. Over the past several years these two supervisors' sections have been head and shoulders above the other six sections on hard measures of performance (number of units produced). This is true despite the almost opposite approaches the two have taken in handling their workers. Henry explained his approach as follows:

> The only way to handle workers is to come down hard on them whenever they make a mistake. In fact, I call them together every once in a while and give them heck whether they deserve it or not, just to keep them on their toes. If they are doing a good job, I tell them that's what they're getting paid for. By taking this approach, all I have to do is walk through my area, and people start working like mad.

Jane explained her approach as follows:

> I don't believe in that human relations stuff of being nice to workers. But I do believe that a worker deserves some recognition and attention from me if he or she does a good job. If people make a mistake, I don't jump on them. I feel that we are all entitled to make some errors. On the other hand, I always do point out what the mistake was and what they should have done, and as soon as they do it right, I let them know it. Obviously, I don't have time to give attention to everyone doing things right, but I deliberately try to get around to people doing a good job every once in a while.

Although Henry's section is still right at the top along with Jane's section in units produced, personnel records show that there has been 3 times more turnover in Henry's section than in Jane's section, and the quality-control records show that Henry's section has met quality standards only twice in the last six years, while Jane has missed attaining quality standards only once in the last six years.

1. Both these supervisors have similar backgrounds. On the basis of learning theory, how can you explain their opposite approaches to handling people?
2. What are some of the examples of punishment, positive reinforcement, and negative reinforcement found in this case? If Jane is using a reinforcement approach, how do you explain this statement: "I don't believe in that human relations stuff of being nice to workers"?
3. How do you explain the performance, turnover, and quality results in these two sections of the production department?

CASE:
Volunteers Can't Be Punished

Ann-Marie Jackson is head of a volunteer agency in a large city. She is in charge of a volunteer staff of over twenty-five people. Weekly, she holds a meeting with this group in order to keep them informed and teach them the specifics of any new laws or changes in state and federal policies and procedures that might affect their work, and she discusses priorities and assignments for the group. This meeting is also a time when members can share some of the problems and concerns for what they are personally doing and what the agency as a whole is doing. The meeting is scheduled to begin at 9 A.M. sharp every Monday. Lately, the volunteers have been filtering in every five minutes or so until almost 10 A.M. Ann-Marie has felt she has to delay the start of the meetings until all the people arrive. The last few weeks the meetings haven't started until 10 A.M. In fact, at 9 A.M., nobody has shown up. Ann-Marie cannot understand what has happened. She feels it is important to start the meetings at 9 A.M. so that they can be over before the whole morning is gone. On the other hand, she feels that her hands are tied because, after all, the people are volunteers and she can't push them or make them get to the meetings on time.

1. What advice would you give Ann-Marie? In terms of reinforcement theory, explain what is happening here and what Ann-Marie needs to do to get the meetings started on time.
2. What learning theories (operant, cognitive, and/or social) could be applied to Ann-Marie's efforts to teach her volunteers the impact of new laws and changes in state and federal policies and procedures?
3. How could someone like Ann-Marie use modeling to train her staff to do a more effective job?

CASE:
Up the Piece Rate

Larry Ames has successfully completed a company training program in O.B. Mod. He likes the approach and has started using it on the workers in his department. Following the O.B. Mod. model, he has identified several performance behaviors, measured and analyzed them, and used a positive reinforcement-extinction intervention strategy. His evaluation has showed a significant improvement in the performance of his department. Over coffee one day he commented to one of the other supervisors, "This contingent reinforcement approach really works. Before, the goody-goody people up in personnel were always telling us to try to understand and be nice to our workers. Frankly, I couldn't buy that. In the first place, I don't think there is anybody who can really *understand* my people—I certainly can't. More important, though, is that under this approach I am only nice *contingently*—contingent upon good performance. That makes a lot more sense, and my evaluation proves that it works." The other supervisor commented, "You are being reinforced for use of the reinforcement technique on your people." Larry said, "Sure I am. Just like the trainer said: 'Behavior that is reinforced will strengthen and repeat itself.' I'm so reinforced that I am starting to use it on my wife and kids at home, and you know what? It works there, too."

The next week Larry was called into the department head's office and was told, "Larry, as you know, your department has shown a substantial increase in performance since you completed the O.B. Mod. program. I have sent our industrial engineer down there to analyze your standards. I have received her report, and it looks like we will have to adjust your rates upward by 10 percent. Otherwise, we are going to have to pay too much incentive pay. I'm sure you can use some of the things you learned in that O.B. Mod. program to break the news to your people. Good luck, and keep up the good work."

1. Do you think Larry's boss, the department head, attended the O.B. Mod. program? Analyze the department head's action in terms of O.B. Mod.
2. What do you think will be Larry's reaction now and in the future? How do you think Larry's people will react?
3. Given the 10 percent increase in standards, is there any way that Larry could still use the O.B. Mod. approach with his people? With his boss? How?

CASE:
A Tardiness
Problem

You have been getting a lot of complaints recently from your boss about the consistent tardiness of your work group. The time-sheet records indicate that your people's average start-up time is about ten minutes late. While you have never been concerned about the tardiness problem, your boss is really getting upset. He points out that the tardiness reduces the amount of production time and delays the start-up of the assembly line. You realize that the tardiness is a type of avoidance behavior—it delays the start of a very boring job. Your work group is very cohesive, and each of the members will follow what the group wants to do. One of the leaders of the group seems to spend a lot of time getting the group into trouble. You want the group to come in on time, but you don't really want a confrontation on the issue because, frankly, you don't think it is important enough to risk getting everyone upset with you. You decide to use an O.B. Mod. approach.

1. Trace through the five steps in the O.B. Mod. model to show how it could be applied to this tardiness problem. Make sure you are specific in identifying the critical performance behaviors and the antecedents and consequences of the functional analysis.
2. Do you think the approach you have suggested in your answer above will really work? Why or why not?

INTEGRATIVE CONTEMPORARY CASE/READING FOR PART 2

The Company Built
Upon the Golden
Rule: Lincoln
Electric

George E. Willis, Chairman and Chief Executive Officer of The Lincoln Electric Company, characterizes our organization as follows: "We're not a marketing company, we're not an R&D company, and we're not a service company. We're a manufacturing company, and I believe that we are the best manufacturing company in the world" (Christensen, Berg, and Salter, 1976, p. 352). That is a bold statement. The fact that a manufacturing company such as ours is probably as well known, worldwide, for its management practices as for its products, is intriguing.

Since 1895, Lincoln Electric has been engaged in creating real products to suit the real needs of real people. It is our conviction that people—employees, customers, and stockholders—are basic to our business and to our profitability. If we produce the finest quality product at the lowest possible price, deliver it on time, and back it up with excellent service, that meets the needs of our customers and by extension, our stockholders. It also meets the fundamental need of our employees to develop their own potential by doing their best. If, as managers, we treat our employees the way that we would like to be treated, we are rewarded with the kind of dedicated, talented and loyal work force that will consistently meet the needs of the marketplace. On all counts, our record shows that the rewards have been ample.

Any successful enterprise can point to a history that rests upon a unique blend of individual talent, certain fortuitous circumstances, and plenty of hard work. In the case of Lincoln Electric, the widely different abilities of two brothers coalesced to meet the demands of a fast-growing industrial base in the heartland of America around the turn of the century.

The Early Years. John C. Lincoln determined while still in high school that electrical engineering would be his life's work. He attended Ohio State University in the 1880s, but left after three years because he could see no advantage in remaining to receive a Bachelor of Arts degree. At the time, the science of engineering was undergoing such rapid change that by the time a book was written on the subject, it was obsolete. Before 1890, John Lincoln had secured the first of what would number fifty-five patents in his name (Moley, 1962, p. 36). It was for an electric brake design for streetcars.

Lincoln's first positions were with Brush Electric Company and the Elliot-Lincoln Electric Company. The latter was so named after Lincoln had developed an innovative electric motor and was elected president of the firm. When Elliot-Lincoln failed in the business panic of 1895, John Lincoln set up a shop in his home to do commission work and develop his own inventions. A commission from Herbert Henry Dow, who later founded the Dow Chemical company, provided him with the $200 he used as capital to start The Lincoln Electric Company. In 1895, Lincoln patented the electric motor he had developed for Dow and made it the basis for his infant company's operations.

Meanwhile, John C.'s brother James F. Lincoln, seventeen years his junior, was working hard at a variety of jobs in order to earn college tuition. By 1902, with the aid of his savings and some loans from his older brother, James F. entered Ohio State

Source: Harry C. Handlin, "The Company Built Upon the Golden Rule: Lincoln Electric," *Journal of Organizational Behavior Management*, vol. 12, no. 1, 1992, pp. 151–163, copyright 1992 by the Haworth Press, Inc. All rights reserved. Reprinted by permission.

University. As had been the case with John, however, Jim Lincoln's studies did not lead to a degree. Illness in his fourth year of college caused him to withdraw from Ohio State. Several years later, the University awarded both of the Lincoln brothers engineering degrees with honors. In 1907, Jim Lincoln entered his brother's employ at the age of twenty-four. He was put on the payroll at a salary of $150 per month, plus a percentage of gross sales. It was immediately apparent that he was aggressive, ambitious, and possessed of unusual management ability.

The working partnership of these two brothers generated unique benefits for the two of them as individuals, and for the fledgling Lincoln Electric Company as a whole. But we spoke above of circumstance. In the early years of the century, the technology of arc welding began to penetrate the industrial scene. The idea of making welding machinery part of the company's product line held its own appeal for each of the Lincoln brothers. John was intrigued by the engineering problems posed by the new process and its application, while Jim Lincoln foresaw the technology's tremendous potential for commercial development. In 1911, Lincoln Electric introduced its first arc welding machine (Moley, 1962). The need for large numbers of transport ships during World War I created the first large-scale demand for welding. Although two giant companies—Westinghouse and General Electric—quickly entered the field, Lincoln Electric had a head start. While we remain a relatively small company, with only 2,600 employees in our U.S. operations, we have never relinquished that lead.

The Birth of Incentive Management. In 1914, the Lincoln Electric plant employed 150 workers, and gross sales had reached $250,000 (Moley, 1962). That year, James F. Lincoln was made vice president and general manager of the company. One of his first innovations was to set up an advisory board comprised of elected representatives from each department of the company. With that simple act, the seeds of Lincoln Electric's famous Incentive Management program were sown. The Advisory board has met once every two weeks ever since.

Jim Lincoln was an acute observer of the world around him. As he witnessed the early activities of the American labor movement, he was struck by the absence of both cooperation and empathy in the stances taken on the one hand by management, and on the other, by labor. He realized that if every Lincoln Electric employee wanted the company to succeed as much as *he* did, success would be inevitable. In searching for the key that would motivate his work force, he decided to start by listening to the employees. In his own words, this is what he learned:

> If those crying loudest about the inefficiencies of labor were put in the position of the wage earner, they would react as he does. The worker is not a man apart. He has the same needs, aspirations and reactions as the industrialist. A worker will not cooperate in any program that will penalize him. *Does any manager?* (Christensen et al., 1976)

The sons of a minister, John C. and James F. Lincoln had been raised with the words "Do unto others as you would have them do unto you" ringing in their ears. It was not difficult for them to adopt the Golden rule as a basic operating premise of their company. And in almost a century of operation, it has never failed us.

Growing with the Twentieth Century. Today, The Lincoln Electric Company is the largest manufacturer of arc welding products in the world, operating twenty plants in fifteen countries. In the early 1920s, it became apparent that arc welding would be the joining technology of the future, and the company committed itself to remaining in the forefront of the field. We still produce industrial motors, but we have emphasized welding technology for the last seven decades.

We attribute our stability, our profitability, and our steady growth to the Incentive Management philosophy (Lincoln, 1951) developed by James F. Lincoln, with able assistance from Lincoln employees, over the period from 1914 to the late 1950s. The basic elements of our management approach were all in place, and had been operating for some time, prior to Jim Lincoln's death in 1967. Our vice chairman, Harry Carlson, likes to point out that "A unique triumph of the company is its survival following the loss of the family leadership which nurtured it for over seventy years. Many, many companies have foundered and ultimately failed in the critical transition from family to professional management." In the case of Lincoln Electric, a loyal work force and the principles of Incentive Management proved to be stellar allies during that transition period.

Incentive Management: How It Really Works. First, let us examine what Incentive Management is not. It is not a "quick fix." It is not a panacea. It is not a static formula—in fact, it demands constant flexibility. Especially in the short run, it is not a particularly easy way to run an organization. That said, we must also point out that this difficult, challenging management approach *works.* It works because by definition, it demands the very best that each of us has to give.

Quality begins at home. At The Lincoln Electric Company, we guarantee our products, and we guarantee our employees' jobs. This gives us a tremendous advantage in the marketplace. To both our customers and our workers, it means that we are in business for the long haul, not the quick buck. We are profoundly aware that profit is the resource that enables us to serve our customers. Therefore, we have developed a management philosophy that directly rewards our employees for turning out high quality products very efficiently while controlling costs. They do this simply because it is in their own best interests.

Responsibility. Our mission is to produce more and more units of the best possible product to sell at the lowest possible price to an ever increasing number of customers. We have been able to fulfill that mission consistently for just one reason: at every level of the organization, Lincoln employees take individual responsibility for the jobs they do. Because our people back up their work, we can offer warranties that exceed the industry standard. This means that every worker must be a manager, and every manager must be a worker. The Harvard Business School case study of the company notes that "Lincoln's organizational hierarchy was flat, with few levels between the bottom and the top. For example . . . the vice president of sales had 37 regional sales managers reporting to him" (Christensen et al., 1976). This is possible because Lincoln employees are self-managers.

In self-management is found the true meaning of efficiency, because nothing increases overhead as quickly and non-productively as extra layers of management. We believe that the ability to be self-managing is latent in all human beings. In developing that potential, Lincoln Electric has found the following practices indispensable:

- Individual accountability for quality.
- Individual accountability for output.
- Wages and bonuses directly tied to quality and output.
- Exact staffing of departments to cut absenteeism and emphasize the importance of each employee's job.
- Maintaining the fewest possible layers of management.

Communications. Under Incentive Management, information is shared with all employees regarding the financial and market position of the organization. This is done with printed reports and orally. In too many organizations, communication moves only one way, from the top down. Incentive Management, with its respect for each individual, demands two-way communication. When employees know what is expected of them, they have the opportunity to do their best. One critically important job of management is to be clear about its expectations. This means consistently communicating those expectations, and also setting a good personal example for employees to follow. This way, effective communication becomes part of the daily life of the organization.

We have found our mission itself to be an asset in this regard. Doing what is best for the customer tends to reduce conflict and can solve many communications problems. Making customers our primary focus is a significant unifying force within the company. In addition to a straightforward mission statement that every employee can understand and take to heart, Incentive Management has given us two more methods for establishing and maintaining good two-way communication. The Advisory Board mentioned above provides a forum for employees to bring issues of concern to top management's attention, to discuss employee relations, to question company policies, and to make suggestions for their improvement. This group has no decision-making status. However, questions receive careful attention and prompt responses. Advisory Board members are elected by their fellow workers for one year, non-successive terms, and they are paid for the time spent serving in this capacity. Any aspect of the company's operations may be brought before the Board for discussion, including such items as general policy, cost reduction, new products, sales, safety, working conditions, and ways to provide better service to the customer. The Advisory Board meets every two weeks, with either the Chairman or the President chairing each meeting.

Next, we have an "Open Door/Open Mind Policy." We believe that a manager who keeps the office door open to employees at all times is the symbol of an open mind. Any employee should feel free to contact any level of supervision or management with a legitimate suggestion, complaint or request at any time. Of course, if the manager is otherwise engaged, the employee may have to wait, or may choose to make an appointment for another time. With a work force made up of responsible, self-managing people, an Open Door/Open Mind Policy is rarely abused. The level of mutual respect it engenders is so healthy for the organization as a whole that it more than offsets any temporary problems that might occur when such a policy is first instituted.

Hiring practices. At Lincoln, we hire very, very carefully, because we expect our employees to make a lifetime commitment to the company. It is essential that we identify candidates who can demonstrate both the *desire* to succeed and *capacity* for growth. Years of experience have taught us that these qualities, more than any other single factor, indicate the potential of a successful new hire. In the long run, they are more important than formal education, work experience, or any particular level of skill. Incentive Management is specifically structured to encourage employees to develop their latent abilities. At Lincoln, the hiring process relies on an extensive series of personal interviews. In each interview, the emphasis is on identifying the job candidate's levels of self-motivation and success orientation. The development that can take place in the new recruit, no matter what the job may be, can and should be far greater after the employee is hired than it was before. That is what Incentive Management can do.

Recognition. Early on, Jim Lincoln realized that recognition is one of the most effective incentives for improved performance. Recognizing the self-motivated, self-managing and highly productive individual will encourage the continuing development of that person's abilities, while also allowing the individual to set a good example for others. Many incentives are more important than money; recognition is a very effective motivator (Lincoln, 1951, pp. 99–104). Key methods of recognizing employees are:

Promotion from within. As the most effective means of recognizing every employee's potential for development, Lincoln maintains a policy of promotion from within whenever possible. This necessarily means that hiring is restricted, with very few exceptions, to entry-level jobs. While it is certainly true that some employees are unlikely to be promoted, a policy of promoting from within recognizes and respects the potential of every worker.

Employee of the year awards. Every employee is considered potentially eligible for these annual awards, without regard to the capacity in which that individual serves the company. If a floor-sweeper performs the tasks and duties of that position in an outstanding manner, that person will be considered for this award.

Rewards. As an organization in business for the long term, we must pay wages and salaries based on local levels whether a particular year has been profitable or not. At Lincoln, our non-union factory work force is paid on a piecework basis. Employees are paid only for good pieces; defects must be corrected on their own time. When the company is profitable, the employees have contributed to creating those profits, and as such, share in them. Determining each individual's fair share according to that worker's contribution to profitability is not simple. Job evaluations to establish base rates and piecework pay, as well as strict control of working hours and the size of the work force, directly affect profitability. To handle this task, a Merit Rating system was developed. Its key points can be summarized as follows.

Each employee is evaluated in the context of a Merit Rating Group, which may consist of a single department, or several small departments combined. Merit ratings are completed twice each year. Each employee receives a set of four Merit Rating cards evaluating that person's performance, compared to all others in the rating group, on the basis of four equal categories or indicators. The cards record performance in these areas:

1. Dependability—This card rates the degree to which supervisors consider the employee to be self-managing. Included in this general performance category are

work safety, orderliness, care of equipment, and the effective use that person makes of his or her own skills.

2. Quality—In addition to rating the quality of the work performed, this card also considers the worker's success in eliminating errors and in reducing inefficiency and waste.

3. Output—This card rates how much productive work has actually been done by the employee within the rating period. It also reflects the individual's record of on-time attendance and willingness to expend consistent effort.

4. Ideas and Cooperation—New ideas and methods are important to our continuing efforts to work safely, reduce costs, increase output, improve quality, and improve our relationship with customers. This card gives credit for ideas, initiative, sharing of knowledge, acceptance of change, and ability to work as part of a team.

Merit ratings actually constitute a numerical grade determined by the relative position of the individual within the rating group. Each rating group is initially averaged to 25 points per person for each category. The hypothetical, perfectly average worker would receive 25 points in each category, for a perfectly average total merit rating of 100 points. Of course, no such person exists. It is entirely possible for a worker to be assigned a Merit Rating of 100, but it is likely that such a person might receive, for instance, 23 points for Dependability, 28 points for Quality, 27 points for Output, and 22 points for the Ideas and Cooperation card.

The guiding principle behind every Merit Rating decision is that of fairness and honesty. At Lincoln, we know we cannot compromise on these issues, because we are striving to increase individual motivation. Although a particular manager's judgement can and will vary, any suggestion of unfairness or dishonesty will damage motivation for a long time. The primary purpose of Merit Rating is to determine each individual's relative contribution to the success of the company in that period. The Merit Rating provides the opportunity for an objective discussion with each employee, ultimately permitting individual bonus calculation. The discussion with the employee includes a frank evaluation of the previous period's performance, resulting in a thorough understanding of the rating, clearly stated ways to improve in the future, and a continuing belief in the fairness of the process.

Security. Since the late 1950s, Lincoln Electric has operated under a policy of Guaranteed Continuous Employment. Our guarantee of employment states that no employee with two years or more of service will be laid off for lack of work. In extraordinary business circumstances, employees' hours may be reduced to 75 percent of the standard forty-hour work week, and we have had to do this occasionally—most recently during the recession of the early 1980s. However, not once in more than thirty years has a Lincoln employee of two years or more standing been terminated for lack of work. While the policy does *not* protect any employee who fails to perform his or her job properly, it *does* emphasize that management is responsible for maintaining a level of business that will keep every employee working productively. The institution of guaranteed employment sprang from our belief that fear is an ineffective motivator. If an employee lives in fear of being laid off, the natural tendency will be to make a job last as long as possible. Relief from such anxiety frees people to do their best work, confident in the knowledge that when one task has been completed, another will be waiting.

Implementing Incentive Management. I have already noted that Incentive Management is not an especially easy way to run an organization. However, at Lincoln we have a long track record that *proves* it works. In case there are readers who are attracted to these ideas, but find the prospect of initiating such a comprehensive program daunting, I will suggest some simple steps that can be taken to implement Incentive Management.

Commitment. Given management commitment and employee involvement, Incentive Management will make any organization more productive and more profitable. Without management commitment, of course, nothing will happen. Management and shareholders should study the principles of Incentive Management carefully. Shareholders must be made aware that this is not an easy practice, or a "quick fix." Only when all aspects of the program have been explored and are thoroughly understood can a consensus be reached concerning which elements should be adopted. A program lacking support from any segment of the organization will not succeed, so only those principles that can be fully supported by everyone should be considered.

Next, employees must be given the opportunity to evaluate the program themselves. Some Incentive Management depends upon the responsible participation of both management and labor, it cannot be imposed against the will of the employees. Enthusiastic supporters of the approach should be encouraged to promote its benefits to their fellow workers.

Finally, with the complete support of the shareholders, management and employees have to make a joint commitment to a comprehensive Incentive Management program. If profitability is elusive, any organization can still adopt, to its benefit, all those aspects of Incentive Management not directly related to bonus distribution. The bonus should be instituted as soon as profits are earned, or the program will quickly lose the support of employees.

Establishing the first advisory board. Two-way communication should be regarded as the foundation for any company's growth. Therefore, the first Advisory Board must set the best possible example for those to follow. The initial Advisory Board should be established by appointment. Management should select those individuals who understand that what is best for the company, both short and long term, is also best for the employees. This is a challenge to the company executives, because an effective Advisory Board will encourage employees to openly speak up, and in many instances, criticize the actions of the executive in charge. Certain decisions may have to be explained far more thoroughly than is the case in other accepted management practices. Remember, though, it works.

Toward the end of the first year of Advisory Board operation, the first of several elections should be held in which employees, by department, select their representatives for the next year's term of service on the Board. Departmental elections should be staggered over a period of months, so that new members joining the Board can benefit from the example and experience of veteran representatives. This will help to provide the continuity necessary to effective Board functioning. At Lincoln, Advisory Board service is for non-successive terms of one year, and representatives are paid a fixed fee for the assistance they render in this capacity. It is highly recommended that minutes of each meeting be promptly published and circulated on bulletin boards for review by all employees.

Advisory Board service should be regarded as a privilege and an important responsibility. Employees are being given an opportunity to contribute directly to the success of the company's manufacturing, marketing, engineering, and administrative functions. Board members are expected to be guided by the best interests of the company, which will also serve the best interests of the employees. Representatives should make an ongoing effort to foster cooperation among workers at every level of the organization. Each employee plays a vital role in the final results of the company.

Bonus determination. If the year has been profitable, it will become the responsibility of the Board of Directors to determine the total amount of the year-end bonus, in which the employees will share according to their Merit Ratings. Of course, there will be variations as to how this particular decision is made. At Lincoln, a bonus is earned only after all expenses are paid, including the wages of shareholders in the form of dividends, and necessary seed money. Incentive Management has been developed at Lincoln Electric over a period of several decades. In fact, it is not static, and like any worthwhile approach, is under more or less continual development. Those who would adopt these principles, however, usually cannot afford the luxury of taking ten or twenty years to develop their own management systems. In the current world marketplace, it is incumbent upon all of us to improve efficiency and provide better service to the customer now.

REFERENCES

Christensen, C. R., Berg, N. A., & Salter, M. S. (1976). The Lincoln Electric Company, Cleveland, Ohio. *Policy Formulation and Administration,* Seventh Edition, Homewood, Illinois: Richard D. Irwin, Inc.

Lincoln, J. F. (1951). *Incentive Management.* Cleveland, Ohio: The Lincoln Electric Company.

Moley, R. (1962). *The American Century of John C. Lincoln.* New York: Duell, Sloan and Pearce.

1. How typical do you think Lincoln Electric is? Obviously, this company has a long, unique history, but is this a type of company that can compete in today's environment?

2. What is Lincoln Electric's incentive management system? How does this fit with the Golden Rule? How does this fit with what you have studied in relation to motivation and reward systems?

3. Sections of this case on Lincoln Electric specifically refer to topics covered in the chapters in Part 2 of the text. Identify these topics and assess how they are being applied at this company. How do you think they could be more effectively applied now and in the future?

EXPERIENTIAL EXERCISES FOR PART 2

EXERCISE: Self-Perception and Development of the Self-Concept*

Goals:

1. To enable the students to consider their own self-concepts and to compare this with how they feel they are perceived by others.
2. To explore how the self-concept in personality is formed largely on the basis of feedback received from others (the reality that we "mirror ourselves in others").
3. To stimulate student thinking about how management of human resources may involve perception and personality.

Implementation:

1. The students take out a sheet of paper and fold it in half from top to bottom.
2. The students write "How I See Myself" and "How I Think Others See Me."
3. The students write down five one-word descriptions (adjectives) under each designation which, in their opinion, best describe how they perceive themselves and how others perceive them.
4. The students then share their two lists with their classmates (in dyads and triads, or the whole class) and discuss briefly. Each person may communicate what he or she is most proud of.
5. The instructor may participate in the exercise by sharing his or her list of adjectives.

EXERCISE: He Works, She Works*

Goal:

To increase your awareness of common stereotypes that exist in many organizations about male and female characteristics.

Implementation:

1. Complete the "He Works, She Works" worksheet shown at the top of the next page. In the appropriate spaces, write what you think the stereotyped responses would be. Do not spend too much time considering any one item. Rather, respond quickly and let your first impression or thought guide your answer.
2. Compare your individual responses with those on the "He Works, She Works" answer sheet provided by your instructor.
3. Compare your individual responses with those of other class members or participants. It is interesting to identify and discuss the most frequently used stereotypes.

* The exercise "Self-Perception and Development of the Self-Concept" was suggested by Philip Van Auken and is used with his permission. The "He Works, She Works" exercise is from Donald D. White and David A. Bednar, *Organizational Behavior*, Allyn and Bacon, Inc., Boston, 1987, pp. 199–200, as adapted from Natasha Josefowitz, *Pathways to Power*, Addison-Wesley, Menlo Park, Calif., 1980.

He Works, She Works (Worksheet)

The family picture is on *his* desk: (e.g., *He's a solid, responsible family man.*)	The family picture is on *her* desk: (e.g., *Her family will come before her career.*)
His desk is cluttered:	*Her* desk is cluttered:
He's talking with coworkers:	*She's* talking with coworkers:
He's not at his desk:	*She's* not at her desk:
He's not in the office:	*She's* not in the office:
He's having lunch with the boss:	*She's* having lunch with the boss:
The boss criticized *him*:	The boss criticized *her*:
He got an unfair deal:	*She* got an unfair deal:
He's getting married:	*She's* getting married:
He's going on a business trip:	*She's* going on a business trip:
He's leaving for a better job:	*She's* leaving for a better job:

EXERCISE: Motivation Questionnaire*

Goals:

1. To experience firsthand the concepts of one of the work-motivation theories—in this case, the popular Maslow hierarchy of needs.
2. To get personal feedback on your opinions of the use of motivational techniques in human resources management.

Implementation:

The following questions for the Motivation Questionnaire on the facing page have seven possible responses:

1. Please mark one of the seven responses by circling the number that corresponds to the response that fits your opinion. For example, if you "strongly agree," circle the number "+3."
2. Complete every item. You have about ten minutes to do so.

* The "Motivation Questionnaire" is reprinted from "Motivation: A Feedback Exercise," in John E. Jones and J. William Pfeiffer (eds.), *The Annual Handbook for Group Facilitators*, University Associates, San Diego, Calif., 1973, pp. 43–45, and is used with permission.

	Strongly Agree	Agree	Slightly Agree	Don't Know	Slightly Disagree	Disagree	Strongly Disagree
	+3	+2	+1	0	−1	−2	−3
1. Special wage increases should be given to employees who do their jobs very well.	+3	+2	+1	0	−1	−2	−3
2. Better job descriptions would be helpful so that employees will know exactly what is expected of them.	+3	+2	+1	0	−1	−2	−3
3. Employees need to be reminded that their jobs are dependent on the company's ability to compete effectively.	+3	+2	+1	0	−1	−2	−3
4. Supervisors should give a good deal of attention to the physical working conditions of their employees.	+3	+2	+1	0	−1	−2	−3
5. Supervisors ought to work hard to develop a friendly working atmosphere among their people.	+3	+2	+1	0	−1	−2	−3
6. Individual recognition for above-standard performance means a lot to employees.	+3	+2	+1	0	−1	−2	−3
7. Indifferent supervision can often bruise feelings.	+3	+2	+1	0	−1	−2	−3
8. Employees want to feel that their real skills and capacities are put to use on their jobs.	+3	+2	+1	0	−1	−2	−3
9. The company retirement benefits and stock programs are important factors in keeping employees on their jobs.	+3	+2	+1	0	−1	−2	−3
10. Almost every job can be made more stimulating and challenging.	+3	+2	+1	0	−1	−2	−3
11. Many employees want to give their best in everything they do.	+3	+2	+1	0	−1	−2	−3
12. Management could show more interest in the employees by sponsoring social events after hours.	+3	+2	+1	0	−1	−2	−3
13. Pride in one's work is actually an important reward.	+3	+2	+1	0	−1	−2	−3
14. Employees want to be able to think of themselves as "the best" at their own jobs.	+3	+2	+1	0	−1	−2	−3
15. The quality of the relationships in the informal work group is quite important.	+3	+2	+1	0	−1	−2	−3
16. Individual incentive bonuses would improve the performance of employees.	+3	+2	+1	0	−1	−2	−3
17. Visibility with upper management is important to employees.	+3	+2	+1	0	−1	−2	−3
18. Employees generally like to schedule their own work and to make job-related decisions with a minimum of supervision.	+3	+2	+1	0	−1	−2	−3
19. Job security is important to employees.	+3	+2	+1	0	−1	−2	−3
20. Having good equipment to work with is important to employees.	+3	+2	+1	0	−1	−2	−3

Scoring:

1. Transfer the numbers you circled in the questionnaire to the appropriate places in the spaces below.

Statement No.	Score	Statement No.	Score
10	____	2	____
11	____	3	____
13	____	9	____
18	____	19	____
Total	____	Total	____
(Self-actualization needs)		(Safety needs)	
6	____	1	____
8	____	4	____
14	____	16	____
17	____	20	____
Total	____	Total	____
(Esteem needs)		(Basic needs)	

Statement No.	Score
5	____
7	____
12	____
15	____
Total	____
(Belongingness needs)	

2. Record your total scores in the following chart by marking an "X" in each row below the number of your total score for that area of needs motivation.

	−12	−10	−8	−6	−4	−2	0	+2	+4	+6	+8	+10	+12
Self-actualization													
Esteem													
Belongingness													
Safety													
Basic													

Low use   High use

By examining the chart, you can see the relative strength you attach to each of the needs in Maslow's hierarchy. There are no right answers here, but most work-motivation theorists imply that most people are concerned mainly with the upper-level needs (that is, belongingness, esteem, and self-actualization).

EXERCISE: Job Design Survey*

Goals:

1. To experience firsthand the job characteristics approach to job design, in this case through the Hackman-Oldham Job Diagnostic Survey (JDS).

2. To get personal feedback on the motivating potential of your present or past job and to identify and compare its critical characteristics.

Implementation:

1. Please describe your present job (or a job you have held in the past) as objectively as you can. Circle the number that best reflects the job.

   a. How much *variety* is there in your job? That is, to what extent does the job require you to do many things at work, using a variety of your skills and talents?

   1----------2----------3-----------4-----------5----------6---------7

Very little; the job requires me to do the same routine things over and over again.	Moderate variety.	Very much; the job requires me to do many different things, using a number of different skills and talents.

   b. To what extent does your job involve doing a *"whole"* and *identifiable piece of work?* That is, is the job a complete piece of work that has an obvious beginning and end, or is it only a small part of the overall piece of work, which is finished by other people or by machines?

   1----------2----------3-----------4-----------5----------6---------7

My job is only a tiny part of the overall piece of work; the results of my activities cannot be seen in the final product or service.	My job is a moderate-sized "chunk" of the overall piece of work; my own contribution can be seen in the final outcome.	My job involves doing the whole piece of work, from start to finish; the results of my activities are easily seen in the final product or service.

   c. In general, *how significant or important* is your job? That is, are the results of your work likely to significantly affect the lives or well-being of other people?

   1----------2----------3-----------4-----------5----------6---------7

Not very significant; the outcomes of my work are *not* likely to have important effects on other people.	Moderately significant.	Highly significant; the outcomes of my work can affect other people in very important ways.

   d. How much *autonomy* is there in your job? That is, to what extent does your job permit you to decide on *your own* how to go about doing the work?

   1----------2----------3-----------4-----------5----------6---------7

Very little; the job gives me almost no personal "say" about how and when the work is done.	Moderate autonomy; many things are standardized and not under my control, but I can make some decisions.	Very much; the job gives me almost complete responsibility for deciding how and when the work is done.

* The "Job Design Survey" is drawn from J. R. Hackman and G. R. Oldham, "Development of the Job Diagnostic Survey," *Journal of Applied Psychology,* vol. 60, 1975, pp. 159–170.

e. To what extent does doing the *job itself* provide you with information about your work performance? That is, does the actual *work itself* provide clues about how well you are doing—aside from any feedback coworkers or supervisors may provide?

1-----------2-----------3------------4------------5-----------6----------7

| Very little; the job itself is set up so that I could work forever without finding out how well I am doing. | Moderately; sometimes doing the job provides feedback to me; sometimes it does not. | Very much; the job is set up so that I get almost constant feedback as I work about how well I am doing. |

2. The five questions above measure your perceived skill variety, task identity, task significance, autonomy, and feedback in your job. The complete JDS uses several questions to measure these dimensions. But to get some idea of the motivating potential, use your scores (1 to 7) for each job dimension and calculate as follows:

$$MPS = \frac{\text{skill variety} + \text{task identity} + \text{task significance}}{3} \times \text{autonomy} \times \text{feedback}$$

Next, plot your job design profile and MPS score on the graphs below. These show the national averages for all jobs. Analyze how you compare and suggest ways to redesign your job.

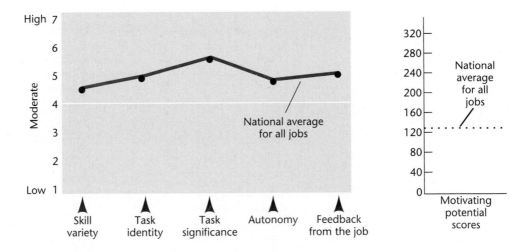

EXERCISE: Role Playing and O.B. Mod.*

Goal: To experience the application of the O.B. Mod. approach to human resources management.

Implementation: This role-playing situation involves two people: Casey, the supervisor of claims processing in a large insurance firm, and Pat, an employee in the

---

* "Role Playing and O.B. Mod." is adapted from Fred Luthans and Mark J. Martinko, *The Power of Positive Reinforcement,* McGraw-Hill, New York, 1978, pp. 35–38.

department. One person will be selected to play the role of Casey, and another will play Pat. The information on, and background for, each of the participants follow. When the participants have carefully read their roles, the supervisor, Casey, will be asked to conduct a performance-related discussion with Pat. Those who are not playing one of the roles should carefully observe the conversation between Casey and Pat and provide the information requested below. The observers should not necessarily read the roles of Casey and Pat.

1. List those words, phrases, or sentences that Casey used that seem particularly reinforcing.
2. List any words, phrases, or sentences used by Casey that may have been punishing.
3. List any suggestions that you have for improving Casey's future conversations with employees.
4. Using the steps of O.B. Mod. (identify, measure, analyze, intervene, and evaluate), how would you (or your group) improve the human performance in this claims department? Be as specific as you can for each step. You may have to fabricate some of the examples.

Role-playing situation for Casey:

After reading the information below, you are to conduct a performance-related discussion with Pat in order to reward increased productivity.

You are the supervisor of twenty people in the claims processing department of a large insurance company. Several weeks ago, you established standards for claims processing and measured each employee's work output. One employee, Pat Nelson, had particularly low output figures and averaged less than 80 percent of standard during the baseline data collection period. Your target for rewarding Pat was an 85 percent average for a one-week period. During the first two weeks, Pat failed to meet this goal. Now, in the third week after you have decided to use this approach, Pat has achieved the new goal. Pat's performance is illustrated in the graph below.

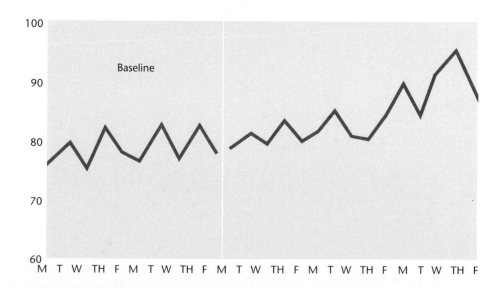

*Role-playing situation
for Pat:*

After reading the information below, you are to be interviewed by your supervisor concerning your performance.

You are Pat Nelson, an employee in the claims processing department of a large insurance company. Recently, your supervisor, Casey Parks, instituted a new system of measuring performance in the department. Most of the other employees have already discussed their performance with Casey, but for some reason Casey has not yet talked with you. Now this morning, Casey wanted to have a talk about your performance. You are somewhat anxious about what Casey will have to say. You know that you are not the best employee in the department, but you do make your best effort. You hope that Casey will recognize this and not be too hard on you.

PART 3

The Dynamics of Organizational Behavior

9 Group Dynamics and Teams

Learning Objectives

- **Describe** the basic nature of groups: the dynamics of group formation and the various types of groups.
- **Discuss** the implications that research on groups has for the practice of management.
- **Explain** the important dynamics of informal groups and organizations.
- **Analyze** the positive and negative attributes of formal work groups such as committees.
- **Present** the newly emerging team concept and practice.

Part 2 is devoted mainly to the micro variables important to organizational behavior. This part is more concerned with the dynamic nature of organizational behavior. This initial chapter approaches organizational behavior dynamics from the perspective of the group—both informal and formal—and the newly emerging team concept and practice.

The first section examines the way groups are formed, the various types of groups, some of the dynamics and functions of groups, and the findings of research on groups. The next section explores the dynamics of informal roles and organization. This discussion is followed by an analysis of formally designated work groups, specifically, the positive and negative attributes of committees. The balance of the chapter is devoted to teams. The distinction is made between work groups and teams, and specific attention is devoted to quality circles and self-managed teams. Finally, the way to make teams more effective through training and evaluation is discussed.

THE NATURE OF GROUPS

The group is widely recognized as an important sociological unit of analysis in the study of organizational behavior. Studying groups is especially valuable when the dynamics are analyzed. Group dynamics is concerned with the interactions and forces among group members in a social situation. When the concept is applied to the study of organizational behavior, the focus is on the dynamics of members of formal or informal work groups and, now, teams in the organization.

Similar to many other areas of organizational behavior, the study and application of groups is undergoing considerable controversy and change. For example, in a recent commentary about the status of groups in the field of organizational behavior, Alderfer noted:

> Groups and group dynamics are a little like the weather—something that nearly everyone talks about and only a few do anything about. Research, practice, and education about group dynamics are currently in a state of ferment. In the world of practice, we hear leaders speaking out to encourage teamwork, to support empowering people, and to establish organizational cultures that promote total quality management. Each of the initiatives depends on understanding groups well and acting effectively with them. Yet the collective behavior that follows the leaders' words often reveals a lack of sophisticated understanding and an inability to take competent action.[1]

The term *group* can be defined a number of different ways, depending on the perspective that is taken. A comprehensive definition would say that if a group exists in an organization, its members:

1. Are motivated to join.
2. Perceive the group as a unified unit of interacting people.
3. Contribute in various amounts to the group processes (that is, some people contribute more time or energy to the group than do others).
4. Reach agreements and have disagreements through various forms of interaction.[2]

Just as there is no one definition of the term "group," there is no universal agreement on what is meant by *group dynamics*. Although Kurt Lewin popularized the term in the 1930s, through the years different connotations have been attached to it. One normative view is that group dynamics describes *how* a group *should* be organized and conducted. Democratic leadership, member participation, and overall cooperation are stressed. Another view of group dynamics is that it consists of a set of *techniques*. Here, role playing, brainstorming, buzz groups, leaderless groups, group therapy, sensitivity training, team building, transactional analysis, and the Johari window are equated with group dynamics. Some of these techniques are covered in the next chapter and in Chapter 20, on organization development. A third view is the closest to Lewin's original conception. Group dynamics is viewed from the perspective of the internal nature of groups, how they form, their structure and processes, and how they function and affect individual members, other groups, and the organization. The following sections are devoted to this third view of group dynamics.

The Dynamics of Group Formation

Why do individuals form into groups? Before discussing some very practical reasons, it would be beneficial to examine briefly some of the classic theories of group formation, or why people affiliate with one another. The most basic theory explaining affiliation is *propinquity*. This interesting word means simply that individuals affiliate with one another because of spatial or geographical proximity. The theory would predict that students sitting next to one another in class, for example, are more likely to form into a group than are students sitting at opposite ends of the room. In an organization, employees who work in the same area of the plant or office or managers with offices close to one another would more probably form into groups than would those who are not physically located together. There is some research evidence to support the propinquity theory, and on the surface it has a great deal of merit for explaining group formation. The drawback is that it is not analytical and does not begin to explain some of the complexities of group formation. Some theoretical and practical reasons need to be explored.

Theories of Group Formation. A more comprehensive theory of group formation than mere propinquity comes from the theory based on activities, interactions, and sentiments.[3] These three elements are directly related to one another. The more activities persons share, the more numerous will be their interactions and the stronger will be their sentiments (how much the other persons are liked or disliked); the more interactions among persons, the more will be their shared activities and sentiments; and the more sentiments persons have for one another, the more will be their shared activities and interactions. This theory lends a great deal to the understanding of group formation and process. The major element is *interaction*. Persons in a group interact with one another, not just in the physical propinquity sense, but also to accomplish many group goals, such as cooperation and problem solving.

There are many other theories that attempt to explain group formation. Most often they are only partial theories, but they are generally additive in nature. One of the more comprehensive is a *balance theory* of group formation.[4] The theory states that persons are attracted to one another on the basis of similar attitudes toward commonly relevant objects and goals. Figure 9.1 shows this balance theory. Individual X will interact and form a relationship/group with individual Y because of common attitudes and values (Z). Once this relationship is formed, the participants strive to maintain a symmetrical balance between the attraction and the common attitudes. If an imbalance occurs, an attempt is made to restore the balance. If the balance cannot be restored, the relationship dissolves. Both propinquity and interaction play a role in balance theory.

FIGURE 9.1
A balance theory of group formation.

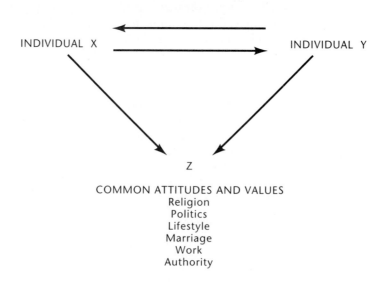

INDIVIDUAL X   INDIVIDUAL Y

Z

COMMON ATTITUDES AND VALUES
Religion
Politics
Lifestyle
Marriage
Work
Authority

Still another theoretical approach to group formation receiving considerable attention is *exchange theory*.[5] Similar to its functioning as a work-motivation theory, discussed in Chapter 6, exchange theory of groups is based upon reward-cost outcomes of interaction. A minimum positive level (rewards greater than costs) of an outcome must exist in order for attraction or affiliation to take place. Rewards from interactions gratify needs, while costs incur anxiety, frustration, embarrassment, or fatigue. Propinquity, interaction, and common attitudes all have roles in exchange theory.

Besides the more established social psychology explanations for group formation, there are also some generally recognized identifiable stages of group development.[6] These stages can be briefly summarized as follows:

1. *Forming.* This initial stage is marked by uncertainty and even confusion. Group members are not sure about the purpose, structure, task, or leadership of the group.
2. *Storming.* This stage of development, as indicated by the term, is characterized by conflict and confrontation. (In the usually emotionally charged atmosphere, there may be considerable disagreement and conflict among the members about roles and duties.)
3. *Norming.* Finally, in this stage the members begin to settle into cooperation and collaboration. They have a "we" feeling with high cohesion, group identity, and camaraderie.
4. *Performing.* This is the stage where the group is fully functioning and devoted to effectively accomplishing the tasks agreed upon in the norming stage.
5. *Adjourning.* This represents the end of the group, which in on going, permanent groups will never be reached. However, on project teams or task forces with a specific objective, once the objective is accomplished, the group will disband or have a new composition, and the stages will start over again.

Practicalities of Group Formation. Besides the conceptual explanations for group formation and development, there are some very practical reasons for joining and/or forming a group. For instance, employees in an organization may form a group for economic, security, or social reasons. Economically, workers may form a group to work on a project that is paid for on a group-incentive plan such as gainsharing,[7] or they may form a union to demand higher wages. For security, joining a group provides the individual with a united front in combating indiscriminant, unilateral treatment. The adage that there is strength in numbers applies in this case. The most important practical reason individuals join or form groups is, however, that groups tend to satisfy the very intense social needs of most people. Workers, in particular, generally have a very strong desire for affiliation. This need is met by belonging to a group. Research going as far back as the Hawthorne studies has found the affiliation motive to have a major impact on human behavior in organizations. Chapter 6 also discusses this motive.

Types of Groups

There are numerous types of groups. The theories of group formation that were just discussed are based partly upon the attraction between two persons—the simple dyad group. Of course, in the real world groups are usually much more complex than the dyad. There are small and large groups, primary and secondary groups, coalitions, membership and reference groups, in- and out-groups, and formal and informal groups. Each type has different characteristics and different effects on its members.

Primary Groups. Often the terms *small group* and *primary group* are used interchangeably. Technically, there is a difference. A small group has to meet only the criterion of small size. Usually, no attempt is made to assign precise numbers, but the accepted criterion is that the group must be small enough for face-to-face interaction and communication to occur. In addition to being small, a primary group must have a feeling of comradeship, loyalty, and a common sense of values among its members. Thus, all primary groups are small groups, but not all small groups are primary groups.

Two examples of a primary group are the family and the peer group. Initially, the primary group was limited to a socializing group, but then a broader conception was given impetus by the results of the Hawthorne studies. Work groups definitely have primary group qualities. Research findings point out the tremendous impact that the primary group has on individual behavior, regardless of context or environmental conditions. An increasing number of companies, such as General Mills, Federal Express, Chaparral Steel, and 3M, have begun to use the power of primary groups by organizing employees into self-managed teams. These teams range from three to thirty members; consist of blue-collar workers, white-collar workers, or both; and arrange schedules, set goals, suggest improvements, hire and fire team members and managers, and even devise strategy.[8] The last part of the chapter discusses this team concept and practice in detail.

Coalitions. In addition to primary groups, coalitions are very relevant to organizations. The concept of a coalition has been used in organizational analysis through the years. Although the concept is used in different ways by different theorists, a recent comprehensive review of the coalition literature suggests that the following characteristics of a coalition be included:

1. Interacting group of individuals
2. Deliberately constructed by the members for a specific purpose
3. Independent of the formal organization's structure
4. Lacking a formal internal structure
5. Mutual perception of membership
6. Issue-oriented to advance the purposes of the members
7. External forms
8. Concerted member action, act as a group[9]

Although the above have common characteristics with other types of groups, coalitions are separate, usually very powerful, and often effective entities in organizations. For example, a recent study found that employees in a large bureaucratic organization formed into coalitions to overcome petty conflicts and ineffective management in order to get the job done.[10]

Other Types of Groups. Besides primary groups and coalitions, there are also other classifications of groups that are important to the study of organizational behavior. Two important distinctions are between membership and reference groups, and between in-groups and out-groups. These differences can be summarized by noting that membership groups are those to which the individual actually belongs. An example would be membership in a craft union. Reference groups are those to which an individual would like to belong—those he or she identifies with. An example would be a prestigious social group. In-groups are those who have or share the dominant values, and out-groups are those on the outside looking in. All these types of groups have relevance to the study of organizational behavior, but the formal and informal types are most directly applicable.

There are many formally designated work groups such as committees in the modern organization. The functional departmental committees (finance, marketing, operations, and human resources) are examples, as are standing committees such as the public affairs committee, grievance committee, or executive committee. Committees as a type of formal group are given detailed attention later in the chapter. Teams, as discussed under primary groups and at the end of the chapter, have emerged as the most important type of group in today's organizations and are being effectively applied in a variety of work situations.

Informal groups form for political, friendship, or common interest reasons. For political purposes, the informal group may form to attempt to get its share of rewards and/or limited resources. Friendship groups may form on the job and carry on outside the workplace. Common interests in sports or ways to get back at management can also bind members into an informal group. The dynamics of these informal groups are examined in more detail in an upcoming section.

Implications from Research on Group Dynamics

Starting with the Hawthorne studies, there has been an abundance of significant research on groups that has implications for organizational behavior and management. Besides the Hawthorne studies, there are numerous research studies on group dynamics which indirectly contribute to the better understanding of organizational behavior.[11] In general, it can be concluded from research over the years that groups have a positive impact on both individual employee effectiveness (help learn about the organization and one's self, gain new skills, obtain rewards not available to individuals, and fulfill important social needs) and organizational effectiveness (strength in numbers of ideas and skills, improved decision making and control, and facilitating change as well as organizational stability).[12]

In addition to the somewhat general conclusions, there are some specific studies in social psychology which seem to have particular relevance to organizational behavior. The seminal work of social psychologist Stanley Schachter seems especially important for the application of group dynamics research to human resources management.

The Schachter Study. In a classic study[13] Schachter and his associates tested the effect that group cohesiveness and induction (or influence) had on productivity under highly controlled conditions. *Cohesiveness* was defined as the average resultant force acting on members in a group. Through the manipulations of cohesiveness and induction, the following experimental groups were created:

1. High cohesive, positive induction (Hi Co, + Ind)
2. Low cohesive, positive induction (Lo Co, + Ind)
3. High cohesive, negative induction (Hi Co, − Ind)
4. Low cohesive, negative induction (Lo Co, − Ind)

The independent variables in the experiment were cohesiveness and induction, and the dependent variable was productivity. Figure 9.2 summarizes the results.

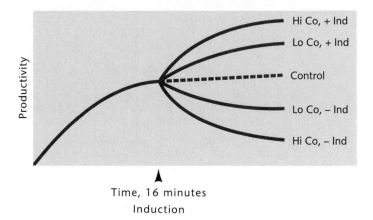

FIGURE 9.2
The "pitchfork" results from the Schachter study.

Although Schachter's experiment did not obtain a statistically significant difference in productivity between the high and low cohesive groups that were positively induced, a follow-up study which used a more difficult task did.[14]

Implications of the Schachter Study. The results of Schachter's study contain some very interesting implications for the study of organizational behavior. The "pitchfork" productivity curves in Figure 9.2 imply that highly cohesive groups have very powerful dynamics, both positive and negative, for human resources management. On the other hand, the low cohesive groups are not so powerful. However, of even more importance to human resources management is the variable of induction. Performance depends largely on how the high or low cohesive group is induced.

At least for illustrative purposes, leadership may be substituted for induction. If this is done, the key variable for the subjects' performance in the Schachter experiment becomes leadership. A highly cohesive group that is given positive leadership will have the highest possible productivity. On the other side of the coin, a highly cohesive group that is given poor leadership will have the lowest possible productivity. A highly cohesive group is analogous to a time bomb in the hands of management. The direction in which the highly cohesive group goes, breaking production records or severely restricting output, depends on how it is led. The low cohesive group is much safer in the hands of management. Leadership will not have a serious negative or positive impact on this group. However, the implication is that if management wishes to maximize productivity, it must build a cohesive group and give it proper leadership and over time this highly cohesive group may become self-managing.

This discussion does not imply that subjects doing a simple task in a laboratory setting can be made equivalent to managing human resources in the modern, complex organization. This, of course, cannot and should not be attempted. On the other hand, there are some interesting insights and points of departure for organizational behavior analysis that can come out of laboratory investigations such as Schachter's. For instance, the results of Schachter's study can be applied in retrospect to the work of Frederick W. Taylor or to the Hawthorne studies. Taylor accounted only for the Hi Co, − Ind productivity curve when he advocated "breaking up the group." If his scientific management methods could be considered + Ind, the best productivity he could obtain would be that of Lo Co, + Ind.

TABLE 9.1 Factors That Increase and Decrease Group Cohesiveness

Factors That Increase Group Cohesiveness	Factors That Decrease Group Cohesiveness
Agreement on group goals	Disagreement on goals
Frequency of interaction	Large group size
Personal attractiveness	Unpleasant experiences
Intergroup competition	Intragroup competition
Favorable evaluation	Domination by one or more members

Source: Andrew D. Szilagyi, Jr., and Marc J. Wallace, Jr., *Organizational Behavior and Performance*, 5th ed., Scott, Foresman/Little, Brown, Glenview, Ill., 1990, pp. 282–283.

In other words, in light of the Schachter study, Taylor's methods could yield only second-best productivity. In the Hawthorne studies, both the relay room operatives and the bank wirers were highly cohesive work groups. As is brought out in Chapter 1, a possible explanation of why one highly cohesive work group (the relay room workers) produced at a very high level and the other highly cohesive group (the bank wirers) produced at a very low rate is the type of induction (supervision) that was applied. Both leadership and group dynamics factors, such as cohesiveness, can have an important impact on group performance in organizations. Table 9.1 briefly summarizes some of the major factors that can increase and decrease group cohesiveness.

The Group's Contribution to Employee Satisfaction and Performance. Besides the work coming out of social psychology, more specific focus on the impact that groups have on employee behavior, especially the contribution to satisfaction and performance, has also received attention. A summary of the way to use groups to enhance satisfaction and performance is the following:

1. Organizing work around intact groups
2. Having groups charged with selection, training, and rewarding of members
3. Using groups to enforce strong norms for behavior, with group involvement in off-the-job as well as on-the-job behavior
4. Distributing resources on a group rather than an individual basis
5. Allowing and perhaps even promoting intergroup rivalry so as to build within-group solidarity[15]

A review of the research literature also determined three factors that seem to play the major role in determining group effectiveness: (1) task interdependence (how closely group members work together); (2) outcome interdependence (whether, and how, group performance is rewarded); and (3) potency (members' belief that the group can be effective).[16]

THE DYNAMICS OF INFORMAL GROUPS

Informal groups play a significant role in the dynamics of organizational behavior. The major difference between formal and informal groups is that the formal group has officially prescribed goals and relationships, whereas the informal one does not. Despite this distinction, it is a mistake to think of formal and informal groups as two distinctly separate entities. The two types of groups coexist and are inseparable. Every formal organization has informal groups, and every informal organization eventually evolves some semblance of formal groups.

Norms and Roles in Informal Groups

With the exception of a single social act such as extending a hand upon meeting, the smallest units of analysis in group dynamics are norms and roles. Many behavioral scientists make a point of distinguishing between the two units, but conceptually they are very similar. *Norms* are the "oughts" of behavior. They are prescriptions for acceptable behavior determined by the group. Norms will be strongly enforced by work groups if they:

1. Aid in group survival and provision of benefits.
2. Simplify or make predictable the behavior expected of group members.
3. Help the group avoid embarrassing interpersonal problems.
4. Express the central values or goals of the group and clarify what is distinctive about the group's identity.[17]

A role consists of a pattern of norms; the use of the term in organizations is directly related to its theatrical use. A role is a position that can be acted out by an individual. The content of a given role is prescribed by the prevailing norms. Probably *role* can best be defined as a position that has expectations evolving from established norms.

Informal Roles and the Informal Organization

Informal roles vary widely and are highly volatile. Table 9.2 summarizes some of the general informal roles that today's employees often assume. These role descriptions are not intended to be stereotypes or to imply that each organizational participant

TABLE 9.2 Informal Roles of Employees

Task-oriented employees: those who have the role of "getting the job done" and are known as those who "deliver the goods"

Technique-oriented employees: the masters of procedure and method

People-oriented employees: those who have the role of patron saint and good Samaritan to people in need

Nay-sayers: those who counterbalance the "yes" persons and who have thick skins and can find fault with anything

Yes-sayers: those who counterbalance the nay-sayers; the "yes" persons who circumvent opposition

Rule enforcers: the "people of the book"; those who are stereotype bureaucrats

Rule evaders: the "operators"; those who know how to get the job done "irrespective"

Rule blinkers: the people who are not against the rules but don't take them seriously

Involved employees: those who are fully immersed in their work and the activities of the organization

Detached employees: slackers who either "go along for the ride" or "call it quits" at the end of regular hours

Regulars: those who are "in," who accept the values of the group and are accepted by the group

Deviants: those who depart from the values of the group—the "mavericks"

Isolates: the true "lone wolves," who are further from the group than the deviants

Newcomers: those who know little and must be taken care of by others; people who are "seen but not heard"

Old-timers: those who have been around a long time and "know the ropes"

Climbers: those who are expected to "get ahead," not necessarily on the basis of ability but on the basis of potential

Stickers: those who are expected to stay put, who are satisfied with life and their position in it

Cosmopolitans: those who see themselves as members of a broader professional, cultural, or political community

Locals: those who are rooted to the organization and local community

Source: Bertram M. Gross, *Organizations and Their Managing,* Free Press, New York, 1968, pp. 242–248.

has only one role. The same person may have one role in one situation (a member of a middle management work group) and another role in another situation (the informal leader of the dissident group on a new project).

With the increasing importance of teams (covered in the last major section) in today's organizations, there is increasing recognition given to the informal team member roles. Here is a summary of four such roles:

1. *Contributor.* This task-oriented team member is seen as very dependable. He or she enjoys providing the team with good technical information and data, is always prepared, and pushes the team to set high performance goals.
2. *Collaborator.* This team member focuses on the "big picture." She or he tries to remind others of the vision, mission, or goal of the team, but is flexible and open to new ideas, is willing to work outside the defined role, and is willing to share the glory with other team members.
3. *Communicator.* This positive, people-oriented team member is process-driven and is an effective listener. He or she plays the role of facilitator of involvement, conflict resolution, consensus building, feedback, and building an informal relaxed atmosphere.
4. *Challenger.* Known for candor and openness, this member questions the team's goals, methods, and even ethics. He or she is willing to disagree with the leader or higher authority and encourages well-conceived risk taking.[18]

Besides the informal roles, the overall informal organization structure also has important dynamics for the study of organizational behavior. The classic Milo study conducted by Melville Dalton remains the best illustration of the power of the informal organization.[19] Figure 9.3*a* represents the formal organization at Milo. Through the use of intimates, interviews, diaries, observation, and socializing, Dalton was able to construct the informal organization chart shown in Figure 9.3*b*. This informal chart shows the actual power, as opposed to the formally designated power and influence, of the various managers at Milo.

Like the formal organization structures discussed in the next part of the book, the informal organization has both functions and dysfunctions. In contrast to formal organization analysis, the dysfunctional aspects of informal organization have received more attention than the functional ones. For example, conflicting objectives, restriction of output, conformity, blocking of ambition, inertia, and resistance to change are frequently mentioned dysfunctions of the informal organization.[20] More recently, however, organizational analysis has begun to recognize the functional aspects as well. For example, the following list suggests some practical benefits that can be derived from the informal organization:

1. Makes for a more effective total system
2. Lightens the workload on management
3. Fills in gaps in a manager's abilities
4. Provides a safety valve for employee emotions
5. Improves communication[21]

Because of the inevitability and power of the informal organization, the functions should be exploited in the attainment of objectives rather than futilely combated by management. As a recent analysis of leadership points out: "informal social networks exert an immense influence which sometimes overrides the formal hierarchy. . . . Leadership goes beyond a person's formal position into realms of informal, hidden, or unauthorized influence."[22]

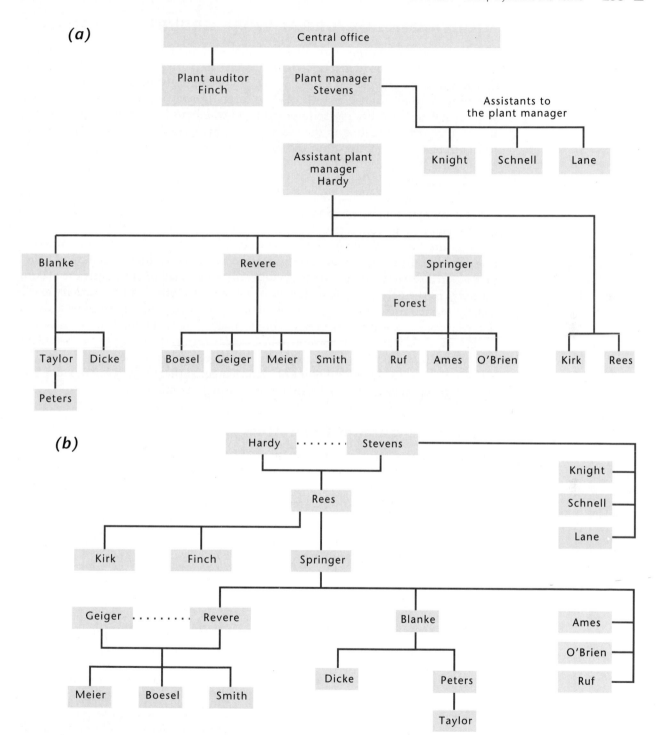

FIGURE 9.3
(*a*) A simplified formal organization chart of Milo.
(*b*) A simplified informal organization chart of Milo.
(*Source*: Melville Dalton, *Men Who Manage*, Wiley, New York, 1959, pp. 21–22.)

THE DYNAMICS OF FORMAL WORK GROUPS

Although informal norms and roles and informal organization are most closely associated with group dynamics, there are also important dynamics in formally designated work groups. Examples of formal work groups include various types of committees, commissions, boards, or task forces. Teams are also a type of formal work group and have become so important and widely used in recent years that they are given separate attention in the last section. This section on formal work groups concentrates on committees, but the discussion would also apply to commissions, boards, and task forces.

Committees are found in all types of organizations. There is a myriad of committees in government, educational, religious, and business organizations. The accompanying Application Example: Agreeing to Greater Productivity illustrates a union-management committee in action at Chrysler. Although they are more frequent at the top of the pyramid, there is usually some type of formal committee on every level of the organization. Committees perform many different functions. They may act in a service, advisory, coordinating, informational, or final decision-making capacity. In the decision-making function, a committee acts in a line capacity and is usually termed a *plural-executive committee*. Many companies have moved to the plural-executive concept rather than a single executive head. Union Carbide is typical of this trend. The company's major policies evolve from the office of the president. This office is composed of the president and three executive vice presidents. This foursome serves as the central point of management authority in the company. This type of group management is becoming increasingly common.

Positive Attributes of Committees

Committee action has many advantages over individual action. Perhaps the greatest attribute of the committee group is the combined and integrated judgment which it can offer. The old adage says that two heads are better than one. To speak optimistically, one would say that committee members bring with them a wide range of experience, knowledge, ability, and personality characteristics. This agglomeration lends itself to the tremendous amount of diverse knowledge that is required to solve modern organizational problems. As the head of the National Bank of Greece recently noted: "Management is about problem solving, and the committee meeting is an instrument designed to solve problems. But effective meetings don't just happen. They happen only when there is an effective person chairing the meeting."[23]

Committees can be a very effective organizational device to help reduce conflict and promote coordination between departments and specialized subunits. Through committee discussion, each member can empathize with the others' purposes and problems. In effect, committees foster horizontal communication. An example is the interdepartmental meeting at which each member receives information and insights about the others' departments. The production department is informed of delivery dates being promised by sales, and sales gets a firsthand look at the problems it may be creating for production scheduling and inventory. As Chapter 15 points out, the committee is about the only formalized vehicle for horizontal communication in most traditional forms of organization structure.

From a human standpoint, the biggest advantage of committees may be the increased motivation and commitment derived from participation. By being involved in the analysis and solution of committee problems, individual members will more

Application Example

Agreeing to Greater Productivity

When committees work together toward a common objective, the benefits can be rewarding for both sides. An agreement between Chrysler and United Auto Workers provides a good example. In the 1980s Chrysler had a difficult time, but recently there are a few product lines that have been big money-makers. One is the minivan, which provides about $2000 profit per unit. Chrysler would like to turn out as many of these vans as possible, and in the latest agreement with the union group, the St. Louis minivan plant is using a three-shift, or near-continuous, operation.

By running three seven-hour shifts instead of two eight-hour shifts six days a week, Chrysler is able to increase its current 108 hours of weekly production to 126. This means that the company will be able to make an additional 50,000 minivans a year. One reason the union agreed to go along with the request is that the only alternative was to retool the existing plant for minivan assembly, which would cost approximately $500 million. Since the firm was strapped for capital, the only way it could pay for this retooling would have been to cut back in other areas and to lay off personnel. Because the union did not want this to happen, it agreed to a round-the-clock type of operation.

Will union-management committees at Chrysler agree to this arrangement at other plants? Such an arrangement is unlikely. The union is convinced that it would eventually lead to big layoffs of its people. On the other hand, continued cooperation between the two committees is likely to be necessary, since round-the-clock operations are bound to create other problems. One such problem is that the line cannot be run hour after hour. Painting booths must be stopped daily for maintenance and filter changes in order to keep a high level of quality; any major breakdown will cut deeply into overall capacity. There are bound to be such occurrences when equipment is run on a continuous basis. Nevertheless, both Chrysler and the union committees may have come out ahead thanks to their willingness to cooperate. With this type of union cooperation and other innovations, such as decreased product development time and improved quality and market appeal, Chrysler has had a dramatic turnaround. For example, in 1993, Chrysler recorded $3.8 billion in pretax operating earnings. Every union member working for Chrysler took home a profit-sharing check of $4300, the highest in auto industry history. Obviously, this cooperative effort turned out to be a "win-win" situation for the company and the union members.

---

readily accept and try to implement what has been decided. A committee can also be instrumental in human development and growth. Group members, especially the young and inexperienced, can take advantage of observing and learning from other members with much experience or with different viewpoints and knowledge. A committee provides the opportunity for personal development that individuals would never receive on their own.

Negative Attributes of Committees

The above discussion points out some definite advantages of committees, but the Application Example: Committees May Not Be the Answer gives some of the problems that are inherent. Traditionally, management theorists have stressed the negative aspects. The classical theorist Luther Gulick wanted to limit the use of committees to abnormal situations because he thought they were too dilatory, irresponsible, and time-consuming for normal administration. The classical theorist

Committees May Not Be the Answer

Most modern management theorists espouse the benefits of getting together in committees to make decisions. It allows individuals to give their input and increases motivation and commitment. However, committees may not be appropriate for all decision-making situations. For example, holding committee meetings may simply be a facade for managers' own insecurities. Afraid to take responsibility for a decision, a manager may call a meeting to make a decision. In doing so, the manager can use the committee as a scapegoat for poor decisions.

Norman Sigband, a management communications professor, uses an example of a meeting he observed at a small plastics manufacturing firm. A committee consisting of a division manager, six department heads, and the heads of three sections was asked to discuss the replacement of an injured secretary. The group spent fifty minutes deciding whether a new person should be hired or a replacement acquired through a temporary service. As a result, the committee ran out of time to discuss the installation of a new fluorescent lighting system. This decision would have affected several departments and required an investment of $28,000. The secretarial decision, on the other hand, affected only one department and should have been made by the division manager. A side effect of such unnecessary meetings is a decline in committee attendance. When asked to address petty issues, members may become apathetic and skip meetings. Thus, when a really important issue needs to be addressed, relevant members may be absent. To overcome such problems, Sigband offers six suggestions for making committee meetings as productive as possible:

1. Only hold meetings for which there is a verifiable need.
2. Decide on an overall purpose and series of objectives each time.
3. Invite only people who can make a definite contribution.
4. Distribute an agenda and necessary handouts to each invitee prior to the session.
5. Make all mechanical arrangements ahead of time (room, projectors, seating, transparencies, etc.).
6. Begin and end every meeting on schedule.

Urwick was an even harsher critic. He listed no less than fourteen faults of committees, the main ones being that committees are often irresponsible, are apt to be bad employers, and are costly. Thus, the classicists tended to emphasize the negative, and through the years a number of well-known jokes have been made up about committees. Here is a sampling:

A camel is a horse designed by a committee.
The best committee is a five-person committee with four members absent.
In a committee, minutes are taken but hours are wasted.
A committee is a collection of the unfit appointed by the unwilling to perform the unnecessary.

In addition to the general negativism and jokes, there are also some specific problems associated with committees.

One very practical disadvantage is that committees are indeed time-consuming and costly. Anyone who has participated in committee meetings can appreciate the satirical definition above, that a committee takes minutes but wastes hours. The nature of a committee is that everyone has an equal chance to speak out, but this takes a great deal of time, and time costs money. A $60,000-per-year manager costs about $30 per hour. Therefore, a five-person committee of this caliber costs the organization $150 per hour. Added to this figure may be transportation, lodging, and staff backup costs.

From an organizational standpoint, there are some potential problems inherent in committees. The most obvious is divided responsibility. This is a saying that in a committee, there is group or corporate but no individual responsibility or accountability. Thus, critics argue, the committee in reality turns out to have no responsibility or accountability. In fact, individuals may use the committee as a shield to avoid personal responsibility for bad decisions or mistakes. One solution to this problem is to make all committee members responsible, and another is to hold the chairperson responsible. Both approaches have many obvious difficulties. For example, if the entire committee is held responsible for a wrong decision, what about the individual members who voted against the majority? Holding them accountable for the committee's decision could have disastrous effects on their morale, but holding only those who voted for a particular decision responsible would create an inhibiting effect that would destroy the value of committee action.

Besides being time-consuming and costly and having divided responsibility, committees may reach decisions that are products of excessive compromise, logrolling, and one-person or minority domination. The comment that the camel is a horse designed by a committee underscores this limitation. It represents the reverse of the advantages of integrated group judgment and the pooling of specialized knowledge. Where unanimity is either formally required or an informal group norm, the difficulties are compounded. The final decision may be so extremely watered down or "compromised to death" that the horse actually does turn out to be a camel. The strength of committee action comes through a synthesis and integration of divergent viewpoints, not through a compromise representing the least common denominator. One way to avoid the problem is to limit the committee to serving as a forum for the exchange of information and ideas. Another possibility is to let the chairperson have the final decision-making prerogative. Yet these solutions are not always satisfactory because when the committee is charged with making a decision, considerable social skill and a willingness to cooperate fully must exist if good-quality decisions are to evolve.

Groupthink: A Major Problem with Committees and Groups

A dysfunction of highly cohesive groups and committees that has received a lot of attention recently has been called *groupthink* by Irving Janis. He defines it as "a deterioration of mental efficiency, reality testing, and moral judgment that results from in-group pressures."[24] Essentially, groupthink results from the pressures on individual members to conform and reach consensus. Committees that are suffering from groupthink are so bent on reaching consensus that there is no realistic appraisal of alternative courses of action in a decision, and deviant, minority, or unpopular views are suppressed.

Janis has concluded that a number of historic fiascos by government policy-making groups (for example, Britain's do-nothing policy toward Hitler prior to World War II, the unpreparedness of U.S. forces at Pearl Harbor, the Bay of Pigs invasion of Cuba, and the escalation of the Vietnam war) can be attributed to groupthink. The Watergate affair during the Nixon administration and the Iran-contra affair during the Reagan administration are also examples. The decision process by which NASA launched the space shuttle *Challenger* on its fateful mission

TABLE 9.3 Symptoms of Groupthink

1. There is the *illusion of invulnerability*. There is excessive optimism and risk taking.
2. There are *rationalizations* by the members of the group to discount warnings.
3. There is an unquestioned belief in the group's *inherent morality*. The group ignores questionable ethical or moral issues or stances.
4. Those who oppose the group are *stereotyped* as evil, weak, or stupid.
5. There is *direct pressure* on any member who questions the stereotypes. Loyal members don't question the direction in which the group seems to be heading.
6. There is *self-censorship* of any deviation from the apparent group consensus.
7. There is the *illusion of unanimity*. Silence is interpreted as consent.
8. There are *self-appointed mindguards* who protect the group from adverse information.

Source: Irving L. Janis, *Groupthink*, 2d ed., Houghton Mifflin, Boston, 1982, pp. 174–175.

can be analyzed in terms of the characteristics of groupthink. For example, conformity pressures were in evidence when NASA officials complained to the contractors about delays. Other symptoms of groupthink shown in Table 9.3—illusions of invulnerability and unanimity and mindguarding—were played out in the *Challenger* disaster by management's treatment and exclusion of input by the engineers.[25]

Although historically notorious news events can be used to dramatically point out the pitfalls of groupthink, it can commonly occur in committees in business firms or hospitals or any other type of organization. To date, there has been at least some partial support of the groupthink model when applied to areas such as leader behavior and decision making.[26] In general, committees should recognize and then avoid, if possible, the symptoms of groupthink identified in Table 9.3. For example, the first symptom leads to the so-called "risky shift phenomenon" of groups. Research going back many years has shown that, contrary to popular belief, a group may make more risky decisions than the individual members would on their own.[27] This conclusion, of course, must be tempered by the values attached to the outcomes, but most of the research over the years finds that groups take more risks than individuals acting alone.

Such symptoms as this risky shift phenomenon and the others found in Table 9.3 should make groups take notice and be very careful that they do not slip into groupthink. To help overcome the potentially disastrous effects of groupthink, free expression of minority and unpopular viewpoints should be encouraged and legitimatized. Companies such as General Electric, Bausch and Lomb, Apple Computer, Ford, Johnson and Johnson, and United Parcel Service are known for not only tolerating, but formally encouraging, conflict and debate during committee meetings.

Although many studies show that successful companies advocate such open conflict and healthy debate among group members, other studies point to the value of consensus. This apparent contradiction may be resolved by recognizing the following:

> Consensus may be preferred for smaller, non-diversified, privately held firms competing in the same industry while larger firms dealing with complex issues of diversification may benefit from the dissent raised in open discussions. Larger firms in uncertain environments need dissent while smaller firms in more simple and stable markets can rely on consensus.[28]

TEAMS IN THE MODERN WORKPLACE

In recent years, teams have emerged as the most important group phenomenon in organizations. The term "team" is not new to organizations, and teamwork has been stressed throughout the years. For example, the well-known quality guru Joseph Juran first took his "Team Approach to Problem Solving" to the Japanese in the 1950s and then in the 1980s to the United States.[29] Today, teams are becoming increasingly popular as a result of advanced information technology and the concern for total quality and organizational learning processes (see Chapter 2). These organizational developments have shifted from a reliance on individual managers and workers to interfunctional management teams and work teams that focus on complex problems and tasks. After first defining what is meant by a team and critically analyzing quality circles and self-managed teams found in today's organizations, the ways to train self-managed teams and make them effective are discussed.

The Nature of Teams

Although the term "team" is frequently used for any group, especially to get them to work together and to motivate them, some team experts are trying to make a distinction between teams and traditional work groups. For example, the authors of a recent book on the use of teams for creating high-performance organizations note that the difference between a work group and a team relates to performance results. They note:

> A working group's performance is a function of what its members do as individuals. A team's performance includes both individual results and what we call 'collective work-products.' A collective work-product is what two or more members must work on together . . . [it] reflects the joint, real contribution of team members.[30]

They go on to make these specific differences between work groups and teams:

1. The work group has a strong, clearly focused leader; the team has shared leadership roles.
2. The work group has individual accountability; the team has individual and mutual accountability.
3. The work group's purpose is the same as the organization; the team has a specific purpose.
4. The work group has individual work-products; the team has collective work-products.
5. The work group runs efficient meetings; the team encourages open-ended, active problem-solving meetings.
6. The work group measures effectiveness indirectly (for example, financial performance of the overall business); the team measures performance directly by assessing collective work-products.
7. The work group discusses, decides, and delegates; the team discusses, decides, and does real work together.[31]

The point is that teams do go beyond traditional formal work groups by having a collective, synergistic (the whole is greater than the sum of its parts) effect.

Teams can be formed for any purpose. One typology breaks the types down into four categories: (1) advice (board, review panels, employee involvement groups); (2) production (manufacturing crews, mining teams, maintenance crews, flight attendant crews, data processing groups); (3) project (research groups, planning teams, engineering teams, task forces); and (4) action (sports teams, entertainment groups, expeditions, negotiating teams, surgery teams, military units).[32] However, the two types of teams that have received the most attention have been, first, quality circles and, more recently, autonomous, or self-managed, teams.

Quality circles, sometimes called quality control circles, were implemented in Japan largely by American quality control experts following World War II. They remain very popular in Japan and are given credit for much of the success of Japanese quality products. As a reaction to this success, American firms began adopting quality circles in the 1970s and 1980s. However, it is generally recognized that after reaching their peak in the 1980s, quality circles have declined in popularity in the United States and have given way to the now more popular self-managed teams.

Quality circles are typically made up of volunteers from the lower levels of operations in manufacturing and offer advice to management on improving quality and productivity. On the other hand, self-managed teams, sometimes called autonomous work teams, are formally designated by management and can be made up of employees from all levels in all types of organizations. Self-managed teams may make decisions and do the real work of the organization. As implied by the term, these teams have no appointed supervisor or manager in charge; they do their own managerial functions, such as planning, scheduling, controlling, and staffing.

The Effectiveness of Teams

Although there is considerable testimonial evidence of the value of both quality circles and self-managed teams, research and documented experience is just starting to emerge. Research evidence on quality circles is generally inconclusive because of the lack of standardized variables (team participation programs of all sizes and shapes have been called quality circles).[33] However, it is generally recognized that in actual practice quality circles generally have had a good track record in Japan, but have run into problems in the United States.[34] One review concluded that this may be a result of poor implementation rather than being the fault of the quality circle concept itself.[35]

Research does continue on quality circles. For example, when new grounding such as systems theory is used to frame the quality circle intervention across organizations, predictions of improved team member attendance and retention have held up.[36] As has been found in other cross-cultural applications of organizational behavior techniques, the reason quality circles are so successful in Japan and not the United States

> . . . does not indicate so much that this approach just won't work across cultures as that historical and cultural values and norms need to be recognized and overcome for such a relatively sophisticated theory and technique to work effectively.[37]

To date, both the research and practice literature has been more favorable to self-managed teams. Similar to that on quality circles, there has been much testimonial evidence on the success of self-managed teams,[38] but supporting research is also starting to emerge. For example, a comprehensive meta-analysis covering seventy studies concluded that self-managed teams had a positive impact on productivity and specific attitudes related to the team, but not on general attitudes, absenteeism, or turnover.[39] This finding on the impact on productivity is impressive, and recent studies also find a more favorable impact on attitudes as well,[40] but there are still practical problems to overcome. For example, a recent in-depth interview survey of 4500 teams at 500 organizations uncovered a host of individual and organizational factors behind team ineffectiveness.[41] Individual problems included the following:

1. Team members aren't willing to give up past practices or set aside power and position.
2. Not all team members have the ability, knowledge, or skill to contribute to the group. Team function slows because some members shoulder more responsibility than others.
3. As team members, workers often face conflicts or challenges to their own personal beliefs. What works for the group often does not work for the individual.[42]

Organizational-level problems uncovered by this survey included compensation and reward systems that still focused solely on individual performance; thus there was little incentive for teams to perform well.[43]

How to Make Teams More Effective

For teams to be more effective, they need to overcome some of the real problems that some, if not most, are currently experiencing. Most suggested guidelines revolve around training and evaluation systems. An example of an effective training approach would be the ten-step model shown in Table 9.4. GE, in its Electrical Distribution and Control Division, has successfully used this training model. According to the

TABLE 9.4 Training Guidelines for Developing Effective Self-Managed Teams

Steps of Training	Summary
1. Establish credibility.	The trainers must first establish their knowledge and believability.
2. Allow ventilation.	The trainees must have their anxieties and unresolved issues cleared before starting.
3. Provide an orientation.	The trainers should give specific verbal directions and provide clear expectations and models of behavior.
4. Invest in the process.	Early on, have the team identify its problems and concerns.
5. Set group goals.	The trainees create, through consensus, their own mission statement and then set goals and specific activities and behaviors to accomplish these goals.
6. Facilitate the group process.	The trainees are taught about how groups function and are given techniques, such as nominal grouping and paired comparison.
7. Establish intragroup procedures.	This involves setting up a meeting format that might include reporting minutes, making announcements, discussing problems and issues, proposing solutions, taking action, and making new assignments.
8. Establish intergroup processes.	Although the team is self-managed, leaders must be selected in order to interact with others, such as supervisors, managers, and other teams.
9. Change the role of the trainers.	As the team becomes more experienced and empowered, the trainers take on a more passive role.
10. End the trainers' involvement.	At this point, the team is on its own and is self-managing.

Source: Paul E. Brauchle and David W. Wright, "Training Work Teams," *Training and Development*, March 1993, pp. 65–68.

trainers, the trained GE teams "are made up of dedicated people who enjoy working together, who maintain high standards, and who demonstrate high productivity and commitment to excellence."[44]

Besides going through the steps of training teams to become effective self-managing entities, team experts agree that they must also be monitored and evaluated on a continuous basis. As noted by one expert:

> At any point, team members can slide back to a lower level of effectiveness if they do not continually work together as a team, listen and communicate effectively, deal with conflict effectively, recognize each other's unique contributions, provide honest feedback and demonstrate other characteristics of an effective team.[45]

She then goes on to specify five key areas of the team that should be closely monitored and periodically measured: (1) team mission, (2) goal achievement, (3) empowerment, (4) open, honest communication, and (5) positive roles and norms.[46] By controlling such key functions, self-managed teams can be effective and contribute to the performance goals of the organization.

Summary

Groups represent an important dynamic for the study and application of organizational behavior. Group formation, types, and processes; the dynamics of informal roles and organization; and formal work groups such as committees and teams are all of particular relevance to the study of organizational behavior. Group formation can be theoretically explained by propinquity; as a relationship between activities, interactions, and sentiments; as a symmetrical balance between attraction and common attitudes; and as a reward-cost exchange. Participants in an organization also form into groups for very practical economic, security, and social reasons. Many different types of groups are found in modern organizations. Conceptually, there are primary groups, coalitions, and others such as membership and reference groups. Groups have been researched over the years, and findings from classic studies such as the one conducted by Schachter have implications for organizational behavior.

The last half of the chapter discusses and analyzes the dynamics of informal and formal groups and teams. Informal norms and roles and the informal organization are very relevant to and often represent the real organization. Informal structure coexists with every formal structure. Traditionally, only the dysfunctional aspects of informal organization have been emphasized. More recently, the functional aspects have also been recognized.

The dynamics of formally designated groups revolve mostly around traditional committees and teams. Although committees can be time-consuming, costly, and conducive to divided responsibility, excessive compromise, and groupthink, they can lead to improved decisions through combined and integrated judgment, reduced conflict, facilitated coordination, and increased motivation and commitment through participation. However, teams, not committees, have recently emerged as the most important formal groups in today's organizations. Initially, most publicity was given to quality circles, but now self-managed teams are in the spotlight. Quality circles have been widely used and quite successful in Japan, but have had problems and have faded in popularity in the United States. Self-managed teams, however, are beginning to become an established form of doing work to meet the high-tech, quality challenges facing both manufacturing and service organizations. To date, self-managed teams have a quite successful track record. To keep them on track, there is a recognized need for training and evaluation of teams.

Questions for Discussion and Review

1. Briefly discuss the major theoretical explanations for group formation. Which explanation do you think is most relevant to the study of organizational behavior? Defend your choice.
2. What implications does the Schachter study have for the study of organizational behavior?
3. What are some functions of the informal organization? What are some dysfunctions?
4. How can the disadvantages of committees be overcome?
5. What are some of the major symptoms of groupthink? Can you give an example from your own experience where groupthink may have occurred?
6. How, if at all, do teams as used in today's organizations differ from traditional work groups?
7. What is the difference between quality circles and self-managed teams? What has been the track record of both?
8. What are two ways to make and maintain self-managed teams' effectiveness?

Footnote References and Supplemental Readings

1. Clayton P. Alderfer, "Editor's Introduction: Contemporary Issues in Professional Work with Groups," *Journal of Applied Behavioral Science*, March 1992, p. 9.
2. John M. Ivancevich and Michael T. Matteson, *Organizational Behavior and Management*, 3d ed., Irwin, Homewood, Ill., 1993, p. 286.
3. George C. Homans, *The Human Group*, Harcourt, Brace & World, New York, 1950, pp. 43–44.
4. Theodore M. Newcomb, *The Acquaintance Process*, Holt, New York, 1961.
5. John W. Thibaut and Harold H. Kelley, *The Social Psychology of Groups*, Wiley, New York, 1959.
6. See Bruce W. Tuckman, "Developmental Sequence in Small Groups," *Psychological Bulletin*, November 1965, pp. 384–399, and Bruce W. Tuckman and Mary Ann C. Jensen, "Stages of Small Group Development Revisited," *Group and Organization Studies*, December 1977, pp. 419–427.
7. Christine L. Cooper, Bruno Dyck, and Norman Frohlich, "Improving the Effectiveness of Gainsharing: The Role of Fairness and Participation," *Administrative Science Quarterly*, December 1992, pp. 471–490.
8. Brian Dumaine, "Who Needs a Boss?" *Fortune*, May 7, 1990, p. 52.
9. William B. Stevenson, Jone L. Pearce, and Lyman Porter, "The Concept of 'Coalition' in Organization Theory and Research," *Academy of Management Review*, April 1985, pp. 261–262.
10. Nancy C. Morey and Fred Luthans, "The Use of Dyadic Alliances in Informal Organization: An Ethnographic Study," *Human Relations*, vol. 44, no. 6, 1991, pp. 597–618.
11. For examples of some recent basic research on work groups, see James E. Driskell, Beckett Olmstead, and Eduardo Salas, "Task Cues, Dominance Cues, and Influence in Task Groups," *Journal of Applied Psychology*, February 1993, pp. 51–60, and Richard Saavedra, P. Christopher Earley, and Linn Van Dyne, "Complex Interdependence in Task-Performing Groups," *Journal of Applied Psychology*, February 1993, pp. 61–72.
12. See David A. Nadler, J. Richard Hackman, and Edward E. Lawler, *Managing Organizational Behavior*, Little, Brown, Boston, 1979, p. 102.
13. Stanley Schachter, Norris Ellertson, Dorothy McBride, and Doris Gregory, "An Experimental Study of Cohesiveness and Productivity," *Human Relations*, August 1951, pp. 229–239.
14. Leonard Berkowitz, "Group Standards, Cohesiveness, and Productivity," *Human Relations*, vol. 7, no. 4, 1954, pp. 509–519.
15. Barry W. Staw, "Organizational Psychology and the

Pursuit of the Happy/Productive Worker," *California Management Review*, Summer 1986, p. 49.

16. Gregory P. Shea and Richard A. Guzzo, "Group Effectiveness: What Really Matters?" *Sloan Management Review*, Spring 1987, p. 25.

17. Don Hellriegel, John W. Slocum, Jr., and Richard W. Woodman, *Organizational Behavior*, 5th ed., West, St. Paul, Minn., 1989, p. 216.

18. Glenn M. Parker, *Team Players and Teamwork*, Jossey-Bass, San Francisco, 1991, pp. 63–64.

19. Melville Dalton, *Men Who Manage*, Wiley, New York, 1959.

20. Ross Webber, *Management*, 2d ed., Irwin, Homewood, Ill., 1979, p. 118.

21. Keith Davis and John W. Newstrom, *Human Behavior at Work*, 7th ed., McGraw-Hill, New York, 1985, p. 311.

22. Louis B. Barnes and Mark P. Kriger, "The Hidden Side of Organizational Leadership," *Sloan Management Review*, Fall 1986, p. 15.

23. Cited in Thomas R. Horton, "In Praise of a Managerial Whipping Boy," *Management Review*, October 1990, p. 32.

24. Irving L. Janis, *Victims of Groupthink*, Houghton Mifflin, Boston, 1972, p. 9.

25. David G. Myers, *Social Psychology*, 3d ed., McGraw-Hill, New York, 1990, p. 297.

26. Carrie R. Leana, "A Partial Test of Janis' Groupthink Model: Effects of Group Cohesiveness and Leader Behavior on Defective Decision Making," *Journal of Management*, vol. 11, no. 1, 1985, pp. 5–17.

27. The original research on risky shift goes back to a master's thesis by J. A. F. Stoner, "A Comparison of Individual and Group Decisions Involving Risk," Massachusetts Institute of Technology, Sloan School of Industrial Management, Cambridge, Mass., 1961.

28. Richard A. Cosier and Charles R. Schwenk, "Agreement and Thinking Alike: Ingredients for Poor Decisions," *Academy of Management Executive*, February 1990, p. 70.

29. Mary Helen Yarborough, "A Team Approach," *HR Focus*, August 1993, p. 17.

30. Jon R. Katzenback and Douglas K. Smith, "The Discipline of Teams," *Harvard Business Review*, March–April 1993, p. 112.

31. Ibid., p. 113.

32. Eric Sundstrom, Kenneth P. DeMeuse, and David Futrell, "Work Teams: Applications and Effectiveness," *American Psychologist*, February 1990, p. 120.

33. See Robert Kreitner and Angelo Kinicki, *Organizational Behavior*, 2d ed., Irwin, Homewood, Ill., 1992, p. 413.

34. Ibid., and Mitchell L. Marks, "The Question of Quality Circles," *Psychology Today*, March 1986, pp. 36–38, 42, 44, 46.

35. Kreitner and Kinicki, loc. cit., and Jeremy Main, "The Trouble with Managing Japanese-Style," *Fortune*, Apr. 2, 1984, pp. 50–51.

36. Kimberly Buch, "Quality Circles and Employee Withdrawal Behaviors: A Cross-Organizational Study," *Journal of Applied Behavioral Science*, March 1992, pp. 62–73.

37. Dianne H. B. Welsh, Fred Luthans, and Steven M. Sommer, "Managing Russian Factory Workers: The Impact of U.S.-Based Behavioral and Participative Techniques," *Academy of Management Journal*, February 1993, pp. 58–79.

38. For example, see Dumaine, loc. cit.

39. See Paul S. Goodman, Rukmini Devadas, and Terri L. Griffith Hughson, "Groups and Productivity: Analyzing the Effectiveness of Self-Managing Teams," in John P. Campbell, Richard J. Campbell, and Associates (eds.), *Productivity in Organizations*, Jossey-Bass, San Francisco, 1988, pp. 295–327.

40. C. A. L. Pearson, "Autonomous Workgroups: An Evaluation at an Industrial Site," *Human Relations*, vol. 45, no. 9, 1992, pp. 905–936.

41. "Work Teams Have Their Work Cut Out for Them," *HR Focus*, January 1993, p. 24.

42. Ibid.

43. Ibid.

44. Paul E. Brauchle and David W. Wright, "Training Work Teams," *Training and Development*, March 1993, p. 68.

45. Victoria A. Hovemeyer, "How Effective Is Your Team?" *Training and Development*, September 1993, p. 68.

46. Ibid., p. 67.

REAL CASE: The Grand Experiment at Saturn

The production of the Saturn is perhaps the most aggressive and visible self-managed-team (SMT) "experiment" in the United States. General Motors established this autonomous division in the mid-1980s to create an innovative, cost competitive, small car. The Saturn strategy was established to: (1) build a car that would compete with domestic and international models in the small-car market, and (2) involve and empower employees in all aspects of decision making (traditionally done by management or functional experts).

A team structure was established (usually from 8–15 members) that was responsible for: selection of team members, production scheduling, quality, staffing (including job assignments, vacations, lunch, and breaks), budgeting, problem-solving, routine maintenance, tooling, safety, working with external suppliers and customers, internal coordination with other teams and departments, and team structure (appointing informal team leaders, and developing specialists or "champions") and training.

Saturn's ultimate goal was to have SMTs utilize the consensus method of decision making. Decisions would be agreed upon by the team utilizing the "70 percent comfort" rule. That is, each team member must feel 70 percent comfortable with any decision. Before production of the Saturn began, extensive training was conducted to ensure new SMT members were prepared for this new operating structure. Each member received 700 hours of training in all aspects of the Saturn philosophy: interpersonal skills, the SMT concept, conflict resolution, and the above-mentioned responsibilities of SMTs. Another unique concept at Saturn is that all employees (SMT members and management) are on salary. In the beginning, compensation is tied to the so-called 5 percent risk and reward plan. This means that employees will only receive 95 percent of their salary and will not receive the other 5 percent unless everyone meets their training goal. Eventually, Saturn will place 20 percent of employees' base salary at risk. This means that every employee will have to meet certain production and quality goals to earn the remaining 20 percent. If the SMTs exceed their goals, they will be eligible for bonuses. Recently, all employees were given a $1000 bonus check for exceeding production and quality goals.

Another unique aspect of the Saturn Corporation is that at each management level and at each staff function, a United Auto Worker counterpart shares decision making equally with Saturn managers. However, the SMT structure is the foundation of Saturn. Each team has an elected leader (SMT coordinator). The next level up in the structure is composed of work-unit module advisors. These advisors serve as troubleshooters or counselors for all SMTs within each business unit (powertrain, body systems, and vehicle systems). These advisors also serve as liaisons to the union representatives and managers who run each of the three business units. A manufacturing advisory committee acts as the "chief overseer" of the Saturn Corporation's three plants. This committee includes union and management representatives from each of the three facilities, and the overall site manager and their union counterpart. At the top of the Saturn structure is the long-range planning and policy making body for the corporation.

Since the Saturn Corporation introduced their first automobiles in 1991, they have made strides in increasing production capacity to meet initial demands for their cars and continue to smooth out operational problems. Because this "grand experiment" cost General Motors approximately $5 billion to develop, GM had considerable interest in ensuring that Saturn would succeed. Perhaps even more important was that American manufacturers' pride was on the line. After considerable pressure from General Motors, Saturn has succeeded in increasing production (adding shifts and opening a new production facility) and eliminating the original annual operating losses of $750 million by mid-1993. But organizational problems still remain.

Because Saturn must hire new employees from existing laid-off General Motors workers (per the United Auto Worker and General Motors collective bargaining agreements), the applicant pool for Saturn is shrinking. This shrinking pool of workers has the potential for recent hires to often be less committed to the SMT philosophy. Second, in an effort to increase productivity, team size is being reduced and 50-hour workweeks have been implemented, causing employee stress and burnout. Third, there is a growing distrust of the union's close ties with Saturn management. In fact, the local United Auto Worker president was narrowly elected in early 1993, defeating a more pro-union candidate. Fourth, there is increasing anger over union member appointments for key positions on the production floor (normally accomplished by the SMTs). The union leadership feels that recent appointments are more sympathetic toward management than to union concerns. Finally, due to pressures for increased production, training is being scaled back (from 700 hours to 175 hours during the first three months of employment).

To date, although Saturn's "grand experiment" has mixed results, on balance this experiment in American manufacturing is a success story. In particular, the use of self-managed teams has been validated. However, the real test will be to see if these same statements hold true in five or ten years.

1. The Saturn example shows how the team concept of self-managed teams can be effectively implemented. How do self-managed teams differ from traditional formal and informal work groups?
2. What impact does the self-managed team concept have on the traditional management structure? Where do middle managers fit in this new structure?
3. As this case shows, Saturn's "grand experiment" does have some drawbacks. As a Saturn manager, what specific recommendations would you give to solve these difficulties? How would you implement your recommendations?

CASE: The Schoolboy Rookie

Kent Sikes is a junior at State University. He has taken a summer job in the biggest factory in his hometown. He was told to report to the warehouse supervisor the first day at work. The supervisor assigned him to a small group of workers who were responsible for loading and unloading the boxcars that supplied the materials and carried away the finished goods of the factory.

After two weeks on the job, Kent was amazed at how little work the workers in his crew accomplished. It seemed that they were forever standing around and talking or, in some cases, even going off to hide when there was work to be done. Kent often found himself alone unloading a boxcar while the other members of the crew were off messing around someplace else. When Kent complained to his coworkers, they made it very plain that if he did not like it, he could quit, but if he complained to the supervisor, he would be sorry. Although Kent has been deliberately excluded from any of the crew's activities, such as taking breaks together or having a Friday afternoon beer after work at the tavern across the street, yesterday he went up to one of the older members of the crew and said, "What gives with you guys, anyway? I am just trying to do my job. The money is good and I just don't give a hang about this place. I will be leaving to go back to school in a few weeks, and I wish I could have gotten to know you all better, but frankly I am sure glad I'm not like you guys." The older worker replied, "Son, if you'd been here as long as I have, you would be just like us."

1. Using some of the theories, explain the possible reasons for the group formation of this work crew. What types of groups exist in this case?
2. Place this work group in the Schachter study. What role does the supervisor play in the performance of this group?
3. What are the major informal roles of the crew members and Kent? What status position does Kent have with the group? Why?
4. Why hasn't Kent been accepted by the group? Do you agree with the older worker's last statement in the case? Why or why not?

**CASE:
The Blue-Ribbon
Committee**

Mayor Sam Small is nearing completion of his first term in office. He feels his record has been pretty good, except for the controversial issue of housing. He has been able to avoid doing anything about housing so far and feels very strongly that this issue must not come to a head before the next election. The voters are too evenly divided on the issue, and he would lose a substantial number of votes no matter what stand he took. Yet with pressure increasing from both sides, he had to do something. After much distress and vacillation, he has finally come upon what he thinks is an ideal solution to his dilemma. He has appointed a committee to study the problem and make some recommendations. To make sure that the committee's work will not be completed before the election comes up, it was important to pick the right people. Specifically, Sam has selected his "blue-ribbon" committee from a wide cross section of the community so that, in Sam's words, "all concerned parties will be represented." He has made the committee very large, and the members range from Ph.D.s in urban planning to real estate agents to local ward committee persons to minority group leaders. He has taken particular care in selecting people who have widely divergent, outspoken, public views on the housing issue.

1. Do you think Sam's strategy of using this committee to delay taking a stand on the housing issue until after the election will work? Why or why not?
2. What are some of the important dynamics of this committee? Do you think the committee will arrive at a good solution to the housing problems facing this city?
3. Do you think this committee will suffer from groupthink?
4. What types of informal roles is Sam exhibiting? Do you think he is an effective manager? Do you think he is an effective politician? Is there a difference?

10 Interactive Conflict and Negotiation Skills

Learning Objectives

- **Describe** intraindividual conflict due to frustration, goals, and roles.
- **Analyze** interpersonal conflict.
- **Explain** intergroup behavior and conflict.
- **Relate** the dimensions of organizational conflict.
- **Discuss** negotiation skills for more effective management.

Interactive behavior can occur at the individual, interpersonal, group, or organizational level. It often results in conflict at all these levels. Although such conflict, especially intraindividual conflict, is very closely related to stress (discussed in Chapter 11), conflict is given separate treatment here because of the emphasis on interactive behavior. Thus, this chapter first analyzes intraindividual conflict stemming from frustration, goals, and roles. Next, interpersonal dynamics and the resulting conflict are examined. The next two sections are concerned with intergroup behavior and conflict and organizational conflict. Potential strategies for managing conflict at each of these levels of analysis of interactive behavior (that is, individual, interpersonal, group, and organizational) are presented throughout. The last section presents some negotiation skills that are increasingly becoming recognized as an effective way to manage.

INTRAINDIVIDUAL CONFLICT

A smooth progression of the need-drive-goal motivational cycle (discussed in Chapter 6) and fulfillment of one's role expectations do not always occur in reality. Within every individual there are usually (1) a number of competing needs and roles, (2) a variety of ways that drives and roles can be expressed, (3) many types of barriers which can occur between the drive and the goal, and (4) both positive and negative aspects attached to desired goals. These complicate the human adaptation process and often result in conflict. Intraindividual forms of conflict can be analyzed in terms of the frustration model, goals, and roles.

Conflict Due to Frustration

Frustration occurs when a motivated drive is blocked before a person reaches a desired goal. Figure 10.1 illustrates what happens. The barrier may be either overt (outward, or physical) or covert (inward, or mental-sociopsychological). An example of a frustrating situation might be that of a thirsty person who comes up against a stuck door and is prevented from reaching a water fountain. Figure 10.2 illustrates this simple frustrating situation. Frustration normally triggers defense mechanisms in the person. Traditionally, psychologists felt that frustration always led to the defense mechanism of aggression. It was thought that, cn becoming frustrated, a person reacts by physically or symbolically attacking the barrier. In the example in Figure 10.2, the person would react by kicking and/or cursing the jammed door.

More recently, aggression has come to be viewed as only one possible reaction. Frustration may lead any of the defense mechanisms used by the human organism. Although there are many such mechanisms, they can be grouped according to four broad categories: aggression, withdrawal, fixation, and compromise. In the illustration of Figure 10.2, backing away from the door and pouting would be an example of withdrawal; pretending the door is not jammed and continually trying to open it would be an example of fixation; and substituting a new goal (drinking a cup of coffee already in the room) or a new direction (climbing out the window) would be an example of compromise.

Although the thirsty person frustrated by the stuck door is a very uncomplicated example, the same frustration model can be used to analyze more complex behavior. One example might be a minority person who comes from a disadvantaged educational and economic background but who still has intense needs for pride and dignity. A goal that may fulfill the individual's needs is meaningful employment. The drive set up to alleviate the need and accomplish the goal would be to search for a good job. The individual in this example who meets barriers (prejudice, discrimination, lack of education, and nonqualification) may become frustrated. Possible reactions to this frustration may be aggression (riot or hate), withdrawal (apathy and unemployment), fixation (pretending the barriers do not exist and continuing to search unsuccessfully for a good job), or compromise (finding expression of pride and dignity in something other than a good job, such as in a militant group).

FIGURE 10.1
A model of frustration.

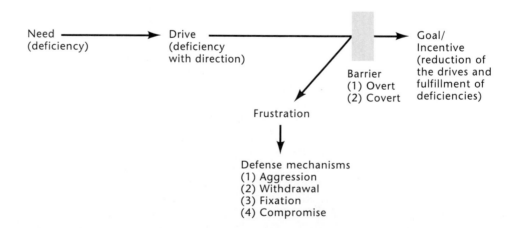

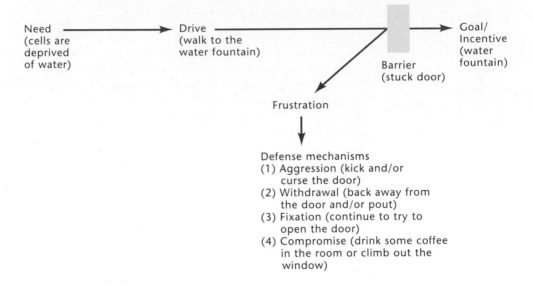

FIGURE 10.2
A simple example of frustration.

The frustration model can be useful in the analysis not only of behavior in general but also of specific aspects of on-the-job behavior. Table 10.1 summarizes some behavioral reactions to frustration that may occur in the formal organization. These examples generally imply that there is a negative impact on the individual's performance and on the organization as a result of frustration. Some of this frustration may actually be translated into real costs to the organization.

Theft of company property and even violence on the job may be a form of an aggressive outcome to job frustration. For example, the Postal Service has received considerable media attention because of a series of several tragic instances of violence over the past decade. Although 34 postal workers met violent deaths during this period, this number represents 0.63 per 100,000 postal workers compared with the average of 0.71 workers nationwide.[1] In addition to aggression, the withdrawal reaction to frustration may be a major explanation for the "motivational problem" of employees. They may be apathetic or have "retired on the job" because they are frustrated, not because they have no motivation. Many employees' motives have been blocked by dead-end jobs, high degrees of job specialization, or supervisors who put up barriers. Also, the fixation reaction to frustration may be used to explain irrational bureaucratic behavior. (The rules become the ends in themselves and the frustrated employee pathetically adapts to the barriers.) Compromise can help explain mid-career changes (frustrated employees go around the barriers) or "living outside the job" (frustrated employees cannot achieve motivated goals on the job, so they seek goals outside the job). These reactions to frustration often cost organizations a great deal because of the dysfunctions associated with aggression, withdrawal, and fixation. In the case of compromise, the employee's motivation is forced outside the organization. Although the discussion so far indicates the dysfunctional nature of frustration, such negativity should not be automatically assumed.

In some cases frustration may actually result in a positive impact on individual performance and organizational goals. An example is the worker or manager who has high needs for competence and achievement and who has a self-concept that includes confidence in being able to do a job well. A person of this type who is frustrated on

TABLE 10.1 Examples of Reactions to Frustration

Adjustive Reactions	Psychological Process	Illustration
Compensation	Devoting oneself to a pursuit with increased vigor to make up for some feeling of real or imagined inadequacy	The zealous, hardworking president of the Twenty-Five Year Club who has never advanced very far in the company hierarchy
Displacement	Redirecting pent-up emotions toward persons, ideas, or objects other than the primary source of the emotion	The supervisor who roughly rejects a simple request from a subordinate after receiving a rebuff from the boss
Fantasy	Daydreaming or engaging in other forms of imaginative activity to provide both an escape from reality and imagined satisfactions	The employee who daydreams of the day in the staff meeting when she corrects the boss's mistakes and is publicly acknowledged as the real leader of the industry
Negativism	Actively or passively resisting, operating unconsciously	The manager who, having been unsuccessful in getting out of a committee assignment, picks apart every suggestion that anyone makes in the meetings
Projection	Protecting oneself from awareness of one's own undesirable traits or unacceptable feelings by attributing them to others	The unsuccessful person who, deep down, would like to block the rise of others in the organization and who continually feels that others are out to "get him"
Rationalization	Justifying inconsistent or undesirable behavior, beliefs, statements, and motivations by providing acceptable explanations for them	The salesperson who pads the expense account because "everybody does it"
Regression	Returning to an earlier and less mature level of adjustment in the face of frustration	The manager who, having been blocked in some administrative pursuit, busies herself with clerical duties or technical details more appropriate for her subordinates
Resignation, apathy, and boredom	Breaking psychological contact with the environment, withholding any sense of emotional or personal involvement	The employee who, receiving no reward, praise, or encouragement, no longer cares whether or not he does a good job
Flight or withdrawal	Leaving the field in which frustration, anxiety, or conflict is experienced, either physically or psychologically	The salesperson who, when a big order falls through, takes the rest of the day off; the older worker who, constantly rebuffed or rejected by superiors and colleagues, is pushed toward being a loner and ignores what friendly gestures are made

Source: Timothy W. Costello and Sheldon S. Zalkind, *Psychology in Administration: A Research Orientation,* Prentice-Hall, Englewood Cliffs, N.J., 1963, pp. 148–149.

the job may react in a traditional defensive manner, but the frustration may result in improved performance. The person may try harder to overcome the barrier or may overcompensate, or the new direction or goal sought may be more compatible with the organization's goals. In addition, it should be remembered that defense mechanisms per se are not bad for the individual. They play an important role in the psychological adjustment process and are unhealthy only when they dominate the individual's personality. Also, those who have successfully overcome frustration in the past by learning that it is possible to surmount barriers or find substitute goals are more tolerant of frustration than those who have never experienced it, or than those who have experienced excesses in frustration.[2] However, in general, a major goal of management should be to eliminate the barriers (imagined, real, or potential) that are or will be frustrating to employees. This goal may be accomplished through job redesign efforts (see Chapter 7) that are more compatible with employee motivation or leadership skills that get the frustrating barriers out of people's way.

Goal Conflict

Another common source of conflict for an individual is a goal which has both positive and negative features, or two or more competing goals. Whereas in frustration a single motive is blocked before the goal is reached, in goal conflict two or more motives block one another. For ease of analysis, three separate types of goal conflict are generally identified:

1. *Approach-approach* conflict, where the individual is motivated to approach two or more positive but mutually exclusive goals.
2. *Approach-avoidance* conflict, where the individual is motivated to approach a goal and at the same time is motivated to avoid it. The single goal contains both positive and negative characteristics for the individual.
3. *Avoidance-avoidance* conflict, where the individual is motivated to avoid two or more negative but mutually exclusive goals.

To varying degrees, each of these forms of goal conflict exists in the modern organization.

Approach-Approach Conflict. This type of goal conflict probably has the least impact on organizational behavior. Although conflict may arise about making a choice between two positive goals, such a situation is preferable to one that involves two negative goals or a goal with both negative and positive characteristics. For example, if both personal and organizational goals are attractive to organizational participants, they will usually make a choice rather quickly and thus eliminate their conflict. A more specific example would be the new college graduate who is faced with two excellent job opportunities or the executive who has the choice between two very attractive offices in which to work. Such situations often cause the person some anxiety but are quickly resolved, and the person, unlike the donkey in the fable, does not "starve between two haystacks."

Approach-approach conflict can be analyzed in terms of the well-known theory of cognitive dissonance.[3] In simple terms, *dissonance* is the state of psychological discomfort or conflict created in people when they are faced with two or more goals or alternatives to a decision. Although these alternatives occur together, they do not belong or fit together. The theory states that the person experiencing dissonance will be highly motivated to reduce or eliminate it and will actively avoid situations and information which would be likely to increase it. For example, the young person faced with two equally attractive job opportunities would experience dissonance. According to this theory, the young person would actively try to reduce the dissonance. The individual may cognitively rationalize that one job is really better than the other one and, once the choice is made, be sincerely convinced that it was the right choice and actively avoid any evidence or argument to the contrary.

Approach-Avoidance Conflict. This type of goal conflict is most relevant to the analysis of organizational behavior. Normally, organizational goals have both positive and negative aspects for organization participants. Accordingly, the organizational goal may arouse a great deal of conflict within a person and may actually cause the person to vacillate anxiously at the point where approach equals avoidance.

Figure 10.3 shows some possible gradients for approach and avoidance. X represents the point of maximum conflict, where the organism may come to a complete stop and vacillate. In order for the organism to progress beyond X, there

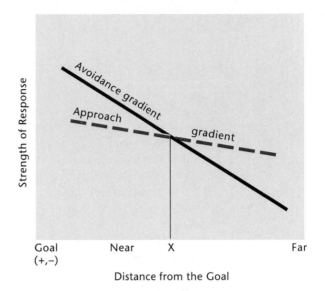

FIGURE 10.3
Gradients of approach-
avoidance conflict.

must be a shift in the gradients so that there is a greater strength of response for approach than for avoidance. The slopes of the gradients shown in Figure 10.3 approximate those obtained from animals who are first trained to approach food at the end of a runway and then are shocked while feeding there. As shown, the pull or effort toward a positive goal is stronger the nearer the goal, but not as strong as the tendency to get away from a negative goal. The slope of the avoidance from the negative goal is steeper than the slope of the approach to reach the positive goal.

The approach-avoidance gradients for humans will not always resemble those found in Figure 10.3. The slopes may be different for different people and different goals. In general, however, it is safe to assume that the positive aspects of a given organizational goal are stronger and more salient at a distance (in time and/or space) than the negative aspects. On the other hand, as a person gets nearer to the goal, the negative aspects become more pronounced, and at some point the individual may hesitate or fail to progress any further. For example, managers engaged in long-range planning typically are very confident of a goal (a strategic plan) they have developed for the future. Yet, as the time gets near to commit resources and implement the plan, the negative consequences seem to appear much greater than they did in the developing stage. Managers in such a situation may reach the point where approach equals avoidance. The result is a great deal of internal conflict and stress, which may cause indecision, ulcers, or even depression.

Such conflict and its aftermath are very common among decision makers and people in responsible positions in the fast-changing "new paradigm" organizations described in the chapters in the introductory part of the text. This era of global competition and downsizing has been depicted as one that involves trying to manage in the midst of chaos. As noted in a recent cover story of *Fortune*, "To the survivors, the revolution feels something like this: scary, guilty, painful, liberating, disorienting, exhilarating, empowering, frustrating, fulfilling, confusing, challenging."[4] In other words, as these terms indicate, many of today's managers are experiencing very mixed feelings, or approach-avoidance reactions. This type of conflict can often be resolved in the same manner as cognitive dissonance, or the gradients may be shifted by the individual so that either the positive or the negative aspects clearly predominate.

Avoidance-Avoidance Conflict. Analogous to approach-approach conflict, this type of conflict does not have a great deal of impact on organizational behavior. Avoidance-avoidance conflict is usually easily resolved. A person faced with two negative goals may not choose either of them and may simply leave the situation. If this can be done, the conflict is quickly resolved. In some situations, however, the person is unable to leave. This would be true of people in nonvoluntary organizations, such as inmates in a prison, patients in a hospital, or members of the armed services. To a lesser extent, most personnel in modern organizations are also restricted from leaving, for example, workers who detest their supervisor and have too much pride to be unemployed. Such workers cannot easily resolve their avoidance-avoidance conflict in a time when jobs are very scarce. This set of circumstances can lead to very dissatisfied workers who feel they have no escape.

Goal Conflict in Perspective. All three types of goal conflict might in certain instances benefit the organization. Approach-approach conflict can be mildly distressing for a person but represent the best of two worlds. Approach-avoidance conflict arising over organizational goals may force very careful planning and forecasting of exact positive and negative outcomes. Even avoidance-avoidance conflict may stimulate the person involved to examine and try to solve the problems causing the conflict. Yet, on balance, except for approach-approach conflicts, management should attempt to resolve goal conflicts. In particular, a major management effort should be devoted to building compatibility, not conflict, between personal and organizational goals.

Role Conflict and Ambiguity

Closely related to the concept of norms (the "oughts" of behavior), *role* is defined as a position that has expectations evolving from established norms. People living in contemporary society assume a succession of roles throughout life. A typical sequence of social roles would be that of child, son or daughter, teenager, college student, boyfriend or girlfriend, spouse, parent, and grandparent. Each of these roles has recognized expectations which are acted out like a role in a play.

Besides progressing through a succession of roles such as those just mentioned, the adult in modern society fills numerous other roles at the same time. It is not uncommon for the adult middle-class male to be simultaneously playing the roles of husband, father, provider, son (to elderly parents), worker or manager, student (in a night program), coach of a Little League baseball team, church member, member of a social club, bridge partner, poker club member, officer of a community group, and weekend golfer. Women, of course, also have numerous, often conflicting, roles. Although all the roles which men and women bring into the organization are relevant to their behavior, in the study of organizational behavior the organizational role is the most important. Roles such as assembly line worker, clerk, supervisor, salesperson, engineer, systems analyst, department head, vice president, and chairperson of the board often carry conflicting demands and expectations. As the accompanying International Application Example: Cultural Conflict shows, sometimes these roles differ by culture and can result in conflict.

International Application Example

Cultural Conflict

Japan's direct investment in the United States has been substantial over the years. This investment has not only brought new plants, technologies, and jobs to America but also has resulted in some conflict. The Japanese-run companies in the United States are an example of how cultural conflict can erupt. For instance, large Japanese companies are known for their lifetime employment policies, which purportedly produce corporate loyalty. Employees often stay in a Japanese company throughout their entire career. American workers, on the other hand, may work for several companies in the course of their career. Asa Jonishi, senior director of Japan's Kyocera Corporation, says, "Most Americans are very, very individualistic—you could almost say egotistic; they are quite different from the way we would like our people to be." Two other important cultural differences are trade unions and women managers. In U.S. industry, both are common. The Japanese, on the other hand, have had little experience with either. As a result, Japanese companies are becoming experienced with lawsuits. For example, former female employees of Sumitomo Corporation of America filed a sex-discrimination suit that alleged that Sumitomo restricted women to clerical positions. Sumitomo settled the suit by promising to increase the number of women in sales and management positions. In another case, the AFL-CIO won a dispute with Toyota and its Japanese contractor. To end the negative publicity of the unions' campaign, Toyota and its contractor agreed to hire union workers to build their new plant.

It should be noted that some of the Japanese cultural values have been readily accepted in the American workplace. For instance, consensus management, which the Japanese are noted for, is being accepted in industries where autocratic leaders once existed. Pat Park, assistant general manager of Haseko, says: "There are many times when I'm the janitor here, picking up rubbish. But there are also many times the major decisions are made because I say so. There's more equity in Japanese companies." Thus, not all cultural differences lead to conflict. As all companies continue to transcend national borders, cultural differences may begin to narrow. However, culture still has a pervasive, but sometimes conflicting, influence on organizational behavior.

There are three types of role conflict.[5] One type is the conflict between the *person and the role*. There may be conflict between the person's personality and the expectations of the role. For example, a production worker and member of the union is appointed to a supervisory position. This new supervisor may not really believe in keeping close control over the workers and it goes against the individual's personality to be hard-nosed, but that is what the head of production expects. A second type is *intrarole* conflict created by contradictory expectations about how a given role should be played. Should a new supervisor be autocratic or democratic in dealing with the workers? Finally, *interrole* conflict results from the differing requirements of two or more roles that must be played at the same time. Work roles and nonwork roles are often in such conflict. For example, a successful executive working for a computer company said that she often worked from 7:30 A.M. to 11:30 P.M. Her long hours led to the breakup of a relationship. When she got word that her mother was seriously ill, she remembered: "I had about five minutes to be upset before the phone started ringing again. You get so far into it, you don't even realize your life has gotten away from you completely."[6]

The first-line supervisor and the fast-climbing executive obviously represent the extreme cases of organizational role conflict. Yet to varying degrees, depending on the individual and the situation, people in every other position in the modern organization also experience one or all three types of conflict. Staff engineers are not sure of their real authority. The clerk in the front office does not know whether to respond to a union organizing drive. The examples are endless. The question is not whether role conflict and ambiguity exist—they do, and they seem inevitable. Rather, the key becomes a matter of determining how role conflict can be resolved or managed.

INTERPERSONAL CONFLICT

Besides the intraindividual aspects of conflict, the interpersonal aspects of conflict are also an important dynamic of interactive behavior. The interrole conflict discussed in the preceding section certainly has interpersonal implications, and so do intergroup and organizational conflict, discussed in the next sections. But this section is specifically concerned with analyzing the conflict that can result when two or more persons are interacting with one another.

Sources of Interpersonal Conflict

Managers who have conflict with subordinates, bosses, or peers most often attribute the cause to a personality problem or defect in the other party. For example, research from attribution theory, presented in Chapter 6, noted that the so-called fundamental attribution error has people attribute others' behavior to personal factors such as intelligence, ability, motivation, attitudes, or personality. Whetten and Cameron, however, go beyond this surface explanation and propose that there are four sources of interpersonal conflict.[7] These can be summarized as follows:

1. *Personal differences.* Everyone has a unique background because of his or her upbringing, cultural and family traditions, and socialization processes. Because no one has the same family background, education, experience, and values, the differences can be a major source of conflict. Disagreements stemming from the differences "often become highly emotional and take on moral overtones. A disagreement about who is factually correct easily turns into a bitter argument over who is morally right."[8]
2. *Information deficiency.* This source of conflict results from communication breakdown in the organization. It may be that the two people in conflict are using different information or that one or both have misinformation. Unlike personal differences, this source of conflict is not emotionally charged and once corrected, there is little resentment.
3. *Role incompatibility.* This type of interpersonal conflict draws from both intra-individual role conflict (discussed in an earlier section) and intergroup conflict (discussed in the next section). Specifically, in today's interfunctional organizations, many managers have functions and tasks that are interdependent. However, the individual roles of these managers may be incompatible. For example, the production manager and the sales manager have interdependent functions: one supports the other. However, the role of the production manager is to cut costs, and one way to do this is to keep inventories low. The sales manager, on the other hand, has the role of increasing revenues through increased sales. The sales manager may make delivery promises to customers that are incompatible with the

low inventory levels kept by production. The resulting conflict from role incompatibility may have to be resolved by higher-level management.

4. *Environmental stress.* The above types of conflict can be amplified by a stressful environment. In environments characterized by scarce or shrinking resources, downsizing, competitive pressures, or high degrees of uncertainty, conflict of all kinds will be more probable. "For example, when a major pet-food manufacturing facility announced that one-third of its managers would have to support a new third shift, the feared disruption of personal and family routines prompted many managers to think about sending out their resumes. In addition, the uncertainty of who was going to be required to work at night was so great that even routine management work was disrupted by posturing and infighting."[9]

Analyzing Interpersonal Conflict

Besides identifying some of the major sources of interpersonal conflict, it is useful to analyze the dynamics of individuals interacting with one another. One way to analyze their confronting others is through the response categories of (1) forcing (assertive, uncooperative); (2) accommodating (unassertive, cooperative); (3) avoiding (uncooperative, unassertive); (4) compromising (between assertiveness and cooperativeness); and (5) collaborating (cooperative, assertive).[10]

Another popular framework for analyzing the dynamics of interpersonal behavior is the Johari window. Developed by Joseph Luft and Harry Ingham (thus the name *Johari*), this model is particularly useful in analyzing interpersonal conflict. As Figure 10.4 shows, the model helps identify several interpersonal styles, shows the characteristics and results of these styles, and suggests ways of interpreting the conflicts that may develop between the self and others.

In simple terms, the self can be thought of as "me," and others can be thought of as "you" in a two-person interaction. There are certain things that the person knows about himself or herself and certain things that are not known. The same is true of others. There are certain things the person knows about the other and certain things that are not known. The following summarizes the four cells in the Johari window:

1. *Open self.* In this form of interaction the person knows about himself or herself and about the other. There would generally be openness and compatibility and

FIGURE 10.4
The Luft and Ingham Johari window for interpersonal relationships.

	The person knows about the other	The person does not know about the other
The person knows about him or herself	1 OPEN SELF	2 HIDDEN SELF
The person does not know about him or herself	3 BLIND SELF	4 UNDISCOVERED SELF

little reason to be defensive. This type of interpersonal relationship would tend to lead to little, if any, interpersonal conflict.

2. *Hidden self.* In this situation the person understands himself or herself but does not know about the other person. The result is that the person remains hidden from the other because of the fear of how the other might react. The person may keep his or her true feelings or attitudes secret and will not open up to the other. There is potential interpersonal conflict in this situation.

3. *Blind self.* In this situation the person knows about the other but not about himself or herself. The person may be unintentionally irritating to the other. The other could tell the person but may be fearful of hurting the person's feelings. As in the hidden self, there is potential interpersonal conflict in this situation.

4. *Undiscovered self.* This is potentially the most explosive situation. The person does not know about himself or herself and does not know about the other. In other words, there is much misunderstanding, and interpersonal conflict is almost sure to result.

The Johari window only points out possible interpersonal styles. It does not necessarily describe, but rather helps analyze, possible interpersonal conflict situations.

One way of decreasing the hidden self and increasing the open self is through the processes of self-disclosure. By becoming more trustful of others and disclosing information about themselves, people may reduce the potential for conflict. On the other hand, such self-disclosure is a risk for the individual, and the outcome must be worth the cost. To decrease the blind self and at the same time increase the open self, the other must give feedback, and the person must use it.

Strategies for Interpersonal Conflict Resolution

There are conflict resolution strategies associated with each of the response categories of forcing, accommodating, avoiding, compromising, and collaborating. For example, an effective strategy would be to use a problem-solving collaborative approach rather than, say, a forcing or avoiding approach. The collaborative approach strives "to find solutions to the causes of the conflict that are satisfactory to both parties rather than to find fault or assign blame."[11] Ways to manage interpersonal conflict can also be found in the Johari analysis. For example, those who find themselves in hidden, blind, or undiscovered interpersonal relations should try to move toward an open relationship to resolve real or potential conflict.

There are also some simple ways of dealing with crises, such as those found in the accompanying Application Example: Dealing with Crises. Additionally, there are rules of thumb, or simple guidelines, that can be followed to manage interpersonal conflict. One such list that can be used by managers to effectively deal with destructive workplace disputes is the following:

1. Model the attitudes and behaviors you want your employees to emulate.
2. Identify the source of conflict, structural or interpersonal.
3. Focus on the task, not personalities.
4. Address conflict in a timely way.
5. Learn from conflict.[12]

Too often when a conflict occurs between supervisor-subordinate pairs, employees-customers, coworkers, or even friends or marriage partners, there tends to be either a fight (personal attacks) or a flight (embarrassed silence or leave)

**Application
Example**

Dealing with Crises

A manager at a small cosmetics company learned that his firm had just been acquired by a large international conglomerate. His staff wanted to know how this would affect the firm's current plans for the new fiscal year. When he asked his boss, he was told, "Don't worry about anything. It's going to be business as usual." The manager had a difficult time accepting this. So did his staff, many of whom were convinced that their jobs were in jeopardy.

This situation is common in industry these days, and the worst part for many managers is that they will not know for several months how everything is going to turn out. In the interim, they need a strategy for dealing with the resulting conflict. What can they do? Psychologists who have studied these situations have concluded that there are two phases to crisis management: (*a*) emotion and (*b*) reason and action. By mentally "walking through" these two phases, psychologists contend, it is possible to get oneself prepared for managing in a crisis. The emotional phase is typically characterized by negative responses. Some managers feel panic brought on by the dismay and confusion caused by the crisis. Most feel some degree of anger, which is then followed by feelings of guilt. However, these feelings are then typically replaced by a take-charge attitude. The manager begins looking for ways of straightening out the situation. This is when the second phase begins. The reason and action phase is characterized by an assessment of the facts, followed by effective decision making. This process entails examining the situation and setting goals, assessing ways of straightening things out, rebuilding confidence among the subordinates, and developing effective two-way communication. At this point the situation is usually well under control.

Whenever there is a setback or disaster, managers are likely to go through these two phases. The better that managers understand their emotional reactions to the crisis, the more effectively they tend to respond—and the more likely it is that they will succeed.

---

response. Neither is an effective way to handle interpersonal conflict. More appropriate for resolving conflict and preserving positive relationships would be to follow this process:

1. Allow time to cool off.
2. Analyze the situation.
3. State the problem to the other person.
4. Leave the person an "out."[13]

Although these simple guidelines for managing interpersonal conflict come from the practitioner literature, there is also some research support for such approaches.[14] However, most conflict resolution (including not only interpersonal, but also intergroup and organizational, covered next) ends up based on three basic strategies. These are the lose-lose, win-lose, and win-win approaches. The win-win strategy is the most effective, but since the other two types are so commonly used, they should also be understood.

Lose-Lose. In a lose-lose approach to conflict resolution, both parties lose. It has been pointed out that this approach can take several forms.[15] One of the more common approaches is to compromise or take the middle ground in a dispute. A second approach is to pay off one of the parties in the conflict. These payments often take the form of bribes. A third approach is to use an outside third party or arbitrator. A final type of lose-lose strategy appears when the parties in a conflict resort to bureaucratic rules or existing regulations to resolve the conflict. In all four of these approaches, both parties in the conflict lose. It is sometimes the only way that conflicts can be resolved, but it is generally less desirable than the win-lose or, especially, the win-win strategy.

Win-Lose. A win-lose strategy is a very common way of resolving conflict in American society. In a competitive type of culture, as is generally found in the United States, one party in a conflict situation attempts to marshal its forces to win, and the other party loses. The following list summarizes some of the characteristics of a win-lose situation:

1. There is a clear we-they distinction between the parties.
2. The parties direct their energies toward each other in an atmosphere of victory and defeat.
3. The parties see the issue from their own point of view.
4. The emphasis is on solutions rather than on the attainment of goals, values, or objectives.
5. Conflicts are personalized and judgmental.
6. There is no differentiation of conflict-resolving activities from other group processes, nor is there a planned sequence of those activities.
7. The parties take a short-run view of the issues.[16]

Examples of win-lose strategies can be found in supervisor-subordinate relationships, line-staff confrontations, union-management relations, and many other conflict situations found in today's organizations. The win-lose strategy can have both functional and dysfunctional consequences for the organization. It is functional in the sense of creating a competitive drive to win, and it can lead to cohesiveness and esprit de corps among the individuals or groups in the conflict situation. On the dysfunctional side, a win-lose strategy ignores other solutions such as a cooperative, mutually agreed-upon outcome; there are pressures to conform, which may stifle a questioning, creative atmosphere for conflict resolution; and highly structured power relationships tend to emerge rapidly. The biggest problem, however, with a win-lose strategy is that someone always loses. Those who suffer the loss may learn something in the process, but losers also tend to be bitter and vindictive. A much healthier strategy is to have both parties in a conflict situation win.

Win-Win. A win-win strategy of conflict resolution is probably the most desirable from a human and organizational standpoint. Energies and creativity are aimed at solving the problems rather than beating the other party. It takes advantage of the functional aspects of win-lose and eliminates many of the dysfunctional aspects. The needs of both parties in the conflict situation are met, and both parties receive rewarding outcomes. A review of the relevant literature revealed that "win-win decision strategies are associated with better judgments, favorable organization experience, and more favorable bargains."[17] Although it is often difficult to accomplish a win-win outcome of an interpersonal conflict, this should be a major goal of the management of conflict.

INTERGROUP BEHAVIOR AND CONFLICT

Conceptually similar to interpersonal behavior is intergroup behavior. The previous chapter concentrates on *intra*group behavior and dynamics. There are also some interesting dynamics and resulting conflict that occur between groups. An understanding of the theoretical framework for intergroup behavior is a prerequisite for examining the conflict that often results.

Intergroup Behavior in Organizations

Social psychologists have been concerned about intergroup conflict and hostility for a number of years. Intergroup behavior is even specifically identified as follows: "Intergroup behavior occurs whenever individuals belonging to one group interact, collectively or individually, with another group or its members in terms of their reference group identification."[18]

Social psychologist Muzafer Sherif's realistic group conflict theory (RGCT) is probably the best known. This theory considers intergroup conflict in a holistic manner, beyond the realm of personality, group psychology, and interpersonal relations. "The basic thesis of RGCT is that intergroup hostility is produced by the existence of conflicting goals (i.e., competition) and reduced by the existence of mutually desired superordinate goals attainable only through intergroup cooperation."[19] The implication of such a theory, especially in the era of interfunctional teams, as discussed in the previous chapter, is that competition may lead to dysfunctional conflict, while cooperation can reduce the conflict and better attain the overall goals of the organization.

A more macro-oriented approach relevant to the understanding of intergroup behavior and conflict is role theory. The chapters in Part 4 of the text deal specifically with organization process and design. One way to look at organizations, however, is in terms of interacting role sets. Instead of depicting an organization as being made up of interacting individuals, one could think of it as consisting of interacting and overlapping role sets.

Interacting and Overlapping Role Sets. The role concept used in analyzing intra-individual conflict can also be used in the understanding of intergroup behavior. In particular, all organizational participants have certain expectations of others and of themselves concerning what is involved in their roles. The organization could be thought of as a set of such roles, and when these roles are in interaction with one another, the organization could more realistically be pictured as a system of overlapping role sets; this often results in conflict.

Robert L. Kahn is most closely associated with the role-set theory of organization. In Kahn's view the organization is made up of overlapping and interlocking role sets. These role sets would normally transcend the boundaries of the classical conception of organizations. Figure 10.5 gives an example of the interacting role-set concept of organization. The figure shows only three possible role sets from a large manufacturing organization. The purchasing agent, executive vice president, and design engineer are called the *focal persons* of the sets shown. The supplier's and consultant's roles are vital in their respective sets but would not be included within traditional organizational boundaries. They are external to the classical organization. The design engineer is a member of the purchasing agent's role set but is also a focal

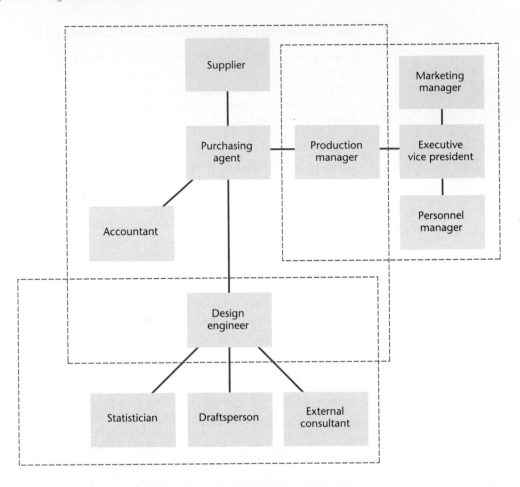

FIGURE 10.5
The organization as
overlapping role sets.

person for another role set. The production manager is shown as a member of two role sets. The overlaps can result in role conflicts and ambiguities. Such dynamics become important in intergroup conflict analysis.

Antecedents to Intergroup Conflict. Several antecedent conditions have been identified for explaining intergroup conflict. These can be summarized as follows:[20]

1. *Competition for resources.* Most organizations today have very limited resources. Groups within the organization vie for budget funds, space, supplies, personnel, and support services.

2. *Task interdependence.* If two groups in the organization depend on one another in a mutual way or even one-way (as in a sequential technological process), there tends to be more conflict than if groups are independent of one another. The more diverse the objectives, priorities, and personnel are of the interdependent groups (for example, research and production), the more conflict there tends to be.

3. *Jurisdictional ambiguity.* This may involve "turf" problems or overlapping responsibilities. For example, conflict might occur when one group attempts to assume more control or take credit for desirable activities, or give up its part and any responsibility for undesirable activities.

4. *Status struggles.* This conflict occurs when one group attempts to improve its status and another group views this as a threat to its place in the status hierarchy. One group may also feel it is being inequitably treated in comparison with another group of equal status in terms of rewards, job assignments, working conditions, privileges, or status symbols. Human resources departments typically feel they are treated inequitably in relation to sales, finance, or production departments.

The Impact of, and Strategies for, Intergroup Conflict

Presenting interacting groups in terms of overlapping role sets and some antecedents provides a better understanding of the dynamics and resulting conflict that can occur. Groups in conflict have much different behavior from that of smoothly cooperating groups. There is evidence that groups in conflict change both internally and in relation to one another. "Unfortunately, these changes generally result in either a continuance or an escalation of the conflict."[21] In particular, after searching the relevant literature, Daft identified the following characteristics of groups in conflict:

1. There is a clear distinction and comparison between "we" (the in-group) and "they" (the out-group).
2. A group that feels it is in conflict with another group becomes more cohesive and pulls together to present a solid front to defeat the other group.
3. The positive feelings and cohesion within the in-group do not transfer to the members of the out-group. The members of the out-group are viewed as the enemy rather than as neutrals.
4. Threatened group members feel superior—they overestimate their strength and underestimate that of members of other groups.
5. The amount of communication between conflicting groups decreases. When there is communication, it is characterized by negative comments and hostility.
6. If a group is losing in a conflict, the members' cohesion decreases and they experience increased tension among themselves. They look for a scapegoat to blame their failure on.
7. The intergroup conflict and resulting hostility are not the result of neurotic tendencies on the part of individual members. These seem to be a product of group interaction, even when individuals in the group are normal and well adjusted.[22]

The above findings from research help describe and provide an understanding of the behavior of conflicting groups in organizations, such as unions and management, production and sales, office personnel and operating personnel, nurses and doctors, and faculty and administrators. There is even some evidence that gender may affect intergroup behavior. Research indicates that although men and women are equally adept at helping groups solve conflict, women tend to seek changes in future behavior while men tend to push for more immediate results.[23]

There is also recent theoretical analysis indicating the importance that the origin of the group (for example, mandated versus voluntary) and the degree of externally imposed task structure (for example, high versus low) may have on the outcomes of intergroup interactions.[24] For example, mandated groups with high external task structure are predicted to have low member satisfaction and minimal quality of output while voluntary groups with low external task structure are predicted to have high member satisfaction and high quality of output. These indications, of course, need to be tested by empirical research, but if the model proves predictive, it could greatly help managers make better decisions in forming and structuring interacting groups.

Flowing out of this profile are a number of strategies that can be employed to reduce the conflict. These can be grouped into four major types:

1. *Avoidance.* This type of strategy attempts to keep the conflict from surfacing at all. Examples would be to simply ignore the conflict or impose a solution. This strategy may be appropriate if the conflict is trivial or if quick action is needed to prevent the conflict from occurring.

2. *Defusion.* Under this strategy, an attempt is made to deactivate the conflict and cool off the emotions and hostilities of the groups involved. Examples would include trying to "smooth things over" by playing down the importance and magnitude of the conflict or of established superordinate goals that need the cooperation of the conflicting groups in order to be accomplished. This strategy is appropriate where a stopgap measure is needed or when the groups have a mutually important goal.

3. *Containment.* Under this strategy, some conflict is allowed to surface, but it is carefully contained by spelling out which issues are to be discussed and how they are to be resolved. To carry out this strategy, the problems and procedures may be structured, and representatives from the conflicting parties may be allowed to negotiate and bargain within the structure established. This strategy is appropriate where open discussions have failed and the conflicting groups are of equal power.

4. *Confrontation.* Under this strategy, which is at the other end of the continuum from avoidance, all the issues are brought into the open, and the conflicting groups directly confront the issues and each other in an attempt to reach a mutually satisfactory solution. This strategy may involve mutual problem solving or even formally redesigning jobs or responsibilities in order to resolve the conflict. Confrontation is most appropriate when there is a minimum level of trust, when time is not critical, and when the groups need to cooperate to get the job done effectively.[25]

There are many other strategies that could be used besides those described above. For example, conflict management techniques such as the following can be used: superordinate goal (a common goal that is appealing to conflicting groups); the reduction of interdependence between the conflicting groups; expanding resources so that competition between the groups is minimized; mutual problem solving to get the conflicting groups together in a face-to-face meeting; creation of a formal appeals system; and merging conflicting groups.[26] In addition, the win-win perspective is important, and many of the organization development techniques presented in Chapter 20 are also applicable.

ORGANIZATIONAL CONFLICT

So far, this chapter has focused, in turn, on intraindividual, interpersonal, and intergroup conflict. All these types of conflict take place within the organizational setting. Now attention is directed at organizational conflict per se, but it must be remembered that intraindividual, interpersonal, and intergroup conflict are all inherent in organizational conflict.

Structural Conflict

Individuals in the organization have many conflicting organizational cross pressures operating on them. For example, in the classical organization there are four predominant types of structural conflict:

1. *Hierarchical conflict.* There may be conflict between the various levels of the organization. The board of directors may be in conflict with top management, middle management may be in conflict with supervisory personnel, or there may be general conflict between management and the workers.
2. *Functional conflict.* There may be conflict between the various functional departments of the organization. Conflict between the production and marketing departments discussed earlier is a classic example.
3. *Line-staff conflict.* There may be conflict between line and staff. It often results from situations in which staff personnel do not formally possess authority over line personnel.
4. *Formal-informal conflict.* There may be conflict between the formal and informal organizations. For example, the informal organization's norms for performance may be incompatible with the formal organization's norms for performance.

These forms of organizational conflict have been given attention in other chapters. However, the example of line-staff conflict is representative of organizational conflict. In particular, the classic research of Melville Dalton is a good example of an analysis of line-staff conflict.[27] Also covered in Chapter 9, his case study of Milo (a pseudonym), a factory of 8000 employees, has become a classic analysis of line-staff conflict. Through detailed observations, Dalton was able to record actual conflict that occurred between line and staff personnel at this plant. One of his major conclusions was that line managers often view staff advice as a threat. An example was the case of R. Jefferson, a staff engineer who devised a new plan for operations. At least two line supervisors admitted privately to Dalton that the plan had merit, but they nevertheless rejected it. One of them, H. Clause, explained why:

> Jefferson's idea was pretty good. But his . . . overbearing manner turned him off with me. He came out here and tried to ram the scheme down our throats. He made me so . . . mad I couldn't see. The thing about him and the whole white-collar bunch that burns me up is the way they expect you to jump when they come around. . . . I been in this plant twenty-two years. I've worked in tool rooms, too. I've forgot more than most of these college punks'll ever know. I've worked with all kinds of schemes and all kinds of people. You see what I mean—I've been around, and I don't need a punk like Jefferson telling me where to head in. I wouldn't take that kind of stuff from my own kid—and he's an engineer too. No, his [Jefferson's] scheme may have some good points, but not good enough to have . . . him lording it over you. He acted like we had to use his scheme . . . that noise! Him and the whole white-collar bunch—I don't mean any offense to you—can go to . . . We've got too . . . many bosses already.[28]

In support of the classic conflict situation, Dalton documented that at Milo the staff personnel were substantially younger and had more formal education than the line supervisors. Combined with social factors, these personal characteristics were given as the major factors explaining the organizational conflicts which existed at Milo. However, in a later study, Dalton found some indication that the traditional line-staff conflict model may be changing, at least in some industries. His study of Transode Corporation, a fictitious name given to an electronics firm that employed a highly technical engineering staff that had no official hierarchy and a group of line officers who were formed into a strict hierarchy, provided insights into how conflict can be reduced. In this situation, friction was decreased by "assigning each individual a specific authority, by obscuring status symbols and by stressing symbols of science, quality, and service that allowed all officers to share the luster of association with a vital product."[29]

A very simple solution to help alleviate line-staff conflict and improve communications would be for all staff personnel to use the approach of "sell before tell" when dealing with line personnel. Taken philosophically and literally, this approach has great merit for improving line-staff relationships and thus resolving organizational conflict.

Besides the classic structural conflicts such as line-staff conflict, more contemporary organization designs (covered in Chapter 17) also contain potential conflict situations. The project and matrix organizations in particular have structurally created conflict. The project manager with responsibility but no authority and the manager in a matrix structure with a functional boss and a project boss present two prominent conflict situations. There is also research evidence to indicate that organizations with limited resources and lowered commitment to the status quo trigger interdepartmental influence attempts that may lead to conflict.[30]

On the other side of the coin, some of the new total quality programs, as presented in Chapter 2, have been shown to reduce interdepartmental conflict and increase cooperation.[31] Also, where conscious attempts of having cooperative goals and open discussions between departments have been tried, there have been significant improvements in customer service, task completion, and effective resource use.[32] However, it should be remembered that reducing or eliminating interorganizational conflict is not necessarily equated with more effective management. Similar to the other types of intraindividual, interpersonal, and intergroup conflict, conflict in modern organization designs can also be healthy. In some cases the modern designs may actually try to promote conflict to benefit the organization.

The Role of Conflict in Today's Organizations

Traditionally, the approach to organizational conflict was very simple and optimistic. It was based on the following assumptions:

1. Conflict is by definition avoidable.
2. Conflict is caused by troublemakers, boat rockers, and prima donnas.
3. Legalistic forms of authority such as "going through channels" or "sticking to the book" are emphasized.
4. Scapegoats are accepted as inevitable.[33]

Management traditionally relied on formal authority and classical organization restructuring to solve their "conflict problem." Individual managers often became hypocritical in order to avoid conflicts from above or below. They tried to either ignore conflict or rationalize it away with the position that there is nothing that can be done about it.

Starting with the wide acceptance of the Argyris thesis that there is a basic incongruence between the needs and characteristics of adult, mature employees and the requirements of the modern formal organization, the behavioral approach to management began to reexamine its assumptions and concerns about conflict. This development has, at least indirectly, been caused by the overall societal concern with conflict on national, organizational, group, and individual bases. The outcome has been a new set of assumptions about organizational conflict, which are almost the exact opposite of the traditional assumptions. Some of the new assumptions about conflict are the following:

1. Conflict is inevitable.
2. Conflict is determined by structural factors such as the physical shape of a building, the design of a career structure, or the nature of a class system.
3. Conflict is integral to the nature of change.
4. A minimal level of conflict is optimal.[34]

Using such assumptions as a starting point, most experts today emphasize the importance of making a cost-benefit analysis of the conflict situation at any level and then setting up dispute systems.[35] Also, experts urge an expanded view of conflict in organizations. For example, it is suggested that conflict be viewed as a cognitive bargaining process that should focus on negotiation as a way to manage and resolve conflict.[36] These negotiation skills have recently emerged as an important area of study and application in the field of organizational behavior.

NEGOTIATION SKILLS

In recent years negotiation has moved from the industrial relations field to the forefront of necessary managerial skills. As Neale and Bazerman noted: "Everyone negotiates. In its various forms, negotiation is a common mechanism for resolving differences and allocating resources." They then define negotiation as "a decision-making process among interdependent parties who do not share identical preferences. It is through negotiation that the parties decide what each will give and take in their relationship."[37]

Although some organizational behavior scholars note that there are similarities between negotiation strategies and conflict management,[38] negotiation can go beyond just resolving conflict and become a managerial skill for personal and organizational success. For example, a manager can successfully negotiate a salary raise or a good price for supplies. After first noting some of the biases or errors that negotiators commonly make and the traditional negotiation techniques that have been used, the remainder of the chapter is devoted to the newly emerging skills needed for successful negotiation.

Traditional Negotiation Approaches

When negotiating, people in general and managers in particular tend to have certain biases and make certain errors, which prevents them from negotiating rationally and getting the most they can out of a situation. The research on these common mistakes can be summarized as follows:

1. Negotiators tend to be overly affected by the frame, or form of presentation, of information in a negotiation.
2. Negotiators tend to nonrationally escalate commitment to a previously selected course of action when it is no longer the most reasonable alternative.
3. Negotiators tend to assume that their gain must come at the expense of the other party and thereby miss opportunities for mutually beneficial trade-offs between the parties.

4. Negotiator judgments tend to be anchored upon irrelevant information, such as an initial offer.

5. Negotiators tend to rely on readily available information.

6. Negotiators tend to fail to consider information that is available by focusing on the opponent's perspective.

7. Negotiators tend to be overconfident concerning the likelihood of attaining outcomes that favor the individual(s) involved.[39]

Besides these common bias problems, negotiators traditionally have taken either a distributive or a positional bargaining approach. Distributive bargaining assumes a "fixed pie" and focuses on how to get the biggest share, or "slice of the pie." The conflict management strategies of compromising, forcing, accommodating, and avoiding, discussed earlier, all tend to be associated with a distributive negotiation strategy. As noted by Whetten and Cameron:

> Compromise occurs when both parties make sacrifices in order to find a common ground. Compromisers are generally more interested in finding an expedient solution. . . . Forcing and accommodating demand that one party give up its position in order for the conflict to be resolved. When parties to a conflict avoid resolution, they do so because they assume that the costs of resolving the conflict are so high that they are better off not even attempting resolution.[40]

Closely related to distributed bargaining is the commonly used positional bargaining approach. This approach to negotiation involves successively taking, and then giving up, a sequence of positions. In its simplest form, this is what happens when one haggles in an open market. However, positional bargaining also happens in international diplomacy. Fisher and Ury note that such positional bargaining can serve a useful purpose: "It tells the other side what you want; it provides an anchor in an uncertain and pressured situation; and it can eventually produce the terms of an acceptable agreement."[41]

Both distributed and positional bargaining have simplistic strategies such as "tough person," or "hard"; "easy touch," or "soft"; or even "split the difference." Characteristics of the "hard" strategy include the following: The goal is victory, distrust others, dig in to your position, make threats, try to win a contest of will, and apply pressure. By contrast, the "soft" strategy includes these characteristics: The goal is agreement, trust others, change your position easily, make offers, try to avoid a contest of will, and yield to pressure.[42] The hard bargainer typically dominates and has intuitive appeal. However, both research[43] and everyday practice are beginning to reveal that more effective negotiation approaches than these traditional strategies are possible.

Newly Emerging Negotiation Skills

There are now recognized alternative approaches to traditionally recognized distributed and positional bargaining and the hard versus soft strategies in negotiation. Whetten and Cameron suggest an integrative approach that takes an "expanding the pie" perspective that uses problem-solving techniques to find win-win outcomes.[44] Based on a collaborating (rather than a compromising, forcing, accommodating, or avoiding) strategy, the integrative approach requires the effective negotiator to use skills such as (a) establishing superordinate goals; (b) separating the people from the problem; (c) focusing on interests, not on positions; (d) inventing options for mutual gain; and (e) using objective criteria.[45]

In addition to the above guidelines for effective negotiation skills, there is an alternative to positional bargaining and soft versus hard strategies that has been developed by the Harvard Negotiation Project. This alternative to traditional negotiation is called the *principled negotiation*, or *negotiation on the merits*, approach. There are four basic elements in this alternative approach to negotiation. Very simply, they are:

1. *People.* Separate the people from the problem.
2. *Interests.* Focus on interests, not positions.
3. *Options.* Generate a variety of possibilities before deciding what to do.
4. *Criteria.* Insist that the result be based on some objective standard.[46]

The principled skills go beyond hard versus soft and change the game to negotiate on the basis of merits. For example, in soft bargaining the participants are friends, in hard bargaining they are adversaries, but in the principled approach they are problem solvers; in soft the approach is to trust others, in hard there is distrust of others, in the principled approach the negotiator proceeds independent of trust; and in the soft approach negotiators make offers, in the hard approach they make threats, in the principled approach they explore common interests.[47] These principled negotiation skills can result in a wise agreement. As noted by Fisher and Ury:

> The method permits you to reach a gradual consensus on a joint decision *efficiently* without all the transactional costs of digging in to positions only to have to dig yourself out of them. And separating the people from the problem allows you to deal directly and empathetically with the other negotiator as a human being, thus making possible an *amicable* agreement.[48]

Along with social, behavioral, leadership, team, and communication skills, these negotiation skills are becoming increasingly recognized as important to effective management of people in today's organizations.

Summary

The dynamics of interactive behavior at individual, interpersonal, group, and organizational levels, and the resulting conflict, play an increasingly important role in the analysis and study of organizational behavior. Although conflict and stress are conceptually and practically similar, especially at the individual level, they are covered separately (Chapter 11 is devoted to stress). Conflict at the intraindividual level involves frustration, goal conflict, and role conflict and ambiguity. Frustration occurs when goal-directed behavior is blocked. Goal conflict can come about from approach-approach, approach-avoidance, or avoidance-avoidance situations. Role conflict and ambiguity result from a clash in the expectations of the various roles possessed by an individual and can take the forms of person and role conflict, intrarole conflict, or interrole conflict.

Interpersonal conflict is first examined in terms of its sources (personal differences, information deficiency, role incompatibility, and environmental stress). Then the analysis of interpersonal conflict is made through the response categories of forcing, accommodating, avoiding, compromising, and collaborating, and the Johari window (open self, hidden self, blind self, and undiscovered self). The strategies for interpersonal conflict resolution include a problem-solving collaborative approach, movement toward an open self, and some simple guidelines. Most strategies for managing not only interpersonal but also intergroup and organizational conflict end up with lose-lose, win-lose, or, the most desirable outcome, win-win approaches.

Intergroup conflict has been studied in social psychology for a number of years. Widely recognized are Sherif's realistic group conflict theory (RGCT) and Kahn's role-set theory. Antecedents to intergroup conflict can be identified (competition for resources, task interdependence, jurisdictional ambiguity, and status struggles). Also, there are a number of strategies to manage intergroup conflict (avoidance, diffusion, containment, and confrontation).

The broader organizational perspective of conflict can be found in both the classical (hierarchical, functional, line-staff, and formal-informal) and modern (project and matrix) structures. Traditionally, the management of organizational conflict was based on simplistic assumptions. Formal authority and classical restructuring were used in attempts to eliminate it. The more modern approach is to assume the inevitability of conflict, recognize that it is not always bad for the organization, and try to manage it effectively rather than merely try to eliminate it.

The last part of the chapter is concerned with negotiation skills. Going beyond industrial relations and conflict management, negotiation skills are becoming increasingly recognized as important to effective management. Traditionally, negotiators have depended on distributed and positional bargaining. Relying on simplistic hard or soft strategies, this traditional approach is now being challenged by more effective alternative negotiation skills. Representative of these newly recognized negotiation skills are the integrative approach, which uses a problem-solving, collaborative strategy, and the principled, or negotiation on the merits, approach, which emphasizes people, interests, options, and criteria. These negotiation skills go beyond hard versus soft strategies and change the game, leading to a win-win, wise agreement.

Questions for Discussion and Review

1. What is frustration? What are some of its manifestations? How can the frustration model be used to analyze organizational behavior?
2. Explain approach-avoidance conflict. Give a realistic organizational example of where it may occur.
3. What are some of the major sources of interpersonal conflict? Which do you think is most relevant in today's organizations?
4. Briefly summarize the four "selfs" in the Johari window. What implications does each have for interpersonal conflict?
5. How do groups in conflict behave? What are the four strategies that can be used to manage intergroup conflict effectively?
6. How do the traditional assumptions about organizational conflict differ from the modern assumptions? What implications do these new assumptions have for the management of organizational conflict?
7. Compare and contrast the traditional versus the new negotiation skills. Why do you think the new skills lead to better agreements?

Footnote References and Supplemental Readings

1. "Postal Service Focuses on Workplace Violence," *Lincoln Journal*, Nov. 18, 1993, p. 6.

2. Spencer A. Rathus, *Psychology*, 4th ed., Holt, Rinehart and Winston, Fort Worth, Tex., 1990, p. 437.

3. Leon Festinger, *A Theory of Cognitive Dissonance*, Stanford University Press, Stanford, Calif., 1957.

4. John Huey, "Managing in the Midst of Chaos," *Fortune*, Apr. 5, 1993, p. 38.

5. See David G. Myers, *Social Psychology*, 3d ed., McGraw-Hill, New York, 1990, pp. 178–179.

6. Brian O'Reilly, "Is Your Company Asking Too Much?" *Fortune*, Mar. 12, 1990, p. 39.

7. David A. Whetten and Kim S. Cameron, *Developing Management Skills*, 2d ed., HarperCollins, New York, 1991, pp. 397–399.

8. Ibid., p. 398.

9. Ibid., p. 399.

10. Ibid., pp. 400–402. These categories are based on some of the original work of Alan C. Filley, *Interpersonal Conflict Resolution*, Scott, Foresman, Glenview, Ill., 1975.

11. Whetten and Cameron, op. cit., p. 402.

12. Yuan-Duen Lee, "Managing Workplace Conflict," *Management Review*, July 1993, p. 57.

13. Corwin P. King, "When People Bite: How to Handle Conflicts," *HR Focus*, January 1993, p. 19.

14. For example, see Sim B. Sitkin and Robert J. Bies, "Social Accounts in Conflict Situations: Using Explanations to Manage Conflict," *Human Relations*, March 1993, pp. 347–370.

15. Alan C. Filley, Robert J. House, and Steven Kerr, *Managerial Process and Organizational Behavior*, 2d ed., Scott, Foresman, Glenview, Ill., 1976, pp. 166–167.

16. Ibid., p. 167.

17. Ibid., p. 177.

18. Jay W. Jackson, "Realistic Group Conflict Theory: A Review and Evaluation of the Theoretical and Empirical Literature," *The Psychological Record*, Summer 1993, p. 397.

19. Ibid.

20. See Gary Yukl, *Skills for Managers and Leaders*, Prentice-Hall, Englewood Cliffs, N.J., 1990, pp. 283–285.

21. James L. Gibson, John M. Ivancevich, and James H. Donnelly, Jr., *Organizations*, 6th ed., Business Publications, Plano, Tex., 1988, p. 314.

22. Richard L. Daft, *Organization Theory and Design*, West, St. Paul, Minn., 1983, pp. 424–425.

23. "Labor Letter," *The Wall Street Journal*, Jan. 10, 1987, p. 1.

24. Janice H. Schopler, "Interorganizational Groups: Origins, Structure, and Outcomes," *Academy of Management Review*, October 1987, pp. 702–713.

25. Daniel C. Feldman and Hugh J. Arnold, *Managing Individual and Group Behavior in Organizations*, McGraw-Hill, New York, 1986, pp. 223–225.

26. See Stephen P. Robbins, *Organization Theory*, 3d ed., Prentice-Hall, Englewood Cliffs, N.J., 1990, pp. 425–431.

27. Melville Dalton, *Men Who Manage*, Wiley, New York, 1959; Melville Dalton, "Conflicts Between Staff and Line Managerial Officers," *American Sociological Review*, June 1950, pp. 342–350; and Melville Dalton, "Changing Staff-Line Relationships," *Personnel Administration*, March–April 1966, pp. 3–5, 40–48.

28. Dalton, *Men Who Manage*, p. 75.

29. Dalton, "Changing Staff-Line Relationships," p. 45.

30. Christopher Gresov and Carroll Stephens, "The Context of Interunit Influence Attempts," *Administrative Science Quarterly*, June 1993, pp. 252–276.

31. Eileen F. N. Collard, "The Impact of Deming Quality Management on Interdepartmental Cooperation," *Human Resource Development Quarterly*, Spring 1993, pp. 71–79.

32. Dean Tjosvold, Valerie Dann, and Choy Wong, "Managing Conflict Between Departments to Serve Customers," *Human Relations*, October 1992, pp. 1035–1054.

33. Joe Kelly, *Organizational Behavior*, rev. ed., Dorsey-Irwin, Homewood, Ill., 1975, p. 555.

34. Ibid.

35. Jeanne M. Brett, Stephen B. Goldberg, and William L. Ury, "Designing Systems for Resolving Disputes in Organizations," *American Psychologist*, February 1990, pp. 162–170.

36. Robin L. Pinkley, "Dimensions of Conflict Frame: Disputant Interpretations of Conflict," *Journal of Applied Psychology*, vol. 75, no. 2, 1990, p. 117.

37. Margaret A. Neale and Max H. Bazerman, "Negotiating Rationally: The Power and Impact of the Negotiator's Frame," *Academy of Management Executive*, August 1992, p. 42.

38. Whetten and Cameron, op. cit., p. 402.

39. Neale and Bazerman, op. cit., p. 43.

40. Whetten and Cameron, op. cit., p. 404.

41. Roger Fisher and William Ury, *Getting to Yes*, Penguin Books, New York, 1983, p. 4.

42. Ibid., p. 9.

43. See Whetten and Cameron, op. cit., p. 404, and recent research such as Laurie R. Weingart, Rebecca J. Bennett, and Jeanne M. Brett, "The Impact of Consideration of Issues and Motivational Orientation on Group Negotiation Process and Outcome," *Journal of Applied Psychology*, June 1993, pp. 504–517.

44. Whetten and Cameron, op. cit., p. 404.

45. Gregory B. Northcraft and Margaret A. Neale, *Organizational Behavior*, Dryden, Chicago, 1990, pp. 247–248.

46. Fisher and Ury, op. cit., p. 11.

47. Ibid., p. 13.

48. Ibid., p. 14.

**REAL CASE:
Do Just the
Opposite**

One of the major reasons for organizational conflict is a downturn in the economy. When things start going bad, most companies cut back their expenses and start laying off people. Recent research shows that this may be the worst strategy of all, because it is too defensive in nature. When things get bad, this may be the time for the company to strike out and take advantage of the situation. Simply put, when times get bad, successful firms do the opposite of what everyone else is doing. A recent analysis put it this way:

> Old reflexes that used to kick in when recession loomed will have to be rethought. Don't expect, for instance, to have the luxury of cutting back heavily on marketing and product development. The experts argue that smart companies will find the funds to *increase* advertising and new-product launches. Says Harvard business school professor John Kotter, "It's a different set of responses. You don't just say, 'It's tough times, let's cut.' You take risks and spend more."

Home Depot is a good example. When the economy began to falter, the owners of the company appeared on the quarterly satellite broadcast to the salespeople and discussed the psychology of selling during a recession. They offered steps in how to increase sales among customers who were likely to be more resistant than ever to spending money.

Other firms have different approaches. At Geico Insurance, the company used the economic turndown to scan its nationwide markets, see where competitors were hurting most, and beef up advertising and cut prices in these locales. Result: Market share in these areas began rising. At GM, Chrysler, and Toyota, new-product development times have been shortened so that new offerings can be brought to market more quickly. Allegheny Ludlum, the Pittsburgh maker of specialty steel, pushed ahead with its $85 million finishing mill that increased capacity by 30 percent. TJ International, maker of windows and specialty building materials, took advantage of the slowdown to tinker with its production facilities and work processes, looking for better ways to manufacture the products. This was not possible when the facilities were being run at full tilt. At Delta Airlines, people were reassigned jobs until there was an upturn in the economy—with some pilots actually unloading baggage from arriving flights. CBS sold some of its holdings and had everyone tighten up spending and become more efficient. Macy's began focusing on improved customer service in order to win back customers who had been wooed away by the competition.

1. The information in this case illustrates what the best firms do to meet a recession. How do their less effective competitors react to such economic frustration? Use Figure 10.1 and Table 10.1 to formulate your answer and discuss three adjustive reactions.
2. A recession would undoubtedly bring about intergroup conflict in the organization. What are some antecedent conditions that would help explain this conflict? Identify and describe three.
3. How do the managers in this case view conflict? How is this view different from the views of their less effective competitors?

**CASE:
Drinking Up the
Paycheck**

James Emery is the father of four children. He was raised in a hardworking immigrant family. His needs for achievement and power were developed while he was growing up. Now he finds himself in a low-paying, dead-end assembly line job with a large manufacturing firm. It is all he can do to get through the day, so he has started daydreaming on the job. On payday he often goes to the tavern across the street and generally spends a lot of money. The next day he is not only hung over but also very depressed because he knows that his wife cannot make ends meet and his children often go without the essentials.

Now he cannot take it any longer. At first he thought of going to his boss for some help and advice, but he really does not understand himself well enough, and he certainly does not know or trust his boss enough to discuss his problems openly with him. Instead, he went to his union steward and told him about his financial problems and how much he hated his job. The steward told James exactly what he wanted to hear. "This darn company is the source of all your problems. The working conditions are not suited for a slave, let alone us. The pay also stinks. We are all going to have to stick together when our present contract runs out and get what we deserve—better working conditions and more money."

1. Explain James's behavior in terms of the frustration model.
2. Cite a specific example of role conflict in this case.
3. What style from the Johari window can explain James's relationship with his boss? With his union steward?
4. What type of conflict resolution strategy is the union steward suggesting? Do you think the real problems facing James are working conditions and pay? Why or why not?
5. What, if anything, can be done to help the James Emerys of the world? Keep your answer in terms of human resources management.

CASE: Arresting the Neighbor's Kid

Barney Kohl is a police officer assigned to the juvenile department of a large city. Part of the oath that Barney took was to uphold the law consistently for all people. The scope of his job includes investigation of youth drug traffic, alcoholism, and vandalism. Barney is also involved in the community outreach program, which works to build greater understanding and cooperation between the police department and the youth of the community.

Last night, Barney ran into one of the most difficult, if not the most dangerous, problems he has ever faced. While on patrol, he received a radio report to investigate some possible vandalism at a junior high school. Upon reaching the scene he found five youths, aged twelve to fifteen, engaged in malicious acts of vandalism. They were throwing rocks through the windows and had splashed paint against the walls. After calling backup units, he proceeded to run down and arrest the vandals. He was successfully holding the group at bay and was waiting for the backup unit to arrive when he noticed that one of the offenders was his neighbor's son. The city has a parents' responsibility law that makes parents financially liable for the damage caused by their children's actions. The damage looked as if it would be considerable, probably running into the thousands of dollars. Barney knows his neighbor can't afford the costs because he has a physical disability and is out of work. He also knows this incident will lead to great problems in their family and, of course, would place a great strain on his own and his family's relationship with the neighbors.

1. What kind of conflict is this police officer experiencing? What should he do?
2. How do you explain the boys' behavior in terms of the frustration model?
3. If you were asked to conduct a training seminar for police officers on the management of conflict, what topics would you cover? What strategies would you suggest?

11 Occupational Stress

Learning Objectives

- **Define** stress by giving attention to what it is not.
- **Identify** the extraorganizational, organizational, and group stressors.
- **Examine** individual dispositions of stress.
- **Discuss** the effects of stress, including physical, psychological, and behavioral problems.
- **Present** both individual and organizational strategies for coping with stress.

A leading expert on stress, cardiologist Robert Eliot, gives the following prescription for dealing with stress: "Rule No. 1 is, don't sweat the small stuff. Rule No. 2 is, it's all small stuff. And if you can't fight and you can't flee, flow."[1] What is happening in today's organizations, however, is that the "small stuff" is getting to employees, and they are not going with the "flow."

Stress has become a major buzzword and legitimate concern of the times. A recent estimate is that stress is costing corporate America a staggering $68 billion annually in lost productivity due to absences from work and stress claims costing up to 10 percent of a company's earnings.[2] Health care professionals are reporting that up to 90 percent of patients complain of stress-related symptoms and disorders.[3] Unlike some of the other topics in organizational behavior, stress directly translates into dollars and cents to the organization and affects the physical and psychological well-being of individual employees.

The previous chapter, on interactive behavior and conflict, can be used as a foundation and point of departure for this chapter's discussion of stress. Although conflict and stress are conceptually close, especially the intraindividual dimensions of conflict, the perspective, variables, and research are treated differently. Since both conflict and stress are such major contemporary problems affecting organizational behavior, they are both given specific attention. This chapter first explores the meaning of stress and why it has emerged as a major topic for the study of organizational behavior and the practice of human resources management. Next, the major causes of stress in jobs today (extraorganizational, organizational, and group, and the individual dispositions) are examined. This discussion is followed by an analysis of the effects that job stress has on both the individual and the organization.

The last part of the chapter is devoted to the coping strategies that can be used at the individual and organizational levels to manage stress effectively.

THE MEANING OF STRESS

Stress is usually thought of in negative terms. It is thought to be caused by something bad (for example, a college student is placed on scholastic probation, a loved one is seriously ill, or the boss gives a formal reprimand for poor performance). This is a form of distress. But there is also a positive, pleasant side of stress caused by good things (for example, a college student makes the dean's list; an attractive, respected acquaintance asks for a date; an employee is offered a job promotion at another location). This is a form of *eu*stress. This latter term was coined by the pioneers of stress research from the Greek *eu*, which means "good." In other words, stress can be viewed in a number of different ways and has been described as the most imprecise word in the scientific dictionary. The word "stress" has also been compared with the word "sin": "Both are short, emotionally charged words used to refer to something that otherwise would take many words to say."[4] After the definition of stress and the relation to burnout are discussed, some of the historical background is presented.

The Definition of Stress and the Relation to Burnout

Although there are numerous definitions and much debate about the meaning of job stress,[5] Ivancevich and Matteson define *stress* simply as "the interaction of the individual with the environment," but then they go on to give a more detailed working definition, as follows: "an adaptive response, mediated by individual differences and/or psychological processes, that is a consequence of any external (environmental) action, situation, or event that places excessive psychological and/or physical demands upon a person."[6] Beehr and Newman define *job stress* as "a condition arising from the interaction of people and their jobs and characterized by changes within people that force them to deviate from their normal functioning."[7] Taking these two definitions and simplifying them for the purposes of this chapter, "stress" is defined as an adaptive response to an external situation that results in physical, psychological, and/or behavioral deviations for organizational participants.

It is also important to point out what stress is *not*:

1. *Stress is not simply anxiety.* Anxiety operates solely in the emotional and psychological sphere, whereas stress operates there and also in the physiological sphere. Thus, stress may be accompanied by anxiety, but the two should not be equated.
2. *Stress is not simply nervous tension.* Like anxiety, nervous tension may result from stress, but the two are not the same. Unconscious people have exhibited stress, and some people may keep it "bottled up" and not reveal it through nervous tension.
3. *Stress is not necessarily something damaging, bad, or to be avoided.* Eustress is not damaging or bad and is something people should seek out rather than avoid. The key, of course, is how the person handles the stress. Stress is inevitable; distress may be prevented or can be effectively controlled.[8]

As far as the increasingly popular term "burnout" is concerned, some stress researchers contend that burnout is a type of stress[9] and others treat it differently. For example, a recent comprehensive review of job burnout says that it is characterized by emotional exhaustion, depersonalization, and diminished personal accomplishment.[10] Burnout is also most closely associated with the so-called helping professions such as nursing, education, and social work.[11] So, even though technically burnout may be somewhat different from stress, the two terms will be treated the same and used interchangeably.

The Background of Stress

Concern about the impact of stress on people has its roots in medicine and specifically in the pioneering work of Hans Selye, the recognized father of stress. In his search for a new sex hormone, he serendipitously (by chance) discovered that tissue damage is a nonspecific response to virtually all noxious stimuli. He called this phenomenon the *general adaptation syndrome* (GAS), and about a decade later he introduced the term "stress" in his writings.

The GAS has three stages: alarm, resistance, and exhaustion. In the alarm stage an outside stressor mobilizes the internal stress system of the body. There are a number of physiological and chemical reactions, such as increased pituitary and adrenaline secretions; noticeable increases in respiration, heart rate, and blood pressure; and a heightening of the senses. If the stressor continues, then the GAS moves into the resistance stage, during which the body calls upon the needed organ or system to deal with the stressor. However, while there may be a great deal of resistance to one stressor during this second stage, there may be little, if any, resistance to other, unrelated stressors. This helps explain why a person going through an emotional strain may be particularly vulnerable to other illness or disease. Finally, if the stressor persists over a long period of time, the reserves of the adaptive mechanisms during the second stage may become drained, and exhaustion sets in. When this happens, there may be a return to the alarm stage, and the cycle starts again with another organ or system, or the "automatic shutoff valve" of death occurs. This GAS process, of course, can be very hard on the person and takes its toll on the human body.

Besides the physiologically oriented approach to stress represented by the classic GAS model, which remains a vital dimension of modern stress research and stress management, attention is also being given to the psychological (for example, mood changes, negative emotions, and feelings of helplessness) and the behavioral (for example, directly confronting the stressors or attempting to obtain information about the stressors) dimensions of stress. All three dimensions (physiological, psychological, and behavioral) are important to the understanding of job stress and coping strategies in modern organizations.

THE CAUSES OF STRESS

The antecedents of stress, or the so-called stressors, affecting today's employees are summarized in Figure 11.1. As shown, these causes come from both outside and inside the organization and from the groups that employees are influenced by and from employees themselves.

Extraorganizational Stressors

Although most analyses of job stress ignore the importance of outside forces and events, it is becoming increasingly clear that these have a tremendous impact. Taking

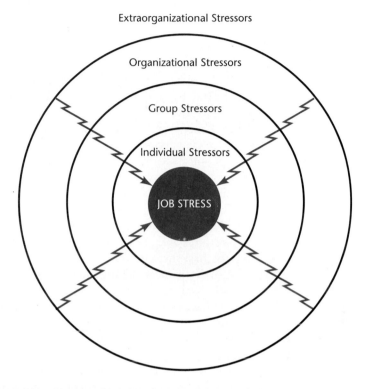

Extraorganizational Stressors

Organizational Stressors

Group Stressors

Individual Stressors

JOB STRESS

FIGURE 11.1
Categories of stressors affecting occupational stress.

an open-systems perspective of an organization (that is, the organization is greatly affected by the external environment), it is clear that job stress is not limited just to things that happen inside the organization, during working hours. Extraorganizational stressors include things such as societal/technological change, the family, relocation, economic and financial conditions, race and class, and residential or community conditions.[12]

The phenomenal rate of social and technical change, which is given detailed attention in Chapter 20, has had a great effect on people's lifestyles, and this of course is carried over into their jobs. Although medical science has increased the life spans of people and has eradicated or reduced the threat of many diseases, the pace of modern living has increased stress and decreased personal *wellness*. The concept of wellness has been defined as "a harmonious and productive balance of physical, mental, and social well-being brought about by the acceptance of one's personal responsibility for developing and adhering to a health promotion program."[13] Because people tend to get caught up in the rush-rush, mobile, urbanized, crowded, on-the-go lifestyle of today, their wellness in general has deteriorated, and the potential for stress on the job has increased.

It is generally recognized that a person's family has a big impact on personality development. A family situation—either a brief crisis, such as a squabble or the illness of a family member, or long-term strained relations with the spouse or children—can act as a significant stressor for employees. There is even research indicating that in dual-career families, a stressed-out husband may transmit this stress to his wife.[14] Relocating the family because of a transfer or a promotion can also lead to stress. For most people in recent years, their financial situation has proved to be a stressor. Many people have been forced to take a second job ("moonlight"), or the spouse has had to enter the work force in order to make ends meet. This situation reduces time for recreational and family activities. The overall effect on the employees is more stress on their primary jobs. Some stress researchers define these personal life stressors as unresolved environmental demands (for example, family or financial problems) requiring adaptive behaviors in the form of social readjustments.[15]

Life's changes may be slow (getting older) or sudden (the death of a spouse). These sudden changes have been portrayed in novels and movies as having a dramatic effect on people, and medical researchers have verified that especially sudden life changes do in fact have a very stressful impact on people.[16] They found a definite relationship between the degree of life changes and the subsequent health of the person. The more change, the poorer the subsequent health. These life changes can also directly influence job performance. One psychologist, Faye Crosby, reports that divorce interferes with work more than any other trauma in a person's life. She says, "During the first three months after a spouse walks out, the other spouse—male or female—usually is incapable of focusing on work."[17]

Sociological variables such as race, sex, and class can also become stressors. Sociologists have noted over the years that minorities may have more stressors than whites. More recently, research has found that women experience more psychological distress than men, but men are more prone to severe physical illness.[18] For professional women, the particular sources of stress have been identified as discrimination, stereotyping, the marriage/work interface, and social isolation.[19] In a recent survey, a significant number of working women report feeling personal or family stress which in turn leads to job stress.[20] In particular, dual family and work roles frequently result in job stress. Also, people in the middle and upper classes may have particular or common stressors. The same is true of the local community or region that one comes from. For example, one researcher identified the condition of housing, convenience of services and shopping, neighborliness, and degree of noise and air pollution as likely stressors.[21]

Organizational Stressors

Besides the potential stressors that occur outside the organization, there are also those associated with the organization itself. Although the organization is made up of groups and individuals, there are also more macro-level dimensions, unique to the organization, that contain potential stressors. Figure 11.2 shows that these macro-level stressors can be categorized into administrative policies and strategies, organizational structure and design, organizational processes, and working conditions. It should be noted that as organizations dramatically change to meet the environmental challenges outlined in Chapter 1 (globalization, information technology explosion, quality obsession, and diversity), there are more and more accompanying stressors for individual employees in their jobs. For example, as noted by one recent analysis of the organizational situation:

> Downsizing has left many companies with fewer people, and those remaining workers have been forced to pick up the slack of the workers who have left. The result often is frantic employees and more stress-related workers' compensation claims.[22]

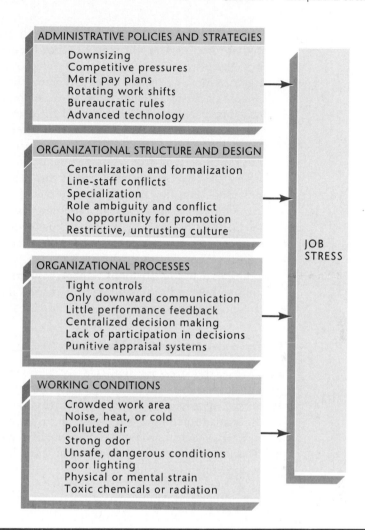

FIGURE 11.2
Macro-level organizational stressors.

In a survey of Fortune 500 CEOs, over three-fourths agreed with the statement that "large U.S. companies will have to push their managers harder if we are to compete successfully with the Japanese and other global competitors."[23] This translates to longer hours and more stress. A recent survey of a large cross section of American employees found almost all work longer than the standard forty-hour workweek and over half put in six to twenty additional hours per week.[24] These respondents were averaging ten-hour days, and some of them put in fifteen hours. Research indicates that such chronic occupational demands can lead to stress.[25] Also, there is evidence that working women with perceived pay inequity and work overload experience more stress.[26]

Group Stressors

Chapters 9 and 10 indicate the tremendous influence that the group has on behavior. The group can also be a potential source of stress. These group stressors can be categorized into three areas:

1. *Lack of group cohesiveness.* Starting with the historically famous Hawthorne studies, discussed in Chapter 1, it has become very clear that cohesiveness, or "togetherness," is very important to employees, especially at the lower levels of organizations. If an employee is denied the opportunity for this cohesiveness because of the task design, because the supervisor does things to prohibit or limit it, or because the other members of the group shut the person out, the resulting lack of cohesiveness can be very stress-producing.

2. *Lack of social support.* Employees are greatly affected by the support of one or more members of a cohesive group. By sharing their problems and joys with others, they are much better off. If this type of social support is lacking for an individual, the situation can be very stressful.

3. *Intraindividual, interpersonal, and intergroup conflict.* This is the topic of Chapter 10. Conflict is very closely conceptually linked to stress. Conflict is normally associated with incompatible or hostile acts between intraindividual dimensions such as personal goals or motivational needs/values, between individuals within a group, and between groups. Chapter 10 goes into the details of these levels of conflict, but for the purposes of this chapter it can be said simply that such conflict can lead to considerable stress for individuals.

Individual Stressors: The Role of Dispositions

In a sense, the stressors discussed so far (extraorganizational, organizational, and group) all eventually get down to the individual level. There is also more research and agreement on possible situational dimensions and individual dispositions which may affect stress outcomes. For example, role conflict, ambiguity, and individual dispositions such as Type A personality patterns, personal control, learned helplessness, self-efficacy, and psychological hardiness may all affect the level of stress someone experiences.

Role Conflict and Ambiguity. Like the conflict at organizational and group levels, role conflict and the closely related concept of role ambiguity are given specific attention in Chapter 10. Individual employees have multiple roles (family, work, professional, recreational, church, club, community, and so on), and these often make conflicting demands and create conflicting expectations. After an extensive search of the empirical research it was concluded that "work schedule, work orientation, marriage, children, and spouse employment patterns may all produce pressures to participate extensively in the work role or the family role."[27] Stress results when the time demands for the work role are incompatible with the time pressures of the family role or vice versa.

Role ambiguity results from inadequate information or knowledge to do a job. This ambiguity may be due to inadequate training, poor communication, or the deliberate withholding or distortion of information by a coworker or supervisor. In any event, the result of role conflict and ambiguity is stress for the individual,[28] and there is a substantial body of research indicating undesirable outcomes for the individual and the organization.[29] Role overload and/or underload (being asked to do too much or too little), which has not received as much attention as role conflict and ambiguity, may be just as stress-provoking.

Type A Characteristics. The discussion of personality in Chapter 5 points out the complexity of, and individual differences in, personality dispositions and traits.

TABLE 11.1 Type A–Type B Self-Test

To determine your Type A or Type B profile, circle the number on the continuums (the verbal descriptions represent endpoints) that best represents your behavior for each dimension.

Am casual about appointments	1 2 3 4 5 6 7 8	Am never late
Am not competitive	1 2 3 4 5 6 7 8	Am very competitive
Never feel rushed, even under pressure	1 2 3 4 5 6 7 8	Always feel rushed
Take things one at a time	1 2 3 4 5 6 7 8	Try to do many things at once; think about what I am going to do next
Do things slowly	1 2 3 4 5 6 7 8	Do things fast (eating, walking, etc.)
Express feelings	1 2 3 4 5 6 7 8	"Sit" on feelings
Have many interests	1 2 3 4 5 6 7 8	Have few interests outside work

Total your score: _____ Multiply it by 3: _____. The interpretation of your score is as follows:

Number of points	Type of personality
Less than 90	B
90 to 99	B+
100 to 105	A−
106 to 119	A
120 or more	A+

Source: R. W. Bortner, "A Short Rating Scale as a Potential Measure of Pattern A Behavior," *Journal of Chronic Diseases*, vol. 22, 1966, pp. 87–91.

Personality traits such as authoritarianism, rigidity, masculinity, femininity, extroversion, supportiveness, spontaneity, emotionality, tolerance for ambiguity, anxiety, and the need for achievement have been uncovered by research as being particularly relevant to individual stress.[30] Most recent attention, however, has centered on the so-called Type A personality.

Although heart researchers have been working on the use of personality types and the resulting behavior patterns in order to predict heart attacks since the 1950s, in the late 1960s Friedman and Rosenman popularized the use of Type A and opposing Type B personalities in the study of stress.[31] These types were portrayed as relatively stable characteristics, and initially Friedman and Rosenman's extensive studies found the Type A profile correlated highly with experienced stress and dangerous physical consequences.

Table 11.1 gives the reader a chance to see whether he or she tends to be a Type A or a Type B personality. A majority of Americans are Type A, and an even higher percentage of managers are Type A; one study found that 60 percent of the managers sampled were clearly Type A and that only 12 percent were Type B.[32]

Friedman and Rosenman define the Type A personality as "an action-emotion complex that can be observed in any person who is aggressively involved in a chronic, incessant struggle to achieve more and more in less and less time, and if required to do so, against the opposing efforts of other things or other persons."[33] Table 11.2 briefly summarizes the Type A and Type B profiles. Obviously, Type A employees (managers, salespersons, staff specialists, secretaries, or rank-and-file operating employees) experience considerable stress. They are the ones who:

1. Work long, hard hours under constant deadline pressures and conditions for overload.

TABLE 11.2 Profiles of Type A and Type B Personalities

Type A Profile	Type B Profile
Is always moving	Is not concerned about time
Walks rapidly	Is patient
Eats rapidly	Doesn't brag
Talks rapidly	Plays for fun, not to win
Is impatient	Relaxes without guilt
Does two things at once	Has no pressing deadlines
Can't cope with leisure time	Is mild-mannered
Is obsessed with numbers	Is never in a hurry
Measures success by quantity	
Is aggressive	
Is competitive	
Constantly feels under time pressure	

2. Often take work home at night or on weekends and are unable to relax.
3. Constantly compete with themselves, setting high standards of productivity that they seem driven to maintain.
4. Tend to become frustrated by the work situation, to be irritated with the work efforts of others, and to be misunderstood by supervisors.[34]

At first, because of Rosenman and Friedman's studies, it was generally thought that Type A's were much more prone to the worst outcome of stress: heart attacks.[35] More recently, however, a number of studies have been unable to confirm their findings.[36] For example, Type A's may release and better cope with their stress than do Type B's. The controversy surrounding the conflicting conclusions are discussed in the accompanying Application Example: Is Being a Type A Dangerous?

The most recent studies seem to indicate that it is not so much the impatience that is closely associated with Type A's, but rather anger and hostility that leads to heart problems. A leading medical researcher noted that the term "Type A" probably has outlived its usefulness. He stated: "Being a workaholic, being in a hurry, interrupting people, are not necessarily bad for your heart. What is bad is if you have high levels of hostility and anger, and you don't bother to hide it when dealing with other people."[37] This conclusion was recently supported by an organizational psychiatrist who, after extensive study of the causes of stress in Japanese, German, and American workers, concluded that "how workers handle their own aggression is the key factor in determining whether they will experience the kind of stress that can lead to heart attacks, high blood pressure and other health problems."[38] However, before completely dismissing the relationship of Type A to severe physical outcomes, it should be noted that anger, hostility, and aggression sometimes goes along with a Type A personality.

Besides the debate surrounding the impact of Type A personality on health is the question of the success of Type A's versus Type B's. It is pretty clear that Type A's are typically on a "fast track" to the top. They are more successful than Type B's. However, at the *very* top they do not tend to be as successful as Type B's, who are more patient and take a broader view of things.[39] The key may be to shift from Type A to Type B behavior, but, of course, most Type A's are unable and *unwilling* to make the shift and/or to cope with their Type A characteristics.

Personal Control and Learned Helplessness. Besides Type A personality patterns, another important disposition is an individual's perception of control. As mentioned

Application Example

Is Being a Type A Dangerous?

The complexities involved in studying behavior are exemplified by the recent controversy surrounding the link between the Type A personality and heart disease. Most people have heard of the Type A personality—competitive, driven, and impatient—and its association with heart disease. Decades of research have supported the link.

Meyer Friedman and Ray Rosenman, California cardiologists, are noted for discovering the link. Their findings were replicated by several larger studies. The most compelling evidence came from the Western Collaborative Group Study (WCGS), an eight-year study ending in 1969. The study showed that Type A men had twice as many heart attacks or other forms of heart disease as anyone else.

However, a seven-year study ending in 1982 found contradictory results. The Multiple Risk Factor Intervention Trial (MRFIT) was sponsored by the National Heart, Lung, and Blood Institute to single out the deadliest risks of heart disease. The results failed to show that Type A men were more likely to develop heart disease than anyone else.

How do researchers explain such conflicting findings? One test is to compare measurement techniques. Both the WCGS and the MRFIT used structured interviews to identify Type A's. The structured interview is considered the most accurate assessment technique for identifying Type A's since it not only evaluates the content of answers but also accounts for tone of voice, facial expressions, and gestures—important indicators of the impatience characteristic of Type A's.

Of importance is not only the technique itself but also how it is used. For example, Larry Scherwitz, a psychologist at the University of California, San Francisco, listened to the interview tapes of both the WCGS and the MRFIT. He noticed that the MRFIT interviewers asked the questions faster than the WCGS interviewers. He believes this could have skewed the MRFIT results.

According to Scherwitz, the fast-paced interviewers come across as cold and uninterested. He believes that the hostile Type A's responded by hiding their hostile feelings—making them appear to be Type B's. The more sensitive Type B's, on the other hand, may have reacted more curtly—responding like Type A's. Such responses may have led to mislabeling, which could have easily confounded the results.

Rosenman also points out an important flaw with the MRFIT. "Type A's are not going to sign up for studies like this, with once-a-week follow-ups and lots of paperwork. You don't get impatient, hostile people volunteering to do this." Rosenman emphasizes the importance of how subjects are selected. However, he does not indicate how subjects were contacted for the WCGS. Although other areas of the studies' designs need to be considered, these two areas show why rigorous methodology is necessary for conclusive findings.

Whether the Type A personality is dangerous is still a subject for debate. Further research with attention to methodology is needed before any conclusions can be made.

in Chapter 5's discussion on job satisfaction, people's feelings about their ability to control the situation will be an important disposition for stress. In particular, if employees feel that they have little control over the work environment and over their own job, they will experience stress.[40] Studies have shown that if employees are given a sense of control over their work environment, such as being given a chance to be involved in the decision-making process that affects them, this will reduce their work stress.[41] Most recently, a large study by Cornell University medical researchers found that those workers who experience a loss of control, especially in relatively low-level jobs, have triple the risk of developing high blood pressure. The researchers concluded that lack of control turns stress into physical problems. They also found that if a high-stress job included latitude to control the situation, there was no increase in blood pressure.[42] A recent study in a hospital setting also found that employee perceptions of the amount of control they experience at work relate to stress which in turn affects physiological outcomes such as blood pressure as well as psychological outcomes such as job satisfaction.[43]

The feeling of loss of control goes back to some of the classic research on learned helplessness conducted by Seligman.[44] In conducting experiments on dogs who could not escape shock, he found that they eventually accepted it and did not even try to escape. Later, when the dogs could learn to escape easily, they did not—they had learned to be helpless. Other studies found that people, too, can learn to be helpless,[45] which helps explain why some employees just seem to have given up and seem to accept stressors in their work environment, even when a change for the better is possible.

Most recently, Seligman and his colleagues have concentrated on people's explanations for their lack of control. Specifically, they suggest that people are most apt to experience helplessness when they perceive the causes of the lack of control:

1. To be related to something about their own personal characteristics (as opposed to outside, environmental forces).
2. As stable and enduring (rather than just temporary).
3. To be global and universal (cutting across many situations, rather than in just one sphere of life).[46]

Further study and research on the sense of control in general and learned helplessness in particular will provide much insight into stress and how to cope with it.

Self-Efficacy. Another important disposition that has recently emerged to help understand stress in the workplace is self-efficacy. (This concept is introduced in Chapter 5 on self theories of personality.) There is increasing evidence that people's self-perception of their capacity to be effective and bring about change may be an important disposition in the ability to withstand stress.[47] For example, Bandura has found that those with high self-efficacy have a relatively low level of physiological arousal (for example, they have less adrenaline in the bloodstream).[48] Yet, those under stress tend to have high physiological arousal. Thus, those with high self-efficacy tend to remain calmer when faced with a stressful situation. As Rathus points out: "Overarousal can impair our ability to solve complex stress-related problems by elevating our motivation well beyond optimal levels and by distracting us from tasks at hand. So, people with higher self-efficacy expectations have biological as well as psychological reasons for remaining calmer."[49]

Psychological Hardiness. Everyone has observed individual differences of people faced with stressors. Some people seem to go to pieces at the slightest provocation, while others seem unflappable in the face of extremely stressful situations. Those able to cope successfully with extreme stressors seem to have a "hardiness" disposition.

Kobasa and her colleagues studied executives under considerable stress who were both hardy and nonhardy. She found that the hardy executives had a lower rate of stress-related illness and were characterized as having commitment (they become very involved in what they were doing); challenge (they believed that change rather than stability was normal); and control (they felt they could influence the events around them).[50] She suggests that the predisposition of psychological hardiness helps those with it to resist stress by providing buffers between themselves and stressors.

Such buffering from hardiness may be an important quality as organizations now and in the future demand more and more from their employees at all levels. As recently noted:

> Why does the job seem so demanding? It isn't just long hours or clumsy direction from above, though there's plenty of that. All sorts of pressure, from the stress of participatory management techniques to the hyperkinesia of two-career marriages to the dismay of finding your workload increasing as you near 50, just when you thought you could adopt a more dignified pace, are working together to squeeze the oomph from heretofore steely-eyed achievers.[51]

Kobasa's research would say that those with hardiness will be able to survive and even thrive in such an environment, but those who do not possess hardiness may suffer the harmful outcomes of stress that are covered next.

THE EFFECTS OF OCCUPATIONAL STRESS

As is pointed out in the introductory comments, stress is not automatically bad for individual employees or their organizational performance. In fact, it is generally recognized that low levels of stress can even enhance job performance. For example, one recent study found that mild stress, such as getting a new supervisor or being involuntarily transferred, may have the positive result of an increased search for information in the job.[52] This may lead employees to new and better ways of doing their jobs. Also, mild stress may get employees' "juices" flowing and lead to increased activity, change, and overall better performance. People in certain jobs, such as in sales or creative fields (for example, newspaper journalists and television announcers who work under time pressures), would seem to benefit from a mild level of stress. People in other jobs, such as police officers or physicians, may not benefit from constant mild stress.

Research is also emerging that indicates that the level of difficulty and nature of the task being performed and personal dispositions (such as Type A, personal control and learned helplessness, self-efficacy, and psychological hardiness, discussed in previous sections) and other psychological dispositions (such as negative affectivity[53] —see Chapter 5) and neuroticism[54] may affect the relationship between stress and performance. However, it is still safe to conclude that:

1. The performance of many tasks is in fact strongly affected by stress.
2. Performance usually drops off sharply when stress rises to high levels.[55]

It is the dysfunctional effects of high levels of stress that should be and are a major concern for contemporary society in general and for effective human resources management in particular. The problems due to high levels of stress can be exhibited physically, psychologically, or behaviorally by the individual.

Physical Problems Due to Stress

Most of the attention and the basic research over the years has been devoted to the impact that stress has on physical health. A high level of stress is accompanied by high blood pressure and high levels of cholesterol and may even result in heart disease,[56] ulcers, and arthritis. There may even be a link between stress and cancer.[57]

Obviously, such serious physical ailments have a drastic effect on the individual; not always so obvious, but just as serious, are the effects that physical problems such as heart disease can have on the organization. Ivancevich and Matteson have provided the following worksheet for computing the costs of replacing employees lost to heart disease in a company employing 4000 people.[58]

1. Number of employees	4000
2. Men in age range forty-five to sixty-five (0.25 × line 1)	1000
3. Estimated deaths due to heart disease per year (0.006 × line 2)	6
4. Estimated premature retirement due to heart problems per year (0.003 × line 2)	3
5. Company's annual personnel losses due to heart disorders (sum of lines 3 and 4)	9
6. Annual replacement cost: the average cost of hiring and training replacements for experienced employees (line 5 × $4300)	$38,700
7. Number of employees who will eventually die of heart disease if present rate continues (0.5 × line 1)	2000

These figures are just estimates, but they dramatically illustrate how heart disease alone can affect costs and sheer numbers of employees in a typical organization. Obviously, not all heart disease can be directly linked to stress; environmental conditions and the person's general state of health, heredity, and medical history can also contribute. However, there seems to be enough evidence that stress can and does contribute to this dreaded disease and to other physical problems as well.

Psychological Problems Due to Stress

While considerable attention has been given to the relationship between stress and physical health, especially within the medical community, not as much has been given to the impact of stress on mental health. Yet, at least indirectly if not directly, the psychological problems resulting from stress may be just as important, if not more important, to day-to-day job performance as the physical problems.

High levels of stress may be accompanied by anger, anxiety, depression, nervousness, irritability, tension, and boredom. A recent study found that stress had the strongest impact on aggressive actions such as sabotage, interpersonal aggression, hostility, and complaints.[59] These types of psychological problems from stress, in turn, are especially relevant to poor job performance, lowered self-esteem,[60] resentment of supervision, inability to concentrate and make decisions, and job dissatisfaction.[61] These outcomes of stress can have a direct cost effect on the organization. For example, the National Centers for Disease Control reported that psychological stress is the source of numerous job-related insurance claims.[62] Recent court cases have also brought stress-related problems stemming from employment under the employer's workers' compensation insurance. Experts are predicting that if the number of stress-related workers' compensation claims continues to grow at current rates, these claims will lead all other claims in this decade.[63]

Of even greater significance, the outcomes of stress can have a subtle, but very real, effect on the styles and effectiveness of managers in key positions. For example, managers who are under constant stress may become very moody, and their subordinates soon learn not to disturb them, even with important information, because they will just "bite your head off." Such managers may also realize, at times, that they are acting this way; they may feel that they are not living up to the expectations of their important position and suffer a loss of self-esteem. In this state they may also procrastinate and continue to put things off and not make needed decisions. And, finally, they may resent their boss for trying to get them back on track and begin to hate the job in general. Coworkers, subordinates, and superiors may become very disgusted with such a manager and explain the behavior away as being the result of a "rotten personality," when in fact the problems are the result of stress. If the manager had a heart attack, everyone would feel sorry and say that he or she was under too much stress, but a manager's moodiness, low self-esteem, inability to make a decision, and dissatisfaction with the boss and the job cause people to get angry and say that the manager is "no darned good" or "can't get along with anyone." Both a heart attack and a psychological problem may have the same cause (too much stress), and although people may react to them differently, the negative effect on performance is the same in the case of a psychological problem, or perhaps even worse.

Behavioral Problems Due to Stress

As has been the case with other topics covered in this text, the *behavioral* unit of analysis may be most helpful—in this case, in analyzing the effects of job stress. Direct behaviors that may accompany high levels of stress include undereating or overeating, sleeplessness, increased smoking and drinking, and drug abuse. When it is realized that 6 percent of the population are alcoholics, that another estimated 10 percent are problem drinkers, and that 6 billion doses of amphetamines and barbiturates are consumed annually,[64] the potential problems for employee behavior caused by alcohol and drug abuse become dramatically clear.

Although problems with alcohol have been recognized for a number of years, severe problems stemming from drug abuse have emerged more recently. For example, Kidder, Peabody, the New York–based investment bank, spent $100,000 on a drug program and many other firms, such as Lockheed and Southern California Rapid Transit, have drug-testing programs for their employees.[65]

One company had such a problem with on-the-job drinking that it bought a breath-alcohol meter to test its employees. The president of the union in this firm stated: "there were a couple of people who came to work drunk every day."[66] Although the meter has not been used as yet, one worker was overheard to say, "I guess I'll have to stop going to the bar at lunchtime."[67] Besides being dangerous, as in this company, which used a lot of saws and punches, these problems may be manifested by tardiness, absenteeism, and turnover.

There is some research evidence indicating a relationship between stress and especially absenteeism and turnover.[68] For example, workers may experience stress and react by getting drunk and staying home from work the next day with a hangover. They then feel bad about this drinking. They may feel that they are letting everyone down "the morning after" and eventually quit or be fired from the job. In the meantime the absenteeism rate climbs, and subsequently the turnover rates increase, both of which are very costly to the organization in terms of filling in for absent workers and replacing those who have left. Staying away from a job that is causing stress or quitting the job is a "flight" reaction to the situation. Actually, this may be a healthier reaction than a "fight" reaction, in which the person may stay on the stress-producing job and become angry and/or aggressive.

Like the psychological problems resulting from stress, the behavioral problems are often not attributed to stress by coworkers or supervisors and generate little sympathy. But, also like the psychological and the physical symptoms of stress, the behavioral problems can be controlled, more effectively managed, and even prevented by the individual and the organization. These coping strategies are discussed next.

**Application
Example**

> ### Taking Time to Manage Time
>
> One of the major causes of stress for managers comes from time pressures. No matter how fast some managers work and how much time they put in, they are still unable to get all their work done. One of the most effective ways of dealing with this problem is the use of time management techniques. Today many organizations from Chase Manhattan to Exxon to Xerox are training their managers how to get more done in less time. Some of the most helpful guidelines for effective time management are the following:
>
> 1. Make out a "to do" list that identifies everything that must be done during the day. This helps keep track of work progress.
> 2. Delegate as much minor work as possible to subordinates.
> 3. Determine when you do the best work—morning or afternoon—and schedule the most difficult assignments for this time period.
> 4. Set time aside, preferably at least one hour, during the day when visitors or other interruptions are not permitted.
> 5. Have the secretary screen all incoming calls in order to turn away those that are minor or do not require your personal attention.
> 6. Eat lunch in the office one or two days a week in order to save time and give yourself the opportunity to catch up on paperwork.
> 7. Discourage drop-in visitors by turning your desk so that you do not have eye contact with the door or hallway.
> 8. Read standing up. The average person reads faster and more accurately when in a slightly uncomfortable position.
> 9. Make telephone calls between 4:30 and 5:00 P.M. People tend to keep these conversations brief so that they can go home.
> 10. Do not feel guilty about those things that have not been accomplished today. Put them on the top of the "to do" list for tomorrow.

COPING STRATEGIES FOR STRESS

Much of the discussion so far in this chapter and, at least indirectly, a lot of the material in previous and subsequent chapters (for example, discussions of job design, goal setting, organizational behavior modification, group dynamics, management of conflict, communication skills, political strategies, leadership styles, organization processes and design, decision-making skills, control techniques, management of change, and organization development techniques) suggests ways to manage and more effectively cope with stress. There are even overall theories being developed on coping with stress.[69] The accompanying Application Example: Taking Time to Manage Time suggests some simple techniques such as time management that can be used to cope with stress. Generally speaking, however, there are two major approaches to dealing with job stress.

First are the individual strategies, which tend to be more reactive in nature. That is, they tend to be ways of coping with stress that has already occurred. Some individual strategies, such as physical exercise, can be both reactive and proactive, but most are geared toward helping the person who is already suffering from stress. The second general approach is to develop a more proactive set of strategies at the organizational level. The idea behind these organizational strategies is to remove existing or potential stressors and thus, like preventive medicine, prevent the onset of stress for individual jobholders.

Individual Coping Strategies

Today, self-help remedies, do-it-yourself approaches, weight-loss clinics and diets, health foods, and physical exercise are being given much attention in the mass media. People are actually taking responsibility, or know they *should* be taking responsibility, for their own wellness. Individual coping strategies for dealing with stress make sense. In other words, most people don't have to be convinced of the value of taking charge and actually making a change in their lives.

Some specific techniques that individuals can use to eliminate or more effectively manage inevitable, prolonged stress are the following:

1. *Exercise.* Today, it is not whether you win or lose, but whether you get some good exercise that counts. People of all ages are walking, jogging, swimming, riding bicycles, or playing softball, tennis, or racquetball in order to get some exercise to combat stress. Although this seems to make a great deal of sense and many laypeople and physicians swear by it, there still is no conclusive evidence that exercise will directly reduce the chances of heart disease or stroke. But there seems little doubt that it can help people better cope with stress, even if only as a result of the side effects, such as relaxation, enhanced self-esteem, and simply getting one's mind off work for a while.

2. *Relaxation.* Whether a person simply takes it easy once in a while or uses specific relaxation techniques such as biofeedback or meditation, the intent is to eliminate the immediately stressful situation or manage a prolonged stressful situation more effectively. Taking it easy may mean curling up with a good book in front of a fireplace or watching something "light" (not a violent program or a sports program) on television. Meditation involves muscle and mental relaxation; the person slowly repeats a peaceful phrase or word or concentrates on a mental picture in a quiet location. There is some research evidence that much meditation can have a desirable physical[70] and mental[71] impact on people. Whether it can have a practical impact on job stress is yet to be determined. However, a number of firms are using it. For example, a stockbroker who regularly uses meditation recently stated: "It's widely known that this industry has a lot of stress. So where a lot of people drink alcohol, we meditate. It's not that we don't feel stress. It just doesn't hit us as much."[72]

3. *Behavioral self-control.* Chapter 8 gives specific attention to behavioral management. By deliberately managing the antecedents and the consequences of their own behavior, people can achieve self-control. For example, sales managers who have a steady stream of customer complaints all day could change the antecedent by having an assistant screen all complaints and allow only exceptions to reach them. They could also manage the consequences by rewarding themselves with an extra break when they remain calm and collected after interacting with a particularly angry customer. Besides managing their own behavior to reduce stress, people can also become more aware of their limits and of "red flags" that signal trouble ahead. They can avoid people or situations that they know will put them under stress. In other words, this strategy involves individuals' controlling the situation instead of letting the situation control them.

4. *Cognitive therapy.* Besides behavioral self-control techniques, a number of clinical psychologists have entered the stress field in recent years with cognitive therapy techniques. Techniques such as Ellis's rational emotive model[73] and Meichenbaum's cognitive behavior modification have been successfully used to reduce test anxiety[74] and have recently been used as an individual strategy for reducing job stress. One study described the approach as follows:

Participants were taught that much of their experienced strain (anxiety, tension, etc.) is caused by their cognitions ("self-talks"). This part of the treatment program, then, consisted of off-line lectures and interactive discussions designed to help participants (a) recognize events at work and what cognitions they elicit; (b) become aware of the effects of such cognitions on their physiological and emotional responses; (c) systematically evaluate the objective consequences of events at work; and (d) replace self-defeating cognitions that unnecessarily arouse strain (e.g., "I'm an incompetent worker who cannot handle the workload") with more adaptive appraisals (e.g., "I handle this workload as well as anyone else," or "the workload is too high and I should approach my supervisor").[75]

When this coping strategy (combined with some simple relaxation techniques) was systematically evaluated by a field experimental design in a social service agency, it was found to have a positive impact on some of both the physiological (epinephrine, a hormone produced by the adrenal glands) and the psychological (depression) variables measured.[76] However, there were no significant effects on some of the other variables measured, and the treatment effects were not replicated in a subsequent intervention on the original control group. Another study evaluated a similar cognitive therapy approach applied to police academy trainees. This study found that in simulated exercises, those who used the cognitive strategy performed more effectively and exhibited greater self-control and less strain than those who did not use the approach.[77] However, there were methodological flaws[78] that probably prevent definitive conclusions at this point on the value of the cognitive approach to managing stress. Yet, as is true of the other strategies discussed so far, there is enough promise to continue its use in trying to cope with stress.

5. *Networking.* One clear finding that has come out of social psychology research over the years is that people need and will benefit from social support. Applied as a strategy to reduce job stress, this would entail forming close associations with trusted empathetic coworkers and colleagues who are good listeners and confidence builders. These friends are there when needed and provide support to get the person through stressful situations. Today, such alliances, especially if deliberately sought out and developed, are called *networks.* Although the relationship between social support and stress reduction appears complicated,[79] there is some research evidence that a networking strategy may be able to help people cope better with job stress[80] and be more effective[81] and successful managers.[82]

Organizational Coping Strategies

Organizational coping strategies are designed by management to eliminate or control organizational-level stressors in order to prevent or reduce job stress for individual employees. Earlier in the chapter, the organizational stressors are categorized in terms of overall policies and strategies, structure and design processes/functions, and working conditions (see Figure 11.2). It logically follows that these areas would be the focus of attention in developing organizational coping strategies. In other words, each of the specific stressors would be worked on in order to eliminate or reduce job stress. For example, in the policy area, attention would be given to making performance reviews and pay plans as equitable and as fair as possible. In the structural area, steps would be taken to back away from high degrees of formalization and specialization. The same would be done in the areas of physical conditions (for example, safety hazards would be removed, and lighting, noise, and temperature would be improved) and processes/functions (for example, communication and information would be improved, and ambiguous or conflicting goals would be clarified or resolved). In addition, the Association for Fitness in Business estimates that 12,000 companies today offer stress-coping programs ranging from counseling services, lunchtime stress management seminars, and wellness publications to elaborate company-run fitness centers where employees can sweat out the tension.[83] There is also evidence that the number of stress management programs is increasing and they are being evaluated more rigorously.[84]

In addition to working on each specific organizational stressor identified in Figure 11.2, more generalized strategies might include the following:

1. *Create a supportive organizational climate.* Unfortunately, most large organizations today continue to be highly formalized with accompanying inflexible, impersonal climates. This type of climate can lead to considerable job stress. A coping strategy would be to make the structure more decentralized and organic, with participative decision making and upward communication flows. In theory, these structural and process changes would create a more supportive climate for employees, give them more control over their jobs, and would prevent or reduce their job stress. The chapters in Part 4 of this text analyze the details of organization structure and processes and the ramifications that they can have for the effective management of stress; however, as a number of reviews of literature on stress have pointed out, "the evidence bearing on relationships between climate factors and stress is speculative and needs to be empirically tested."[85]

2. *Enrich the design of tasks.* Chapter 7 is devoted specifically to job design. As is brought out there, enriching jobs either by improving job content factors (such as responsibility, recognition, and opportunities for achievement, advancement, and growth[86]) or by improving core job characteristics (such as skill variety, task identity, task significance, autonomy, and feedback[87]) may lead to motivational states or experienced meaningfulness, responsibility, and knowledge of results. Presumably, these enriched tasks will eliminate the stressors found in more routine, structured jobs. However, as Chapter 7 points out, not all people respond favorably to enriched job designs; and therefore, at least with some people some of the time, the enriched job may actually lead to increased job stress. For example, an individual with low growth needs, low self-efficacy, lack of hardiness, and/or fear of failure may experience increased stress in an enriched job. Overall, however, careful managing of task design may be an effective way to cope with stress.

3. *Reduce conflict and clarify organizational roles.* Role conflict and ambiguity was identified earlier as a major individual stressor. It is up to management to reduce the conflict and clarify *organizational* roles so that this cause of stress can be eliminated or reduced. Each job should have clear expectations and the necessary information and support so that the jobholder is not left with conflicting demands or an ambiguous understanding of what he or she is to do. A specific role clarification strategy might be to have the person occupying a role obtain a list of expectations from each role sender. This list would then be compared with the focal person's expectations, and any differences would be openly discussed to clarify ambiguities and negotiated to resolve conflict.[88]

4. *Plan and develop career paths and provide counseling.* Traditionally, organizations have shown only passing interest in the career planning and development of their employees. Individuals are left to decide career moves and strategies on their own and, at most, get paternalistic advice once in a while from a supervisor. This situation is analogous to that of students at a large university who are simply

names on an adviser's computer printout sheet, which contains the names of hundreds of advisees. This situation obviously can be a source of considerable uncertainty and stress for both the students and the professor. The same is true for members of any large organization; the stress is created by not knowing what their next move is or how they are going to make it.

Summary

This chapter examines occupational stress. Although not always bad for the person (for example, the father of stress, Hans Selye, feels that complete freedom from stress is death[89]) or the organization (low levels of stress may lead to performance improvement), stress is still one of the most important and serious problems facing the field of organizational behavior. Defined as an adaptive response to an external situation that results in physical, psychological, and/or behavioral deviations for organizational participants, stress was first studied in terms of Selye's general adaptation syndrome. The three stages of GAS are alarm, resistance, and exhaustion. Since this beginning, which concentrated mainly on the physiological dimensions of stress, attention has also been focused on the psychological and behavioral dimensions.

The causes of stress can be categorized into extraorganizational, organizational, and group stressors, and individual stressors and dispositions. In combination or singly, they represent a tremendous amount of potential stress impinging upon today's jobholder—at every level and in every type of organization. The effects of such stress can create physical problems (heart disease, ulcers, arthritis, and maybe even cancer), psychological problems (mood changes, lowered self-esteem, resentment of supervision, inability to make decisions, and job dissatisfaction), and/or behavioral problems (tardiness, absenteeism, turnover, and accidents). A number of individual and organizational strategies have been developed to cope with these stress-induced problems. Exercise, relaxation, behavioral self-control techniques, cognitive therapy techniques, and networking are some potentially useful coping strategies that individuals can apply to help combat existing stress. Taking a more proactive approach, management of organizations could create a more supportive climate, enrich tasks, reduce conflict, and clarify roles. Whether on an individual or an organizational level, steps need to be taken to prevent or reduce job stress.

Questions for Discussion and Review

1. How is stress defined? Is it always bad for the individual? Explain.
2. What is the general adaptation syndrome? What are the stages?
3. What are the general categories of stressors that can affect job stress? Give some examples of each.
4. What are some of the dispositions that may influence an individual's reaction to stress? Give an example of each.
5. Job stress can have physiological, psychological, and behavioral effects. Give an example of each and cite some research findings on the relationship between job stress and these outcomes.
6. Coping strategies for job stress are given for both the individual and the organizational levels. Summarize and evaluate these various strategies for preventing and/ or more effectively managing stress.

Footnote References and Supplemental Readings

1. "Stress: Can We Cope?" *Time*, June 6, 1983, p. 48.
2. Virginia M. Gibson, "Stress in the Workplace: A Hidden Cost Factor," *HR Focus*, January 1993, p. 15.
3. Ibid.
4. John M. Ivancevich and Michael T. Matteson, *Organizational Behavior and Management*, Business Publications, Plano, Tex., 1987, p. 211.
5. See Terry A. Beehr, "The Current Debate About the Meaning of Job Stress," *Journal of Organizational Behavior Management*, Fall/Winter 1986, pp. 5–18.
6. John M. Ivancevich and Michael T. Matteson, *Organizational Behavior and Management*, 3d ed., Irwin, Homewood, Ill., 1993, p. 244.
7. T. A. Beehr and J. E. Newman, "Job Stress, Employee Health, and Organizational Effectiveness: A Facet Analysis, Model, and Literature Review," *Personnel Psychology*, Winter 1978, pp. 665–699.
8. This summary is based on Hans Selye, *Stress Without Distress*, Lippincott, Philadelphia, 1974, and James C. Quick and Jonathan D. Quick, *Organizational Stress and Preventative Management*, McGraw-Hill, New York, 1984, pp. 8–9.
9. Daniel C. Ganster and John Schaubroeck, "Work, Stress and Employee Health," *Journal of Management*, vol. 17, 1991, pp. 235–271.
10. Cynthia L. Cordes and Thomas W. Dougherty, "A Review and an Integration of Research on Job Burnout," *Academy of Management Review*, October 1993, pp. 621, 623–624. Also see C. Maslach, *Burnout: The Cost of Caring*, Prentice-Hall, Englewood Cliffs, N.J., 1982.
11. Brian K. Evans and Donald G. Fischer, "The Nature of Burnout: A Study of the Three-Factor Model of Burnout in Human Service and Non-Human Service Samples," *Journal of Occupational and Organizational Psychology*, March 1993, pp. 29–38.
12. John M. Ivancevich and Michael T. Matteson, *Stress and Work*, Scott, Foresman, Glenview, Ill., 1980, p. 145.
13. Robert Kreitner, "Personal Wellness: It's Just Good Business," *Business Horizons*, May–June 1982, p. 28.
14. Fiona Jones and Ben C. Fletcher, "An Empirical Study of Occupational Stress Transmission in Working Couples," *Human Relations*, July 1993, pp. 881–903.
15. Rabi S. Bhagat and Stephen M. Allie, "Organizational Stress, Personal Life Stress, and Symptoms of Life Strains: An Examination of the Moderating Role of Sense of Competence," *Journal of Vocational Behavior*, vol. 35, 1989, p. 233.
16. T. H. Holmes and R. H. Rahe, "Social Readjustment Rating Scale," *Journal of Psychosomatic Research*, vol. 11, 1967, pp. 213–218.
17. *The Wall Street Journal*, Dec. 23, 1986, p. 1.
18. Todd D. Jick and Linda F. Mitz, "Sex Differences in Work Stress," *Academy of Management Review*, July 1985, pp. 408–420.
19. Debra L. Nelson and James C. Quick, "Professional Women: Are Distress and Disease Inevitable?" *Academy of Management Review*, April 1985, pp. 206–218.
20. Genevieve Soter Capowski, "Stress and the Working Woman," *Management Review*, August 1993, p. 5.
21. R. Marens, "The Residential Environment," in A. Campbell, P. E. Converse, and W. L. Rodgers (eds.), *The Quality of American Life*, Russell Sage, New York, 1976.
22. Charlene Marmer Solomon, "Working Smarter: How HR Can Help," *Personnel Journal*, June 1993, p. 54.
23. Sally Solo, "Stop Whining and Get Back to Work," *Fortune*, Mar. 12, 1990, p. 49.
24. Solomon, op. cit., p. 56.
25. John Schaubroeck and Daniel C. Ganster, "Chronic Demands and Responsivity to Challenge," *Journal of Applied Psychology*, February 1993, pp. 73–85.
26. "Study Pinpoints the Causes of Stress for Working Women," *HR Focus*, September 1993, p. 24.
27. Jeffrey H. Greenhaus and Nicholas J. Beutell, "Sources of Conflict Between Work and Family Roles," *Academy of Management Review*, January 1985, p. 80.
28. John Schaubroeck, Daniel C. Ganster, Wesley E. Sime, and David Ditman, "A Field Experiment Testing Supervisory Role Clarification," *Personnel Psychology*, Spring 1993, pp. 1–25.
29. For example, see R. L. Kahn, D. M. Wolfe, R. P. Quinn, J. D. Snoeck, and R. A. Rosenthal, *Organizational Stress: Studies in Role Conflict and Ambiguity*, Wiley, New York, 1964; Robert H. Miles, "An Empirical Test of Causal Inference Between Role Perceptions of Conflict and Ambiguity and Various Personal Outcomes," *Journal of Applied Psychology*, June 1975, pp. 334–339; Robert H. Miles, "Role Requirements as Sources of Organizational Stress," *Journal of Applied Psychology*, April 1976, pp. 172–179; Andrew D. Szilagyi, Henry P. Sims, and Robert T. Keller, "Role Dynamics, Locus of Control and Employee Attitudes and Behavior," *Academy of Management Journal*, June 1976, pp. 259–276; and Arthur G. Bedeian and Achilles A. Armenakis, "A Path-Analytic Study of the Consequences of Role Conflict and Ambiguity," *Academy of Management Journal*, June 1981, pp. 417–424.
30. Arthur P. Brief, Randall S. Schuler, and Mary Van Sell, *Managing Job Stress*, Little, Brown, Boston, 1981, p. 94.

31. Meyer Friedman and Ray H. Rosenman, *Type A Behavior and Your Heart*, Knopf, New York, 1974.

32. John H. Howard, David A. Cunningham, and Peter A. Rechnitzer, "Health Patterns Associated with Type A Behavior: A Managerial Population," *Journal of Human Stress*, March 1976, pp. 24–31.

33. Friedman and Rosenman, loc. cit.

34. Brief, Schuler, and Van Sell, op. cit., pp. 11–12.

35. R. Rosenman and M. Friedman, "The Central Nervous System and Coronary Heart Disease," *Hospital Practice*, vol. 6, 1971, pp. 87–97.

36. "Unraveling Stress," *The Economist*, April 13, 1985, p. 82, and Jerry E. Bishop, "Prognosis for the 'Type A' Personality Improves in a New Heart Disease Study," *The Wall Street Journal*, Jan. 14, 1988, p. 29.

37. "Heart Disease, Anger Linked Research Shows," *Lincoln Journal*, Jan. 17, 1989, p. 4.

38. "Some Workers Just Stress-Prone," *The New York Times*, reported in *Lincoln Journal Star*, Oct. 3, 1993, p. 3E.

39. Richard M. Steers, *Introduction to Organizational Behavior*, 2d ed., Scott, Foresman, Glenview, Ill., 1984, p. 518.

40. Ronald E. Riggio, *Introduction to Industrial/Organizational Psychology*, Scott, Foresman/Little, Brown, Glenview, Ill., 1990, p. 204.

41. S. E. Jackson, "Participation in Decision Making as a Strategy for Reducing Job Related Strain," *Journal of Applied Psychology*, vol. 68, 1983, pp. 3–19.

42. "Jobs with Little Freedom Boost Heart Risk," *Lincoln Journal*, Apr. 11, 1990, p. 1.

43. Marilyn L. Fox, Deborah J. Dwyer, and Daniel C. Ganster, "Effects of Stressful Job Demands and Control on Physiological and Attitudinal Outcomes in a Hospital Setting," *Academy of Management Journal*, April 1993, pp. 289–318.

44. M. E. P. Seligman, *Helplessness: On Depression, Development, and Death*, Freeman, San Francisco, 1975.

45. S. Mineka and R. W. Henderson, "Controllability and Predictability in Acquired Motivation," *Annual Review of Psychology*, vol. 36, 1985, pp. 495–529.

46. See L. Y. Abrahamson, J. Garber, and M. E. P. Seligman, "Learned Helplessness in Humans: An Attributional Analysis," in J. Garber and M. E. P. Seligman (eds.), *Human Helplessness: Theory and Applications*, Academic Press, New York, 1980; summarized in Robert S. Feldman, *Understanding Psychology*, 2d ed., McGraw-Hill, New York, 1990, p. 525. Also see Mark J. Martinko and William L. Gardner, "Learned Helplessness: An Alternative Explanation for Performance Deficits," *Academy of Management Review*, vol. 7, 1982, pp. 413–417.

47. Spencer A. Rathus, *Psychology*, 4th ed., Holt, Rinehart and Winston, Fort Worth, Tex., 1990, pp. 440–441.

48. A. Bandura, C. B. Taylor, S. L. Williams, I. N. Medford, and J. D. Barchas, "Catecholamine Secretion as a Function of Perceived Coping Self-Efficacy," *Journal of Consulting and Clinical Psychology*, vol. 53, 1985, pp. 406–414.

49. Rathus, op. cit., p. 441.

50. S. C. Kobasa, "Stressful Life Events, Personality, and Health: An Inquiry into Hardiness," *Journal of Personality and Social Psychology*, vol. 37, 1979, pp. 1–11, and S. C. Kobasa, S. R. Maddi, and S. Kahn, "Hardiness and Health: A Perspective Study," *Journal of Personality and Social Psychology*, vol. 42, 1982, pp. 168–177.

51. Brian O'Reilly, "Is Your Company Asking Too Much?" *Fortune*, Mar. 12, 1990, p. 39.

52. Howard M. Weiss, Daniel R. Ilgen, and Michael E. Sharbaugh, "Effects of Life and Job Stress on Information Search Behaviors of Organizational Members," *Journal of Applied Psychology*, February 1982, pp. 60–62.

53. See Michael J. Burke, Arthur P. Brief, and Jennifer M. George, "The Role of Negative Affectivity in Understanding Relations Between Self-Reports of Stressors and Strains: A Comment on the Applied Psychology Literature," *Journal of Applied Psychology*, June 1993, pp. 402–412, and John Schaubroeck, Daniel C. Ganster, and Marilyn L. Fox, "Dispositional Affect and Work-Related Stress," *Journal of Applied Psychology*, vol. 77, no. 3, 1992, pp. 322–335.

54. Jenny Firth-Cozens, "Why Me? A Case Study of the Process of Perceived Occupational Stress," *Human Relations*, vol. 45, no. 2, 1992, pp. 131–142.

55. Robert A. Baron, *Behavior in Organizations*, 2d ed., Allyn and Bacon, Boston, 1986, p. 223.

56. Thomas G. Cummings and Cary L. Cooper, "A Cybernetic Framework for Studying Occupational Stress," *Human Relations*, May 1979, pp. 395–418.

57. K. Bammer and B. H. Newberry (eds.), *Stress and Cancer*, Hogrefe, Toronto, 1982.

58. Ivancevich and Matteson, *Stress and Work*, p. 92.

59. Peter Y. Chen and Paul E. Spector, "Relationships of Work Stressors with Aggression, Withdrawal, Theft and Substance Use: An Exploratory Study," *Journal of Occupational and Organizational Psychology*, September 1992, pp. 177–184.

60. J. E. McGrath, "Stress and Behavior in Organizations," in M. D. Dunnette (ed.), *Handbook of Industrial and Organizational Psychology*, Rand McNally, Chicago, 1976.

61. Beehr and Newman, loc. cit.; A. A. McLean, *Work Stress*, Addison-Wesley, Reading, Mass., 1980; and Cary L. Cooper and Judi Marshall, "Occupational

Sources of Stress," *Journal of Occupational Psychology*, March 1976, pp. 11–28.

62. "Job Stress Said a 'Substantial Health Problem,'" *Lincoln Journal*, Oct. 6, 1986, p. 15.

63. David S. Allen, "Less Stress, Less Litigation," *Personnel*, January 1990, p. 33.

64. Ivancevich and Matteson, *Stress and Work*, p. 96.

65. *The Wall Street Journal*, Oct. 14, 1986, p. 1, and *The Wall Street Journal*, Nov. 11, 1986, p. 35.

66. "Firm Hopes Breath Meter Curbs Workers' Drinking," *Lincoln Journal*, June 11, 1983, p. 13.

67. Ibid.

68. For example, see Lyman W. Porter and Richard M. Steers, "Organizational, Work, and Personal Factors in Employee Turnover and Absenteeism," *Psychological Bulletin*, August 1973, pp. 151–176; Richard M. Steers and Susan R. Rhodes, "Major Influences on Employee Attendance: A Process Model," *Journal of Applied Psychology*, August 1978, pp. 391–407; and W. H. Mobley, R. W. Griffeth, H. H. Hand, and B. M. Meglino, "Review and Conceptual Analysis of the Employee Turnover Process," *Psychological Bulletin*, May 1979, pp. 493–522.

69. Jeffrey R. Edwards, "A Cybernetic Theory of Stress, Coping, and Well-Being in Organizations," *Academy of Management Review*, April 1992, pp. 238–274.

70. Robert K. Wallace and Herbert Benson, "The Physiology of Meditation," *Scientific American*, February 1972, pp. 84–90.

71. Terri Schultz, "What Science Is Discovering About the Potential Benefits of Meditation," *Today's Health*, April 1972, pp. 34–37.

72. "Executives Meditating to Success," *Omaha World-Herald*, Feb. 11, 1986, p. 9.

73. A. Ellis, *Reason and Emotion in Psychotherapy*, Lyle Stuart, New York, 1962.

74. D. H. Meichenbaum, "Cognitive Modification of Test-Anxious College Students," *Journal of Consulting and Clinical Psychology*, vol. 39, 1972, pp. 370–378.

75. Daniel C. Ganster, Bronston T. Mayes, Wesley E. Sime, and Gerald D. Tharp, "Managing Organizational Stress: A Field Experiment," *Journal of Applied Psychology*, October 1982, p. 536.

76. Ibid., pp. 533–542.

77. I. G. Sarson, J. H. Johnson, J. P. Berberich, and J. S. Siegel, "Helping Police Officers to Cope with Stress: A Cognitive Behavioral Approach," *American Journal of Community Psychology*, vol. 7, 1979, pp. 593–603.

78. Ganster, Mayes, Sime, and Tharp, op. cit., p. 534.

79. Anson Seers, Gail W. McGee, Timothy T. Serey, and George B. Graen, "The Interaction of Job Stress and Social Support: A Strong Inference Investigation," *Academy of Management Journal*, June 1983, pp. 273–284.

80. McLean, loc. cit.

81. John Kotter, *The General Managers*, Free Press, New York, 1982.

82. Fred Luthans, Stuart A. Rosenkrantz, and Harry W. Hennessey, "What Do Successful Managers Really Do? An Observation Study of Managerial Activities," *Journal of Applied Behavioral Science*, vol. 21, no. 3, 1985, pp. 255–270.

83. Laurie Hays, "But Some Firms Try to Help," *The Wall Street Journal*, Apr. 24, 1987, p. 16D. Also see Helene Cooper, "Offering Aerobics, Karate, Aquatics, Hospitals Stress Business of 'Wellness,'" *The Wall Street Journal*, Aug. 9, 1993, pp. B1, B3.

84. John M. Ivancevich, Michael T. Matteson, Sara M. Freedman, and James S. Phillips, "Worksite Stress Management Interventions," *American Psychologist*, February 1990, pp. 252–261; John C. Erfurt, Andrea Foote, and Max A. Heirich, "The Cost-Effectiveness of Worksite Wellness Programs for Hypertension Control, Weight Loss, Smoking Cessation, and Exercise," *Personnel Psychology*, Spring 1992, pp. 5–28; and Shirley Reynolds, Emma Taylor, and David A. Shapiro, "Session Impact in Stress Management Training," *Journal of Occupational and Organizational Psychology*, June 1993, pp. 99–113.

85. Ivancevich and Matteson, *Stress and Work*, p. 212. Also see Newman and Beehr, loc. cit.

86. F. Herzberg, B. Mausner, and B. Snyderman, *The Motivation to Work*, Wiley, New York, 1959.

87. J. Richard Hackman and Greg R. Oldham, "Motivation Through the Design of Work: Test of a Theory," *Organizational Behavior and Human Performance*, August 1976, pp. 250–279.

88. J. R. P. French and R. D. Caplan, "Psychosocial Factors in Coronary Heart Disease," *Industrial Medicine*, vol. 39, 1970, pp. 383–397.

89. Selye, loc. cit.

REAL CASE: **Getting Along** **without the Boss**	The impact of stress on entrepreneurs and other self-starters has long been an area of concern to both researchers and practitioners. For example, when Everett Suters started his own business, he never realized that his personality and disposition had not prepared him for the rigors of the task he was undertaking. Suters is a high achiever and, like most

of these people, he believed strongly in the old maxim, "If you want something done right, do it yourself." The problem, however, was that within a short period of time his health began to be affected.

Suters started out working in the sales area of a large corporation. He was very successful at this job because he quickly realized that the most important thing in selling is hard work. If he called on a customer and the individual was not interested in buying his product, he would go on to another location and call on another customer. The more people he called on, the higher his sales volume. His success was determined by how long and how hard he worked.

However, when he started his own business, Suters soon realized that his previous success strategy would not work. As his computer-service business increased its customer base, more and more work fell on Suters's shoulders. He found himself scurrying from one project to the next. There never was any time for planning for the future. The entire day was spent handling rush projects. His appointment calendar was so filled with things to do he even found himself having trouble handling emergency situations. At the same time he began getting angry at his personnel, whom he saw as not working as hard as he nor being as concerned with the success of the operation as he was.

Exhausted and burned out after two years, Suters decided to take a month's vacation. It was the only way of ensuring that his health did not totally break down. When he returned, refreshed and ready to start again, Suters found that things were running smoothly. With him out of the way, the staff were able to plan more projects, get things organized, and not have to wait until they got an okay from the boss on everything. Quite obviously, Suters had been burning himself out with overwork and proving ineffective in the process.

Now aware that his stress was caused by inefficient management practices and an overcommitment to working harder rather than smarter, Suters began changing his operational methods. He began delegating more authority to his staff and refusing to handle busywork projects that could easily be managed by someone else. He stopped agreeing to help customers with all their problems and began to face the fact that many of his clients were making unreasonable demands on the company. This freed up a great deal of personal time for more important projects. He also began setting and reviewing organizational priorities so that he knew where the company was going and how it would get there. In summarizing his new approach, Suters pointed to three important steps: *(a)* plan to do more than you can do; *(b)* prioritize what you plan to do by importance and urgency; and *(c)* commit yourself to *less* than you can do and *only* to those projects that are the most important or urgent. In summing up what he has learned as president of his company, Suters says:

> This is not to suggest that it's easy to maintain this management style. As with most addicts, reformed overachievers have to be on the alert constantly to keep from backsliding. Over the course of any year, my company hires new people, and the old syndrome starts to creep back. Even experienced people begin to depend too much on me. So every year I take the cure: three weeks away to prove to myself and to the members of my staff that they can get along without me.

1. What caused Suters's job stress? (Use Figure 11.2 in formulating your answer.)
2. What were some of the individual coping strategies Suters employed to help him deal with his stress problem?
3. What lessons can be learned by managers from Suters's personal experience? Identify and describe three of them.

CASE:
Sorry, No Seats Are Left; Have a Nice Flight

Jim Miller has been a ticket agent for Friendly Airlines for the past three years. This job is really getting to be a hassle. In order to try to reduce the mounting losses that Friendly has suffered in recent months, management have decided to do two things: (1) over-book their flights so that every seat possible will be filled and (2) increase their service to their customers and live up to their name. Jim, of course, is at the point of application of this new policy. When checking in passengers, he is supposed to be very courteous and friendly, and he has been instructed to end every transaction with the statement, "Have a nice flight." The problem, of course, is that sometimes there are more passengers holding confirmed reservations checking in than there are seats on the plane. Rightfully, these people become extremely upset with Jim and sometimes scream at him and even threaten him. During these confrontations Jim becomes "unglued." He breaks into a sweat, and his face turns bright red. The company guidelines on what to do in these situations are very vague. When Jim called his supervisor for advice, he was simply told to try to book passengers on another flight, but be friendly.

1. Is Jim headed for trouble? What would be some physical, psychological, and behavioral outcomes of this type of job stress?
2. What could the company do to help reduce the stress in Jim's job?
3. What individual coping strategies could Jim try in this situation?

CASE:
A Gnawing Stomachache

Sandy Celeste was thirty years old when her divorce became final. She was forced to go to work to support her two children. Sandy got married right after graduating from college and had never really held a full-time job outside the home. Nevertheless, because of her enthusiasm, education, and maturity, she impressed the personnel manager at Devon's Department Store and was immediately hired. The position involves supervising three departments of men's and women's clothing. Sandy's training consisted of approximately two months at another store in the Devon chain. She spent this training period both selling merchandise and learning the supervisor's responsibilities. On the first day of her supervisory job, Sandy learned that, because of size constraints at the store, eight clothing departments are all located in the same area. In addition to Sandy, there are two other supervisors in the other departments. These three supervisors share the service of twenty-eight full- and part-time salespeople. Since the various departments are so jammed together, all the salespeople are expected to know each department's merchandise. Devon's merchandising philosophy is that it will not finish one department or store-wide sale without starting another. Both the clerks and the supervisors, who work on a commission and salary basis, are kept busy marking and remarking the merchandise as one sale stops and another starts. To make matters worse, Devon's expects the employees to remark each item just prior to closing time the night after a big sale. The pressure is intense, and customers are often neglected. However, all the salespeople realize that when the customer suffers, so do their commissions. As a supervisor, Sandy is expected to enforce the company's policy rigidly. Soon after taking the position as supervisor, Sandy began to experience severe headaches and a gnawing stomachache. She would like to quit her job, but realistically she can't because the pay is good and she needs to support her children.

1. To what do you attribute Sandy's health problems? What are some possible extra-organizational, organizational, group, and individual stressors?
2. Is there anything that this company could do to alleviate stress for its supervisors? What individual coping strategies could Sandy try?

12 Power and Politics

Learning Objectives

- **Define** power and its relationship to authority and influence.
- **Identify** the various classifications of power.
- **Discuss** the contingency approach to power.
- **Explain** a macro view of power.
- **Relate** the political implications of power.
- **Present** some political strategies for power acquisition in modern organizations.

Over the years, groups, informal organization, interactive behavior, conflict, and stress have received considerable attention as important dynamics of organizational behavior; power and politics, however, have not. As Rosabeth Kanter observed a number of years ago, "Power is America's last dirty word. It is easier to talk about money—and much easier to talk about sex—than it is to talk about power."[1] Yet, it is becoming clear, and anyone who has spent any time in a formal organization can readily verify, that organizations are highly political and power is the name of the game. Power and politics must be brought "out of the closet" and recognized as an important dynamic in organizational behavior. For example, the dynamics of power—how to use it and how to abuse it—were discovered by Joseph O'Donnell, who was abruptly fired from his high-level executive position with JWT Group Inc. when he proposed stripping the CEO and chairman Don Johnston of his day-to-day operating duties. In other cases, however, such a grab for power has worked. Lewis Glucksman, for instance, pushed Peter Peterson from the head of Lehman Brothers a few years ago,[2] and every day, in organizations at all levels, power plays and political moves take place.

The first part of the chapter defines what is meant by power and describes how power is related to authority and influence. The next part concentrates on the various classifications of power. Particular attention is given to the French and Raven classification of the sources of power. After an examination of some of the research results on power types, attention is given to some contingency approaches (for example, the influenceability of the target and an overall contingency model of power). Next, a more macro perspective of power is presented. Structured determinants of power are emphasized. The last part is concerned with organizational politics. Particular attention is given to a political perspective of power in today's organizations and to some specific political strategies for the acquisition of power.

THE MEANING OF POWER

Although the concepts in the field of organizational behavior seldom have universally agreed upon definitions, *power* may have even more diverse definitions than most. Almost every author who writes about power defines it differently. Going way back, for example, the famous pioneering sociologist Max Weber defined power as "the probability that one actor within a social relationship will be in a position to carry out his own will despite resistance."[3] More recently, a search of the literature on power found it referred to as the ability to get things done despite the will and resistance of others or the ability to "win" political fights and outmaneuver the opposition. The power theorists stress the positive sum of power, suggesting it is the raw ability to mobilize resources to accomplish some end without reference to any organized opposition.[4] Pfeffer, the organizational behavior theorist perhaps most closely associated with the study of power, recently simply defined power as a potential force and in more detail "as the potential ability to influence behavior, to change the course of events, to overcome resistance, and to get people to do things that they would not otherwise do."[5]

Usually, definitions of power are intertwined with the concepts of authority and influence. For example, the definition above uses the word *influence* in describing power, the pioneering theorist Chester Barnard defined power in terms of "informal authority," and many modern organizational sociologists define authority as "legitimate power."[6] These distinctions between concepts need to be cleared up in order to understand power.

The Distinctions Between Power, Authority, and Influence

In Chapter 6 the power motive is defined as the need to manipulate others and have superiority over them. Extrapolating from this definition of the need for power, "power" itself can be defined as the ability to get an individual or group to do something—to get the person or group to change in some way. The person who possesses power has the ability to manipulate or change others. Such a definition of power distinguishes it from authority and influence.

Authority legitimatizes and is a source of power. Authority is the right to manipulate or change others. Power need not be legitimate. In addition, the distinction must be made between top-down classical, bureaucratic authority and Barnard's concept of bottom-up authority based upon acceptance. In particular, Barnard defined *authority* as "the character of a communication (order) in a formal organization by virtue of which it is accepted by a contributor to or 'member' of the organization as governing the action he contributes."[7]

Such an acceptance theory of authority is easily differentiated from power. Grimes notes: "What legitimizes authority is the promotion or pursuit of collective goals that are associated with group consensus. The polar opposite, power, is the pursuit of individual or particularistic goals associated with group compliance."[8]

Influence is usually conceived of as being broader in scope than power. It involves the ability to alter other people in general ways, such as by changing their satisfaction and performance. Influence is more closely associated with leadership than power is, but both obviously are involved in the leadership process. Thus, authority is different from power because of its legitimacy and acceptance, and influence is broader than power, but it is so conceptually close that the two terms can be used interchangeably.

The above discussion points out that an operational definition of power is lacking, and this vagueness is a major reason power has been largely ignored in the study of organizational behavior. Yet, especially when it is linked to the emerging concern for organizational politics, the study of power can greatly enhance the understanding of organizational behavior.

The Classifications of Power

Any discussion of power usually begins and sometimes ends with the five categories of the sources of power identified by social psychologists John French and Bertram Raven.[9] Describing and analyzing these five classic types of power (reward, coercive, legitimate, referent, and expert) serves as a necessary foundation and point of departure for the entire chapter. Most of the examples and applications to organizational behavior come from these five types of power.

Reward Power. This source of power depends on the person's having the ability and resources to reward others. In addition, the target of this power must value these rewards. In an organizational context, managers have many potential rewards, such as pay increases, promotions, favorable work assignments, more responsibility, new equipment, praise, feedback, and recognition, available to them. In operant learning terms, this means that the manager has the power to administer positive reinforcers. In expectancy motivation terms, this means that the person has the power to provide positive valences and that the other person perceives this ability.

To understand this source of power more completely, one must remember that the recipient holds the key. If managers offer subordinates what they think is a reward (for example, a promotion with increased responsibility), but subordinates do not value it (for example, they are insecure or have family obligations that are more important to them than a promotion), then managers do not really have reward power. By the same token, managers may not think they are giving a reward to subordinates (they calmly listen to chronic complainers), but if subordinates perceive this as rewarding (the managers are giving them attention by intently listening to their complaining), the managers nevertheless have reward power. Also, managers may not really have the rewards to dispense (they may say that they have considerable influence with top management to get their people promoted, but actually they don't), but as long as their people think they have it, they do indeed have reward power.

Coercive Power. This source of power depends on fear. The person with coercive power has the ability to inflict punishment or aversive consequences on the other person or, at least, to make threats that the other person believes will result in punishment or undesirable outcomes. This form of power has contributed greatly to the negative connotation that power has for most people. In an organizational context, managers frequently have coercive power in that they can fire or demote subordinates or dock their pay, although the legal climate and unions have stripped away some of this power. Management can also directly or indirectly threaten an employee with these punishing consequences. In operant learning terms, this means that the person has the power to administer punishers or negatively reinforce (terminate punishing consequences, which is a form of negative control). In expectancy motivation terms, this means that power comes from the expectation on the part of the other persons that they will be punished if they do not conform to the powerful person's desires. For example, there is fear of punishment if they do not follow the rules, directives, or policies of the organization. It is probably this fear that gets most people to come to work on time and look busy when the boss walks through the area. In other words, much of organizational behavior may be explained in terms of coercive power rather than reward power.

Legitimate Power. This power source, identified by French and Raven, stems from the internalized values of the other persons which give the legitimate right to the agent to influence them. The others feel they have the obligation to accept this power. It is almost identical to what is usually called authority and is closely aligned with both reward and coercive power because the person with legitimacy is also in a position to reward and punish. However, legitimate power is unlike reward and coercive power in that it does not depend on the relationships with others but rather on the position or role that the person holds. For example, people obtain legitimacy because of their title (captain or executive vice president) or position (oldest in the family or officer of a corporation) rather than their personalities or how they affect others.

Legitimate power can come from three major sources. First, the prevailing cultural values of a society, organization, or group determine what is legitimate. For example, in some societies, the older people become, the more legitimate power they possess. The same may be true for certain physical attributes, gender, or job. In an organizational context, managers generally have legitimate power because employees believe in the value of private property laws and in the hierarchy where higher positions have been designated to have power over lower positions. The same holds true for certain functional positions in an organization. An example of the latter would be engineers who have legitimacy in the operations area of a company, while accountants have legitimacy in financial matters. The prevailing values within a group also determine legitimacy. For example, in a street gang the toughest member may have legitimacy, while in a work group the union steward may have legitimacy.

Second, people can obtain legitimate power from the accepted social structure. In some societies there is an accepted ruling class. But an organization or a family may also have an accepted social structure that gives legitimate power. For example, when blue-collar workers accept employment from a company, they are in effect accepting the hierarchical structure and granting legitimate power to their supervisors.

A third source of legitimate power can come from being designated as the agent or representative of a powerful person or group. Elected officials, a chairperson of a committee, and a member of the board of directors of a corporation or a union or management committee would be examples of this form of legitimate power.

Each of these forms of legitimate power creates an obligation to accept and be influenced. But, in actual practice, there are often problems, confusion, or disagreement about the range or scope of this power. Consider the following:

> An executive can rightfully expect a supervisor to work hard and diligently; may he also influence the supervisor to spy on rivals, spend weekends away from home, join an encounter group? A coach can rightfully expect [her] players to execute specific plays; may [she] also direct their life styles outside the sport? A combat officer can

rightfully expect his men to attack on order; may he also direct them to execute civilians whom he claims are spies? A doctor can rightfully order a nurse to attend a patient or observe an autopsy; may [she] order [him or] her to assist in an abortion against [his or] her own will?[10]

These gray areas point to the real concern that many people in contemporary society have regarding the erosion of traditional legitimacy. These uncertainties also point to the complex nature of power.

Referent Power. This type of power comes from the desire on the part of the other persons to identify with the agent wielding power. They want to identify with the powerful person, regardless of the outcomes. The others grant the person power because he or she is attractive and has desirable resources or personal characteristics.

Advertisers take advantage of this type of power when they use celebrities, such as movie stars or sports figures, to do testimonial advertising. The buying public identifies with (finds attractive) certain famous people and grants them power to tell them what product to buy. For example, a review of research has found that arguments, especially emotional ones, are more influential when they come from beautiful people.[11]

Timing is an interesting aspect of the testimonial advertising type of referent power. Only professional athletes who are in season (for example, baseball players in the summer and early fall, football players in the fall and early winter, and basketball players in the winter and early spring) are used in the advertisements, because then they are very visible, they are in the forefront of the public's awareness, and consequently they have referent power. Out of season the athlete is forgotten and has little referent power. Exceptions, of course, are the handful of superstars (for example, George Foreman, Michael Jordan, Joe Montana, and Magic Johnson) who transcend seasons and have referent power all year long, and even after they have retired.

In an organizational setting, referent power is much different from the other types of power discussed so far. For example, managers with referent power must be attractive to subordinates so that subordinates will want to identify with them, regardless of whether the managers later have the ability to reward or punish or whether they have legitimacy. In other words, the manager who depends on referent power must be personally attractive to subordinates.

Expert Power. The last source of power identified by French and Raven is based on the extent to which others attribute knowledge and expertise on the power seeker. Experts are perceived to have knowledge or understanding only in certain well-defined areas. All the sources of power depend on the target's perceptions, but expert power may be even more dependent on this than the others. In particular, the target must perceive the agent to be credible, trustworthy, and relevant before expert power is granted.

Credibility comes from having the right credentials; that is, the person must really know what he or she is talking about and be able to show tangible evidence of this knowledge. For example, if a highly successful football coach gives an aspiring young player some advice on how to do a new block, he will be closely listened to—he will be granted expert power. The coach has expert power in this case because he is so knowledgeable about football. His evidence for this credibility is the fact that he is a former star player and has coached championship teams. If this coach tried to give advice on how to play basketball or how to manage a corporation, he would have no credibility and thus would have no expert power. For avid football fans or players, however, this coach might have general referent power (that is, he is very attractive to them), and they would be influenced by what he has to say on any subject—basketball or corporate management.

In organizations, staff specialists have expert power in their functional areas, but not outside. For example, engineers are granted expert power in production matters but not in personnel or public relations problems. The same holds true for other staff experts, such as computer experts or accountants. For example, the computer person in a small office may be the only one who really understands the computer and how to use it, and this knowledge gives him or her considerable power.

As already implied, however, expert power is highly selective, and, besides credibility, the agent must also have trustworthiness and relevance. By trustworthiness, it is meant that the person seeking expert power must have a reputation for being honest and straightforward. In the case of political figures, scandals could undermine their expert power in the eyes of the voting public. In addition to credibility and trustworthiness, a person must have relevance and usefulness to have expert power. Going back to the earlier example, if the football coach gave advice on world affairs, it would be neither relevant nor useful, and therefore the coach would not have expert power.

It is evident that expertise is the most tenuous type of power, but managers, and especially staff specialists, who seldom have the other sources of power available to them, often have to depend upon their expertise as their only source of power. As organizations become increasingly technologically complex and specialized, the expert power of organization members at all levels may become more and more important. This is formally recognized by some companies that deliberately include lower-level staff with expert power in top-level decision making. For example, the president of a high-tech firm stated: "In general, the faster the change in the know-how on which a business depends, the greater the divergence between knowledge and position power is likely to be. Since our business depends on what it knows to survive, we mix 'knowledge-power people' with 'position-power people' daily, so that together they make the decisions that will affect us for years to come."[12] Some organizations are using their expertise to fend off the competition. The International Application Example: Keeping the Inside Track illustrates how Intourist, the giant Russian tourism agency, is trying to use experience rather than expertise to hold off competition.

It must also be remembered that French and Raven did recognize that there may be other sources of power. For instance, some organizational sociologists such as Crozier[13] recognize the source of power of task interdependence (where two or more organizational participants must depend on one another). An example would be an executive who has legitimate power over a subordinate, but because the executive must depend on the subordinate to get the job done correctly and on time, the subordinate also has power over the executive.[14] There is research evidence that subordinates in such an interdependent relationship with their boss receive better pay raises.[15] French and Raven also point out that the sources are interrelated (for example, the use of coercive power by managers may reduce their referent power), and the same person may exercise different types of power under different circumstances and at different times. The latter point has recently led to some contingency models of power in organizations.

Keeping the Inside Track

Recent elections in Russia have led the government to reduce the pace at which it is introducing economic changes. However, this backtracking does not affect the degree of competition that Russian firms will feel from their foreign rivals. In the case of Intourist, which for decades monopolized foreign tourism in Russia, this competitive threat is being managed through the use of expert power that is helping the company survive and recently compete successfully domestically and against foreigners. The two biggest internal competitors are Intourbureau and Sputnik. Intourbureau was set up in 1967 to handle trade-union exchange programs, and in recent years it has ventured into commercial travel. Today, it has hotels in twenty-five cities and hosts about 200,000 foreign visitors annually. Sputnik handles tours for young Russians (thirty-five years of age or under) who want to visit other locales around the country.

The biggest problem that Intourist faces is its past poor reputation. The agency was famous for lost reservations, lackadaisical tour guides, dingy rooms, and rude employees. On the other hand, Intourist still has the necessary infrastructure to compete. For years, tourists to Russia have learned to call Intourist and have it take care of all their reservations, which helps explain why the agency handles about 2 million of the nation's 2.5 million foreign tourists each year and arranges Russian travel abroad. Moreover, Intourist owns 110 hotels and is affiliated with more than 800 travel agents in other countries. And it is now expanding operations so that by the end of the 1990s it is estimated that the agency will have five times as many rooms as it did at the beginning.

Will past experience help overcome a bad reputation in Intourist's competitive battles? Experience alone will probably not be enough to ensure Intourist's success, especially given the influx of foreign competitors who are attempting to lure tourists to their own facilities. Examples are Radisson Hotels, the Sheraton, and Pan American, all of which, either individually or in joint-venture arrangements, are getting into the tourism business in Russia. In some cases, they are teaming up with competitors of Intourist; in other cases, they are dealing directly with Russian cities—as in the case of the Sheraton Moscow Hotel, a partnership with the city of Moscow. Thus, while Intourist will continue to be a major player in the tourism business, its power is beginning to erode in the face of competition and its past problems.

Contingency Approaches to Power

As in other areas of organizational behavior and management, contingency approaches to power are beginning to emerge. For example, Pfeffer simply says that power comes from being in the "right" place. He describes the right place or position in the organization as one where the manager has:

1. Control over resources such as budgets, physical facilities, and positions that can be used to cultivate allies and supporters.
2. Control over or extensive access to information—about the organization's activities, about the preferences and judgments of others, about what is going on, and who is doing it.
3. Formal authority.[16]

There is some research support[17] for such insightful observations, and there are also research findings that lead to contingency conclusions such as the following:

1. The greater the professional orientation of group members, the greater relative strength referent power has in influencing them.

2. The less effort and interest high-ranking participants are willing to allocate to a task, the more likely lower-ranking participants are to obtain power relevant to this task.[18]

Besides these overall contingency observations, there is increasing recognition of the moderating impact of the control of strategic contingencies such as organizational interdependence and the extent to which a department controls critical operations of other departments[19] or the role of influence behaviors in the perception of power.[20] Also, the characteristics of influence targets (that is, their influenceability) have an important moderating impact on the types of power that can be successfully used. An examination of these characteristics of the target and an overall contingency model is presented next.

Influenceability of the Targets of Power. Most discussions of power imply a unilateral process of influence from the agent to the target. It is becoming increasingly clear, however, that power involves a reciprocal relationship between the agent and the target, which is in accordance with the overall social learning perspective taken in other chapters of the text. The power relationship can be better understood by examining some of the characteristics of the target. The following characteristics have been identified as being especially important to the influenceability of targets.[21]

1. *Dependency.* The greater the targets' dependency on their relationship to agents (for example, when a target cannot escape a relationship, perceives no alternatives, or values the agent's rewards as unique), the more targets are influenced.
2. *Uncertainty.* Experiments have shown that the more uncertain people are about the appropriateness or correctness of a behavior, the more likely they are to be influenced to change that behavior.
3. *Personality.* There have been a number of research studies showing the relationship between personality characteristics and influenceability. Some of these findings are obvious (for example, people who cannot tolerate ambiguity or who are highly anxious are more susceptible to influence, and those with high needs for affiliation are more susceptible to group influence), but some are not (for example, both positive and negative relationships have been found between self-esteem and influenceability).
4. *Intelligence.* There is no simple relationship between intelligence and influenceability. For example, highly intelligent people may be more willing to listen, but, because they also tend to be held in high esteem, they also may be more resistant to influence.
5. *Gender.* Although traditionally it was generally acknowledged that women were more likely to conform to influence attempts than men because of the way they were raised, there is now evidence that this is changing.[22] As women's and society's views of the role of women are changing, there is less of a distinction by gender of influenceability.
6. *Age.* Social psychologists have generally concluded that susceptibility to influence increases in young children up to about the age of eight or nine and then decreases with age until adolescence, when it levels off.
7. *Culture.* Obviously, the cultural values of a society have a tremendous impact on the influenceability of its people. For example, some cultures, such as Western cultures, emphasize individuality, dissent, and diversity, which would tend to decrease influenceability, while others, such as many in Asia, emphasize cohesiveness, agreement, and uniformity, which would tend to promote influenceability.

Taking as Long as It Takes

In recent years many American firms doing business internationally have found, to their chagrin, that their overseas hosts have been using the agenda to gain power over visiting dignitaries. Here is a story related by a business lawyer who recently returned from Japan.

"I went to Japan to negotiate a licensing agreement with a large company there. We had been in contact with these people for three months and during that time had hammered out a rough agreement regarding the specific terms of the contract. The president of the firm thought that it would be a good idea if I, the corporate attorney, went to Tokyo and negotiated some of the final points of the agreement before we signed. I arrived in Japan on a Sunday with the intention of leaving late Friday evening. When I got off the plane, my hosts were waiting for me. I was whisked through customs and comfortably ensconced in a plush limousine within 30 minutes.

"The next day began with my host asking me for my return air ticket so his secretary could take care of confirming the flight. I was delighted to comply. We then spent the next four days doing all sorts of things—sightseeing, playing golf, fishing, dining at some of the finest restaurants in the city. You name it, we did it. By Thursday I was getting worried. We had not yet gotten around to talking about the licensing agreement. Then on Friday morning we had a big meeting. Most of the time was spent discussing the changes my hosts would like to see made in the agreement. Before I had a chance to talk, it was time for lunch. We finished eating around 4 P.M. This left me only four hours before I had to leave for the airport. During this time I worked to get them to understand the changes we wanted made in the agreement. Before I knew it, it was time to head for the airport. Halfway there my host pulled out a new contract. 'Here are the changes we talked about,' he said. 'I have already signed for my company. All you have to do is sign for yours.' Not wanting to come home empty-handed, I signed. It turned out that the contract was much more favorable to them than to us. In the process, I learned a lesson. Time is an important source of power. When you know the other person's agenda, you have an idea of what the individual's game plan must be and can work it to your advantage. Since this time, I have all my reservations and confirmations handled stateside. When my guest asks me how long I will be staying, I have a stock answer, 'As long as it takes.'"

As the accompanying International Application Example: Taking as Long as It Takes indicates, controlling the agenda and time in foreign cultures may be used to gain power and influenceability. These individual differences in targets greatly complicate the effective use of power and point up the need for contingency models.

An Overall Contingency Model for Power. Many other contingency variables in the power relationship besides the target could be inferred from the discussion of the various types of power, for example, credibility and surveillance. All these variables can be tied together and related to one another in an overall contingency model.

The classic work on influence processes, by social psychologist Herbert Kelman,[23] can be used to structure an overall contingency model of power. The model in Figure 12.1 incorporates the French and Raven sources of power with Kelman's sources of power, which in turn support three major processes of power.

According to the model, the target will *comply* in order to gain a favorable reaction or avoid a punishing one from the agent. This is the process that most

Required Sources of Power	Process of Power	Target's Influenceability	Required Conditions
Reward Coercive Means-ends-control	Compliance	Wants to gain a favorable reaction; wants to avoid a punishing one from the agent	The agent must have surveillance over the target
Referent Attractiveness	Identification	Finds a self-satisfying relationship with the agent; wants to establish and maintain a relationship with the agent	The agent must have salience; the agent must be in the forefront of the target's awareness
Expert Legitimate Credibility	Internalization	Goes along with the agent because of consistency with internal values	The agent must have relevance

FIGURE 12.1

An overall contingency model of power based on the French/Raven and Kelman theories.

supervisors in work organizations must rely upon. But in order for compliance to work, supervisors must be able to reward and punish (that is, have control over the means to their subordinates' ends) and keep an eye on their subordinates (that is, have surveillance over them).

People will *identify*, not in order to obtain a favorable reaction from the agent, as in compliance, but because it is self-satisfying to do so. But in order for the identification process to work, the agent must have referent power—be very attractive to the target—and be salient. For example, a research study by Kelman found that students were initially greatly influenced by a speech given by a very handsome star athlete; that is, they identified with him. However, when the students were checked six months after the speech, they were not influenced. The handsome athlete was no longer salient; that is, he was no longer in the forefront of their awareness, and his words carried no influence. As discussed earlier, except for the handful of superstars, athletes are soon forgotten and have no power over even their most avid fans. Once they have graduated or are out of season, they lose their salience and, thus, their power.

Finally, people will *internalize* because of compatibility with their own value structure. But, as Figure 12.1 shows, in order for people to internalize, the agent must have expert or legitimate power (credibility) and, in addition, be relevant. Obviously, this process of power is most effective. Kelman, for example, found that internalized power had a lasting impact on the subjects in his studies.

This model of power has considerable relevance to how and under what conditions supervisors and managers influence their subordinates. Many must depend on compliance because they are not attractive or do not possess referent power for identification to work. Or they lack credibility or do not have expert or legitimate power for internalization to occur. Kelman's research showed that internalization had the longest-lasting impact and as shown in the model does not need surveillance nor salience. In other words, what is generally considered to be leadership (covered in the next chapter) is more associated with getting people not just to comply but also to identify with the leader and, even better, to internalize what the leader is trying to accomplish in the influence attempt. This internalization would be especially desirable in today's highly autonomous, open organizations.

The Two Faces of Power

Besides the sources and situational, or contingency, nature of power, there are also different types of power that can be identified. Social psychologist David McClelland has, as Chapter 6 points out, done considerable work on the impact of the motivational need for power (what he calls *n Pow*). His studies indicate that there are two major types of power, one negative and one positive.

As the introductory comments point out, over the years power has often had a negative connotation. The commonly used term "power-hungry" reflects this negative feeling about power. According to McClelland, power

> . . . is associated with heavy drinking, gambling, having more aggressive impulses, and collecting "prestige supplies" like a convertible. . . . People with this personalized power concern are more apt to speed, have accidents, and get into physical fights. If . . . possessed by political officeholders, especially in the sphere of international relations, the consequences would be ominous.[24]

McClelland feels that this negative use of power is associated with *personal power*. He feels that it is primitive and does indeed have negative consequences.

The contrasting "other face" of power identified by McClelland is *social power*. It is characterized by a "concern for group goals, for finding those goals that will move people, for helping the group to formulate them, for taking some initiative in providing members of the group with the means of achieving such goals, and for giving group members the feeling of strength and competence they need to work hard for such goals."[25] Under this definition of social power, the manager may often be in a precarious position of walking a fine line between an exhibition of personal dominance and the more socializing use of power. McClelland has accumulated some empirical evidence that social power managers are quite effective. In some ways this role power may play in organizational effectiveness is in opposition to the more humanistic positions, which emphasize the importance of democratic values and participative decision making. There is also recent empirical evidence that would counter McClelland's view. One study found that those with a high need for power may suppress the flow of information, especially information that contradicts their preferred course of action, and thus have a negative impact on effective managerial decision making.[26] But regardless of some of the controversy surrounding power, it is clear that power is inevitable in today's organizations. How power is used and what type of power is used can vitally affect human performance and organizational goals.

A More Macro View of Power

Although the discussion of power so far has organizational implications (especially the contingency models), there is a view from organization theory that structure actually determines power. For example, Pfeffer states:

> The design of an organization, its structure, is first and foremost the system of control and authority by which the organization is governed. . . . Thus, organizational structures create formal power and authority by designating certain persons to do certain tasks and make certain decisions and create informal power through the effect on information and communication structures within the organization.[27]

The position one occupies in the structure also is a determinant of power. For example, those at the top of the hierarchical structure (that is, upper-level management) have power sources such as formal position, resources, and control of decision premises, while lower-level managers may get their power from physical location or information flow.[28] There is also evidence that as organizations go international, they are using structure to facilitate or inhibit the power of their foreign subsidiaries.[29]

Besides the power implications from organizational structuring, there are also power differentials found in the formal positions in the hierarchy. In particular, even though the heads of the various functions of a business firm are on the same level, they do not possess the same power. For example, which functional department head—production, marketing, or finance—has the most power will depend on the type of firm. In a manufacturing concern, production and engineering have the most power, but in a big oil company, marketing may have the most power. These horizontal power differentials, of course, will be contingent on a number of environmental factors, such as the technology and the economy. In recent years, because of the economic and political climate, the financial and legal departments of many American organizations have become very powerful, but in Japan the operations, quality control, and personnel functions are more powerful. In other words, like the more micro analysis of power, the macro analysis of power must also recognize the contingency approach. Some recently suggested contingency variables—to summarize what has just been discussed—are areas such as organizational environment, culture, structure, and process.[30]

POLITICAL IMPLICATIONS OF POWER

Power and politics are very closely related concepts. A popular view of organizational politics is how one can pragmatically get ahead in an organization. Alvin Toffler, the noted author of *Future Shock*, *The Third Wave*, and *Powershift*, observed that "companies are always engaged in internal political struggles, power struggles, infighting, and so on. That's normal life."[31] Another view, however, deals with the acquisition of power. In this latter view, power and politics become especially closely intertwined. A recognition of the political realities of power acquisition in today's organizations and an examination of some specific political strategies for acquiring power are of particular interest for understanding the dynamics of organizational behavior.

A Political Perspective of Power in Organizations

As Chapter 17 discusses in detail, the classical organization theorists portrayed organizations as highly rational structures in which authority meticulously followed the chain of command and in which managers had legitimatized power. The discussion in Chapter 9 of informal managerial roles and organization portrays another, more realistic view of organizations. It is in this more realistic view of organizations that the importance of the political aspects of power comes to the forefront. As Pfeffer notes: "Organizations, particularly large ones, are like governments in that they are fundamentally political entities. To understand them, one needs to understand organizational politics, just as to understand governments, one needs to understand governmental politics."[32]

The political perspective of organizations departs from the rational, idealistic model. For example, Walter Nord dispels some of the dreams of ideal, rationally structured and humanistic organizations by pointing out some of the stark realities of political power. He suggests four postulates of power in organizations that help focus on the political realities:

1. Organizations are composed of coalitions which compete with one another for resources, energy, and influence.
2. Various coalitions will seek to protect their interests and positions of influence.
3. The unequal distribution of power itself has dehumanizing effects.
4. The exercise of power within organizations is one very crucial aspect of the exercise of power within the larger social system.[33]

In other words, the political power game is very real in today's organizations. Researchers on organizational politics conclude that

> . . . politics in organizations is simply a fact of life. Personal experience, hunches, and anecdotal evidence for years have supported a general belief that behavior in and of organizations is often political in nature. More recently, some conceptual and empirical research has added further support to these notions.[34]

Some of today's large corporations have even formalized their political nature by creating political action committees (PACs) to support certain government positions. For example, the president of NBC, Robert Wright, created a stir when he proposed the network create a PAC and purportedly suggested that employees who don't contribute "should question their own dedication to the company and their expectations."[35] But like other aspects of organizational dynamics, politics is not a simple process; it can vary from organization to organization and even from one subunit of an organization to another. A comprehensive definition drawing from the literature is that "organizational politics consists of intentional acts of influence undertaken by individuals or groups to enhance or protect their self-interest when conflicting courses of action are possible."[36] The political behavior of organizational participants tends to be opportunistic for the purpose of maximizing self-interest.[37]

Research on organizational politics has identified several areas that are particularly relevant to the degree to which organizations are political rather than rational. These areas can be summarized as follows:

1. *Resources.* There is a direct relationship between the amount of politics and how critical and scarce the resources are. Also, politics will be encouraged when there is an infusion of new, "unclaimed" resources.
2. *Decisions.* Ambiguous decisions, decisions on which there is lack of agreement, and uncertain, long-range strategic decisions lead to more politics than routine decisions.
3. *Goals.* The more ambiguous and complex the goals become, the more politics there will be.
4. *Technology and external environment.* In general, the more complex the internal technology of the organization, the more politics there will be. The same is true of organizations operating in turbulent external environments.
5. *Change.* A reorganization or a planned organization development (OD) effort (see Chapter 20, on various OD techniques) or even an unplanned change brought about by external forces will encourage political maneuvering.[38]

The above implies that some organizations and subunits within the organization will be more political than others. By the same token, however, it is clear that most of today's organizations meet the above requirements for being highly political. That is, they have very limited resources; make ambiguous, uncertain decisions; have very unclear yet complex goals; have increasingly complex technology; and are undergoing drastic change. This existing situation facing organizations makes them more political, and the power game becomes increasingly important. Miles states: "In short, conditions that *threaten* the status of the powerful or *encourage* the efforts of those wishing to increase their power base will stimulate the intensity of organizational politics and increase the proportion of decision-making behaviors that can be classified as political as opposed to rational."[39] For example, with the political situation of today's high-tech, radically innovative firms, it has been suggested that medieval structures of palace favorites, liege lordship, and fiefdoms may be more relevant than the more familiar rational structures.[40] The next section presents some political strategies for power acquisition in today's organizations.

Specific Political Strategies for Power Acquisition

Once it is understood and accepted that contemporary organizations are in reality largely political systems, some very specific strategies can be identified to help organization members more effectively acquire power.

For over twenty years, various political strategies for gaining power in organizations have been suggested. Table 12.1 gives a representative summary of these strategies. Research is also being done on political tactics. For example, Yukl and Falbe recently derived eight political, or influence, tactics that are commonly found in today's organizations. These tactics are identified in Table 12.2. Yukl and his colleagues found that the consultation and rational persuasion tactics were used most frequently[41] and along with inspirational appeal were most effective.[42] Some modern organization theorists take more analytical approaches than most of the strategies

TABLE 12.1 Political Strategies for Attaining Power in Organizations

Taking counsel
Maintaining maneuverability
Promoting limited communication
Exhibiting confidence
Controlling access to information and persons
Making activities central and nonsubstitutable
Creating a sponsor-protégé relationship
Stimulating competition among ambitious subordinates
Neutralizing potential opposition
Making strategic replacements
Committing the uncommitted
Forming a winning coalition
Developing expertise
Building personal stature
Employing trade-offs
Using research data to support one's own point of view
Restricting communication about real intentions
Withdrawing from petty disputes

TABLE 12.2 Political Tactics Derived from Research

Tactics	Description
Pressure tactics	The use of demands, threats, or intimidation to convince you to comply with a request or to support a proposal.
Upward appeals	Persuading you that the request is approved by higher management, or appeals to higher management for assistance in gaining your compliance with the request.
Exchange tactics	Making explicit or implicit promises that you will receive rewards or tangible benefits if you comply with a request or support a proposal, or remind you of a prior favor to be reciprocated.
Coalition tactics	Seeking the aid of others to persuade you to do something or using the support of others as an argument for you to agree also.
Ingratiating tactics	Seeking to get you in a good mood or to think favorably of the influence agent before asking you to do something.
Rational persuasion	Using logical arguments and factual evidence to persuade you that a proposal or request is viable and likely to result in the attainment of task objectives.
Inspirational appeals	Making an emotional request or proposal that arouses enthusiasm by appealing to your values and ideals, or by increasing your confidence that you can do it.
Consultation tactics	Seeking your participation in making a decision or planning how to implement a proposed policy, strategy, or change.

Source: Adapted from Gary Yukl and Cecilia M. Falbe, "Influence Tactics and Objectives in Upward, Downward, and Lateral Influence Attempts," *Journal of Applied Psychology,* vol. 75, 1990, p. 133. Used with permission.

suggested in Table 12.1 and Table 12.2, and they depend more on concepts such as uncertainty in their political strategies for power. For example, Pfeffer's strategies include managing uncertainty, controlling resources, and building alliances.[43] Others take a more pragmatic approach, such as the recent analysis that suggests that successful political behavior involves keeping people happy, cultivating contacts, and wheeling and dealing.[44]

One of the more comprehensive and relevant lists of strategies for modern managers comes from DuBrin.[45] A closer look at a sampling of his suggested strategies provides important insights into power and politics in modern organizations.

Maintain Alliances with Powerful People. As has already been pointed out, the formation of coalitions (alliances) is critical to the acquisition of power in an organization. An obvious coalition would be with members of other important departments or with members of upper-level management. Not so obvious but equally important would be the formation of an alliance with the boss's secretary or staff assistant, that is, someone who is close to the powerful person. An ethnographic study of a city bus company found that a series of dyadic alliances went beyond the formal system and played an important role in getting the work done both within and between departments.[46] For example, alliances between supervisors and certain drivers got the buses out on the worst winter snow days, and kept them running during sparse summer vacation periods.

Embrace or Demolish. Machiavellian principles can be applied as strategies in the power game in modern organizations. One management writer has applied these principles to modern corporate life. For example, for corporate takeovers, he draws on Machiavelli to give the following advice:

The guiding principle is that senior managers in taken-over firms should either be warmly welcomed and encouraged or sacked; because if they are sacked they are powerless, whereas if they are simply downgraded they will remain united and resentful and determined to get their own back.[47]

Divide and Rule. This widely known political and military strategy can also apply to the acquisition of power in a modern organization. The assumption, sometimes unwarranted, is that those who are divided will not form coalitions themselves. For example, in a business firm the head of finance may generate conflict between marketing and production in hopes of getting a bigger share of the limited budget from the president of the company.

Manipulate Classified Information. The observational studies of managerial work have clearly demonstrated the importance of obtaining and disseminating information.[48] The politically astute organization member carefully controls this information in order to gain power. For example, the purchasing agent may reveal some new pricing information to the design engineer before an important meeting. Now the purchasing agent has gained some power because the engineer owes the purchasing agent a favor.

Make a Quick Showing. This strategy involves looking good on some project or task right away in order to get the right people's attention. Once this positive attention is gained, power is acquired to do other, usually more difficult and long-range projects. For example, an important, but often overlooked, strategy of a manager trying to get acceptance of a total quality management program (see Chapter 2) is to show some quick, objective improvements in the quality of a product, service, or process.

Collect and Use IOUs. This strategy says that the power seeker should do other people favors but should make it clear that they owe something in return and will be expected to pay up when asked. The "Godfather" in the famous book and movie of that name very effectively used this strategy to gain power.

Avoid Decisive Engagement (Fabianism). This is a strategy of going slow and easy—an evolutionary rather than a revolutionary approach to change. By not "ruffling feathers," the power seeker can slowly but surely become entrenched and gain the cooperation and trust of others.

Progress One Step at a Time (Camel's Head in the Tent). This strategy involves taking one step at a time instead of trying to push a whole major project or reorganization attempt. One small change can be a foothold that the power seeker can use as a basis to get other, more major things accomplished.

Wait for a Crisis (Things Must Get Worse Before They Get Better). This strategy uses the reverse of "no news is good news"; that is, bad news gets attention. For example, many deans in large universities can get the attention of central administration and the board of regents or trustees only when their college is in trouble, for instance, if their accreditation is threatened. Only under these crisis conditions can they get the necessary funding to move their college ahead.

Take Counsel with Caution. Finally, this suggested political strategy is concerned more with how to keep power than with how to acquire it. Contrary to the traditional prescriptions concerning participative management and empowerment of employees, this suggests that at least some managers should avoid "opening up the gates" to their subordinates in terms of shared decision making. The idea here is that allowing subordinates to participate and to have this expectation may erode the power of the manager.

A Final Word on Power and Politics

Obviously, the strategies discussed above are only representative, not exhaustive, of the many possible politically based strategies for acquiring power in organizations. Perhaps even more than in the case of many of the other topics covered in the text, there is little research backup for these ideas on power and, especially, politics. There is also a call for a framework and guidelines to evaluate the ethics of power and politics in today's organizations. This ethical concern goes beyond the notions of success or effectiveness. As one analysis pointed out: "When it comes to the ethics of organizational politics, respect for justice and human rights should prevail for its own sake."[49] Besides the possible ethical implications of power and politics carried to the extreme, there may be dysfunctional effects such as morale being weakened, victors and victims being created, and energy and time being spent on planning attacks and counterattacks instead of concentrating on getting the job done.[50] There is some empirical evidence that those managers who are observed to engage in more political activity are relatively more successful in terms of promotions, but are relatively less effective in terms of subordinate satisfaction and commitment and the performance of their unit.[51]

One thing about power and politics, however, is certain: Modern, complex organizations tend to create a climate that promotes power seeking and political maneuvering. It is a fact of modern organizational life, and it is hoped that future research will be forthcoming that will help managers better understand the dynamics, meaning, and successful application of power and politics.

Summary

This chapter examines one of the most important and realistic dynamics of organizational behavior—power and politics. "Power" and "politics" have a number of different meanings. Power can be distinguished from authority and influence, but most definitions subsume all three concepts. Most of the attention given to power over the years has centered on the French and Raven classification of power types: reward, coercive, legitimate, referent, and expert. More recently, some contingency models for power have been developed, which take into consideration the influence-ability of the targets of power (that is, their dependency, uncertainty, personality, intelligence, gender, age, and culture). Overall contingency models are also beginning to emerge. Closely related to the contingency models of the French and Raven power types is the view of power by McClelland. McClelland suggests that there are two faces of power: negative personal power and positive social power. Finally, a more macro view of power in organizations is needed for comprehensive understanding. Both vertical and horizontal structural arrangements have implications for power in organizations.

Politics is very closely related to power. This chapter gives particular attention to a political perspective of power in modern organizations, in terms of resources, decisions, goals, technology, external environment, and change, and to strategies for the acquisition of power. Some specific political strategies are to maintain alliances with powerful people, embrace or demolish, divide and rule, manipulate classified information, make a quick showing, collect and use IOUs, avoid decisive engagement, progress one step at a time, wait for a crisis, and take counsel with caution. Above all, it should be remembered that both power and politics represent the realities of modern organizational life. The study of these important dynamics can significantly improve the understanding of organizational behavior.

Questions for Discussion and Review

1. How would you define "power" in your own words? How does power differ from authority? From influence?
2. Identify, briefly summarize, and give some realistic examples of each of the French and Raven power types.
3. Using the contingency model of power, who would you use to advertise products in the fall, winter, spring, and summer? Explain your choices.
4. In the chapter it is stated: "The political power game is very real in today's organizations." Explain this statement in terms of the discussion in the chapter and any firsthand experience you have had to verify it.
5. Identify three or four of the political strategies that are discussed in the chapter. Explain how these might actually help someone acquire power in a modern organization.

Footnote References and Supplemental Readings

1. Rosabeth Moss Kanter, "Power Failure in Management Circuits," *Harvard Business Review*, July–August 1979, p. 65.
2. "Trying a Palace Coup Can Be Hazardous to an Executive's Career," *The Wall Street Journal*, Feb. 17, 1987, p. 1.
3. Max Weber, *The Theory of Social and Economic Organization*, A. M. Henderson and Talcott Parsons (trans. and ed.), Free Press, New York, 1947, p. 152.
4. David Krackhardt, "Assessing the Political Landscape: Structure, Cognition, and Power in Organizations," *Administrative Science Quarterly*, vol. 35, 1990, p. 343.
5. Jeffrey Pfeffer, *Managing with Power*, Harvard Business School Press, Boston, 1992, p. 30.
6. A. J. Grimes, "Authority, Power, Influence and Social Control: A Theoretical Synthesis," *Academy of Management Review*, October 1978, p. 725.
7. Chester I. Barnard, *The Functions of the Executive*, Harvard University Press, Cambridge, Mass., 1938, p. 163.
8. Grimes, op. cit., p. 726.
9. John R. P. French, Jr., and Bertram Raven, "The Bases of Social Power," in D. Cartwright (ed.), *Studies in Social Power*, University of Michigan, Institute for Social Research, Ann Arbor, 1959.
10. H. Joseph Reitz, *Behavior in Organizations*, 3d ed., Irwin, Homewood, Ill., 1987, p. 435.
11. David G. Myers, *Social Psychology*, 3d ed., McGraw-Hill, New York, 1990, p. 240.
12. Andrew S. Grove, "Breaking the Chains of Command," *Newsweek*, Oct. 3, 1983, p. 23.
13. M. Crozier, *The Bureaucratic Phenomenon*, University of Chicago Press, Chicago, 1964.
14. Gregory B. Northcraft and Margaret A. Neale, *Organizational Behavior*, Dryden, Chicago, 1990, pp. 342–343.
15. Kathryn M. Bartol and David C. Martin, "When Politics Pays: Factors Influencing Managerial Compensation Decisions," *Personnel Psychology*, vol. 43, 1990, p. 599.
16. Pfeffer, op. cit., p. 69.

17. For example, see Herminia Ibarra and Steven B. Andrews, "Power, Social Influence, and Sense Making: Effects of Network Centrality and Proximity on Employee Perceptions," *Administrative Science Quarterly*, June 1993, pp. 277–303.

18. Stephen P. Robbins, *Organizational Behavior*, Prentice-Hall, Englewood Cliffs, N.J., 1979, p. 276.

19. Carol Stoak Saunders, "The Strategic Contingencies Theory of Power: Multiple Perspectives," *Journal of Management Studies*, January 1990, p. 4.

20. Daniel J. Brass and Marlene E. Burkhardt, "Potential Power and Power Use: An Investigation of Structure and Behavior," *Academy of Management Journal*, June 1993, pp. 441–470.

21. Adapted from Reitz, op. cit., pp. 441–443.

22. Ibid., pp. 442–443.

23. See Herbert C. Kelman, "Compliance, Identification, and Internalization: Three Processes of Attitude Change," *Journal of Conflict Resolution*, March 1958, pp. 51–60.

24. David C. McClelland, "The Two Faces of Power," *Journal of International Affairs*, vol. 24, no. 1, 1970, p. 36.

25. Ibid., p. 41.

26. Eugene M. Fodor and Terry Smith, "The Power Motive as an Influence on Group Decision Making," *Journal of Personality and Social Psychology*, January 1982, pp. 178–185.

27. Jeffrey Pfeffer, "The Micropolitics of Organizations," in Marshall W. Meyer et al. (eds.), *Environments and Organizations*, Jossey-Bass, San Francisco, 1978, pp. 29–50. Also see Jeffrey Pfeffer, *Power in Organizations*, Pitman, Marshfield, Mass., 1981.

28. Richard L. Daft, *Organization Theory and Design*, West, St. Paul, Minn., 1983, pp. 384–385, 389. Also see Stephen P. Robbins, *Organization Theory*, 3d ed., Prentice-Hall, Englewood Cliffs, N.J., 1990, pp. 265–270.

29. Carol K. Jacobson, Stefanie A. Lenway, and Peter S. Ring, "The Political Embeddedness of Private Economic Transactions," *Journal of Management Studies*, May 1993, pp. 453–478.

30. Anthony T. Cobb, "Political Diagnosis: Applications in Organizational Development," *Academy of Management Review*, July 1986, p. 490.

31. Alvin Toffler, "Powership—In the Workplace," *Personnel*, June 1990, p. 21.

32. Jeffrey Pfeffer, "Understanding Power in Organizations," *California Management Review*, Winter 1992, p. 29.

33. Walter Nord, "Dreams of Humanization and the Realities of Power," *Academy of Management Review*, July 1978, pp. 675–677.

34. Gerald R. Ferris and K. Michele Kacmar, "Perceptions of Organizational Politics," *Journal of Management*, vol. 18, no. 1, 1992, p. 93.

35. "Labor Letter," *The Wall Street Journal*, Dec. 23, 1986, p. 1.

36. Barbara Gray and Sonny S. Ariss, "Politics and Strategic Change Across Organizational Life Cycles," *Academy of Management Review*, October 1985, p. 707.

37. Patricia M. Fandt and Gerald R. Ferris, "The Management of Information and Impressions: When Employees Behave Opportunistically," *Organizational Behavior and Human Decision Processes*, vol. 45, 1990, p. 140. Also see Martin Gargiulo, "Two-Step Leverage: Managing Constraint in Organizational Politics," *Administrative Science Quarterly*, March 1993, pp. 1–19.

38. Robert H. Miles, *Macro Organizational Behavior*, Goodyear, Santa Monica, Calif., 1980, pp. 182–184.

39. Ibid., p. 182.

40. Jone L. Pearce and Robert A. Page, Jr., "Palace Politics: Resource Allocation in Radically Innovative Firms," *The Journal of High Technology Management Research*, vol. 1, 1990, pp. 193–205.

41. Gary Yukl and Cecilia M. Falbe, "Influence Tactics and Objectives in Upward, Downward, and Lateral Influence Attempts," *Journal of Applied Psychology*, vol. 75, 1990, pp. 132–140.

42. Gary Yukl and J. Bruce Tracey, "Consequences of Influence Tactics Used with Subordinates, Peers, and the Boss," *Journal of Applied Psychology*, August 1992, pp. 525–535.

43. Jeffrey Pfeffer, "Power and Resource Allocation in Organizations," in Barry M. Staw and Gerald R. Salancik (eds.), *New Directions in Organizational Behavior*, St. Clair, Chicago, 1977, pp. 255–260.

44. Andrew Kakabadse, "Organizational Politics," *Management Decision*, vol. 25, no. 1, 1987, pp. 35–36.

45. These strategies are discussed fully in Andrew J. DuBrin, *Human Relations*, Reston, Reston, Va., 1978, pp. 113–122; DuBrin, in turn, abstracted them from the existing literature on power and politics. Also see Andrew J. DuBrin, *Winning Office Politics*, Prentice-Hall, Englewood Cliffs, N.J., 1990, Chap. 8 and 9.

46. Nancy C. Morey and Fred Luthans, "The Use of Dyadic Alliances in Informal Organization: An Ethnographic Study," *Human Relations*, vol. 44, 1991, pp. 597–618.

47. Anthony Jay, *Management and Machiavelli*, Holt, New York, 1967, p. 6.

48. Fred Luthans, Richard M. Hodgetts, and Stuart A. Rosenkrantz, *Real Managers*, Ballinger, Cambridge, Mass., 1988.

49. Gerald F. Cavanagh, Dennis J. Moberg, and Manuel Velasquez, "The Ethics of Organizational Politics," *Academy of Management Review*, July 1981, p. 372.

50. Robert P. Vecchio, *Organizational Behavior*, Dryden, Chicago, 1988, p. 270.

51. Luthans, Hodgetts, and Rosenkrantz, loc. cit.

**REAL CASE:
Fighting Back**

One of the areas in which organizations are finding power to be an extremely important consideration is that of patent protection. When a firm secures a patent, it gains power over the marketplace. However, if this patent cannot be defended against violators, it has little value. A good example of a patent protection battle is that of Fusion Systems, a small, high-tech American firm, and Mitsubishi, the giant Japanese conglomerate.

A few years ago, Fusion developed a core technology that allowed it to manufacture high-intensity ultraviolet lamps powered by 500 to 6000 watts of microwave energy. The company obtained patents in the United States, Europe, and Japan. One of its first big orders came from the Adolph Coors Company for lamp systems to dry the printed decoration on beer cans. Other customers included Hitachi, IBM, 3M, Motorola, Sumitomo, Toshiba, NEC, and Mitsubishi. The last purchased Fusion's lamp system and immediately sent it to the research and development lab to be reverse engineered. Once Mitsubishi had stripped down the product, it began filing patent applications that copied and surrounded Fusion's high-intensity microwave lamp technology. Fusion was unaware of what was going on until it began investigating and found that Mitsubishi had filed nearly 300 patent applications directly related to its own lamp technology. When Fusion tried to settle the matter through direct negotiations, the firm was unsuccessful. In addition, Mitsubishi hired the Stanford Research Institute to study the matter and the Institute concluded that the Japanese company's position was solid. However, the chairman of the applied physics department at Columbia University, who was hired by Fusion, disagreed and—after reviewing the patent materials from both companies—concluded that Mitsubishi had relied heavily on technology developed at Fusion and that Mitsubishi's lamp represented no significant additional breakthrough.

Mitsubishi then offered Fusion a deal: Mitsubishi would not sue Fusion for patent infringement if Fusion would pay Mitsubishi a royalty for the privilege of using "its" patents in Japan. Mitsubishi would then get a royalty-free, worldwide cross license of all of Fusion's technology. Fusion responded by going to the Office of the U.S. Trade Representative and getting help. The company also found a sympathetic ear from the Senate Finance Committee and the House Republican Task Force on Technology Transfer, as well as from the Secretary of Commerce and the American ambassador to Japan. At present the dispute continues, but Mitsubishi is beginning to give ground in the face of political pressure. At the same time, Fusion is continuing to develop innovations in its core field of expertise and remains the leader in both Japanese and worldwide markets. The company believes that as long as it maintains the exclusive rights to this technology, competitors will not be able to erode its market power.

1. What type of power does a patent provide to a company? Is this the same kind of power that people within a firm attempt to gain?
2. What types of political strategies has Mitsubishi used to try to gain power over Fusion? Using the material in Table 12.1, identify and describe three.
3. How has Fusion managed to retaliate successfully? Using the material in Table 12.2, identify and describe three tactics it has employed.

CASE:
Throwing Away
a Golden
Opportunity

Roger Allen was a man on the move. Everyone in the firm felt that someday he would be company president. To listen to his boss, Harry Walden, it was only a matter of time before Roger would be at the helm.

The current president of the firm was a marketing person. She had worked her way up from field salesperson to president by selling both the product and her competency to customers and the company alike. In a manner of speaking, the marketing department was the "well-oiled" road to the top. Roger was the number one salesperson and, according to the grapevine, was due to get Harry Walden's job when the latter retired in two years. However, Roger was not sure that he wanted to be vice president of marketing. Another slot was opening up in foreign sales. Roger knew nothing about selling to Europe, but this was the firm's first venture outside the United States, and he thought he might like to give it a try. He talked to Harry about it, but the vice president tried to discourage him. In fact, Harry seemed to think that Roger was crazy to consider the job at all. "Rog," he said, "that's no place for you. Things are soft and cozy back here. You don't have to prove yourself to anyone. You're number one around here. Just sit tight and you'll be president. Don't go out and make some end runs. Just keep barreling up the middle for four yards on each carry, and you'll score the big touchdown." Roger was not convinced. He thought perhaps it would be wise to discuss the matter with the president herself. This he did. The president was very interested in Roger's ideas about international marketing. "If you really think you'd like to head up this office for us, I'll recommend you for the job."

After thinking the matter over carefully, Roger decided that he would much rather go to Europe and try to help establish a foothold over there than sit back and wait for the stateside opening. He told his decision to Harry. "Harry, I've talked to the president, and she tells me that this new opening in foreign sales is really going to get a big push from the company. It's where the action is. I realize that I could sit back and take it easy for the next couple of years, but I think I'd rather have the international job." Harry again told Roger that he was making a mistake. "You're throwing away a golden opportunity. However, if you want it, I'll support you."

A week later, when the company selected someone else from sales to head the international division, Roger was crushed. The president explained the situation to him in this way: "I thought you wanted the job and I pushed for you. However, the other members of the selection committee voted against me. I can tell you that you certainly didn't sell Harry very strongly on your idea. He led the committee to believe that you were really undecided about the entire matter. In fact, I felt rather foolish telling them how excited you were about the whole thing, only to have Harry say he'd talked to you since that time and you weren't that sure at all. When Harry got done, the committee figured you had changed your mind after talking to me, and they went on to discuss other likely candidates."

1. Who had power in this organization? What type of power did Harry Walden have?
2. Do you think Roger played company politics well? If so, why didn't he get the international sales job?
3. At this point, what would you do if you were Roger? What political strategies could be used?

13 Leadership: Background and Processes

Learning Objectives

- **Define** leadership.
- **Present** the background and classic studies of leadership.
- **Discuss** the established theories of leadership, including the trait, group and exchange, contingency, and path-goal approaches.
- **Identify** other emerging theoretical frameworks for leadership, such as charismatic, transformational, social learning, and substitutes for leadership.

This chapter on leadership theory and the next on leadership application are an appropriate conclusion to the dynamics of organizational behavior. Leadership is the focus and conduit of most of the other areas of organizational behavior. The first half of the chapter deals with the definition and classical background. The last half then presents the major theoretical processes of leadership. Particular attention is devoted to both established and emerging theories of leadership.

WHAT IS LEADERSHIP?

Leadership has probably been written about, formally researched, and informally discussed more than any other single topic. For example, it has even been humorously proposed that leadership succession depends on birthdays. The discovery was made while developing a list of birth dates of famous people. It seems that the heads of some large corporations often shared the same birthday as their successor. For instance, Edward G. Jefferson and his predecessor at Du Pont Corporation, Irving S. Shapiro, share a July 15 birthday. Although astrologers would suggest that companies need leaders with the same "sun signs" that influence their styles, the companies vigorously deny considering the calendar in making leadership appointments.[1]

Despite all this attention given to leadership, there is still considerable controversy. Some organizational behavior theorists do not even recognize leadership. For example, a recent academic article started with this assumption: "The social construct of leadership is viewed as a myth that functions to reinforce existing social beliefs and structures about the necessity of hierarchy and leaders in organizations."[2] Yet, throughout history the difference between success and failure, whether in a war, a business, a protest movement, or a basketball game, has been attributed to leadership. The intensity of today's concern about leadership is pointed out by recent observations such as the following:

> Business in America has lost its way, adrift in a sea of managerial mediocrity, desperately needing leadership to face worldwide economic competition. Once the dominant innovator in technology, marketing, and manufacturing, American business has lost ground to foreign competition.[3]

Regardless of all the attention given to leadership and its recognized importance, it does remain pretty much of a "black box," or unexplainable concept. It is known to exist and to have a tremendous influence on human performance, but its inner workings and specific dimensions cannot be precisely spelled out. Despite these inherent difficulties there are still many attempts over the years to define leadership. Unfortunately, almost everyone who studies or writes about leadership defines it differently. About the only commonality is the role that influence plays in leadership.

In recent years, many theorists and practitioners emphasize the difference between managers and leaders. For example, as Bennis recently noted: "To survive in the twenty-first century, we are going to need a new generation of leaders—leaders, not managers. The distinction is an important one. Leaders conquer the context—the volatile, turbulent, ambiguous surroundings that sometimes seem to conspire against us and will surely suffocate us if we let them—while managers surrender to it."[4] He then goes on to point out his thoughts on some specific differences between leaders and managers, as shown in Table 13.1. Obviously, these are not scientifically derived differences, but it is probably true that an individual can be a leader without being a manager and a manager without being a leader.

Although many specific definitions could be cited, most would depend on the theoretical orientation taken. Besides influence, leadership has been defined in terms of group processes, personality, compliance, particular behaviors, persuasion, power, goal achievement, interaction, role differentiation, initiation of structure, and combi-

TABLE 13.1 Some Characteristics of Managers Versus Leaders in the Twenty-First Century

Manager Characteristics	Leader Characteristics
Administers	Innovates
A copy	An original
Maintains	Develops
Focuses on systems and structure	Focuses on people
Relies on control	Inspires trust
Short-range view	Long-range perspective
Asks how and when	Asks what and why
Eye on the bottom line	Eye on the horizon
Imitates	Originates
Accepts the status quo	Challenges the status quo
Classic good soldier	Own person
Does things right	Does the right thing

Source: Warren G. Bennis, "Managing the Dream: Leadership in the 21st Century," *Journal of Organizational Change Management*, vol. 2, no. 1, 1989, p. 7.

nations of two or more of these.[5] The specific definition is not important. What is important is to interpret leadership in terms of the specific theoretical framework and to realize that leadership, however defined, does make a difference.

THE BACKGROUND AND CLASSIC STUDIES ON LEADERSHIP

Unlike many other topics in the field of organizational behavior, there are a number of studies and a considerable body of knowledge on leadership. A review of the better-known classic studies can help set the stage for the established and emerging theories of leadership.

The Iowa Leadership Studies

A series of pioneering leadership studies conducted in the late 1930s by Ronald Lippitt and Ralph K. White under the general direction of Kurt Lewin at the University of Iowa have had a lasting impact. Lewin is recognized as the father of group dynamics and as an important cognitive theorist. In the initial studies, hobby clubs for ten-year-old boys were formed. Each club was submitted to all three different styles of leadership—authoritarian, democratic, and laissez faire. The authoritarian leader was very directive and allowed no participation. This leader tended to give individual attention when praising and criticizing but tried to be friendly or impersonal rather than openly hostile. The democratic leader encouraged group discussion and decision making. This leader tried to be "objective" in giving praise or criticism and to be one of the group in spirit. The laissez faire leader gave complete freedom to the group; this leader essentially provided no leadership.

Unfortunately, the effects that styles of leadership had on productivity were not directly examined. The experiments were designed primarily to examine patterns of aggressive behavior. However, an important by-product was the insight that was gained into the productive behavior of a group. For example, the researchers found that the boys subjected to the autocratic leaders reacted in one of two ways: either aggressively or apathetically. Both the aggressive and apathetic behaviors were deemed to be reactions to the frustration caused by the autocratic leader. The researchers also pointed out that the apathetic groups exhibited outbursts of aggression when the autocratic leader left the room or when a transition was made to a freer leadership atmosphere. The laissez faire leadership climate actually produced the greatest number of aggressive acts from the group. The democratically led group fell between the one extremely aggressive group and the four apathetic groups under the autocratic leaders.

Sweeping generalizations on the basis of the Lippitt and White Studies are dangerous. Preadolescent boys making masks and carving soap are a long way from adults working in a complex, formal organization. Furthermore, from a viewpoint of modern behavioral science research methodology, many of the variables were not controlled. Nevertheless, these leadership studies have important historical significance. They were the pioneering attempts to determine, experimentally, what effects styles of leadership have on a group. Like the Hawthorne studies, the Iowa studies are too often automatically discounted or at least deemphasized because they were experimentally crude. The values of the studies were that they were the first to analyze leadership from the standpoint of scientific methodology, and, more important, they showed that different styles of leadership can produce different, complex reactions from the same or similar groups.

The Ohio State Leadership Studies

In 1945, the Bureau of Business Research at Ohio State University initiated a series of studies on leadership. An interdisciplinary team of researchers from psychology, sociology, and economics developed and used the Leader Behavior Description Questionnaire (LBDQ) to analyze leadership in numerous types of groups and situations. Studies were made of Air Force commanders and members of bomber crews; officers, noncommissioned personnel, and civilian administrators in the Navy Department; manufacturing supervisors; executives of regional cooperatives; college administrators; teachers, principals, and school superintendents; and leaders of various student and civilian groups.

The Ohio State studies started with the premise that no satisfactory definition of leadership existed. They also recognized that previous work had too often assumed that *leadership* was synonymous with *good leadership*. The Ohio State group was determined to study leadership, regardless of definition or of whether it was effective or ineffective.

In the first step, the LBDQ was administered in a wide variety of situations. In order to examine how the leader was described, the answers to the questionnaire were then subjected to factor analysis. The outcome was amazingly consistent. The same two dimensions of leadership continually emerged from the questionnaire data. The were *consideration* and *initiating structure*. These two factors were found in a wide variety of studies encompassing many kinds of leadership positions and contexts. The researchers carefully emphasize that the studies show only *how* leaders carry out their leadership function. Initiating structure and consideration are very similar to the time-honored military commander's functions of mission and concern with the welfare of the troops. In simple terms, the Ohio State factors are task or goal orientation (initiating structure) and recognition of individual needs and relationships (consideration). The two dimensions are separate and distinct from each other.

The Ohio State studies certainly have value for the study of leadership. They were the first to point out and emphasize the importance of *both* task and human dimensions in assessing leadership. This two-dimensional approach lessened the gap between the strict task orientation of the scientific management movement and the human relations emphasis, which had been popular up to that time. However, on the other side of the coin, the rush for empirical data on leadership led to a great dependence on questionnaires in the Ohio State studies to generate data about leadership behaviors, and this may not have been justified. For example, Schriesheim and Kerr concluded after a review of the existing literature that "the Ohio State scales cannot be considered sufficiently valid to warrant their continued uncritical usage in leadership research."[6] In addition to the validity question is the almost unchallenged belief that these indirect questionnaire methods are in fact measuring leadership *behaviors* instead of simply measuring the questionnaire respondent's behavior and/ or perceptions of, and attitudes toward, leadership. A multiple measures approach, especially observation techniques, seems needed and has been used in recent years.

The Early Michigan Leadership Studies

At about the same time that the Ohio State studies were being conducted, a group of researchers from the Survey Research Center at the University of Michigan began their studies of leadership. In the original study at the Prudential Insurance Company, twelve high-low productivity pairs were selected for examination. Each pair represented a high-producing section and a low-producing section, with other variables, such as type of work, conditions, and methods, being the same in each pair. Nondirective interviews were conducted with the 24 section supervisors and 419 clerical workers. Results showed that supervisors of high-producing sections were significantly more likely to be general rather than close in their supervisory styles and be employee-centered (have a genuine concern for their people). The low-producing section supervisors had essentially opposite characteristics and techniques. They were found to be close, production-centered supervisors. Another important, but sometimes overlooked, finding was that employee satisfaction was *not* directly related to productivity.

The general, employee-centered supervisor, described above, became the standard-bearer for the traditional human relations approach to leadership. The results of the Prudential studies were always cited when human relations advocates were challenged to prove their theories. The studies have been followed up with hundreds of similar studies in a wide variety of industrial, hospital, governmental, and other organizations. Thousands of employees, performing unskilled to highly professional and scientific tasks, have been analyzed. Rensis Likert, the one-time director of the Institute for Social Research of the University of Michigan, presented the results of the years of similar research in his books and became best known for his "System 4" leadership style, which is covered in the next chapter.

ESTABLISHED THEORIES OF LEADERSHIP

The Iowa, Ohio State, and Michigan studies are three of the historically most important leadership studies for the study of organizational behavior. Unfortunately, they are still heavily depended upon, and leadership research has not surged ahead from this relatively auspicious beginning. Before analyzing the current status of leadership research, it is important to look at the theoretical development that has occurred through the years.

There are several distinct theoretical bases for leadership. At first, leaders were felt to be born, not made. This so-called "great person" theory of leadership implied that some individuals are born with certain traits that allow them to emerge out of any situation or period of history to become leaders. This evolved into what is now known as the *trait theory* of leadership. The trait approach is concerned mainly with identifying the personality traits of the leader. Dissatisfied with this approach, and stimulated by research such as the Ohio State studies, researchers switched their emphasis from the individual leader to the group being led. In the group approach, leadership is viewed more in terms of the leader's behavior and how such behavior affects and is affected by the group of followers.

In addition to the leader and the group, the situation began to receive increased attention in leadership theory. The situational approach was initially called *Zeitgeist* (a German word meaning "spirit of the time"); the leader is viewed as a product of the times and the situation. The person with the particular qualities or traits that a situation requires will emerge as the leader. The International Application Example: Yeltsin Speaks illustrates a current example of such a leader. This view has much historical support as a theoretical basis for leadership and serves as the basis for situational—and now, contingency—theories of leadership. Fiedler's contingency theory, which suggests that leadership styles must fit or match the situation in order to be effective, is the best known. A more recent situational, or contingency, theory takes some of the expectancy concepts of motivation that are discussed in Chapter 6 and applies them to leadership and situations. Called the path-goal theory of leadership, it is an attempt to synthesize motivational and leadership concepts. The following sections examine these established trait, group, contingency, and path-goal theories of leadership.

International Application Example

Yeltsin Speaks

Mikhail Gorbachev was the best-known leader in the crumbling Soviet Union, but Boris Yeltsin emerged as the most effective. An early ally of Gorbachev, Yeltsin resigned from the Soviet Politburo in 1987 and broke with the Communist party in 1989. At the time, it appeared that any hopes he had of playing a role in Soviet history were at an end. However, if nothing else, Yeltsin was an effective leader. Once in opposition, he quickly earned a reputation as a combative advocate of a faster road to democracy. For the next three years, he cleverly baited Gorbachev for failing to act decisively. As a result, he became identified as a man with both vision and boldness. In May 1990, over the opposition of Gorbachev, he was elected chairman of the Russian Federation's 252-member Supreme Soviet after a campaign in which he pledged to hold Russian law "juridically higher" than Soviet law—a statement that, in essence, amounted to a declaration of independence for Russia.

Once in power, Yeltsin wasted no time setting up a tough and independent-minded government. He attracted some of the best young, talented technocrats from the old Soviet system. One Western diplomat who was familiar with the Yeltsin team noted: "These guys look like the student council at Berkeley in the Sixties—young, tough, and radical. This is the kind of government perestroika needs." The team was made up of such members as market-oriented economist Yegor Gaidar and Boris Fyodorov, a 32-year-old finance minister, who was an expert on international banking. Another was Grigori Yavlinsky, 38, an economist and deputy prime minister who echoed the feelings of many Russians when he said: "Our goal is to get out of the bottomless pit we find ourselves in. In the entire history of human existence, no one has thought of anything more efficient than the free market. By mastering it, we will free ourselves from the abyss and gain the capacity to draw on the achievements of world civilization."

Since taking over in Russia, Yeltsin has survived two major crises. He came out victorious not only in the coup attempt in December of 1991 but also in the hardliners' resistance in October of 1993. However, as of 1994 the situation looks quite bleak for Yeltsin and Russia. The economy is in shambles and the people are upset. Many of Yeltsin's original team of economic reformers, such as Yegor Gaidar and Boris Fyodorov, have resigned in frustration over the lack of progress. Only time will tell what the eventual outcome will be for Yeltsin and Russia. Whatever lies ahead, there is little argument that Yeltsin did demonstrate the leadership necessary for the situation in surviving the coup attempt and in putting down the hardliners. Whether he has the leadership to pull Russia out of the economic doldrums is yet to be seen.

Trait Theories of Leadership

The scientific analysis of leadership started off by concentrating on leaders themselves. The vital question that this theoretical approach attempted to answer was, what characteristics or traits make a person a leader? The earliest trait theories, which can be traced back to the ancient Greeks and Romans, concluded that leaders are born, not made. The "great person" theory of leadership said that individuals are born either with or without the necessary traits for leadership. Famous figures in history—for example, Napoleon—were said to have had the "natural" leadership abilities to rise out of any situation and become great leaders.

Eventually, the "great person" theory gave way to a more realistic trait approach to leadership. Under the influence of the behavioristic school of psychological thought, researchers accepted the fact that leadership traits are not completely inborn but can also be acquired through learning and experience. Attention turned to the search for universal traits possessed by leaders. The results of this voluminous research effort were generally very disappointing. Only intelligence seemed to hold up with any degree of consistency. When these findings are combined with those of studies on physical traits, the conclusion seems to be that leaders are bigger and brighter than those being led, but not too much so.

When the trait approach is applied to organizational leadership, the result is even cloudier. One of the biggest problems is that all managers think they know what the qualities of a successful leader are. Obviously, almost any adjective can be used to describe a successful leader. Recognizing these semantic limitations and realizing that there is no cause-and-effect relationship between observed traits and successful leadership, there is some evidence to suggest that empathy or interpersonal sensitivity and self-confidence are desirable leadership traits.[7]

In general, research findings do not agree on which traits are generally found in leaders or even on which ones are more important than others. Similar to the trait theories of personality, the trait approach to leadership has provided some descriptive insight but has little analytical or predictive value. The trait approach is still alive, but now the emphasis has shifted away from personality traits and toward job-related skills. Katz has identified the technical, conceptual, and human skills needed for effective management.[8] Yukl includes skills such as creativity, organization, persuasiveness, diplomacy and tactfulness, knowledge of the task, and the ability to speak well.[9] These skills have become very important in the application of organizational behavior and are given specific attention in the next chapter.

Group and Exchange Theories of Leadership

The group theories of leadership have their roots in social psychology. Classic exchange theory, in particular, serves as an important basis for this approach. Discussed in Chapters 6 and 9, this means simply that the leader provides more benefits/rewards than burdens/costs for followers. There must be a positive exchange between the leaders and followers in order for group goals to be accomplished. Chester Barnard applied such an analysis to managers and subordinates in an organizational setting more than a half-century ago. More recently, this social exchange view of leadership has been summarized as follows:

> Exchange theories propose that group members make contributions at a cost to themselves and receive benefits at a cost to the group or other members. Interaction continues because members find the social exchange mutually rewarding.[10]

The above quotation emphasizes that leadership is an exchange process between the leader and followers. Social psychological research can be used to support this notion of exchange. In addition, the original Ohio State studies and follow-up studies through the years, especially the dimension of giving consideration to followers, give support to the group perspective of leadership.

Followers' Impact on Leaders. A few important research studies indicate that followers/subordinates may actually affect leaders as much as leaders affect followers/subordinates. For example, one study found that when subordinates were not performing very well, the leaders tended to emphasize initiating structure, but when subordinates were doing a good job, leaders increased their emphasis on consideration.[11] In a laboratory study it was found that group productivity had a greater impact on leadership style than leadership style had on group productivity,[12] and in another study it was found that in newly formed groups, leaders may adjust their supportive behavior in response to the level of group cohesion and arousal already present.[13] In other words, such studies seem to indicate that subordinates affect leaders and their behaviors as much as leaders and their behaviors affect subordinates. Some practicing managers, such as the vice president of Saga Corporation, feel that subordinates lack followership skills, and there is growing evidence that the newer generation of managers is increasingly reluctant to accept a followership role.[14] Moreover, it is probably not wise to ignore followership. Most managers feel that subordinates have an obligation to follow and support their leader. As the CEO of Commerce Union Corporation noted: "Part of a subordinate's responsibility is to make the boss look good."[15]

The Vertical Dyad Linkage Model. Relevant to the exchange view of leadership is the vertical dyad linkage (VDL) approach,[16] more recently called leader-member exchange (LMX).[17] The VDL or LMX theory says that leaders treat individual subordinates differently. In particular, leaders and subordinates develop dyadic (two-person) relationships which affect the behavior of both leaders and subordinates. For example, subordinates who are committed and who expend a lot of effort for the unit are rewarded with more of the leader's positional resources (for example, information, confidence, and concern) than those who do not display these behaviors.

Over time, the leader will develop an "in-group" of subordinates and an "out-group" of subordinates and treat them accordingly. Thus, for the same leader, research has shown that in-group subordinates report fewer difficulties in dealing with the leader and perceive the leader as being more responsive to their needs than out-group subordinates do.[18] Also, leaders spend more time "leading" members of the in-group (that is, they do not depend on formal authority to influence them), and they tend to "supervise" those in the out-group (that is, they depend on formal roles and authority to influence them).[19] Finally, there is evidence that subordinates in the in-group (those who report a high-quality relationship with their leader) assume greater job responsibility, contribute more to their units, and are rated as higher performers than those reporting a low-quality relationship.[20]

This exchange theory has been around for some time now, and although it is not without criticism,[21] in general, the research continues to be relatively supportive. However, at present, VDL or LMX seems to be more descriptive of the typical process of role making by leaders, rather than prescribing the pattern of downward exchange relations optimal for leadership effectiveness.[22] Research is also using more sophisticated methodologies[23] and suggests that task characteristics moderate the LMX-performance relationship.[24] The identification of leader-follower relationships which are best suited to specific environmental contingencies is still needed.[25]

Contingency Theory of Leadership

After the trait approach proved to fall short of being an adequate overall theory of leadership, attention turned to the situational aspects of leadership. Social psychologists began the search for situational variables that affect leadership roles, skills, behavior, and followers' performance and satisfaction. Numerous situational variables were identified, but no overall theory pulled it all together until Fred Fiedler proposed a widely recognized situation-based, or contingency, theory for leadership effectiveness.

Fiedler's Contingency Model of Leadership Effectiveness. To test the hypothesis he had formulated from previous research findings, Fiedler developed what he called a *contingency model of leadership effectiveness*. This model contained the relationship between leadership style and the favorableness of the situation. Situational favorableness was described by Fiedler in terms of three empirically derived dimensions:

1. The *leader-member relationship*, which is the most critical variable in determining the situation's favorableness
2. The *degree of task structure*, which is the second most important input into the favorableness of the situation
3. The *leader's position power* obtained through formal authority, which is the third most critical dimension of the situation[26]

Situations are favorable to the leader if all three of the above dimensions are high. In other words, if the leader is generally accepted by followers (high first dimension), if the task is very structured and everything is "spelled out" (high second dimension), and if a great deal of authority and power is formally attributed to the leader's position (high third dimension), the situation is favorable. If the opposite exists (if the three dimensions are low), the situation will be very unfavorable for the leader. Fiedler was convinced that the favorableness of the situation in combination with the leadership style determines effectiveness.

Through the analysis of research findings, Fiedler was able to discover that under very favorable *and* very unfavorable situations, the task-directed, or hard-nosed, type of leader was most effective. However, when the situation was only moderately favorable or unfavorable (the intermediate range of favorableness), the human relations, or lenient, type of leader was most effective. Figure 13.1 summarizes this relationship between leadership style and the favorableness of the situation.

Why is the task-directed leader successful in very favorable situations? Fiedler offered the following explanation:

> In the very favorable conditions in which the leader has power, informal backing, and a relatively well-structured task, the group is ready to be directed, and the group expects to be told what to do. Consider the captain of an airliner in its final landing approach. We would hardly want him to turn to his crew for a discussion on how to land.[27]

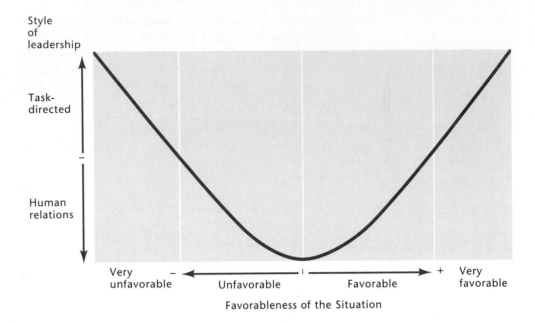

FIGURE 13.1
Fiedler's contingency model of leadership.

As an example of why the task-oriented leader is successful in a highly unfavorable situation, Fiedler cited

> . . . the disliked chairman of a volunteer committee which is asked to plan the office picnic on a beautiful Sunday. If the leader asks too many questions about what the group ought to do or how he should proceed, he is likely to be told that "we ought to go home."[28]

The leader who makes a wrong decision in this highly unfavorable type of situation is probably better off than the leader who makes no decision at all.

Figure 13.1 shows that the human relations leader is effective in the intermediate range of favorableness. An example of such situations is the typical committee or unit. In these situations, the leader may not be wholly accepted by the other members of the group, the task may not be completely structured, and some authority and power may be granted to the leader. Under such a relatively unfavorable, but not extremely unfavorable, situation, the model predicts that a human relations, lenient type of leader will be most effective. The same would be true of a moderately favorable situation.

Research Support for the Contingency Model. As is true of any widely publicized theoretical development, Fiedler's model has stimulated a great deal of research. Not surprisingly, the results are mixed and a controversy has been generated. Fiedler and in particular his students have provided almost all the support for the model over the years. For example, to defend the validity of his theory, he cites thirty studies in a wide variety of teams and organizations (Navy teams, chemical research teams, shop departments, supermarkets, heavy machinery plant departments, engineering groups, hospital wards, public health teams, and others) and concludes that "the theory is highly predictive and that the relations obtained in the validation studies are almost identical to those obtained in the original studies."[29] With one exception, which Fiedler explains away, he maintains that the model correctly predicted the correlations that should exist between the leader's style and performance in relation to the identified favorableness of the situation. As predicted, his studies show that in very unfavorable and very favorable situations, the task-oriented leader performs best. In a moderately favorable and moderately unfavorable situation, the human relations–oriented leader is more effective. Although Fiedler recognizes that there is increasing criticism of his conclusions, he still maintains that "methodologically sound validation studies have on the whole provided substantial support for the theory,"[30] and some comprehensive reviews support this contention,[31] but others do not.

Critical Analysis of the Contingency Model. Although there is probably not as much criticism of Fiedler's work as there is, for example, of Herzberg's motivation theory, a growing number of leadership researchers do not wholly agree with Fiedler's interpretations or conclusions. For example, Graen and his colleagues initially raised some criticisms of the procedures and statistical analysis of the studies used to support the validity of the model.[32] Schriesheim and his colleagues have been especially critical of the reliability and validity of Fiedler's measurement instrument.[33] Fiedler[34] and his colleagues[35] have answered these criticisms to their satisfaction, but most summaries remain critical. For example, Yukl recently concluded—after reviewing the research—that the model has serious conceptual deficiencies limiting its utility for explaining leadership effectiveness, deficiencies such as its narrow focus on a single leader trait, ambiguity about what is really measured, and the absence of explanatory processes.[36]

Applications of Fiedler's Work. In addition to the conceptual and methodological questions, there is also the criticism of Fiedler's extension of the model to the actual practice of human resources management. On the basis of the model, Fiedler suggests that management would be better off engineering positions so that the requirements fit the leader instead of using the more traditional technique of selecting and developing leaders to fit into existing jobs.[37] With this in mind, Fiedler and his colleagues then developed a self-programmed training manual (called *Leader Match*), which includes a series of questionnaires that identify the person's leadership style and the situational dimensions of his or her job (task structure, leader-member relations, and position power).[38] Then the trainee is given a series of short problems with several alternative solutions.

Under Fiedler's leadership effectiveness training, the trainee is taught (on the basis of feedback compatible with the contingency model) ways to diagnose the situation so as to change it and optimize the leader style–leader situation match. Some of the suggested ways to modify leader-member relations are spending more (or less) informal time with subordinates and suggesting or effecting transfers of particular subordinates into or out of the unit. To decrease task structure, the leader may ask for new or unusual problems; to increase task structure, the leader may ask for more instructions and prepare a detailed plan. To raise position power, the leader could become an expert on the job, or to lower position power, the leader could call on subordinates to participate in planning and decision making.[39]

Most of the support for this Leader Match training has come from Fiedler and his students/colleagues. After a review of five studies conducted in civilian organizations and seven conducted in military settings, Fiedler concluded that all twelve studies yielded statistically significant results supporting Leader Match training.[40] He claims that these studies also support "the contested point that leaders are able to modify their leadership situations to a degree sufficient to increase their effectiveness."[41] Other, more recent research is critical of Leader Match as not being very consistent with what the contingency model should predict.[42]

Fiedler's Contingency Theory in Perspective. Overall, there seems little question that Fiedler has provided one of the major breakthroughs for leadership theory and practice. Although much of the criticism is justified, there are several reasons Fiedler's model has made a contribution:

1. It was the first highly visible leadership theory to present the contingency approach.
2. It emphasized the importance of both the situation and the leader's characteristics in determining leader effectiveness.
3. It stimulated a great deal of research, including tests of its predictions and attempts to improve on the model, and inspired the formulation of alternative contingency theories.
4. It led to the development of the Leader Match program that applies the model to actual leadership situations.[43]

At the very least, Fiedler has done and continues to do considerable empirical research, and in recent years he has proposed a new contingency theory.[44]

In the cognitive resource theory (CRT), Fiedler identifies the situations under which a leader's cognitive resources, such as intelligence, experience, and technical expertise, relate to group and organizational performance. Based on Fiedler and his colleagues' research, CRT predicts:

1. More intelligent leaders develop better plans, decisions, and action strategies than less intelligent leaders.
2. Intelligence contributes more strongly to group performance if the leader is directive and the group members are motivated and supportive of the leader.
3. Interpersonal stress distracts the leader from the task and the leader's intelligence will contribute more highly if the leader has relatively stress-free relationships with superiors and subordinates.[45]

As is the case with his original contingency model, CRT has been criticized,[46] but also will generate more research and, one hopes, make meaningful linkages to practice.

Path-Goal Leadership Theory

The other widely recognized theoretical development from a contingency approach is the path-goal theory derived from the expectancy framework of motivation theory. Although Georgopoulos and his colleagues at the University of Michigan's Institute for Social Research used path-goal concepts and terminology many years ago for analyzing the impact of leadership on performance, the modern development is usually attributed to Martin Evans and Robert House, who wrote separate papers on the subject.[47] In essence, the path-goal theory attempts to explain the impact that leader behavior has on subordinate motivation, satisfaction, and performance. The

House version of the theory incorporates four major types, or styles, of leadership.[48] Briefly summarized, these are:

1. *Directive leadership.* This style is similar to that of the Lippitt and White authoritarian leader. Subordinates know exactly what is expected of them, and the leader gives specific directions. There is no participation by subordinates.
2. *Supportive leadership.* The leader is friendly and approachable and shows a genuine concern for subordinates.
3. *Participative leadership.* The leader asks for and uses suggestions from subordinates but still makes the decisions.
4. *Achievement-oriented leadership.* The leader sets challenging goals for subordinates and shows confidence that they will attain these goals and perform well.

This path-goal theory—and here is how it differs in one respect from Fiedler's contingency model—suggests that these various styles can be and actually are used by the same leader in different situations.[49] Two of the situational factors that have been identified are the personal characteristics of subordinates and the environmental pressures and demands facing subordinates. With respect to the first situational factor, the theory asserts:

> Leader behavior will be acceptable to subordinates to the extent that the subordinates see such behavior as either an immediate source of satisfaction or as instrumental to future satisfaction.[50]

And with respect to the second situational factor, the theory states:

> Leader behavior will be motivational (e.g., will increase subordinate effort) to the extent that (1) it makes satisfaction of subordinate needs contingent on effective performance, and (2) it complements the environment of subordinates by providing the coaching, guidance, support, and rewards which are necessary for effective performance and which may otherwise be lacking in subordinates or in their environment.[51]

Using one of the four styles contingent upon the situational factors as outlined above, the leader attempts to influence subordinates' perceptions and motivate them, which in turn leads to their role clarity, goal expectancies, satisfaction, and performance. This is specifically accomplished by the leader as follows:

1. Recognizing and/or arousing subordinates' needs for outcomes over which the leader has some control
2. Increasing personal payoffs to subordinates for work-goal attainment
3. Making the path to those payoffs easier to travel by coaching and direction
4. Helping subordinates clarify expectancies
5. Reducing frustrating barriers
6. Increasing the opportunities for personal satisfaction contingent on effective performance[52]

In other words, by doing the above, the leader attempts to make the path to subordinates' goals as smooth as possible. But to accomplish this path-goal facilitation, the leader must use the appropriate style contingent on the situational variables present. Figure 13.2 summarizes this path-goal approach.

As is true of the expectancy theory of motivation, there has been a surge of research on the path-goal theory of leadership. So far, most of the research has

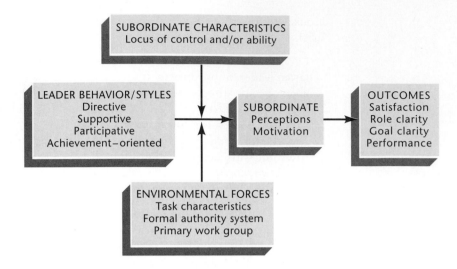

FIGURE 13.2
A summary of path-goal relationships.

concentrated on only parts of the theory rather than on the entire theory. For example, a sampling of the research findings indicates the following:

1. Studies of seven organizations have found that *leader directiveness is* (a) positively related to satisfactions and expectancies of subordinates engaged in ambiguous tasks and (b) negatively related to satisfactions and expectancies of subordinates engaged in clear tasks.
2. Studies involving ten different samples of employees found that *supportive leadership* will have its most positive effect on satisfaction for subordinates who work on stressful, frustrating, or dissatisfying tasks.
3. In a major study in an industrial manufacturing organization, it was found that in nonrepetitive, ego-involving tasks, employees were more satisfied under *participative leaders* than under nonparticipative leaders.
4. In three separate organizations it was found that for subordinates performing ambiguous, nonrepetitive tasks, the higher the *achievement orientation of the leader*, the more subordinates were confident that their efforts would pay off in effective performance.[53]

The more recent reviews of the research on the path-goal theory are not as supportive as the above. For example, Schriesheim and DeNisi note that only a couple of hypotheses have really been drawn from the theory, which means that it may be incapable of generating meaningful predictions.[54] Another note of pessimism offered by these reviewers is that only one of the two hypotheses has received consistent empirical support. Research has generally substantiated the hypothesis that the higher the task structure (repetitiveness) of the jobs performed by subordinates, the higher the relationship between supportive leader behavior/style and subordinate satisfaction. On the other hand, the second hypothesis—that the higher the task structure, the lower the correlation between instrumental (directive) leader behavior and subordinate satisfaction—has received, at best, mixed research support. Schriesheim and DeNisi then report results of their own research, which indicates that the path-goal theory is capable of producing meaningful and testable predictions beyond the two task structure hypotheses.[55] Also, a recent comprehensive review of forty-eight studies demonstrated that the mixed results of the individual studies, when cumulated, were transformed into support for continued testing of path-goal theory.[56]

Overall, the path-goal theory, like the other established theories presented in this chapter, seems to need more research, but it certainly warrants further attention in the coming years. One recent analysis concluded that leaders will be perceived most favorably by their subordinates, and succeed in exerting most influence over them, when they behave in ways that closely match (1) the needs and values of subordinates and (2) the requirements of a specific work situation.[57] In other words, the path-goal theory, like the expectancy theory in work motivation, may help better explain the complexities of the leadership process.

EMERGING THEORETICAL FRAMEWORKS FOR LEADERSHIP

Despite a relative degree of acceptance of the contingency and path-goal theories of leadership and the great (at least relative to other areas in organizational behavior) amount of research that has been conducted, few would disagree today that leadership is still in trouble. Leadership is currently being attacked on all fronts—in terms of theories relating to it, research methods for studying it, and applications.[58] For example, John Miner was very critical of leadership theory and then proposed that it be dropped altogether,[59] and Schriesheim and Kerr are quite critical of the traditional methods used in leadership research.[60] The time has come for alternative theories, research methods, and applications for leadership studies.

Besides the established trait, group, contingency, and path-goal theories of leadership, a number of other theories have emerged in recent years. These include the charismatic, transformational, social learning, and substitutes theories of leadership. An overview of each of these provides better understanding of the complex leadership process.

Charismatic Leadership Theories

Charismatic leadership is a throwback to the old conception of leaders as being those who "by the force of their personal abilities are capable of having profound and extraordinary effects on followers."[61] Although the charismatic concept, or charisma, goes as far back as the ancient Greeks and is cited in the Bible, its modern development is attributed to the work of Robert House.[62] On the basis of the analysis of political and religious leaders, House suggests that charismatic leaders are characterized by self-confidence and confidence in subordinates, high expectations for subordinates, ideological vision, and the use of personal example. Followers of charismatic leaders identify with the leader and the mission of the leader, exhibit extreme loyalty to and confidence in the leader, emulate the leader's values and behavior, and derive self-esteem from their relationship with the leader.[63] More recently, Bass extended the profile of charismatic leaders by including business leaders such as Lee Iacocca or women who have broken through the glass ceiling to be top-level executives, discussed in the accompanying Managing Diversity in Action: Breaking the Glass Ceiling with Charisma. In particular, he notes that

**Managing
Diversity
in Action**

Breaking the Glass Ceiling with Charisma

If charismatic leaders have technical expertise, and are able to foster attitudinal, behavioral, and emotional changes in their followers, then Mary Kay Ash is certainly a charismatic leader. Since founding her firm, Mary Kay Cosmetics, in 1963, she has served as a role model for thousands of employees, who both admire and emulate her leadership style. However, she is not alone. A few other businesses have top-level women executives who have been able to break through the glass ceiling largely on the basis of their charismatic leadership.

A good example is Jill Barad, president and chief executive officer of Mattel. When Barad took over the reins in 1988, sales were stagnant. In five years she doubled revenues. Her strategy involves encouraging her marketing and research staffs to develop new twists for established products. She also pitches in and helps out by spending almost one-third of her time traveling and talking to retailers and kids about what they want to see the company offer. This direct contact with customers puts her in an ideal position to discuss strategy changes with the marketing and production staffers and jointly work with them in implementing product ideas. As she put it: "You don't develop the kinds of brands we've developed without a very coordinated effort. I'm into team building."

Another good example is provided by Judy Lewent, chief financial officer at Merck, the pharmaceutical giant. When she took over her position in 1988 as an executive in the financial group, her objective was to make it economically feasible for the firm to maintain its long-standing commitment to research and development. She was convinced that R&D was needed for the creation of blockbuster drugs. In pursuing her objectives, Lewent has put Merck into a number of joint ventures with firms such as Du Pont, Johnson & Johnson, and Astra, a Swedish pharmaceutical company. At the same time she has worked hard to create a climate of innovation for the 500 employees in her group. Recently, for example, she implemented a new program that emphasizes inventive ways to finance and reward staffers who consistently come up with creative solutions to problems. As she puts it: "I saw right away that creativity was the key to success in the financial area here."

Still another example of a successful women business leader is Ruth Owades, founder and president of Calyx and Corolla, which delivers fresh, often exotic, flowers overnight directly from growers in Florida and Hawaii. Owades's core strategy is to establish strong links between her firm and the growers and delivery service people. In achieving this success and maintaining the company's advantage over the competition, Owades relies heavily on her people to help identify and solve problems. Through the use of action-oriented meetings, where all staff personnel have a chance to give their input, the staffers are able to participate directly in running the business. This approach has worked so well that there has been no management turnover in recent years. The personnel enjoy working at Calyx and Corolla because they feel that they are a part of a winning team.

charismatic leaders have superior debating and persuasive skills and technical expertise, and foster attitudinal, behavioral, and emotional changes in their followers.[64]

Because of the effects that charismatic leaders have on followers, the theory predicts that charismatic leaders will produce in followers performance beyond expectations as well as strong commitment to the leader and his or her mission. House and his colleagues provide beginning support for charismatic theory,[65] but as with the other leadership theories, more research is needed. Also, extensions of the theory are being proposed. For example, Conger and Kanungo treat charisma as an attributional phenomenon and propose that it varies with the situation.[66] Leader traits that foster charismatic attributions include self-confidence, impression-management skills, social sensitivity, and empathy. Situations that promote charismatic leadership include a crisis requiring dramatic change, or followers who are very dissatisfied with the status quo.

Included in the extensions of charismatic leadership is also the recognition of a dark side.[67] Charismatic leaders tend to be portrayed as wonderful heroes, but as Table 13.2 shows, there can also be unethical characteristics associated with charismatic leaders. With regard to meeting the challenge of being ethical, it has been noted that charismatic leaders

> . . . deserve this label only if they create transformations in their organizations so that members are motivated to follow them and to seek organization objectives not simply because they are ordered to do so, and not merely because they calculate that such compliance is in their self-interest, but because they voluntarily identify with the organization, its standards of conduct and willingly seek to fulfill its purpose.[68]

This transformation idea is also picked up by Bass, who suggests that charismatic leadership is really just a component of the broader-based transformational leadership, covered next.[69]

Transformational Leadership Theory

Identifying charismatic characteristics of leaders can become very important as organizations transform traditional ways of being led to meet the challenge of dramatic change. It is this transformation process that has led to the transformational theory.

Burns identified two types of political leadership: transactional and transformational.[70] The more traditional transactional leadership involves an exchange relationship between leaders and followers, but transformational leadership is based more on leaders' shifting the values, beliefs, and needs of their followers. Table 13.3 summarizes the characteristics and approaches of transactional versus transformational leaders. On the basis of his research findings, Bass concludes that in many instances (such as relying on passive management by exception), transactional leadership is a prescription for mediocrity and that transformational leadership leads to superior performance in organizations facing demands for renewal and change. He

TABLE 13.2 Ethical and Unethical Characteristics of Charismatic Leaders

Ethical Charismatic Leader	Unethical Charismatic Leader
■ Uses power to serve others	■ Uses power only for personal gain or impact
■ Aligns vision with followers' needs and aspirations	■ Promotes own personal vision
■ Considers and learns from criticism	■ Censures critical or opposing views
■ Stimulates followers to think independently and to question the leader's view	■ Demands own decisions be accepted without question
■ Open, two-way communication	■ One-way communication
■ Coaches, develops, and supports followers; shares recognition with others	■ Insensitive to followers' needs
■ Relies on internal moral standards to satisfy organizational and societal interests	■ Relies on convenient, external moral standards to satisfy self-interests

Source: Jane M. Howell and Bruce J. Avolio, "The Ethics of Charismatic Leadership: Submission or Liberation?" *Academy of Management Executive*, May 1992, p. 45. Used with permission.

TABLE 13.3 Characteristics and Approaches of Transactional Versus Transformational Leaders

Transactional Leaders

1. *Contingent reward:* Contracts exchange of rewards for effort, promises rewards for good performance, recognizes accomplishments.
2. *Management by exception* (active): Watches and searches for deviations from rules and standards, takes corrective action.
3. *Management by exception* (passive): Intervenes only if standards are not met.
4. *Laissez faire:* Abdicates responsibilities, avoids making decisions.

Transformational Leaders

1. *Charisma:* Provides vision and sense of mission, instills pride, gains respect and trust.
2. *Inspiration:* Communicates high expectations, uses symbols to focus efforts, expresses important purposes in simple ways.
3. *Intellectual stimulation:* Promotes intelligence, rationality, and careful problem solving.
4. *Individual consideration:* Gives personal attention, treats each employee individually, coaches, advises.

Source: Bernard M. Bass, "From Transactional to Transformational Leadership: Learning to Share the Vision," *Organizational Dynamics*, Winter 1990, p. 22. Used with permission.

suggests that fostering transformational leadership through policies of recruitment, selection, promotion, training, and development will pay off in the health, well-being, and effective performance of today's organizations.[71]

Most of the research on transformational leadership to date has relied on Bass's questionnaire, which has received some criticism,[72] or qualitative research that simply describes leaders through interviews. An example of the latter were the interviews with top executives of major companies conducted by Tichy and Devanna. They found that effective transformational leaders share the following characteristics:

1. They identify themselves as change agents.
2. They are courageous.
3. They believe in people.
4. They are value-driven.
5. They are lifelong learners.
6. They have the ability to deal with complexity, ambiguity, and uncertainty.
7. They are visionaries.[73]

Only recently has empirical research begun to support these characteristics. For example, field studies have shown that transformational leaders more frequently employ legitimating tactics and engender higher levels of identification and internalization[74] (see Chapter 12) and have better performance.[75] In addition, other theories are also starting to gain attention to help explain the complex process of leadership.

A Social Learning Approach

Just as social learning theory was shown in Chapter 1 to provide the basis for an overall conceptual framework for organizational behavior,[76] social learning theory can provide a model for the continuous, reciprocal interaction between the leader (including his or her cognitions), the environment (including subordinates/followers and macro variables), and the behavior itself.[77] These interactions are shown in Figure 13.3. This would seem to be a comprehensive and viable theoretical foundation for understanding leadership.[78]

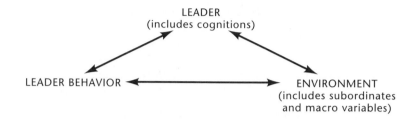

FIGURE 13.3
A social learning
approach to leadership.

Any of the other theoretical approaches, standing alone, seem too limiting. For example, the one-sided, cognitively based trait theories suggest that leaders are causal determinants that influence subordinates independent of subordinates' behaviors or the situation. The contingency theories are a step in the right direction, but even they for the most part have a unidirectional conception of interaction, in which leaders and situations somehow combine to determine leadership behavior. Even those leadership theories which claim to take a bidirectional approach (either in the exchange sense between the leader and the subordinate group or in the contingency sense between the leader and the situation) actually retain a unidirectional view of leadership behavior. In these theories, the causal input into the leader's behavior is the result of the interdependent exchange, but the behavior itself is ignored as a leadership determinant.

As far as leadership application for the social learning approach is concerned, the four-term contingency S-O-B-C (situation-organism-behavior-consequence) model introduced in Chapter 1 can be used by leaders to perform a functional analysis. Unlike the more limited A-B-C (antecedent-behavior-consequence) functional analysis used in O.B. Mod. (see Chapter 8), the variables in the S-O-B-C functional analysis can be either overt (observable), as in the operant view, or covert (unobservable), as recognized in the social learning view, and, of course, recognition is given to the role of cognitive mediating processes by the insertion of the O. The successful application of this S-O-B-C functional analysis to human resources management "depends upon the leader's ability to bring into awareness the overt or covert antecedent cues and contingent consequences that regulate the leader's and subordinate's performance behavior."[79] More specifically, in this leadership application, the subordinates are actively involved in the process, and together with the leader they concentrate on their own and one another's *behaviors*, the environmental contingencies (both antecedent and consequent), and their mediating cognitions. Some examples of this approach are the following:

1. The leader becomes acquainted with the macro and micro variables that control his or her own behavior.
2. The leader works with the subordinate to discover the personalized set of behavioral contingencies that regulate the subordinate's behavior.
3. The leader and the subordinate jointly attempt to discover ways in which they can manage their individual behavior to produce more mutually reinforcing and organizationally productive outcomes.[80]

In such an approach, the leader and the subordinate have a negotiable, interactive relationship and are consciously aware of how they can modify (influence) each other's behavior by giving or holding back desired rewards.

Although work has been done on the theoretical development of a social learning approach to leadership, research and application are just getting under way.[81] Only time will tell whether it will hold up as a viable, researchable approach to leadership. However, because of its growing importance as a theoretical foundation for the fields of psychology and organizational behavior as a whole and because it recognizes the interactive nature of all the variables of previous theories, a social learning approach to leadership would seem to have potential for the future.

Substitutes for Leadership

Because of dissatisfaction with the progress of leadership theory and research in explaining and predicting the effects of leader behavior on performance outcomes, some of the basic assumptions about the importance of leadership per se are being challenged. In particular, Kerr and Jermier propose that there may be certain "substitutes" for leadership that make leader behavior unnecessary and redundant, and "neutralizers" which prevent the leader from behaving in a certain way or which counteract the behavior.[82] These substitutes or neutralizers can be found in subordinate, task, and organization characteristics. Figure 13.4 gives specific examples of

FIGURE 13.4
Kerr and Jermier's substitutes and neutralizers for leadership.

SUBORDINATE CHARACTERISTICS		IMPACT ON LEADERSHIP
Experience, ability, and training	⟶	Substitute for instrumental leadership
Professional orientation	⟶	Substitute for instrumental and supportive leadership
Indifference toward organizational rewards	⟶	Neutralizes instrumental and supportive leadership
TASK CHARACTERISTICS		
Structured and routine task	⟶	Substitute for instrumental leadership
Feedback within the task	⟶	Substitute for instrumental leadership
Intrinsically satisfying task	⟶	Substitute for supportive leadership
ORGANIZATION CHARACTERISTICS		
Cohesive work groups	⟶	Substitute for instrumental and supportive leadership
Low position power of leader	⟶	Neutralizes instrumental and supportive leadership
Formalization	⟶	Substitute for instrumental leadership
Inflexibility	⟶	Neutralizes instrumental leadership
Leader physically isolated from subordinates	⟶	Neutralizes instrumental and supportive leadership

possible substitutes and neutralizers according to supportive/relationship leadership and instrumental/task leadership.

As shown, subordinate experience, ability, and training may substitute for instrumental/task leadership. For example, craftspersons or professionals such as accountants or engineers may have so much experience, ability, and training that they do not need instrumental/task leadership to perform well and be satisfied. Those subordinates who don't particularly care about organizational rewards (for example, professors or musicians) will neutralize both supportive/relationship and instrumental/task leadership attempts. Tasks that are highly structured and automatically provide feedback substitute for instrumental/task leadership, and those which are intrinsically satisfying (for example, teaching) do not need supportive/ relationship leadership. There are also a number of organizational characteristics that substitute for or neutralize leadership.

There has been further analysis of the leader substitutes concept,[83] and Kerr and Jermier have provided some empirical support from field studies of police officers.[84] They found that substitutes such as feedback from the task being performed had more impact on certain job-related activities than leader behaviors did. Other studies have also been interpreted (post hoc) to support organizational characteristics such as formalization as leader substitutes.[85] More recent direct tests have yielded mixed results. One study using hospital personnel with a wide variety of skills and backgrounds and in a wide variety of professions found several potential substitutes to predict subordinate satisfaction and commitment, but only one of the single substitutes (organizational formalization) rendered leadership impossible and/ or unnecessary.[86] A follow-up study found that worker professionalism was an important moderator variable. It also found that professionals differed from nonprofessionals in that intrinsically satisfying work tasks and importance placed on organizational rewards were strong substitutes for leaders' support.[87]

Overall, the substitutes notion puts leadership back into proper perspective and may help explain the relatively poor track record of leadership research. In particular, the leadership situation (subordinate, task, or organization) may replace or counteract the leader's behavior in affecting subordinate satisfaction and performance. It has recently been noted that "the idea of leadership substitutes and neutralizers helps to account for the largely mixed results of research on most leadership theories. Studies of leadership that ignore the effect of neutralizers and substitutes may fail to uncover hypothesized relationships because the particular leadership process is irrelevant, rather than because the theory is invalid."[88]

In other words, some things are beyond leaders' control; leaders do not have mystical powers over people. The situation does play a role. By the same token, leaders can have a considerable impact. The substitutes idea does not negate leadership; it just puts a more realistic boundary on what leadership is capable of achieving from subordinates. Some styles and skills of leadership are more effective than others. The next chapter examines these leadership styles and skills.

Summary

This chapter presents and analyzes various theoretical aspects of leadership. The classic research studies on leadership set the stage for the theoretical development of leadership. The trait theories concentrate on the leaders themselves but, with the possible exception of intelligence and empathy/interpersonal sensitivity and self-confidence, really do not come up with any agreed upon traits of leaders. In recent times the trait approach has surfaced in terms of skills, which are covered in the next chapter.

The group and exchange theories emphasize the importance of followers, and although the vertical dyad linkage (VDL or LMX) model is still quite popular and is generating considerable research, the group and exchange theories in general are recognized to be only partial theories. Today, the widely recognized theories of leadership are situationally based. In particular, Fiedler's contingency model makes a significant contribution to leadership theory and potentially to the practice of human resources management. The path-goal approach is also an important contribution to leadership theory. It incorporates expectancy motivation concepts.

All the established theories of leadership continue to provide understanding and a foundation for the practice of leadership in today's organizations. However, in recent years a number of alternative theories have emerged to supplement and, in some cases, facilitate better understanding of the various processes of leadership. In particular, the charismatic, transformational, social learning, and substitutes approaches have received attention in recent years. Charismatic leaders (characterized as having qualities beyond the usual appointed leader) get extraordinary commitment and performance from followers. The charismatic leaders, however, as a group are considered only a subsection of the larger group of transformational leaders characterized by charisma, inspiration, and intellectual and individualized stimulation. These transformational leaders are felt to be especially suited to today's organizations as they experience dramatic change. The social learning theory of leadership incorporates the leader, the situation, and the behavior itself. This social learning approach emphasizes the importance of behavior and the continuous, interacting nature of all the variables in leadership. Finally, the substitutes approach recognizes that certain subordinate, task, and organizational characteristics may substitute for or neutralize the impact that leader behavior has on subordinate performance and satisfaction.

Questions for Discussion and Review

1. Briefly summarize the findings of the three classic leadership studies.
2. How do the group theories differ from the trait theories of leadership?
3. What are the three critical situational variables identified by Fiedler? If these are very favorable, what is the most effective style to use?
4. In simple terms, what is the path-goal theory of leadership? What is the leader's function in this conceptualization?
5. What are the major differences between traditional transactional leaders and emerging transformational leaders? Can you clarify these differences in how today's organizations are led?
6. What are the three variables in the social learning approach to leadership? How do they relate to one another? How can this approach be applied to the practice of human resources management?
7. What is meant by "substitutes for," and "neutralizers of," leadership? Give some subordinate, task, and organizational examples of these substitutes and neutralizers.

Footnote References and Supplemental Readings

1. Andrea Rothman, "Maybe Your Skills Aren't Holding You Back; Maybe It's a Birthday," *The Wall Street Journal*, Mar. 19, 1987, p. 35.
2. Gary Gemmill and Judith Oakley, "Leadership: An Alienating Social Myth?" *Human Relations*, vol. 45, no. 2, 1992, p. 113.
3. Abraham Zaleznik, "The Leadership Gap," *Academy of Management Executive*, February 1990, p. 9.
4. Warren G. Bennis, "Managing the Dream: Leadership in the 21st Century," *Journal of Organizational Change Management*, vol. 2, no. 1, 1989, p. 7.
5. Bernard M. Bass, *Bass and Stogdill's Handbook of Leadership*, 3d ed., Free Press, New York, 1990, p. 11.
6. Chester A. Schriesheim and Steven Kerr, "Theories and Measures of Leadership: A Critical Appraisal of Current and Future Directions," in James G. Hunt and Lars L. Larson (eds.), *Leadership: The Cutting Edge*, Southern Illinois University Press, Carbondale, 1977, p. 22.
7. H. Joseph Reitz, *Behavior in Organizations*, 3d ed., Irwin, Homewood, Ill., 1987, p. 469.
8. Robert Katz, "Skills of an Effective Administrator," *Harvard Business Review*, September–October 1974, pp. 90–101.
9. Gary A. Yukl, *Leadership in Organizations*, Prentice-Hall, Englewood Cliffs, N.J., 1981, p. 70.
10. Bass, op. cit., p. 48.
11. Charles N. Greene, "The Reciprocal Nature of Influence Between Leader and Subordinate," *Journal of Applied Psychology*, vol. 60, 1975, pp. 187–193.
12. J. C. Barrow, "Worker Performance and Task Complexity as Causal Determinants of Leader Behavior Style and Flexibility," *Journal of Applied Psychology*, vol. 61, 1976, pp. 433–440.
13. Charles N. Greene and Chester A. Schriesheim, "Leader-Group Interactions: A Longitudinal Field Investigation," *Journal of Applied Psychology*, February 1980, pp. 50–59.
14. Keith Davis and John Newstrom, *Human Behavior at Work: Organizational Behavior*, 7th ed., McGraw-Hill, New York, 1985, pp. 160, 182, and Ann Howard and James A. Wilson, "Leadership in a Declining Work Ethic," *California Management Review*, Summer 1982, pp. 33–46.
15. Larry Reibstein, "Follow the Leader: Workers Face Dilemma When Boss Is Sinking," *The Wall Street Journal*, Mar. 10, 1987, p. 29.
16. F. Dansereau, Jr., G. Graen, and W. J. Haga, "A Vertical Dyad Linkage Approach to Leadership Within Formal Organizations: A Longitudinal Investigation of the Role Making Process," *Organizational Behavior and Human Performance*, February 1975, pp. 46–78.
17. G. Graen, M. Novak, and P. Sommerkamp, "The Effects of Leader-Member Exchange and Job Design and Productivity and Satisfaction: Testing a Dual Attachment Model," *Organizational Behavior and Human Performance*, vol. 30, 1982, pp. 109–131.
18. Dansereau, Graen, and Haga, loc. cit.
19. Fred Dansereau, Jr., Joseph A. Alutto, Steven E. Markham, and MacDonald Dumas, "Multi-plexed Supervision and Leadership: An Application of Within and Between Analysis," in James G. Hunt, Uma Sekaran, and Chester A. Schriesheim (eds.), *Leadership: Beyond Establishment Views*, Southern Illinois University Press, Carbondale, 1982, pp. 81–103.
20. Robert C. Liden and George Graen, "Generalizability of the Vertical Dyad Linkage Model of Leadership," *Academy of Management Journal*, September 1980, pp. 451–465.
21. Robert P. Vecchio, "A Further Test of Leadership Effects Due to Between-Group Variation and Within-Group Variation," *Journal of Applied Psychology*, April 1982, pp. 200–208, and Richard M. Dienesch and Robert C. Liden, "Leader-Member Exchange Model of Leadership: A Critique and Further Development," *Academy of Management Review*, July 1986, pp. 618–634.
22. Gary Yukl, "Managerial Leadership: A Review of Theory and Research," *Journal of Management*, vol. 15, no. 2, 1989, p. 266.
23. Francis J. Yammarino and Alan J. Dubinsky, "Superior-Subordinate Relationships: A Multiple Levels of Analysis Approach," *Human Relations*, vol. 45, no. 6, 1992, pp. 575–600.
24. Kenneth J. Dunegan, Dennis Duchon, and Mary Uhl-Bien, "Examining the Link Between Leader-Member Exchange and Subordinate Performance: The Role of Task Analyzability and Variety of Moderators," *Journal of Management*, vol. 18, no. 1, 1992, pp. 59–76.
25. Patrick T. Gibbons, "Impacts of Organizational Evolution on Leadership Roles and Behaviors," *Human Relations*, vol. 45, no. 1, 1992, pp. 1–18.
26. Fred E. Fiedler, *A Theory of Leadership Effectiveness*, McGraw-Hill, New York, 1967, pp. 13–144.
27. Ibid., p. 147.
28. Ibid.
29. Fred Fiedler and Martin M. Chemers, *Leadership and Effective Management*, Scott, Foresman, Glenview, Ill., 1974, p. 83.
30. Fred E. Fiedler and Linda Mahar, "The Effectiveness

of Contingency Model Training: A Review of the Validation of Leader Match," *Personnel Psychology*, Spring 1979, p. 46.

31. Michael J. Strube and Joseph E. Garcia, "A Meta-Analytic Investigation of Fiedler's Contingency Model of Leadership Effectiveness," *Psychological Bulletin*, September 1981, pp. 307–321.

32. George Graen, D. Alvares, J. B. Orris, and J. A. Martella, "Contingency Model of Leadership Effectiveness: Antecedent and Evidential Results," *Psychological Bulletin*, October 1970, pp. 285–296, and George Graen, James B. Orris, and Kenneth M. Alvares, "Contingency Model of Leadership Effectiveness: An Evaluation," *Organizational Behavior and Human Performance*, June 1973, pp. 339–355.

33. Schriesheim and Kerr, loc. cit., and Chester A. Schriesheim, Brendan D. Bannister, and William H. Money, "Psychometric Properties of the LPC Scale: An Extension of Rice's Review," *Academy of Management Review*, April 1979, pp. 287–290.

34. Fred E. Fiedler, "A Rejoinder to Schriesheim and Kerr's Premature Obituary of the Contingency Model," in Hunt and Larson, op. cit., pp. 45–51.

35. Robert W. Rice, "Reliability and Validity of the LPC Scale: A Reply," *Academy of Management Review*, April 1979, pp. 291–294.

36. Yukl, "Managerial Leadership," p. 266.

37. Fred E. Fiedler, "Engineer the Job to Fit the Manager," *Harvard Business Review*, September–October 1965, pp. 115–122.

38. Fred E. Fiedler, Martin M. Chemers, and Linda Mahar, *Improving Leadership Effectiveness: The Leader Match Concept*, Wiley, New York, 1976.

39. Ibid., pp. 154–158.

40. Fiedler and Mahar, loc. cit.

41. Ibid., p. 61.

42. Arthur G. Jago and James W. Ragan, "The Trouble with Leader Match Is That It Doesn't Match Fiedler's Contingency Model," *Journal of Applied Psychology*, vol. 71, no. 4, 1986, pp. 555–559.

43. Ronald E. Riggio, *Introduction to Industrial/Organizational Psychology*, Scott, Foresman/Little, Brown, Glenview, Ill., 1990, p. 293.

44. F. E. Fiedler, "The Contribution of Cognitive Resources to Leadership Performance," *Journal of Applied Social Psychology*, vol. 16, 1986, pp. 532–548, and F. E. Fiedler and J. E. Garcia, *New Approaches to Leadership: Cognitive Resources and Organizational Performance*, Wiley, New York, 1987.

45. Fred E. Fiedler, Susan E. Murphy, and Frederick W. Gibson, "Inaccurate Reporting and Inappropriate Variables: A Reply to Vecchio's Examination of Cognitive Resource Theory," *Journal of Applied Psychology*, vol. 77, 1992, pp. 372–374.

46. Robert P. Vecchio, "Cognitive Resource Theory: Issues for Specifying a Test of the Theory," *Journal of Applied Psychology*, vol. 77, 1992, pp. 375–376.

47. Basil S. Georgopoulos, Gerald M. Mahoney, and Nyle W. Jones, "A Path-Goal Approach to Productivity," *Journal of Applied Psychology*, December 1957, pp. 345–353; Martin G. Evans, "The Effect of Supervisory Behavior on the Path-Goal Relationship," *Organizational Behavior and Human Performance*, May 1970, pp. 277–298; and Robert J. House, "A Path-Goal Theory of Leader Effectiveness," *Administrative Science Quarterly*, September 1971, pp. 321–338.

48. Robert J. House and Terence R. Mitchell, "Path-Goal Theory of Leadership," *Journal of Contemporary Business*, Autumn 1974, pp. 81–97.

49. Ibid.

50. Ibid.

51. Alan C. Filley, Robert J. House, and Steven Kerr, *Managerial Process and Organizational Behavior*, 2d ed., Scott, Foresman, Glenview, Ill., 1976, p. 254.

52. House and Mitchell, loc. cit.

53. Filley, House, and Kerr, op. cit., pp. 256–260.

54. Chester A. Schriesheim and Angelo DeNisi, "Task Dimensions as Moderators of the Effects of Instrumental Leadership: A Two Sample Applicated Test of Path-Goal Leadership Theory," *Journal of Applied Psychology*, October 1981, pp. 589–597. Also see Schriesheim and Kerr, op. cit.

55. Ibid., pp. 103–105.

56. Julie Indvik, "Path-Goal Theory of Leadership: A Meta-Analysis," *Academy of Management Best Papers Proceedings*, 1986, pp. 189–192.

57. Robert A. Baron, *Behavior in Organizations*, 2d ed., Allyn and Bacon, Boston, 1986, p. 292.

58. Representative of the critical analysis of leadership theory and research would be Charles N. Greene, "Disenchantment with Leadership Research: Some Causes, Recommendations, and Alternative Directions," in Hunt and Larson (eds.), *Leadership: The Cutting Edge*, pp. 57–67; Schriesheim and Kerr, loc. cit.; Barbara Karmel, "Leadership: A Challenge to Traditional Research Methods and Assumptions," *Academy of Management Review*, July 1978, pp. 475–482; and James S. Phillips and Robert G. Lord, "Notes on the Practical and Theoretical Consequences of Implicit Leadership Theories for the Future of Leadership Measurement," *Journal of Management*, vol. 12, no. 1, 1986, pp. 31–41.

59. John B. Miner, "The Uncertain Future of the Leadership Concept: An Overview," in James G. Hunt and Lars L. Larson (eds.), *Leadership Frontiers*, Kent State University, Comparative Administration Resources Institute, Kent, Ohio, 1975, pp. 197–208.

60. Schriesheim and Kerr, loc. cit.

61. R. J. House and J. L. Baetz, "Leadership: Some

Empirical Generalizations and New Research Directions," in B. M. Staw (ed.), *Research in Organizational Behavior*, vol. 1, JAI Press, Greenwich, Conn., 1979, p. 399.

62. Robert J. House, "A 1976 Theory of Charismatic Leadership," in Hunt and Larson (eds.), *Leadership: The Cutting Edge*, pp. 189–207.

63. Ibid.

64. Bernard M. Bass, *Leadership and Performance Beyond Expectations*, Free Press, New York, 1985, pp. 54–61.

65. R. J. House, J. Woycke, and E. M. Fodor, "Charismatic and Non Charismatic Leaders: Differences in Behavior and Effectiveness," in J. A. Conger and R. M. Kanungo (eds.), *Charismatic Leadership: The Elusive Factor in Organizational Effectiveness*, Jossey-Bass, San Francisco, 1988, pp. 98–121, and Robert J. House, William D. Spangler, and James Woycke, "Personality and Charisma in the U.S. Presidency: A Psychological Theory of Leadership Effectiveness," *Academy of Management Best Papers Proceedings*, 1990, pp. 216–219.

66. J. A. Conger and R. Kanungo, "Toward a Behavioral Theory of Charismatic Leadership in Organizational Settings," *Academy of Management Review*, vol. 12, 1987, pp. 637–647, and J. A. Conger and R. M. Kanungo, "Behavioral Dimensions of Charismatic Leadership," in J. A. Conger and R. M. Kanungo (eds.), *Charismatic Leadership: The Elusive Factor in Organizational Effectiveness*, Jossey-Bass, San Francisco, 1988, pp. 78–97.

67. Jane M. Howell and Bruce J. Avolio, "The Ethics of Charismatic Leadership: Submission or Liberation?" *Academy of Management Executive*, May 1992, pp. 43–54.

68. Ibid., p. 52. Also see F. Bird and J. Gandz, *Good Management: Business Ethics in Action*, Prentice-Hall, Toronto, 1991, p. 166.

69. Bass, *Bass & Stogdill's Handbook*, p. 221.

70. J. M. Burns, *Leadership*, Harper & Row, New York, 1978.

71. Bernard M. Bass, "From Transactional to Transformational Leadership: Learning to Share the Vision," *Organizational Dynamics*, Winter 1990, pp. 19–31.

72. Yukl, op. cit., pp. 272–273.

73. Noel M. Tichy and Mary Anne Devanna, *The Transformational Leader*, Wiley, New York, 1986, and Noel M. Tichy and Mary Anne Devanna, "The Transformational Leader," *Training and Development Journal*, July 1986, pp. 30–32.

74. Bennett J. Tepper, "Patterns of Downward Influence and Follower Conformity in Transactional and Transformational Leadership," *Academy of Management Best Papers Proceedings*, 1993, pp. 267–271.

75. Robert T. Keller, "Transformational Leadership and the Performance of Research and Development Project Groups," *Journal of Management*, vol. 18, 1992, pp. 489–501.

76. See Tim R. V. Davis and Fred Luthans, "A Social Learning Approach to Organizational Behavior," *Academy of Management Review*, April 1980, pp. 281–290.

77. See Fred Luthans, "Leadership: A Proposal for a Social Learning Theory Base and Observational and Functional Analysis Techniques to Measure Leader Behavior," in J. G. Hunt and L. L. Larson (eds.), *Crosscurrents in Leadership*, Southern Illinois University Press, Carbondale and Edwardsville, Ill., 1979, pp. 201–208; Fred Luthans and Tim R. V. Davis, "Operationalizing a Behavioral Approach to Leadership," *Proceedings of the Midwest Academy of Management*, 1979, pp. 144–155; and Tim R. V. Davis and Fred Luthans, "Leadership Reexamined: A Behavioral Approach," *Academy of Management Review*, April 1979, pp. 237–248.

78. See Luthans, loc. cit., for an expanded discussion.

79. Davis and Luthans, "Leadership Reexamined," p. 244.

80. Ibid., p. 245.

81. See Fred Luthans and Tim R. V. Davis, "Behavioral Self-Management: The Missing Link in Managerial Effectiveness," *Organizational Dynamics*, Summer 1979, pp. 42–60; Tim R. V. Davis and Fred Luthans, "Defining and Researching Leadership as a Behavioral Construct: An Idiographic Approach," *Journal of Applied Behavioral Science*, vol. 20, no. 3, 1984, pp. 237–251; and, most recently, Henry P. Sims, Jr., and Peter Lorenzi, *The New Leadership Paradigm: Social Learning and Cognition in Organizations*, Sage, Newbury Park, Calif., 1992.

82. Steven Kerr and John M. Jermier, "Substitutes of Leadership: Their Meaning and Measurement," *Organizational Behavior and Human Performance*, December 1978, pp. 375–403. Also see Steven Kerr, "Substitutes for Leadership: Some Implications for Organizational Design," *Organization and Administrative Sciences*, vol. 8, no. 1, 1977, p. 135, and Jon P. Howell, Peter Dorfman, and Steven Kerr, "Moderator Variables in Leadership Research," *Academy of Management Review*, vol. 11, no. 1, 1986, pp. 88–102.

83. J. Jermier and L. Berkes, "Leader Behavior in a Police Command Bureaucracy: A Closer Look at the Quasi-Military Model," *Administrative Science Quarterly*, March 1979, pp. 1–23, and S. Kerr and J. W. Slocum, Jr., "Controlling the Performances of People in Organizations," in P. C. Nystrom and W. H. Starbuck (eds.), *Handbook of Organizational Design*, Oxford, New York, 1981, pp. 116–134.

84. Kerr and Jermier, loc. cit.

85. Robert H. Miles and M. M. Petty, "Leader Effective-

ness in Small Bureaucracies," *Academy of Management Journal*, June 1977, pp. 238–250.

86. Jon P. Howell and Peter W. Dorfman, "Substitutes for Leadership: Test of a Construct," *Academy of Management Journal*, December 1981, pp. 714–728.

87. Jon P. Howell and Peter W. Dorfman, "Leadership and Substitutes for Leadership Among Professionals and Nonprofessional Workers," *Journal of Applied Behavioral Science*, vol. 22, no. 1, 1986, pp. 29–46.

88. Robert P. Vecchio, *Organizational Behavior*, Dryden, Chicago, 1988, p. 309.

REAL CASE:
The Teflon Leader

Most often the media and general public focus on the current president. For example, President Clinton has been referred to as "Slick Willy" by his detractors, while his supporters note his "putting people first" approach and leadership style. However, in the study of leadership, past presidents often provide more interesting insights because their entire presidency can be viewed as a composite and their leadership style analyzed in light of historical hindsight. In particular, Ronald Reagan was an interesting case study for leadership. Commonly referred to as the "Teflon president" because nothing (no problems or embarrassments) stuck to him, he was popular with some people and unpopular with others. But all agree on one basic fact: He had a leadership style that was interesting and in some ways unique. Close observers have concluded that some of the basic approaches that exemplified Reagan's style were the following:

1. He always put a great deal of emphasis on being able to communicate well. In fact, when his speechwriters would hand him their material, the president would go over it and change some of their examples to ones he liked better and felt were more appropriate to his audience.
2. He always tried to convey an upbeat message. If things were not going well, his emphasis would be on how they could be improved.
3. He identified his major goals and continued moving toward them during his terms in office. He did not change his mind in midstream and begin shifting toward different major objectives. This consistency of behavior made it easier for him to keep his programs heading in a consistent direction.
4. He repeated his national goals over and over again, so everyone knew what he wanted done. In particular, those who supported him were able to line up behind him. Having heard the message often enough, they became part of his cheering squad—something every effective leader needs.
5. He tried to compromise on those issues where he realized he would be unable to achieve all he was seeking. For example, if he wanted $100 million for a program and could get only 70 percent of that amount, he would take it and then work on getting the other 30 percent the next fiscal year. He did not get himself caught up in an "all or nothing" strategy.
6. He focused on the major issues without getting bogged down in the day-to-day decision making. This was left for others who were more skilled than he at implementation.
7. During Cabinet meetings he encouraged people to speak their minds; if they disagreed with the majority, they should say so. In this way, Reagan was able to get input on both sides of the issue under discussion.
8. He believed that the most important thing a leader could do was surround himself with the best possible talent. Then he could delegate authority and let these people carry out the overall policy that had been agreed upon.

In the years ahead, a great deal of additional research is likely to be conducted regarding Ronald Reagan's leadership style. However, for the time being at least, most experts believe that his approach to leadership worked pretty well for him.

1. How can Fiedler's contingency model of leadership be used to explain the success of President Reagan's style?
2. How can the path-goal theory of leadership be used in explaining the President's approach? Cite an example in your answer.
3. Was Reagan a charismatic leader? Support your answer? How does he compare and contrast to more recent presidents, such as Clinton?

CASE:
The Missing
Ingredient

When Cecil Schmidt took over the helm of Rugersby Insurance, a large brokerage firm in the Northeast, he knew that things were in bad shape. The industry had been suffering massive losses and most insurers had come to realize that their rates were too low. Premiums had to be raised and the price-cutting strategies of earlier years had to be abandoned if the firm was to survive.

Cecil was brought in with the mandate to "straighten things out and get our profitability up." It took him almost three years to get things turned around. First, he stopped all hiring except for replacements and encouraged voluntary retirement. Second, all nonessential personnel were let go and their work was redistributed to others. Third, all marginally profitable accounts were dropped and the focus of attention was placed on the money-makers. Fourth, in-house operating and maintenance costs were cut to the bone.

As a result of these efficiency and marketing-related measures, monthly losses dropped from $30,000 to under $2000 within three months. A year after he assumed the helm, Cecil was able to tell the board that the company was operating at its break-even point. The next year profits were in excess of $200,000; for the three years following, they doubled every year. Rugersby was now in the top half of the industry in terms of profitability for a firm its size. Cecil attributed a great deal of this success to his draconian measures of cost cutting and heavy emphasis on efficiency.

Unfortunately, a year ago, profits started to decline. There appear to be two major reasons for this. One is that the company's revenues have increased 207 percent since Cecil has come on board, while the number of personnel has declined by 24 percent. Many people feel that they are overworked and have begun looking for positions elsewhere. To make matters worse, the company has been having trouble hiring new people. A second reason is that overall efficiency is declining. Many of the cost-cutting steps taken by Cecil appear to have been short-run. For example, managers used to take the overnight flight from New York to San Francisco. Since they were in first class, they would be well fed, see a movie, and sleep. When they arrived in San Francisco the next morning, they were ready to begin work. Now that they must travel coach, the managers take a day flight, which means that they lose one day of work going out and another coming back. When Cecil asked them to fly at night, they told him that they cannot sleep in coach because it is too uncomfortable. As a result, they have to fly out during the day in order to ensure that they get a good night's sleep and are prepared for work the next day; the same is true for the return flight.

Earlier this week the board of directors of Rugersby met and decided to ask for Cecil's resignation. The chairperson summed up the feelings of the committee by saying: "Cecil has done a good job, but it's time for a change. If we don't do something, we'll be back where we were when Cecil arrived. We want to bring in someone who is less cost-focused and more people-oriented. We think that this is the missing ingredient that is causing our problems."

1. Why are Cecil's cost-cutting efforts now losing their effectiveness?
2. Is the board correct in its assessment of the situation? Why or why not?
3. What leadership lessons can be learned from this case? Cite and describe two.

**CASE:
He Sure Looked
Good**

Mannion Inc. started looking for a new corporate president almost eighteen months ago. The process was slow; for a while, it appeared that none of the applicants would make the final list. However, after interviewing over thirty executives from both inside and outside the company, the selection committee recommended that five people be considered for the position. In its report to the board of directors, the committee said that each of the five finalists was "equal to the task and any one of them can provide us the leadership needed for the twenty-first century."

The board reviewed the list and unanimously agreed that there were two individuals who warranted initial consideration. If either was deemed superior to the other after the interviews, this person would be offered the job and the second would be kept as a backup. Only if both individuals proved unacceptable or could not be hired would the board move on and consider the remaining three candidates.

The first person to be interviewed was Mark Schlaiffer. Mark, forty-four, has worked for a major competitor for fourteen years. He currently is senior production vice president and is considered one of the most effective managers in the industry. As a result of a strategic plan he developed, his company was able to cut costs by 22 percent and emerge as one of the low cost producers in the world. It is likely that Mark will be made president of his company if he remains.

The other person was Margaret Hutchins, forty-five, vice president of operations at a large high-tech company. Although Mannion Inc. is not in the high-tech business, Margaret's success in nurturing and developing research and development projects is well known in the industry and she is considered a first-rate leader. Much of the success of her company is attributed, by insiders as well as industry analysts, to Margaret's skills and abilities. She has been offered the presidency of three companies over the last five years, and in each case she has declined. However, she has indicated that she would take the job at Mannion if it were offered.

Yesterday, the board met and made its decision. The offer was made to Mark. In explaining why they chose him, the board members noted five reasons that seemed to outweigh the others. They were these:

- He is distinguished looking; he has a "presidential" look.
- He is tall (6 feet 6 inches), which helps him convey an image of power and authority.
- He is affable and friendly.
- He is a good public speaker.
- He is extremely intelligent.

There were also many positive comments made about Margaret, including her fine operating performance. However, the board was unanimous in deciding to make the first offer to Mark. If he did not accept, they planned to invite two more individuals to be interviewed and then choose between them and Margaret in deciding whom to offer the job to next.

1. On what basis did the company make its choice?
2. On the basis of your answer to the above question, do you think the board made a mistake?
3. What recommendations would you make to them based on their decision and the comments supporting it?

14 Leadership Styles, Activities, and Skills

- **Relate** the style implications from the classic studies and modern theories of leadership.
- **Present** the widely recognized styles of leadership, including those from the managerial grid, the life-cycle approach, and Likert's systems.
- **Discuss** the findings on leadership roles and activities.
- **Examine** the relationship that activities have with successful and effective leaders.
- **Identify** and **analyze** the skills needed for effective leadership of today's organizations.

The preceding chapter presented the background and the established and emerging theoretical frameworks for leadership. Analogous to the earlier treatment of motivation and learning in the previous part of the text, this chapter serves as the follow-up application of leadership theories. This application chapter deals mainly with the various styles, roles and activities, and skills of leaders/managers.

First, the style implications from the classic studies and theories of the preceding chapter are examined. Then, the main part of the chapter presents and analyzes the widely recognized styles of leadership. This discussion is followed by an examination of roles and activities, with special attention given to successful and effective leaders/managers. The last part of the chapter gives attention to the leadership skills that are increasingly being recognized as needed for today's dramatically changing organizations. Very simply, the differences between styles, activities, and skills are that leadership styles deal with the *way* leaders influence followers, roles and activities are *what* leaders do, and skills are concerned with *how* leaders can be effective.

In this chapter the terms "leaders" and "managers" are used interchangeably, although the preceding chapter pointed out the distinction between managers and leaders, and there is even empirical evidence that there may be a difference.[1] Nevertheless, as Richard Teerlink, the highly successful CEO of Harley-Davidson recently noted: "In the business environment of the future, everyone will be in a leadership role."[2] Thus, this chapter on *leadership* styles, roles and activities, and skills is also on *management* styles, roles and activities, and skills.

LEADERSHIP STYLES

The classic leadership studies and the various leadership theories discussed in the preceding chapter all have direct implications for what style the manager or supervisor uses in human resources management. The word "style" is very vague. Yet, it is widely used to describe successful leaders. For example, the leadership style of Steve Jobs, a founder of Apple Computer and now of Next Computer Inc., was recently described as follows:

> Sometimes it's hard to tell whether Steve Jobs is a snake-oil salesman or a bona fide visionary, a promoter who got lucky or the epitome of the intrepid entrepreneur. What's indisputable is that he possesses consummate charm, infectious enthusiasm, and an overdose of charisma.[3]

This vivid description also points out the difficulty of attaching a single style to a leader. Styles also differ from one culture to another, as shown by the accompanying TQM in Action: First Japan, Now Korea. The following sections describe how leadership styles have been studied and evaluated over the years.

TQM in Action

First Japan, Now Korea

When America's quality products began to slide in comparison with Japan's, American management professors and practitioners looked toward Japanese total quality management for answers. It was found that Japanese total quality management gave extra attention to human resources. Since then, American managers have adopted many of the Japanese practices. Quality circles come quickly to mind. Recently, however, another success story is gaining America's attention. South Korea, not Japan, has been winning the competitive battle in many areas. Korean-run businesses such as Lucky-Goldstar, Samsung, Hyundai, and Daewoo have had much success. They have posed a new threat to American business leadership. Thus, Americans are now looking toward the Koreans as well as the Japanese for the answers.

In some ways the Koreans are similar to the Japanese. For instance, Korean managers espouse teamwork, employee participation, minimal hierarchies, and emphasis on the employee's personal needs. However, when the Koreans come to run their operations in the United States, they are more flexible than the Japanese. As a result, Koreans have adjusted better to American ways. For instance, although managers in Korea sit in open-air offices, Korean managers in America separate themselves with lightly tinted glass. Also, Americans are not asked to sing a company song or to take exercise breaks. Thomas G. Dimmick, a manager with the Korean firm Samsung, comments on the inflexibility of the Japanese: "The Japanese are from a homogeneous society, so they are less accepting of anything that is not Japanese. Korea is a land of division, so the people are willing to listen and not get their feet stuck in concrete."

The Korean-run plants in the United States have experienced considerable success. The average American worker at a Korean-run plant produces more quality goods compared with American-owned companies. However, American workers at Japanese-run plants still produced the most. Yet, management experts predict that the gap between Japanese and Korean plants will narrow. After all, Korean managers tend to work more hours than their Japanese or American counterparts. The diligence of the Koreans should pay off in the long run. If the Korean-run plants continue to succeed, Korean management may replace Japanese management as a model for total quality management.

Style Implications of the Classic Studies and the Modern Theories

Chapter 1 discusses the major historical contributions to the study of organizational behavior. Most of this discussion has indirect or direct implications for leadership style. For example, the Hawthorne studies were interpreted in terms of their implications for supervisory style. Also relevant is the classic work done by Douglas McGregor, in which his Theory X represents the old, authoritarian style of leadership and his Theory Y represents the enlightened, humanistic style. The studies discussed at the beginning of the preceding chapter are directly concerned with style. The Iowa studies analyzed the impact of autocratic, democratic, and laissez faire styles, and the studies conducted by the Michigan group found the employee-centered supervisor to be more effective than the production-centered supervisor. The Ohio State studies indentified consideration (a supportive type of style) and initiating structure (a directive type of style) as being the major functions of leadership. The trait and group theories have indirect implications for style, and the human relations and task-directed styles play an important role in Fiedler's contingency theory. The path-goal conceptualization depends heavily upon directive, supportive, participative, and achievement-oriented styles of leadership.

The same is true of the charismatic and transformational leaders. They have an inspirational style with vision, and they "do the right thing" for their people. Table 14.1 summarizes the charismatic leader style according to three major types of behavior, with illustrative actions. An example of such a style in recent times would be Paul O'Neil of ALCOA. He espoused a clear vision for his firm, anchored on quality, safety, and innovation. He made his vision compelling and central to the company, set high expectations for his management team and employees throughout the organization, and provided continuous support and energy for his vision through meetings, task forces, videotapes, and extensive personal contact.[4]

A rough approximation of the various styles derived from the studies and theories discussed so far can be incorporated into the continuum shown in Table 14.2. For ease of presentation, the styles listed may be substituted for the expressions "boss-centered" and "subordinate-centered" used by Tannenbaum and Schmidt in

TABLE 14.1 Nadler and Tushman's Charismatic Leadership Styles

Types of Charismatic Leadership Styles	Meaning	Examples
Envisioning	Creating a picture of the future—or a desired future state—with which people can identify and which can generate excitement	Articulating a compelling vision Setting high expectations
Energizing	Directing the generation of energy, the motivation to act, among members of the organization	Demonstrating personal excitement and confidence Seeking, finding, and using success
Enabling	Psychologically helping people act or perform in the face of challenging goals	Expressing personal support Empathizing

TABLE 14.2 Summary Continuum of Leadership Styles Drawn from the Classic Studies and Theories of Leadership

Boss-centered	Subordinate-centered
Theory X ⟷	Theory Y
Autocratic ⟷	Democratic
Production-centered ⟷	Employee-centered
Close ⟷	General
Initiating structure ⟷	Consideration
Task-directed ⟷	Human relations
Directive ⟷	Supportive
Directive ⟷	Participative

their classic leadership continuum shown in Figure 14.1. The verbal descriptions and the relationship between authority and freedom found in Figure 14.1 give a rough representation of the characteristics of the various styles of leadership. This depiction can serve as background for a more detailed examination of the specific application of styles to the practice of human resources management.

One thing is certain: Leadership style can make a difference. For example, a survey found that senior executives view their companies' leadership styles as pragmatic rather than conceptual, and conservative rather than risk taking. These same executives felt that to meet their current and future challenges, the styles should be the other way around.[5] As Bennis has noted: "Never before has American business faced so many challenges, and never before have there been so many choices in how to face those challenges. We must look now at what it is going to take not just to regain global leadership, but simply to stay a player in the game."[6] The following sections examine the widely recognized leadership styles available to today's managers to meet these challenges.

FIGURE 14.1
The Tannenbaum and Schmidt continuum of leadership behavior.

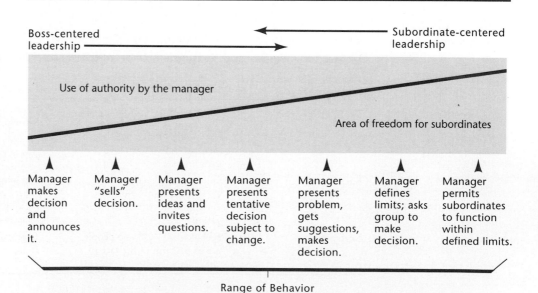

Managerial Grid Styles

One very popular approach to identifying leadership styles of practicing managers is Blake and Mouton's classic managerial grid. Figure 14.2 shows that the two dimensions of the grid are "concern for people" along the vertical axis and "concern for production" along the horizontal axis. These two dimensions are equivalent to the consideration and initiating structure functions identified by the Ohio State studies and the employee-centered and production-centered styles used in the Michigan studies.

The five basic styles identified in the grid represent varying combinations of concern for people and production. The 1,1 manager has minimum concern for people and production; this style is sometimes called the "impoverished" style. The opposite is the 9,9 manager. This individual has maximum concern for both people and production. The implication is that the 9,9 is the best style of leadership, and Blake and Mouton have stated in no uncertain terms: "There should be no question about which leadership style is the most effective. It's that of the manager whom we call, in the terminology of the Managerial Grid, a 9,9 team builder."[7] Blake and Mouton provided empirical evidence that their interactive notion of leadership style (that is, concern for people interacting with concern for production) has more predictive validity than additive situational approaches.[8] The 5,5 manager is the "middle-of-the-roader," and the other two styles represent the extreme concerns for people (1,9, "country club" manager) and production (9,1 "task" manager). A

FIGURE 14.2
The Blake and Mouton managerial grid.

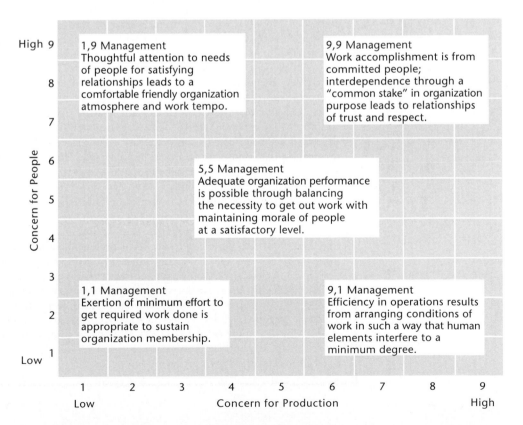

manager's position on the grid can be determined by a questionnaire developed by Blake and Mouton and can play an important role in organization development. The International Application Example: Balancing People and Profits offers an example of the managerial grid approach to international negotiations.

Balancing People and Profits

One of the most interesting examples of current leadership practices is provided by those individuals in the international arena who are negotiating business deals. Quite often, they fit into one of two groups: business people from other countries who are seeking opportunities to invest, and national leaders who are seeking to attract investment. For example, Lou Gerstner, the current head of beleaguered IBM, is working closely with Toshiba of Japan to develop a series of technological projects related to memory chips and liquid crystal displays, and John Welch, of greatly admired General Electric, is expanding operations into China, India, Mexico, and other developing nations. Each would like to enter into a contract that enhances his position, and this is where effective leadership enters the picture.

These chief executive officers (CEOs) are not alone. In recent years Russia and the other republics of the former Soviet Union have worked very hard to attract foreign investment. CEOs from PepsiCo, Archer Daniels Midland, United Telecommunications, and Chevron, to name but a few, have all recently gone to talk with the Russians and others about investment opportunities there. The problem for many of these business leaders is that the political power base continues to change and thus there is considerable risk. On the one hand, they must talk to the head of the Russian government, but on the other hand, other senior-level government officials in Russia and especially the other republics have local authority and can block decisions made in Moscow. Moreover, leaders on both sides of these international negotiations must balance a concern for the local people with a concern for the work to be done and the profits which must be earned in order to attract the initial foreign investment.

In the case of Russia, these leaders must find investments to attract American capital. As mentioned above, major U.S. leaders such as Don Kendall of PepsiCo, Dwayne Andreas of Archer Daniels Midland, Bill Esrey of United Telecommunications, and Den Derr of Chevron all went to Russia in an effort to find out what the country had to offer and where the government would allow them to invest. Given that Russia is in major need of investment capital, it would seem that anything these business leaders wanted to do would be acceptable. However, this was not true. On the one hand, the Russian leaders talked about the need for investment, while on the other, they offered no immediate promise of return on investment. The picture is no different in other countries seeking to attract investors. Leaders on both sides of the negotiating table are finding that they must balance a concern for people with a concern for work.

In the case of Russia, negotiators must find investments that will help improve the lifestyle of the country (concern for people) while also ensuring that the investors have the freedom needed to operate efficiently and to repatriate their profits (concern for work). American leaders need to convince the leaders of Russia that their country will not be highly attractive unless a definition of property ownership rights is clarified, control of operations is ensured, and the ruble is convertible into dollars or other desirable foreign currency (concern for work), while also illustrating that such investments will help improve the standard of living in the country (concern for people). Quite obviously, both sides are learning that a 9,9 leadership style is not restricted to the confines of one's own organization.

Hersey and Blanchard's Life-Cycle, or Situational, Approach

Another popular approach to management style training and development is the *life-cycle* (later termed the *situational*) approach to leadership.[9] It is an extension of the managerial grid approach. Following the original Ohio State studies and the grid approach, Hersey and Blanchard's approach identifies two major styles:

1. *Task style.* The leader organizes and defines roles for members of the work group; the leader explains the tasks that members are to do and when, where, and how they are to do them.
2. *Relationship style.* The leader has close, personal relationships with the members of the group, and there is open communication and psychological and emotional support.

Taking the lead from some of Fiedler's work on situational variables, Hersey and Blanchard incorporated the maturity of the followers into their model. The level of maturity is defined by three criteria:

1. Degree of achievement motivation
2. Willingness to take on responsibility
3. Amount of education and/or experience

Although they recognize that there may be other important situational variables, Hersey and Blanchard focus only on this maturity level of work group members in their model.

Figure 14.3 summarizes the situational approach. The key for leadership effectiveness in this model is to match up the situation with the appropriate style. The following summarizes the four basic styles:

1. *Telling style.* This is a high-task, low-relationship style and is effective when followers are at a very low level of maturity.
2. *Selling style.* This is a high-task, high-relationship style and is effective when followers are on the low side of maturity.
3. *Participating style.* This is a low-task, high-relationship style and is effective when followers are on the high side of maturity.
4. *Delegating style.* This is a low-task, low-relationship style and is effective when followers are at a very high level of maturity.

Like the grid approach, Hersey and Blanchard's approach includes a questionnaire instrument which presents twelve situations that generally depict the various levels of maturity of the group; respondents answer how they would handle each situation. These responses follow the four styles. How closely respondents match the situation with the appropriate style will determine their effectiveness score.

The theoretical rationale is generally criticized as being "weak, because Hersey and Blanchard have neglected to provide a coherent, explicit rationale for the hypothesized relationships."[10] They also, by their own admission, highly oversimplify the situation by giving only surface recognition to follower maturity. Also, as in the grid approach, there is a noted absence of any empirical tests of the model. One review of all facets of the approach was particularly critical of the instrument that Hersey and Blanchard used to measure leader effectiveness,[11] and a recent empirical test did not find support for the underlying assumptions or predictions.[12] Overall, as

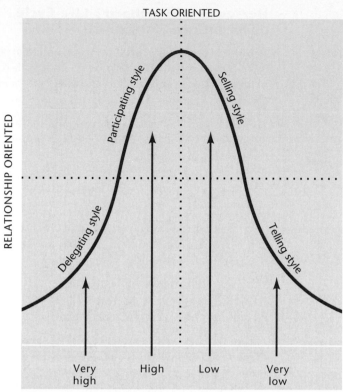

TASK ORIENTED

Participating style

Selling style

RELATIONSHIP ORIENTED

Delegating style

Telling style

| Very high | High | Low | Very low |

Maturity Level of Followers
(need for achievement, willingness to accept
responsibility, and education/experience)

FIGURE 14.3
Hersey and Blanchard's
situational leadership
model.

is true of the other style approaches, this situational approach seems to be of some value in training and development work in that it can point out the need for flexibility and take into consideration the different variables affecting leaders, but this type of approach has limited utility for identifying leadership effectiveness.

Likert's Four Systems of Management

The grid and situational approaches are both highly descriptive and at this time lack empirically validated research backup. In contrast, Rensis Likert proposed four basic systems, or styles, of organizational leadership that evolved from the many years of research by the Michigan group. Table 14.3 summarizes these four styles, called *systems of management leadership*.

The manager who operates under a system 1 approach is very authoritarian and actually tries to exploit work group members. The system 2 manager is also authoritarian but in a paternalistic manner. This benevolent autocrat keeps strict control and never delegates authority to work group members, but he or she "pats them on the head" and "does it for their best interests." The system 3 manager uses a consultative style. This manager asks for and receives participative input from work group

TABLE 14.3 Likert's Systems of Management Leadership

Leadership Variable	System 1 (Exploitive Autocratic)	System 2 (Benevolent Autocratic)	System 3 (Participative)	System 4 (Democratic)
Confidence and trust in subordinates	Manager has no confidence or trust in subordinates.	Manager has condescending confidence and trust, such as a master has in a servant.	Manager has substantial but not complete confidence and trust; still wishes to keep control of decisions.	Manager has complete confidence and trust in subordinates in all matters.
Subordinates' feeling of freedom	Subordinates do not feel at all free to discuss things about the job with their superior.	Subordinates do not feel very free to discuss things about the job with their superior.	Subordinates feel rather free to discuss things about the job with their superior.	Subordinates feel completely free to discuss things about the job with their superior.
Superiors' seeking involvement with subordinates	Manager seldom gets ideas and opinions of subordinates in solving job problems.	Manager sometimes gets ideas and opinions of subordinates in solving job problems.	Manager usually gets ideas and opinions and usually tries to make constructive use of them.	Manager always asks subordinates for opinions and always tries to make constructive use of them.

members but maintains the right to make the final decision. The system 4 manager uses a democratic style. This manager gives some direction to work group members but provides for total participation and decision by consensus and majority.

To give empirical research backup on which style is more effective, Likert and his colleagues asked thousands of managers to describe, on an expanded version of the format shown in Table 14.3, the highest- and lowest-producing departments with which they had had experience. Quite consistently, the high-producing units were described according to systems 3 and 4, and the low-producing units fell under systems 1 and 2. These responses were given irrespective of the manager's field of experience or of whether the manager was in a line or staff position.[13]

The Impact of Intervening Variables and Time. An important refinement of Likert's work is the recognition of three broad classes of variables that affect the relationship between leadership and performance in a complex organization.[14] They are briefly summarized as follows:

1. *Causal variables.* These are the independent variables that determine the course of developments and results of an organization. They include only those variables which are under the control of management; for example, economic conditions are *not* causal variables in this sense. Examples would be organization structure and management's policies and decisions and their leadership styles, skills, and behavior.
2. *Intervening variables.* These reflect the internal climate of the organization. Performance goals, loyalties, attitudes, perceptions, and motivations are some important intervening variables. They affect interpersonal relations, communication, and decision making in the organization.
3. *End-result variables.* These are the dependent variables, the outcomes of the organization. Examples would be productivity, service, costs, quality, and earnings.

Likert points out that there is not a direct cause-and-effect relationship between, for example, leadership style (a causal variable) and earnings (an end-result variable). The intervening variables must also be taken into consideration. For example, moving to a system 1 style of management may lead to an improvement in profits but a deterioration of the intervening variables (that is, a decline in attitudes, loyalty, and motivation). In time, these intervening variables may lead to a decrease in profits. Thus, although on the surface it appeared that system 1 was increasing profits, because of the impact on the intervening variables, in the long run system 1 may lead to a decrease in profits. The same can be said for the application of a system 4 style. In the short run, profits may dip, but because of the impact on intervening variables, there may be an increase in profit over time. Obviously, the time lag between intervention and the impact on end-result variables becomes extremely important to Likert's scheme. On the basis of some research evidence, Likert concludes: "Changes in the causal variables toward System 4 apparently require an appreciable period of time before the impact of the change is fully manifest in corresponding improvement in end-result variables."[15]

An Example of Time Lag. Likert's "time lag" helps explain the following relatively common sequence of events. A system 1 manager takes over an operation and may have continuing good performance results. In the meantime, however, the intervening variables are declining. Because of the good results, the system 1 manager is promoted. A system 4 manager now takes over the operation. Because of the time lag, the intervening variables, which were affected by the system 1 manager, now start to affect performance. Under the system 4 manager, performance starts to decline, but the intervening variables start to improve. However, top management see that when the system 4 manager took over, performance started to decline. The system 4 manager is replaced by a system 1 manager to "tighten up" the operation. The intervening variables affected by the system 4 manager now start to affect performance, and the cycle repeats itself. Figure 14.4 depicts this situation. In other words, the cause-and-effect relationships that appear on the surface may be very misleading because of the time lag impact of the intervening variables. As in the example, top management evaluations often credit the wrong manager (the system 1

FIGURE 14.4
A hypothetical example depicting Likert's time lag impact of intervening variables on performance.

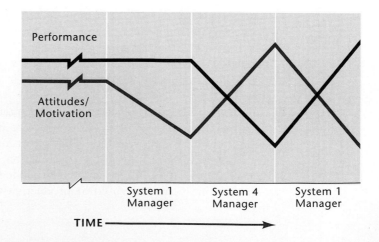

manager in this case) for improving performance and unjustly blame the wrong manager (the system 4 manager in the example) for poor performance. Some organizations may be guilty of this never-ending cycle of rewarding and punishing the wrong managers because of the time lag effect of intervening variables.

Analysis of Likert's Approach. One of the major criticisms of Likert's work concerns its overdependence on survey questionnaire measures for gathering data to develop the theory and application of system 4 management. Sole dependence on Likert scale (continuums of dimensions as shown in Table 14.3) questionnaire responses is not enough. As has been pointed out a number of times in this text, there is increasing criticism of data gathered only by questionnaires and interviews. Multiple measures of behaviorally oriented variables in organizations are needed. More use of archival information (existing records kept by every organization for other uses, for example, government reports, personnel records, and performance data) and data gathered through observation are needed.

Although ethical standards must always be maintained, subject awareness must be minimized to increase the reliability and validity of data that are gathered for research purposes. Both questionnaires and interviews have a great deal of subject awareness or intrusiveness. Archival analysis and some naturalistic observational techniques minimize subject awareness and are called *unobtrusive measures*.[16] Not only Likert's work but also much of the other research reported in this text is based upon indirect questionnaire measures. What is needed is to supplement these measures with other measures, such as observations and archival data. As Chapter 1 points out, the use of multiple measures increases tremendously the chance of getting better, more accurate, and more valid data.

Another problem inherent in Likert's scheme, besides the real and potential measurement problems, is the implication of the universality of the system 4 approach. Although Likert points out that "differences in the kind of work, in the traditions of the industry, and in the skills and values of the employees of a particular company will require quite different procedures and ways to apply appropriately the basic principles of system 4 management,"[17] he still implies that system 4 will *always* be more effective than system 1. Proponents of situational, or contingency, leadership theories and their research findings would, of course, counter this generalization.

Convincing arguments can be made for directive, rather than system 4, styles of leadership. This position has been stated as follows:

> The inescapable fact is that many, many organizations who are less than "excellent" in the caliber of their people and support systems simply can't afford to have their managers be participative without a commensurate dose of direction. That is, in the vast majority of actual leadership situations democratic behaviors must be tempered with a measure of direction or follow-up to assure that organizational goals are accomplished efficiently and effectively.[18]

This position on leadership effectiveness was essentially ignored by Likert.

Leadership Styles in Perspective

Blake and Mouton's managerial grid, Hersey and Blanchard's life cycle, and Likert's four systems represent the established approaches to leadership style. These have been around for a number of years, but are still relevant in the prescriptive sense of what managers should do, even in today's emerging organizations. However, except for Likert's scheme, which still has methodological problems as discussed above, there is a general lack of research support. Yet, there is accumulating evidence that a leader's style can make a difference. For example, recent studies have found that the leader's style is the key to the formulation and implementation of strategy[19] and even plays an important role in work group members' creativity.[20] In other words, there is little doubt that the *way* (style) leaders influence work group members can make a difference in their own and their people's performance.

In recent years, however, except for the continued use as a training vehicle, the concern for styles of leadership has given way to the importance of the roles and activities of leadership and the skills of effective leaders. The rest of the chapter is concerned with this *what* (roles and activities) and *how* (skills) of leadership.

THE ROLES AND ACTIVITIES OF LEADERSHIP

In answer to the question of what do leaders really do, observational studies by Henry Mintzberg and the author (Luthans) were conducted. These studies provide direct empirical evidence of the roles (Mintzberg) and activities (Luthans) of leaders/ managers.

Leader/Manager Roles

On the basis of his direct observational studies (as opposed to the questionnaire/ interview studies so commonly used in leadership research), Mintzberg proposes the three types of managerial roles shown in Figure 14.5.[21] The *interpersonal roles* arise directly from formal authority and refer to the relationship between the manager and others. By virtue of the formal position, the manager has a *figurehead role* as a symbol of the organization. Most of the time spent as a figurehead is on ceremonial duties such as greeting a touring class of students or taking an important customer to lunch. The second interpersonal role is specifically called the *leader role*. In this role the manager uses his or her influence to motivate and encourage subordinates to accomplish organizational objectives. In the third type of interpersonal role the manager undertakes a *liaison role*. This role recognizes that managers often spend more time interacting with others outside their unit (with peers in other units or those completely outside the organization) than they do working with their own superiors and subordinates.

Besides the interpersonal roles flowing from formal authority, Figure 14.5 shows that managers also have important *informational roles*. Most observational studies find that managers spend a great deal of time giving and receiving information. As *monitor*, the manager is continually scanning the environment and probing subordinates, bosses, and outside contacts for information; as *disseminator*, the manager distributes information to key internal people; and as *spokesperson*, the manager provides information to outsiders.

In the *decisional role*, the manager acts upon the information. In the *entrepreneurial role* in Mintzberg's scheme, the manager initiates the development of a project and assembles the necessary resources. The *disturbance handler*, on the other hand, instead of being proactive like the entrepreneur, is reactive to the problems and pressures of the situation. The disturbance handler has a crisis management type of role; for example, the employees are about to strike, or a major subcontractor is threatening to pull out. As *resource allocator* the manager decides who gets what in

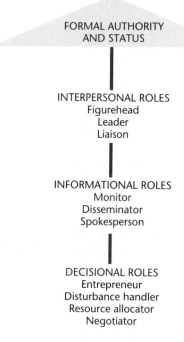

FORMAL AUTHORITY
AND STATUS

INTERPERSONAL ROLES
Figurehead
Leader
Liaison

INFORMATIONAL ROLES
Monitor
Disseminator
Spokesperson

DECISIONAL ROLES
Entrepreneur
Disturbance handler
Resource allocator
Negotiator

FIGURE 14.5
Mintzberg's managerial
roles.

his or her department. Finally, the *negotiator* decisional role recognizes the time managers spend at all levels in the give-and-take of negotiating with subordinates, bosses, and outsiders. For example, a production manager may have to negotiate a grievance settlement with the union business agent, or a supervisor in a social services department may have to negotiate certain benefit payments that one of the counselors wants to give a client.

These informal managerial roles suggested by Mintzberg get much closer to describing what managers/leaders really do than the formally described and prescribed functions. Mintzberg's work has definitely shed some light on what leaders do, but as he stated in a retrospective commentary about the ten roles: "We remain grossly ignorant about the fundamental content of the manager's job and have barely addressed the major issues and dilemmas in its practice."[22] More recent studies have used leadership roles such as vision setter, motivators, analyzer, and task master.[23] These roles were then tested concerning their relationships to three dimensions of firm performance. The results were that leaders with high behavioral complexity— the ability to play multiple, competing roles—produce the best performance, particularly with respect to business performance (growth and innovation) and organizational effectiveness.[24]

The Activities of Successful and Effective Leaders

Closely related to the study and identification of leader/manager roles are their day-to-day activities. The author (Luthans) and his colleagues conducted a comprehensive study to answer three major questions: (1) What do managers do? (2) What do successful real managers do? and (3) What do effective real managers do?[25] Answers to these questions can provide insights and specific descriptions of the daily activities of successful (those promoted relatively rapidly in their organizations) and effective (those with satisfied and committed subordinates and high-performing units) managers or leaders.

What Do Managers Do? The so-called Real Managers Study first used trained observers to freely observe and record in detail the behaviors and activities of forty-four managers from all levels and types of Midwest organizations (retail stores, hospitals, corporate headquarters, a railroad, government agencies, insurance companies, a newspaper office, financial institutions, and manufacturing plants). The voluminous data gathered from the free observation logs were then reduced through the Delphi technique (described in Chapter 16) into twelve categories with observable behavioral descriptors, as shown in Table 14.4. These empirically derived behavioral descriptors were then conceptually collapsed into the four managerial activities shown in Figure 14.6. Briefly summarized, these activities are as follows:

1. *Communication.* This activity consists of exchanging routine information and processing paperwork. Its observed behaviors include answering procedural questions, receiving and disseminating requested information, conveying the results of meetings, giving or receiving routine information over the phone, processing mail, reading reports, writing reports/memos/letters, routine financial reporting and bookkeeping, and general desk work.
2. *Traditional management.* This activity consists of planning, decision making, and controlling. Its observed behaviors include setting goals and objectives, defining tasks needed to accomplish goals, scheduling employees, assigning tasks, providing routine instructions, defining problems, handling day-to-day operational crises, deciding what to do, developing new procedures, inspecting work, walking around inspecting the work, monitoring performance data, and doing preventive maintenance.
3. *Human resources management.* This activity contains the most behavioral categories: motivating/reinforcing, disciplining/punishing, managing conflict, staffing, and training/developing. Because it was not generally permitted to be observed, the disciplining/punishing category was subsequently dropped from the analysis. The observed behaviors for this activity include allocating formal rewards, asking for input, conveying appreciation, giving credit where due, listening to suggestions, giving positive feedback, providing group support, resolving conflict between work group members, appealing to higher authorities or third parties to resolve a dispute, developing job descriptions, reviewing applications, interviewing applicants, filling in where needed, orienting employees, arranging for training, clarifying roles, coaching, mentoring, and walking work group members through a task.
4. *Networking.* This activity consists of socializing/politicking and interacting with outsiders. The observed behaviors associated with this activity include nonwork-related chitchat; informal joking around; discussing rumors, hearsay, and the grapevine; complaining, griping, and putting others down; politicking and gamesmanship; dealing with customers, suppliers, and vendors; attending external meetings; and doing/attending community service events.

The above lists of activities empirically answer the question of what managers really do. The activities include some of the classic activities identified by pioneering theorists such as Henri Fayol[26] (the traditional activities), as well as more recent views by modern leadership theorists such as Henry Mintzberg[27] (the communica-

TABLE 14.4 Managerial Activities and Behavioral Descriptors Derived from Free Observation of Real Managers

1. **Planning/Coordinating**
   a. setting goals and objectives
   b. defining tasks needed to accomplish goals
   c. scheduling employees, timetables
   d. assigning tasks and providing routine instructions
   e. coordinating activities of each work group member to keep work running smoothly
   f. organizing the work

2. **Staffing**
   a. developing job descriptions for position openings
   b. reviewing applications
   c. interviewing applicants
   d. hiring
   e. contacting applicants to inform them of being hired or not
   f. "filling in" where needed

3. **Training/Developing**
   a. orienting employees, arranging for training seminars, etc.
   b. clarifying roles, duties, job descriptions
   c. coaching, mentoring, walking work group members through task
   d. helping work group members with personal development plans

4. **Decision Making/Problem Solving**
   a. defining problems
   b. choosing between two or more alternatives or strategies
   c. handling day-to-day operational crises as they arise
   d. weighing the trade-offs; cost-benefit analyses
   e. actually deciding what to do
   f. developing new procedures to increase efficiency

5. **Processing Paperwork**
   a. processing mail
   b. reading reports, in-box
   c. writing reports, memos, letters, etc.
   d. routine financial reporting and bookkeeping
   e. general desk work

6. **Exchanging Routine Information**
   a. answering routine procedural questions
   b. receiving and disseminating requested information
   c. conveying results of meetings
   d. giving or receiving routine information over the phone
   e. staff meetings of an informational nature (status update, new company policies, etc.)

7. **Monitoring/Controlling Performance**
   a. inspecting work
   b. walking around and checking things out, touring
   c. monitoring performance data (e.g., computer printouts, production, financial reports)
   d. preventive maintenance

8. **Motivating/Reinforcing**
   a. allocating formal organizational rewards
   b. asking for input, participation
   c. conveying appreciation, compliments
   d. giving credit where due
   e. listening to suggestions
   f. giving positive performance feedback
   g. increasing job challenge
   h. delegating responsibility and authority
   i. letting work group members determine how to do their own work
   j. sticking up for the group to managers and others, backing a work group member

9. **Disciplining/Punishing**
   a. enforcing rules and policies
   b. nonverbal glaring, harassment
   c. demotion, firing, layoff
   d. any formal organizational reprimand or notice
   e. "chewing out" a work group member, criticizing
   f. giving negative performance feedback

10. **Interacting with Outsiders**
    a. public relations
    b. customers
    c. contacts with suppliers, vendors
    d. external meetings
    e. community-service activities

11. **Managing Conflict**
    a. managing interpersonal conflict between work group members or others
    b. appealing to higher authority to resolve a dispute
    c. appealing to third-party negotiators
    d. trying to get cooperation or consensus between conflicting parties
    e. attempting to resolve conflicts between a work group member and self

12. **Socializing/Politicking**
    a. nonwork related chitchat (e.g., family or personal matters)
    b. informal "joking around," B.S.
    c. discussing rumors, hearsay, grapevine
    d. complaining, griping, putting others down
    e. politicking, gamesmanship

Source: Fred Luthans and Diane Lee Lockwood, "Toward an Observation System for Measuring Leader Behavior in Natural Settings," in J. G. Hunt, D. Hosking, C. Schriesheim, and R. Stewart (eds.), *Leaders and Managers*, Pergamon Press, New York, 1984, p. 122.

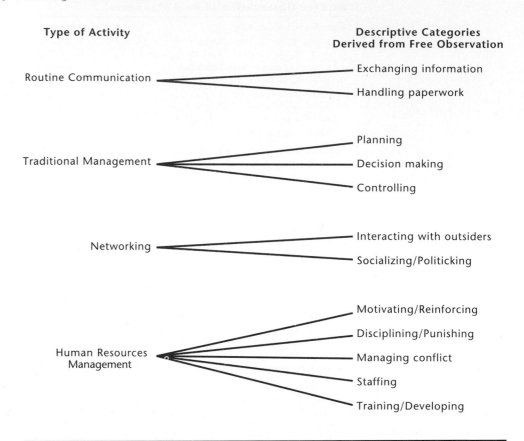

Type of Activity	Descriptive Categories Derived from Free Observation
Routine Communication	Exchanging information
	Handling paperwork
Traditional Management	Planning
	Decision making
	Controlling
Networking	Interacting with outsiders
	Socializing/Politicking
Human Resources Management	Motivating/Reinforcing
	Disciplining/Punishing
	Managing conflict
	Staffing
	Training/Developing

FIGURE 14.6
Luthans' conceptual categories of real managers' activities.

tion activities) and John Kotter[28] (the networking activities). As a whole, however, especially with the inclusion of human resources management activities, this view of real managers' activities is more comprehensive than previous studies of leader/manager activities.

After the nature of managerial activities was determined through the free observation of the 44 managers, the next phase of the study was to determine the relative frequency of these activities. Data on another sample of 248 real managers (not the 44 used in the initial portion of this study but from similar organizations) were gathered. Trained participant observers filled out a checklist based on the managerial activities shown in Table 14.4 at a random time, once every hour, over a two-week period. As shown in Figure 14.7, the managers were found to spend about a third of their time and effort in communication activities, a third in traditional management activities, a fifth in human resources management activities, and a fifth in networking activities. This relative-frequency analysis—based on observational data of a large sample—provides a fairly confident answer to the question of what real managers do.

What Do Successful Real Managers Do? Important though it is to get an empirical answer to the basic question of what leaders/managers do, of even greater interest is determining what successful and effective leaders/managers do. Success was defined in terms of the speed of promotion within an organization. A success index on the sample in the study was calculated by dividing the managers' levels in their respective

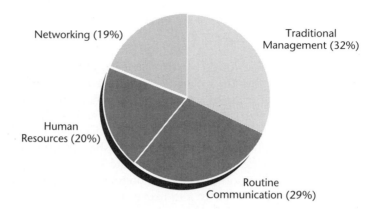

FIGURE 14.7
Relative distribution of real managers' activities. (*Source*: Fred Luthans, Richard M. Hodgetts, and Stuart A. Rosenkrantz, *Real Managers*, Ballinger, Cambridge, Mass., 1988, p. 27. Used with permission.)

organizations by their tenure (length of service) there. Thus, a manager at the fourth level of management who has been with the organization for five years would be rated more successful than a manager at the third level who had been at that level for twenty-five years. Obviously, there are some potential problems with such a measure of success, but for the large sample of managers, this was an objective and useful measure.

To answer the question of what successful managers do, several types of analyses were conducted. In all these analyses, the importance of networking in real managers' success was very apparent. Of the four major activities, only networking had a statistically significant relationship with success.[29] Overall, it was clear that networking made the biggest relative contribution to manager success and, importantly, human resources management activities made the least relative contribution.

What does this mean? It means that in this study of real managers, using speed of promotion as the measure of success, it was found that successful managers spend relatively more time and effort socializing, politicking, and interacting with outsiders than did their less successful counterparts. Perhaps equally important, the successful managers did not give relatively as much time or attention to the traditional management activities of planning, decision making, and controlling or to the human resources management activities of motivating/reinforcing, staffing, training/developing, and managing conflict. In other words, for the real managers in this study, networking seems to be the key to success (as defined by rapid promotion).

What Do Effective Real Managers Do? Although the operational measure of success used in the study was empirical and direct, the definition and measurement of effectiveness was more indirect and perceptual. The vast literature on managerial effectiveness offers little agreement on criteria or measures. To overcome as many of the obstacles and disagreements as possible, for a sample of the real managers, the study used a combined effectiveness index that represented the two major—and generally agreed upon—criteria of both leadership theory/research and practice: (1) getting the job done through high quantity and quality standards of performance, and (2) getting the job done through people, requiring their satisfaction and commitment.

In particular, an organizational effectiveness questionnaire[30] that measures the unit's quality and quantity of performance, a job satisfaction questionnaire,[31] and an organizational commitment questionnaire[32] were used. This multiple-measure index was employed in the study to answer the most important question of what effective managers do. It was found that communication and human resources management activities made by far the largest relative contribution to the managers' effectiveness, and that the traditional management activities, and especially the networking activities, made by far the least relative contribution. In other words, if effectiveness is defined as the perceived quantity and quality of the performance of a manager's unit and his or her work group members' satisfaction and commitment, then the biggest relative contribution to leadership effectiveness comes from the human-oriented activities—communication and human resources management.

Another intriguing finding from this part of the study was that the least relative contribution to the managers' measured effectiveness came from the networking activity. This, of course, is in stark contrast to the results of the successful manager analysis. Networking activity had by far the strongest relative relationship to success, but the weakest to effectiveness. On the other hand, human resources management activities had a strong relationship to effectiveness (second only to also human-oriented communication activities), but had the weakest relative relationship to success. In other words, the successful managers in this study did not do the same activities as the effective managers (in fact, they did almost the opposite). These contrasting profiles may have significant implications for understanding the current performance problems facing today's organizations.

Implications of the Real Managers Study. The Real Managers Study is obviously bound by the definitions that were used, and, of course, one could question the generalizability of the findings and conclusions to all managers. As far as generalizability goes, it is interesting to note that a replication of this study that observed Russian managers in a large textile factory found very similar results.[33] Chapter 19 gives details of this Russian study, but for now it can be said that the study provides at least beginning evidence that the activities identified for the successful and effective U.S. managers may hold across cultures. However, much more evidence is needed to draw any definitive conclusions about generalizability. In addition, as was recently pointed out, knowing *what* leaders do, which was the purpose of the Real Managers Study, must be supplemented with *why* they are doing it.[34]

Despite the limitations, there seem to be a number of implications from the Real Managers Study for the application of leadership in today's organizations. Probably the major implication stems from the significant difference between the activities of successful and effective managers. The most obvious implication from this finding is that more attention may need to be given to formal reward systems so that effective managers are promoted. Organizations need to tie formal rewards (especially promotions) to performance, in order to move ahead and meet the challenges that lie ahead. This can be accomplished most pragmatically in the short run by performance-based appraisal and reward systems and in the long run by developing cultural values that support and reward effective performance, not just successful socializing and politicking. An important goal to meet the challenges of the years ahead might be as simple as making effective managers successful.

Besides the implications for performance-based appraisal and reward systems and organizational culture, much can be learned from the effective managers in the study. In particular, it is important to note the relative importance that they gave to the human-oriented activities of communication and human resources management. The effective managers' day-to-day activities revolved around their people—keeping them informed, answering questions, getting and giving information, processing information, giving feedback and recognition, resolving conflicts, and conducting training and development. In other words, these effective managers provide some answers to how to meet the challenges that lie ahead. Human-oriented leadership skills may be of considerable value in meeting the challenges of global competition, of information, and of quality service. The next section focuses on these leadership skills.

LEADERSHIP SKILLS

As the preceding chapter indicates, there is now recognition in both leadership theory and practice of the importance of skills, *how* leaders behave and perform effectively. Both styles and roles/activities are closely related to skills and can be used as a point of departure for the discussion of skills. First, some of the commonly recognized leadership skills are identified; then, training, job redesign, and behavioral management skills (discussed in previous chapters) are suggested as effective leadership techniques.

What Skills Do Leaders Need?

As mentioned in Chapter 13, the research for leader traits has given way to attempts to identify leader skills. There are many lists of such skills in the practitioner-oriented literature. For example, a recent list of suggested leadership skills critical to success in the global economy includes the following:[35]

1. *Cultural flexibility.* In international assignments this skill refers to cultural awareness and sensitivity. In domestic organizations the same skill could be said to be critical for success in light of the increasing diversity. Leaders must have the skills not only to manage but also to recognize and celebrate the value of diversity in their organizations.
2. *Communication skills.* Effective leaders must be able to communicate, in written form, orally, and nonverbally.
3. *HRD skills.* Since human resources are so much a part of leadership effectiveness, leaders must have human resource development (HRD) skills of developing a learning climate, designing training programs, transmitting information and experience, assessing results, providing career counseling, creating organizational change, and adapting learning materials.[36]
4. *Creativity.* Problem solving, innovation, and creativity provide the competitive advantage in today's global marketplace. Leaders must possess the skills to not only be creative themselves but also provide a climate that encourages creativity and assist their people to be creative.
5. *Self-management of learning.* This skill refers to the need for continuous learning of new knowledge and skills. In this time of dramatic change and chaos, leaders must undergo continuous change themselves. They must be self-learners.

This list is up to date and is as good as any other; however, as an academic analysis recently noted: "The prevailing conceptualizations of skills required for successful managerial performance hinders our understanding of the phenomenon."[37] To get around this problem, Whetten and Cameron provide a more empirical derivation of effective leadership skills. On the basis of an interview study of over 400 highly effective managers, the ten skills most often identified were the following:

1. Verbal communication (including listening)
2. Managing time and stress
3. Managing individual decisions
4. Recognizing, defining, and solving problems
5. Motivating and influencing others
6. Delegating
7. Setting goals and articulating a vision
8. Self-awareness
9. Team building
10. Managing conflict[38]

Follow-up studies and related research have found skills similar to the ten above. Through statistical techniques, the results of the various research studies were combined into the following four categories of effective leadership skills:

1. Participative and human relations (for example, supportive communication and team building)
2. Competitiveness and control (for example, assertiveness, power, and influence)
3. Innovativeness and entrepreneurship (for example, creative problem solving)
4. Maintaining order and rationality (for example, managing time and rational decision making)[39]

Commenting on these various leadership skills identified through research, Whetten and Cameron note three characteristics:

1. The skills are behavioral. They are not traits nor, importantly, styles. They consist of an identifiable set of actions that leaders perform and that result in certain outcomes.
2. The skills, in several cases, seem contradictory or paradoxical. For example, they are neither all soft- nor all hard-driving, neither oriented toward teamwork and interpersonal relations exclusively nor individualism and entrepreneurship exclusively.
3. The skills are interrelated and overlapping. Effective leaders do not perform one skill or one set of skills independent of others. In other words, effective leaders are multiskilled.[40]

On the basis of this background, Whetten and Cameron then develop models for both personal and interpersonal leadership skills. Figure 14.8 and Figure 14.9

FIGURE 14.8
Whetten and Cameron model of personal skills. (*Source*: David A. Whetten and Kim S. Cameron, *Developing Management Skills*, 2d ed., Harper-Collins, New York, 1991, p. 17. Used with permission.)

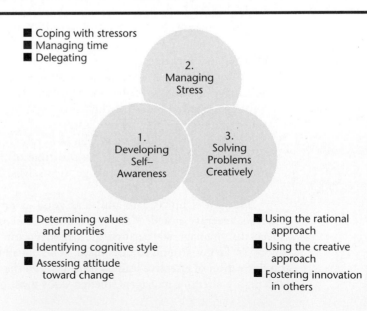

■ Coping with stressors
■ Managing time
■ Delegating

2. Managing Stress

1. Developing Self–Awareness

3. Solving Problems Creatively

■ Determining values and priorities
■ Identifying cognitive style
■ Assessing attitude toward change

■ Using the rational approach
■ Using the creative approach
■ Fostering innovation in others

FIGURE 14.9
Whetten and Cameron model of interpersonal skills.
(*Source*: David A. Whetten and Kim S. Cameron, *Developing Management Skills*, 2d ed., Harper-Collins, New York, 1991, p. 16. Used with permission.)

show these models. As shown, the personal skills of developing self-awareness, managing stress, and solving problems creatively overlap with one another, and so do the interpersonal skills of communicating supportively, gaining power and influence, motivating others, and managing conflict. These models not only can be used to summarize what skills were found to be important in effective leaders but also can serve as guidelines for needed skill development in the future.

Other Techniques for Leadership Effectiveness

Besides the skills discussed above, other techniques involving training, job design, and behavioral management, discussed in previous chapters, can also be used by effective leaders. For example, leaders can undergo personal growth training that may involve a combination of psychological exercises and outdoor adventures. This approach is aimed at empowering participants to take greater responsibility for their own lives and ultimately their organizations.[41] As revealed in the following reflection of a personal growth training participant, these currently popular programs may be wrongly equating the thrills involved with effective leadership:

> I peer over the edge of the cliff, trying to be logical. The harness to which I am attached seems sturdy. I have just watched several other participants jump. Although they appeared anxious at first, they not only survived the leap—they seemed to enjoy it. I also trust the safety of the system because I trust that the training company does not want me to die. Okay, given that assessment, let's take the risk. It might even be fun. And somehow, I might become a better leader. So off the edge I go.[42]

Although such personal growth training is controversial, there is no question that leaders need to use training techniques with their people. The Japanese, of course, have placed a high priority on training of all kinds, which is a major reason for their tremendous success. Recently, however, premier American corporations have also become committed to the importance of training. For example, all employees at the highly successful Quad Graphics firm spend considerable time every week in training sessions—on their own time—to improve themselves and make their company more competitive. A major component of the Motorola "quality revolution" was that spending on employee training went to $100 million per year, with 40 percent directly devoted to the skills and procedures needed to produce a no-defect product or to provide timely, error-free, courteous service to internal and external customers. Old job-rotation training programs have also come to life at companies such as McDonnell Douglas, where this firm's policy follows the adage that there is no training experience better than "walking a mile in the other person's shoes." The same goes for cross-training and the newer "pay for knowledge" approaches that an increasing number of U.S. firms are beginning to implement.

Besides training, job redesign is another important technique leaders can use effectively. Covered in Chapter 7, this approach attempts to manage the job rather than the extremely complex person that holds the job. From enriching the job by building in more responsibility, the more recent approach is to concentrate on the characteristics of identity, variety, significance, autonomy, and feedback identified by Hackman and his colleagues and covered in Chapter 7. There has been a stream of research to support the concept that when employees perceive these characteristics in their job, they do high-quality work. Leaders need to give special attention to the autonomy and feedback characteristics of their people's jobs. Autonomy involves empowering their subordinates to make decisions and solve their own problems, in other words, giving them more control over their own job. Feedback can be built into some jobs, but leaders also must provide specific, immediate performance feedback to their people.

Finally, the behavioral management approach, covered in Chapter 8, can be effectively used by leaders to meet the challenges ahead. The organizational behavior modification (O.B. Mod.) techniques based on the principles of operant conditioning and social learning theory were shown in Chapter 8 to have dramatic results on human performance in organizations. It is important to note that O.B. Mod. interventions have used mainly nonfinancial rewards—feedback systems and contingent recognition/attention in both manufacturing and service organizations.

The intent of this discussion is not to give an exhaustive list of leadership skills and techniques. All the styles and roles/activities discussed in this chapter and the theories in the preceding chapter, plus the techniques discussed in the motivation and learning chapters, are relevant and can be effective. Obviously, there are many other leadership skills and techniques that can also be effectively used. In total, how leaders apply their skills and techniques can and will make a difference in the challenges that lie ahead.

Summary

This chapter is concerned with leadership styles (the way leaders/managers influence followers/subordinates), roles and activities (what leaders/managers do in their day-to-day jobs), and skills (how leaders/managers can be effective). Leadership styles have been studied the longest and are derived from both the classic leadership studies and the modern theories. Examples of well-known approaches to leadership styles include Blake and Mouton's managerial grid; Hersey and Blanchard's situational, or life-cycle, model; and Likert's four systems. Each of these approaches to style has been around for a long time, but still has implications for the practice of leadership.

The grid is valuable mainly because it allows managers to describe their styles. Hersey and Blanchard's approach shows how well managers can match the appropriate style with the maturity level of the group being led, and Likert's work has implications for organizational effectiveness. Likert's recognition of intervening variables and their time lag effects has significant implications for practice. However, all these approaches to style need more and better research in order to make meaningful contributions to the actual practice of leadership.

The shift in attention from styles to roles and activities reflects a more empirical emphasis on what leaders really do. Through observational methodology, Mintzberg identified interpersonal (figurehead, leader, liaison), informational (monitor, disseminator, spokesperson), and decisional (entrepreneur, disturbance handler, resource allocator, negotiator) roles. Closely related is the observational study of leader/manager activities. The author's (Luthans) Real Managers Study investigated the question of what leaders/managers do in their day-to-day activities and what successful and effective leaders/managers do. It was found that the managers spend about a third of their time and effort in communication activities, a third in traditional management activities, a fifth in human resources management activities, and a fifth in networking activities. The analysis of successful managers (those rapidly promoted) found that networking made the biggest relative contribution to their rise and human resources management activities the least. In contrast, however, the analysis of effective managers (those with satisfied and committed subordinates and high-performing units) found that communication and human resources management activities made the largest relative contribution and networking the least. This difference between successful and effective managers has considerable implications for how one gets ahead in an organization (networking involves socializing/politicking and interacting with outsiders) and the reward systems of organizations (the effective managers may not be promoted as fast as the politically savvy ones).

The last part of the chapter is concerned with leadership skills, how leaders behave and perform effectively. Although there are many skills, such as cultural flexibility, communication, HRD, creativity, and self-management of learning, the more research-based skills identified by Whetten and Cameron seem most valuable. Their personal skills model, involving developing self-awareness, managing stress, and solving problems creatively, and the interpersonal skills model, involving communicating supportively, gaining power and influence, motivating others, and managing conflict, are especially comprehensive and useful. Finally, the more widely recognized organizational behavior techniques found in other chapters (for example, training, job design, and behavioral management) can also be effectively used by leaders.

Questions for Discussion and Review

1. What are some styles of charismatic leadership? What do they mean? Give an example.
2. Briefly identify the major styles from Blake and Mouton's grid, from Hersey and Blanchard's life-cycle model, and from Likert's four systems. How can the wrong manager be rewarded under the Likert scheme?
3. What are the major categories of roles identified by Mintzberg? What are some of the subroles when leaders/managers give and receive information?

4. Use the Real Managers Study to briefly answer the following: What do managers do? What do successful managers do? What do effective managers do?

5. What are some of the needed skills for leaders/managers to be effective? What are the three major characteristics of these skills?

Footnote References and Supplemental Readings

1. Avis Johnson and Fred Luthans, "The Relationship Between Leadership and Management: An Empirical Assessment," *Journal of Managerial Issues*, Spring 1990, pp. 13–25.

2. "Harley-Davidson: Going Whole Hog to Provide Stakeholder Satisfaction," *Management Review*, June 1993, p. 55.

3. Alan Deutschman, "Steve Jobs' Next Big Gamble," *Fortune*, Feb. 8, 1993, p. 99.

4. David A. Nadler and Michael L. Tushman, "Beyond the Charismatic Leader: Leadership and Organizational Change," *California Management Review*, Winter 1990, p. 83.

5. "Changing Perspectives," *The Wall Street Journal*, Nov. 25, 1986, p. 1.

6. Warren G. Bennis, "Managing the Dream: Leadership in the 21st Century," *Journal of Organizational Change Management*, vol. 2, no. 1, 1989, p. 6.

7. Robert Blake and Jane S. Mouton, "Should You Teach There's Only One Best Way to Manage?" *Training HRD*, April 1978, p. 24.

8. Robert Blake and Jane S. Mouton, "Management by Grid Principles or Situationalism: Which?" *Group and Organization Studies*, December 1981, pp. 439–455.

9. Paul Hersey and Kenneth H. Blanchard, *Management of Organizational Behavior*, 4th ed., Prentice-Hall, Englewood Cliffs, N.J., 1982.

10. Gary A. Yukl, *Leadership in Organizations*, Prentice-Hall, Englewood Cliffs, N.J., 1981, pp. 143–144.

11. Claude L. Graeff, "The Situational Leadership Theory: A Critical View," *Academy of Management Review*, April 1983, pp. 285–291.

12. Warren Blank, John R. Weitzel, and Stephen G. Green, "A Test of the Situational Leadership Theory," *Personnel Psychology*, vol. 43, 1990, pp. 579–597.

13. Rensis Likert, *The Human Organization*, McGraw-Hill, New York, 1967, pp. 3, 11.

14. Ibid., pp. 26, 29.

15. Ibid., pp. 80–81.

16. Eugene J. Webb, Donald T. Campbell, Richard D. Schwartz, and Lee Sechrest, *Unobtrusive Measures: Nonreactive Research in the Social Sciences*, Rand McNally, Chicago, 1966.

17. Likert, op. cit., p. 192.

18. Jan P. Muczyk and Bernard C. Reimann, "The Case for Directive Leadership," *The Academy of Management Executive*, November 1987, p. 309.

19. Afsaneh Nahavandi and Ali R. Malekzadeh, "Leader Style in Strategy and Organizational Performance: An Integrative Framework," *Journal of Management Studies*, May 1993, pp. 405–426.

20. Matthew R. Redmond and Michael D. Mumford, "Putting Creativity to Work: Effects of Leader Behavior on Subordinate Creativity," *Organizational Behavior and Human Decision Processes*, June 1993, pp. 120–151.

21. The figure and following discussion are based on Henry Mintzberg, "The Managers' Job: Folklore and Fact," *Harvard Business Review*, July–August 1975, pp. 49–61.

22. Henry Mintzberg, "Retrospective Commentary on 'The Manager's Job: Folklore and Fact,'" *Harvard Business Review*, March–April 1990, p. 170.

23. Stuart L. Hart and Robert E. Quinn, "Roles Executives Play: CEOs, Behavioral Complexity, and Firm Performance," *Human Relations*, May 1993, pp. 543–575.

24. Ibid.

25. The following sections are drawn from Fred Luthans, Richard M. Hodgetts, and Stuart A. Rosenkrantz, *Real Managers*, Ballinger, Cambridge, Mass., 1988, and Fred Luthans, "Successful vs. Effective Real Managers," *Academy of Management Executive*, May 1988, pp. 127–132. The very extensive study took place over a four-year period.

26. See Henri Fayol, *General and Industrial Management*, Constance Storrs (trans.), Pitman, London, 1949.

27. See Henry Mintzberg, *The Nature of Managerial Work*, Harper & Row, New York, 1973, and Henry Mintzberg, "The Manager's Job: Folklore and Fact," pp. 49–61.

28. See John Kotter, *The General Managers*, Free Press, New York, 1982, and John Kotter, "What Do Effective General Managers Really Do?" *Harvard Business Review*, November–December 1982, pp. 156–167.

29. Fred Luthans, Stuart Rosenkrantz, and Harry Hennessey, "What Do Successful Managers Really Do?" *Journal of Applied Behavioral Science*, August 1985, pp. 255–270.

30. Paul E. Mott, *The Characteristics of Effective Organizations*, Harper & Row, New York, 1972.
31. P. C. Smith, L. M. Kendall, and C. L. Hulin, *The Measurement of Satisfaction in Work and Retirement*, Rand McNally, Chicago, 1969.
32. Richard T. Mowday, L. W. Porter, and Richard M. Steers, *Employee-Organizational Linkages: The Psychology of Commitment, Absenteeism, and Turnover*, Academic Press, New York, 1982.
33. Fred Luthans, Dianne H. B. Welsh, and Stuart A. Rosenkrantz, "What Do Russian Managers Really Do? An Observational Study with Comparisons to U.S. Managers," *Journal of International Business Studies*, Fourth Quarter, 1993, pp. 741–761.
34. Manfred F. R. Kets de Vries, Danny Miller, and Alain Noel, "Understanding the Leader-Strategy Interface: Application of the Strategic Relationship Interview Method," *Human Relations*, January 1993, pp. 5–21.
35. Michael J. Marquart and Dean W. Engel, "HRD Competencies for a Shrinking World," *Training and Development*, May 1993, pp. 62–64.
36. Ibid., p. 63.
37. Rabindra M. Kanungo and Sasi Misra, "Managerial Resourcefulness: A Reconceptualization of Management Skills," *Human Relations*, December 1992, pp. 1311–1332.
38. David A. Whetten and Kim S. Cameron, *Developing Management Skills*, HarperCollins, New York, 1991, p. 8.
39. Ibid., p. 11.
40. Ibid., pp. 8–11.
41. Jay A. Conger, "Personal Growth Training: Snake Oil or Pathway to Leadership?" *Organizational Dynamics*, Summer 1993, pp. 19–30.
42. Ibid., p. 19.

REAL CASE: A New Breed of Business Leaders

There is renewed controversy about the best way to lead today's dramatically changing organizations. In the popular press, there are suggestions for a new breed of leaders. One list suggests that this new breed of leaders are those (a) who think of themselves as sponsors, team leaders, or internal consultants rather than as individuals who are charged with managing others; (b) who believe the decision-making process should involve the other members of the team rather than being carried out by the leader only; (c) who share information with their people; (d) who focus efforts on getting results from their people, rather than on how many hours the people are working; and (e) who go outside the chain of command, if this will get things done.

In practice, there is some evidence that this new breed of leadership is actually being put into practice. A good example is Lawrence Bossidy, president of Allied Signal, a $12-billion-a-year manufacturer of aerospace equipment, auto parts, and other products. Bossidy recently expressed his leadership philosophy as follows: Hire the best possible people to help run the business and then get out of their way. He also strongly advocates breaking down the barriers between departments and getting everyone to work as a team. He feels that when workers feel empowered, they do more; when they feel threatened, they do less. Using these ideas, Bossidy is working hard to increase productivity and profits.

Another example of the new breed of leadership in action is provided by William Weiss of Ameritech, an $11-billion-a-year Bell operating company that serves 12 million customers, mostly in the Midwest. Weiss's leadership style focuses on getting people to accept and adjust to change. When he took over the firm, it was burdened with a slow-moving bureaucracy. Realizing that the marketplace was changing too fast to allow the old ways of doing things to work, he began working to identify a vision for the firm and putting risk takers into high management positions. Also, he dramatically changed the structure. A few years ago Ameritech was organized on the basis of geographic regions; now it is organized on the basis of customer segmentation. Under this new structure, the company responds to the needs of its customers and continually makes changes so that it is responding appropriately to these needs. At the same time, Weiss is continuing to downsize the organization, but empower and reassure those who remain. In a recent year the company made record profits, and Weiss announced a 7 percent reduction in the managerial work force. In the process, the employees are beginning to learn how to live with change and adjust to market conditions.

Michael Walsh, chief executive officer of Tenneco, a $14-billion-a-year conglomerate that sells natural gas and farm and construction equipment, uses a similar approach. Walsh believes that good leaders not only are risk takers but also are willing to make themselves vulnerable. He also believes that this approach has to be followed by managers throughout the organization. Commenting on these ideas, he says: "Every person in a key position has to see himself or herself as a mini-CEO. They have to conceptualize what has to be done, in the same way the CEO has. Then it cascades." Does this style work at Tenneco? If the financial statements are any indication, it certainly does. Over the last five years the firm has cut its debt-to-capital ratio by more than 20 points while producing a $1.1 billion swing in operating earnings, and the company feels that it is only halfway to where it wants to go in unleashing its potential productivity. Clearly, Walsh is operationalizing a new breed of leadership that is helping his firm realize its true potential.

1. According to the leadership styles discussed in this chapter, which one is closest to the business leaders in this case?
2. In terms of the managerial grid (see Figure 14.2), how would you describe these business leaders?
3. How do you think these business leaders spend their day in terms of the managerial activities identified in Table 14.4?

CASE:
The Puppet

Rex Justice is a long-term employee of the Carfax Corporation, and for the last several years he has been a supervisor in the financial section of the firm. He is very loyal to Carfax and works hard to follow the company policies and procedures and the orders of the managers above him. In fact, upper-level management think very highly of him; they can always count on Rex to meet any sort of demand that the company places on him. He is valued and well liked by all the top managers. His employees in the financial section have the opposite opinion of Rex. They feel that he is too concerned with pleasing the upper-level brass and not nearly concerned enough with the needs and concerns of the employees in his department. For example, they feel that Rex never really pushes hard enough for a more substantial slice of the budget. Relative to other departments in the company, they feel they are underpaid and overworked. Also, whenever one of them goes to Rex with a new idea or suggestion for improvement, he always seems to have five reasons why it can't be done. There is considerable dissatisfaction in the department, and everyone thinks that Rex is just a puppet for management. Performance has begun to suffer because of his style and leadership. Upper-level management seem to be oblivious to the situation in the finance section.

1. How would you explain Rex's leadership style in terms of one or more of the approaches discussed in the chapter?
2. What advice would you give Rex to improve his approach to leadership?
3. Could a leadership training program be set up to help Rex? What would it consist of?

INTEGRATIVE CONTEMPORARY CASE/READING FOR PART 3

The New Non-
Manager Managers

It's still open season on the American middle manager, and big guns continue to bag their daily limit without difficulty. Hardly a day passes without some formerly blue-chip outfit like GM, IBM, or Sears dispatching another couple of thousand or so to the corporate afterlife. The American Management Association reports that while middle managers are only about 5% of the work force at the 836 companies it surveyed, they account for a plump 22% of the past year's layoffs.

The reasons are no mystery. Middle managers have always handled two main jobs: supervising people, and gathering, processing, and transmitting information. But in growing numbers of companies, self-managed teams are taking over such standard supervisory duties as scheduling work, maintaining quality, even administering pay and vacations. Meanwhile, the ever-expanding power and dwindling cost of computers have transformed information handling from a difficult, time-consuming job to a far easier and quicker one. Zap! In an instant, historically speaking, the middle manager's traditional functions have vaporized.

That's bad enough. At the same time, competition is forcing many companies to squeeze costs without mercy. Guess who looks like a big, fat target? Says Cynthia Kellams, a management consultant at Towers Perrin: "If you can't say why you actually make your company a better place, you're out."

Knowing precisely what middle managers won't be doing much of anymore is only so useful. What *will* they, or their late Nineties equivalents, be doing? For an answer, look at those who are prospering. Call them the new managers, or—better yet—the new, non-manager managers. Many, perhaps most, are baby-boomers who bring a radically new set of values to the workplace. The 78 million Americans born between 1946 and 1964 tend to be an irreverent bunch. Many don't see the CEO as much of a hero. In fact, they often think the big guy gets in the way. They like to call themselves leaders, facilitators, sponsors—anything but managers.

More significantly, boomer managers want something other than the reassuring routine of the organization man. They want challenging and meaningful work. Says Lou Lenzi, a general manager at RCA who helped create ProScan, a successful new line of televisions: "For me there is a certain amount of professional pride, the satisfaction of making something happen."

For a closer glimpse of tomorrow's manager, consider Cindy Ransom, 37, a middle manager—er, sponsor—passionate about her job at Clorox. Three years ago Ransom asked her workers at a 100-person plant in Fairfield, California, to redesign the plant's operations. As she watched, intervening only to answer the occasional question, a team of hourly workers established training programs, set work rules for absenteeism, and reorganized the once traditional factory into five customer-focused business units. As the workers took over managerial work, Ransom used her increasing free time to attend to the needs of customers and suppliers.

Last year Clorox named Ransom's plant the most improved in the company's household products division, its largest. Did money spur her to help work the change? That certainly doesn't hurt, but she cites a more compelling reason: to see the people who work with her succeed. Says she: "When I read about America losing its competitive edge, it really pisses me off. It gets me motivated to make a

Source: Brian Dumaine, "The New Non-Manager Managers," *Fortune,* Feb. 22, 1993, pp. 80–84. Copyright 1993, Time Inc. All rights reserved. Reprinted by permission from Time.

difference in my little corner, to make my factory competitive enough so my people can be employed here until they retire." For her reward, Ransom won't move up in the hierarchy, but instead will get to apply her skills at a Clorox plant overseas, which suits her just fine.

Managers like Ransom, committed to coaching, sponsoring—heck, why not use the term—empowering their people, are still rare. Says James Champy, CEO of CSC Index, a consulting firm in Cambridge, Massachusetts, that specializes in reengineering organizations: "We won't see them in great numbers for another five to ten years. But corporate America is definitely going in that direction."

Another reason the new manager is coming into vogue: Middle managers who master skills such as team building and intrapreneurship and who acquire broad functional expertise will likely be in the best position to get tomorrow's top corporate jobs. That's because the role of the top executive is becoming more like that of a team player and broker of others' efforts, not that of an autocrat.

Look at Drypers, a small but fast-growing maker of disposable diapers. This profitable Houston company, whose sales last fiscal year grew 25% to $140 million, operates with an office of the chief executive that consists of five managing directors, all with equal power. The five, each of whom has a functional responsibility like finance, marketing, and manufacturing, work much like a middle management team, sharing information and kicking around ideas. No major decision is made until the five managing directors arrive at consensus. A lone CEO might be able to make a decision faster, but at Drypers, once a decision is made, all functions feel they own it, which helps wonderfully their inclination to put it into effect swiftly.

For example, the company last year developed and launched technologically advanced, disposable training pants called Big Boy and Big Girl in six months, fast by industry standards. After only a half year on the market, the new line has an impressive 20% market share in southeastern Texas. Says managing director David Pitassi: "When you have a shared vision, it's a very powerful thing."

In companies that have adopted advanced organizational structures and systems—flattened hierarchies, self-managed teams, cutting-edge pay and performance systems—a number of variants on the new manager are emerging.

The Socratic Manager. An old-school manager often told people what to do, how to do it, and when. A new-style manager asks the questions that will get people to solve problems and make decisions on their own. Dee Zalneraitis, 37, the information group manager at a Hudson, Massachusetts, division of R.R. Donnelley & Sons, America's largest printer, is a good example.

Old Manager	New Manager
■ Thinks of self as a manager or boss	■ Thinks of self as a sponsor, team leader, or internal consultant
■ Follows the chain of command	■ Deals with anyone necessary to get the job done
■ Works within a set organizational structure	■ Changes organizational structures in response to market change
■ Makes most decisions alone	■ Invites others to join in decision making
■ Hoards information	■ Shares information
■ Tries to master one major discipline, such as marketing or finance	■ Tries to master a broad array of managerial disciplines
■ Demands long hours	■ Demands results

Her division began converting to self-managed teams last year. Zalneraitis's new role is to teach, train, cajole, and comfort her 40 people until they feel confident enough to do the things she now does—hiring, firing, scheduling vacations, and the like. Once Zalneraitis feels her people can handle the responsibility, she hopes to move on to another equally challenging post in the company, somewhat like an internal consultant might. Says she: "I'd like to manage my way out of my current job in two years."

One of the hardest things about being this kind of manager, Zalneraitis found, is letting people figure things out on their own when she knows the answer. But it's the only way people can really learn, she says. A worker once went on vacation without scheduling someone to cover for her. Although Zalneraitis saw the problem right away, she had to sit and listen to the phones ring until her people figured it out.

Another of Zalneraitis's goals is to bring as many of her people as possible into decision-making. This entails decisions. "You always have to ask yourself, should I invite them to participate in the process?" she says. Under the old system, Zalneraitis at budget time would spend a week and a half behind closed doors feeling harassed. Now she shows all her people the budget and asks them how they can save money. They respond: An employee helped her balance the budget by suggesting they do away with some scheduled trips to an unreasonably demanding customer, for instance. Says Zalneraitis: "It takes a lot more time explaining things. You really have to enjoy helping them learn." If she does her job right, her hourly people will soon take over budgeting.

Even more than line managers, staff people must adopt new roles as teachers. Example: When he was head of human resources at S.C. Johnson Wax, the $3-billion-a-year maker of household products like Raid and Pledge, Earl VanderWielen redefined the job of the human resources manager. In a traditional system, an HR person is often divorced from day-to-day business, spending his time supervising companywide pay systems and making sure everyone adheres to government regulations. By contrast, VanderWielen knows the business inside out—he spent ten years as a manufacturing manager—and gets deeply involved in operations. When the company decided to move toward self-managed teams about eight years ago, VanderWielen and his small staff worked long hours on the factory floor, teaching line managers and workers about such management techniques as statistical analysis and pay-for-skills. In one instance, a team of workers figured out how to switch a line from liquid floor wax to a stain remover in 13 minutes instead of three days. Overall results have been startling. At its plant in Racine, Wisconsin, Johnson Wax has increased productivity 30% in the past eight years while reducing the number of middle managers from 140 to 37.

The Open Manager. Self-managed teams like those at R.R. Donnelley and Johnson Wax work only when all members have the same information, and lots of it. That's something Kevin Grundy, a director of manufacturing and engineering at Next Computer, believes in deeply. While Next, which sells high-performance workstations mostly to the government and universities, has been struggling financially, it is still admired as one of America's most open and freewheeling companies. To be competitive, founder and CEO Steve Jobs believes, every employee must contain the company's DNA and therefore must be privy to crucial information like profits, sales, and strategic plans.

But Next takes openness a step further: Everyone knows everyone else's salary and stockholdings, or at least can find out just by asking. Says Grundy, who believes sharing pay information helps morale: "The availability of salaries ensures that most inequities in the system get resolved. You don't want a lot of secret deals going on and one guy making more than the guy sitting next to him because he's a good negotiator."

At Grundy's factory, he and the human resources staffer have a list of what everyone makes. Anyone can come and look anytime. Grundy used to post the salaries but found that some people would look at the list and walk away in a lather. The idea now is to make sure the person with the list is trained to offer explanations about pay discrepancies. A very good engineer who was busting his back on a project saw that his compensation was lower than someone else's on the team. Grundy said to him: "I realize it's unfair but I just can't go and change it. Give me some time to get you where you need to be. You have to trust me." It worked. The engineer remained a productive member of the team, knowing that he'd eventually get his raise. In another instance one of Grundy's people asked, "Why don't I get paid more?" Grundy didn't think he deserved more. Says he: "You have to sit down with someone like that and talk about where he needs improvement. If he's only working eight hours a day and everyone else is putting in 12, you have to highlight the difference."

Interestingly, Grundy found that few people ask to see the list. He guesses they figure they can't do much about their pay anyway.

The Renaissance Manager. Remember the heyday of the general manager 20 or 30 years ago? Many executives, consultants, and academics believed then that a good manager could manage anything—a sharp insurance executive could shape up a machine-tool company in no time. The new manager also has broad skills but sticks to his industry or core technology, such as microchips, pharmaceuticals, or financial services. His breadth of knowledge is in the different functions within his industry or technology: sales, marketing, manufacturing, finance.

You'll find one of these corporate Renaissance men in Indianapolis at the U.S. headquarters of France's Thomson Consumer Electronics, maker of RCA televisions. Louis Lenzi, head of industrial design in the television division, wears conservative clothes and a no-fuss haircut, but he's no Fifties organization man. When asked how he motivates people, Lenzi will point to a life-size poster in his office of the Punisher, a horrific Marvel comic character, and then pick up a toy machine gun and start spraying the room.

Responding more seriously, Lenzi, 35, says the trick to working with people to get things done—especially when you have no direct authority over them—is to win their respect. He does this by showing them he has a thorough understanding of their jobs, skills, and needs.

Example: Over the past couple of years Lenzi has served on the cross-functional team of managers—marketers, engineers, manufacturing experts—that developed ProScan, a successful high-end line of TVs. Because each manager took turns being team leader, no one was really the boss. This meant Lenzi had to win his teammates' respect by demonstrating a broad knowledge of the business. In other words, he was not just some designer to be called on when deciding the color or shape of the new ProScan TV; he was a real player. Lenzi's carefully planned background, which included assignments that taught him about marketing, manufacturing, and engineering, helped immeasurably. He spent nine months on the road, interviewing TV retailers and customers, sat in endless meetings with engineers and manufacturers working out technical details for the new set, and even helped work up the marketing campaign.

Not only is the line a success, but all the team members subsequently moved on to bigger and better things. Says Lenzi: "It made us all better generalists."

The hardest thing about being a new manager, says Lenzi, is that you're often handling two jobs at once. While working on the ProScan team, he also had to handle his day-to-day job managing 37 people designing other RCA products. Says he: "I had to build trust and confidence. Part of the trick is showing up only when crucially needed. If my people had an issue with the factory on, say, whether to paint the back of a TV—which the designers thought was a great idea and the manufacturers thought insane—I'd go to a meeting and raise hell where I had to raise hell and cajole where I had to cajole."

The Radical Manager. Consultants say any new manager worth his or her low-sodium salt substitute must learn to create new businesses swiftly in response to fast and fickle markets. Anthony Lombardo, 45, general manager at Sony Medical, has found a formula for rapid-fire innovation. Sony Medical makes color printers and other peripherals for use with medical imaging equipment like ultrasound machines. A sort of entrepreneurial laboratory, the company has at least a half-dozen new seed ventures going at all times. Lombardo and his people spend lots of time with doctors and HMOs—their key customers—and constantly scan the rest of Sony for technologies that might serve those customers. Once they hit on one, they start a small cell of about ten people from different disciplines and let them run with it. The idea is to experiment constantly, move fast, see if the idea works, and if it doesn't, move on to the next.

An example: Using Sony's touchscreen and laser-disk-player technology, Lombardo last year worked with the Foundation for Informed Medical Decision Making to create an interactive system that helps patients in a hospital or doctor's office learn about their afflictions. Sales of the system should total $40 million within four to six years.

The key, says Lombardo, is constantly creating, juggling, shifting, and finally destroying organizations as the market demands. Says he: "We're not bound by the shape of the car. We can change the shape of the car. We have people who go around the corporation and look for new technologies and ideas that will constantly drive change in our business."

The Scavenger Manager. When times were flush in corporate America, a manager who wanted to create a new product would simply ask for resources—people, technology, money—and with luck, get them. Today, with budgets tight, the new manager must beg, borrow, and steal anything he can. A master scavenger is Okidata's John Ring, 55, who with no staff, little money, and very little authority, got six stubborn divisions spread over three continents to pool their resources on a project. The result: Doc-it, a new desktop printer, fax, scanner, and copier that an industry consulting group named product of the year last September.

A Brit with gray hair and mustache, Ring looks a bit weary as he recounts the Doc-it odyssey—understandably so. When he had the idea to combine all those features in early 1988, his compatriots at Okidata, an American subsidiary of Oki, a large Japanese maker of semiconductors, telecommunication equipment, and computer printers, said it couldn't be done.

Undaunted, Ring traveled to Japan and Europe to get the Oki people not only to buy into the idea but also to share their technological know-how. In Japan, for instance, Oki's fax and printer businesses were in different divisions.

Through sheer perseverance Ring eventually got the divisions to pool technologies and money. "To influence people you have to prove you're right, and then keep hammering away," he says. "I've been bloodied by this product, but I've given as good as I've got." When naysayers at headquarters in Japan said you couldn't get a printer in a box that small, Ring and a colleague went off to a garage in Cherry Hill, New Jersey, broke up an Oki printer, jammed the innards in nearly half the space, and glued the cut-up box back together. The printer worked.

Getting people to do things when you can't order them around, says Ring, is like living in some sort of Dadaesque world with no black or white and a thousand shades of gray: "You have to live with uncertainty. You never get the total green light. One day you wake up and say, 'I've done it.' It's all incremental."

The Humane Manager. In a world of unceasing change, the new manager must balance the tremendous demands of work with demands from the rest of his life—and help others do the same. It isn't easy. No one knows that better than Rick Hess, 40, of M/A-Com, a Lowell, Massachusetts, defense company that makes microwave communications equipment and is trying to build business in the private sector. M/A-Com's chief operating officer said to the staff in April, "I went home last night and told my wife the next year will be hell. I suggest you go home and tell yours. It's tough times."

A typical day for Hess starts at 7 A.M. and ends at 7 P.M. He goes home, tucks his four young kids in, and then does paperwork until bed, typically about 11. He tries to leave weekends for his family. It helps, he found, to keep his work in perspective. "I'm a fairly patient person," he says. "I get angry but don't display it. I try to look at the long term. I always have a goal, and I focus on that and don't get upset with the day to day."

Hess knows his people are under a lot of stress, too, and that part of the new manager's job is to make sure they avoid burnout. He stays close to them, takes them to lunch, tries to find out what's going on in their lives. He plays softball and basketball with them one night a week. "I want to know if someone's wife is having a baby so I don't give him a job that requires him to work an 80-hour week. The worst thing I can do is give someone an assignment he's bound to fail."

To motivate his people Hess constantly tries to get them to challenge themselves, another important skill of the new manager. "Don't rule people out because they don't have experience," he says. "Don't trap people in cubbies. Give people a reach if they have potential. Let a technical guy go and talk with customers and grow." Hess likes ambitious people because he understands that he won't be able to go to his next job until someone is ready to take his.

Being a new manager is hard. Practically no one has been trained for it, and many companies still aren't sure what to make of the phenomenon. If you want to feel noble about it, reflect that this new generation of smart, aggressive, entrepreneurial managers likely holds the key to America's future prosperity. And if nobility is a little higher than you're aiming, remember that in today's marketplace, with today's workers, the new non-manager manager has the best chance of producing the results that will advance his or her career.

1. What are some of the major reasons middle management ranks have been so hard hit by layoffs and the restructuring of employment?
2. Briefly summarize the major differences between the traditional manager and the so-called new nonmanager.
3. Of the various types of new managers identified in the article, which one do you think will be most needed and successful in the organizational environment that is emerging now and in the future?
4. This part of the text deals with groups and teams, conflict, stress, power and politics, and leadership. How does the new nonmanager relate to these dynamics of organizational behavior?

EXPERIENTIAL EXERCISES FOR PART 3

EXERCISE: Groups and Conflict Resolution*

Goals:

1. To compare individual versus group problem solving and decision making
2. To analyze the dynamics of groups
3. To demonstrate conflict and ways of resolving it

Implementation:

1. Divide any number of people into small groups of four or five.
2. Take about fifteen minutes for individual responses and thirty minutes for group consensus.
3. Each individual and group should have a worksheet. Pencils, a flip chart (newsprint or blackboard), marker pens, or chalk may also be helpful to the groups.

Process:

1. Each individual has fifteen minutes to read the story and answer the eleven questions about the story. Each person may refer to the story as often as needed but may not confer with anyone else. Each person should circle "T" if the answer is clearly true, "F" if the answer is clearly false, and "?" if it isn't clear from the story whether the answer is true or false.
2. After fifteen minutes each small group makes the same decisions using group consensus. Allow thirty minutes for group consensus. No one should change his or her answers on the individual questions. The ground rules for group decisions are as follows:
   a. Group decisions should be made by consensus. It is illegal to vote, trade, average, flip a coin, etc.
   b. No individual group member should give in only to reach agreement.
   c. No individual should argue for his or her own decision. Instead, each person should approach the task using logic and reason.
   d. Every group member should be aware that disagreements may be resolved by facts. Conflict can lead to understanding and creativity if it does not make group members feel threatened or defensive.

Scoring:

1. After thirty minutes of group work, the exercise leader should announce the correct answers. Scoring is based on the number of correct answers out of a possible total of eleven. Individuals are to score their own individual answers, and someone should score the group decision answers. The exercise leader should then call for:
   a. The group-decision score in each group.
   b. The average individual score in each group.
   c. The highest individual score in each group.

Source: Alan Filley, *Interpersonal Conflict Resolution*, Scott, Foresman, Glenview, Ill., 1975, pp. 139–142, as adapted from William H. Haney, *Communication and Organizational Behavior*, Irwin, Homewood, Ill., 1967, pp. 319–324.

2. Responses should be posted on the tally sheet. Note should be taken of those groups in which the group score was (1) higher than the average individual score or (2) higher than the best individual score. Groups should discuss the way in which individual members resolved disagreements and the effect of the ground rules on such behavior. They may consider the obstacles experienced in arriving at consensus agreements and the possible reasons for the difference between individual and group decisions.

The story: A businessman had just turned off the lights in the store when a man appeared and demanded money. The owner opened a cash register. The contents of the cash register were scooped up, and the man sped away. A member of the police force was notified promptly.

Statements about the story:

1. A man appeared after the owner had turned off his store lights.	T	F	?
2. The robber was a man.	T	F	?
3. A man did not demand money.	T	F	?
4. The man who opened the cash register was the owner.	T	F	?
5. The store owner scooped up the contents of the cash register and ran away.	T	F	?
6. Someone opened a cash register.	T	F	?
7. After the man who demanded the money scooped up the contents of the cash register, he ran away.	T	F	?
8. While the cash register contained money, the story does *not* state *how much.*	T	F	?
9. The robber demanded money of the owner.	T	F	?
10. The story concerns a series of events in which only three persons are referred to: the owner of the store, a man who demanded money, and a member of the police force.	T	F	?
11. The following events in the story are true: someone demanded money, a cash register was opened, its contents were scooped up, and a man dashed out of the store.	T	F	?

Tally Sheet

Group Number	Group Score	Average Individual Score	Best Individual Score	Group Score Better Than Average Indiv.?	Group Score Better Than Best Indiv.?

EXERCISE: NASA Moon Survival Task*

Goals:

The challenge in decision making is to obtain the best information within limits of time and other resources. This is often very difficult because information does not exist in pure form. It is always filtered through people who may or may not get along with each other and who might not even care about a good decision. This exercise is a means to help you look at the process of gathering information, working out group procedures, analyzing different contributions, and handling conflict and motivation. The exercise is intended to help you examine the strengths and weaknesses of individual decision making versus group decision making.

Instructions:

You are a member of a space crew originally scheduled to rendezvous with another ship on the lighted surface of the moon. Because of mechanical difficulties, however, your ship was forced to land at a spot some 200 miles from the rendezvous point. During landing, much of the equipment aboard was damaged, and, because survival depends on reaching the main ship, the most critical items available must be chosen for the 200-mile trip.

Implementation:

1. On the next page are listed the fifteen items left intact and undamaged after the landing. Your task is to rank them in terms of their importance to your crew in reaching the rendezvous point.
2. In the first column (step 1) place the number 1 by the most important item, the number 2 by the second most important, and so on, through number 15, the least important. You have fifteen minutes to complete this phase of the exercise.
3. After the individual rankings are completed, participants should be formed into groups having from four to seven members.
4. Each group should then rank the fifteen items as a team. This group ranking should be a consensus after a discussion of the issues, not just the average of each individual ranking. While it is unlikely that everyone will agree exactly on the group ranking, an effort should be made to reach at the least a decision that everyone can live with. It is important to treat differences of opinion as a means of gathering more information and clarifying issues and as an incentive to force the group to seek better alternatives.
5. The group ranking should be listed in the second column (step 2).
6. The third phase of the exercise consists of the instructor's providing the expert's rankings, which should be entered in the third column (step 3).

Scoring:

1. Each participant should compute the difference between the individual ranking (step 1) and the expert's ranking (step 3), and between the group ranking (step 2) and the expert's ranking (step 3).
2. Then add the two "difference" columns—the smaller the score, the closer the ranking is to the view of the experts.

Source: This exercise was developed by Jay Hall, Teleometrics International, and was adapted by J. B. Ritchie and Paul Thompson, *Organization and People*, 2d ed., West, St. Paul, Minn., 1980, pp. 238–239. Also see James B. Lau and A. B. Shani, *Behavior in Organizations*, 4th ed., Irwin, Homewood, Ill., 1988, pp. 94–99.

NASA Tally Sheet

Items	Step 1 Your individual ranking	Step 2 The team's ranking	Step 3 Survival expert's ranking	Step 4 Difference between Steps 1 and 3	Step 5 Difference between Steps 2 and 3
Box of matches					
Food concentrate					
50 feet of nylon rope					
Parachute silk					
Portable heating unit					
Two .45 calibre pistols					
One case dehydrated Pet milk					
Two 100-lb. tanks of oxygen					
Stellar map (of the moon's constellation)					
Life raft					
Magnetic compass					
5 gallons of water					
Signal flares					
First aid kit containing injection needles					
Solar-powered FM receiver-transmitter					
TOTAL				Your score	Team score

(The lower the score, the better)

EXERCISE: TGIF (Thank God It's Friday!)

Goals:

This exercise provides an opportunity to experience and explore several facets of group dynamics. While the activity itself is recreational in nature, it reflects many of the same challenges faced by managerial groups and contemporary empowered and self-managed teams. That is, the exercise calls upon decision-making and interpersonal behavior skills necessary to effectively manage a collaborative work effort.

Implementation:

The activity itself involves the spelling out of a list of common or well-known phrases and items. Each quotation includes a number, and that number is the clue to solving the puzzle. For example, the sample puzzle is presented as "7 D. of the W."

The number 7 is part of the phrase and provides the clue that the saying is "7 days of the week." Another common item is "12 E. in a D." which stands for "12 eggs in a dozen."

Source: Professor Steven M. Sommer, University of Nebraska-Lincoln, developed the exercise around the two anonymous activity sheets. Used with permission.

Activity Sheet A

Instructions:

Each equation below contains the initials of words that will make it correct. Finish the missing words. For example:

7 - D. of the W.   Would be *7 days of the week.*

1. 26 - L. of the A.   _____

2. 7 - W. of the A. W.   _____

3. 1001 - A. N.   _____

4. 54 - C. in a D. (with the J.)   _____

5. 12 - S. of the Z.   _____

6. 9 - P. in the S. S.   _____

7. 13 - S. of the A. F.   _____

8. 88 - P. K.   _____

9. 18 - H. on a G. C.   _____

10. 32 - D. F. at which W. F.   _____

11. 90 - D. in a R. A.   _____

12. 200 - D. for P. G. in M.   _____

13. 8 - S. on a S. S.   _____

14. 3 - B. M. (S. H. T. R.)   _____

15. 4 - Q. in a G.   _____

16. 24 - H. in a D.   _____

17. 1 - W. on a U.   _____

18. 5 - D. in a Z. C.   _____

19. 57 - H. V.   _____

20. 11 - P. on a F. T.   _____

21. 1000 - W. that a P. is W.   _____

22. 29 - D. in F. in a L. Y.   _____

23. 64 - S. on a C. B.   _____

24. 40 - D. and N. of the G. F.   _____

Procedure:

1. (Five minutes). Students should break up into groups of four or five.
2. Do not read the discussion questions before doing the task.
3. (Twenty to thirty minutes). The groups solve as many items on one of the following activity sheets (A or B) as possible.
4. (Five minutes). The instructor reads off the answers to the list. Groups may propose alternative solutions.
5. (Fifteen minutes). In a class forum, the groups discuss and compare their experiences by responding to the discussion questions.

Activity Sheet B

1. EZ / iiiiiiii	2. T O U C H	3. Moth cry cry cry	4. Black coat
5. Time Time	6. L A N D	7. Hurry ↑	8. Me Quit
9. Le vel	10. Knee / light	11. Man / Board	12. He's / Himself
13. R|ea|di|ng	14. AGES	15. R ROAD A D	16. O / M.A. B.A. PH.D.
17. WEAR / LONG	18. DICE DICE	19. ECNALG	20. CYCLE CYCLE CYCLE
21. CHAIR	22. T O W N	23. ii ii O O	24. Stand / I

6. As a follow-up activity, use the alternate list. The follow-up may be used to show effective group development, effective teamwork (after discussing problems that may have surfaced with the first list), or the power of groups over individuals (have students complete the list on their own, then as a group).

Discussion questions:

1. How did the group try to solve the list? Did you plan out your approach? Did you explore answers as a group, divide parts among individuals? Or did each member try to solve the entire list individually and then pool answers? Did people take on different roles? Recorder? Encourager? Idea generator? Spy?

2. How important was it for the group to solve all twenty-four puzzles? Did the team initially set a goal to finish the list? How challenging was this exercise? What happened as you approached completion? Did commitment go up? As the last few unsolved items became frustrating, did the group start to lose its desire?

3. Describe the climate or personality of the group. Was everyone in agreement about how hard to work? How many to finish? Did members begin to react differently to the frustrations of getting the list completed? Did some argue to finish? Did others tell the team to quit?

4. Did some members try to dominate the process? The suggested solutions? How well did you get along in doing the exercise? Was there conflict? Did members fight fair in debating different answers? Was each discovery of a correct answer a source of excitement and pride? Or was it a sense of relief, a step closer to getting it over with?

5. Did the group develop any rules to regulate behavior? Was there a process of group development in which members discussed the assignment before beginning to tackle it? What changes in behaviors or expectations occurred as time progressed and the group became more or less focused on the activity? Did a form of self-discipline emerge to keep the team focused, to prevent being embarrassed in relation to other groups?

6. To what extent did public evaluation of performance become important? Did you begin to monitor how well other groups were doing? Did your group try to spy on their answers? Did you negotiate any trades?

EXERCISE: Power and Politics*

Goals:

1. To gain some insights into your own power needs and political orientation

2. To examine some of the reasons people strive for power and what political strategies can be used to attain it

Implementation:

Answer each question below with "mostly agree" or "mostly disagree," even if it is difficult for you to decide which alternative best describes your opinion.

Source: Reprinted with permission from Andrew J. DuBrin, *Human Relations*, Reston, Reston, Va., 1978, pp. 122–123.

	Mostly Agree	Mostly Disagree
1. Only a fool would correct a boss's mistakes.	_____	_____
2. If you have certain confidential information, release it to your advantage.	_____	_____
3. I would be careful not to hire a subordinate with more formal education than myself.	_____	_____
4. If you do a favor, remember to cash in on it.	_____	_____
5. Given the opportunity, I would cultivate friendships with powerful people.	_____	_____
6. I like the idea of saying nice things about a rival in order to get that person transferred from my department.	_____	_____
7. Why not take credit for someone else's work? They would do the same to you.	_____	_____
8. Given the chance, I would offer to help my boss build some shelves for his or her den.	_____	_____
9. I laugh heartily at my boss's jokes, even when they are not funny.	_____	_____
10. I would be sure to attend a company picnic even if I had the chance to do something I enjoyed more that day.	_____	_____
11. If I knew an executive in my company was stealing money, I would use that against him or her in asking for favors.	_____	_____
12. I would first find out my boss's political preferences before discussing politics with him or her.	_____	_____
13. I think using memos to zap somebody for his or her mistakes is a good idea (especially when you want to show that person up).	_____	_____
14. If I wanted something done by a coworker, I would be willing to say, "If you don't get this done, our boss might be very unhappy."	_____	_____
15. I would invite my boss to a party at my house, even if I didn't like him or her.	_____	_____
16. When I'm in a position to, I would have lunch with the "right people" at least twice a week.	_____	_____
17. Richard M. Nixon's alleged bugging of the Democratic headquarters would have been a clever idea if he hadn't been caught.	_____	_____
18. Power for its own sake is one of life's most precious commodities.	_____	_____
19. Having a high school named after you would be an incredible thrill.	_____	_____
20. Reading about job politics is as much fun as reading an adventure story.	_____	_____

Scoring:

Each statement you check "mostly agree" is worth one point toward your power and political orientation score. If you score 16 or over, it suggests that you have a strong inclination toward playing politics. A high score of this nature would also suggest that you have strong needs for power. Scores of 5 or less would suggest that you are not inclined toward political maneuvering and that you are not strongly power driven.

A caution is in order. This questionnaire is designed primarily to encourage you to think carefully about the topic of power and politics. It lacks the scientific validity of a legitimate, controlled test.

EXERCISE: Leadership Questionnaire*

Goal: To evaluate oneself in terms of the leadership dimensions of task orientation and people orientation.

Implementation:
1. Without prior discussion, fill out the Leadership Questionnaire. Do *not* read the rest of this until you have completed the test.
2. In order to locate yourself on the Leadership Style Profile Sheet, you will score your own questionnaire on the dimensions of task orientation (T) and people orientation (P).

Scoring: The scoring is as follows:

1. Circle the item number for items 8, 12, 17, 18, 19, 30, 34, and 35.
2. Write the number 1 in front of a *circled item number* if you responded S (seldom) or N (never) to that item.
3. Also write a number 1 in front of *item numbers not circled* if you responded A (always) or F (frequently).
4. Circle the number 1's which you have written in front of the following items: 3, 5, 8, 10, 15, 18, 19, 22, 24, 26, 28, 30, 32, 34, and 35.
5. *Count the circled number 1's.* This is your score for the level of your concern for people. Record the score in the blank following the letter P at the end of the questionnaire.
6. *Count the uncircled number 1's.* This is your score for your concern for the task. Record this number in the blank following the letter T.
7. Next, look at the Leadership Style Profile Sheet on p. 412 and follow the directions.

Variations:
1. Participants can predict how they will appear on the profile prior to scoring the questionnaire.
2. Paired participants already acquainted can predict each other's scores. If they are not acquainted, they can discuss their reactions to the questionnaire items to find some bases for this prediction.
3. The leadership styles represented on the profile sheet can be illustrated through role playing. A relevant situation can be set up, and the "leaders" can be coached to demonstrate the styles being studied.
4. Subgroups can be formed of participants similarly situated on the shared leadership scale. These groups can be assigned identical tasks to perform. The work generated can be processed in terms of morale and productivity.

Source: Reprinted with permission from J. William Pfeiffer and John E. Jones (eds.), *A Handbook of Structured Experiences for Human Relations Training,* vol. 1, University Associates, San Diego, Calif., 1974. The questionnaire was adapted from Sergiovanni, Metzeus, and Burden's revision of the Leadership Behavior Description Questionnaire, *American Educational Research Journal,* vol. 6, 1969, pp. 62–79.

Leadership Questionnaire

Name _____ Group _____

Directions: The following items describe aspects of leadership behavior. Respond to each item according to the way you would most likely act if you were the leader of a work group. Circle whether you would most likely behave in the described way always (A), frequently (F), occasionally (O), seldom (S), or never (N). Once the test is completed, go back to number 2 under Implementation.

A F O S N	1. I would most likely act as the spokesperson of the group.
A F O S N	2. I would encourage overtime work.
A F O S N	3. I would allow members complete freedom in their work.
A F O S N	4. I would encourage the use of uniform procedures.
A F O S N	5. I would permit the members to use their own judgment in solving problems.
A F O S N	6. I would stress being ahead of competing groups.
A F O S N	7. I would speak as a representative of the group.
A F O S N	8. I would needle members for greater effort.
A F O S N	9. I would try out my ideas in the group.
A F O S N	10. I would let the members do their work the way they think best.
A F O S N	11. I would be working hard for a promotion.
A F O S N	12. I would tolerate postponement and uncertainty.
A F O S N	13. I would speak for the group if there were visitors present.
A F O S N	14. I would keep the work moving at a rapid pace.
A F O S N	15. I would turn the members loose on a job and let them go to it.
A F O S N	16. I would settle conflicts when they occur in the group.
A F O S N	17. I would get swamped by details.
A F O S N	18. I would represent the group at outside meetings.
A F O S N	19. I would be reluctant to allow the members any freedom of action.
A F O S N	20. I would decide what should be done and how it should be done.
A F O S N	21. I would push for increased production.
A F O S N	22. I would let some members have authority which I could keep.
A F O S N	23. Things would usually turn out as I had predicted.
A F O S N	24. I would allow the group a high degree of initiative.
A F O S N	25. I would assign group members to particular tasks.
A F O S N	26. I would be willing to make changes.
A F O S N	27. I would ask the members to work harder.
A F O S N	28. I would trust the group members to exercise good judgment.
A F O S N	29. I would schedule the work to be done.
A F O S N	30. I would refuse to explain my actions.
A F O S N	31. I would persuade others that my ideas are to their advantage.
A F O S N	32. I would permit the group to set its own pace.
A F O S N	33. I would urge the group to beat its previous record.
A F O S N	34. I would act without consulting the group.
A F O S N	35. I would ask that group members follow standard rules and regulations.
T_____	P_____

T-P Leadership Style Profile Sheet

Name _____ Group _____

Directions: To determine your style of leadership, mark your score on the concern for task dimension (T) on the left-hand arrow below. Next, move to the right-hand arrow and mark your score on the concern for people dimension (P). Draw a straight line that intersects the P and T scores. The point at which that line crosses the shared leadership arrow indicates your score on that dimension.

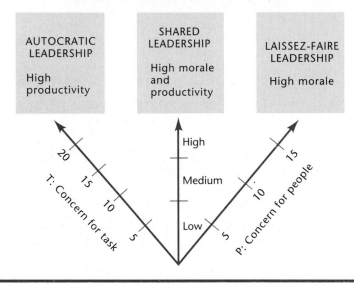

Shared leadership results from balancing
concern for task and concern for people

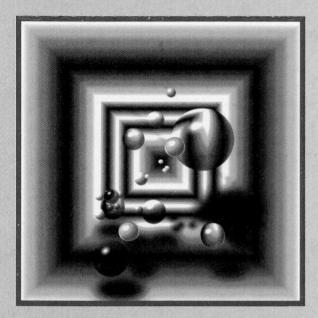

PART 4

A Macro Perspective of Organizational Behavior

15 Communication Technology and Interpersonal Processes

Learning Objectives

- **Relate** the perspective, historical background, and meaning of the communication process in organizations.
- **Describe** modern communication technology.
- **Identify** the dimensions of nonverbal communication.
- **Discuss** the specific downward, upward, and horizontal (interactive) interpersonal communication processes.

Communication is one of the most frequently discussed dynamics in the entire field of organizational behavior, but it is seldom clearly understood. In practice, effective communication is a basic prerequisite for the attainment of organizational goals, but it has remained one of the biggest problems facing modern management. Communication is an extremely broad topic and of course is not restricted to the organizational behavior field. Some estimates of the extent of its use go up to about three-fourths of an active human being's life, and even higher proportions of a typical manager's time. The comprehensive study reported in Chapter 14 that directly observed a wide cross section of what were called "real managers" in their day-to-day behaviors found that they devote about a third of their activity to routine communication—exchanging routine information and processing paperwork.[1] More important, however, is the finding that the communication activity made the biggest relative contribution to effective managers. Figure 15.1 summarizes these findings.

There seems little doubt that communication plays an important role in managerial and organizational effectiveness. Yet, on the other side of the same coin, communication is commonly cited as being at the root of practically all the problems of the world. It is given as the explanation for lovers' quarrels, ethnic prejudice, war between nations, the generation gap, industrial disputes, and organizational conflict. These examples are only representative of the numerous problems attributed to ineffective communication. Obviously, this thinking can go too far: communication can become a convenient scapegoat or crutch. Not all organization and interpersonal difficulties are the result of communication breakdown. Other matters discussed in this book—motivation, decision making, stress, organization structure, to name but a few—can also contribute to problems. Yet it is also true that the communication process is a central problem in most human and organizational activities.

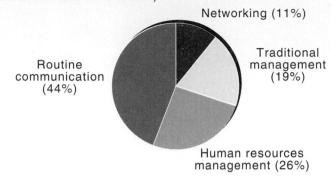

CONTRIBUTION TO REAL MANAGER'S EFFECTIVENESS
(N = 178, drawn from participant observation data related to combined effectiveness measure of unit performance and subordinate satisfaction and commitment)

FIGURE 15.1
The contribution of communication activities to real managers' effectiveness.
(*Source*: Fred Luthans, Richard M. Hodgetts, and Stuart A. Rosenkrantz, *Real Managers*, Ballinger, Cambridge, Mass., 1988, p. 68. Used with permission.)

First, the historical background of the role of communication in management and organizational behavior is briefly discussed. This discussion is followed by a precise definition of communication and presentation of the two communication extremes—advanced communication technology and simple nonverbal communication. In communication technology, both management information systems (MIS) and the telecommunications revolution are given detailed attention. In the other extreme, that of nonverbal communication, body language and paralanguage are covered. The remainder of the chapter, the heart of the chapter, is concerned with interpersonal communication (downward, upward, and horizontal or interactive). An interpersonal process, as opposed to a linear information flow perspective of communication, is taken throughout.

HISTORICAL BACKGROUND OF THE ROLE OF COMMUNICATION

Early discussions of management gave very little emphasis to communication. Although communication was implicit in the managerial function of command and the structural principle of hierarchy, the early theorists never fully developed or integrated it into management theory. At the same time, they did generally recognize the role of informal communication in relation to the problem of supplementing the formal, hierarchical channels. But the pioneering management theorist Henri Fayol was about the only one who gave a detailed analysis of, and supplied a meaningful solution to, the problem of communication.

Fayol's Contribution

Figure 15.2 shows how Fayol presented a simplified version of the formal organization. If the formal channels in this organization were strictly followed and F wanted to communicate with P, the communication would have to go through E—D—C—B—A—L—M—N—O—P and back again. In other words, F would have to go through a total of twenty positions. On the other hand, if F could lay a "gangplank" to P, it would, in the words of Fayol,

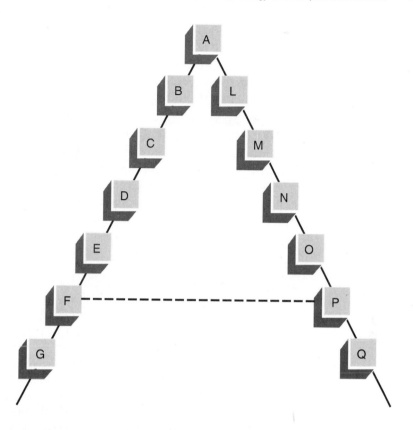

FIGURE 15.2
Fayol's gangplank
concept.

. . . allow the two employees F and P to deal at one sitting, and in a few hours, with
some question or other which via the scalar chain would pass through twenty
transmissions, inconvenience many people, involve masses of paper, lose weeks or
months to get to a conclusion less satisfactory generally than the one which could
have been obtained via direct contact as between F and P.[2]

This gangplank concept has direct implications for horizontal communication
systems in modern formal organizations. Unfortunately, such classical insights were
few and far between.

Barnard's Contribution

It was largely Chester Barnard in the late 1930s who meaningfully developed
communication as a vital dynamic of organizational behavior. He was convinced that
communication is the major shaping force in the organization. He ranked it with
common purpose and willingness to serve as one of the three primary elements of the
organization. To him, communication both makes the organization cooperative
system dynamic and links the organization purpose to the human participants.
Communication techniques, which he considered to be written and oral language,
were deemed not only necessary to attain organization purpose but also a potential
problem area for the organization. In Barnard's words: "The absence of a suitable
technique of communication would eliminate the possibility of adopting some
purposes as a basis of organization. Communication technique shapes the form and
the internal economy of organization."[3]

Barnard also interwove communication into his concept of authority. He emphasized that meaning and understanding must occur before authority can be communicated from manager to subordinate. He listed seven specific communication factors which are especially important in establishing and maintaining objective authority in an organization. He believed them to be, in brief, the following:

1. The channels of communication should be definitely known.
2. There should be a definite formal channel of communication to every member of an organization.
3. The line of communication should be as direct and short as possible.
4. The complete formal line of communication should normally be used.
5. The persons serving as communication centers should be competent.
6. The line of communication should not be interrupted while the organization is functioning.
7. Every communication should be authenticated.[4]

Modern Perspective

Since the original contributions by Fayol and Barnard, the dynamics of communication have been one of the central concerns, if not *the* central concern, of organizational behavior and management theorists. Except in the principles of those management textbooks which still rely heavily on a classical process framework, communication is given major attention. In addition, there has been a deluge of books and articles which deal specifically with interpersonal and organizational communication. Unfortunately, practically all this vast literature gives only a surface treatment of the subject and is seldom based upon systematic research findings. For example, there have been complaints about an uncritical acceptance of the effectiveness of open communication, when a contingency perspective would be more in line with the evidence.[5]

One exception was the Real Managers Study, reported in Chapter 14 and mentioned in the introductory comments of this chapter. One part of this study combined direct observation of managers in their natural setting with self-report measures to try to determine how they communicated.[6] The model shown in Figure 15.3 gives the results. The first dimension of the managerial communication model represents a continuum ranging from the humanistic interactor (who frequently interacts both up and down the organization hierarchy and exhibits human-oriented activities) to the mechanistic isolate (who communicates very little, except on a formal basis). The other dimension describes a continuum from the informal developer (who communicates spontaneously in all directions and exhibits activities related to developing his or her people) to the formal controller (who uses formally scheduled communication interaction and exhibits monitoring/controlling activities).[7] This empirically derived model describes two major dimensions of managerial communication. It provides a framework for *how* managers communicate on a day-to-day basis and can be used as a point of departure for formally defining communication and the interpersonal processes of communication in today's organizations.

The Definition of Communication

The term *communication* is freely used by everyone in modern society, including members of the general public, organizational behavior scholars, and management practitioners. In addition, as noted earlier, the term is employed to explain a multi-

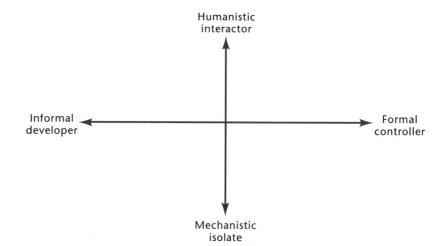

FIGURE 15.3
Managerial communication model: How managers communicate. (*Source*: Fred Luthans and Janet K. Larsen, "How Managers Really Communicate," *Human Relations*, vol. 39, no. 2, 1986, p. 175.)

tude of sins both in the society as a whole and in work organizations. Despite this widespread usage, very few members of the general public—and not a great many more management people—can precisely define the term. Part of the problem is that communication experts have not agreed upon a definition themselves.

Most definitions of "communication" used in organizational behavior literature stress the use of symbols to transfer the meaning of information. For example, a recent analysis stresses that communication is the understanding, not of the visible, but of the invisible and hidden. These hidden and symbolic elements embedded in the culture give meaning to the visible communication process.[8] Equally, if not of more importance, however, is the fact that communication is a personal process that involves the exchange of behaviors. The personal aspects have been noted in no uncertain terms by most organizational behavior scholars. For example, Ivancevich and Matteson recently noted that "communication among people does not depend on technology but rather on forces in people and their surroundings. It is a process that occurs within people."[9]

In addition to being a personal process, communication has other implications. A communication expert emphasizes the *behavioral* implications of communication by pointing out that "the only means by which one person can influence another is by the behaviors he performs—that is, the communicative exchanges between people provide the sole method by which influence or effects can be achieved."[10] In other words, the behaviors that occur in an organization are vital to the communication process. This personal and behavioral exchange view of communication takes many forms.

The continuum in Figure 15.4 can be used to identify the major categories of communication that are especially relevant to the study of organizational behavior.

FIGURE 15.4
The continuum of communication in organizational behavior.

| Communication technology | Interpersonal communication | Nonverbal communication |

On the one extreme is sophisticated communication technology, and on the other extreme is relatively simple nonverbal communication. The middle ground is occupied by interpersonal approaches, which represent the perspective taken in this chapter. An overview of the communication technology and nonverbal approaches is necessary to put the discussion of the interpersonal communication process into proper perspective.

COMMUNICATION TECHNOLOGY

Chapter 2 covers the newly emerging advanced information technology found in today's organizations. Not only has this technology had a flattening effect on organization structure, it has also had an impact on the communication process. When information technology is applied to the communication process in organizations, the term "management information systems," or MIS, is commonly used.

Management Information Systems (MIS)

Although management information systems do not have to be computerized, normally they are. With the common use of personal computers today and the emergence of the so-called information superhighway, almost all information processing is done by computers. MIS involves generating, processing, and transmitting information. The system itself involves not only computer hardware and software but also data and people—both MIS personnel and users.

Although MIS is usually associated with integrated networks of information that support management decision making,[11] MIS can also be used for strategic planning[12] (for example, American Hospital Supply used MIS to change the perspective and direction of the company), improved customer service (for example, some airlines are providing gate agents with relevant information to personalize service at the gate),[13] and for communication per se. The next chapter, on decision making, devotes attention to how computerized systems, especially artificial intelligence and expert systems, can support decision making, but for now it can be said that MIS can be used as part of the interpersonal and organizational communication systems. For example, managers can get on the system to ask others for information about solving problems or can use the system to monitor the literature on particular technological developments.

Telecommunications

Closely related to computerized MIS is the telecommunications explosion. In fact, the boundaries between computing and communicating are becoming very blurred. Today, computers communicate and telecommunication networks compute.[14] In addition to computers, telecommunications use telephone and television technologies and both a wireless system of portable phones and a wired system built around fiber-optic links.

The wireless communication technology can eventually replace phones anchored by copper wires. This new wireless technology is expected to reach millions of new customers and offer prices half those of cellular services. However, there may be a price paid by working people. One observer recently noted that wireless communication

. . . could be a mixed blessing, freeing people from their desks yet chaining them to their jobs. Indeed, cellular companies are already building computerized systems that can automatically track a person's movements anywhere in North America, so the same telephone number will reach a person's desk phone or pocket phone wherever he or she roams. People will run, but they may not be able to hide.[15]

This recent communications technology explosion, sometimes called "a second communication revolution,"[16] is not confined to North America or to phones. For instance, cross-border telephone circuit traffic exceeded 30 billion minutes world-wide in 1990; in 1991, it reached 36 billion; and it is estimated to rise to 60 or 70 billion in 1995. The annual growth rate of outbound traffic of the United States is 18 percent (excluding to Mexico and Canada); of Germany, 14 percent; of Japan, 23 percent; and of Taiwan, 31 percent.[17]

Going beyond mere phones, the telecommunications revolution, or "personal communications services" (PCS), uses digital electronics of computers capable of sending data, images, and even video to

. . . an expanding family of nomadic computing devices—palm-size computers, electronic notepads and what some people call mutant devices that combine the features of a telephone, computer and pager.[18]

This blurring between audio, video, and computer technology is also found in the increasingly popular CD-ROMs, which stands for Compact Disc Read-Only Memory (you can't record on them). They are related to the shiny silvery discs that revolutionized the music business. From a communications standpoint, the key distinguishing feature of CD-ROMs is that they have enormous capacity. They can hold the equivalent of hundreds of floppy disks. For example, one CD-ROM could contain all the phone numbers in the United States or a whole set of encyclopedias that can combine audio and video with the text. For example, with a CD-ROM one could read about a composer such as Beethoven, see his picture, and hear his music all at the personal computer terminal. The thirty-four leading CD-ROM software producers sold more than $50 million in products during the first half of 1993, and the number of CD-ROM titles reached 3000 by the end of 1993, up from 800 the year before.[19]

In the wired world of fiber optics, information is transmitted as pulses of laser light through ultrapure glass fibers. Here is a description of what this fiber-optic system can do:

The most advanced system today can transmit information at the rate of 3.4 billion bits per second, or the equivalent of 48,000 telephone conversations on a single pair of fibers. Of course, fiber optics will be important not so much for its role in accommodating voice traffic as for its role in accommodating the explosively growing traffic generated by facsimile, computer networking, and video.[20]

In other words, whether wireless or over fiber optics, the telephone, television, and computer will combine to form a very powerful, but user-friendly, communication system.

Some of the telecommunication techniques already widely used to communicate in today's organizations are telephone caller ID, electronic mail, voice messaging, and electronic bulletin boards. Caller ID displays the number of the person calling. This number can be connected to a computer for many uses. American Express, for example, uses such a system at its customer relations center. When customers call, the computer uses the number to retrieve their name and bring up the

AMEX file to the screen *before* the customer representative even picks up the phone.[21]

Electronic Mail and Voice Messaging

As discussed in Chapter 2, electronic mail (E-mail) uses electronic circuitry to transmit written messages via computer terminals instantaneously to other people within the organization or to those in other organizations around the world. Through the Internet (the fast-growing interconnection of computer networks around the globe), millions of people can now obtain information on virtually anything and potentially communicate with anyone who has a computer. In addition to sending messages, E-mail can be used for transferring computer files (spreadsheets, database files, and address lists) as well as for electronic data interchange (EDI), an automated form of ordering and inventory control. E-mail providers may also be hooked into various computer databases that give users access to up-to-the-minute news and financial information, credit reports, airline schedules, electronic banking, and even home shopping.[22]

In voice messaging, the computer acts as a sophisticated answering machine. The computer answers the phone, relays memos, gives out information, and takes messages. For example, Plunkett, Gibson, & Allen, a large law firm in Texas, receives an average of a thousand incoming calls per day. The firm was having trouble with the volume of calls and client service suffered. So the firm installed a voice-message system and clients are now promptly greeted with personal messages from their attorney and have the option of leaving a detailed, confidential message. Attorneys can get their messages from inside or outside the office, twenty-four hours a day. When they return calls, they already have all the information necessary to assist the client. Research indicates that the average business phone call lasts four to five minutes, but the average voice message is less than a minute. Plunkett, Gibson, & Allen's voice-message system resulted in a 60 percent reduction in the number of internal calls and a reduction also in the amount of paperwork. The system also resulted in greatly improved client service.[23]

Whereas E-mail and voice messaging tend to be for individual users, electronic bulletin boards are like the traditional corkboard in public access areas except that electronic bulletin boards use a computer and a modem instead of paper and thumbtacks. Electronic boards use computers to communicate routine information or to reduce paperwork and filing by storing policy manuals, job descriptions, telephone directory listings, and other documents to which managers and employees can gain access. Besides those for internal use in an organization, there are an increasing number of general public-access bulletin boards that are run by commercial database companies and are organized around a particular interest, such as software or a professional group. Besides making contacts, electronic bulletin boards can also become important to a firm's daily operations. For example, at Language Exchange Inc., a language teaching and translation service based in Washington, D.C., translators dial into the Language Exchange Bulletin Board to pick up documents that have been scanned into the system. They make their translations and send them back to the bulletin board, where the documents are then edited, proofread, typeset, or sent directly to the client. The company estimates it can handle ten times the former business with this bulletin-board system.[24]

There seems to be no limit to the role that communication technology will play in the future. There is tremendous growth in the use of all areas of the technology. As one business executive noted: "Sooner or later, everybody will be using telecommunication technology and the world will be a better place, or at least a simpler place."[25]

NONVERBAL COMMUNICATION

The opposite end of the continuum from sophisticated communication technology is nonverbal communication. Although verbal communication has long been recognized as being important, nonverbal communication has only recently been given attention in the study of communication. Sometimes called the "silent language," *nonverbal communication* can be defined as "nonword human responses (such as gestures, facial expressions) *and* the perceived characteristics of the environment through which the human verbal and nonverbal messages are transmitted."[26] Thus, whether a person says something or, equally important, does *not* say anything, communication still can take place.

Body Language and Paralanguage

There are many forms of nonverbal communication. Probably the most widely recognized is body language. Body movements convey meanings and messages. This form includes facial expressions and what people do with their eyes, feet, hands, and posture. For example, good salespeople, advertisers, and even poker players capitalize on their knowledge of people's eyes. As explained by Preston:

> . . . when an individual is excited or aroused, the pupils of the eyes will dilate. When haggling over a price, a buyer will unconsciously signal an alert seller that a particular price is acceptable. . . . Some colors or shapes cause more excitement than others, and the reaction registers in the shopper's eyes. With this research information, marketing people redesign their products to better appeal to buyers in a competitive environment. Good poker players watch the eyes of their fellow players as new cards are dealt. The pupil dilation very often will show if the card being dealt improves the player's hand.[27]

Besides the obvious meanings attached to things such as a firm handshake or touching the other person when making an important point, at least one communication expert believes that what the person does with the lower limbs is the key to body language. He explains:

> That is where the tension and anxiety show. The person may claim to be relaxed, yet the legs are crossed tightly, and one foot thrusts so rigidly in the air that it appears to be on the verge of breaking off. *Insight:* People concentrate on hiding their tension from the waist up. Their real state is revealed in their legs and feet.[28]

As Chapter 4, on impression management, points out, even a person's clothing can become important in body language. For example, in his best-selling book *Dress for Success*, John Molloy points out: "The most authoritative pattern is the pinstripe, followed in descending order by the solid, the chalk stripe and the plaid. If you need to be more authoritative, stick with dark pinstripes."[29] In addition to dress, physical appearance in general seems important. From her research with clients, one consultant concluded that physical attractiveness is "the single most important quality in determining your success at every stage in your life. People who are attractive are judged to be nicer people, more intelligent, more capable, more desirable mates and better employees."[30]

Besides the truly silent dimensions of nonverbal communication such as body language, time (for example, being late or early), or space (for example, how close one gets during a conversation or seating arrangements in a committee meeting), there are also *ways* in which people verbalize that are an important dimension of nonverbal communication. Sometimes called *paralanguage*, these include things such as voice quality, volume, speech rate, pitch, nonfluencies (saying "ah," "um," or "uh"), laughing, and yawning.[31] Also, *who* says a word (for example, whether the boss or a coworker asks for "volunteers") and in what *environmental context* it is said (for example, in the boss's office or out on the golf course) makes a difference.

Improving Nonverbal Effectiveness

As with other forms of communication, there are specific guidelines that can be used to increase the accuracy of interpreting others' nonverbal behavior. Here are some suggestions to improve nonverbal communication:

1. *Look at what is happening in the situation.* When nonverbal behavior is an emotional response, it reflects what is going on at the moment and can be used to better understand the person's nonverbal behavior.
2. *Consider the discrepancies between the nonverbal behavior and the verbal statements.* If there is a mismatch, then this should be a signal for closer examination of what is going on. Sometimes the nonverbal signals are more accurate than the verbals.
3. *Watch for subtleties in the nonverbal behavior.* For example, the difference between a real smile and a fake one can usually be detected.[32]

Cultural differences can also play an important role in effective nonverbal communication. The following are a few guidelines affecting communication in foreign cultures: Expect more physical closeness in Latin America; the use of "thumbs up" is fine almost anywhere except Australia; and take your hands out of your pockets when meeting a Japanese person. The accompanying International Application Example: Nonverbal and Verbal Communication gives some further guidelines for both nonverbal and verbal communication in foreign cultures. Overall, nonverbal dimensions are extremely important to interpersonal communication and must be given as much recognition as the more technical transmissions from the advanced communication technology.

INTERPERSONAL COMMUNICATION

As shown in the continuum in Figure 15.4, interpersonal communication represents the middle ground between communication technology on the one extreme and nonverbal communication on the other. For the study of organizational behavior, interpersonal communication is most relevant.

In interpersonal communication, the major emphasis is on transferring information from one person to another. Communication is looked upon as a basic

International Application Example

Nonverbal and Verbal Communication

One of the best ways of coping with foreign cultures and customs is to be careful in the use of both verbal and nonverbal communication. This means saying and doing the right things and, perhaps even more important, not saying or doing the wrong things. Here are some guidelines that American managers are finding useful in treading their way through the intercultural maze of foreign countries:

1. In Europe, act as if you are calling on a rich old aunt. Dress well, do not chew gum, do not smoke without first seeking permission, do not use first names unless invited to do so by the other party, be punctual to meetings, and, if you are unsure of the proper dress, err on the side of conservatism.
2. When in France, speak English to your hosts. They know how to speak English and typically are appalled at the performance of foreigners trying to communicate in their tongue. Stick to the language you know best. Also, be on time for all engagements. The French are sticklers for promptness.
3. Remember that the Germans differ from the French in a number of ways. One of these is that they are even bigger sticklers for promptness. Also, remember that gentlemen walk and sit to the left of all women and men of senior business rank. Do not get on the wrong side.
4. In Britain, social events are not used for discussing business. This is left at the office. Also, remember that the British religiously keep engagement calendars, so if you are inviting some people to lunch or dinner, send your invitation well in advance or you are likely to find that date already filled in your prospective guest's calendar. If you are attending a formal dinner, it is common to toast Her Majesty's health after the main course. This is the signal that you may now smoke. Do not light up prior to this time. Also, remember that while promptness is valued, if you are invited to dinner at 8 P.M., you may show up five or ten minutes late, but it is not good manners to show up early.
5. In Italy, it is common to shake hands with everyone. However, do not expect them to remember your name. No one does on the first introduction. Also, get in the habit of calling people by their title. For example, university graduates often prefer to be addressed as such, and there are different titles depending on the individual's field of study.
6. In Spain, punctuality is taken seriously only when attending a bullfight. Most offices and shops close for siesta from 1:30 P.M. to 4:30 P.M., and restaurants do not usually reopen until after 9 P.M. or get into full swing before 11 P.M. An early dinner in Spain often ends around midnight; a late dinner goes into the wee hours of the morning. If you are invited to dinner and are unaccustomed to late hours, take an afternoon nap. You are going to need it if you hope to last through dessert.

method of effecting behavioral change, and it incorporates the psychological processes (perception, learning, and motivation) on the one hand and language on the other. However, it must be noted that the explosion of advanced communication technology is also having an impact on this human interaction process. For example, a recent analysis noted: "Human communication has always been central to organizational action. Today, the introduction of various sophisticated electronic communication technologies and the demand for faster and better forms of interaction are visibly influencing the nature of [interpersonal] communication."[33] On the other extreme, listening sensitivity and nonverbal communications are also closely associated with interpersonal communication. For example, Bill Marriott, Jr., of the hotel chain, spends nearly half his time listening and talking to front-line employees. It is important to note that he listens and then talks to his people.[34]

The Importance of Feedback to Interpersonal Communication

The often posed philosophical question that asks, Is there a noise in the forest if a tree crashes to the ground but no one is there to hear it? demonstrates some of the important aspects of interpersonal communication.[35] From a communications perspective, the answer is no. There are sound waves but no noise because no one perceives it. There must be both a sender and a receiver in order for interpersonal communication to take place. The sender is obviously important to communication, but so is the neglected receiver who gives feedback to the sender.

The importance of feedback cannot be overemphasized because effective interpersonal communication is highly dependent on it. Proper follow-up and feedback require establishing an informal and formal mechanism by which the sender can check on how the message was actually interpreted. Feedback makes communication a two-way process.[36]

Table 15.1 summarizes some characteristics of effective and ineffective feedback for employee performance. The following list explains these characteristics in more detail:

1. *Intention*. Effective feedback is directed toward improving job performance and making the employee a more valuable asset. It is not a personal attack and should not compromise the individual's feeling of self-worth or image. Rather, effective feedback is directed toward aspects of the job.
2. *Specificity*. Effective feedback is designed to provide recipients with specific information so that they know what must be done to correct the situation. Ineffective feedback is general and leaves questions in the recipients' minds. For example, telling an employee that he or she is doing a poor job is too general and will leave the recipient frustrated in seeking ways to correct the problem.
3. *Description*. Effective feedback can also be characterized as descriptive rather than evaluative. It tells the employee what he or she has done in objective terms, rather then presenting a value judgment.
4. *Usefulness*. Effective feedback is information that an employee can use to improve performance. It serves no purpose to berate employees for their lack of skill if they do not have the ability or training to perform properly. Thus, the guideline is that if it is not something the employee can correct, it is not worth mentioning.

TABLE 15.1 Luthans and Martinko's Characteristics of Feedback for Effective and Ineffective Interpersonal Communication in Human Resources Management

Effective Feedback	Ineffective Feedback
1. Intended to help the employee	1. Intended to belittle the employee
2. Specific	2. General
3. Descriptive	3. Evaluative
4. Useful	4. Inappropriate
5. Timely	5. Untimely
6. Considers employee readiness for feedback	6. Makes the employee defensive
7. Clear	7. Not understandable
8. Valid	8. Inaccurate

5. *Timeliness.* There are also considerations in timing feedback properly. As a rule, the more immediate the feedback, the better. This way the employee has a better chance of knowing what the supervisor is talking about and can take corrective action.

6. *Readiness.* In order for feedback to be effective, employees must be ready to receive it. When feedback is imposed or forced upon employees, it is much less effective.

7. *Clarity.* Effective feedback must be clearly understood by the recipient. A good way of checking this is to ask the recipient to restate the major points of the discussion. Also, supervisors can observe facial expressions as indicators of understanding and acceptance.

8. *Validity.* In order for feedback to be effective, it must be reliable and valid. Of course, when the information is incorrect, the employee will feel that the supervisor is unnecessarily biased, or the employee may take corrective action which is inappropriate and only compounds the problem.[37]

Other Important Variables in Interpersonal Communication

Besides feedback, other variables, such as trust, expectations, values, status, and compatibility, greatly influence the interpersonal aspects of communication. If the subordinate does not trust the boss, there will be ineffective communication. The same is true of the other variables mentioned. People perceive only what they expect to perceive; the unexpected may not be perceived at all. The growing generation gap can play havoc with interpersonal communication; so can status differentials and incompatibilities of any sort. Giving attention to, and doing something about, these interpersonal variables can spell the difference between effective and ineffective communication.

Because there are so many variables inherent in the interpersonal communication process, there is a need for a conceptual framework. One such framework to study interpersonal communication is in terms of the downward, upward, and interactive processes.

DOWNWARD COMMUNICATION

Traditionally, one of the dominant themes of organizational communication has been the so-called downward process. However, when a personal perspective replaces a linear information flow perspective, the downward process is more accurately portrayed as interpersonal linkages, not just information flows, in the downward system.

The Purposes and Methods of Downward Communication

Katz and Kahn have identified five general purposes of top to bottom communication in an organization:

1. To give specific task directives about job instructions
2. To give information about organizational procedures and practices
3. To provide information about the rationale of the job
4. To tell subordinates about their performance
5. To provide ideological information to facilitate the indoctrination of goals[38]

In the past, most organizations have concentrated on and accomplished only the first two of these purposes; to a large extent, this is still the case today. In general, downward communication on job performance and the rationale-ideological aspects of jobs has been neglected.

A communication process that gives only specific directives about job instructions and procedures and fails to provide information about job performance or rationale-ideological information about the job has a negative organizational impact. This type of downward orientation promotes an authoritative atmosphere which tends to inhibit the effectiveness of the upward and horizontal processes of communication. Communicating the rationale for the job, the ideological relation of the job to the goals of the organization, and information about job performance to employees can, if properly handled, greatly benefit the organization. As Katz and Kahn point out: "If people know the reasons for their assignment, this will often insure their carrying out the job more effectively; and if they have an understanding of what their job is about in relation to their subsystem, they are more likely to identify with organizational goals."[39] This does not imply that management should tell assembly line workers that their jobs are extremely important to the success of the company—that the company would fold unless they put on a bolt right or welded a part properly. Obviously, this type of communication can backfire. The workers would justifiably reason: "Who are they trying to kid? My job isn't *that* important. It is just another hypocritical con job by management." What is meant is that providing *full* information about the job, its ramifications for the rest of the organization, and the quality of the employee's performance in it should be an important function of downward communication. Providing as much information as possible can be especially important in dealing with employees who are not native born, as seen in the International Application Example: Different Cultures, Different Meanings.

Media Used for Downward Communication

Besides the increasing use of the communication technology discussed earlier, traditionally, downward communication systems relied on many types of print and oral media to disseminate information. Some examples of written media are organizational handbooks, manuals, magazines, newspapers, and letters sent to the home or distributed on the job; bulletin-board items, posters, and information displays; and standard reports, descriptions of procedures, and memos. For example, United Airlines has a daily *Employee Newsline* and a monthly employee newspaper. Of particular interest, however, is its biweekly *Supervisors' Hotlines*, which both informs supervisors and encourages them to communicate accurate information in the *Hotline* to those who report to them.[40]

Examples of oral media used in the system are direct orders or instructions from managers, speeches, meetings, closed-circuit television programs, public address systems, and telephones. Arthur Morrissette, president and founder of Interstate Van Lines in Springfield, Virginia, has key managers address their employees every morning and extensively every couple of weeks; he even has a sing-along where employees belt out the lyrics to the company anthem.[41]

The numerous types of media give an indication of the avalanche of information that is descending on personnel from the downward system. An example would be the manager of a metal-fabricating division of a large firm:

**International
Application
Example**

Different Cultures, Different Meanings

As more and more organizations do business in the international arena, communication is going to become a growing problem. This is true not only for oral and written communication but for nonverbal communication as well. For example, many Americans are accustomed to conveying information by shrugging their shoulders, raising their eyebrows, clenching their fist with the thumb out and extended or placing the thumb and index finger together to form an "O." Do international business people understand these nonverbal gestures? If so, do they give the gestures the same interpretation as do Americans?

One recent research study showed pictures of twenty gestures such as those described in the paragraph above and asked people from various countries to identify them. The respondents were asked to write out their answers so that the responses could be compared both within and between international groups. If the response had no meaning, they were to indicate this also. In all, there were seven groups of respondents: Colombian, Venezuelan, Peruvian, Jamaican, Indian, Thai, and Japanese. The researchers found that of the twenty pictures, only one had the same meaning for all groups. Overall, the respondents identified 40 percent of the gestures the same way as in the United States and 40 percent differently. There were mixed responses on the remaining 20 percent. The results showed that the Thai and Japanese respondents agreed with the American meanings on fewer than half of the gestures, while the Venezuelan and Jamaican respondents agreed on about two-thirds of them.

This research points to the importance of communication in the international arena. There are people from many parts of the world who have very different meanings for the same nonverbal communications. For example, the "A-okay" sign that is conveyed by placing the thumb and forefinger in an "O" shape is an obscene gesture in Latin America and the Middle East, but a very common and positive gesture in the United States. Unless business people are aware of the fact that nonverbal communications can differ radically from one part of the world to the next, there will continue to be communication breakdowns and, in some cases, considerable embarrassment.

He received six hundred pages of computer printout each day detailing the output of each production line, the location of various materials, and other indexes of the operation. He said that it would take him approximately three full days to simplify the information into usable form. Instead, he found an empty storage room, stacked the printouts there, and subcontracted with a trash removal firm to remove the printouts, untouched, once a month.[42]

Unfortunately, this is not an extreme example. The author observed that in the basement of one large organization, the trash bin used for miscellaneous throwaway items was always neatly stacked and never full. However, next to it was a bin marked for discarded computer printout paper that was always overflowing into the aisle and was stacked dangerously high, literally threatening to become a dangerous avalanche at any time.

Ways to Improve Downward Communication

Quality of information has often been sacrificed for quantity. Also, social psychology experiments over the years have clearly demonstrated people's willingness to ignore useful information and use useless information.[43] Some organizations have tried to solve their downward communication problems by the use of the communication technology discussed earlier. For example, the New York Transit Authority has an information system whereby if one of its buses breaks down, six months of service records are immediately available on a computer monitor at the service depot.[44] These emerging technologies help solve some of the information overload problem of the downward system. In addition, a research study found that although decision makers who perceive information overload may be more satisfied than those who perceive information underload, they may not perform as well.[45]

The biggest problem, however, is ignoring the importance of the receiver. This problem, of course, is symptomatic of taking a linear (in this case, downward) information flow perspective, as opposed to a personal perspective. After an extensive review of the literature, one communications researcher concluded that the downward flow of information can affect receivers in the following ways:

1. People's interpretations of communications follow the path of least resistance.
2. People are more open to messages which are consonant with their existing image, their beliefs, and their values.
3. Messages which are incongruent with values tend to engender more resistance than messages which are incongruent with rational logic.
4. To the extent that people positively value need fulfillment, messages which facilitate need fulfillment are more easily accepted than messages which do not.
5. As people see the environment changing, they are more open to incoming messages.
6. The total situation affects communication; a message interpreted as congruent in one situation may be interpreted as incongruent in another.[46]

If managers understand these impacts of communication on subordinates and do something about them, communication can become more effective. There is a series of studies indicating that if employees do get needed information (that is, if downward communication is effective), they perform better as individuals and in groups.[47] Unfortunately, there is recent research evidence that indicates that managers are still not communicating very effectively with their people.[48]

UPWARD COMMUNICATION

Just as downward communication becomes a dynamic interpersonal process, upward communication also becomes an interpersonal process. In the traditional view, the classical organization structure formally provided for vertical information flows, downward and upward. However, in practice, except for feedback controls, the downward system completely dominated the upward system. Whereas the downward process is highly directive—giving orders, instructions, information, and procedures—the upward process is characteristically nondirective in nature. While bureaucratic authority facilitates a directive atmosphere, a free, participative, empowered approach is necessary for effective upward communication.

Traditionally, bureaucratic authority has prevailed over the more participative, empowered styles, with the result that upward communication has often been outwardly stifled, badly misused, or conveniently ignored by management. Too often, employees simply fear to give upward communication, especially if it is bad news. An example would be the "computer company president who had to tell his chairperson—a substantial shareholder—and the assembled directors that results wouldn't be up to plan. The exec went about it the right way, providing a full explanation and detailed plans for getting back on track. The chairperson fired him on the spot anyway."[49]

Methods of Improving the Effectiveness of Upward Communication

The hierarchical structure is about the only formal method that the classical approach used to communicate upward, and, as has been pointed out, in practice this has not worked out well. Other techniques and channels for upward communication are necessary. The following are some possible ways to promote more effective upward communications:

1. *The grievance procedure.* Provided for in most collective bargaining agreements, the grievance procedure allows employees to make an appeal upward beyond their immediate manager. It protects individuals from arbitrary action by their direct manager and encourages communication about complaints. A growing number of companies, such as Federal Express, General Electric, and Borg-Warner, have been instituting peer-review boards to resolve grievances.[50] These boards consist of three peers (those on the same level or below) and two management representatives, and their decisions are binding on both parties.
2. *The open-door policy.* Taken literally, this means that the manager's door is always open to employees. It is a continuous invitation for employees to come in and talk about anything that is troubling them. Unfortunately, in practice the open-door policy is more fiction than fact. The manager may slap the employee on the back and say, "My door is always open to you," but in many cases both the employee and the manager know the door is really closed. It is a case where the adage "actions speak louder than words" applies.
3. *Counseling, attitude questionnaires, and exit interviews.* The personnel department can greatly facilitate upward communication by conducting nondirective, confidential counseling sessions; periodically administering attitude questionnaires; and holding meaningful exit interviews for those who leave the organization. Much valuable information can be gained from these forms of communication.
4. *Participative techniques.* Participative decision techniques can generate a great deal of communication. This may be accomplished by either informal involvement of employees or formal participation programs such as the use of junior boards, union-management committees, suggestion boxes, and quality circles. There is also empirical research evidence indicating that participants in communication networks are generally more satisfied with their jobs, are more committed to their organizations, and are better performers than those who are not involved in the communication process.[51]
5. *The ombudsperson.* A largely untried but potentially significant technique to enable management to obtain more upward communication is the use of an ombudsperson. The concept has been used primarily in Scandinavia to provide an outlet for persons who have been treated unfairly or in a depersonalized manner by large, bureaucratic government. It has more recently gained popularity in American state governments, military posts, and universities. Although it is just

being introduced in a few business organizations, if set up and handled properly, it may work where the open-door policy has failed. As business organizations become larger and more diverse, the ombudsperson may fill an important void that exists under these conditions.

Perhaps the best and simplest way to improve upward communication is for managers to develop good listening habits and systems for listening. For example, the top managers of a Canadian forest products company felt they were great communicators until an employee survey revealed differently. Here is what they did to solve the problem:

> The two owners undertook a series of thirty dinners in the course of the next year. Ten employees and their spouses, eventually including everyone at the mill, went to dinner with their bosses. After the meal, there was a sociable and often long and intense question-and-answer session, "We all wanted to be listened to," says the president. "By the end of the evening, I'd often see a remarkable change in attitude on the part of even the crustiest of the union guys."[52]

Some practical guidelines to facilitate active listening are (1) maintaining attention; (2) using restatement; (3) showing empathy; (4) using probes to draw the person out; (5) encouraging suggestions; and (6) synchronizing the interaction by knowing when to enter a conversation and when to allow the other person to speak.[53]

Types of Information for Upward Communication

Overall, employees can supply basically two types of information: (1) personal information about ideas, attitudes, and performance and (2) more technical feedback information about performance, a vital factor for the control of any organization. The personal information is generally derived from what employees tell their managers. Some examples of such information are:

1. What the persons have done
2. What those under them have done
3. What their peers have done
4. What they think needs to be done
5. What their problems are
6. What the problems of the unit are
7. What matters of organizational practice and policy need to be reviewed[54]

A growing number of innovative organizations are building upward feedback systems into their policies and practices. Here is what some representative firms are doing:[55]

1. *AT&T.* As part of the performance management program, questionnaires are developed and given organization-wide. These questionnaires are given to personnel in a unit and tap areas such as respect for the individual, dedication to helping customers, teamwork, innovation, and high standards of integrity. The manager receives the results as feedback about his or her unit. The manager then discusses the results in a one-on-one meeting with a facilitator and later in a meeting with her or his team.
2. *Massmutual Insurance.* Over a four-year period, everyone from the CEO to first-level managers received 360-degree feedback (from bosses, those working for them, and peers). A scientifically derived skills profile containing eight categories

is filled out on each manager. At first, only the target manager saw the results, but now management are also able to review the feedback.

3. *AMOCO Corporation.* Managers can voluntarily ask for feedback from their direct employees on a questionnaire concerning communication, teamwork, and leadership skills. Another questionnaire instrument called "the profiler," which can be filled out anonymously from one's computer terminal, provides feedback to managers participating in a training program called the Leadership Development Process.

4. *Deloitte & Touche.* This professional services firm offers its office managers a standard questionnaire that they can either use as is or customize. Members of the work group fill out the questionnaire, reflecting their attitudes and opinions. The results go only to the person being reviewed. Recently, however, some officers are providing the feedback results to the manager's advisor or mentor who in turn helps set the manager's annual goal plan.

The other type of upward information, feedback for control purposes, such as accounting data, is necessary if the organization is to survive. As has been pointed out: "Decision centers utilize information feedback to appraise the results of the organization's performance and to make any adjustments to insure the accomplishment of the purposes of the organization."[56] The role that feedback communication plays is stressed earlier in this chapter. Its role in the decision process is covered in Chapter 16.

INTERACTIVE COMMUNICATION IN ORGANIZATIONS

The classical hierarchical organization structure gives formal recognition only to vertical communication. Nevertheless, most of the classical theorists saw the need to supplement the vertical with some form of horizontal system, as Fayol did with his gangplank concept. Horizontal communication is required to make a coordinated effort in achieving organizational goals. The horizontal requirement becomes more apparent as the organization becomes larger, more complex, and more subject to the downsizing and the flattening of structures, covered in Chapter 2. Well-known companies such as General Electric, Du Pont, Motorola, and Xerox have recently moved to such a horizontal model of organization.[57] These and other modern organization designs such as project and matrix, discussed in Chapter 17, formally incorporate horizontal flows into the structure. However, as is the case with vertical (downward and upward) flows in the organization structure, the real key to horizontal communication is found in people and behaviors. Because of the dynamic, interpersonal aspects of communication, the *interactive* form seems more appropriate than just the *horizontal* form. The horizontal flows of information (even in a horizontal structure) are only part of the communication process that takes place across an organization.

The Extent and Implications of Interactive Communication

Most management experts today stress the important but overlooked role that interactive communication plays in organizations. In most cases the vertical communication process overshadows the horizontal. For example, the recent study of "real managers" reported at the beginning of the chapter found that approximately 100 interactions per week reportedly occurred between managers and their employees (both to them and from them). "While there was far more communication downward (between managers and their employees) than upward (between managers and top managers above them in the organization), there were no specific differences determined by initiation of interaction."[58] The horizontal communication in this study was mainly represented by the networking activity (socializing/politicking and interacting with outsiders) that was shown to be related to successful managers (those promoted relatively fast) more than any other activity.[59] Other studies have also found a relationship, although complex, between communication activities and leadership.[60]

Just as in other aspects of organizational communication, there are many behavioral implications contained in the interactive process. Communication with peers, that is, with persons of relatively equal status on the same level of an organization, provides needed social support for an individual. People can more comfortably turn to a peer for social support than they can to those above or below them. The result can be good or bad for the organization. If the support is couched in terms of task coordination to achieve overall goals, interactive communication can be good for the organization. On the other hand, "if there are no problems of task coordination left to a group of peers, the content of their communication can take forms which are irrelevant to or destructive of organizational functioning."[61] In addition, interactive communication among peers may be at the sacrifice of vertical communication. Persons at each level, giving social support to one another, may freely communicate among themselves but fail to communicate upward or downward. In fact, in the study of "real managers," Figure 15.1 showed that networking had the least relative relationship with effective managers (those with satisfied and committed employees and high-performing units), but routine communication activities (exchanging information and processing paperwork) had the highest.[62]

The Purposes and Methods of Interactive Communication

Just as there are several purposes of vertical communication in an organization, there are also various reasons for the need for interactive communication. Basing his inquiry on several research studies, a communications scholar has summarized four of the most important purposes of interactive communication:

1. *Task coordination.* The department heads may meet monthly to discuss how each department is contributing to the system's goals.
2. *Problem solving.* The members of a department may assemble to discuss how they will handle a threatened budget cut; they may employ brainstorming techniques.
3. *Information sharing.* The members of one department may meet with the members of another department to give them some new data.
4. *Conflict resolution.* The members of one department may meet to discuss a conflict inherent in the department or between departments.[63]

The examples for each of the major purposes of interactive communication traditionally have been departmental or interdepartmental meetings, but in recent years, they include teams. Such meetings and now teams that exist in most organizations have been the major methods of interactive communication. In addition, most organizations' procedures require written reports to be distributed across departments and to teams. The quantity, quality, and human implications discussed in relation to the vertical communication process are also inherent in interactive communication.

Also like downward communication, communication technology via computers, telephones, and television has had a tremendous impact on interactive communication. Via their computer terminals, members of an organization at the same location or dispersed throughout the world can communicate with one another. For example, to stimulate sharing ideas and technological developments among its engineers, Hewlett-Packard has about sixty computer conferences running simultaneously.[64] Live interactive television hookups can also be used to hold meetings with participants at various geographical locations. This is less costly and time-consuming than bringing everyone into one location and, because it is face-to-face and interactive, it improves communication over traditional telephone conferencing.

Because of the failure of the classical structures to meet the needs of interactive communication, not only have new organizational forms emerged, but the informal organization and groups have been used to fill the void. Informal contacts with others on the same level are a primary means of interactive communication. The informal system of communication can be used to spread false rumors and destructive information, or it can effectively supplement the formal channels of communication. It can quickly disseminate pertinent information that assists the formal systems to attain goals. However, whether the informal system has negative or positive functions for the organization depends largely on the goals of the person doing the communicating. Like any communication system, the entire informal system has a highly personal orientation, and, as has been pointed out earlier, personal goals may or may not be compatible with organizational goals. The degree of compatibility that does exist will have a major impact on the effect that the grapevine has on organizational goal attainment.

Some organization theorists are critical of the grapevine because its speed makes control of false rumors and information difficult to manage. By the same token, however, this speed factor may work to the advantage of the organization. Since the informal system is so personally based and directed, it tends to be much faster than the formal downward system of information flow. Important relevant information that requires quick responsive action by lower-level personnel may be more effectively handled by the informal system than by the formal system. Thus, the informal system is a major way that interactive communication is accomplished. The formal horizontal and upward systems are often either inadequate or completely ineffective. The informal system is generally relied upon to coordinate the units horizontally on a given level.

Summary

At every level of modern society, communication is a problem. One of the problems when applied to organizations has been the failure to recognize that communication involves more than just linear information flows; it is a dynamic, interpersonal process that involves behavior exchanges. Management information systems, telecommunication, and nonverbal approaches are also important to communication in today's organizations. MIS involves generating, processing, and transmitting information, and telecommunication involves an interaction between telephone (both wireless and fiber-optic), television, and of course, computers. Developments such as the Internet, CD-ROMs, and electronic mail are having a huge impact on communication in organizations. Yet, communication is still a dynamic, interpersonal process. The three major dimensions of communication from this perspective are downward, upward, and interactive processes. Each has varied purposes and methods. The downward system is generally adequate in providing information, but better techniques are needed to improve the upward and horizontal systems. All three processes in organizations can greatly benefit from increased attention given to the dynamic, interpersonal aspects of communication.

Questions for Discussion and Review

1. Explain Fayol's "gangplank" concept. What are some of its advantages and disadvantages?
2. Compare and contrast the various telecommunication techniques for effective communication. What applications may CD-ROMs have in organizations?
3. Why is feedback so important to communication? What are some guidelines for the effective use of feedback?
4. What are some of the major purposes and methods of downward communication?
5. What are some techniques for improving upward communication?
6. What are the major purposes and methods of interactive communication?

Footnote References and Supplemental Readings

1. Fred Luthans, Richard M. Hodgetts, and Stuart A. Rosenkrantz, *Real Managers*, Ballinger, Cambridge, Mass., 1988, p. 27 and Chap. 6.
2. Henri Fayol, *General and Industrial Management*, Constance Storrs (trans.), Pitman, London, 1949, p. 35.
3. Chester I. Barnard, *The Functions of the Executive*, Harvard University Press, Cambridge, Mass., 1938, p. 90.
4. Ibid., pp. 175–181.
5. Eric M. Eisenberg and Marsha G. Witten, "Reconsidering Openness in Organizational Communication," *Academy of Management Review*, July 1987, pp. 418–426.
6. Fred Luthans and Janet K. Larsen, "How Managers Really Communicate," *Human Relations*, vol. 39, no. 2, 1986, pp. 161–178.
7. Ibid.
8. Bernard J. Reilly and Joseph A. Di Angelo, Jr., "Communication: A Cultural System of Meaning and Value," *Human Relations*, February 1990, p. 129.
9. John M. Ivancevich and Michael T. Matteson, *Organizational Behavior and Management*, 3d ed., Irwin, Homewood, Ill., 1993, p. 633.
10. Aubrey Fisher, *Small Group Decision Making*, McGraw-Hill, New York, 1974, p. 23.
11. David H. Holt, *Management*, Prentice-Hall, Englewood Cliffs, N.J., 1987, p. 55.
12. See Albert L. Lederer and Raghu Nath, "Making Strategic Information Systems Happen," *Academy of Management Executive*, August 1990, pp. 76–83.
13. See Blake Ives and Richard O. Mason, "Can Information Technology Revitalize Your Customer Service?" *Academy of Management Executive*, November 1990, pp. 52–69.
14. Randall L. Tobias, "Telecommunications in the 1990s," *Business Horizons*, January–February 1990, p. 81.
15. "Wireless-Communication Technology Exploding," *The New York Times*, reported in *Omaha World Herald*, Sept. 21, 1993, p. 1.
16. Jan A. G. M. Van Dijk, "Communication Networks and Modernization," *Communication Research*, June 1993, p. 384.
17. Ibid.
18. "Wireless-Communication Technology Exploding," loc. cit.
19. "Trade Show to Tout CD-ROMs," *Omaha World Herald*, Nov. 15, 1993, p. 15.
20. Tobias, op. cit., p. 82.
21. Jeffery Ferry, "The Wired World," *Vis a Vis*, May 1990, p. 25.
22. Jill MacNeice, "Calls by Computer," *Nation's Business*, July 1990, p. 29.
23. Mike Bransby, "Voice Mail Makes a Difference," *The Journal of Business Strategy*, January/February 1990, p. 8.
24. MacNeice, loc. cit.

25. Ferry, loc. cit.

26. Don Hellriegel, John W. Slocum, Jr., and Richard W. Woodman, *Organizational Behavior*, 4th ed., West, St. Paul, Minn., 1986, p. 221.

27. Paul Preston, *Communication for Managers*, Prentice-Hall, Englewood Cliffs, N.J., 1979, p. 161.

28. Martin G. Groder, "Incongruous Behavior: How to Read the Signals," *Bottom Line*, Mar. 30, 1983, p. 13.

29. John T. Molloy, *Dress for Success*, Warner Books, New York, 1975, p. 46.

30. V. Hale Starr, quoted in "Expert: Non-Verbal Body Language Counts," *Omaha World Herald*, Dec. 20, 1982, p. 2.

31. Dalmor Fisher, *Communication in Organizations*, West, St. Paul, Minn., 1981.

32. See Robert S. Feldman, *Understanding Psychology*, 2d ed., McGraw-Hill, New York, 1990, pp. 329–330.

33. Joanne Yates and Wanda J. Orlikowski, "Genres of Organizational Communication: A Structural Approach to Studying Communication and Media," *Academy of Management Review*, April 1992, p. 299.

34. James L. Heskett, *Managing in the Service Economy*, Harvard Business School Press, Boston, 1986, p. 127.

35. Peter F. Drucker, *Management*, Harper & Row, New York, 1974, p. 483.

36. Andrew D. Szilagyi, Jr., and Marc J. Wallace, Jr., *Organizational Behavior and Performance*, Scott, Foresman, Glenview, Ill., 1987, p. 410.

37. Fred Luthans and Mark J. Martinko, *The Practice of Supervision and Management*, McGraw-Hill, New York, 1979, pp. 180–182.

38. Daniel Katz and Robert Kahn, *The Social Psychology of Organizations*, 2d ed., Wiley, New York, 1978, p. 440.

39. Ibid., p. 443.

40. Heskett, loc. cit.

41. Nelson W. Aldrich, Jr., "Lines of Communication," *Inc.*, June 1986, p. 142.

42. Szilagyi and Wallace, op. cit., p. 408.

43. See David G. Myers, *Social Psychology*, 3d ed., McGraw-Hill, New York, 1990, p. 117.

44. "Manager's On-Line Design Keeps New Yorkers Rolling," *Computerworld*, Dec. 10, 1984, p. 8.

45. Charles A. O'Reilly, "Individuals and Information Overload in Organizations," *Academy of Management Journal*, December 1980, pp. 684–696.

46. Donald F. Roberts, "The Nature of Communication Effects," in Wilbur Schramm and Donald F. Roberts (eds.), *The Process and Effects of Mass Communication*, rev. ed., University of Illinois Press, Chicago, 1971, pp. 368–371.

47. Charles A. O'Reilly, "Supervisors and Peers as Information Sources, Group Supportiveness, and Individual Performance," *Journal of Applied Psychology*, October 1977, pp. 632–635, and Charles A. O'Reilly and Karlene H. Roberts, "Task Group Structure, Communication, and Effectiveness in Three Organizations," *Journal of Applied Psychology*, December 1977, pp. 674–681.

48. For example, see Victor J. Callan, "Subordinate-Manager Communication in Different Sex Dyads: Consequences for Job Satisfaction," *Journal of Occupational and Organizational Psychology*, March 1993, pp. 13–27.

49. Walter Kiechel, III, "Breaking Bad News to the Boss," *Fortune*, Apr. 9, 1990, p. 111.

50. Larry Reibstein, "More Firms Use Peer Review Panel to Resolve Employees' Grievances," *The Wall Street Journal*, Dec. 3, 1986, p. 25.

51. Karlene H. Roberts and Charles A. O'Reilly, "Some Correlations of Communication Roles in Organizations," *Academy of Management Journal*, March 1979, pp. 42–57.

52. Tom Peters, *Thriving on Chaos: Handbook for a Management Revolution*, Knopf, New York, 1987, p. 305.

53. Gary Yukl, *Skills for Managers and Leaders*, Prentice-Hall, Englewood Cliffs, N.J., 1990, pp. 111–115.

54. Katz and Kahn, op. cit., p. 446.

55. Catherine Romano, "Fear of Feedback," *Management Review*, December 1993, pp. 40–41.

56. William G. Scott and Terence R. Mitchell, *Organization Theory*, rev. ed., Irwin, Homewood, Ill., 1972, p. 147.

57. John A. Byrne, "The Horizontal Corporation," *Business Week*, Dec. 20, 1993, pp. 76–81.

58. Luthans and Larsen, op. cit., p. 168.

59. Fred Luthans, Stuart A. Rosenkrantz, and Harry W. Hennessey, "What Do Successful Managers Really Do? An Observational Study of Managerial Activities," *Journal of Applied Behavioral Science*, vol. 21, no. 3, 1985, pp. 255–270.

60. J. Fulk and E. R. Wendler, "Dimensionality of Leader-Subordinate Interactions: A Path-Goal Investigation," *Organizational Behavior and Human Performance*, vol. 30, 1982, pp. 241–264, and Larry E. Penley and Brian Hawkins, "Studying Interpersonal Communication in Organizations: A Leadership Application," *Academy of Management Journal*, June 1985, pp. 309–326.

61. Katz and Kahn, op. cit., p. 445.

62. Luthans, Hodgetts, and Rosenkrantz, op. cit., Chap. 4.

63. Gerald M. Goldhaber, *Organizational Communication*, Wm. C. Brown, Dubuque, Iowa, 1974, p. 121.

64. Henry C. Mishkoff, "The Network Nation Emerges," *Management Review*, August 1986, pp. 29–31.

REAL CASE:
800 to the Rescue

One of the major trends that has changed American industry over the last five years has been the rise of consumer demands for higher-quality goods and services. It is becoming tougher and tougher to please customers, and yet those firms that fail to do so are finding themselves losing market share. How can companies keep up with these demands? One way is by developing strategies that help them communicate with their customers and quickly respond to problem areas.

One of the best examples is provided by the rise in toll-free telephone numbers that give the customer twenty-four hour service. This approach has proved so popular that over the last ten years AT&T's 800-line network has grown from 1.5 billion to 8 billion customers. These lines are extremely important in providing companies with feedback regarding how well they are serving their customers and how they can improve. Take the case of Cadillac, which has added twenty-two toll-free numbers since 1984. As a result of this feedback, the company has eliminated the deductibles on warranties and has become the first American carmaker to institute 24-hour roadside service. In fact, the company's emphasis on service plus improvements in the quality of its cars helped it win the Malcolm Baldrige Award in 1990.

General Electric is another good example. Its 800-number network, first installed in 1982 and receiving 1000 calls weekly, now handles 65,000 calls a week. The firm has found this channel of communication to be so important that it recently raised its requirements for the 150 phone reps that staff these phones. Now they must have a college degree and sales experience. They also have to be able to spot trends in consumer complaints and then alert the appropriate division to take swift action. For example, when the reps started receiving calls from mothers complaining that the end-of-the-cycle signal on clothes dryers disturbed their napping babies, the company responded by changing the signal so that it now can be turned off by the user.

Colgate-Palmolive uses its 800 line to poll consumers and learn how they feel about the company's products. This information helps the firm identify problems and make changes necessary to meet customer needs. As the company president puts it: "Our customers want a specific product that does a specific job, and they are less willing to settle for the happy medium. We must interact with them to fill their needs."

1. How important is communication feedback to these firms?
2. In addition to the use of 800-line networks, how else can firms improve their communication with customers?
3. What can organizations do to ensure that internal barriers are overcome so that proper action is taken with regard to customer concerns?

CASE:
Doing My Own Thing

Rita Lowe has worked for the same boss for eleven years. Over coffee one day, her friend Sara asked her, "What is it like to work for old Charlie?" Rita replied, "Oh, I guess it's okay. He pretty much leaves me alone. I more or less do my own thing." Then Sara said, "Well, you've been at that same job for eleven years. How are you doing in it? Does it look like you will ever be promoted? If you don't mind me saying so, I can't for the life of me see that what you do has anything to do with the operation." Rita replied, "Well, first of all, I really don't have any idea of how I am doing. Charlie never tells me, but I've always taken the attitude that no news is good news. As for what I do and how it contributes to the operation around here, Charlie mumbled something when I started the job about being important to the operation, but that was it. We really don't communicate very well."

1. Analyze Rita's last statement: "We really don't communicate very well." What is the status of manager-subordinate communication in this work relationship? Katz and

Kahn identified five purposes of the manager-subordinate communication process. Which ones are being badly neglected in this case?

2. It was said in this chapter that communication is a dynamic, personal process. Does the situation described verify this contention? Be specific in your answer.

3. Are there any implications in this situation for upward communication and for interactive communication? How could feedback be used more effectively?

CASE:
Bad Brakes

Michelle Adams is the maintenance supervisor of a large taxicab company. She had been very concerned because the cabdrivers were not reporting potential mechanical problems. Several months ago she implemented a preventive maintenance program. This program depended upon the drivers' filling out a detailed report when they suspected any problem. But this was not happening. On a number of occasions a cab left the garage with major problems that the previous driver was aware of but had not reported. Calling out the field repair teams to fix the breakdown was not only costing the company much time and trouble but also was very unsafe in some cases and created a high degree of customer ill will. The drivers themselves suffered from a loss of fares and tips, and in some cases their lives were endangered by these mechanical failures. After many oral and written threats and admonishments, Michelle decided to try a new approach. She would respond directly to each report of a potential mechanical problem sent in by a driver with a return memo indicating what the maintenance crew had found wrong with the cab and what had been done to take care of the problem. In addition, the personal memo thanked the driver for reporting the problem and encouraged reporting any further problems with the cabs. In less than a month the number of field repair calls had decreased by half, and the number of turned-in potential problem reports had tripled.

1. In communications terms, how do you explain the success of Michelle's follow-up memos to the drivers?

2. Explain and give examples of the three communications processes in this company (that is, downward, upward, and interactive).

16 Decision Making

Learning Objectives

- **Define** the phases in the decision-making process.
- **Identify** some models of behavioral decision making.
- **Present** the behaviorally oriented participative decision-making techniques.
- **Discuss** the creative process and group decision-making techniques.

In this chapter, the important processes of decision making are given attention. A *process* is any action which is performed by management to achieve organizational objectives. Thus, decision making is an organizational process because it transcends the individual and has an effect on organizational goals. First, the overall nature of the decision-making process is explored. Then, the models of behavioral decision making are described. Next, the traditional and modern participative techniques are presented as behaviorally oriented decision techniques. Finally, the creative process and group decision-making techniques are given attention.

THE NATURE OF DECISION MAKING

Decision making is almost universally defined as choosing between alternatives. It is closely related to all the traditional management functions. For example, when a manager plans, organizes, and controls, he or she is making decisions. The classical theorists, however, did not generally present decision making this way. Classical theorists such as Fayol and Urwick were concerned with the decision-making process only to the extent that it affects delegation and authority, while Frederick W. Taylor alluded to the scientific method only as an ideal approach to making decisions. Like most other aspects of modern organization theory, the beginning of a meaningful analysis of the decision-making process can be traced to Chester Barnard. In *The Functions of the Executive*, Barnard gave a comprehensive analytical treatment of decision making and noted: "The processes of decision . . . are largely techniques for narrowing choice."[1]

Most discussions of the decision-making process break it down into a series of steps. For the most part, the logic can be traced to the ideas developed by Herbert A.

Simon, the well-known Nobel Prize–winning organization and decision theorist, who conceptualizes three major phases in the decision-making process:

1. *Intelligence activity.* Borrowing from the military meaning of "intelligence," Simon describes this initial phase as consisting of searching the environment for conditions called for decision making.
2. *Design activity.* During the second phase, inventing, developing, and analyzing possible courses of action take place.
3. *Choice activity.* The third and final phase is the actual choice—selecting a particular course of action from among those available.[2]

Closely related to these phases, but with a more empirical basis (that is, tracing actual decisions in organizations), are the stages of decision making of Mintzberg and his colleagues:

1. *The identification phase*, during which *recognition* of a problem or opportunity arises and a *diagnosis* is made. It was found that severe, immediate problems did not have a very systematic, extensive diagnosis but that mild problems did.
2. *The development phase*, during which there may be a *search* for existing standard procedures or solutions already in place or the *design* of a new, tailormade solution. It was found that the design process was a groping, trial-and-error process in which the decision makers had only a vague idea of the ideal solution.
3. *The selection phase*, during which the choice of a solution is made. There are three ways of making this selection: by the *judgment* of the decision maker, on the basis of experience or intuition rather than logical analysis; by *analysis* of the alternatives on a logical, systematic basis; and by *bargaining* when the selection involves a group of decision makers and all the political maneuvering that this entails. Once the decision is formally accepted, an *authorization* is made.[3]

Figure 16.1 summarizes these phases of decision making based on Mintzberg's research.

Whether expressed in Simon's or Mintzberg's phases, there seem to be identifiable, preliminary steps leading to the choice activity in decision making. Also, it should be noted that decision making is a dynamic process, and there are many feedback loops in each of the phases. "Feedback loops can be caused by problems of timing, politics, disagreement among managers, inability to identify an appropriate alternative or to implement the solution, turnover of managers, or the sudden appearance of a new alternative."[4] The essential point is that decision making is a dynamic process. This dynamic process has both strategic[5] and behavioral implications for organizations. What has become known as behavioral decision making is especially relevant to the study and application of organizational behavior.

FIGURE 16.1
Mintzberg's empirically based phases of decision making in organizations.

BEHAVIORAL DECISION MAKING

Why does a decision maker choose one alternative over another? The answer to this question has been a concern of organizational behavior theorists as far back as March and Simon's classic book, *Organizations*, in 1958. Subsequently, however, the field became more interested in such topics as motivation and goal setting, and emphasis on decision making waned. The field of behavioral decision making was mainly developed outside the mainstream of organizational behavior theory and research by cognitive psychologists and decision theorists in economics and information science. Very recently, however, there has been a resurgence of interest in behavioral decision making and it has moved back into the mainstream of the field of organizational behavior.[6]

Whereas classical decision theory operated under the assumption of rationality and certainty, the new behavioral decision theory does not. Behavioral decision-making theorists argue that individuals have cognitive limitations and, because of the complexity of organizations and the world in general, they must act under uncertainty and often ambiguous and incomplete information.[7] Yet, as the Application Example: Management Decisions shows, sometimes the decisions under uncertainty work out and sometimes they do not. Because of this real-world uncertainty and

Application Example

Management Decisions

Decision making is recognized as an important organization and management process for effective performance. Managers who make good decisions can contribute to goals; those who do not can create dire consequences for the organization. An example of an effective decision maker is David Glass. He has taken over from the deceased Sam Walton to continue to successfully lead Wal-Mart in the retail industry. However, one does not have to look at just the large, visible companies to find examples of effective decision makers. Take the case of Sheridan Garrison, founder of American Freight-ways, a relatively small trucking firm. For over a decade, Garrison effectively ran his company. However, when the trucking industry was deregulated in the late 1970s, he realized it was time to get out of the business. He made the decision to sell the firm and then sat back to watch what happened. Many of the trucking firms in the local area soon began to have financial problems as he sat on the sidelines. However, by the early 1980s Garrison knew the time was ripe to reenter the industry. It is important to note that his decision was not to compete head-to-head with the competition, but rather to offer better service than was currently available. By promising to make pickups and deliveries in towns where the amount of business did not currently justify such service, and by picking up and delivering at all times of the day, his company began to capture market share. Within two years he had the company in the black, and by the end of the decade the firm's profits had reached an all-time high.

Unfortunately, decisions such as those made by Sheridan Garrison do not always work out. Sometimes managers miscalculate and make the wrong decision. Take the case of Jaguar, which is now owned by Ford Motor. Ford management's objective in buying Jaguar was to provide Ford entry into the upscale market. However, things have not worked out very well. A weak worldwide market for luxury cars has ensured that Jaguar will not make a profit until well into the 1990s. In addition to needing to redesign the car to make it more appealing and to keep operating costs down, Jaguar has been having quality-related problems. As a result, Ford is now investing more than $5 billion in overhauling Jaguar and trying to get it back on track. Ford is hoping that these latest decisions will prove to be the right ones.

ambiguity, a number of models of decision making have emerged over the years. The foundation and point of departure for developing and analyzing the various models of behavioral decision making remains the degree and meaning of rationality.

Decision Rationality

The most often used definition of *rationality* in decision making is that it is a means to an end. If appropriate means are chosen to reach desired ends, the decision is said to be rational. However, there are many complications to this simple test of rationality. To begin with, it is very difficult to separate means from ends because an apparent end may be only a means for some future end. This idea is commonly referred to as the *means-ends chain* or *hierarchy*. Simon points out that "the means-end hierarchy is seldom an integrated, completely connected chain. Often the connection between organization activities and ultimate objectives is obscure, or these ultimate objectives are incompletely formulated, or there are internal conflicts and contradictions among the ultimate objectives, or among the means selected to attain them."[8]

Besides the complications associated with the means-ends chain, it may even be that the concept is obsolete. Decision making relevant to the national economy supports this position. Decision makers who seek to make seemingly rational adjustments in the economic system may in fact produce undesirable, or at least unanticipated, end results. Simon also warns that a simple means-ends analysis may have inaccurate conclusions.

One way to clarify means-ends rationality is to attach appropriate qualifying adverbs to the various types of rationality. Thus, *objective* rationality can be applied to decisions that maximize given values in a given situation. *Subjective* rationality might be used if the decision maximizes attainment relative to knowledge of the given subject. *Conscious* rationality might be applied to decisions in which adjustment of means to ends is a conscious process. A decision is *deliberately* rational to the degree that the adjustment of means to ends has been deliberately sought by the individual or the organization; a decision is *organizationally* rational to the extent that it is aimed at the organization's goals; and a decision is *personally* rational if it is directed toward the individual's goals.[9]

Models of Behavioral Decision Making

There are many descriptive models of behavioral decision making. In effect, these have become models for much of management decision-making behavior. The models attempt to describe theoretically and realistically how practicing managers make decisions. In particular, the models strive to determine to what degree management decision makers are rational. The models range from complete rationality, as in the case of the *economic rationality* model, to complete irrationality, as in the case of the *social* model. Figure 16.2 summarizes on a continuum the two major extremes and the in-between models of Simon's bounded rationality and the judgmental heuristics and biases model coming out of cognitive psychology. These models deal specifically with management decision-making behavior.

The Economic Rationality Model. This model comes from the classical economic model, in which the decision maker is perfectly and completely rational in every way. Regarding decision-making activities, the following conditions are assumed:

FIGURE 16.2
The continuum of decision-making behavior.

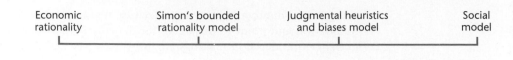

1. The decision will be completely rational in the means-ends sense.
2. There is a complete and consistent system of preferences which allows a choice among the alternatives.
3. There is complete awareness of all the possible alternatives.
4. There are no limits to the complexity of computations that can be performed to determine the best alternatives.
5. Probability calculations are neither frightening nor mysterious.[10]

With this almost infallible ability, the decision maker always strives to maximize outcomes in the business firm, and decisions will be directed to the point of maximum profit where marginal cost equals marginal revenue (MC = MR).

Most economists and quantitative decision theorists do not claim that this depiction is a realistic descriptive model of modern decision-making behavior. But because this rational model and its accompanying quantitative methods have traditionally been embraced by the business schools, many of today's managers still equate "good" management decision making with this approach. Adherence to this approach, however, may be dangerous and may be a leading cause of many of today's problems. As Peters and Waterman observed: "The numerative, rationalist approach to management dominates the business schools. It seeks detached, analytical justification for all decisions. It is right enough to be dangerously wrong, and it has arguably led us seriously astray."[11]

Obviously, Peters and Waterman are not saying "throw the rascal out," nor are other critics of the rational model. It has made and will continue to make a significant contribution to effective decision making. For example, the most successful consumer marketers, such as Procter & Gamble, Chesebrough-Pond's, and Ore-Ida, are known for their rational approach and accompanying quantitative backup. The point that Peters and Waterman are making is that the rational model is not the be-all and end-all of effective decision making and that, if carried to the extreme, it can actually be harmful to the decision-making process.

New Rational Techniques: ABC and EVA. Recently, traditional accounting and finance techniques based on the economic rationality model have been undergoing radical change. For example, well-known companies such as Chrysler, Union Carbide, Hewlett-Packard, and General Electric have moved to a new type of accounting. To better manage costs, they now use activity-based costing, or what has become known as ABC.[12] Traditionally, accounting identified costs according to the category of expense (for example, salaries, supplies, and fixed costs). ABC, on the other hand, determines costs according to what is paid for the different tasks employees perform. Under ABC, costs associated with activities such as processing sales orders, expediting supplier and/or customer orders, resolving supplier quality and/or problems, and retooling of machines are calculated. Both the traditional and ABC methods reach the same bottom-line costs, but ABC provides decision makers a much more accurate breakdown of the cost data. For instance, at Hewlett-Packard when ABC showed that testing new designs and parts was extremely expensive, engineers changed their plans on the spot to favor components that required less testing, thus greatly lowering costs.[13]

Another example of rethinking the traditional economic rationality used by management decision makers is the finance technique of economic value added, or EVA.[14] A long-standing tenet of the economic model has been that a rational decision is one which resulted in earnings higher than the cost of capital. Traditionally, the cost of capital has simply been equated with the interest paid on borrowed capital. Under EVA, however, the true cost of all capital is determined. For example, the true cost of equity capital (the money provided by the shareholders) is the opportunity cost (what shareholders could earn in price appreciation and dividends if they invested in a similar company). Also, what a firm spends on research and development or employee training has been traditionally treated as expenses, but under EVA, it is treated as capital investments and is added into the cost of capital. The EVA is determined by subtracting this total cost of capital from the after-tax operating profit.

Firms with a positive EVA are making rational decisions; those with a negative EVA are destroying capital and are in trouble. When CSX, Briggs and Stratton, and Coca-Cola moved to an EVA approach, the common stock value of these companies greatly increased.[15] Such needed refinements as ABC and EVA have made the economic rationality model a viable, effective approach to management decision making.

The Social Model. At the opposite extreme from the economic rationality model is the social model of psychology. Sigmund Freud presented humans as bundles of feelings, emotions, and instincts, with their behavior guided largely by their unconscious desires. Obviously, if this were an accurate description, people would not be capable of making effective decisions.

Although most contemporary psychologists would take issue with the Freudian description of humans,[16] almost all would agree that social influences have a significant impact on decision-making behavior. Furthermore, social pressures and influences may cause managers to make irrational decisions. The well-known conformity experiment by Solomon Asch demonstrates human irrationality.[17] His study used several groups of seven to nine subjects each. They were told that their task was to compare the lengths of lines. All except one of the "subjects" in each group had prearranged with the experimenter to give clearly wrong answers on twelve of the eighteen line-judgment trials. About 37 percent of the 123 naive subjects yielded to the group pressures and gave incorrect answers to the twelve test situations. In other words, more than one-third of the experimental subjects conformed to a decision they knew was wrong.

If over one-third of Asch's subjects conformed under "right and wrong," "black and white" conditions of comparing the lengths of lines, a logical conclusion would be that the real, "gray" world is full of irrational conformists. It takes little imagination to equate Asch's lines with the alternatives of a management decision. There seems to be little doubt of the importance of social influences in decision-making behavior.

There is still much to be learned about the impact of social processes on decision-making behavior. Social processes even have an impact in the international arena, as shown in the accompanying International Application Example: Some Basic Rules of Protocol. In addition, there are many psychological dynamics. For example,

Some Basic Rules of Protocol

There are many rules of protocol that Americans serving in foreign assignments should recognize. Some are confusing; most are not. In any event, it is important to know these guidelines in order to be as effective as possible. Here are the most useful rules:

1. In many countries of the world, a person's name denotes social rank or family status. A mistake can be an outright insult. So American managers who are going to be meeting some important nationals should find out who they are beforehand and write their names out and memorize them for correct pronunciation.

2. Keep in mind that there are different rules of protocol in different cultures. For example, in Latin America people's names are a combination of the father's and the mother's, but only the father's name is used in conversation. In Spanish-speaking countries, the father's name comes first. For example, Carlos Migoya-Gutierrez is called Mr. Migoya. However, in Portuguese-speaking countries, it is the other way around, i.e., Mr. Gutierrez. To make it even more confusing, in Asia the rules often vary by country. For example, in Korea which of a man's names to use is determined by whether he is the first son or the second son. In Japan, people should be addressed by their surname, while in Thailand you should call people by their given name, i.e., Mr. Ho Chin would be called Mr. Ho. How can an American manager be sure of not making a mistake? The one best way is to ask your host.

3. In the United States it is acceptable to bypass food you do not like. When overseas, however, you should take whatever is put on your plate and make a valiant effort to eat it regardless of taste. If it's something you have never had before, do not ask what it is. You may be unpleasantly surprised.

4. Before getting to the destination, find out the types of clothes that people wear. Remember that color is as important as fashion. If the American male manager is in doubt, a conservative business suit will usually be acceptable, although in the Philippines a barong (a loose, frilly, usually white or cream-colored shirt with tails out) is proper dress, and in Latin countries a guayabera (similar to a barong) will get him through. For women there would be different rules.

5. Despite what is commonly heard about locals in other countries wanting Americans to speak their language, English is still the primary tongue in the international arena. Most educated people understand this language, and many speak it fluently. Unless American managers are absolutely sure of what they are going to say in a foreign tongue, they should stick with English.

there seems to be a tendency on the part of many decision makers to stick with a bad decision alternative, even when it is unlikely that things can be turned around. Staw and Ross[18] have identified four major reasons why this phenomenon of escalation of commitment might happen:

1. *Project characteristics.* This is probably the primary reason for escalation decisions. Task or project characteristics such as delayed return on investment or obvious temporary problems may lead the decision maker to stick with or increase the commitment to a wrong course of action.

2. *Psychological determinants.* Once the decision goes bad, the manager may have information processing errors (use biased facts or take more risks than are justified). Also because the decision maker is now ego-involved, negative information is ignored, and defensive shields are set up.

3. *Social forces.* There may be considerable peer pressure put on decision makers and/or they may need to save face, so they continue or escalate their commitment to a wrong course of action.
4. *Organizational determinants.* Not only may the project or task characteristics lend themselves to the escalation of bad decisions, so may a breakdown in communication, dysfunctional politics, and resistance to change.

Certainly, the completely irrational person depicted by Freud is too extreme to be useful. However, escalation of commitment and other human dynamics covered throughout this text point out that there is little question of the important role that human behavior can and does play in management decision making. Some management behavior is irrational but still very realistic. For example, the author and a colleague conducted two studies that showed that subjects in both laboratory and field settings who did not have computer experience were more influenced in their decision activities by information presented on computer printout paper than they were by information presented on regular paper.[19] On the other hand, for those subjects with computer experience, the reverse was true. In other words, decision makers are influenced in their choice activities even by the type of format in which information is presented to them. Managers without computer experience may be in awe of the computer and place more value on computer-generated information than is justified, while those with computer experience may be highly skeptical and may underrate the importance of computer-generated information.

Simon's Bounded Rationality Model. To present a more realistic alternative to the economic rationality model, Herbert Simon proposed an alternative model. He felt that management decision-making behavior could best be described as follows:

1. In choosing between alternatives, managers attempt to *satisfice*, or look for the one which is satisfactory or "good enough." Examples of satisficing criteria would be adequate profit or share of the market and fair price.
2. They recognize that the world they perceive is a drastically simplified model of the real world. They are content with this simplification because they believe the real world is mostly empty anyway.
3. Because they satisfice rather than maximize, they can make their choices without first determining all possible behavior alternatives and without ascertaining that these are in fact all the alternatives.
4. Because they treat the world as rather empty, they are able to make decisions with relatively simple rules of thumb or tricks of the trade or from force of habit. These techniques do not make impossible demands upon their capacity for thought.[20]

In comparison with the economic rationality model, Simon's model is also rational and maximizing, but it is bounded. Decision makers end up satisficing because they do not have the ability to maximize. The case against maximizing behavior has been summed up by noting that objectives are dynamic rather than static; information is seldom perfect; there are obvious time and cost constraints; alternatives seldom lend themselves to quantified preference ordering; and the effect of environmental forces cannot be disregarded.[21] Simon's model recognizes these limitations. The traditional economic rationality model's assumptions are viewed as unrealistic. But in the final analysis, the difference between the economic rationality model and Simon's model is one of degree because, under some conditions, satisficing approaches maximizing, whereas in other conditions, satisficing and maximizing are very far apart.

Many economic, social, and organizational variables influence the degree to which satisficing becomes maximizing. An example of an economic variable is market structure. The more competitive the market, the more satisficing may approach maximizing. In an agricultural products market, satisficing will by necessity become maximizing. Economists generally recognize that in a purely competitive environment, profit maximization lends itself to the very survival of the firm. Thus, the decision maker must make maximizing decisions. In an oligopolistic market (for example, the automobile and steel industries), satisficing is different from maximizing. Oligopolistic firms can survive on the basis of adequate profit or share of the market. They do not have to operate at the point where marginal cost equals marginal revenue, and, in fact, they may be unavoidably prevented from maximizing.

Besides the economic market constraints, there are many socially based obstacles which prevent maximization in practice. Some of these social barriers are not consciously recognized by the management decision maker. Examples are resistance to change, desire for status, concern for image, organizational politics, and just plain stupidity. On the other hand, the decision maker may in some cases consciously avoid maximizing. Examples of the latter behavior include decisions which discourage competitive entry or antitrust investigation, restrain union demands, or maintain consumer goodwill. However, in the increasingly competitive global economy, maximizing decisions are becoming more necessary.

Judgmental Heuristics and Biases Model. Although Simon's bounded rationality model and the concept of satisficing are an important extension of the wholly economic rationality model, as Bazerman points out, it does not describe *how* judgment will be biased.[22] Thus, taking the bounded rationality model one step further, a model which identifies specific systematic biases that influence judgment has recently emerged.

The judgmental heuristics and biases model is drawn mostly from Kahneman and Tversky, cognitive decision theorists, who suggested that decision makers rely on heuristics (simplifying strategies or rules of thumb).[23] Such judgmental heuristics reduce the information demands on the decision maker and realistically help in the following ways:

1. Summarize past experiences and provide an easy method to evaluate the present
2. Substitute simple rules of thumb or "standard operating procedures" for complex information collection and calculation
3. Save considerable mental activity and cognitive processing[24]

However, even though these cognitive heuristics simplify and help the decision maker, under certain conditions, their use can lead to errors and systematically biased outcomes. Three major biases are identified that help explain how people's judgment deviates from a fully rational process. The following questions will help you better understand and will provide examples for the biases:

1. Are there more words in the English language that (*a*) begin with the letter "r" or (*b*) have "r" as the third letter?
2. On one day in a large metropolitan hospital, eight births were recorded by gender in the order of their arrival. Which of the following orders of births (B = boy, G = girl) was most likely to be reported?
   a. BBBBBBBB   b. BBBBGGGG   c. BGBBGGGB

3. A newly hired engineer for a computer firm in the Boston metropolitan area has four years of experience and good all-around qualifications. When asked to estimate the starting salary for this employee, my secretary (knowing very little about the profession or the industry) guessed an annual salary of $23,000. What is your estimate?

$ _____ per year.[25]

Here are the three biases:

1. *The availability heuristic.* This cognitive input into judgment refers to decision makers' tendencies to assess the frequency, probability, or likelihood of an event occurring by how readily they can remember it.[26] "An event that evokes emotions and is vivid, easily imagined, and specific will be more 'available' from memory than will an event that is unemotional in nature, bland, difficult to imagine, or vague."[27] An example would be a human resource manager's assessment of the probability of the effectiveness of a newly hired skilled worker from the local technical school, based on her recollection of the successes and failures of those graduates she has hired in recent years. This heuristic can be very valuable to decision makers because events that happen most frequently or are most vivid tend to lead to accurate judgments. By the same token, however, errors or bias results from this heuristic when the ease of recall is influenced by factors unrelated to the frequency of an event's occurrence.[28] For example, the most common response to question 1 above is (a), that there are more words that start with the letter "r." However the correct answer, by far, is (b); there are many more words with "r" as the third letter.[29] This is explained by the availability bias. More people can recall words that start with "r" and it is difficult to think of those that have "r" as the third letter, so they falsely conclude that there must be more words that start with "r." In other words, those words that start with "r" are more readily available in the typical person's memory, but this is a case where the remembered information is wrong and an error in judgment results.

2. *The representativeness heuristic.* This second major heuristic uses decision rules of thumb based on the likelihood of an event's occurrence as judged by the similarity of that occurrence to stereotypes of similar occurrences. Managers would be using a representativeness heuristic when they predict the success of a new product on the basis of the similarity of that product to past successful and unsuccessful product types.[30] However, as with the availability heuristic, this representativeness thinking can be biased and lead to errors. For example, most people choose response (c) for question 2 above because it appears to be most random. The reasoning is that both (a) and (b) are too ordered and are unlikely to occur. However, this is faulty logic. The correct response is that all three of the options are equally likely to occur. As explained by Northcraft and Neale, "the problem here is that we believe that a sequence of independent events (such as eight births) generated from a random process should resemble the essential characteristics of a random process, even when the sequence is too short for that process to express itself statistically. Decision makers expect a few examples of a random event to behave in the same way as large numbers of the event."[31]

3. *The anchoring and adjustment heuristic.* In this heuristic, the decision maker makes a judgment by starting from an initial value or anchor and then adjusts to make the final decision. As Bazerman goes on to explain: "The initial value, or

starting point, may be suggested from historical precedent, from the way in which a problem is presented, or from random information. For example, managers make salary decisions by adjusting from an employee's past year's salary."[32] However, as with the others, bias and resulting error in judgment can creep into this decision rule. For example, in question 3 above most people do not think they are affected by the secretary's estimate. Yet, Bazerman clearly found that they are. When he raised the secretary's estimate to $80,000, individuals give much higher estimates, on average, than when the secretary's estimate was at $23,000.[33] In other words, people use the secretary's estimate as an anchor (even though it is irrelevant information) and adjust from there.

Overall, even though the judgmental heuristics and biases model is based on relatively complex cognitive processing, it is quite descriptive of how managers actually make decisions. Despite the fact that this cognitive approach has only recently emerged in the mainstream of organizational behavior, there is a sound theoretical base and a growing stream of research.[34]

In the final analysis, all the decision models presented are appropriate under certain conditions and are used in combination with one another. This last one, however, has been largely ignored up to very recent times. Obviously, it has to be taken into consideration for understanding decision making in today's organizations. Besides the heuristics and biases model, the behavioral techniques discussed next can also be helpful for not only understanding decision making, but making it more effective.

BEHAVIORALLY ORIENTED DECISION-MAKING TECHNIQUES

Most of the behavioral techniques, at least traditionally, have revolved around participation. Used as a technique, participation involves individuals or groups in the decision-making process. It can be formal or informal, and it entails intellectual and emotional as well as physical involvement. The actual amount of participation in making decisions ranges from one extreme of no participation, wherein the superior makes the decision and asks for no help or ideas from anyone, to the other extreme of full participation, where everyone connected with, or affected by, the decision is completely involved. In practice, the degree of participation will be determined by factors such as the experience of the person or group and the nature of the task. The more experience and the more open and unstructured the task, the more participation there will tend to be.

In today's organizations there is an awakened interest in participation. As was recently noted: "Interest in participation among American managers, unions, and workers has been spurred by the competitive assault on U.S. companies by companies with more participatory industrial relations systems, by the challenges of new production technologies, and by the disappointing productivity performance of American companies."[35] Participative techniques have been talked about ever since the early human relations movement, and now some organizations and individual managers are actually trying them.

Application and Research on Participation

Participation techniques can be applied informally on an individual or a group basis or formally on a program basis. Individual participation techniques are those in which an employee somehow affects the decision making of a manager. Group participation utilizes consultative and democratic techniques. Under consultative participation, managers ask for and receive involvement from their employees, but the managers maintain the right to make the decision. In the democratic form, there is total participation, and the group, not the individual head, makes the final decision by consensus or majority vote.

Although participation has long been discussed and advocated, only recently has there been research support that it enhances employee performance. As a recent comprehensive review of the research literature concluded: "Participation generally fosters a sense of identification with the firm, a positive quality of working life, and enhanced mental health as needs for autonomy, responsibility, and material well-being are fulfilled. Participation has been shown to result in higher productivity, decreased turnover, and increased job satisfaction."[36] Research continues on participation in decision making and the findings reveal complex relationships with antecedents, moderators, and outcomes.[37]

Examples of formal programs of participation range all the way from the classic Scanlon Plan and widely used suggestion plans or boxes to the more recent quality circles popularized by the Japanese and teams or self-managed work groups.

Traditional Participative Techniques

The Scanlon Plan is a pioneering form of labor-management cooperation. The plan, originated by Joseph Scanlon (who was at first with the steelworkers' union and later with MIT) about fifty years ago, consists of a system of committees which encourage labor to participate in management decisions. The unique feature of the Scanlon Plan is that the rewards for an individual's successful suggestion are divided equally among all members of the group. A comprehensive analysis of the Scanlon Plan tested several hypotheses derived from the extensive literature on the plan during the preceding thirty years. After examining twenty-three firms that had the Scanlon Plan in operation, researchers concluded that success was positively related to (1) the average level of participation in decision making reported by employees, (2) the number of years the company had been using the plan, and (3) management's—especially the CEO's—attitudes toward, and expectations of, the plan.[38]

Commonly used suggestion plans or boxes are also a traditional participation program. At A&P grocery stores, the company cut back wages but gives bonuses for suggestions and inputs to its participation program. In the Philadelphia area alone, A&P paid out $10 million in bonuses in a five-year period.[39] Suggestion systems in general are commonly thought to be seldom used and of little value to the companies using them and the employees who participate. Yet an estimate of a recent year was that suggestion box ideas saved companies $2.2 billion and paid out $160 million to those making the suggestions.[40] If employee responses are properly handled and adequately rewarded, the suggestion box can be a very effective method of obtaining participation in the decision-making process from anyone in the organization.

Modern Participative Techniques

Modern participative techniques revolve around participative decision making pushed down to the worker level in terms of empowerment, discussed in Chapter 2, and the use of work groups or self-managed teams, discussed in Chapter 9. These techniques have been used extensively overseas for a number of years, but are also becoming popular in more enlightened U.S. firms. Table 16.1 summarizes the applications abroad and what Hewlett-Packard does with these techniques in the United States.

These modern participative techniques are recognized as successful by both practicing organizations (for example, General Mills claims that since it implemented participative teams, productivity has increased 40 percent[41]) and the recent research literature.[42] Some specific examples of money-saving ideas and innovations that came out of Chevron's participative program are the following:

- A transportation supervisor proposed that Chevron quit providing lube oil, lubricants, and hydraulic oil to chartered boats. Eliminating these provisions resulted in significant yearly savings, and no increase in vessel rates. Research with other companies taking similar actions verified that boat rates did not increase.
- A mechanical supervisor recognized that sending excess valves to an outside vendor for machining and lapping was a "resource loss." He designed and built a valve-lapping machine that eliminated the need for sending valves to vendors.
- A production supervisor noticed that the workboat assigned to his offshore field and the workboat assigned to an adjacent field together averaged more than twenty-four hours per day of standby time. He developed a plan to release one boat and share the other between fields.[43]

The best-known group participative technique is the quality circle. Quality circles, discussed in Chapter 9, really started in this country but were developed and, as indicated in Table 16.1, are widely used in Japan. Recently they have been imported back to this country. Quality circles "typically are small groups of volunteers from the same work areas who meet regularly to identify, analyze, and solve quality and related problems in their area of responsibility. Members of a group choose a particular problem to study, gather data, and use such methods as brainstorming, Pareto analysis, histograms, and control charts to form a recommendation that can be presented to management."[44] In recent years in the United States, quality circles have given way to self-managed teams as the major participative approach (see Chapter 9). These teams are trained in communication and problem-solving skills and in quality/measurement strategies and techniques.[45]

Participative Techniques in Perspective

There are many positive and negative attributes of the participative techniques of decision making. Balancing these attributes in evaluating the effectiveness of participative decision making is difficult because of moderating factors such as leadership style or personality of the parties involved and situational, environmental, contextual factors,[46] and ideology.[47] Also, even though there is general research support, as is pointed out in the introductory comments, an extensive review of research found that the different forms of participative techniques had markedly different outcomes. For example, informal participation was found to have a positive effect on employee productivity and satisfaction; representative participation had a positive impact on

TABLE 16.1 Applications and Use of Modern Participative Techniques Across Cultures

Type of Participative Technique	Japanese Firms	Spanish Co-ops	Swedish Auto Firms	Hewlett-Packard
Decision making at the worker level	Widespread quality circles with the power to change the deployment of workers within workshops and the way jobs are concluded.	Experiments with shop-floor redesigns, small work teams, and quality circles along Japanese and Swedish lines are being diffused among the co-ops.	Workers design and organize their own jobs within a team framework to accomplish their common assignment. The design of the factory supports their self-paced teamwork.	700 quality circles at peak. Implementing self-directed work teams. Cooperative product design. Quality program.
Team of self-managed groups	Organization structures, such as broad job specification, group responsibility, and job rotation, require and promote teamwork.	Experiments with small work teams and quality circles along Japanese and Swedish lines are being diffused among the co-ops.	Self-directed assembly groups with frequent job rotation and enrichment.	Units kept small. Communication emphasized. Participative decision-making practiced. Implementing self-directed work teams in new factories.

Source: Adapted from David I. Levine, "Participation, Productivity, and the Firm's Environment," *California Management Review*, Summer 1990, p. 88. Copyright © 1990 by the Regents of the University of California. Reprinted from the *California Management Review*, vol. 32, no. 4. By permission of the Regents.

satisfaction, but not on productivity; and short-term participation was ineffective by both criteria.[48]

One problem is the tendency toward pseudoparticipation. Many managers ask for participation, but whenever subordinates take them up on it by making a suggestion or trying to give some input into a decision, they are put down or never receive any feedback. In some cases managers try to get their subordinates involved in the task but not in the decision-making process. This can lead to a boomerang effect regarding employee satisfaction. If the manager claims to want participation from subordinates but never lets them become intellectually and emotionally involved and never uses their suggestions, the results may be disastrous. Also, participation can be very time-consuming, and it has the same general disadvantages of committees. From a behavioral standpoint, however, the advantages far outweigh the disadvantages. Most of the benefits are touched upon throughout this text. Perhaps the biggest advantage is that the participative techniques recognize that each person can make a meaningful contribution to the attainment of organizational objectives.

CREATIVITY AND GROUP DECISION MAKING

By far, the most advances that have been made in decision making over the past several years have been quantitative in nature. Management science techniques and computerized decision support systems (DSS) are increasingly being used to help managers make better decisions. As Chapter 2 points out, such information-based approaches have had considerable impact and success. Yet, there are some recent research findings that indicate DSS may not be the end-all solution to effective decision making. For example, one recent study found that more information was provided and exchanged by a group using DSS, but when compared with a group without DSS, no better decisions were made.[49] In another study, although the DSS improved the organization of the decision-making process, the DSS also led to less thorough and critical discussion.[50] In other words, there is still a critical need for nonquantitative, behaviorally oriented decision-making techniques. Unfortunately, only the participative behavioral techniques discussed so far have been available to managers, and there have been only a few scattered attempts to develop new techniques for helping make more creative and problem-solving types of decisions. Yet it is these creative decisions which are the major challenge facing modern management.[51]

The Process of Creativity

A key challenge for organizations in the years ahead is to have more creativity and innovation. A recent analysis noted that creativity is "the gift and discipline that provides the competitive edge—in marketing, production, finance and all of the other aspects of an organization."[52] An example of a highly successful creative firm is Raychem Corporation, which on its twenty-fifth anniversary had developed over 200,000 products, more than 900 U.S. patents with some 300 pending, and 3000 foreign patents with another 9000 pending.[53] Unfortunately, such creative companies are still the exception rather than the rule.

Creative ideas from both individuals and groups are scarce. One of the problems may be that students educated in business schools know how to crunch numbers and develop models, but they have no knowledge of the creative process or how to develop creative solutions to problems. For example, General Foods held a competition in which student teams from prestigious business schools were given the charge to develop a new marketing plan that would stem the plunging sales of Sugar-Free Kool-Aid. Although they used models and the right terminology, they offered very few original ideas that the company could or would be able to use. The marketing manager concluded, "There were a couple of ideas that were of interest, but nothing we haven't looked at before."[54] A starting point for getting around this problem would be to understand the meaning and dimensions of creativity.

A simple, but generally recognized definition of *creativity* is that it involves combining responses or ideas of individuals or groups in novel ways.[55] The creative process is very complex. Creative solutions to even the simplest problems have wide variation. For instance, how would you respond to the problem of coming up with as many uses for a newspaper as possible? Compare your solution with the following proposed by a ten-year-old boy:

> You can read it, write on it, lay it down and paint a picture on it. . . . You could put it in your door for decoration, put it in the garbage can, put it on a chair if the chair is messy. If you have a puppy, you put newspaper in its box or put it in your backyard for the dog to play with. When you build something and you don't want anyone to see it, put newspaper around it. Put newspaper on the floor if you have no mattress, use it to pick up something hot, use it to stop bleeding, or to catch the drips from drying clothes. You can use a newspaper for curtains, put it in your shoe to cover what is hurting your foot, make a kite out of it, shade a light that is too bright. You can wrap fish in it, wipe windows, or wrap money in it. . . . You put washed shoes in newspaper, wipe eyeglasses with it, put it under a dripping sink, put a plant on it, make a paper bowl out of it, use it for a hat if it is raining, tie it on

your feet for slippers. You can put it on the sand if you have no towel, use it for bases in baseball, make paper airplanes with it, use it as a dustpan when you sweep, ball it up for the cat to play with, wrap your hands in it if it is cold.[56]

Obviously, this boy describing the uses of a newspaper was very creative, but what caused his creativity?

Feldman points out that it is much easier to provide examples of creativity than it is to identify causes. However, he identifies two major dimensions that can help explain the creative process:

1. *Divergent thinking.* This refers to a person's ability to generate novel, but still appropriate, responses to questions or problems. This is in contrast to convergent thinking which leads to responses that are based mainly on knowledge and rational logic. In the newspaper problem, convergent thinking would answer, "you read it," but divergent thinking would say, "make a kite out of it." The latter—divergent thinking—is considered more creative.
2. *Cognitive complexity.* This refers to a person's use of and preference for elaborate, intricate, and complex stimuli and thinking patterns. Creative people tend to have such cognitive complexity and display a wide range of interests, are independent, and are interested in philosophical or abstract problems. It is important to note, however, that creative people are not necessarily more intelligent (if intelligence is defined by standard tests of intelligence or grades in school, which tend to focus more on convergent thinking skills).[57]

There are some techniques that managers can use to help them make more creative decisions. For example, a national survey of highly creative top managers found that they use techniques such as guided imagery, self-hypnosis, journal keeping, and lateral styles of thinking.[58] Not only does encouraging creativity help the organization, it may also help the employees. On the basis of interviews in several major Japanese companies, it was found that employee creativity is managed through deliberate structural means, not to effect direct economic outcomes to the organization, but to develop the employees' motivation, job satisfaction, and teamwork.[59] In other words, even though the Japanese are not known for their creative breakthroughs in product development or technology, they effectively structure their organizations to allow their people to creatively apply their ideas. These creative ideas include methods for improved quality, efficiency, and flexibility, such as "Just in Time" (JIT), "Statistical Process Controls" (S.P.C.), and "Quality Control Circles" (QCC).[60]

Group Decision Making

Creativity in decision making can apply to individuals or groups. Since individual decision making has largely given way to group decision making in today's organizations, an understanding of group dynamics and teams, as discussed in Chapter 9, becomes relevant to decision making. For example, that chapter's discussion of groupthink problems and phenomena such as the risky shift (that a group may make more risky decisions than individual members on their own) helps one better understand the complexity of group decision making. In fact, a number of social decision schemes have emerged from social psychology research in recent years.

These schemes or rules can predict the final outcome of group decision making on the basis of the individual members' initial positions. Rathus has summarized these as follows:

1. *The majority-wins scheme.* In this commonly used scheme, the group arrives at the decision that was initially supported by the majority. This scheme appears to guide decision making most often when there is no objectively correct decision. An example would be a decision about what car model to build when the popularity of various models has not been tested in the "court" of public opinion.

2. *The truth-wins scheme.* In this scheme, as more information is provided and opinions are discussed, the group comes to recognize that one approach is objectively correct. For example, a group deciding whether to use SAT scores in admitting students to college would profit from information about whether these scores actually predict college success.

3. *The two-thirds majority scheme.* This scheme is frequently adopted by juries, who tend to convict defendants when two-thirds of the jury initially favors conviction.

4. *The first-shift rule.* In this scheme, the group tends to adopt the decision that reflects the first shift in opinion expressed by any group member. If a car-manufacturing group is equally divided on whether or not to produce a convertible, it may opt to do so after one group member initially opposed to the idea changes her mind. If a jury is deadlocked, the members may eventually follow the lead of the first juror to change his position.[61]

Besides the above schemes, there are also other phenomena such as the status quo tendency (when individuals or groups are faced with decisions, they resist change and will tend to stick with existing goals or plans) which affect group decision making. Suggestions such as the following can be used to help reduce and combat the status quo tendency and thus make more effective group decisions:

- When things are going well, decision makers should still be vigilant in examining alternatives.
- It can help to have separate groups monitor the environment, develop new technologies, and generate new ideas.
- To reduce the tendency to neglect gathering negative long-term information, managers should solicit worst-case scenarios as well as forecasts that include long-term costs.
- Build checkpoints and limits into any plan.
- When limits are reached, it may be necessary to have an outside, independent, or separate review of the current plan.
- Judge people on the way they make decisions and not only on outcomes, especially when the outcomes may not be under their control.
- Shifting emphasis to the quality of the decision process should reduce the need of the decision maker to appear consistent or successful when things are not going well.
- Organizations can establish goals, incentives, and support systems that encourage experimenting and taking risks.[62]

In addition to simple guidelines such as the above, group decision techniques such as Delphi and nominal grouping can also be used to help eliminate the dysfunctions of groups and help them make more effective decisions.

The Delphi Technique

Although Delphi was first developed by N. C. Dalkey and his associates in 1950 at the Rand Corporation's Think Tank, it has only recently become popularized as a group decision-making technique, for example, for long-range forecasting. Today, numerous organizations in business, education, government, health, and the military are using Delphi. No decision technique will ever be able to predict the future completely, but the Delphi technique seems to be as good a crystal ball as is currently available.

The technique, named after the oracle at Delphi in ancient Greece, has many variations, but generally it works as follows:

1. A group (usually of experts, but in some cases nonexperts may deliberately be used) is formed, but, importantly, the members are not in face-to-face interaction with one another. Thus, the expenses of bringing a group together are eliminated.
2. Each member is asked to make anonymous predictions or input into the problem decision the panel is charged with.
3. Each panel member then receives composite feedback from what the others have inputted. In some variations the reasons are listed (anonymously), but mostly just a composite figure is used.
4. On the basis of the feedback, another round of anonymous inputs is made. These iterations take place for a predetermined number of times or until the composite feedback remains the same, which means everyone is sticking with his or her position.

A major key to the success of the technique lies in its anonymity. Keeping the responses of panel members anonymous eliminates the problem of "saving face" and encourages the panel experts to be more flexible and thus to benefit from the estimates of others. In the traditional interacting group decision-making technique, the experts may be more concerned with defending their vested positions than they are with making a good decision.

Many organizations testify to the success they have had so far with the Delphi technique. McDonnell Douglas Aircraft has used the technique to forecast the future uncertainties of commercial air transportation. Weyerhaeuser, a building supply company, has used it to predict what will happen in the construction business, and Smith, Kline, Beecham, a drug manufacturer, has used it to study the uncertainties of medicine. TRW, a highly diversified, technically oriented company, has fourteen Delphi panels averaging seventeen members each. The panels suggest products and services which have marketing potential and predict technological developments and significant political, economic, social, and cultural events. Besides business applications, the technique has been used successfully on various problems in government, education, health, and the military. In other words, Delphi can be applied to a wide variety of program planning and decision problems in any type of organization.

The major criticisms of the Delphi technique center on its time consumption, cost, and Ouija-board effect. The third criticism implies that, much like the parlor game of that name, Delphi can claim no scientific basis or support. To counter this criticism, Rand has attempted to validate Delphi through controlled experimentation. The corporation set up panels of nonexperts who use the Delphi technique to answer questions such as, "How many popular votes were cast for Lincoln when he first ran for President?" and "What was the average price a farmer received for a bushel of apples in 1940?" These particular questions were used because the average person does not know the exact answers but knows something about the subjects. The result of these studies showed that the original estimates by the panel of nonexperts were reasonably close to being correct, but with the Delphi technique of anonymous feedback, the estimates greatly improved.

The Nominal Group Technique

Closely related to Delphi is the nominal group approach to group decision making. The nominal group has been used by social psychologists in their research for many years. A nominal group is simply a "paper group." It is a group in name only because no verbal exchange is allowed between members. In group dynamics research, social psychologists would pit a fully interacting group against a nominal group (a group of individuals added together on paper but not interacting verbally). In terms of number of ideas, uniqueness of ideas, and quality of ideas, research has found nominal groups to be superior to real groups. The general conclusion is that interacting groups have certain dysfunctions that inhibit creativity. For example, a recent study found that the performance of participants in interacting groups was more similar, more conforming, than the performance of those in nominal groups.[63] Yet, except for idea generation, the interactive effect of group members is known to have a significant positive effect on other variables. The latter type of effect is given attention in Chapter 9, on group dynamics and teams.

When the pure nominal group approach is expanded into a specific technique for decision making in organizations, it is labeled the *nominal group technique* (NGT) and consists of the following steps:

1. Silent generation of ideas in writing
2. Round-robin feedback from group members, who record each idea in a terse phrase on a flip chart or blackboard
3. Discussion of each recorded idea for clarification and evaluation
4. Individual voting on priority ideas, with the group decision being mathematically derived through rank ordering or rating[64]

The difference between this approach and Delphi is that the NGT members are usually acquainted with one another, have face-to-face contact, and communicate with one another directly in the third step. Although more research is needed, there is some evidence that NGT-led groups come up with many more ideas than traditional interacting groups and may do as well as, or slightly better than, groups using Delphi.[65] A study also found that NGT-led groups performed at a level of accuracy that was equivalent to that of the most proficient member.[66] However, another study found that NGT-led groups did not perform as well as interacting groups whose participants were pervasively aware of the problem given the group and when there were no dominant persons who inhibited others from communicating ideas.[67] Thus, as is true of most of the techniques discussed in this text, there are moderating effects. A review of the existing research literature on Delphi and NGT concluded:

> In general, the research on both Delphi and nominal group techniques suggests that they can help improve the quality of group decisions because they mitigate the problems of interacting groups—individual dominance and groupthink. A skillful

chairperson, therefore, may adapt these techniques to particular decision-making situations.[68]

Summary

This chapter has been devoted to the process of decision making. Decision making is defined as choosing between two or more alternatives. However, viewed as a process, the actual choice activity is preceded by gathering information and developing alternatives. The models of behavioral decision making include the completely economic rationality model on one extreme, Herbert Simon's bounded rationality model and the judgmental heuristics and biases model in the middle range, and the irrationally based social model on the other extreme. Each of these models gives insights into decision-making rationality. For example, even the traditional accounting and finance techniques under the economic rationality model of decision making have recently given way in some companies to more effective activity-based costing (ABC) and economic value added (EVA) techniques. The same is true of the social models on the other extreme. Understanding human dynamics such as escalation of commitment gives more credibility to the social model of decision making. However, Simon's bounded rationality and more recently the judgmental model from cognitive psychology have emerged as having the biggest impact on behavioral decision-making theory and practice.

The techniques for decision making have been dominated mainly by quantitative models. The behavioral techniques do not begin to approach the sophistication of the quantitative techniques. Yet it is the creative, problem-solving management decisions which are crucial for organizational success. Understanding of the traditional (Scanlon Plan and suggestion plan or boxes) and modern (decision making at the worker level, team/self-managed groups, and quality circles) participative techniques and the creative and group decision-making process and techniques (Delphi and nominal grouping) can lead to more effective decision making for the future.

Questions for Discussion and Review

1. What are the three steps in Simon's decision-making process? Relate these steps to an actual decision.
2. Compare and contrast the economic rationality model and the social model. What are some recent refinements of these two extreme models?
3. Describe the major characteristics of Simon's bounded rationality model. Do you think this model is descriptive of practicing executives?
4. Identify the three major judgmental biases. How do they differ from one another? Give an example of each in management decision making.
5. What are the traditional and modern participative techniques? If you were in charge of the production department at a manufacturing plant, which technique or techniques would you implement and why?
6. What is the difference between divergent and convergent thinking, and what is their relationship to the process of creativity?
7. Explain a hypothetical situation in which Delphi and/or NGT could be used.

Footnote References and Supplemental Readings

1. Chester I. Barnard, *The Functions of the Executive*, Harvard University Press, Cambridge, Mass., 1938, p. 14.

2. Herbert A. Simon, *The New Science of Management Decision*, Harper, New York, 1960, p. 2.

3. Henry Mintzberg, Duru Raisin-ghani, and André Theoret, "The Structure of 'Unstructured' Decision Processes," *Administrative Science Quarterly*, June 1976, pp. 246–275.

4. Richard L. Daft, *Organization Theory and Design*, West, St. Paul, Minn., 1983, pp. 357–358.

5. For example, see Paul J. H. Schoemaker, "Strategic Decisions in Organizations: Rational and Behavioural Views," *Journal of Management Studies*, January 1993, pp. 107–130.

6. See Max H. Bazerman, *Managerial Decision Making*, 2d ed., Wiley, New York, 1990.

7. See James L. Bowditch and Anthony F. Buono, *A Primer on Organizational Behavior*, 2d ed., Wiley, New York, 1990, p. 99.

8. Herbert A. Simon, *Administrative Behavior*, 2d ed., Macmillan, New York, 1957, p. 64.

9. Ibid., pp. 76–77.

10. Ibid., p. xxiii.

11. Thomas J. Peters and Robert H. Waterman, Jr., *In Search of Excellence: Lessons from America's Best-Run Companies*, Harper & Row, New York, 1982, p. 29.

12. Terence P. Pare, "A New Tool for Managing Costs," *Fortune*, June 14, 1993, pp. 124–129.

13. Ibid., p. 128.

14. Shawn Tully, "The Real Key to Creating Wealth," *Fortune*, Sept. 20, 1993, pp. 38–50.

15. Ibid., p. 38.

16. Paul Gray, "The Assault on Freud," *Time*, Nov. 29, 1993, pp. 47–51.

17. Solomon E. Asch, "Opinions and Social Pressure," *Scientific American*, November 1955, pp. 31–35.

18. Barry M. Staw and Jerry Ross, "Understanding Behavior in Escalation Situations," *Science*, October 1989, pp. 216–220.

19. Fred Luthans and Robert Koester, "The Impact of Computer-Generated Information on the Choice Activity of Decision Makers," *Academy of Management Journal*, June 1976, pp. 328–332, and Robert Koester and Fred Luthans, "The Impact of the Computer on the Choice Activity of Decision Makers: A Replication with Actual Users of Computerized MIS," *Academy of Management Journal*, June 1979, pp. 416–422.

20. Simon, *Administrative Behavior*, pp. xxv-xxvi.

21. E. Frank Harrison, *The Managerial Decision-Making Process*, Houghton Mifflin, Boston, 1975, p. 69.

22. The analysis of the judgmental heuristics model comes largely from Bazerman, *Managerial Decision Making*.

23. For example, see D. Kahneman and A. Tversky, "Subjective Probability: A Judgment of Representativeness," *Cognitive Psychology*, vol. 3, 1972, pp. 430–454; D. Kahneman and A. Tversky, "On the Psychology of Prediction," *Psychological Review*, vol. 80, 1973, pp. 237–251; D. Kahneman and A. Tversky, "Prospect Theory: An Analysis of Decision Under Risk," *Econometrica*, vol. 47, 1979, pp. 263–291; A. Tversky and D. Kahneman, "Availability: A Heuristic for Judging Frequency and Probability," *Cognitive Psychology*, vol. 5, 1973, pp. 207–232; and A. Tversky and D. Kahneman, "Judgment Under Uncertainty: Heuristics and Biases," *Science*, vol. 185, 1974, pp. 1124–1131.

24. See Gregory B. Northcraft and Margaret A. Neale, *Organizational Behavior*, Dryden, Chicago, 1990, p. 184.

25. See Max H. Bazerman, *Judgment in Management Decision Making*, Wiley, New York, 1986, 1990, 1994.

26. Tversky and Kahneman, "Availability: A Heuristic," loc. cit., and Tversky and Kahneman, "Judgment Under Uncertainty," loc. cit.

27. Bazerman, *Managerial Decision Making*, p. 7.

28. Northcraft and Neale, op. cit., p. 185.

29. Kahneman and Tversky, "On the Psychology of Prediction," loc. cit.

30. Bazerman, *Managerial Decision Making*, p. 7.

31. Northcraft and Neale, op. cit., p. 187.

32. Bazerman, *Managerial Decision Making*, p. 7.

33. Ibid., p. 28.

34. For example, see issues of the *Journal of Behavioral Decision Making* and the *Journal of Risk and Uncertainty*, as well as the standard journals such as *Organizational Behavior and Human Decision Processes*. Scott T. Allison, Anne Marie R. Jordan, and Carole E. Yeatts, "Cluster-Analytic Approach Toward Identifying Structure and Content of Human Decision Making," *Human Relations*, vol. 45, 1992, pp. 49–72.

35. David L. Levine, "Participation, Productivity, and the Firm's Environment," *California Management Review*, Summer 1990, p. 86.

36. Barry A. Macy, Mark F. Peterson, and Larry W. Norton, "A Test of Participation Theory in a Work Re-design Field Setting: Degree of Participation and Comparison Site Contrasts," *Human Relations*, vol. 42, 1989, p. 1110.

37. For example, see Brian K. Evans and Donald G. Fischer, "A Hierarchical Model of Participatory Decision Making, Job Autonomy, and Perceived Control," *Human Relations*, November 1992, pp. 1169–1190.

38. J. Kenneth White, "The Scanlon Plan: Causes and Correlates of Success," *Academy of Management Journal*, June 1979, pp. 292–312.

39. "Worker Participation at A&P Stores Gives the Chain a Boost," *The Wall Street Journal*, Jan. 6, 1987, p. 1.

40. Labor Letter, *The Wall Street Journal*, Sept. 12, 1989, p. A1.

41. Brian Dumaine, "Who Needs a Boss?" *Fortune*, May 7, 1990, p. 52.

42. Eric Sundstrom, Kenneth P. DeMeuse, and David Futrell, "Work Teams," *American Psychologist*, February 1990, pp. 120–133.

43. Kevin J. Lewis, "HR Keeps Chevron Well Oiled," *Personnel*, January 1990, p. 18.

44. George Munchus, "Employer-Employee Based Quality Circles in Japan: Human Resource Policy Implications for American Firms," *Academy of Management Review*, April 1983, p. 255.

45. See Paul E. Brauchle and David W. Wright, "Training Work Teams," *Training and Development*, March 1993, pp. 65–69, and Jon R. Katzenbach and Douglas K. Smith, "The Discipline of Teams," *Harvard Business Review*, March–April 1993, pp. 111–120.

46. David M. Schweiger and Carrie R. Lena, "Participation in Decision Making," in Edwin A. Locke (ed.), *Generalizing from Laboratory to Field Settings*, Lexington Books, Lexington, Mass., 1986, p. 148.

47. Stewart Black and Newton Margulies, "An Ideological Perspective on Participation: A Case for Integration," *Journal of Organizational Change Management*, vol. 2, no. 1, 1989, pp. 13–34, and L. Alan Witt, "Exchange Ideology as a Moderator of the Relationships Between Importance of Participation in Decision Making and Job Attitudes," *Human Relations*, vol. 45, 1992, pp. 73–86.

48. John L. Cotton, David A. Vollrath, Kirk L. Froggatt, Mark L. Lengnick-Hall, and Kenneth R. Jennings, "Employee Participation: Diverse Forms and Different Outcomes," *Academy of Management Review*, January 1988, pp. 8–22.

49. Alan R. Dennis, "Information Processing in Group Decision Making: You Can Lead a Group to Information, But You Can't Make It Think," *Academy of Management Best Papers Proceedings*, 1993, pp. 283–287.

50. Marshall Scott Poole, Michael Holmes, Richard Watson, and Gerardine DeSanctis, "Group Decision Support Systems and Group Communication," *Communication Research*, April 1993, pp. 176–213.

51. Walter Kiechel, "How We Will Work in the Year 2000," *Fortune*, May 17, 1993, pp. 38–52.

52. Joseph V. Anderson, "Weirder Than Fiction: The Reality and Myths of Creativity," *Academy of Management Executive*, November 1992, p. 40.

53. William Taylor, "The Business of Innovation," *Harvard Business Review*, March–April 1990, p. 97.

54. Trish Hall, "When Budding MBAs Try to Save Kool-Aid, Original Ideas Are Scarce, *The Wall Street Journal*, Nov. 25, 1986, p. 31.

55. M. D. Mumford and S. B. Gustafson, "Creativity Syndrome: Integration, Application, and Innovation," *Psychological Bulletin*, vol. 103, 1988, pp. 27–43.

56. This description is part of a study reported in W. C. Ward, N. Kogan, and E. Pankove, "Incentive Effects in Children's Creativity," *Child Development*, vol. 43, 1972, pp. 669–676, and is found in Robert S. Feldman, *Understanding Psychology*, 2d ed., McGraw-Hill, New York, 1990, p. 243.

57. Feldman, op. cit., pp. 242–243.

58. Weston H. Agor, "Use of Intuitive Intelligence to Increase Productivity," *HR Focus*, September 1993, p. 9.

59. Min Basadur, "Managing Creativity: A Japanese Model," *Academy of Management Executive*, May 1992, pp. 29–42.

60. Ibid., p. 29.

61. Spencer A. Rathus, *Psychology*, 4th ed., Holt, Rinehart and Winston, Fort Worth, Tex., 1990, pp. 634–635.

62. William S. Silver and Terence R. Mitchell, "The Status Quo Tendency in Decision Making," *Organizational Dynamics*, Spring 1990, pp. 45–46.

63. Paul B. Paulus and Mary T. Dzindolet, "Social Influence Processes in Group Brainstorming," *Journal of Personality and Social Psychology*, April 1993, pp. 575–586.

64. Andre L. Delbecq, Andrew H. Van deVen, and David H. Gustafson, *Group Techniques for Program Planning*, Scott, Foresman, Glenview, Ill., 1975, p. 8.

65. A. H. Van deVen, *Group Decision-Making Effectiveness*, Kent State University Center for Business and Economic Research Press, Kent, Ohio, 1974.

66. John Rohrbaugh, "Improving the Quality of Group Judgment: Social Judgment Analysis and the Nominal Group Technique," *Organizational Behavior and Human Performance*, October 1981, pp. 272–288.

67. Thad B. Green, "An Empirical Analysis of Nominal and Interacting Groups," *Academy of Management Journal*, March 1975, pp. 63–73.

68. David R. Hampton, Charles E. Summer, and Ross A. Webber, *Organizational Behavior and the Practice of* *Management*, 5th ed., Scott, Foresman, Glenview, Ill., 1987, p. 274.

REAL CASE:
Getting
Additional
Information

Access to information is changing the way more and more people do things, from children in the classroom to executives in the boardroom. In particular, managers are now beginning to realize one important fact about decision making: the more information they can gather on a particular area or problem, the more likely it is that they can make a good decision. The result has been the mushrooming of the information processing business.

As early as the 1970s, many entrepreneurs with a close eye on what was needed in management decision making and control were forecasting an "information market" boom. They believed that both business firms and consumers would be willing to pay to have information provided to them. For example, General Motors might want to know the most recent articles or news releases on cars with front-wheel drive. One way to get this information would be to have someone in the public relations department cut and clip every piece of information found in all the newspapers and journals that the company purchased. An easier way, however, would be to subscribe to a news retrieval service that would provide all this same information for the asking. All subscribers have to do is use the computer to tell the retrieval service the types of information they want. The computer will then search its files and print out everything related to the topic areas requested by the customer.

Today, a number of firms are providing information services to clients. Examples are the following:

- Dow Jones News/Retrieval accumulates information collected by the company's news organization, divides it into categories such as financial data, stock prices, and international news, and sells each separately to subscribers.
- Reuters, the news agency, sells software that allows currency and commodities traders to spot opportunities based on their own strategies. The data used by the software are obtained from Reuters's database.
- The Institute for Scientific Information scans approximately 7000 scientific and medical journals and indexes them for 300,000 customers.
- Telerate sells financial information on such things as money market and foreign currency rates.

In addition to the examples above, a number of other new information services are springing up. One is Strategic Intelligence Systems (SIS) Inc., which has built databases on eighteen separate industries. These data include economic trends, product development, and other information useful for strategy formulation and implementation. By interviewing its clients and finding out the kinds of information they need, SIS helps client managers make better decisions. Another service is CompuServe Inc., which provides its subscribers everything from airline schedules to stock reports to electronic shopping services to games. As management finds itself needing more and more timely information for decision making, computerized information services are likely to become increasingly important.

1. When managers use the services to provide themselves with information, what phase of the decision-making process are they focusing on?
2. Of what value are information services to today's decision makers? Do these services allow the manager to make decisions along the line of the economic rationality model?
3. Are we likely to see greater use of these information services in the future? Why or why not?

**CASE:
Harry Smart
or Is He?**

Harry Smart, a very bright and ambitious young executive, was born and raised in Boston and graduated from a small New England college. He met his future wife, Barbra, who was also from Boston, in college. They were married the day after they both graduated cum laude. Harry then went on to Harvard, where he received an MBA, and Barbra earned a law degree from Harvard. Harry is now in his seventh year with Brand Corporation, which is located in Boston, and Barbra has a position in a Boston law firm.

As part of an expansion program, the board of directors of Brand has decided to build a new branch plant. The president personally selected Harry to be the manager of the new plant and informed him that a job well done would guarantee him a vice presidency in the corporation. Harry was appointed chairperson, with final decision-making privileges, of an ad hoc committee to determine the location of the new plant. At the initial meeting, Harry explained the ideal requirements for the new plant. The members of the committee were experts in transportation, marketing, distribution, labor economics, and public relations. He gave them one month to come up with three choice locations for the new plant.

A month passed and the committee reconvened. After weighing all the variables, the experts recommended the following cities in order of preference: Kansas City, Los Angeles, and New York. Harry could easily see that the committee members had put a great deal of time and effort into their report and recommendations. A spokesperson for the group emphasized that there was a definite consensus Kansas City was the best location for the new plant. Harry thanked them for their fine job and told them he would like to study the report in more depth before he made his final decision.

After dinner that evening he asked his wife, "Honey, how would you like to move to Kansas City?" Her answer was quick and sharp, "Heavens, no!" she said. "I've lived in the East all my life, and I'm not about to move out into the hinterlands. I've heard the biggest attraction in Kansas City is the stockyards. That kind of life is not for me." Harry weakly protested, "But, honey, my committee strongly recommends Kansas City as the best location for my plant. Their second choice was Los Angeles and the third was New York. What am I going to do?" His wife thought a moment and then replied, "Well, I would consider relocating to or commuting from New York, but if you insist on Kansas City, you'll have to go by yourself!"

The next day Harry called his committee together and said, "You should all be commended for doing an excellent job on this report. However, after detailed study, I am convinced that New York will meet the needs of our plant better than Kansas City or Los Angeles. Therefore, the decision will be to locate the new plant in New York. Thank you all once again for a job well done."

1. Did Harry make a rational decision?
2. What model of behavioral decision making does this incident support?
3. What decision techniques that were discussed in the chapter could be used by the committee to select the new plant site?

17 Organization Theory and Design

Learning Objectives

- **Analyze** the characteristics, dysfunctions, and current status of the bureaucratic model.
- **Discuss** the classic organization concepts and structural characteristics of centralization/decentralization, flat/tall, departmentation, and line/staff.
- **Explain** the modern organization theories of open systems, information processing, contingency, ecology, and learning.
- **Present** the modern project, matrix, network, virtual, and horizontal designs of organizations.

In this chapter, the inductive conceptual framework moves to the extreme macro level of analysis for organizational behavior. This chapter is concerned with organization theory and design. Organization structure represents the skeletal framework for organizational behavior. As the discussion of the conceptual framework in Chapter 1 points out, the organization structure is the dominant environmental factor that interacts with the person and the behavior. This chapter presents the organization from the viewpoint of classical and modern theory and design. The bureaucratic model of organization dominates the classical approach. After presenting and discussing this model, the chapter gives an overview and analysis of some of the extensions and modifications represented by the concepts of centralization and decentralization, flat and tall structures, departmentation, and line and staff.

Although the classical approach is still much in evidence today, as Chapter 2 points out, information technology, global competition, and the concern for total quality have had a dramatic impact on organization structure. New theories, designs, and networks have emerged to meet the contemporary situation. For example, very recently well-known companies, such as General Electric, have been eliminating vertical structure and adopting a horizontal design, and Xerox now develops new products through multidisciplinary teams that work in a single process instead of vertical functions or departments.[1] In general, the modern approach to organization theory and design is more flexible and recognizes the interaction of technology and people. For example, one modern organization theorist has noted: "Organization structure is more than boxes on a chart; it is a pattern of interactions and coordination that links the technology, tasks, and human components of the organization to ensure that the organization accomplishes its purposes."[2] There is also a renewed recognition for the role that structure (or lack of structure) plays in innovation, change, and learning in today's and tomorrow's organizations.

Before getting into the newer organization theories and designs, there is a need to have a thorough understanding of classical concepts. First, the bureaucratic model is presented and analyzed. This discussion is followed by a description of the widely recognized concepts of centralization/decentralization, flat/tall, departmentation, and line/staff. These classical concepts serve as a point of departure for examining the modern organization theories (open systems, information processing, contingency, ecology, and learning) and designs (project, matrix, network, virtual, and horizontal).

CLASSICAL ORGANIZATION THEORY AND DESIGN

The classical organization is most often associated with bureaucracy. Even though organizations are undergoing dramatic, some would say radical, changes, bureaucracies still exist and must be understood to move toward and interpret some of the new theories and designs. For example, even though IBM has undergone a total reorganization and has implemented some of the newest structural designs, a recent critical analysis concludes that "IBM's stifling corporate bureaucracy remains a barrier to change."[3] The starting point of any analysis of organization theory and design still remains the bureaucratic model.

The Bureaucratic Model

Bureaucratic theory and design are attributed to Max Weber, one of the pioneers of modern sociology. He formulated this approach to organization in the early 1900s, and his work was first translated from German to English in the 1940s. Weber presented what he thought was an ideal organization structure that he called a bureaucracy. His concern for the ideal was a natural extension of his interest in the development and change of Western society. Specifically, Weber believed that rationalization is the most persistent cultural value of Western society. On an organizational level, the bureaucracy represented a completely rational form.

Weber specified several characteristics of his ideal organization structure. The four major ones are the following:

1. *Specialization and division of labor*. Weber's bureaucracy contained "a specified sphere of competence. This involves (a) a sphere of obligations to perform functions which has been marked off as part of a systematic division of labor (b) The provision of the incumbent with the necessary authority . . . (c) That the necessary means of compulsion are clearly defined and their use is subject to definite conditions."[4] This statement implies that Weber recognized the importance of having the authority and power to carry out assigned duties. In addition, the bureaucrats must know the precise limit of their sphere of competence so as not to infringe upon those of others.

2. *Positions arranged in a hierarchy*. Weber stated: "The organization of offices follows the principle of hierarchy: that is, each lower office is under the control and supervision of a higher one."[5] This bureaucratic characteristic forces control over every member in the structure. Some organization theorists, such as Herbert Simon, have pointed out that hierarchy is the natural order of things. An example

lies in the biological subsystems, such as the digestive and circulatory systems; these are composed of organs, the organs are composed of tissues, and the tissues are composed of cells. Each cell is in turn hierarchically organized into a nucleus, cell wall, and cytoplasm. The same is true of physical phenomena such as molecules, which are composed of electrons, neutrons, and protons.[6] In a manner analogous to the biological and physical structures, hierarchy is a basic characteristic of complex organization structures.

3. *A system of abstract rules.* Weber felt a need for "a continuous organization of official functions bound by rules."[7] A rational approach to organization requires a set of formal rules to ensure uniformity and coordination of effort. A well-understood system of regulations also provides the continuity and stability that Weber thought were so important. Rules persist, whereas personnel may frequently change. They may range from no smoking in certain areas to the need for board approval for multi-thousand-dollar capital expenditures.

4. *Impersonal relationship.* It was Weber's belief that the ideal official should be dominated by "a spirit of formalistic impersonality, without hatred or passion, and hence without affection or enthusiasm."[8] Once again, Weber was speaking from the viewpoint of ideal rationality and not of realistic implementation. He felt that in order for bureaucrats to make completely rational decisions, they must avoid emotional attachment to subordinates and clients/customers.

The four characteristics just described are not the only ones recognized and discussed by Weber. Another important aspect of the ideal bureaucracy is that employment is based on technical qualifications. The bureaucrat is protected against arbitrary dismissal, and promotions are made according to seniority and/or achievement. In total, it must be remembered that Weber's bureaucracy was intended to be an ideal construct: no real-world organization exactly follows the Weber model. The widely recognized organization theorist Peter M. Blau summarizes Weber's thinking as follows:

> Weber dealt with bureaucracy as what he termed an ideal type. This methodological concept does not represent an average of the attributes of all existing bureaucracies (or other social structures), but a pure type, derived by abstracting the most characteristic aspects of all known organizations.[9]

It has been pointed out that the classical, rational approach to structure is of value to managers of formal work organizations that have no conflict or whose subordinates have no power,[10] but, of course, this is the ideal, not reality. In this age of complex, highly conflicting relationships, and empowered employees, this bureaucratic model is only the starting point, not the end, of organizational analysis.

Bureaucratic Dysfunctions

With the exception of Weber, sociologists and philosophers have been very critical of bureaucracies. For example, Karl Marx believed that bureaucracies are used by the dominant capitalist class to control the other, lower social classes. According to Marx, bureaucracies are characterized by strict hierarchy and discipline, veneration of authority, incompetent officials, lack of initiative and imagination, fear of responsibility, and a process of self-aggrandizement.[11] This interpretation of bureaucracy is basically exactly opposite to what Weber proposed. The Weber model can serve equally well in analyzing either the functional or the dysfunctional ramifications of classical organization structure.

The Dysfunctions of Specialization. The Weber bureaucratic model emphasizes that specialization enhances productivity and efficiency. The model ignores, but can be used to point out, the dysfunctional qualities of specialization. Empirical investigation has uncovered both functional and dysfunctional consequences. In other words, specialization has been shown to lead to increased productivity and efficiency but also to create conflict between specialized units, to the detriment of the overall goals of the organization. For example, specialization may impede communication between units. The management team of a highly specialized unit has its own terminology and similar interests, attitudes, and personal goals. Because "outsiders are different," the specialized unit tends to withdraw into itself and not fully communicate with units above, below, or horizontal to it. Performing a highly specialized job is also a major cause of employee boredom and burnout—blue-collar blues and white-collar woes.

The Dysfunctions of Hierarchy. What was said of specialization also holds true for the other characteristics of a bureaucracy. The functional attributes of a hierarchy are that it maintains unity of command, coordinates activities and personnel, reinforces authority, and serves as a formal system of communication. In theory, the hierarchy has both a downward and an upward orientation, but in practice, it has often turned out to have only a downward emphasis. Thus, individual initiative and participation are often blocked, upward communication is impeded, and there is no formal recognition of horizontal communication. Personnel who follow only the formal hierarchy may waste a great deal of time and energy.

The Dysfunctions of Rules. Bureaucratic rules probably have the most obvious dysfunctional qualities. Contributing to the bureaucratic image of red tape, rules often become the ends in themselves, rather than the means for more effective goal attainment. The famous management consultant Peter Drucker cites the following common misuses of rules that require reports and procedures:

First is the mistaken belief that procedural rules are instruments of morality. They should not determine what is right or wrong conduct.

Second, procedural rules are sometimes mistakenly substituted for judgment. Bureaucrats should not be mesmerized by printed forms; forms should be used only in cases where judgment is not required.

The third and most common misuse of procedural rules is as a punitive control device from above. Bureaucrats are often required to comply with rules that have nothing to do with their jobs—for example, plant managers who have to accurately fill out numerous forms for staff personnel and corporate management which they cannot use in obtaining their own objectives.[12]

Drucker would like to see every procedural rule put on trial for its life at least every five years. He cites the case of an organization in which all reports and forms were totally done away with for two months. At the end of the suspension, three-fourths of the reports and forms were deemed unnecessary and were eliminated.[13]

The Dysfunctions of Impersonal Characteristics. The impersonal quality of the bureaucracy has even more dysfunctional consequences than specialization, hierarchy, and rules. Behaviorally oriented organization theorists and researchers have given a great deal of attention to the behavioral dysfunctions of bureaucratic structures. Much discussion in this text is critical of the impersonal characteristic of bureaucracies. The same is true of today's consumers and employees. Everyone has horror stories and everyday irritations dealing with impersonal bureaucracies.

The Modern View of Bureaucracies

The acknowledged bureaucratic dysfunctions have led most people to readily accept Parkinson's popular "laws" (for example, bureaucratic staffs increase in inverse proportion to the amount of work done[14]) and the popular "Peter principle" (managers rise to their level of incompetence in bureaucracies[15]). These laws and principles have received wide public acceptance because everyone has observed and experienced what Parkinson and Peter wrote about. But as one organizational scholar has noted:

> These two writers have primarily capitalized on the frustrations toward government and business administration felt by the general public, which is not familiar with the processes necessitated by large-scale organization. Parkinson and Peter made a profit on their best sellers; they added little to the scientific study of organizations.[16]

In addition to the popularized criticisms of bureaucracy, a more academic analysis also uncovers many deficiencies. Bennis summarized some of them as follows:

1. Bureaucracy does not adequately allow for personal growth and the development of mature personalities.
2. It develops conformity and groupthink.
3. It does not take into account the informal organization and the emergent and unanticipated problems.
4. Its systems of control and authority are hopelessly outdated.
5. It has no juridical process.
6. It does not possess adequate means for resolving differences and conflicts between ranks and, most particularly, between functional groups.
7. Communication and innovative ideas are thwarted or distorted as a result of hierarchical divisions.
8. The full human resources of bureaucracy are not being utilized because of mistrust, fear of reprisals, etc.
9. It cannot assimilate the influx of new technology or scientists entering the organization.
10. It modifies personality structure in such a way that the person in a bureaucracy becomes the dull, gray, conditioned "organization man."[17]

Parkinson, Peter, and Bennis represent the extreme critics of bureaucratic organization. Nevertheless, during the past few years popular writers, scholars, practitioners, and the general public have felt increasing dissatisfaction and frustration with classical bureaucratic structures. This discontent is reflected in the consumerism movement, which is largely a grassroots reaction to the impersonality of large bureaucracies, and the tremendous appeal of best-selling books such as *In Search of Excellence: Lessons from America's Best-Run Companies*[18] and *Reengineering the Corporation*,[19] whose basic theme is that organizations must be more flexible and less bureaucratic, and must undergo constant change and learning. For example, another recent book, *Transforming Organizations*, argues that

> . . . without continuous systemic organizational change, the competitiveness or even survival of many organizations may be at risk. Continuous change implies that the organization has a capacity to learn from its environment, its various stakeholders,

and itself. Systemic change implies that its major components—strategies, technologies, human resources, and internal structures—require simultaneous transformation.[20]

Obviously, such needed organizational change cannot be handled by the traditional bureaucratic form and may call for drastic action. For example, in Tom Peters's latest book, he colorfully describes how he would like managers to engage in bureaucracy bashing:

> Rant and rave. Tear up papers. Refuse to read them. Don't attend meetings. . . . Be outrageous. Get rid of all your file cabinets. . . . Put big cardboard boxes around your desk, and throw all the junk you receive into them—unread. Put a big red label on the boxes: "This week's unread paperwork."[21]

He recognizes that such radical behavior may jeopardize one's career, but feels that unless it is done, organizations depending on bureaucratic structuring—especially those which use vertical processing of information—will not be competitive or even, in the long run, survive.

Taken in perspective, the argument is not necessarily that the classical bureaucratic model is completely wrong but, rather, that the times have rendered many of those concepts and principles irrelevant. Bureaucratic organization is thought to be too inflexible to adapt readily to the dynamic nature and purpose of many of today's organizations and public needs. Flexibility, adaptability, and learning are necessary requirements for modern organization structures. The increasing size of organizations (as a result of both mergers and internal growth), information technology, the concern for total quality, globalization, and the huge social and economic upheavals in recent years are but a few of the things which have contributed to a new organizational environment. There has even been a call for Mikhail Gorbachev's concept of perestroika (openness) to be applied to restructuring American corporations.[22] One thing is certain, the traditional bureaucratic organization structure has not been able to deal with these dramatic changes. Something else is needed. The rest of this chapter discusses this "something else" besides bureaucratic principles that can be and is being used to structure today's organizations.

MODIFICATIONS OF BUREAUCRATIC STRUCTURING

The classical bureaucratic model has served as a point of departure for modified vertical and horizontal structural arrangements. Vertical analysis concentrates on centralization versus decentralization and on flat versus tall structuring. These characteristics represent modifications of the classical principles of delegation of authority and limited span of control. Decentralization expands the principle of delegation to the point of an overall philosophy of organization and management. A *tall* organization structure means a series of narrow spans of control, and a *flat* structure incorporates wide spans. The bureaucratic principle of hierarchy is also closely related to the vertical concept.

Horizontal structural analysis is concerned with organizing one level of the hierarchy. The concepts of departmentation and of line and staff represent this approach. They are derived chiefly from the bureaucratic doctrine of specialization. Departmentation concentrates on organizing each level to attain optimum benefit from high degrees of specialization. The staff concept attempts to resolve the vertical and horizontal conflicts that appeared in the classical scheme. In general, the concepts discussed next carry the bureaucratic concepts one step further. They give greater weight to the human element and recognize that simple, mechanistic structural arrangements are not satisfactory for modern organizations.

Centralization and Decentralization

The terms *centralization* and *decentralization* are freely tossed about in the management and organization theory literature and in actual management and organization design. Most often, both the scholar and the practitioner neglect to define what they mean by the concept.

Types and Meaning.   There are three basic types of centralization and decentralization. The first type is *geographic*, or *territorial*, concentration (centralization) or dispersion (decentralization) of operations. For example, the term "centralized" can be used to refer to an organization that has all its operations under one roof or in one geographic region. On the other hand, the dispersion of an organization's operations throughout the country or the world is a form of decentralization. This type of centralization-decentralization has become particularly relevant as organizations today begin to create international structures.[23] The word "geographic" is often not stated, which adds to the confusion.

The second type is *functional* centralization and decentralization. A good example is the human resources function of an organization. A separate human resources department that performs functions such as selection or training for the other departments is said to be centralized. However, if the various functional departments (for example, marketing, production, and finance) handle their own human resources functions, then human resources is considered decentralized. Both *geographic* and *functional centralization* and *decentralization* are descriptive terms rather than analytical terms.

The third type is the only analytical use of the concept. This is where the terms "centralization" and "decentralization" refer to the retention or delegation of decision-making prerogatives or command. From an organization theory and analysis standpoint, this third type is the most relevant use of the concepts of centralization and decentralization. They are relative concepts because every organization structure contains both features, and the concepts differ only in degree.

Contrary to common belief, it is not possible to determine whether an organization is centralized or decentralized merely by looking at the organization chart. The determining factor is how much of the decision making is retained at the top and how much is delegated to the lower levels. This amount of retention or delegation is not reflected on the organization chart.

Optimum Degree of Decentralization.   Traditionally, the implication has been that decentralization is somehow better than centralization. In truth, neither concept is an ideal or intrinsically good or bad. Generally speaking, decentralization is much more compatible with the behavioral aspects of management. This relevancy is due in part to the lower-level participation in decision making and the currently popular notion of empowerment of employees that results from decentralization. Increased motivation is an extremely important by-product. Besides the behavioral benefits, more effective decisions are possible because of the speed and firsthand knowledge that decentralization provides. Decentralization also affords invaluable experience in decision making for lower-level executives. Finally, it allows more time for top management to concentrate on policymaking and creative innovation. In other words, the concept of decentralization, which has been around for a number of years, is very much a part of the highly touted new organizational forms that are associated with empowerment and pushing the decision making down to the lowest level possible.

Many organizations are still experiencing success in moving from centralization to decentralization. For example, under the leadership of General W. L. (Bill) Creech, the Tactical Air Command (TAC) moved from a highly centralized to a highly decentralized structure. By making subunits more autonomous and creating pride of ownership, he was able to turn the Air Force's worst command into its best.[24] As a result of his success, the Pentagon now gives commanders new authority to abolish regulations, streamline procedures, and do whatever is necessary to get the job done.

In business, a good example is Johnson & Johnson, the highly successful and largest U.S. pharmaceutical firm, with 165 units worldwide. Each unit has considerable autonomy. Although corporate headquarters in New Jersey sets overall corporate policies on financial and certain administrative matters, the unit presidents, many in their late thirties and early forties, have full responsibility for their unit's research and development, manufacturing, marketing, and sales. For example, Johnson & Johnson sent thirty-eight-year-old Carl Spalding to head up its consumer products unit in South Africa. He not only independently ran the business but also had to hire, train, and promote black employees, even build housing for them, often in violation of local traditions.[25] This is decentralization in action.

It is fair to say that, overall, decentralization has supported, and in some cases has stimulated, the behavioral approach to management. At the same time, there is little doubt that a wide discrepancy exists between the theory of decentralization and its practice. Yet, because of its wide acceptance, decentralization has had a definite impact on developing a managerial attitude favoring the implementation of behavioral concepts in organizations. However, it is now recognized that a third dimension such as cooperation may also be structurally needed, in addition to centralization and decentralization. Teamwork or cooperation may even be added to create a triangular design so that the organization becomes a function of three variables—autonomy (decentralization), control (centralization), and cooperation (teamwork).[26] It is these cooperative, team-oriented organizations that have emerged in recent years.

Flat and Tall Structures

Chapter 2 discusses the impact that information technology has had on the flattening of organizations. In addition to the impact of information technology, there is also rethinking on the span of control (the number of subordinates directly reporting to a manager) which has a direct impact on the number of levels of structure. A recent analysis noted:

> The conventional theory is that an executive can only adequately supervise five or six direct reports; today this concept is being rethought as companies consider whether staffing subordinate functions with better quality talent, and charged with clear responsibility and authority, will reduce the extent of executive oversight required of subordinates, thus enabling senior officers to exercise a much wider control horizon.[27]

In organizational analysis, the terms *flat* and *tall* are used to describe the total pattern of spans of control and levels of management. Whereas the classical principle of span of control is concerned with the number of subordinates one superior can effectively manage, the concept of flat and tall is more concerned with the vertical structural arrangements for the entire organization. The nature and scope are analogous to the relationship between delegation and decentralization. In other words, span of control is to flat and tall structures as delegation is to decentralization.

The tall structure has very small or narrow spans of control whereas the flat structure has large or wide spans. In tall structures, the small number of subordinates assigned to each manager allows for tight controls and strict discipline. Classical bureaucratic structures are typically very tall.

Advantages and Disadvantages. Tall structures assume a role in assessing the value of flat structures similar to that of centralization in assessing the relative merits of decentralization. Tall structures are often viewed negatively in modern organizational analysis. More accurately, there are advantages and disadvantages to both flat and tall structures. Furthermore, flat and tall are only relative concepts; there are no absolutes.

Both flat and tall structures could have the same number of personnel. However, the tall structure could have four levels of management, and the flat one only two levels. The tall structure has the definite advantage of facilitating closer control over subordinates. Notice that the term "closer," not "better," was used. The classicists, of course, equated closer with better; the more behaviorally oriented theorists do not. The very nature of flat structures implies that managers cannot possibly keep close control over many subordinates. Therefore, they are almost forced to delegate a certain amount of the work. Thus, wide spans structurally encourage decentralization. The behavioral theorists would say that this opens up the opportunities for individual initiative and self-control.

Behavioral Implications of Flat Versus Tall Structures. One behavioral implication that is often overlooked in analyzing flat versus tall structures is the opportunity that tall structures offer for more personal contact between managers and subordinates. This contact is generally assumed to be negative and conflicting, but it need not be. In a tall structure, the manager may create a positive rapport with his or her subordinates that may not be possible in a flat structure.

Another consideration besides personal contact is the levels of communication in the two structures. In the flat structure there are few levels, which means that both downward and upward communication are simplified. There should be less distortion and inaccuracy. The red tape and endless communication channels associated with a bureaucratic tall structure are not present in a flat structure. On the other hand, the increased equality that exists between subordinates in a flat structure may lead to communication problems. If no status or authority differentials are structurally created, a heavy burden is placed upon horizontal communications. As Chapter 15 brings out, the horizontal communication system is notably deficient in most organizations. The problem may be compounded in flat organizations, where more dependence is placed on this type of communication, but it is not structurally facilitated. For example, the chief financial officer of IBM recently noted that "the key management problem at IBM is horizontal communications across a highly complex company."[28] Also, coordination may be seriously impaired by a flat structure for the same reason.

Overall, the flat structure, at least from a behavioral standpoint, is generally preferable to the tall structure. It can take advantage of the positive attributes of decentralization and personal satisfaction and growth. Although managers who have wide spans will have to give a great deal of attention to selecting and training subordinates, a flat structure has the advantage of providing a wealth of experience in decision making.

Together with these advantages, however, it must be remembered that flat structures only encourage decentralization and individual responsibility and initiative. The supervisor of a small span does not always keep close control and may occasionally decentralize, and the supervisor of a large span does not always create an atmosphere of self-control and decentralization. The degree of centralization or its reverse depends on the overall management and organization philosophy and policies and on individual leadership style and personality. All a flat or a tall arrangement does is structurally promote, not determine, centralization or decentralization and the approach taken toward the behavioral aspects of managing.

Departmentation

Departmentation is concerned with horizontal organization on any one level of the structure, and it is closely related to the classical bureaucratic principle of specialization. There are several types of departmentation. Traditionally, however, the functional and product have dominated.

Functional Departmentation. By far the most widely used and recognized type of departmentation is functional in nature and may be found in all types of organizations. For example, in a manufacturing organization the major functions usually are production, marketing, and finance—the vital functions that enable a manufacturing concern to operate and survive. On the other hand, in a railroad organization the major functions may be operations, traffic, and finance, and in a general hospital they may be medical service, housekeeping, dietetics, and business. Although the titles are different, the railroad and hospital functions are nevertheless analogous to the manufacturing functions in terms of importance and purpose. The titles of various functional departments may differ among industries and even in organizations within the same industry. All businesses, hospitals, universities, government agencies, and religious organizations, as well as the military, contain vital functions and can be functionally departmentalized.

The greatest single advantage of functional departmentation is that it incorporates the positive aspects of specialization. Theoretically, functionalism should lead to the greatest efficiency and the most economical utilization of employees. In practice, however, certain dysfunctions that were discussed with regard to specialization may also negate the advantages of functional departmentation. For example, functional empires may be created that conflict to the point of detracting from overall goal attainment.

A typical case is that of the salesperson who is guided by the sales department goal of maximizing the number of units sold. In order to sell 2000 units to a customer, this salesperson may have to promise delivery by the end of the week and require no money down. The production department, on the other hand, has a goal of keeping costs as low as possible and therefore does not carry a very large inventory. It cannot possibly supply the customer with 2000 units by the end of the week. Finance has still another goal. It must keep bad-debt expense at a minimum and therefore must require substantial down payments and thorough credit checks on every customer. In this situation, the sales department is in conflict with production and finance. If the salesperson goes ahead and makes the sale under the conditions in the example, the customer may not receive the order on time, and if and when it is received, the customer may not be able to pay the bill. In either outcome, the company goals of customer goodwill and minimization of bad-debt expense will suffer because of the salesperson's action.

It is easy to place the blame in the above example on the individual salesperson or on the lack of management coordination and communication. They are both definitely contributing factors. However, an equal, if not overriding, difficulty is the subgoal loyalties that are fostered by functionalization. A true story told by Peter Drucker provides an example of this mentality:

> A commuter train company reported a $20,000 per year cost item for broken glass doors in their passenger stations. Upon investigation it was found that a young accountant had "saved" the company $200 by limiting each station to one key for the rest room. Naturally, the key was always lost and the replacement cost only 20 cents. The catch, however, was that the key cost was set up by financial control to be a capital expenditure which required approval from the home office. This home office approval accompanied by the appropriate paperwork took months to accomplish. On the other hand, emergency repairs could be paid immediately out of the station's cash account. What bigger emergency than not being able to get into the bathroom? Each station had an axe and the result was $20,000 for broken bathroom glass doors.[29]

The presentation of such examples does not imply that conflict is always bad for the organization. In fact, as Chapter 10 points out, many modern organization theorists think that conflict has a good effect on the organization that, in fact, outweighs the bad. Yet, as in the cases cited above, where functionalization creates conflict that hinders overall goal attainment, conflict is detrimental. This negative aspect has led an increasing number of organizations to abandon functionalization for a series of processes. This new perspective was recently stated as viewing the business "as a set of activities that collectively produce value to customers, rather than as an aggregation of functional departments."[30] The old idea of doing one's job in a specialized function and then "throwing it over the wall" to the next function is being replaced by the network and horizontal organization, which are covered at the end of the chapter.

Product Departmentation. At the primary level, many organizations have chosen to organize along product or unit rather than along functional lines. The product form of departmentation is particularly adaptable to the tremendously large and complex modern organizations. It goes hand in hand with profit-centered decentralization. It allows the giant corporations, such as General Motors, General Electric, and Du Pont, to be broken down into groups of self-contained, smaller product organizations. Thus, the advantages of both large and small size can occur in one large organization.

The classical principle of specialization was earlier said to be the greatest benefit derived from functional departmentation. Although often ignored, specialization can also be applied to product departmentation. This was brought out as follows: "The executive who heads a battery manufacturing department generally knows more about production than other functional executives, but he also knows more about batteries than other production executives."[31] However, a greater advantage of organization on a product basis is the matter of control. Because of their self-contained nature, product departments are very adaptable to accounting-control techniques and management appraisal. Product department performance, measured according to several different criteria, can usually be objectively determined. Another advantage is that product departments can be readily added or dropped with a minimum of disruption to the rest of the organization.

As a structural form, product departmentation is very compatible with the behavioral approach. Many of the conflicts that exist in the upper level under functional departmentation are generally resolved by product departmentation. Under product organization, however, the functional conflicts may disappear at the upper levels but reappear in the lower levels that are functionalized. Yet, from the standpoint of overall organizational goals, functional conflict at lower levels may be preferable. Besides reducing the potential for conflict, product division can provide many of the same behavioral advantages offered by decentralization and flat structures. These include more opportunity for personal development, growth, and self-control. Once again, this is not a universal truth, because the advantages still depend on many other personal and organizational variables. All in all, however, product or unit organization, because of its self-contained characteristics, is potentially more structurally adaptable to the behavioral aspects of organization than functional departmentation is.

The Staff Concept of Organization

Staff organization goes way back in history. The military is given credit for its development. As early as the seventeenth century, Gustavus Adolphus of Sweden used a military general staff. The Prussians, with some influence from the French, refined the theory and practice of this concept. At the beginning of the twentieth century, the European version of military staff was installed in the U.S. armed forces. However, it was not until after the Great Depression that the staff concept was widely adapted to American business and industry.

Staff is not a clear-cut organizational concept. It often creates confusion and problems for the organization. Many of the problems stem from conflicting definitions regarding line and staff and the hybrid forms of staff used by many organizations. The military has escaped some of these problems because it has precisely defined and successfully implemented a pure staff system. Under the "pure" military approach, line carries command or decision-making responsibilities, whereas staff gives advice.

Almost every type of modern American organization has attempted to adopt to some degree the military staff concept. In contrast to the military, however, business, hospital, educational, and government organizations have not given proper attention to defining operationally the difference between line and staff. In the military, there definitely exists an informal, implied staff authority, but everyone understands the system and realizes that conflicts can be resolved by reverting to pure line-staff relationships. Unfortunately, this is generally not the case in other types of organizations. What usually develops is a lack of understanding of the line-staff roles and relationships, which often results in a breakdown of communication and open conflict. A typical example is the business corporation which has a myriad of line-staff roles and relationships. It is not unusual to find many lower and middle managers who do not really know whether and when they are line or staff. One reason is that they generally wear more than one hat. Normally, managers are line within their own departments and become line or staff when dealing with outside departments. The manager's functional authority is often not spelled out in the policies of the organization. As a result, personal conflicts and dual-authority situations are rampant. Chapter 10 gives specific attention to the problems of role ambiguity and conflict that can result from such line-staff relationships.

Although these weaknesses exist in a hybrid staff concept, benefits have also been derived. The larger, more technologically complex organizations depended a great deal on staff specialization during the 1970s. However, in manufacturing in the 1980s and in the service sector in the 1990s, many of these staff positions have been eliminated through downsizing, in many cases permanently replaced by information technology. For example, Peters and Waterman noted that their "excellently managed" companies had comparatively few corporate staff personnel. Emerson Electric has 54,000 employees, but fewer than 100 in its corporate headquarters; Dana has 35,000 employees, but decreased its corporate staff from about 500 in 1970 to around 100 today; and Schlumberger, a $6 billion diversified oil service company, runs its worldwide empire with a corporate staff of 90.[32] Because of the success of these companies with small staffs and the need to cut back on personnel costs as a result of the poor economy, all companies today are taking a hard look at their need for corporate staff personnel, and many continue to drastically reduce them.[33] They are beginning to look at more radical alternatives, rather than just modifications of classical structures. The next section presents these alternative ways of theorizing and of structuring organizations.

MODERN ORGANIZATION THEORY

There are some recent arguments that Weber's view of the classical bureaucratic model was mistranslated and that he really did not intend for it to be an ideal type of structure. Instead, he was merely using bureaucracy as an example of the structural form taken by the political strategy of rational-legal domination.[34] In other words, some of the original theories of classical structure may contain underpinnings for modern organization theory.

Historical Roots

The real break with classical thinking on organizational structure is generally recognized to be the work of Chester Barnard. In his significant book, *The Functions of the Executive*, he defined a *formal organization* as a system of consciously coordinated activities of two or more persons.[35] It is interesting to note that in this often cited definition, the words "system" and "persons" are given major emphasis. People, not boxes on an organization chart, make up a formal organization. Barnard was critical of the existing classical organization theory because it was too descriptive and superficial.[36] He was especially dissatisfied with the classical bureaucratic view that authority should come from the top down. Barnard, using a more analytical approach, took an opposite viewpoint. As Chapter 12 points out, he maintained that authority really came from the bottom up.

Besides authority, Barnard stressed the cooperative aspects of organizations. This concern reflects the importance that he attached to the human element in organization structure and analysis. It was Barnard's contention that the existence of a cooperative system is contingent upon the human participant's ability to communicate and their willingness to serve and strive toward a common purpose.[37] Under such a premise, the human being plays the most important role in the creation and perpetuation of formal organizations.

From this auspicious beginning, modern organization theory has evolved in several directions. The first major development in organization theory was to view the organization as a system made up of interacting parts. The open-systems concept, especially, which stresses the input of the external environment, has had a tremendous impact on modern organization theory. This development was followed by an analysis of organizations in terms of their ability to process information in order to reduce the uncertainty in managerial decision making. The next development in organization theory is the contingency approach. The premise of the contingency approach is that there is no single best way to organize. The organizational design must be fitted to the existing environmental conditions. The cultural environment even plays a role in organization structure. The accompanying International Application Example: Organization Epigrams by Country humorously depicts this cultural impact in its hypothetical structures by country.

One of the newer theoretical approaches is a natural selection—or ecological—view of organizations. This organizational ecology theory challenges the contingency approach. While the contingency approach suggests that organizations change through internal transformation and adaptation, the ecological approach says that it is more a process of the "fittest survive"; there is a process of organizational selection and replacement.[38]

Finally, the newest theoretical approach that has emerged is organizational learning. Covered in Chapter 2, the learning organization is based largely on systems theory, but emphasizes the importance of generative over adaptive learning in fast-changing environments. All these modern theories serve as a foundation for the actual designs of practicing organizations, which are covered at the end of this chapter.

The Organization as an Open System

Both the closed- and open-systems approaches are utilized in modern organization theory and practice. However, in today's dramatically changing environment an open-systems approach is becoming much more relevant and meaningful. The key for viewing organizations as open systems is the recognition of the external environment as a source of significant input. In systems terminology, the boundaries of the organization are permeable to the external environment (social, legal, technical, economic, and political).

The simplest open system consists of an input, a transformation process, and an output, which is depicted thus:

$$\text{Input} \rightarrow \text{transformation process} \rightarrow \text{output}$$

A system cannot survive without continuous input, the transformation process, and output.

There are many types of inputs, transformation processes, and outputs. For example, one kind of input actually enters the open system in the "closed" sense. In other words, this type of input has a direct effect on the internal system rather than an outside effect—in systems jargon, it loads the system. Another type of input affects the system in an "open" sense. Generally, this input would consist of the entire environmental influence on the system. Still another kind of input takes the

Organization Epigrams by Country

An epigram typically is a poem or line of verse that is witty and/or satirical. Some international business managers have taken this idea one step further and created what today are called organization epigrams. These are charts that humorously depict the organization structure by country in which they operate. The following figures show some of them along with the logic behind the specific structure. Remember that each contains considerable exaggeration and humor, but perhaps also some degree of insight into how things are really organized.

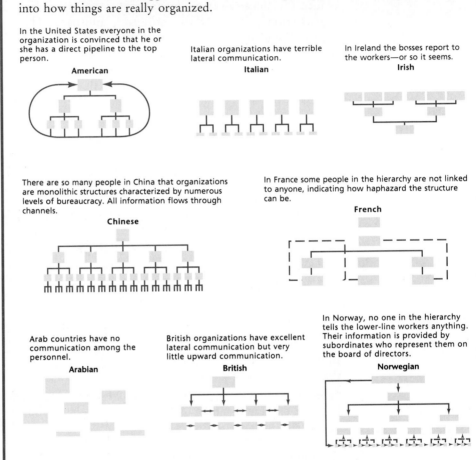

form of replacement or recycling. When a component of the system is ejected or leaves, the replacement becomes an input. This recycling process perpetuates the system. Specific examples of inputs into a business organization include monetary, material, and human resources.

At the heart of the open system are the processes, operations, or channels which transform the inputs into outputs. Here is where the internal organization design plays an important role. The transformation process consists of a logical network of subsystems, which lead to the output. The subsystems are translated into a complex systems network that transforms the inputs into the desired outputs.

The third and final major component of any simple open system is the output. This is represented by the product, result, outcome, or accomplishment of the system. Specific examples of the outputs of a business organization system that correspond to the inputs of monetary, material, and human resources are profit or loss, product sales, and role behaviors.

The simple open-systems concept has universal applicability. Any biological, human, social, economic, or technical phenomenon can be conceptualized in open-systems terms. As has been shown, an economic institution receives inputs of people, raw materials, money, laws, and values. The system then transforms these inputs via complex organizational subsystems into outputs, such as products, services, taxes, dividends, and pollution. From an organization structure standpoint, the critical factor is the design of the transformation process. Oddly, this transformation design involves a closed-systems analysis. In other words, the closed system is a subsystem of the open system. The closed-systems aspects of the transformation process are concerned with the interrelated and interdependent organizational subsystems of structure, processes, and technology. These subsystems must be organized in such a way that they will lead to maximum goal attainment or output.

Although the approach has decreased in popularity in recent years, it has been pointed out that, to date, very little research on organizations has been guided by open-systems thinking.[39] It is not that the open-systems approach has proved to be wrong or lacking in some way but rather that "in order to most fruitfully utilize the systems paradigm of organizations, scholars in the field must re-examine their beliefs about the paradigm and, perhaps, re-educate themselves about how they should think about and study organizations as systems."[40] As has been pointed out, a new type of systems thinking has resurfaced recently in terms of organizational learning. As Peter Senge recently noted:

> What is changing today is the scope of systems thinking skills required. As power and authority are distributed more widely, it becomes increasingly important that people throughout the organization be able to understand how their actions influence others. To do so, local actors need better information systems so they can be aware of systemwide conditions.[41]

This need for information is reflected in the organization theory discussed next.

Information Processing View of Organizations

The view of organizations as information processing systems facing uncertainty serves as a transition between systems theory, which has just been discussed, and contingency theory, which is discussed next. The information processing view makes three major assumptions about organizations.[42] First, organizations are open systems that face external, environmental uncertainty (for example, technology or the economy) and internal, work-related task uncertainty. Jay Galbraith defines task uncertainty as "the difference between the amount of information required to perform the task and the amount of information already possessed by the organization."[43] The organization must have mechanisms and be structured in order to diagnose and cope with this environmental and task uncertainty. In particular, the organization must be able to gather, interpret, and use the appropriate information to reduce the uncertainty. Thus, the second assumption is as follows: "Given the various sources of uncertainty, a basic function of the organization's structure is to create the most appropriate configuration of work units (as well as the linkages between these units) to facilitate the effective collection, processing, and distribution of information."[44] In other words, organizations are information processing systems.

The final major assumption of this view deals with the importance of the subunits or various departments of an organization. Because the subunits have different degrees of differentiation (that is, they have different time perspectives, goals, technology, and so on), the important question is not what the overall organization design should be but, rather, "(a) What are the optimal structures for the different subunits within the organization (e.g., R&D, sales, manufacturing); (b) What structural mechanisms will facilitate effective coordination among differentiated yet interdependent subunits?"[45]

Taking the answers to these questions as a point of departure, Tushman and Nadler draw on the extensive relevant research to formulate the following propositions about an information processing theory of organizations:

1. The tasks of organization subunits vary in their degree of uncertainty.
2. As work-related uncertainty increases, so does the need for increased amount of information, and thus the need for increased information processing capacity.
3. Different organizational structures have different capacities for effective information processing.
4. An organization will be more effective when there is a match between the information processing requirements facing the organization and the information processing capacity of the organization's structure.
5. If organizations (or subunits) face different conditions over time, more effective units will adapt their structures to meet the changed information processing requirements.[46]

The above propositions summarize the current state of knowledge concerning the information processing view of organizations. "The key concept is information, and the key idea is that organizations must effectively receive, process, and act on information to achieve performance."[47] Although the focal point of this approach is the interface between environmental uncertainty—both external and internal—and information processing, it is very closely related to systems, contingency, and organizational learning theories, and some organization theorists would argue that it could even be subsumed under one of these.

Contingency, Ecological, and Learning Organization Theories

The most recent organization theories focus even more on the environment than do the open systems and information processing views. However, the modern contingency, ecological, and learning organization theories treat the environment differently. Contingency theories are proactive and are analogous to the development of contingency management as a whole; they relate the environment to specific organization structures. More specifically, the contingency models relate to how the organization structure adjusts to fit with both the internal environment, such as work technology,[48] and the external environment, such as the economy or legal regulations.[49]

Some organization theorists feel that contingency theory should be replaced by an ecological view.[50] This new approach is best represented by what is called "population-ecology."[51] Very simply, this population-ecology approach can be summarized as follows:

1. It focuses on groups or populations of organizations rather than individual ones. For example, for the population of grocery organizations after World War II, there was an even split between "mom and pop" stores and supermarkets. The environment selected out the small "mom and pop" operations because they were not efficient and only the supermarkets survived.
2. Organizational effectiveness is simply defined as survival.
3. The environment is assumed to be totally determining. At least in the short or intermediate term, management is seen to have little impact on an organization's survival.
4. The carrying capacity of the environment is limited. Therefore, there is a competitive arena where some organizations will succeed and others will fail.[52]

Obviously, this ecology theory is a much different view of organizations than the classical or even modern approaches. A more rational, proactive approach to management that is able to adapt the organization structure to fit the changing demands of the environment is more accepted and practical than environmental determination. Yet, in recent years, many organizations have not been able to keep up with the dramatic changes they are facing. For example, a recent widely read cover story in *Fortune*, called "Dinosaurs?" about General Motors, IBM, and Sears would support the ecological view of organizations.[53]

The key to understanding the potential organizational dinosaurs of recent years is not necessarily that they did not change nor attempt to adapt to their new environment. For example, no one can accuse GM, IBM, and Sears of not changing in the late 1980s and early 1990s. But the key is that these firms and most others were in a reactive mode; they did not anticipate change or stay ahead of change. In terms of organizational learning, discussed in Chapter 2, the potential dinosaurs exhibited only single-loop, or adaptive, learning, not double-loop, or generative, learning.[54] In order for today's organizations to gain a competitive advantage and, according to ecological theory, to even survive in the long run, they must be able to learn how to learn (double-loop) and through generative learning be creative and innovative to be ahead of and anticipate change.

This double-loop, generative learning view has emerged as the latest widely accepted view of organization theory. However, other theories such as radical humanism and chaos also have advocates claiming the best understanding of today's organizations. For example, a radical humanist argument would use a neo-Marxist conceptualization to give workers significant control or empowerment over their own environments and working conditions.[55] Chaos theory would argue that prediction and control of systems behavior is unobtainable, even in extremely simple and deterministic structures, let alone in the increasingly complex and changing organizations of modern times.[56]

Obviously, all the theories discussed so far have merit. However, they also point out that it is very difficult to have a unified theory in the study of organizations. In addition, recent studies have shown that ideology influences organization structure[57] as do recent pragmatic developments such as mergers and acquisitions,[58] diversification strategies,[59] and downsizing.[60] All these factors have impeded scientific progress in the field because, as Pfeffer recently pointed out: "The study of organizations is arguably paradigmatically not well developed, in part because of values that emphasize representativeness, inclusiveness, and theoretical and methodological diversity."[61]

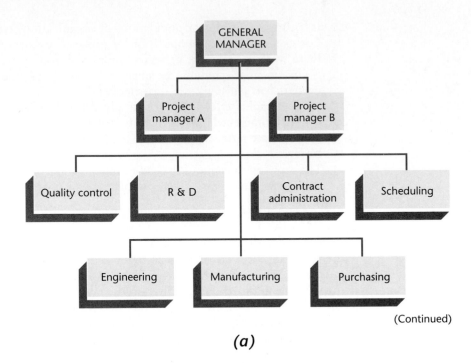

FIGURE 17.1(*a*)
Types of project
designs.

(a)

(Continued)

MODERN ORGANIZATION DESIGNS

Along with organization theorists, many practicing managers are becoming disenchanted with traditional ways of designing their organizations. Up until a few years ago, most managers attempted only timid modifications of classical structures and balked at daring experimentation and innovation. However, many of today's managers have finally overcome this resistance to making drastic organizational changes. They realize that the simple solutions offered by the classical theories are no longer adequate for many of their complex problems. In particular, the needs for flexibility, adaptability to change, creativity, innovation, and the ability to overcome environmental uncertainty are among the biggest challenges facing a growing number of modern organizations.

At first, the alternatives to the bureaucratic model of organization structure included project and matrix designs. More recently, network, virtual, and horizontal structures have emerged. The following sections describe and analyze these modern organization designs.

Project Designs

From a rather restricted beginning in the aerospace industry and in those firms having contracts with the Department of Defense, the use of project designs has increased in all organizations that require a great deal of planning, research, and coordination. In addition to the aerospace industry, project designs are becoming widely used in other industrial corporations and also in financial institutions, health care facilities, government agencies, and educational institutions. Projects of various degrees of importance and magnitude are always under way in modern organizations. The project structure is created when management decide to focus a great amount of talent and resources for a given period on a specific project goal.

There are different ways in which the project approach can be designed. Figure 17.1(*a*) shows that the project managers under this design have no activities or personnel reporting directly to them. The project manager, along with the heads of quality control, research and development, contract administration, and scheduling, acts in a staff capacity to the general manager. The project manager must rely on influence and persuasion in performing a monitoring role, with direct line authority exercised only by the general manager.

Another type is shown in Figure 17.1(*b*). Here, project managers have all the personnel necessary for the project. They have staff and functional line personnel reporting directly to them. Figure 17.1(*b*) shows that the project managers under the aggregate design have full authority over the entire project. In reality, the aggregate project organization is very similar to the traditional product or unit form of departmentation, which is presented earlier in the chapter.

There are other possible variations besides the two shown in Figure 17.1, and the project organization almost always coexists with the more traditional functional structure. But project experts stress that even though there are many similarities between project and functional organizations, project managers must take a new approach to their jobs:

1. They must become reoriented away from the purely functional approach to the management of human and nonhuman resources.

FIGURE 17.1(*b*)
Types of project designs.

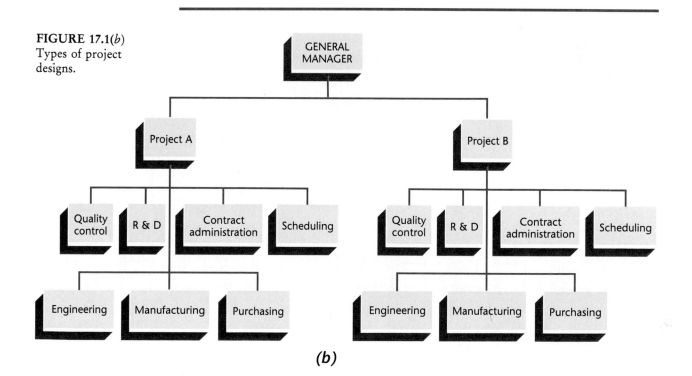

(b)

2. They must understand that purposeful conflict may very well be a necessary way of life as they manage their project across many vertical organizational lines.
3. They must recognize that project management is a dynamic activity in which major changes are almost the order of the day.[62]

These three statements make it clear that the project concept is a philosophy of management as well as a form of structural organization. The same is true of its behavioral perspective. Here are some suggestions for putting a project team together: "Don't put on the team an expert who will dominate its deliberations. And make sure that service on the project represents a career plus, that people detailed to it go on to jobs better than the ones they left."[63] In other words, the project viewpoint is quite different from the functional one.

Matrix Designs

When a project structure is superimposed on a functional structure, the result is a matrix. Sometimes the matrix organization is considered a form of project organization, and the terms are used interchangeably. However, a more accurate portrayal would show that the matrix organization is a project organization *plus* a functional organization. Figure 17.2 shows a very simplified matrix organization. Here, the functional department heads have line authority over the specialists in their departments (vertical structure). The functional specialists are then assigned to given projects (horizontal structure). These assignments are usually made at the beginning

FIGURE 17.2
An example of a matrix design.

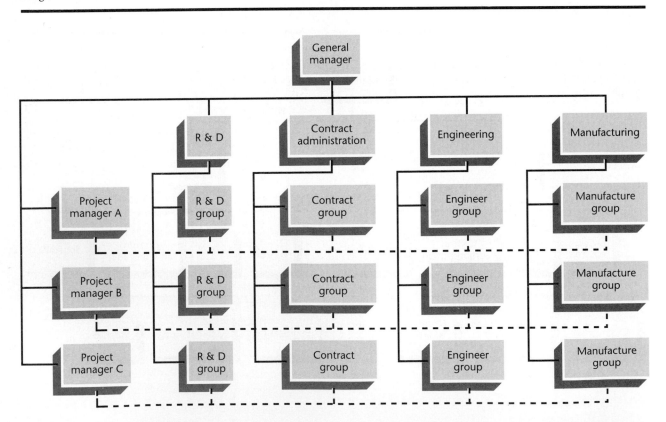

TABLE 17.1 Determinants of the Evolutionary Stages of Matrix Designs

Organization Design	Determinants
Functional $\longrightarrow$	1. Efficiency is the major objective. 2. Competitive advantage is along a single parameter such as technology, price, performance, or delivery. 3. Markets are relatively stable and predictable. 4. There is a narrow range of products with long-term perspectives.
Project $\longrightarrow$	1. There are several simultaneous objectives (for example, performance, cost, price, schedule, technology, and efficiency). 2. There is moderate market change. 3. There are differentiated clients/customers and markets. 4. There is a moderate number of products or projects. 5. There are specific time horizons for each client/customer or project. 6. There is interconnectedness between outside and local organizations.
Product/matrix $\longrightarrow$	1. Innovation is the major objective. 2. There are differentiated products, markets, and customers/clients. 3. High variability and uncertainty characterize the product-market mix. 4. The time perspective for products varies from medium to long.
Matrix $\longrightarrow$	1. There are the same determinants as for product/matrix.

Source: Adapted from Harvey F. Kolodny, "Evolution to a Matrix Organization," *Academy of Management Review*, October 1979, p. 551. Used with permission.

of each project by a collaboration between the appropriate functional and project managers.

It has been argued that the matrix structure evolves as shown in Table 17.1. Once the company has reached the matrix stage, there are also stages or degrees of this form of organization. This first stage of the matrix is usually just a temporary task force; this is followed by the creation of permanent teams or committees organized around specific needs or problems. The last stage occurs when a manager is appointed and held responsible for coordinating the activities and inputs of the teams or committees.[64] Similar to a project manager, the matrix manager needs negotiation skills and a high tolerance for ambiguous power relationships.[65] There is also recent support for the use of matrix designs as being appropriate and responsive to the strategies of diversified multinational corporations.[66]

Direct Violation of Classical Principles. Matrix designs violate the classical organizational principles. The hierarchy principle and the principle of unity of command are flagrantly violated. Furthermore, the matrix concept does not coincide with the usual line-staff arrangements discussed earlier in the chapter. Obviously, a great deal of conflict is generated in matrix organizations. An organizational specialist with IBM has observed that besides fostering conflict, the matrix structure discourages informal groups and the nurturing of supervisor-subordinate relations. After ten years of experience with the transition from traditional hierarchical to matrix organizations, he concluded that the matrix structure "has seemingly reduced participant motivation for all but the most aggressive personalities and has reduced corporate loyalty and identification with the organization."[67] An extensive empirical investigation of the engineering division of an aircraft manufacturing firm found that the matrix structure led to a decrease in the quality of communication and negative effects on relevant role perceptions, work attitudes, and coordination.[68] These disadvantages are balanced by many positive aspects of the matrix organization.

Advantages of Matrix Designs. The matrix organization attempts to combine the best of both worlds. In an eclectic manner, it includes the positive aspects of both the functional and the project designs. These advantages can be summarized as follows:

1. The project is emphasized by designating one individual as the focal point for all matters pertaining to it.
2. Utilization of personnel can be flexible because a reservoir of specialists is maintained in functional organizations.
3. Specialized knowledge is available to all programs on an equal basis; knowledge and experience can be transferred from one project to another.
4. Project people have a functional home when they are no longer needed on a given project.
5. Responsiveness to project needs and customer desires is generally faster because lines of communication are established and decision points are centralized.
6. Management consistency between projects can be maintained through the deliberate conflict operating in the project-functional environment.
7. A better balance between time, cost, and performance can be obtained through the built-in checks and balances (the deliberate conflict) and the continuous negotiations carried on between the project and the functional organizations.[69]

Theorists who advocate a matrix structure maintain that these advantages outweigh the inherent disadvantages.[70] In particular, "Matrix organizations tend to have high levels of performance in dealing with complex, creative work products. Also, because of the amount of interaction among members in matrix structures, and the high levels of responsibility they possess, matrix organizations usually have greater worker job satisfaction."[71]

Many contemporary organizations which are facing tremendous structural and technical complexity have no choice but to move to a matrix arrangement. The critical need for coordination and functional interrelationships can be met by adding a horizontal dimension to the functional structure.

Network Designs

The newly emerging network designs go beyond matrix structures and totally abandon the classical, hierarchical, functional structure of organization. The classical model worked fine in the previous era when there was less competition and more stable and expansive market conditions. Specifically, the classical model "worked well for GM, before Honda; for AT&T, before deregulation; for GE, before Sony; for Siemans, before German unification; for Xerox, before Canon; for IBM, before Fujitsu and Microsoft."[72] To meet the challenge of revolutionary changes, these and other organizations are moving toward network structures.

Network organizations have been discussed in the academic literature for a number of years. For example, organization theorists Miles and Snow identified what they call the *dynamic network*. This involves a unique combination of strategy, structure, and management processes. They also suggest that new insights and terminology, such as vertical desegregation, internal and external brokering, and full-disclosure information systems, will become commonplace.[73]

With the advent of teams and outsourcing (concentrating on core competencies and forming outside partnerships to do the peripheral activities and functions of the organization),[74] network designs are actually being used by practicing organizations. Tapscott and Caston note that such networked organizations are "based on cooperative, multidisciplinary teams and businesses networked together across the enterprise. Rather than a rigid structure, it is a modular organizational architecture in which business teams operate as a network of what we call client and server functions."[75] Table 17.2 compares the various dimensions and characteristics of the traditional, hierarchical organization with this newly emerging network organization.

The Virtual Organization

Closely related to the network organization is the so-called virtual organization.[76] The term "virtual" as used here does not come from the popular "virtual reality," but from "virtual memory," which has been used to describe a way of making a computer's memory capacity appear to be greater than it really is. The virtual organization is a temporary network of companies that come together quickly to exploit fast-changing opportunities.

Different from traditional mergers and acquisitions, the partners in the virtual organization share costs, skills, and access to international markets. Each partner contributes to the virtual organization what it is best at. Briefly summarized, here are the key attributes of the virtual organization:

1. *Technology.* Informational networks will help far-flung companies and entrepreneurs link up and work together from start to finish. The partnerships will be based on electronic contracts to keep the lawyers away and speed the linkups.
2. *Opportunism.* Partnerships will be less permanent, less formal, and more opportunistic. Companies will band together to meet all specific market opportunities and, more often than not, fall apart once the need evaporates.
3. *No borders.* This new organizational model redefines the traditional boundaries of the company. More cooperation among competitors, suppliers, and customers makes it harder to determine where one company ends and another begins.

TABLE 17.2 Traditional Hierarchical Versus the New Network Organization

Dimension/ Characteristic	Traditional Organization	New Network Organization
Structure	Hierarchical	Networked
Scope	Internal/closed	External/open
Resource focus	Capital	Human, information
State	Static, stable	Dynamic, changing
Personnel focus	Managers	Professionals
Key drivers	Reward and punishment	Commitment
Direction	Management commands	Self-management
Basis of action	Control	Empowerment to act
Individual motivation	Satisfy superiors	Achieve team goals
Learning	Specific skills	Broader competencies
Basis for compensation	Position in hierarchy	Accomplishment, competence level
Relationships	Competitive (my turf)	Cooperative (our challenge)
Employee attitude	Detachment (it's a job)	Identification (it's my company)
Dominant requirements	Sound management	Leadership

Source: Don Tapscott and Art Caston, *Paradigm Shift*, McGraw-Hill, N.Y, 1993, p. 11. Used with permission of McGraw-Hill.

4. *Trust.* These relationships make companies far more reliant on each other and require far more trust than ever before. They'll share a sense of "co-destiny," meaning that the fate of each partner is dependent on the other.

5. *Excellence.* Because each partner brings its "core competence" to the effort, it may be possible to create a "best-of-everything" organization. Every function and process could be world-class—something that no single company could achieve.[77]

This type of organization has already arrived at companies such as AT&T, MCI, and Motorola, but will undoubtedly become even more popular in the new environment facing organizations.

Horizontal Organizations

All the modern designs, whether matrix or network, emphasize the importance of horizontal over traditional vertical structuring of the organization. The advanced information technology and total quality emphasis, discussed in Chapter 2, also suggest the use of horizontal structure to facilitate cooperation, teamwork, and a customer rather than a functional orientation. The accompanying Application Example: Managing Across Rather Than Up and Down gives some of the background and applications of this newly emerging horizontal type of organization.

Frank Ostroff, a McKinsey & Company consultant, along with colleague Douglas Smith, is given credit for developing some of the guiding principles that define the horizontal organization design:[78]

1. *Organization revolves around the process, not the task.* Instead of creating a structure around the traditional functions, the organization is built around its three to five core processes. Each process has an "owner" and specific performance goals.

2. *The hierarchy is flattened.* To reduce levels of supervision, fragmented tasks are combined, work that fails to add value is eliminated, and activities within each process are cut to the minimum.

3. *Teams are used to manage everything.* Self-managed teams are the building blocks of the organization. The teams have a common purpose and are held accountable for measurable performance goals.

4. *Customers drive performance.* Customer satisfaction, not profits or stock appreciation, is the primary driver and measure of performance.

5. *Team performance is rewarded.* The reward systems are geared toward team results, not just individual performance. Employees are rewarded for multiple skill development rather than just specialized expertise.

6. *Supplier and customer contact is maximized.* Employees are brought into direct, regular contact with suppliers and customers. Where relevant, supplier and customer representatives may be brought in as full working members of in-house teams.

7. *All employees need to be fully informed and trained.* Employees should be provided all data, not just sanitized information on a "need to know" basis. However, they also need to be trained how to analyze and use the data to make effective decisions.

Implementing such principles in the actual design of an organization is happening, but to date only on a limited basis. For example, some AT&T units are doing

**Application
Example**

Managing Across Rather Than Up and Down

Since the turn of the century organizations' structures have been hierarchical. (The Chinese are really given credit for inventing hierarchy in ancient times.) Under a traditional hierarchy, subordinates report to managers who, in turn, report to higher-level managers and so on up the structure. Now, there is a new organizational trend under way: the so-called horizontal organization, which does away with hierarchy and is designed around processes rather than tasks. For example, instead of bringing a new product to market by first having the people in research and development design it, and then having the people in manufacturing build it, and finally having those in marketing sell it, a team of representatives from all these functions will be brought together and will work collectively and in harmony from beginning to end. Moreover, in the past many firms would build products in-house and then bring them to market in the hope that there were interested buyers. The horizontal organization sidesteps this potential huge problem by conducting marketing research and finding out the type of product customers want to see designed and built. Other characteristics of the horizontal organization include establishing close working relationships with suppliers and other outsiders, training and involving personnel in all key aspects of the project, and perhaps most important, rewarding team performance.

The horizontal organization represents the wave of the future, but there are a number of firms that are already using such an approach. For example, AT&T's Network Systems Division has reorganized its entire business around processes and awards bonuses to employees on the basis of customer evaluations. General Electric has scrapped the vertical structure that was in place in its lighting business and replaced the design with a horizontal structure that is characterized by over 100 different processes and programs. The Government Electronics group at Motorola has redesigned its supply management organization so that it is now a process structure geared toward serving external customers. At Xerox new products are now developed through the use of multidisciplinary teams; the vertical approach that had been used over the years is now gone. Ryder Systems follows a similar pattern, typified by the approach it now uses in handling vehicle leasing. In the past there were fourteen to seventeen separate departments that had to sign off on documents that slowly made their way through the bureaucratic hierarchy. Now, at Ryder the entire process has been redesigned, the work flow shortened, the number of sign-offs reduced, and the time needed to lease vehicles has been cut by 33 percent.

Most firms still use a hierarchical functional approach to their organization structure. However, the horizontal organization offers so many advantages in terms of quality demands, flexibility, and response time that its popularity is likely to continue, and more and more firms are going to find that their old hierarchical structures are no longer able to compete with those firms using a horizontal approach.

---

budgets not based on functions, but on processes such as the maintenance of a worldwide telecommunications network. However, as discussed in the Application Example and the end of part Integrative Contemporary Case/Reading, AT&T is also rewarding its people based on customer evaluations of the teams performing these processes, and Motorola, Xerox, and Ryder, among other leading firms, are moving toward the principles of the horizontal design of organization.[79] This is an entirely new way of organizing and may eventually replace the traditional structures.

Summary

Bureaucracy dominates classical organization theory and structure. Weber's bureaucratic model consists of specialization, hierarchy, rules, and impersonal relationships. Weber believed that this model was an ideal organization structure that would lead to maximum efficiency. Unfortunately, it does not always turn out this way in practice. In fact, there are probably as many dysfunctions as there are functions of bureaucracy. Specialization or hierarchy can lead to organizational efficiencies, but either can provoke detrimental conflict and impede the communication process. Rules often become ends in themselves rather than means toward goal attainment, and everyone can attest to the dysfunctional consequences of the impersonal characteristic of bureaucracies. Because of these and a number of other dysfunctions, many of today's theorists are predicting the decline and fall of the classical bureaucratic form of organization.

Decentralization, flat structures, departmentation, and staff organization have developed to extend and modify the pure bureaucratic classical principles of organization. In general, the behavioral approach is more compatible with the modified structural concepts, but the dramatic changes that have occurred in recent years have led to the search for new, alternative ways to organize.

Modern organization theory is presented from the perspective of systems, information processing, contingency, ecological, and learning approaches. Systems theory emphasizes the impact of the external environment. The information processing approach views the importance of information flows in an organization to cope with internal differentiation and external environmental uncertainty. Contingency theory gives specific attention to adapting to the environment by relating it to organization structure and design. The ecological theory assumes environmental determinism; there is a natural selection and replacement of organizations. The most recent theoretical foundation for the learning organization draws upon systems theory and emphasizes the importance of not only adaptive learning but also generative learning, leading to creativity, innovation, and staying ahead of change.

Modern organization designs are a marked departure from the classical models. The more established project and matrix structures combine both hierarchical, functional elements and the newer horizontal, interfunctional dimensions. These modern designs flagrantly violate classical principles such as unity of command and equal authority and responsibility. However, to even better meet the new environment's needs for flexibility and change are the network, virtual, and horizontal organization designs. These make a total departure from classical structures. Only time will tell whether the new structural forms are suitable replacements for the classical structure. On the other hand, there seems little doubt that the new approaches have already proved themselves valuable enough to become a significant part of organization theory and practice.

Questions for Discussion and Review

1. What are the major characteristics of Weber's bureaucratic model? Discuss the functions and dysfunctions of each.
2. What are the various kinds of centralization and decentralization? Which one is most relevant to organizational analysis? Why?
3. Critically analyze functional versus product (unit) departmentation.

4. Why are many companies today cutting back on their corporate staff? What will happen to the specialized functions they performed for line managers?
5. What was Chester Barnard's contribution to organization theory?
6. How does the open-systems theory differ from the information processing, contingency, ecological, and learning approaches? How does the open-systems concept apply to organizations? How does the information processing concept apply to organizations? How does the contingency concept apply to organizations? How does the ecological concept apply to organizations? How does the learning concept apply to organizations?
7. What are two different types of project structures? How does the project manager differ from the traditional functional manager?
8. The matrix design of organization is variously said to rest on classical, behavioral, systems, information processing, and contingency bases. Explain how each of these approaches could serve as the basis for the matrix design.
9. Briefly define the network, virtual, and horizontal organization designs. How do these differ from the classical design? How do they better meet the challenges of the new environment?

Footnote References and Supplemental Readings

1. John A. Byrne, "The Horizontal Corporation," *Business Week*, Dec. 20, 1993, pp. 78–79.
2. Robert Duncan, "What's the Right Organization Structure?" *Organizational Dynamics*, Winter 1979, p. 59.
3. "A Spanner in the Works," *The Economist*, Oct. 23, 1993, p. 76.
4. A. M. Henderson and Talcott Parsons (trans. and ed.), *Max Weber: The Theory of Social and Economic Organization*, Free Press, New York, 1947, p. 330.
5. Ibid., p. 331.
6. Herbert A. Simon, *The New Science of Management Decision*, Harper, New York, 1960, pp. 40–41.
7. Henderson and Parsons, loc. cit.
8. Ibid., p. 340.
9. Peter M. Blau, *Bureaucracy in Modern Society*, Random House, New York, 1956, p. 34.
10. Gregory K. Dow, "Configuration and Coactivational View of Organization Structure," *Academy of Management Review*, January 1988, p. 61.
11. Rolf E. Rogers, *Organizational Theory*, Allyn and Bacon, Boston, 1975, p. 4.
12. Peter Drucker, *The Practice of Management*, Harper, New York, 1954, pp. 133–134.
13. Ibid., p. 135.
14. C. Northcote Parkinson, *Parkinson's Law and Other Studies in Administration*, Houghton Mifflin, Boston, 1957.
15. Laurence J. Peter, *The Peter Principle*, Morrow, New York, 1969.
16. Rogers, loc. cit.
17. Warren Bennis, "Beyond Bureaucracy," *Trans-Action*, July–August 1965, p. 33.
18. Thomas J. Peters and Robert H. Waterman, Jr., *In Search of Excellence: Lessons from America's Best-Run Companies*, Harper & Row, New York, 1982.
19. Michael Hammer and James Champy, *Reengineering the Corporation*, Harper Business, New York, 1993.
20. Thomas A. Kochan and Michael Useem, *Transforming Organizations*, Oxford University Press, New York, 1992, p. vii.
21. Tom Peters, *Thriving on Chaos: Handbook for a Management Revolution*, Knopf, New York, 1987, p. 459.
22. Hal O'Carroll, "Perestroika in the American Corporation," *Organizational Dynamics*, Spring 1990, pp. 5–21.
23. Saul W. Gellerman, "In Organizations, as in Architecture, Form Follows Function," *Organizational Dynamics*, Winter 1990, p. 64.
24. Jay Finegan, "Four-Star Management," *Inc.*, January 1987, pp. 48, 51.
25. Jeremy Main, "Wanted: Leaders Who Can Make a Difference," *Fortune*, Sept. 28, 1987, p. 94.
26. Robert W. Keidel, "Triangular Design: A New Organization Geometry," *Academy of Management Executive*, November 1990, pp. 21–37.
27. Paul Firstenberg, "Downsizing: What's Your Game Plan?" *Management Review*, November 1993, p. 49.
28. "A Spanner in the Works," loc. cit.
29. Drucker, op. cit., p. 125.
30. Firstenberg, op. cit., pp. 46–47.

31. Henry H. Albers, *Principles of Management*, 4th ed., Wiley, New York, 1974, p. 95.

32. Peters and Waterman, op. cit., p. 311.

33. Thomas Moore, "Goodbye, Corporate Staff," *Fortune*, Dec. 21, 1987, p. 65.

34. Richard M. Weiss, "Weber on Bureaucracy: Management Consultant or Political Theorist?" *Academy of Management Review*, April 1983, pp. 242–248.

35. Chester I. Barnard, *The Functions of the Executive*, Harvard, Cambridge, Mass., 1938, p. 73.

36. Ibid., p. vii.

37. Ibid., p. 82.

38. Glen R. Carroll, "Organizational Ecology in Theoretical Perspective," in Glen R. Carroll (ed.), *Ecological Models of Organizations*, Ballinger, Cambridge, Mass., 1988, pp. 1–2.

39. Donde P. Ashmos and George P. Huber, "The Systems Paradigm in Organization Theory: Correcting the Record and Suggesting the Future," *Academy of Management Review*, October 1987, pp. 607–621.

40. Ibid., p. 618.

41. Peter M. Senge, "Transforming the Practice of Management," *Human Resource Development Quarterly*, Spring 1993, p. 12.

42. These assumptions are identified in Michael L. Tushman and David A. Nadler, "Information Processing as an Integrating Concept in Organization Design," *Academy of Management Review*, July 1978, pp. 614–615.

43. Jay Galbraith, *Designing Complex Organizations*, Addison-Wesley, Reading, Mass., 1973, p. 5.

44. Tushman and Nadler, op. cit., p. 614.

45. Ibid., p. 615.

46. Ibid.

47. James L. Gibson, John M. Ivancevich, and James H. Donelly, Jr., *Organizations*, 6th ed., Business Publications, Plano, Tex., 1988, p. 513.

48. For a recent summary of this research, see Minoo Tehrani, John R. Montanari, and Kenneth P. Carson, "Technology as a Determinant of Organization Structure: A Meta-Analytic Review," *Academy of Management Best Papers Proceedings*, 1990, pp. 180–184.

49. See Derek S. Pugh and David J. Hickson, *Writers on Organizations*, Sage, Newbury Park, Calif., 1989. Chapter 2 provides all the major environmental models of organization.

50. Carroll, loc. cit.

51. For the original presentation of this model, see Michael T. Hannon and John J. Freeman, "The Population Ecology of Organizations," *American Journal of Sociology*, March 1977, pp. 929–964.

52. Stephen P. Robbins, *Organization Theory*, 3d ed., Prentice-Hall, Englewood Cliffs, N.J., 1990, p. 226.

53. Carol J. Loomis, "Dinosaurs?" *Fortune*, May 1993, pp. 36–42.

54. See Chris Argyris and Donald Schon, *Organizational Learning*, Addison-Wesley, Reading, Mass., 1978; Peter M. Senge, *The Fifth Discipline: The Art and Practice of the Learning Organization*, Doubleday, New York, 1991; and Peter M. Senge, "The Leader's New Work: Building Learning Organizations," *Sloan Management Review*, Fall 1990, pp. 7–23.

55. Omar Aktouf, "Management and Theories of Organizations in the 1990s: Toward a Critical Radical Humanism?" *Academy of Management Review*, July 1992, pp. 407–431.

56. Hal Gregersen and Lee Sailer, "Chaos Theory and Its Implications for Social Science Research," *Human Relations*, July 1993, pp. 777–802.

57. Susan C. Schneider, "Conflicting Ideologies: Structural and Motivational Consequences," *Human Relations*, January 1993, pp. 45–64.

58. Sue Cartwright and Cary L. Cooper, "The Psychological Impact of Merger and Acquisition on the Individual: A Study of Building Society Managers," *Human Relations*, March 1993, pp. 327–347.

59. Michael Goold and Kathleen Luchs, "Why Diversify? Four Decades of Management Thinking," *Academy of Management Executive*, August 1993, pp. 7–25.

60. Wayne F. Cascio, "Downsizing: What Do We Know? What Have We Learned?" *Academy of Management Executive*, February 1993, pp. 95–104.

61. Jeffrey Pfeffer, "Barriers to the Advance of Organizational Science: Paradigm Development as a Dependent Variable," *Academy of Management Review*, October 1993, pp. 599–620.

62. David I. Cleland and William R. King, *Systems Analysis and Project Management*, McGraw-Hill, New York, 1968, p. 152.

63. Robert H. Waterman, Jr., quoted in Walter Kiechel, "The Organization That Learns," *Fortune*, Mar. 12, 1990, pp. 134–136.

64. Don Hellriegel, John W. Slocum, Jr., and Richard W. Woodman, *Organizational Behavior*, West, St. Paul, Minn., 1986, p. 417.

65. H. F. Kolodny, "Managing in a Matrix," *Business Horizons*, March–April 1981, pp. 17–35.

66. Jay R. Galbraith and Robert K. Kazanjian, "Organizing to Implement Strategies of Diversity and Globalization: The Role of Matrix Designs," *Human Resource Management*, Spring 1986, pp. 37–54.

67. Michael V. Fiore, "Out of the Frying Pan into the Matrix," *Personnel Administration*, July–August 1979, p. 6.

68. William F. Joyce, "Matrix Organization: A Social Experiment," *Academy of Management Journal*, September 1986, pp. 536–561.

69. Cleland and King, op. cit., p. 172.

70. Robert C. Ford and W. Alan Randolph, "Cross-Functional Structures: A Review and Integration of

Matrix Organization and Project Management," *Journal of Management*, vol. 18, 1992, pp. 267–294.

71. Ronald E. Riggio, *Introduction to Industrial/Organizational Psychology*, Scott, Foresman/Little, Brown, Glenview, Ill., 1990, p. 344.

72. Don Tapscott and Art Caston, *Paradigm Shift*, McGraw-Hill, New York, 1993, p. 32.

73. Raymond E. Miles and Charles C. Snow, "Organizations: New Concepts for New Forms," *California Management Review*, Spring 1986, p. 62. Also see Raymond E. Miles and Charles C. Snow, "Causes of Failure in Network Organizations," *California Management Review*, Summer 1992, pp. 53–72.

74. See Timm Runnion, "Outsourcing Can Be a Productivity Solution for the '90s," *HR Focus*, November 1993, p. 23.

75. Tapscott and Caston, op. cit., p. 75. Also see Shawn Tully, "The Modular Corporation," *Fortune*, February 8, 1993, pp. 106–115.

76. See William H. Davidow and Michael S. Malone, *The Virtual Corporation*, Harper Business, New York, 1992.

77. See "The Virtual Corporation," *Business Week*, Feb. 8, 1993, pp. 98–102.

78. See Byrne, loc. cit.

79. Ibid., p. 78.

REAL CASE:
Two Out of Three "Bite the Dust"

Ten years ago, GM, IBM, and General Electric were all viewed as premier companies. In the mid-1990s only one of the three, GE, still has this reputation. What happened to the other two? Part of the answer is found in the way they structured their organization.

General Motors was once the envy of the world auto industry, with a domestic market share in excess of 50 percent. By 1993 this share had slipped to around 31 percent, while Ford's and Chrysler's shares were rebounding and stood at 25 and 15 percent, respectively. What went wrong? One thing was a structure that encouraged bureaucracy and failed to respond quickly to market demands. By 1993 the cost of building a car at GM was higher than that of a similar model at either Ford or Chrysler. Recently, the head of GM, John Smith, has been trying to reduce this bureaucracy, promote teamwork, and take steps to drive down costs. Will it work? Many observers believe that if he is successful, it will be in spite of an entrenched bureaucracy that continues to drag its feet and try to do things the way they were done back in the 1970s and 1980s.

In many ways, IBM's problems are similar to those of GM. For many years the company was simply the best computer firm in the world. However, as clones entered the marketplace during the 1980s and competitors challenged IBM's position in every market niche from software to service, the company found itself in a structure that was unable to respond appropriately. As a result, both market share and profit margins dropped. By 1993 IBM's profit margin was no higher than the industry average, and its costs in many areas were higher. In an effort to turn things around, the new CEO, Louis Gerstner, has set up an eleven-member executive committee to promote greater corporate cooperation and has formed a thirty-four-member worldwide management council to discuss operating results and company practices and problems. The firm is also introducing a new compensation program that rewards managers for company-wide performance rather than an individual unit's performance. These decisions are designed to reduce the bureaucracy and create teamwork throughout the structure. If IBM can accomplish all this, it may once again be the premier firm in the industry.

In contrast to the above, GE has not suffered from an outdated structure. Under the leadership of CEO Jack Welch, the firm has carefully monitored its environment and changed accordingly. GE has continually examined its strengths and weaknesses and carefully designed a structure and strategy that have allowed it to become one of the most profitable large firms in the world. In particular, GE has focused on introducing and implementing organizational concepts that have revolutionized the firm. Some of these are as follows: (a) the number of levels in the hierarchy has been reduced; (b) there has been a broadening of incentive systems to include more and more of the personnel; (c) cross-functional teams have been formed for the purpose of breaking down departmental walls and developing intracompany teamwork; (d) project teams have been used to focus on specific undertakings and ensure that they do not get lost in the shuffle; (e) GE customers and suppliers have been incorporated into the decision-making process, in an effort to better serve the external market; and (f) customer service is continually monitored and the results used to make additional changes. These ideas have worked out so well for General Electric that the firm recently reported record annual revenues and profits.

1. Why do you think GM's old bureaucratic structure is not working well? Identify and describe some of the major reasons.
2. In what way is IBM an open system? How will the company have to be restructured in order to adjust to this open system?
3. Why do you think GE's organization design is so effective?

**CASE:
The Grass Is
Greener—or Is It?**

Alice Jenkins had been a supervisor of caseworkers in the county social services department for nine years. The bureaucratic procedures and regulations became so frustrating that she finally decided to look for a job in private industry. She had an excellent education and employment record and soon landed a supervisory position in the production end of a large insurance firm. After a few weeks on her new job she was having coffee with one of the supervisors of another department. She said, "I just can't win for losing. I quit my job with the county because I was being strangled by red tape. I thought I could escape that by coming to work in private industry. Now I find out that it is even worse. I was under the illusion that private industry did not have the bureaucratic problems that we had in social services. Where can I go to escape these insane rules and the impersonal treatment?"

1. Is Alice just a chronic complainer, or do you think her former job was as intolerable as her present job, as she indicates? Do you think Alice is typical of most employees in similar types of positions?
2. How would you answer Alice's last question? Can you give an example of a large organization that you are familiar with that is not highly bureaucratized? Does the county social services department or the insurance company have to be bureaucratized?
3. Can the concepts of decentralization, flat structures, departmentation, and staff be used in a social services department or in the clerical area of a large insurance company? Give some examples if possible.

**CASE:
The Outdated
Structure**

Jake Harvey has a position on the corporate planning staff of a large company in a high-technology industry. Although he has spent most of his time on long-range, strategic planning for the company, he has been appointed to a task force to reorganize the company. The president and board of directors are concerned that they are losing their competitive position in the industry because of an outdated organization structure. Being a planning expert, Jake convinced the task force that they should proceed by first determining exactly what type of structure they have now, then determining what type of environment the company faces now and in the future, and then designing the organization structure accordingly. In the first phase they discovered that the organization is currently structured along classical bureaucratic lines. In the second phase they found that they are competing in a highly dynamic, rapidly growing, and uncertain environment that requires a great deal of flexibility and response to change.

1. What type or types of organization design do you feel this task force should recommend in the third and final phase of the approach to their assignment?
2. Explain how the systems, information processing, contingency, ecological, and learning theories of organization can each contribute to the analysis of this case.
3. Do you think Jake was correct in his suggestion of how the task force should proceed? What types of problems might develop as by-products of the recommendation you make in question 1?

18 Organizational Culture

Learning Objectives

- **Define** organizational culture and its characteristics.
- **Relate** how an organizational culture is created.
- **Describe** how an organizational culture is maintained.
- **Explain** some ways of changing organizational culture.

This chapter is concerned with organizational culture. The cultural concept has been a mainstay in the field of anthropology from its beginnings and even was given attention in the early development of organizational behavior.[1] However, only in recent years has organizational culture been recognized as a major dimension for the understanding and practice of organizational behavior. As one recent analysis noted: "In the decade since the culture perspective burst on to the organizational studies scene, the perspective has waxed and waned in influence and vitality."[2] Another analysis concluded: "Now, in the 1990s, we realize that corporate culture is pervasive, important to corporate success, and difficult to change."[3] Although very sparse to date,[4] there are the beginnings of sophisticated research evidence indicating that variations in cultural values may have a significant impact on employee turnover and possibly employees' job performance.[5]

After first defining what is meant by organizational culture and identifying its major characteristics, this chapter examines some of the different types. Then the remainder of the chapter is devoted to creating, maintaining, and changing organizational culture.

THE NATURE OF ORGANIZATIONAL CULTURE

People are affected by the culture in which they live. For example, a person growing up in a middle-class family will be taught the values, beliefs, and expected behaviors common to that family. The same is true for organizational participants. An individual working for 3M, PepsiCo, Wal-Mart, or any other organization with a firmly established culture will be taught the values, beliefs, and expected behaviors of that organization. Society has a *social* culture; where people work has an *organizational* culture.

Definition and Characteristics

When people join an organization, they bring with them the values and beliefs they have been taught. Quite often, however, these values and beliefs are insufficient for helping the individual succeed in the organization. The person needs to learn how the particular enterprise does things. A good example is the U.S. Marine Corps. During boot camp, drill instructors teach recruits the "Marine way." The training attempts to psychologically strip down the new recruits and then restructure their way of thinking. They are taught to think and act like Marines. Anyone who has been in the Marines or knows someone who has will verify that the Corps generally accomplishes its objective. In a less dramatic way, organizations do the same thing.

Edgar Schein, who is probably most closely associated with the study of organizational culture, defines it as

> . . . a pattern of basic assumptions—invented, discovered, or developed by a given group as it learns to cope with its problems of external adaptation and internal integration—that has worked well enough to be considered valuable and, therefore, to be taught to new members as the correct way to perceive, think, and feel in relation to those problems.[6]

More recently, Joanne Martin emphasizes the differing perspectives of cultures in organizations. She notes:

> As individuals come into contact with organizations, they come into contact with dress norms, stories people tell about what goes on, the organization's formal rules and procedures, its formal codes of behavior, rituals, tasks, pay systems, jargon, and jokes only understood by insiders, and so on. These elements are some of the manifestations of organizational culture.[7]

However, she adds that there is another perspective of culture as well:

> When cultural members interpret the meanings of these manifestations, their perceptions, memories, beliefs, experiences, and values will vary, so interpretations will differ—even of the same phenomenon. The patterns or configurations of these interpretations, and the ways they are enacted, constitute culture.[8]

In other words, organizational culture is quite complex. Although there are a number of problems and disagreements associated with the conceptualization of organizational culture,[9] most definitions, including the above, recognize the importance of shared norms and values that guide organizational participants' behavior. In fact, there is research evidence that not only are these cultural values taught to newcomers, but newcomers seek out and want to learn about their organization's culture.[10]

Organizational culture has a number of important characteristics. Some of the most readily agreed upon are the following:

1. *Observed behavioral regularities.* When organizational participants interact with one another, they use common language, terminology, and rituals related to deference and demeanor.
2. *Norms.* Standards of behavior exist, including guidelines on how much work to do, which in many organizations come down to "Do not do too much; do not do too little."
3. *Dominant values.* There are major values that the organization advocates and expects the participants to share. Typical examples are high product quality, low absenteeism, and high efficiency.

4. *Philosophy.* There are policies that set forth the organization's beliefs about how employees and/or customers are to be treated.
5. *Rules.* There are strict guidelines related to getting along in the organization. Newcomers must learn those "ropes" in order to be accepted as full-fledged members of the group.
6. *Organizational climate.* This is an overall "feeling" that is conveyed by the physical layout, the way participants interact, and the way members of the organization conduct themselves with customers or other outsiders.

Each of the above characteristics has controversies surrounding it and varying degrees of research support. For example, there is controversy in the academic literature over the similarities and differences between organizational culture and organizational climate.[11] However, there is empirical support for some of the characteristics, such as the important role that physical layout plays in organizational culture. Here is a real-world illustration:

> Nike Inc. serves as an excellent example of a company that successfully revealed its corporate culture through corporate design. Set on 74 sprawling acres amid the pine groves of Beaverton, Oregon, the Nike World campus exudes the energy, youth and vitality that have become synonymous with Nike's products. The campus is almost a monument to Nike's corporate values: the production of quality goods and, of course, fitness. Included in the seven-building campus is an athletic club with a track, weight rooms, aerobic studios, tennis, racquetball and squash courts, and a basketball court.[12]

The six characteristics of culture are not intended to be all-inclusive. For example, a recent study examined why the companies listed in Table 18.1 were rated as most and least admired. Statistical analysis was conducted that compared the findings from a subjective opinion survey of reputation with what one might expect perceptions to be if they were based solely on financial performance. The financial measures that correlated most closely with the opinion of a firm's "reputation" were, in order, ten-year annual return to shareholders, profits as a percent of assets, total profits, and stock market value.[13] As the head of Coca-Cola, one of the most admired companies for the fourth year in a row, declared: "I get paid to make the owners of Coca-Cola Co. increasingly wealthy with each passing day. Everything else is just fluff."[14] In other words, the importance of bottom-line financial performance remains an important characteristic of American corporate culture. Obviously, the most admired firms have a strong organizational culture and their financial performance plays a big role in their cultural values and how others perceive them.

Uniformity of Culture

A common misconception is that an organization has a uniform culture. However, at least as anthropology uses the concept, it is probably more accurate to treat organizations "as if" they had a uniform culture. "All organizations 'have' culture in the sense that they are embedded in specific societal cultures and are part of them."[15] According to this view, an organizational culture is a common perception held by the organization's members. Everyone in the organization would have to share this perception. However, all may not do so to the same degree. As a result, there can be a dominant culture as well as subcultures throughout a typical organization.

A *dominant culture* is a set of core values shared by a majority of the organization's members. For example, most employees at Southwest Airlines seem to subscribe to such values as hard work, company loyalty, and the need for customer

TABLE 18.1 The Most and Least Admired Companies in America

Top Ten The Most Admired		Bottom Ten The Least Admired	
Rank	**Company**	**Rank**	**Company**
1	Merck (Pharmaceuticals)	311	Wang Laboratories (Computers, office equipment)
2	Rubbermaid (Rubber and plastic products)	310	Continental Airlines Hold. (Transportation)
3	Wal-Mart (Retailing)	309	Glenfed (Savings institution)
4	3M (Scientific, photo, and control equipment)	308	LTV (Metals)
5	Coca-Cola (Beverages)	307	Dime Savings Bank (Savings institution)
6	Procter & Gamble (Soaps, cosmetics)	306	CalFed (Savings institution)
7	Levi Strauss Associates (Apparel)	305	Crystal Brands (Apparel)
8	Liz Claiborne (Apparel)	304	Unisys (Computers, office equipment)
9	J. P. Morgan (Commercial banking)	303	Bethlehem Steel (Metals)
10	Boeing (Aerospace)	302	Hartmarx (Apparel)

Source: Jennifer Reese, "America's Most Admired Corporations," *Fortune*, Feb. 8, 1993, p. 45.

service. At Hewlett-Packard, most of the employees seem to share a concern for product innovativeness, product quality, and responsiveness to customer needs. At Wal-Mart stores, the associates—a term Wal-Mart uses for its employees that is very symptomatic of its culture—share a concern for customer service, hard work, and company loyalty. These values create a dominant culture in these organizations that helps guide the day-to-day behavior of employees.

Important, but often overlooked, are the subcultures in an organization. A *subculture* is a set of values shared by a minority, usually a small minority, of the organization's members. Subcultures typically are a result of problems or experiences that are shared by members of a department or unit. For example, after the AT&T breakup several years ago, the Consumer Products Division, which has its own subculture in the huge corporation, was in deep trouble. It was rapidly losing market share of residential phones to innovative competitors. Division losses were in eight-digit figures. Top-level corporate management gave the mandate: either turn the division around quickly or it would be dropped. This obviously spurred the division into action. The division managers felt that it was unthinkable for their company—that grew out of Alexander Graham Bell's invention over a hundred years ago—to cease making phones. They slashed the division's bureaucracy, reducing seven layers to four, moved manufacturing offshore, and in less than two years, AT&T's Consumer Products Division became the industry's most ferocious competitor.[16]

Subcultures can weaken and undermine an organization if they are in conflict with the dominant culture and/or the overall objectives. Successful firms, however, find that this is not always the case. Most subcultures are formed to help the members of a particular group deal with the specific day-to-day problems with which they are confronted. The members may also support many, if not all, of the core values of the dominant culture. In the case of AT&T's Consumer Products

Division, the subculture became a model for the cultural changes that top-level management were trying to accomplish for the whole corporation.[17]

Strong and Weak Cultures

Some organizational cultures could be labeled "strong," others "weak." As shown in the Application Example: Strong Managers, Strong Cultures, strong organizational cultures are often shaped by strong leaders. However, besides this leadership factor, there seem to be two major factors that determine the strength of an organizational culture: sharedness and intensity. *Sharedness* refers to the degree to which the organizational members have the same core values. *Intensity* is the degree of commitment of the organizational members to the core values.

The degree of sharedness is affected by two major factors: orientation and rewards. In order for people to share the same cultural values, they must know what these values are. Many organizations begin this process with an orientation program. New employees are told about the organization's philosophy and method of operating. This orientation continues on the job where their boss and coworkers share these values through both word of mouth and day-to-day work habits and example. Sharedness is also affected by rewards. When organizations give promotions, raises, recognition, and other forms of reward to those who adhere to the core values, these actions help others better understand these values. Some organizations have been

Application Example

Strong Managers, Strong Cultures

Successful companies have strong cultures. However, they also have strong managers who introduce, reinforce, and/or nurture those cultures. During the 1980s, many CEOs were successful in taking over a firm that had problems, cutting the work force, and whipping it into shape. The successful managers of the 1990s are using a much different approach. Rather than relying on firings, fear, and guilt to rebuild the organization, these managers are working to create pride and enthusiasm in the firm. These individuals set themselves up as role models who establish overall direction and then work long hours to help the company reach agreed-upon goals. The personnel, influenced by this example, join in and help turn the firm around. There are many examples of managers who are using this approach: Barry Gibbons of Burger King; Richard Mayer of General Foods USA; Stephen Berkley, head of Quantum, a disk-drive maker; Leo McKernan of Clark Equipment; Robert Allen at AT&T; and Roberto Goizueta at Coca-Cola.

What are some of the specific techniques they employ? One is the use of positive ideas. They continually talk about how things can be done more efficiently or differently, and they encourage the personnel to think in positive terms as well. Second, they meet with managers throughout the company to get this message across to them, so that everyone understands that the organization is going to spare no effort to turn out the best possible product or service. Third, they look for the best people, many of whom have been bypassed for promotions, and give these individuals the jobs for which they are best suited. This serves as a strong incentive for others who want to help, but who have been limited in their efforts by previous managers who had discouraged teamwork and creative ideas. Fourth, they work to develop pride in their people. Do these ideas really work? Experience has shown that when headhunters are asked to find managers who can turn losing companies into winners, individuals who exhibit these four behaviors are at the top of the list of candidates.

labeled "the best to work for" because the rewards that they give to their people are exemplary and help reinforce commitment to core values. For example, Hallmark Cards Inc. is listed in *The 100 Best Companies to Work for in America*. Hallmark rewards its employees through profit sharing and an ownership plan. Today, employees own one-third of Hallmark's stock. In addition, the company reinforces the importance of cultural values related to the employee's family through programs such as parental leave, adoption assistance, family care choices, sick child care, and parents' noontime and Saturday seminars.[18]

The degree of intensity is a result of the reward structure. When employees realize that they will be rewarded for doing things "the organization's way," their desire to do so increases. Conversely, when they are not rewarded or they feel there is more to be gained by not doing things the organization's way, commitment to core values diminishes. Although recognition and other nonfinancial rewards are important, money still plays an important role. For example, Westinghouse and Red Lobster allocate merit budgets in order to reward those who carry out the cultural values of cooperation and serving internal and external customers.[19]

Table 18.2 provides an example of how an organization can determine whether it has a strong or weak culture. Notice from the answer key that such highly successful companies as Procter & Gamble, PepsiCo, and Coca-Cola all have strong cultures.

Types of Cultures

Many models have been constructed to describe organizational culture. One of the most comprehensive and widely known is that by Deal and Kennedy.[20] Table 18.3 describes the four basic types of cultural profiles they uncovered. Each is characterized by a combination of two factors: the type of risks managers assume and the type of feedback that results from their decisions.

Most organizations are some hybrid of these cultural profiles; they do not fit neatly into any one of them. However, within the organization there are subcultures that do tend to fit into one of these four profiles. For example, according to Table 18.3, Apple's cultural profile would be that of a "work hard/play hard" company. However, because the corporation is so large and has so many different departments, this overall profile describes the enterprise in general terms only. On the other hand, people in the sales area would most certainly fit into this profile. This is in contrast to personnel in the software development area who would be operating in a subculture perhaps best described in Table 18.3 as "bet your company."

CREATING AND MAINTAINING A CULTURE

Some organizational cultures may be the direct, or at least indirect, result of actions taken by the founders. However, this is not always the case. Sometimes founders create weak cultures, and if the organization is to survive, a new top manager must be installed who will sow the seeds for the necessary strong culture. Thomas Watson, Sr., of IBM is a good example. When he took over the CTR Corporation, it was a small firm manufacturing computing, tabulating, and recording equipment. Through his dominant personality and the changes he made at the firm, Watson created a culture that propelled IBM to be one of the biggest and best companies in the world. However, in recent years, IBM's collapse is also largely attributed to its outdated

TABLE 18.2 Computing an Organizational Culture Socialization Score

Respond to the items below as they apply to the handling of professional employees. Upon completion, compute the total score. For comparison, scores for a number of strong, intermediate, and weak culture firms are to be found at the bottom of the page.

	Not True of This Company				Very True of This Company
1. Recruiters receive at least one week of intensive training.	1	2	3	4	5
2. Recruitment forms identify several key traits deemed crucial to the firm's success, traits are defined in concrete terms and interviewer records specific evidence of each trait.	1	2	3	4	5
3. Recruits are subjected to at least four in-depth interviews.	1	2	3	4	5
4. Company actively facilitates de-selection during the recruiting process by revealing minuses as well as pluses.	1	2	3	4	5
5. New hires work long hours, are exposed to intensive training of considerable difficulty and/or perform relatively menial tasks in the first months.	1	2	3	4	5
6. The intensity of entry-level experience builds cohesiveness among peers in each entering class.	1	2	3	4	5
7. All professional employees in a particular discipline begin in entry-level positions regardless of prior experience or advanced degrees.	1	2	3	4	5
8. Reward systems and promotion criteria require mastery of a core discipline as a precondition of advancement.	1	2	3	4	5
9. The career path for professional employees is relatively consistent over the first six to ten years with the company.	1	2	3	4	5
10. Reward systems, performance incentives, promotion criteria and other primary measures of success reflect a high degree of congruence.	1	2	3	4	5
11. Virtually all professional employees can identify and articulate the firm's shared values (i.e., the purpose or mission that ties the firm to society, the customer or its employees).	1	2	3	4	5
12. There are very few instances when actions of management appear to violate the firm's espoused values.	1	2	3	4	5
13. Employees frequently make personal sacrifices for the firm out of commitment to the firm's shared values.	1	2	3	4	5
14. When confronted with trade-offs between systems measuring short-term results and doing what's best for the company in the long term, the firm usually decides in favor of the long-term.	1	2	3	4	5
15. This organization fosters mentor-protégé relationships.	1	2	3	4	5
16. There is considerable similarity among high potential candidates in each particular discipline.	1	2	3	4	5

Compute your score: _____

For comparative purposes:

	Scores	
Strongly socialized firms	65–80	IBM, P&G, Morgan Guaranty
	55–64	ATT, Morgan Stanley, Delta Airlines
	45–54	United Airlines, Coca-Cola
	35–44	General Foods, PepsiCo.
	25–34	United Technologies, ITT
Weakly socialized firms	Below 25	Atari

Source: Richard Pascale, "The Paradox of Corporate Culture: Reconciling Ourselves to Socialization." Copyright © by the Regents of the University of California. Reprinted from the *California Management Review*, vol. 27, no. 2, Winter 1985, pp. 39, 40. By permission of the Regents.

TABLE 18.3 Organizational Culture Profiles

Name of the culture	TOUGH-PERSON	WORK HARD/ PLAY HARD	BET YOUR COMPANY	PROCESS
Type of risks that are assumed	High	Low	High	Low
Type of feedback from decisions	Fast	Fast	Slow	Slow
Typical kinds of organizations that use this culture	Construction, cosmetics, television, radio, venture capitalism, management consulting	Real estate, computer firms, auto distributors, door-to-door sales operations, retail stores, mass consumer sales	Oil, aerospace, capital goods manufacturers, architectural firms, investment banks, mining and smelting firms, military	Banks, insurance companies, utilities, pharmaceuticals, financial-service organizations, many agencies of the government
The ways survivors and/or heroes in this culture behave	They have a tough attitude. They are individualistic. They can tolerate all-or-nothing risks. They are superstitious.	They are super salespeople. They often are friendly, hail-fellow-well-met types. They use a team approach to problem solving. They are non-superstitious.	They can endure long-term ambiguity. They always double-check their decisions. They are technically competent. They have a strong respect for authority.	They are very cautious and protective of their own flank. They are orderly and punctual. They are good at attending to detail. They always follow established procedures.
Strengths of the personnel/culture	They can get things done in short order.	They are able to quickly produce a high volume of work.	They can generate high-quality inventions and major scientific breakthroughs.	They bring order and system to the workplace.
Weaknesses of the personnel/culture	They do not learn from past mistakes. Everything tends to be short-term in orientation. The virtues of cooperation are ignored.	They look for quick-fix solutions. They have a short-term time perspective. They are more committed to action than to problem solving.	They are extremely slow in getting things done. Their organizations are vulnerable to short-term economic fluctuations. Their organizations often face cash-flow problems.	There is lots of red tape. Initiative is downplayed. They face long hours and boring work.
Habits of the survivors and/or heroes	They dress in fashion. They live in "in" places. They like one-on-one sports such as tennis. They enjoy scoring points off one another in verbal interaction.	They avoid extremes in dress. They live in tract houses. They prefer team sports such as touch football. They like to drink together.	They dress according to their organizational rank. Their housing matches their hierarchical position. They like sports such as golf, in which the outcome is unclear until the end of the game. The older members serve as mentors for the younger ones.	They dress according to hierarchical rank. They live in apartments or no-frills homes. They enjoy process sports like jogging and swimming. They like discussing memos.

Source: Adapted from Terence E. Deal and Allan A. Kennedy, *Corporate Cultures: The Rites and Rituals of Corporate Life*, © 1982, Addison-Wesley, Reading, Mass. Excerpts from Chap. 6. Used with permission.

culture.[21] After Watson and his son, the leaders of IBM made some minor changes and modifications that had little impact and eventually left the company in bad shape. However, the current CEO, Lou Gerstner, recently revealed a bold new strategy that changes IBM from top to bottom. A recent observation is that "Mr. Gerstner is convinced that all the cost-cutting in the world will be unable to save IBM unless it upends the way it does business."[22]

IBM is an example of an organization wherein a culture must be changed because the environment changes and the previous core cultural values are not in step with those needed for survival. IBM competitor Apple Computer is another good example. When Steve Jobs and his partner started Apple, they wanted to create a culture in which people could be creative, work on projects that interested them, and turn out a product that would be innovative. However, as they began broadening their horizons and trying to appeal to both the educational and the business market, the firm began to run into trouble. Its culture was not designed to compete in an increasingly cutthroat market. Steve Jobs was a thinker and creator, not an organizer and a manager. Apple began to lose money. A change in leadership and culture was needed. Jobs left Apple and directed his talents in starting a new venture, Next, Inc.[23] The following sections take a close look at how organizational cultures get started, maintained, and changed.

How Organizational Cultures Start

While organizational cultures can develop in a number of different ways, the process usually involves some version of the following steps:

1. A single person (founder) has an idea for a new enterprise.
2. The founder brings in one or more other key people and creates a core group that shares a common vision with the founder. That is, all in this core group believe that the idea is a good one, is workable, is worth running some risks for, and is worth the investment of time, money, and energy that will be required.
3. The founding core group begins to act in concert to create an organization by raising funds, obtaining patents, incorporating, locating space, building, and so on.
4. At this point, others are brought into the organization, and a common history begins to be built.[24]

Most of today's successful corporate giants in all industries basically followed these steps. Three well-known representative examples are Motorola, McDonald's, and Wal-Mart.

- *Motorola.* Paul V. Galvin started the company in 1928. The founding product, a battery eliminator, was already on its way to total obsolescence in the first year of the firm. The founder had to have a new product within a year or two to survive. This constant renewal has become a core cultural value for Motorola. At age seven Robert Galvin accompanied his father on business trips, and in 1940 Robert began working full-time for Motorola. In 1956 Bob Galvin became president and in 1964, chairman and CEO. He is given credit for being the architect for Motorola's quality efforts that resulted in a Malcolm Baldrige National Quality Award in 1988. Galvin described the cultural value of quality and customer service as follows: "The paramount idiom in our company (and it's not different than in a lot of other companies) is total customer satisfaction. And total in our case means total. It doesn't mean a lot, it doesn't mean best in class. It means everything."[25] Such cultural values have made Motorola a, if not the, recognized quality leader in the world. The Galvins, father and son, have contributed much to this success. Characteristically, however, Bob Galvin recently noted: "Motorola is a thousand times bigger than when I came in as a kid. Not because I'm here. We all made it happen. I helped a little."[26]

- *McDonald's.* Ray Kroc worked for many years as a salesperson for a food supplier (Lily Tulip Cup). He learned how retail food operations were conducted. He also had an entrepreneurial streak and began a sideline business with a partner. They sold multimixers, machines that were capable of mixing up to six frozen shakes at a time. One day Kroc received a large order for multimixers from the McDonald brothers. The order intrigued Kroc, and he decided to look in on the operation the next time he was in their area. When he did, Kroc became convinced that the McDonald's fast-food concept would sweep the nation. He bought the rights to franchise McDonald's units and eventually bought out the brothers. At the same time, he built the franchise on four basic concepts: quality, cleanliness, service, and price. In order to ensure that each unit offers the customer the best product at the best price, franchisees are required to attend McDonald University, where they are taught how to manage their business. Here they learn the McDonald cultural values and the proper way to run the franchise. This training ensures that franchisees all over the world are operating their units in the same way. Kroc died several years ago, but the culture he left behind is still very much alive in McDonald's franchises across the globe. In fact, new employees receive videotaped messages from the late Mr. Kroc. Some of the more interesting of his pronouncements that reflect and carry on his values are his thoughts on cleanliness: "If you've got time to lean, you've got time to clean." On the competition he says: "If they are drowning to death, I would put a hose in their mouth." And on expanding he declares: "When you're green, you grow; when you're ripe, you rot."[27] So even though he has not been involved in the business for many years, his legacy lives on. Even his office at corporate headquarters is preserved as a museum, his reading glasses untouched in their leather case on the desk.

- *Wal-Mart.* Sam Walton, founder of Wal-Mart Stores, Inc., opened his first Wal-Mart store in 1962. Focusing on the sale of discounted name-brand merchandise in small-town markets, he began to set up more and more stores in the Sun Belt. At the same time, he began developing effective inventory control systems and marketing techniques. Today, Wal-Mart has overtaken Sears as the largest retailer in the country with annual sales of well over $60 billion. Although Sam died a few years ago, his legacy and cultural values continue. For example, Walton himself stressed, and the current management staff continues to emphasize, the importance of encouraging associates to develop new ideas that will increase their store's efficiency. If a policy does not seem to be working, the company quickly changes it. Executives continually encourage associates to challenge the current system and look for ways to improve it. Those who do these things are rewarded; those who do not perform up to expectations are encouraged to do better. The operating philosophy and environment at Wal-Mart is so attractive that it is consistently rated by *Fortune* at or near the top of the most admired and best-managed corporations in America. Walton's founding values permeate the organization. To make sure the cultural values get out to all associates, the company has a communication network worthy of the Pentagon. It includes everything from a six-channel satellite system to a private air force of numerous planes.[28] Everyone is taught this culture and is expected to operate within the core cultural values of hard work, efficiency, and customer service.

Maintaining Cultures Through Steps of Socialization

Once an organizational culture is started and begins to develop, there are a number of practices that can help solidify the acceptance of core values and ensure that the culture maintains itself. These practices can be described in terms of several socialization steps. Figure 18.1 illustrates the sequence of these steps.

Selection of Entry-Level Personnel. The first step is the careful selection of entry-level candidates.[29] Using standardized procedures and seeking specific traits that tie to effective performance, trained recruiters interview candidates and attempt to screen out those whose personal styles and values do not make a "fit" with the organization's culture. There is accumulating evidence that those who have a realistic preview (called realistic job preview or RJP) of the culture will turn out better.[30]

Placement on the Job. The second step occurs on the job itself, after the person with a fit is hired. New personnel are subjected to a carefully orchestrated series of different experiences whose purpose is to cause them to question the organization's norms and values and to decide whether or not they can accept them. For example, many organizations with strong cultures make it a point to give newly hired personnel more work than they can handle. Sometimes these assignments are beneath the individual's abilities. At Procter & Gamble, for example, new personnel may be

FIGURE 18.1
Steps of organization culture socialization. (*Source:* Richard Pascale, "The Paradox of Corporate Culture: Reconciling Ourselves to Socialization," Copyright © by the Regents of the University of California. Reprinted from the *California Management Review*, vol. 27, no. 2, Winter 1985, p. 38. By permission of the Regents.)

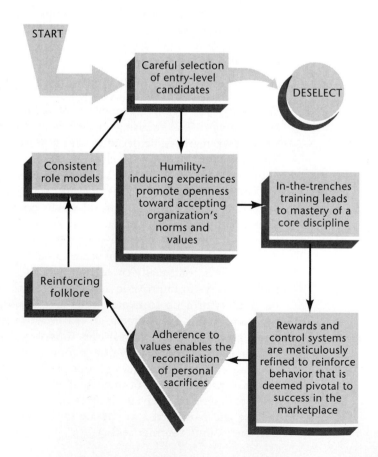

required to color in a sales territory map. The experience is designed to convey the message, "While you're smart in some ways, you're in kindergarten as far as what you know about this organization." The objective is also to teach the new entrant into the culture the importance of humility. These experiences are designed to make newly hired personnel vulnerable and to cause them to move closer emotionally to their colleagues, thus intensifying group cohesiveness. Campus fraternities and the military have practiced this approach for years.

Job Mastery. Once the initial "cultural shock" is over, the next step is mastery of one's job. This is typically done via extensive and carefully reinforced field experience. For example, Japanese firms typically put new employees through a training program for several years. As personnel move along their career path, their performance is evaluated and additional responsibilities are assigned on the basis of progress. Quite often companies establish a step-by-step approach to this career plan, which helps reduce efforts by the personnel to use political power or to take shortcuts in order to get ahead at a faster pace. As Pascale notes, "Relationships, staying power, and a constant proven track record are the inescapable requirements of advancement" during this phase.[31]

Measuring and Rewarding Performance. The next step of the socialization process consists of meticulous attention to measuring operational results and to rewarding individual performance. These systems are comprehensive and consistent, and they focus on those aspects of the business that are most crucial to competitive success and to corporate values. For example, at Procter & Gamble there are three factors that are considered most important: building volume, building profit, and making changes that increase effectiveness or add satisfaction to the job. Operational measures are used to track these three factors, and performance appraisals are tied to milestones. Promotions and merit pay are determined by success in each of these critical areas. Motorola personnel are taught to adhere to the core cultural values through careful monitoring of team performance and through continual training programs. Typically, in companies with a strong culture, those who violate cultural norms, such as overzealousness against the competition or harsh handling of a subordinate, are sent to the "penalty box." This typically involves a lateral move to a less desirous location. For example, a branch manager in Chicago might be given a nebulous staff position at headquarters in New York. This individual is now off-track, which can slow his or her career progress.

Adherence to Important Values. The next step involves careful adherence to the firm's most important values. Identification with these values helps employees reconcile personal sacrifices brought about by their membership in the organization. They learn to accept these values and to trust the organization not to do anything that would hurt them. As Pascale observes: "Placing one's self 'at the mercy' of an organization imposes real costs. There are long hours of work, missed weekends, bosses one has to endure, criticism that seems unfair, job assignments and rotations that are inconvenient or undesirable."[32] However, the organization attempts to overcome these costs by connecting the sacrifices to higher human values such as serving society with better products and/or services. Companies such as Honda Motors do this very effectively. Honda took American technical specialists and their families at great expense and sacrifice to Japan for two to three years. Teaching these Americans the Honda culture firsthand has paid off.

The North American Task Group, as it was called, saved millions of dollars by helping design the '94 Accord so it can be manufactured easily at Honda's Marysville, Ohio, plant. The Americans brainstormed with Japanese designers and reviewed preliminary sketches—up to two years earlier in the process than ever before. [The Americans] did learn a few things: Don't be forceful, don't show emotion, and, if you request a design change, you'd better back it up.[33]

The Japanese organizational cultural values are given in detail and contrasted with traditional American organizational cultural values in the accompanying International Application Example: Theory Z in Action. Ouchi's Theory Z cultural values became very well known by American managers in the 1980s, but in recent years have diminished in popularity as the Japanese became less mysterious and experienced economic problems like the rest of the world.

Reinforcing the Stories and Folklore. The next step involves reinforcing organizational folklore. This entails keeping alive stories that validate the organization's culture and way of doing things. The folklore helps explain why the organization does things a particular way. One of the most common forms of folklore is stories with morals the enterprise wants to reinforce. For example, at Procter & Gamble there is a story about the outstanding brand manager who was fired for overstating the features of a product. The moral of the story is that ethical claims are more important than making money. At AT&T there are numerous stories about field employees who made sacrifices to keep the phones working and operators who stayed on the line when people called in and asked for emergency help because they had suffered a physical calamity. The moral of such stories is that these types of sacrifices are all in the line of duty for telephone employees, who must view their primary responsibility as that of helping the customer.

Recognition and Promotion. The final step is the recognition and promotion of individuals who have done their jobs well and who can serve as role models to new people in the organization. By pointing out these people as winners, the organization encourages others to follow their example. Role models in strong-culture firms are regarded as the most powerful ongoing training program of all. Morgan Stanley, the financial services firm, chooses role models on the basis of energy, aggressiveness, and team play. Procter & Gamble looks for people who exhibit extraordinary consistency in such areas as toughmindedness, motivational skills, energy, and the ability to get things done through others.[34]

Changing Organizational Culture

Sometimes an organization determines that its culture has to be changed. For example, the external environment has undergone drastic change and the organization must either adapt to these new conditions or it may not survive. However, changing old cultures can be quite difficult: a case can even be made that it really can't be done successfully.[35] Predictable obstacles include entrenched skills, staffs, relationships, roles, and structures that work together to reinforce traditional cultural patterns. In addition, powerful stakeholders such as unions, management, or even customers may support the existing culture.[36]

Despite the significant barriers and resistance to change, cultures can be managed and changed over time. This attempt to change culture can take many different forms. Simple guidelines such as developing a sense of history, creating a sense of

**International
Application
Example**

Theory Z in Action

William Ouchi's book *Theory Z: How American Business Can Meet the Japanese Challenge* was one of the first to point out the importance of organizational culture. Many American managers have studied Ouchi's book in order to gain insights regarding how the successful Japanese systems are different from their own and how their firm might successfully modify its culture by drawing on these concepts. In particular, there are seven characteristics that have traditionally been used by the Americans (Theory A) and the Japanese (Theory J). Ouchi's Theory Z is a combination of these theories designed, in most cases, to modify American corporate culture and help firms compete more effectively with the Japanese. Here is how Theory Z modifies Theory A by drawing upon Theory J concepts.

Characteristics	Theory A (American)	Theory J (Japanese)	Theory Z (Modified)
Employment with a firm	Usually short-term; layoffs are quite common.	Especially in some of the large firms, it is for life. Layoffs are rare.	Fairly long-term; this will help develop a loyal semipermanent work force.
Evaluation and promotion of the personnel	Very fast; individuals who are not promoted rapidly often seek employment elsewhere.	Very slow; big promotions are generally not given out for years.	Slower; more emphasis is given to training and evaluation than to promotion.
Career paths	Very specialized; people tend to stay in one area (accounting, finance, sales, etc.) for their entire career.	Very general; personnel are rotated from one area to another and become familiar with all areas of operations.	More general; emphasis is on job rotation and more broadly based training in order to give the person a better feel for the entire organization.
Decision making	Carried out by the individual manager.	Carried out via group decision making.	Carried out with more emphasis on group participation and consensus.
Control	Very explicit; people know exactly what to control and how to do it.	Very implicit and informal; people rely heavily on trust and goodwill.	More attention to informal control procedures coupled with explicit performance measures.
Responsibility	Assigned on an individual basis.	Shared collectively by the group.	Assigned on an individual basis.
Concern for the personnel	Organization is concerned primarily with the worker's work life only.	Organization is concerned with the whole life of the worker, business, and social.	Organization's concern is expanded to include more aspects of the worker's whole life.

oneness, promoting a sense of membership, and increasing exchange among members are helpful.[37] Also, organizations attempting to change their culture must be careful not to abandon their roots and blindly copy the so-called "successful" or "excellent" companies.[38] Pragmatically changing an organization culture affects almost every aspect of the business. Procter & Gamble and AMOCO are examples of firms that have successfully undergone or are undergoing cultural change.

Changing the Culture at Procter & Gamble. For years the culture at P&G had supported steady growth and profits. In recent years, however, the company found itself under a great deal of pressure from the external competitive environment. For example, Kimberly-Clark had cut deeply into P&G's disposable-diaper market, one of the company's most lucrative market niches. At the same time, Lever Brothers was making inroads into P&G's share of the soap and detergent market. On the new-product development front, things were no better. The company was having disappointing results with its Pringles potato chips and was suffering financial losses on its Coldsnap Homemade Ice Cream Mix, Wondra hand cream, and Rely Tampons. These setbacks were reflected on the company's bottom line as pretax earnings fell for the first time in over thirty years. At the same time the firm was having union problems. Its Kansas City plant voted to unionize, and the company went through a long fight with worker representatives in its efforts to change work practices and improve efficiency.

These developments led P&G to make changes in its organizational culture. Some of these were the following:

1. The work team concept, in which production and maintenance workers—called "technicians"—are required to master and use a second skill, was extended throughout P&G's operations.
2. The lifetime-job tradition that once made P&G workers the envy of their blue-collar counterparts elsewhere gave way to layoffs.
3. The corporate paternalism of the past yielded to some hard practicalities as executives and workers alike were put on notice that plants that didn't measure up on productivity, cost, and quality would be shut down.
4. A determined management vigorously resisted attempts by organized labor to dictate how P&G's operations should be run.[39]

In addition to the above, P&G trimmed its work force by 5 percent on the plant floor and 4 percent company-wide. This was accomplished through reduced hiring, early retirement, and, in some cases, layoffs. Changing conditions had led P&G to change its culture.[40]

Changing the Culture at AMOCO. With over 50,000 employees in more than forty countries, AMOCO is a leading petroleum and chemical multinational corporation. For a company with over a hundred years of relative success, there had to be a number of conditions for the cultural change process to occur. Briefly summarized, these have been identified as the following:[41]

1. *Felt need.* An oil price collapse and employee survey data that identified a number of problem areas got everyone's attention.
2. *Management commitment.* Top management commitment was obtained and demonstrated when they understood that the change effort was a long-term process, not a short-term program, and when they believed that the change initiative would have a bottom-line impact.
3. *Shared mindset.* The facilitators worked hard on getting everyone focused on understanding where the company was trying to go in the future and what that meant to their individual roles.
4. *Employee involvement.* Management commitment was not enough; all employees had to get involved to make the change become a reality.

5. *Focused training.* Although the company had plenty of training, now it had to be geared to the requirements of the change initiative and rewarded accordingly.
6. *Accountability.* There was a need not only for training and communication but also for specifying what the employees needed to do differently and for following up to see that it actually was happening.

These conditions set the stage for the actual change process. This process was broken down into strategic direction, organizational assessments, and work improvement/HR practices. Although AMOCO had focused on financial and operational goals in its strategic planning over the years, this was now expanded to include the following:

1. Mission: What is our business?
2. Vision: What do we want to be?
3. Values: What do we believe and how will we act?
4. Goals: What will we accomplish in the long term?
5. Strategies: How will we get there?[42]

This strategic direction was then assessed through surveys. The information from these surveys was fed back to employees and managers to audit how well they were progressing on the strategic direction. In the third and final phase, the initial increased workload was reexamined to determine where unnecessary work could be eliminated. The outcome of this phase was becoming more adaptable and flexible for customer requirements.

AMOCO wanted to institute change in five major systems: strategy, structure, processes, rewards, and people. For example, a strategic plan was developed at the corporate level and filtered down through the rest of the company. Line managers were responsible for communicating the new cultural values. Nonfinancial rewards were emphasized and systems for pay for performance and tying rewards to strategy were developed. The structure of the company was decentralized.

Only time will tell if this cultural change effort at AMOCO is successful. However, the company continues to face many environmental changes and the processes for handling change seem to be in place. One thing is certain: If companies like AMOCO do not change, and do not attempt to systematically manage this change, they will not survive in the turbulent years ahead.

Summary

Organizational culture is a pattern of basic assumptions that are taught to new personnel as the correct way to perceive, think, and act on a day-to-day basis. Some of the important characteristics of organizational culture are observed behavioral regularities, norms, dominant values, philosophy, rules, and organizational climate.

While everyone in an organization will share the organization's culture, not all may do so to the same degree. There can be a dominant culture, but also a number of subcultures. A dominant culture is a set of core values that is shared by a majority of the organization's members. A subculture is a set of values shared by a small percentage of the organization's members.

Some organizations have strong cultures; others have weak cultures. The strength of the culture will depend on sharedness and intensity. Sharedness is the degree to which the organizational members have the same core values. Intensity is the degree of commitment of the organizational members to the core values.

A culture typically is created by a founder or top-level manager who forms a core group that shares a common vision. This group acts in concert to create the cultural values, norms, and climate necessary to carry on this vision. In maintaining this culture, enterprises typically carry out several steps such as the following: careful selection of entry-level candidates; on-the-job experiences to familiarize the personnel with the organization's culture; mastery of one's job; meticulous attention to measuring operational results and to rewarding individual performance; careful adherence to the organization's most important values; a reinforcing of organizational stories and folklore; and, finally, recognition and promotion of individuals who have done their jobs well and who can serve as role models to new personnel in the organization.

In some cases organizations find that they must change their culture in order to remain competitive and even survive in their environment. The cultural change process at Procter & Gamble and AMOCO demonstrates how this may work.

Questions for Discussion and Review

1. What is meant by the term "organizational culture"? Define it and give some examples of its characteristics. What role may financial performance play in a firm's culture?
2. How does a dominant culture differ from a subculture? In your answer be sure to define both terms.
3. How do strong cultures differ from weak cultures? What two factors determine the strength of the culture?
4. In what way do risk taking and feedback help create basic types of organizational culture profiles? Explain, being sure to include a discussion of these profiles in your answer.
5. How do organizational cultures develop? What four steps commonly occur?
6. How do organizations go about maintaining their cultures? What steps are involved? Describe them.

Footnote References and Supplemental Readings

1. Nancy C. Morey and Fred Luthans, "Anthropology: The Forgotten Behavioral Science in Management History," *Academy of Management Best Papers Proceedings*, 1987, pp. 128–132.
2. Daniel R. Denison, "What Is the Difference Between Organizational Culture and Organizational Climate?" *Academy of Management Best Papers Proceedings*, 1993, p. 207.
3. Warren Wilhelm, "Changing Corporate Culture—or Corporate Behavior? How to Change Your Company," *Academy of Management Executive*, November 1992, p. 72.
4. See Andrew M. Pettigrew, "Organizational Climate and Culture: The Constructs in Search of a Role," in Ben Schneider (ed.), *Organizational Climate and Culture*, Jossey-Bass, San Francisco, 1990, p. 417.
5. John E. Sheridan, "Organizational Culture and Employee Retention," *Academy of Management Journal*, December 1992, pp. 1036–1056.
6. Edgar H. Schein, *Organizational Culture and Leadership*, Jossey-Bass, San Francisco, 1985, p. 9.
7. Joanne Martin, *Cultures in Organizations*, Oxford University Press, New York, 1992, p. 3.
8. Ibid.
9. For example, see Mary Jo Hatch, "The Dynamics of Organizational Culture," *Academy of Management Review*, October 1993, pp. 657–693.
10. Elizabeth Wolfe Morrison, "Longitudinal Study of

the Effects of Information Seeking on Newcomer Socialization," *Journal of Applied Psychology*, April 1993, pp. 173–183.

11. Denison, loc. cit., and E. Thomas Moran and J. Fredericks Volkwein, "The Cultural Approach to the Formation of Organizational Climate," *Human Relations*, vol. 45, 1992, pp. 19–48.

12. Genevieve Soter Capowski, "Designing a Corporate Identity," *Management Review*, June 1993, p. 37.

13. Jennifer Reese, "America's Most Admired Corporations," *Fortune*, Feb. 8, 1993, p. 44.

14. Ibid.

15. Nancy C. Morey and Fred Luthans, "Refining the Displacement of Culture and the Use of Scenes and Themes in Organizational Studies," *Academy of Management Review*, April 1985, p. 221.

16. John J. Keller, "Bob Allen Is Turning AT&T into a Live Wire," *Business Week*, Nov. 6, 1989, p. 140.

17. Ibid.

18. Karen Matthes, "Greetings from Hallmark," *HR Focus*, August 1993, p. 12.

19. Mark R. Edwards, "Integrating Fiefdoms and Subcultures into Organization Networks," in Richard Bellingham, Barry Cohen, Mark Edwards, and Judd Allen (eds.), *The Corporate Culture Sourcebook*, Human Resource Development Press, Amherst, Mass., 1990, p. 1975.

20. Terence E. Deal and Allan A. Kennedy, *Corporate Cultures: The Rites and Rituals of Corporate Life*, Addison-Wesley, Reading, Mass., 1982.

21. Carol J. Loomis, "Dinosaurs?" *Fortune*, May 3, 1993, pp. 36–42.

22. "A Spanner in the Works," *The Economist*, Oct. 23, 1993, p. 75.

23. See Alan Deutschman, "Steve Jobs NEXT Big Gamble," *Fortune*, Feb. 8, 1993, pp. 99–102.

24. Schein, op. cit., p. 210.

25. Kenneth R. Thompson, "A Conversation with Robert W. Galvin," *Organizational Dynamics*, Spring 1992, p. 58.

26. Ibid., p. 69.

27. Robert Johnson, "McDonald's Combines a Dead Man's Advice with Lively Strategy," *The Wall Street Journal*, Dec. 18, 1987, p. 1.

28. Sarah Smith, "Quality of Management," *Fortune*, Jan. 29, 1990, p. 46.

29. This process is described in Richard Pascale, "The Paradox of 'Corporate Culture': Reconciling Ourselves to Socialization," *California Management Review*, Winter 1985, pp. 29–38.

30. See Gregory B. Northcraft and Margaret A. Neale, *Organizational Behavior*, Dryden, Chicago, 1990, pp. 460–461, for a review of this literature, and Robert Vandenberg and Vida Scarpello, "The Matching Model: An Examination of the Processes Underlying Realistic Job Previews," *Journal of Applied Psychology*, February 1990, pp. 60–67, for some recent research.

31. Pascale, op. cit., p. 31.

32. Ibid., p. 32.

33. Karen Lowry Miller, "How a Team of Buckeyes Helped Honda Save a Bundle," *Business Week*, Sept. 13, 1993, p. 68.

34. For more on this process, see Richard Pascale, "Fitting New Employees into the Company Culture," *Fortune*, May 18, 1984, pp. 28–43.

35. See Stephen P. Robbins, *Organization Theory*, 3d ed., Prentice-Hall, Englewood Cliffs, N.J., 1990, pp. 456–457.

36. Michael Beer and Elise Walton, "Developing the Competitive Organization," *American Psychologist*, February 1990, p. 157.

37. Warren Gross and Shula Shichman, "How to Grow an Organizational Culture," *Personnel*, September 1987, p. 52.

38. Alan L. Wilkins and Nigel J. Bristow, "For Successful Organization Culture, Honor Your Past," *Academy of Management Executive*, August 1987, pp. 221–228.

39. Thomas M. Rohan, "P&G Fights Back," *Industry Week*, Oct. 15, 1984, pp. 65–66.

40. Jolie B. Solomon and John Bussey, "Pressed by Its Rivals, Procter & Gamble Co. Is Altering Its Ways," *The Wall Street Journal*, May 20, 1985, p. 22.

41. Benson L. Porter and Warrington S. Parker, Jr., "Culture Change," *Human Resource Management*, Spring–Summer 1992, pp. 47–49.

42. Ibid., p. 49.

**REAL CASE:
Yo-Yo Impacts on
Organizational
Culture**

One of the major developments that cause a change in organizational culture is the expansion or contraction of company operations. American Airlines has been like a yo-yo in recent years because of the need to expand coupled with the need to contract because of losses incurred by increasing expenses and recurring union problems.

During most of the 1980s, less than 10 percent of American's revenues were generated by global operations. However, in the latter part of the decade, the firm expanded by increasing its overseas business and, in 1990, it bought Eastern Airline's Latin American route system. Now operating out of a strong Miami hub, American is catering strongly to this southern market. These efforts pushed international revenues to over 20 percent of its total, and the firm projects that by the year 2000 it will be generating 30 percent of all revenues from overseas business.

One of the primary ways in which American is changing is through its efforts to cater to these foreign markets. For example, international fliers care a lot more about inflight service than American realized. When flight attendants warmed the mixed nuts accompanying their cocktails to the precisely correct temperature (98°F), passengers noticed and commented favorably. The airline also learned that many business passengers like to eat soon after the plane is airborne so that they can then sleep or work undisturbed for the rest of the flight; and they prefer simple, not sumptuous, meals.

American Airlines has also adjusted its service features to national preferences. For example, German passengers are particular about the use of titles such as "Herr Doktor." Japanese passengers dislike being touched. Latin passengers like a main course that consists of beef and French wine.

The company also relies heavily on computer technology to keep ahead of the competition. For example, American's Sabre reservation system is the best in the industry. There currently are more than 85,000 Sabre terminals in use throughout the world, and the system helps ensure that travel agents will book their people on American in more cases than not. As a result of these changes in its organization American should be doing well. Yet, despite these strategic and globalization initiatives, as of the middle of the 1990s the airline is still having problems. In 1993 there was a threat of a major walkout and American lost money in the very tough airline industry.

1. How did American Airlines' international expansion cause changes in its organizational culture?
2. Using Figure 18.1 as a point of reference, determine which step in the culture model would be most important to top managers at American Airlines. Why?
3. Using Figure 18.1 as a point of reference, determine which step would be most important in helping ensure that the company continues to adjust its service features to national cultures.
4. Why does this company still have problems? What further changes in its culture would you suggest are needed?

CASE:
Out with the Old,
In with the New

The Anderson Corporation was started in 1962 as a small consumer products company. During the first twenty years the company's research and development (R&D) staff developed a series of new products that proved to be very popular in the marketplace. Things went so well that the company had to add a second production shift just to keep up with the demand. During this time period the firm expanded its plant on three separate occasions. During an interview with a national magazine, the firm's founder, Paul Anderson, said, "We don't sell our products. We allocate them." This comment was in reference to the fact that the firm had only twenty-four salespeople and was able to garner annual revenues in excess of $62 million.

Three years ago Anderson suffered its first financial setback. The company had a net operating loss of $1.2 million. Two years ago the loss was $2.8 million, and last year it was $4.7 million. The accountant estimates that this year the firm will lose approximately $10 million.

Alarmed by this information, Citizen's Bank, the company's largest creditor, insisted that the firm make some changes and start turning things around. In response to this request, Paul Anderson agreed to step aside. The board of directors replaced him with Mary Hartmann, head of the marketing division of one of the country's largest consumer products firms.

After making an analysis of the situation, Mary has come to the conclusion that there are a number of changes that must be made if the firm is to be turned around. The three most important are as follows:

1. More attention must be given to the marketing side of the business. The most vital factor for success in the sale of the consumer goods produced by Anderson is an effective sales force.
2. There must be an improvement in product quality. Currently, 2 percent of Anderson's output is defective as against 0.5 percent for the average firm in the industry. In the past the demand for Anderson's output was so great that quality control was not an important factor. Now it is proving to be a very costly area.
3. There must be reduction in the number of people in the operation. Anderson can get by with two-thirds of its current production personnel and only half of its administrative staff.

Mary has not shared these ideas with the board of directors, but she intends to do so. For the moment she is considering the steps that will have to be taken in making these changes and the effect that all of this might have on the employees and the overall operation.

1. What is wrong with the old organizational culture? What needs to be done to change it?
2. Why might it be difficult for Mary to change the existing culture?
3. What specific steps does Mary need to take in changing the culture? Identify and describe at least two.

**CASE:
Keeping Things
the Same**

Metropolitan Hospital was built two years ago and currently has a work force of 235 people. The hospital is small, but because it is new, it is extremely efficient. The board has voted to increase its capacity from 60 beds to 190 beds. By this time next year, the hospital will be over three times as large as it is now in terms of both beds and personnel.

The administrator, Clara Hawkins, feels that the major problem with this proposed increase is that the hospital will lose its efficiency. "I want to hire people who are just like our current team of personnel—hard-working, dedicated, talented, and able to interact well with patients. If we triple the number of employees, I don't see how it will be possible to maintain our quality patient care. We are going to lose our family atmosphere. We will be inundated with mediocrity and we'll end up being like every other institution in the local area—large and uncaring!"

The chairman of the board is also concerned about the effect of hiring such a large number of employees. However, he believes that Clara is overreacting. "It can't be that hard to find people who are like our current staff. There must be a lot of people out there who are just as good. What you need to do is develop a plan of action that will allow you to carefully screen those who will fit into your current organizational culture and those who will not. It's not going to be as difficult as you believe. Trust me. Everything will work out just fine."

As a result of the chairman's comments, Clara has decided that the most effective way of dealing with the situation is to develop a plan of action. She intends to meet with her administrative group and determine the best way of screening incoming candidates and then helping those who are hired to become socialized in terms of the hospital's culture. Clara has called a meeting for the day after tomorrow. At that time she intends to discuss her ideas, get suggestions from her people, and then formulate a plan of action. "We've come too far to lose it all now," she told her administrative staff assistant. "If we keep our wits about us, I think we can continue to keep Metropolitan as the showcase hospital in this region."

1. What can Clara and her staff do to select the type of entry-level candidates they want? Explain.
2. How can Clara ensure that those who are hired come to accept the core cultural values of the hospital? What steps would you recommend?
3. Could Clara use this same approach if another 200 people were hired a few years from now?

INTEGRATIVE CONTEMPORARY CASE/READING FOR PART 4

The Horizontal
Corporation

*WANTED: Bureaucracy basher,
willing to challenge convention,
assume big risks, and rewrite the
accepted rules of industrial order.*

It's a job description that says nothing about your skills in manufacturing, finance, or any other business discipline. And as seismic changes continue to rumble across the corporate landscape, it's the kind of want ad the 21st century corporation might write.

Skeptical? No matter where you work, it's likely that your company has been, in today's vernacular, "downsized" and "delayered." It has chopped out layers of management and supposedly empowered employees with greater responsibility. But you're still bumping up against the same entrenched bureaucracy that has held you back before. The engineers still battle manufacturing. Marketing continues to slug it out with sales. And the financial naysayers fight everyone.

Source: John A. Byrne, "Horizontal Corporation," *Business Week*, Dec. 20, 1993. Copyright © 1993 by McGraw-Hill, Inc. Reprinted by special permission.

Seven of the Key Elements of the Horizontal Corporation

Simple downsizing didn't produce the dramatic rises in productivity many companies hoped for. Gaining quantum leaps in performance requires rethinking the way work gets done. To do that, some companies are adopting a new organization model. Here's how it might work:

1. *Organize Around Process, Not Task.* Instead of creating a structure around functions or departments, build the company around its three to five "core processes," with specific performance goals. Assign an "owner" to each process.
2. *Flatten Hierarchy.* To reduce supervision, combine fragmented tasks, eliminate work that fails to add value, and cut the activities within each process to a minimum. Use as few teams as possible to perform an entire process.
3. *Use Teams to Manage Everything.* Make teams the main building blocks of the organization. Limit supervisory roles by making the team manage itself. Give the team a common purpose. Hold it accountable for measurable performance goals.
4. *Let Customers Drive Performance.* Make customer satisfaction—not stock appreciation or profitability—the primary driver and measure of performance. The profits will come and the stock will rise if the customers are satisfied.
5. *Reward Team Performance.* Change the appraisal and pay systems to reward team results, not just individual performance. Encourage staffers to develop multiple skills rather than specialized know-how. Reward them for it.
6. *Maximize Supplier and Customer Contact.* Bring employees into direct, regular contact with suppliers and customers. Add supplier or customer representatives as full working members of in-house teams when they can be of service.
7. *Inform and Train All Employees.* Don't just spoon-feed sanitized information on a "need to know" basis. Trust staffers with raw data, but train them in how to use it to perform their own analyses and make their own decisions.

Companies Moving Toward the Horizontal Model

AT&T.   Network Systems Div. reorganized its entire business around processes; now sets budgets by process and awards bonuses to employees based on customer evaluations.

Eastman Chemical.   Kodak unit has over 1,000 teams; ditched senior v-ps for administration, manufacturing, and R&D in favor of self-directed teams.

General Electric.   Lighting business scrapped vertical structure, adopting horizontal design with more than 100 processes and programs.

Lexmark International.   Former IBM division axed 60% of managers in manufacturing and support in favor of cross-functional teams worldwide.

Motorola.   Government Electronics group redesigned its supply management organization as a process with external customers at the end; team members are now evaluating peers.

Xerox.   Develops new products through multi-disciplinary teams that work in a single process, instead of vertical functions or departments.

That's because, despite the cutbacks, you probably still work in the typical vertical organization, a company in which staffers look up to bosses instead of out to customers. You and your colleagues feel loyalty and commitment to the functional fiefdoms in which you work, not to the overall corporation and its goals. And even after all the cutting, too many layers of management still slow decision-making and lead to high coordination costs.

Mere downsizing, in other words, does little to change the fundamental way that work gets done in a corporation. To do that takes a different organizational model, the horizontal corporation. Already, some of Corporate America's biggest names, from American Telephone & Telegraph and DuPont to General Electric and Motorola, are moving toward the idea. In the quest for greater efficiency and productivity, they're beginning to redraw the hierarchical organization charts that have defined corporate life since the Industrial Revolution.

"Wave of the Future." Some of these changes have been under way for several years under the guise of "total quality management" efforts, reengineering, or business-process redesign. But no matter which buzzword or phrase you choose, the trend is toward flatter organizations in which managing across has become more critical than managing up and down in a top-heavy hierarchy.

The horizontal corporation, though, goes much further than these previous efforts: It largely eliminates both hierarchy and functional or departmental boundaries. In its purest state, the horizontal corporation might boast a skeleton group of senior executives at the top in such traditional support functions as finance and human resources. But virtually everyone else in the organization would work together in multidisciplinary teams that perform core processes, such as product development or sales generation. The upshot: The organization might have only three or four layers of management between the chairman and the staffers in a given process.

If the concept takes hold, almost every aspect of corporate life will be profoundly altered. Companies would organize around process—developing new products, for example—instead of around narrow tasks, such as forecasting market demand for a given new product. Self-managing teams would become the building blocks of the new organization. Performance objectives would be linked to customer satisfaction rather than profitability or shareholder value. And staffers would be rewarded not just for individual performance but for the development of their skills and for team performance.

For most companies, the idea amounts to a major cultural transformation—but one whose time may be at hand. "It's a wave of the future," declares M. Anthony Burns, chairman of Ryder System Inc., the truck-leasing concern. "You just can't summarily lay off people. You've got to change the processes and drive out the unnecessary work, or it will be back tomorrow." Such radical changes hold the promise for dramatic gains in productivity, according to Lawrence A. Bossidy, chairman of Allied Signal Inc. "There's an awful lot more productivity you're going to see in the next few years as we move to horizontally organized structures with a focus on the customer," says Bossidy.

How so? Just as a light bulb wastes electricity to produce unwanted heat, a traditional corporation expends a tremendous amount of energy running its own internal machinery—managing relations among departments or providing information up and down the hierarchy, for example.

A horizontal structure eliminates most of those tasks and focuses almost all of a company's resources on its customers. That's why proponents of the idea say it can deliver dramatic improvements in efficiency and speed. "It can get you from 100 horsepower to 500 horsepower," says Frank Ostroff, a McKinsey & Co. consultant. With colleague Douglas Smith, he coined the term "the horizontal organization" and developed a series of principles to define the new corporate model.

The idea is drawing attention in corporate and academic circles. In the past year, Ostroff has given talks on the horizontal organization before sizable gatherings of corporate strategic planners, quality experts, and entrepreneurs. He has also carried the message to MBAs and faculty at the University of Pennsylvania and Yale University, and he boasts invitations from Harvard University and several leading European business schools.

Process and Pain. But this is much more than just another abstract theory making the B-school lecture rounds. Examples of horizontal management abound, though much of the movement is occurring at lower levels in organizations. Some AT&T units are now doing annual budgets based not on functions or departments but on processes such as the maintenance of a worldwide telecommunications network. They're even dishing out bonuses to employees based on customer evaluations of the teams performing those processes. DuPont Co. has set up a centralized group this year to nudge the chemical giant's business units into organizing along horizontal lines. Chrysler Corp. used a process approach to turn out its new Neon subcompact quickly for a fraction of the typical development costs. Xerox Corp. is employing what it calls "microenterprise units" of employees that have beginning-to-end responsibility for the company's products.

In early December, nearly two dozen companies—including such international giants as Boeing, British Telecommunications, Stockholm-based L. M. Ericsson, and Volvo Europe—convened in Boston under the auspices of Mercer Management Consulting, another consulting shop peddling the idea, to swap stories on their efforts to adopt horizontal management techniques. Indeed, nearly all of the most prominent consulting firms are now raking in tens of millions of dollars in revenues by advising companies to organize their operations horizontally.

What those consultants' clients are quickly discovering, however, is that eliminating the neatly arranged boxes on an organization chart in favor of a more horizontal structure can often be a complex and painful ordeal. Indeed, simply defining the processes of a given corporation may prove to be a mind-boggling and time-consuming exercise. Consider AT&T. Initially, the company's Network Services Div., which has 16,000 employees, tallied up some 130 processes before it narrowed them down to 13 core ones.

After that comes the challenge of persuading people to cast off their old marketing, finance, or manufacturing hats and think more broadly. "This is the hardest damn thing to do," says Terry M. Ennis, who heads up a group to help DuPont's businesses organize along horizontal lines. "It's very unsettling and threatening for people. You find line and function managers who have been honored and rewarded for what they've done for decades. You're in a white-water zone when you change."

Some management gurus, noting the fervor with which corporate chieftains embrace fads, express caution. "The idea draws together a number of fashionable trends and packages them in an interesting way," says Henry Mintzberg, a management professor at McGill University. "But the danger is that an idea like this can generate too much enthusiasm. It's not for everyone." Mintzberg notes that there is no one solution to every organization's problems. Indeed, streamlined vertical structures may suit some mass-production industries better than horizontal ones.

Already, consultants say, some companies are rushing to organize around processes without linking them to the corporation's key goals. Before tinkering with its organization chart, Ostroff says, a company must understand the markets and the customers it wants to reach and complete an analysis of what it will take to win them. Only then should the company begin to identify the most critical core processes to achieve its objectives—whether they're lowering costs by 30% or developing new products in half the time it normally required.

Different Climate. In the days when business was more predictable and stable, companies organized themselves in vertical structures to take advantage of specialized experts. The benefits are obvious: Everyone has a place, and everyone understands his or her task. The critical decision-making power resides at the top. But while gaining clarity and stability, such organizations make it difficult for anyone to understand the task of the company as a whole and how to relate his or her work to it. The result: Collaboration among different departments was often a triumph over formal organization charts.

To solve such problems, some companies turned to so-called matrix organizations in the 1960s and 1970s. The model was built around specific projects that cut across departmental lines. But it still kept the hierarchy intact and left most of the power and responsibility in the upper reaches of the organization.

Heightened global competition and the ever increasing speed of technological change have since altered the rules of the game and have forced corporate planners to seek new solutions. "We were reluctant to leave the command-and-control structure because it had worked so well," says Philip Engel, president of CNA Corp., the Chicago-based insurance company that is refashioning its organization. "But it no longer fit the realities."

Indeed, many companies are moving to this new form of corporate organization after failing to achieve needed productivity gains by simple streamlining and consolidation. "We didn't have another horse to ride," says Kenneth L. Garrett, a senior vice-president at AT&T's Network Systems Div. "We weren't performing as well as we could, and we had already streamlined our operations."

In all cases, the objective of the horizontal corporation is to change the narrow mind-sets of armies of corporate specialists who have spent their careers climbing a vertical hierarchy to the top of a given function. As DuPont's Terry Ennis puts it: "Our goal is to get everyone focused on the business as a system in which the functions are seamless." DuPont executives are trying to do away with what Ennis calls the "disconnect" and "handoffs" that are so common between functions and departments. "Every time you have an organizational boundary, you get the potential for a disconnect," Ennis says. "The bigger the organization, the bigger the functions, and the more disconnects you get."

Speedier Cycles. The early proponents of the horizontal corporation are claiming significant gains. At General Electric Co., where Chairman John F. Welch Jr. speaks of building a "boundaryless" company, the concept has reduced costs, shortened cycle times, and increased the company's responsiveness to its customers. GE's $3 billion lighting business scrambled a more traditional structure for its global technology organization in favor of one in which a senior team of 9-to-12 people oversees nearly 100 processes or programs worldwide, from new-product design to improving the yield on production machinery. In virtually all the cases, a multidisciplinary team works together to achieve the goals of the process.

The senior leadership group—composed of managers with "multiple competencies" rather than narrow specialists—exists to allocate resources and ensure coordination of the processes and programs. "They stay away from the day-to-day activities, which are managed by the teams themselves," explains Harold Giles, manager of human resources in GE's lighting business.

The change forced major upheavals in GE's training, appraisal, and compensation systems. To create greater allegiance to a process, rather than a boss, the company has begun to put in place so-called "360-degree appraisal routines" in which peers and others above and below the employee evaluate the performance of an individual in a process. In some cases, as many as 20 people are now involved in reviewing a single employee. Employees are paid on the basis of the skills they develop rather than merely the individual work they perform.

Ryder System is another convert. The company had been organized by division—each with its own functions—based on product. But it wanted an organization that would reduce overhead while being more responsive to customers. "We were reaching the end of the runway looking for cost efficiencies, as most companies have," says J. Ernie Riddle, senior vice-president for marketing. "So we're looking at processes from front to back."

To purchase a vehicle for leasing, for instance, required some 14 to 17 handoffs as the documents wended their way from one functional department to another at a local, and then a national, level. "We passed the baton so many times that the chances of dropping it were great," says Riddle. By viewing this paperwork flow as a single process from purchasing the vehicle to providing it to a customer, Ryder has reduced the handoffs to two from five. By redesigning the work, weeding out unnecessary approvals, and pushing more authority down the organization, the company cut its purchasing cycle by a third, to four months.

"A Clean Sheet." Some startups have opted to structure themselves as horizontal companies from the get-go. One such company is Astra/Merck Group, a new stand-

alone company formed to market antiulcer and high-blood-pressure drugs licensed from Sweden's Astra. Instead of organizing around functional areas, Astra/Merck is structured around a half-dozen "market-driven business processes," from drug development to product sourcing and distribution. "We literally had a clean sheet of paper to build the new model company," says Robert C. Holmes, director of strategic planning. "A functional organization wasn't likely to support our strategic goals to be lean, fast, and focused on the customer."

Congratulations. You're Moving to a New Pepperoni

If the 21st century corporation goes horizontal, what will its organization chart look like? That's right, organization charts—those dull, lifeless templates that reduce power relationships to a confusing mass of boxes and arrows. As a growing number of planners try to turn a management abstraction into a pragmatic reality, organization charts are beginning to look stranger and stranger.

Consider Eastman Chemical Co., the Eastman Kodak Co. division spun off as a separate company in January. "Our organization chart is now called the pizza chart because it looks like a pizza with a lot of pepperoni sitting on it," says Ernest W. Deavenport Jr., who as president is the pepperoni at the center of the pie. "We did it in circular form to show that everyone is equal in the organization. No one dominates the other. The white space inside the circles is more important than the lines."

Each pepperoni typically represents a cross-functional team responsible for managing a business, a geographic area, a function, or a "core competence" in a specific technology or area such as innovation. The white space around them is where the collaborative interaction is supposed to occur.

Eastman Chemical's pizza isn't the only paper representation of the horizontally inclined corporation. PepsiCo flipped its pyramidal organization chart upside-down. To help focus on customers, Pepsi put its field reps at the top. Chief Executive Craig Weatherup now calls Pepsi-Cola, the huge beverage unit of PepsiCo, "the right-side-up company." Astra/Merck Group—nearly a pure horizontal company—boasts a chart with a stack of six elongated rectangles, each representing a core process of the pharmaceutical startup. Across the top are a series of functional boxes, or "skill centers," that drive down through the processes with arrows.

Wild Shamrocks. For its own conceptual model of what the horizontal organization should look like, McKinsey & Co., the consulting firm, came up with a fairly abstract rendering of three boxes floating above a trio of core processes. Each process is represented by a bar with three circles on the surface. The circles symbolize the multidisciplinary teams in charge of a specific process.

This is not the first time organizational theorists have tried to come up with a workable alternative to the vertical structure that has dominated business for a century or more. Some have been as wild as the shamrock image promoted by Charles Handy, a lecturer at the London Business School. Its three leaves symbolize the joining forces of core employees, external contractors, and part-time staffers. James Brian Quinn, a Dartmouth B-school prof, thought up the starburst to reflect the company that splits off units like shooting stars.

But these experimental designs are really just metaphors for the 21st-century corporation, not pragmatic structures that any company has actually adopted. And for every upside-down pyramid, you'll still find thousands of conventional charts.

Just browse through the Conference Board's repository of organization charts, a collection that features the latest diagrams of 450 corporations, from Advance Bank Australia to Xerox. The New York-based organization has been selling charts, at $14

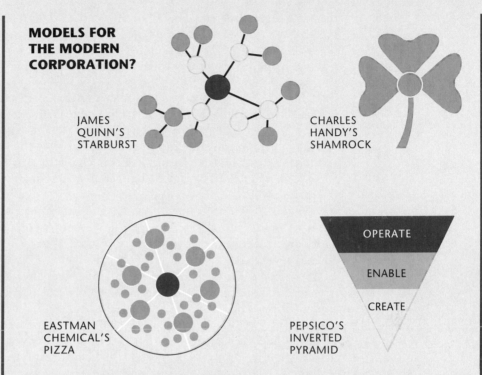

MODELS FOR THE MODERN CORPORATION?

JAMES QUINN'S STARBURST

CHARLES HANDY'S SHAMROCK

EASTMAN CHEMICAL'S PIZZA

PEPSICO'S INVERTED PYRAMID

OPERATE

ENABLE

CREATE

apiece, for nearly a decade. Over that time, the organizational diagrams have gotten flatter, with fewer reporting levels, and they've become more decentralized, too. More recently, in response to heightened concern over corporate governance, some companies such as Mobil Oil Corp. and Ford Motor Co. have put shareholders and the board of directors in boxes above the top dog. But they still favor the old vertical, command-and-control hierarchy.

All of the Conference Board's best-sellers—BankAmerica, Ford, General Electric, IBM, and Motorola—are pretty much what you would expect: plenty of boxes connected by lines in steep pyramids. Indeed, under Ford's office of the chief executive, there are a mind-boggling 59 boxes of divisions, departments, and functions.

Only a few of the charts reflect the trend toward horizontal organization. Why? For one thing, it's simply too early. "Organization charts lag what's happening," says Douglas Smith, a consultant who helped develop the horizontal idea. "And a lot of people can't figure out how to draw it any other way." For another, most of the more dramatic changes along horizontal lines are occurring at divisional or subsidiary levels. That's where—at PepsiCo and Eastman Kodak, at least—those pizzas and inverted pyramids are symbols that the business-as-usual days are long gone.

Some fairly small companies are also finding the model appealing. Consider Modicon Inc., a North Andover (Mass.) maker of automation-control equipment with annual revenues of $300 million. Instead of viewing product development as a task of the engineering function, President Paul White defined it more broadly as a process that would involve a team of 15 managers from engineering, manufacturing, marketing, sales, and finance.

By working together, Modicon's team avoided costly delays from disagreements and misunderstandings. "In the past," says White, "an engineering team would have worked on this alone with some dialogue from marketing. Manufacturing wouldn't get involved until the design was brought into the factory. Now, all the business issues are right on the table from the beginning."

Team Hats. The change allowed Modicon to bring six software products to market in one-third the time it would normally take. The company, a subsidiary of Germany's Daimler Benz, still has a management structure organized by function. But many of the company's 900 employees are involved in up to 30 teams that span several functions and departments. Predicts White: "In five years, we'll still have some formal functional structure, but people will probably feel free enough to spend the majority of their time outside their functions."

So far, the vast majority of horizontal experimentation has been at the lower levels of organizations. Increasingly, however, corporations are overhauling their entire structures to bear a closer resemblance to the horizontal model defined by consultants Ostroff and others. Eastman Chemical Co., the $3.5 billion unit of Eastman Kodak Co. spun off as a stand-alone company on Jan. 1, replaced several of its senior vice-presidents in charge of the key functions with "self-directed work teams." Instead of having a head of manufacturing, for example, the company uses a team consisting of all its plant managers. "It was the most dramatic change in the company's 70-year history," maintains Ernest W. Deavenport Jr., president of Eastman Chemical. "It makes people take off their organizational hats and put on their team hats. It gives people a much broader perspective and forces decision-making down at least another level."

In creating the new organization, the 500 senior managers agreed that the primary role of the functions was to support Eastman's business in chemicals, plastics, fibers, and polymers. "A function does not and should not have a mission of its own," insists Deavenport. Common sense? Of course. But over the years, the functional departments had grown strong and powerful, as they have in many organizations, often at the expense of the overall company as they fought to protect and build turf. Now, virtually all of the company's managers work on at least one cross-functional team, and most work on two or more on a daily basis. For example, Tom O. Nethery, a group vice-president, runs an industrial-business group. But he also serves on three other teams that deal with such diverse issues as human resources, cellulose technology, and product-support services.

These changes in the workplace are certain to dramatically alter titles, career paths, and the goals of individuals, too. At AT&T's Network Systems Div., each of 13 core processes boasts an "owner" and a "champion." While the owners focus on the day-to-day operations of a process, the champions ensure that the process remains linked with overall business strategies and goals. Through it all, collaboration is key. "An overriding challenge is how you get marketing people to talk to finance people when they've thrown rocks at each other for decades," says Gerald Ross, co-founder of ChangeLab International, a consulting firm that specializes in cultural transformation. "Your career will be dependent on your ability to work across boundaries with others very different from you."

Don't rush to write the obituary for functional management, however. No companies have completely eliminated functional specialization. And even advocates of the new model don't envision the end of managers who are experts in manufacturing, finance, and the like. "It's only the rarest of organizations that would choose to be purely vertical or horizontal," says consultant Douglas Smith. "Most organizations will be hybrids."

Still, the horizontal corporation is an idea that's gaining currency and one that will increasingly demand people who think more broadly and thrive on change, who manage process instead of people, and who cherish teamwork as never before.

1. What are some of the major problems with the traditional vertical organization?
2. What are the major characteristics of the newly emerging horizontal organizations? Give some specific examples.
3. How does the horizontal organization affect communication, decision making, and organizational culture?

EXPERIENTIAL EXERCISES FOR PART 4

EXERCISE: Organizations*

Goals:
1. To identify some of the important organizations in your life
2. To determine relevant, specific characteristics of organizations
3. To describe some of the important functions of management in organizations

Implementation:
Read the "Overview" and "Procedure" sections. Complete the "Profile of Organizations" form, which follows these sections.

Overview:
Undoubtedly, you have had recent experiences with numerous organizations. Ten to fifteen minutes of reflective thinking should result in a fairly large list of organizations. Don't be misled by thinking that only large organizations, such as your college or General Motors, are relevant for consideration. How about the clinic, with the doctors, nurses, and secretary/bookkeeper? Or the corner garage or service station? The local tavern, McDonald's, and the neighborhood theater are all organizations. You should have no difficulty listing several organizations with which you have had recent contact.

The second part of the exercise, however, is tougher. Describe several of the key characteristics of the organizations that you have listed. One of the major issues in studying and describing organizations is deciding *what* characteristics or factors are important. Some of the more common characteristics considered in the analysis of organizations are:

1. Size (small to very large)
2. Degree of formality (informal to highly structured)
3. Degree of complexity (simple to complex)
4. Nature of goals (what the organization is trying to accomplish)
5. Major activities (what tasks are performed)
6. Types of people involved (age, skills, educational background, etc.)
7. Location of activities (number of units and their geographic location)

You should be able to develop a list of characteristics that you think are relevant for each of your organizations.

Now to the third, final, and most difficult task. Think about what is involved in the management of these organizations. For example, what kinds of functions do their managers perform? How does one learn the skills necessary to be an effective manager? Would you want to be a manager in any of these organizations?

In effect, in this exercise you are being asked to think specifically about organizations you have been associated with recently, develop your own conceptual model for looking at their characteristics, and think more specifically about the managerial functions in each of these organizations. You

---

Source: Reprinted with permission from Fremont E. Kast and James E. Rosenzweig, "Our Organizational Society," in *Experiential Exercises and Cases in Management*, McGraw-Hill, New York, 1976, pp. 13–15.

probably already know a great deal more about organizations and their management than you think. This exercise should be useful in getting your thoughts together.

Procedure:

Step 1. Prior to class, list up to ten organizations (for example, work, living group, club) in which you have been involved or with which you have had recent contact.

Step 2. Enter five organizations from your list on the following form.

1. List the organization.
2. Briefly outline the characteristics that you consider most significant.
3. Describe the managerial functions in each of these organizations.

Step 3. During the class period, meet in groups of five or six to discuss your list of organizations, the characteristics you consider important, and your descriptions of their management. Look for significant similarities and differences across organizations.

Step 4. Basing your selections on this group discussion, develop a list entitled "What we would like to know about organizations and their management." Be prepared to write this list on the blackboard or on big sheets of paper and to share your list with other groups in the class.

Profile of Organizations

Organization	Key Characteristics	Managerial Functions
1. _____	_____	_____
	_____	_____
	_____	_____
	_____	_____
2. _____	_____	_____
	_____	_____
	_____	_____
	_____	_____
3. _____	_____	_____
	_____	_____
	_____	_____
	_____	_____
4. _____	_____	_____
	_____	_____
	_____	_____
	_____	_____
5. _____	_____	_____
	_____	_____
	_____	_____
	_____	_____

EXERCISE: Paper Plane Corporation

Goals:

1. To work on an actual organizational task
2. To experience the managerial functions of organizing, decision making, and control

Implementation:

Unlimited groups of six participants each are used in this exercise. These groups may be directed simultaneously in the same room. Approximately a full class period is needed to complete the exercise. Each person should have assembly instructions and a summary sheet, which are shown on pages 529 and 530, and ample stacks of paper (8 ½ by 11 inches). The physical setting should be a room large enough so that the individual groups of six can work without interference from the other groups. A working space should be provided for each group.

1. The participants are doing an exercise in production methodology.
2. Each group must work independently of the other groups.
3. Each group will choose a manager and an inspector, and the remaining participants will be employees.
4. The objective is to make paper airplanes in the most profitable manner possible.
5. The facilitator will give the signal to start. This is a ten-minute, timed event utilizing competition among the groups.
6. After the first round, everyone should report his or her production and profits to the entire group. Each person also should note the effect, if any, of the manager in terms of the performance of the group.
7. This same procedure is followed for as many rounds as time allows.

Paper Plane Corporation: Data Sheet

Your group is the complete work force for Paper Plane Corporation. Established in 1943, Paper Plane has led the market in paper plane production. Presently under new management, the company is contracting to make aircraft for the U.S. Air Force. You must establish an efficient production plant to produce these aircraft. You must make your contract with the Air Force under the following conditions:

1. The Air Force will pay $20,000 per airplane.
2. The aircraft must pass a strict inspection made by the facilitator.
3. A penalty of $25,000 per airplane will be subtracted for failure to meet the production requirements.
4. Labor and other overhead will be computed at $300,000.
5. Cost of materials will be $3000 per bid plane. If you bid for ten but make only eight, you must pay the cost of materials for those which you failed to make or which did not pass inspection.

INSTRUCTIONS FOR AIRCRAFT ASSEMBLY

  STEP 1: Take a sheet of paper and fold it in half, then open it back up.

  STEP 2: Fold upper corners to the middle.

  STEP 3: Fold the corners to the middle again.

  STEP 4: Fold in half.

  STEP 5: Fold both wings down.

STEP 6: Fold tail fins up.

  COMPLETED AIRCRAFT

Summary Sheet:

Round 1:

Bid: _____ Aircraft @ $20,000 per aircraft = _____

Results: _____ Aircraft @ $20,000 per aircraft = _____

Less: $300,000 overhead

_____ × $3000 cost of raw materials

_____ × $25,000 penalty

Profit: _____

Round 2:

Bid: _____ Aircraft @ $20,000 per aircraft = _____

Results: _____ Aircraft @ $20,000 per aircraft = _____

Less: $300,000 overhead

_____ × $3000 cost of raw materials

_____ × $25,000 penalty

Profit: _____

Round 3:

Bid: _____ Aircraft @ $20,000 per aircraft = _____

Results: _____ Aircraft @ $20,000 per aircraft = _____

Less: $300,000 overhead

_____ × $3000 cost of raw materials

_____ × $25,000 penalty

Profit: _____

PART 5

Horizons for
Organizational Behavior

19

International Organizational Behavior

Learning Objectives

- **Examine** the role and impact that different cultures have on organizational behavior.
- **Present** the research on organizational behavior across cultures.
- **Discuss** the international implications of interpersonal communication.
- **Analyze** the international implications of employee motivation.
- **Explain** the international implications of managerial leadership.

Just as businesses around the world have ignored the international context except in recent years, so has the field of organizational behavior. For example, up to recent years organizational behavior textbooks did not even include an international chapter such as this one. However, just as it is becoming increasingly clear that the world is shrinking and requires new business strategies,[1] it is also becoming increasingly evident that organizational behavior[2] and human resources management[3] play an important role in this globalization process. For example, a recent analysis noted: "Many companies that rushed into cross-border mergers and acquisitions in the late '80s now realize that such projects are more complicated than they appeared. The missing element is the human factor."[4]

Although there is a trend toward similar clothes, entertainment, and material possessions, and even a growing acceptance of English as the international business language, there are still important differences in the ways in which people think and behave around the world. There are even differences in the way in which knowledge about organizational behavior is accumulated. For example, it has been pointed out that the European behavioral scientists tend to be more cognitive and/or psychoanalytically based, while their American counterparts are more behavioristic and/or humanistically oriented.[5] In understanding and applying organizational behavior concepts in other countries around the world, one must be aware of the similarities and differences.

For example, a recent study conducted by Welsh, Luthans, and Sommer found that U.S.-based extrinsic rewards and behavioral management approaches significantly improved the productivity of workers in a Russian factory, but a participative technique did not.[6] A follow-up critique concluded:

What this study shows is that there are both potential benefits and problems associated with transporting U.S.-based human resource management theories and techniques to other cultures. On the one hand, the findings confirmed that the use of valued extrinsic rewards and improved behavioral management techniques may have a considerable impact on productivity among Russian workers in ways that are similar to American workers. On the other hand, participation had a counterproductive effect on Russian workers' performance.[7]

Another example would be that in some countries managers prefer to use—and may be more effective with—an autocratic leadership style than with the typical U.S. manager's leadership style. Germany is a visible example. Typical U.S. managers who are transferred to Germany may find their leadership style to be too participative. German subordinates may expect them to make more decisions and to consult with them less. Research on obedience to authority (discussed in Chapter 5) found a higher percentage of Germans were obedient than were their U.S. counterparts.[8] Similarly, a U.S. manager in Japan who decides to set up a performance-based incentive system that gives a weekly bonus to the best worker in each work group may be making a mistake. Japanese workers do not like to be singled out for individual attention and go against the group's norms and values. Perhaps this impact of similarities and differences across cultures was best stated by the cofounder of Honda Motor, T. Fujisawa, when he stated: "Japanese and American management is 95 percent the same, and differs in all important aspects."[9]

This chapter examines organizational behavior from an international perspective and within an international context. It starts by using the previous chapter, on organizational culture, as a point of departure for examining the impact that different cultures can have on organizational behavior. This discussion gives attention both to how cultures vary and to how the behaviors within these cultures can differ. The remainder of the chapter analyzes the familiar organizational behavior topics of communication, motivation, and leadership—in an international context.

THE IMPACT OF CULTURE ON INTERNATIONAL ORGANIZATIONAL BEHAVIOR

The previous chapter deals specifically with *organizational* culture, which is a somewhat narrower concept than the culture of a society. *Culture* per se can be defined as the acquired knowledge that people use to interpret experience and generate social behavior. It is important to recognize that culture is learned and helps people in their efforts to interact and communicate with others in the society. When placed in a culture where values and beliefs are different, some people have a great deal of difficulty adjusting.[10] This is particularly true when U.S. business people are assigned to a foreign country. These expatriates quickly learn that the values of U.S. culture are often quite different from those of their host country. Not as well publicized is the fact that those who enter the United States also suffer cultural shock. Consider the following scenario:

> Around a conference table in a large U.S. office tower, three American executives sat with their new boss, Mr. Akiro Kusumoto, the newly appointed head of a Japanese firm's American subsidiary, and two of his Japanese lieutenants. The meeting was called to discuss ideas for reducing operating costs. Mr. Kusumoto began by outlining his company's aspiration for its long-term U.S. presence. He then turned to the current budgetary matter. One Japanese manager politely offered one suggestion,

and an American then proposed another. After gingerly discussing the alternatives for quite some time, the then exasperated American blurted out: "Look, *that* idea is just not going to have much impact. Look at the numbers! We should cut *this* program, and I think we should do it as soon as possible!" In the face of such bluntness, uncommon and unacceptable in Japan, Mr. Kusumoto fell silent. He leaned back, drew air between his teeth, and felt a deep longing to "return East." He realized his life in this country would be filled with many such jarring encounters, and lamented his posting to a land of such rudeness.[11]

In other words, cultural differences are a two-way street. Cultural differences must be understood and managers must be sensitive to them in order to be successful in the global economy.

How Do Cultures Vary?

There are several basic dimensions that differentiate cultures. The following sections examine the most important of these.

How People See Themselves. In some countries of the world, people are viewed as basically honest and trustworthy. In others, people are regarded with suspicion and distrust. For example, a reason some Third World people regard the United States with suspicion and distrust may result from the way these people view themselves. They assume others are like them, that is, prepared to cut corners if they can get away with it. On the other hand, many other people of Third World countries are just the opposite. They do not lock their doors; they are very trusting and assume that no one will break in. It is forbidden to take the property of another person, and the people adhere strictly to that cultural value. In the United States, people also have a mixed view of other people. Most people from the United States still view others as basically honest but also believe that it is important to be alert for any sign of trouble.

When people travel outside their home country, they carry their values with them just like their baggage. This sometimes results in their being surprised over the way they are treated. The following is an example:

> A young Canadian in Sweden found summer employment working in a restaurant owned by Yugoslavians. As the Canadian explained, "I arrived at the restaurant and was greeted by an effusive Yugoslavian man who set me to work at once washing dishes and preparing the restaurant for the June opening.
>
> "At the end of the first day, I was brought to the back room. The owner took an old cash box out of a large desk. The Yugoslavian owner counted out my wages for the day and was about to return the box to the desk when the phone rang in the front room. The owner hesitated: should he leave me sitting in the room with the money or take it with him? Quite simply, could he trust me?
>
> "After a moment, the man got up to answer the phone, leaving me with the open money box. I sat there in amazement; how could he trust me, someone he had known for less than a day, a person whose last name and address he didn't even know."[12]

People's Relationship to Their World. In some societies people attempt to dominate their environment. In other societies they try to live in harmony with it or are subjugated by it. People from the United States and Canada, for example, attempt to dominate their environment. In agriculture they use fertilizers and insecticides to increase crop yields. Other societies, especially those Asia, work in harmony with the environment by planting crops in the right places and at the right time. In still other societies, most notably Third World countries, no action is taken regarding the subjugation of nature, so, for example, when the floods come, there are no dams or irrigation systems for dealing with the impending disaster. Also, when the Berlin Wall crumbled and Eastern Europe opened up, it was found that there was an ecological disaster there. For example, it was found that almost all the rivers were heavily polluted, in some areas 90 percent of the children suffered from respiratory and other pollution-related diseases, and sewage treatment was in a terrible state almost everywhere.[13]

Individualism Versus Collectivism. Some countries of the world encourage individualism. The United States, Great Britain, and Canada are examples. In other countries collectivism, or group orientation, is important. Japan, China, and the Israeli kibbutzim emphasize group harmony, unity, commitment, and loyalty. The differences reflect themselves in many ways, such as in hiring practices. In countries where individualism is important, job applicants are evaluated on the basis of personal, educational, and professional achievements. In group-oriented societies applicants are evaluated on the basis of trustworthiness, loyalty, and compatibility with coworkers. Also in high collectivism cultures, employees tend to show considerable commitment to their organization, while in high individualism cultures, managers tend to be more mobile, going from job to job.[14]

The Time Dimension. In some societies people are oriented toward the past. In others they tend to be more focused on the present. Still others are futuristic in their orientation. People from the United States and Canada are most interested in the present and the near future. Business people in these countries are particularly interested in where their companies are today and where they will be in five to ten years. People who are hired and do not work out are often let go in short order. They seldom last more than one or two years. Most Europeans place more importance on the past than do North Americans. They believe in preserving history and continuing traditions. They are concerned with the past, present, and future. Many Asian countries are futuristic in their approach. The Japanese, for example, have very long-term future-oriented time horizons. When large Japanese firms hire employees, they often retain them for a long time, even for life. The firms will spend a great deal of money to train them, and there is a strong, mutual commitment on both sides. Researchers have even developed ways to measure the time dimensions of organizational members.[15] Scales include those measuring punctuality, allocation, awareness, schedules and deadlines, work pace, and future orientation.

Public and Private Space. Some cultures promote the use of public space; others favor private space. For example, in Japan bosses often sit together with their employees in the same large room. The heads of some of the biggest Japanese firms may leave their chauffeur-driven limousines at home and ride the crowded public subways to work in the morning so that they can be with their workers. In the Middle East there are often many people present during important meetings. These cultures have a public orientation. In contrast, North Americans prefer private space. The more restricted or confined a manager is, the more important the individual is assumed to be. Anyone coming to see the person must first go past a secretary (and sometimes more than one) before being admitted to the manager's presence.

TABLE 19.1 Major Concepts in the Comparative Analysis of U.S. and Japanese Management

Expressions Commonly Used in Management	Principal Meanings, Interpretations, and Images	
	In United States	In Japan
Company	Team in sport	Family in village
Business goal	To win	To survive
Employees	Players in a team	Children in a family
Human relations	Functional	Emotional
Competition	Cutthroat	Cooperation or sin
Profit motivation	By all means	Means to an end
Sense of identification	Job pride	Group prestige
Work motivation	Individual income	Group atmosphere
Production	Productivity	Training and diligence
Personnel	Efficiency	Maintenance
Promotion	According to abilities	According to year of service
Pay	Service and results	Considered an award for patience and sacrifice

Source: Adapted from Motofusa Murayama, "A Comparative Analysis of U.S. and Japanese Management Systems," in Sang M. Lee and Gary Schwendiman (eds.), *Management by Japanese Systems*, Praeger, a division of Greenwood Press, Inc., New York, 1982, p. 237. Copyright © 1982 by Praeger Publishers. Used with permission.

When comparing societies in terms of the dimensions discussed above, it becomes obvious that there are major differences between the ways in which business is done in one corner of the world and another. Table 19.1, for example, provides a summary comparative analysis of U.S. and Japanese management in terms of some major business-related areas.

Behavior across Cultures

Just as there are many ways that culture per se varies, there are also many ways in which behavior varies across cultures. Tables 19.2 and 19.3 provide insights into the degree to which managers agree (or disagree) regarding the value of a hierarchical structure and the necessity of bypassing that structure in getting things done. Table 19.4 shows how important management feel it is to have a precise answer to subordinate questions about work-related activities. Quite obviously, the way managers function and behave appears to be influenced by their culture.

TABLE 19.2 The Main Reason for a Hierarchical Structure Is so That Everybody Knows Who Has Authority over Whom

	Agreement Rate Across Countries to the Above Statement (Least to Greatest)
United States	18%
Germany	24
Great Britain	38
Netherlands	38
France	45
Italy	50
Japan	52
Indonesia	86

Source: Adapted from Andre Laurent, "The Cultural Diversity of Western Conceptions of Management," *International Studies of Management and Organization*, Spring–Summer 1983, p. 82. Used with permission.

TABLE 19.3 In Order to Have Efficient Work Relationships, It Is Often Necessary to Bypass the Hierarchical Line

	Disagreement Rate Across Countries to the Above Statement (Least to Greatest)
Sweden	22%
Great Britain	31
United States	32
Netherlands	39
France	42
Germany	46
Italy	75

Source: Adapted from Andre Laurent, "The Cultural Diversity of Western Conceptions of Management," *International Studies of Management and Organization*, Spring–Summer 1983, p. 86. Used with permission.

TABLE 19.4 It Is Important for a Manager to Have at Hand Precise Answers to Most of the Questions That Subordinates May Raise About Their Work

	Agreement Rate Across Countries to the Above Statement (Least to Greatest)
Sweden	10%
Netherlands	17
United States	18
Great Britain	27
Germany	46
France	53
Italy	66
Indonesia	73
Japan	78

Source: Based on Andre Laurent, "The Cultural Diversity of Western Conceptions of Management," *International Studies of Management and Organization*, Spring–Summer 1983, p. 86. Used with permission.

Dimensions of Cultural Difference

One way of examining organizational behavior across cultures and explaining the differences that exist is to look at important dimensions such as those identified by Geert Hofstede, a well-known Dutch researcher. In a huge study involving 116,000 respondents, he found highly significant differences in the behavior and attitudes of employees from seventy countries who worked for subsidiaries of IBM.[16] Because all his data were collected from one company, the study has been criticized for not being representative of the various countries. However, Hofstede has recently countered such criticism by arguing that

> . . . samples for cross-national comparison need not be representative, as long as they are functionally equivalent. IBM employees are a narrow sample, but very well matched. . . . The only thing that can account for systematic and consistent differences between national groups *within* such a homogenous multinational population is nationality itself—the national environment in which people were brought up *before* they joined this employer. Comparing IBM subsidiaries therefore shows national cultural differences with unusual clarity.[17]

Two of these cultural differences were in individualism/collectivism and in power distance. The following sections take a close look at these and other cultural differences important to organizational behavior. However, a word of caution is still necessary when reading the results of Hofstede's classic study. It must be remembered that "the position of a culture along a dimension is based on the averages for all the respondents in that particular country. Characterizing a national work culture does not mean that every person in the nation has all the characteristics ascribed to that culture—there are bound to be many individual variations."[18] In other words, care must be taken not to stereotype an entire country on the basis of this study. There are numerous subcultures and individual differences.

Individualism/Collectivism and Power Distance. Individualism is the tendency to take care of oneself and one's immediate family. Collectivism is characterized by a tight social framework in which people distinguish between their own group and other groups. Power distance is the extent to which less powerful members of organizations accept the unequal distribution of power, that is, the degree to which employees accept that their boss has more power than they do.

When Hofstede examined employees from fifty countries in terms of individualism and power distance, he found four basic clusters. Figure 19.1 shows that the United States has high individualism and small power distance (employees do not

FIGURE 19.1

The position of selected countries on power distance and individualism.
(*Source*: Adapted from Geert Hofstede, "The Culture Relativity of Organizational Practices and Theories," *Journal of International Business Studies*, Fall 1983, p. 82. Used with permission.)

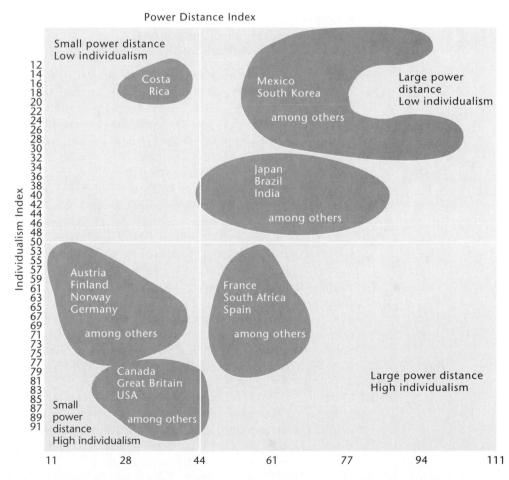

grant their boss much power). This is in contrast, for example, to Mexico, which has high collectivism (tight group) and large power distance (a lot of power granted to the boss). Countries that are in the same circled-in area tend to be similar in terms of individualism/collectivism and power distance. Figure 19.1 illustrates that U.S. multinational firms doing business in Mexico would encounter much greater cultural differences than they would in France and still less if they operated in Great Britain.

In general, Hofstede found that wealthy countries have higher individualism scores and poorer countries have higher collectivism. An exception would be Japan and, since Hofstede gathered his data, the other newly industrialized Asian countries, which have relatively high collectivism, but are now quite well off. The collectivism cultural dimension would be more compatible with the new emphasis on teams in the workplace and might help explain why they work so well in Japan, but may not in the United States. However, small power distance cultures such as that of the United States may be more compatible with newly emerging decentralization, flat structures, and empowerment dimensions of today's organizations.

Uncertainty Avoidance. Another dimension of cultural difference is uncertainty avoidance. Uncertainty avoidance is the extent to which people feel threatened by ambiguous situations and the degree to which they try to avoid these situations by doing such things as:

- Providing greater career stability.
- Establishing more formal rules.
- Rejecting deviant ideas and behavior.
- Accepting the possibility of absolute truths and the attainment of expertise.[19]

In Japan, for example, where lifetime employment exists in at least the large companies, there is high uncertainty avoidance. In the United States, by contrast, where there traditionally has been relatively high job mobility, there is low uncertainty avoidance. Also in Japan, as shown in the accompanying International Application Example: New Rules in Japan Are on the Way, the government has traditionally tried to reduce the uncertainty for business. However, as is the case with lifetime employment, this uncertainty avoidance climate for businesses in Japan may be changing as the Japanese try to recover from their economic downturn and attempt to have a more ethical trade relationship with the United States and other countries.

Figure 19.2 shows the position of selected countries on power distance and uncertainty avoidance. Countries like Great Britain, which has weak uncertainty avoidance and small power distance, tend to have less hierarchy and more interaction between people. Additionally, risk taking is both expected and encouraged. Employees in large power distance and weak uncertainty avoidance cultures such as India tend to think of their organizations as traditional families. Employees in countries such as Mexico and Brazil tend to think of their organizations as pyramids of people rather than as families. Employees in countries such as Austria and Finland tend to work in organizations that are highly predictable without needing a strong hierarchy. Roles and procedures are clearly defined in these cultures.

Masculinity/Femininity. Hofstede also measured the impact of masculinity/ femininity. Masculinity is the extent to which the dominant values of a society emphasize assertiveness and the acquisition of money and other material things.

New Rules in Japan Are on the Way

Over the years, the Japanese government-business relationship has been much different from that in the United States. The Japanese government has long protected local businesses from foreign competition and has proactively helped them sell abroad. Now it appears that there is going to be a dramatic change in this protectionist position of the Japanese government. There appear to be two major reasons for this change in Japanese government-business relations.

First, Japanese customers have long paid higher retail prices than any other major industrial power because the lack of foreign competition allowed local firms to set extremely high prices. For example, a six-pack of beer in Japan in 1993 cost around $13. Moreover, while this type of situation might attract local competition in the United States, in Japan the government requires that breweries produce at least 525,000 gallons annually. So small brewers cannot challenge the major beer makers. Now, however, it appears that the government is going to radically change the monopoly hold that large firms have on local buyers. Examples of some of the changes the Japanese government is considering that will affect local business include (a) the removal of load limits on trucks, so that larger vehicles can haul more produce at a cheaper price; (b) an end to mandatory leasing of cellular phones, so that customers can now buy the units directly and save money in the long run; (c) an extension of supermarket hours, so that large units can compete more effectively with their small, higher-priced competitors; and (d) an easing of restrictions on imported building materials.

Second, there is going to be a dramatic change in the way Japan conducts foreign trade. The U.S. government, in particular, is making it clear that it will no longer wait for the Japanese to slowly open their markets to foreign competition. There is going to be a more fair exchange arrangement under which access to U.S. markets will be dictated, at least in part, by access to Japanese markets. This marks a clear break with the past, when the U.S. government was content to merely try to persuade the Japanese to remove their very restrictive import trade barriers.

Many Japanese people and small businesses confess that they do not understand why foreign governments are continuing to put pressure on them to change their business practices. However, large Japanese multinational firms see the problem quite clearly and know that their restrictive policies have long been regarded as at least being unfair, if not downright unethical, in the eyes of other countries. As a result, there will have to be major changes made if Japan hopes to continue its winning ways. As one observer recently put it: "At last, the U.S. is singing out of one hymn book on trade. Japan may not like the words, but there's no mistaking the melody."

Femininity is the term used by Hofstede that refers to the extent to which the dominant values in a society emphasize relationships among people, concern for others, and interest in quality of work life. As shown in Figure 19.3, in masculine societies with strong uncertainty avoidance such as Japan, the managers tend to be very assertive and materialistic. In feminine societies such as Scandinavian countries like Norway the work force in factories is concerned with quality of work life.

Overall Categories for Employee Attitudes Worldwide. Figures 19.1, 19.2, and 19.3 show how countries tend to cluster on the basis of particular cultural differences. On an overall employee attitude basis, one comprehensive analysis using eight empirical studies concluded that there are eight basic clusters in which most countries

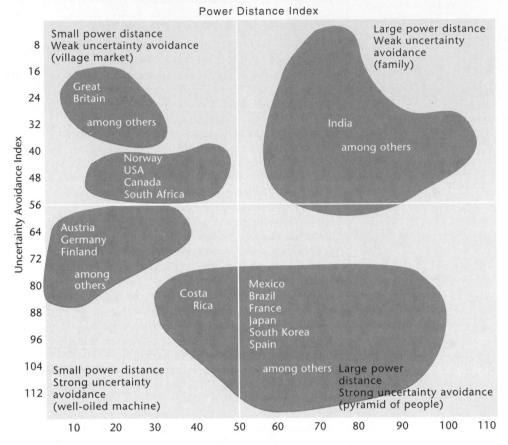

Power Distance Index

Uncertainty Avoidance Index

Small power distance
Weak uncertainty avoidance
(village market)

Great
Britain

among others

Norway
USA
Canada
South Africa

Large power distance
Weak uncertainty
avoidance
(family)

India

among others

Austria
Germany
Finland

among
others

Costa
Rica

Mexico
Brazil
France
Japan
South Korea
Spain

among others

Small power distance
Strong uncertainty
avoidance
(well-oiled machine)

Large power
distance
Strong uncertainty avoidance
(pyramid of people)

FIGURE 19.2
The position of selected countries on power distance and uncertainty avoidance.
(*Source*: Adapted from Geert Hofstede, "The Cultural Relativity of Organizational Practices and Theories," *Journal of International Business Studies*, Fall 1983, p. 84. Used with permission.)

of the world can be placed. These country clusters are shown in Figure 19.4. Countries which do not fit into one of the clusters include Brazil, Japan, India, and Israel. These countries appear in different clusters in different studies so, at least for the time being, more research will have to be conducted before they can be assigned to any specific cluster.[20]

As one would guess, the general attitudes of U.S. employees (work goals, values, needs, and job attitudes) are most culturally similar to those of employees in other "Anglo" countries—Canada, Australia, New Zealand, United Kingdom, Ireland, and South Africa. In addition, the theories and application techniques of organizational behavior discussed in the U.S.-based literature will probably be relevant in the Anglo countries. However, when U.S. managers are dealing with employees from other clusters—Germanic, Nordic, Near Eastern, Arab, Far Eastern, Latin American, or Independent—they must recognize there will be differences.

There is accumulating research on various dimensions of organizational behavior that supports both similarities and differences across cultures. For example, one recent study found that cultural factors do not explain the differences in modesty bias in self-ratings of performance (self-ratings that were lower than supervisory ratings).[21] However, the majority of recent studies do find that culture plays a dominant role in organizational behavior. For example, recent cross-cultural studies have

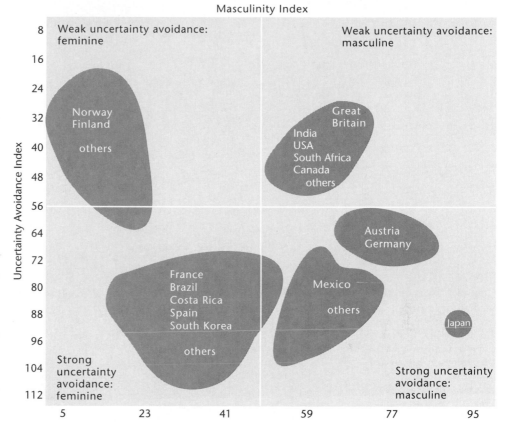

FIGURE 19.3
The position of selected countries on uncertainty avoidance and masculinity/femininity. *(Source*: Adapted from Geert Hofstede, "The Cultural Relativity of Organizational Practices and Theories," *Journal of International Business Studies*, Fall 1983, p. 86. Used with permission.)

shown a cultural impact on Eastern values,[22] stress,[23] performance in groups,[24] participation in decision making,[25] and executive reward systems.[26]

Before leaving the discussion of the impact of culture on organizational behavior, one should note that the differences associated with the cultural groupings identified by Hofstede and the country clusters in Figure 19.4 are changing with time. For instance, countries such as Japan and Korea may be moving closer to the Anglo cluster. There is already considerable evidence that this is happening with Japanese consumers, who are increasingly upset that their standard of living doesn't reflect Japan's national wealth.[27] This frustration is being carried over to the workplace as well. The following story told by a Japanese management expert when he went to a nearly empty barber shop in downtown Tokyo on a Saturday afternoon is very revealing about the changing attitudes of Japanese workers:

"Not many customers today, are there?" I said, relieved that I did not have to wait.
"That's right. Lately, business has been off Saturdays."
"When are you busiest?"
"Well, these days, around eleven, then around two or three in the afternoon on weekdays."
"But everyone around here must be working then. You mean during working hours?" I asked in disbelief.

FIGURE 19.4
Country clusters based on employee attitude. (*Source*: Simcha Ronen and Oded Shenkar, "Clustering Countries on Attitudinal Dimensions: A Review and Synthesis," *Academy of Management Review*, July 1985, p. 449. Used with permission.)

"That's right. People these days don't want to spend their *own time* on things like haircuts."

"And in the past?"

"Well, a decade ago, we'd be busiest during the luncheon break and after five o'clock. Customers would rush to finish in less than 40 minutes."[28]

The recent widespread violent strikes and political protests in Korea, where workers and students are demanding their share of the economic gains, also are indicative of shifting attitudes and values in that fast-developing country.[29]

The rest of this chapter examines whether the cross-cultural similarities and differences do or will have an impact on the generally recognized organizational behavior areas of communication, motivation, and leadership.

COMMUNICATION IN AN INTERNATIONAL ENVIRONMENT

Although Chapter 15 discusses all dimensions of communication, communication can be used here to demonstrate the impact of the international context. For example, the people at the home office of a multinational corporation (MNC) and the nationals in the foreign branch or subsidiary may not have the same meanings for the same words. An example is that Japanese managers rarely come out with a direct "no" to another's request. A way they avoid saying "no" is to say "yes" and then follow the affirmative answer with a detailed explanation which in effect means "no."[30] The following sections examine some of the breakdowns in and ways to improve communication across cultures.

Communication Breakdown across Cultures

There are a number of contributing factors leading to communication breakdown across cultures. Perhaps the best way to get at the root causes of this breakdown is through the concepts of perception, stereotyping, and ethnocentrism.

Perceptual Problems. Chapter 4 is devoted specifically to perception, which is simply portrayed as a person's interpretation of reality and is said to be learned. People are taught to "see" things in a given way. For example, a U.S. manager who sees the wife of a Latin American host enter the door of the kitchen assumes that the woman is putting the finishing touches on the meal. Unknown to the manager perhaps is the fact that the woman actually is supervising the cooking of the food and is checking to see that everything is in order. If the American were to tell the host's wife, "You're a terrific cook," the comments probably would be greeted with a smile because the hosts would realize the U.S. manager did not mean to be rude. However, a fellow Latin guest would never say this to the wife for it would imply that the hosts were too poor to afford a cook.

Stereotyping Problems. Another barrier to communication is stereotyping, also covered in Chapter 4, which is the tendency to perceive another person as belonging to a single class or category. Stereotyping is a very simple, widely used way of constructing an assumed overall profile of other people. For example, ask people from the United States which people try to "keep a stiff upper lip during trying times" and the most common answer is the British. Ask people from the United States what country of the world is famous for its auto engineering and the most common answer is Germany. Whether or not these are accurate stereotypes is immaterial. Most people from the United States believe them. Similarly, those from other countries have their own stereotyped views of people in the United States. Table 19.5 provides some examples. Note from the table that those in the United States are regarded as energetic and industrious by most nations and none of these countries stereotype people in the United States as being lazy.

Ethnocentric Problems. Ethnocentrism refers to the sense of superiority that members of a particular culture have. Those from many countries, for example, claim that people in the United States believe they are the best in everything regardless of what area is under discussion. To the extent that this is true, it is an example of ethnocentrism in action. All societies promote ethnocentrism through their value structures and nationalistic spirit. People are taught the "right" way to do things, and, at least for them, it is regarded as the "best" way as well. When people interact with each other on an international basis, ethnocentrism can cause communication problems. Here is an example:

> U.S. executives who consider English to be the "best" or the "most logical" language will not apply themselves to learn a foreign language which they consider "inferior" or "illogical." And if they consider their nonverbal system to be the most "civilized" system, they will tend to reject other systems as "primitive." In this sense, ethnocentrism can constitute a formidable block to effective empathy and can lead not only to a complete communication breakdown but also to antagonism, or even hostility.[31]

TABLE 19.5 How Those in the United States Are Seen by People of Other Countries

Characteristics Most Often Associated with Those in the United States:		
France	**Japan**	**Germany**
Industrious	Nationalistic	Energetic
Energetic	Friendly	Inventive
Inventive	Decisive	Friendly
Decisive	Rude	Sophisticated
Friendly	Self-indulgent	Intelligent

Characteristics Least Often Associated with Those in the United States:		
France	**Japan**	**Germany**
Lazy	Industrious	Lazy
Rude	Lazy	Sexy
Honest	Honest	Greedy
Sophisticated	Sexy	Rude

Characteristics Most Often Associated with Those in the United States:		
Great Britain	**Brazil**	**Mexico**
Friendly	Intelligent	Industrious
Self-indulgent	Inventive	Intelligent
Energetic	Energetic	Inventive
Industrious	Industrious	Decisive
Nationalistic	Greedy	Greedy

Characteristics Least Often Associated with Those in the United States:		
Great Britain	**Brazil**	**Mexico**
Lazy	Lazy	Lazy
Sophisticated	Self-indulgent	Honest
Sexy	Sexy	Rude
Decisive	Sophisticated	Sexy

Source: Newsweek, July 11, 1983, p. 50.

Ethnocentrism can lead to ethical problems and disputes between countries. As the accompanying International Application Example: Reaching a Win-Win Solution in China points out, the United States and China have had some serious disagreements over a number of issues in recent years. Because of their ethnocentric views, each side thinks it is right in areas such as human rights and selling armaments.

Improving Communication Effectiveness across Cultures

How can people doing business in other countries sensitize themselves to the culture of these nations and avoid making mistakes? One of the most effective ways is by learning about the culture of that country before going there. Some firms have developed "cultural assimilator" training programs. These programmed learning approaches ask the participants to read about a particular situation and then choose one of four courses of action or type of language that they would use. After the participants have made the choice, they then immediately learn if it was right or wrong, along with an explanation. By being put through a couple of hundred situations that they are likely to encounter in the foreign country, they become somewhat sensitized to the culture of that country and are able to communicate more effectively. There is even evidence that speaking the language correctly is not enough. Pronunciation and accent are even important. More and more foreign-born man-

Reaching a Win-Win Solution in China

Dealing with other countries can present a number of ethical problems for people in the United States. China (PRC) provides a good example. A number of countries, including the United States, not only have been very concerned about human rights issues in China but also have been insisting that it is unethical for the Chinese to sell armaments to other nations. The issue of selling armaments is of such importance to the U.S. that if the matter is not resolved satisfactorily, there is the real possibility of economic sanctions. If this were as clear-cut as it appears on the surface, the armament issue would lead the United States to employ the sanctions and the rest of the world would applaud. However, there is another side to the issue. While it is true that the Chinese have sold armaments to Pakistan, it is equally true that the U.S. government approved the sale of F-17 jet fighters to Taiwan, a decision that the Chinese mainland government had vigorously opposed. So it seems that there is something of a stalemate here, with each side accusing the other of questionable ethical behavior.

Although the armament issue appears to be at the political level, there are some business firms that are caught in the middle. AT&T and Cray Research Inc. are two such companies. AT&T would like to sell telephone equipment to the Chinese. There is a very attractive multi-billion-dollar market in China for AT&T products. Cray needs to sell its large supercomputers and the Chinese appear quite willing to buy. However, if the U.S. government applies trade sanctions against the Chinese, these and other U.S. business deals will dry up. Although the resolution of such issues is beyond any one business firm, the firms must still plan for the contingencies. They can also urge political leaders on both sides to resolve such issues equitably. For the moment, any retaliatory action by one can easily be met by the other and each side will be the economic loser. The best way to handle the situation appears to be through continued dialogue and improved communication effectiveness to get to a win-win solution.

agers' careers are being stalled because they have thick accents, even though their grammar and vocabulary skills are good.[32]

A second, and often complementary, approach is to provide the trainee with educational background material on the country, including social structure, religion, values, language, and history. In particular, these training programs are designed to help managers going to a foreign assignment create the right climate between themselves and those with whom they will be communicating. Table 19.6 provides an example of some of the behaviors U.S. managers typically are taught to help build a climate of trust with their subordinates in a host country and those behaviors which should be avoided. Recent research indicates that both types of training methods have additive benefits in preparing managers for intercultural work assignments[33] and that cross-cultural training in general is quite effective.[34] As the Dutch leader of successful workshops on "multicultural" management recently concluded:

> If you don't figure out basics of a foreign culture, you won't get much accomplished. And if your biases lead you to think of foreign ways as childish, the foreigners may well respond by acting childish.[35]

MOTIVATION ACROSS CULTURES

Besides communication, motivation is of central importance in the study and application of international organizational behavior. After first examining the question of whether motivation theories and approaches hold across cultures, this

TABLE 19.6 Managing Cultural Climate

Behaviors That Help *Build* a Trust Climate	Behaviors That Help *Preclude* a Trust Climate
1. Express your doubts, concerns, and feelings in an open, natural way. Encourage your subordinates to do so also.	1. Look on expressions of feelings and doubts as signs of weakness.
2. When subordinates express their doubts, concerns, and feelings, accept them supportively and discuss them thoroughly.	2. Be sarcastic, but cleverly so.
3. Set honesty as one standard that will not be compromised. Demand it from yourself and from your staff.	3. Let your subordinates know that you expect them to "stretch the truth" a little if it will make the organization look good.
4. Be clear about your expectations when assigning work or eliciting opinions. Explain your reasons, wherever possible, behind requests and directions.	4. Be secretive. Never let them really be sure what's on your mind. This keeps them on their toes.
5. Encourage subordinates to look at you as a possible resource in accomplishing results, but develop and reinforce independence.	5. Discourage subordinates from coming to you for help. After all, they should be "stem-winders" and "self-starters."
6. When something goes wrong, determine what happened, not "who did it."	6. When something goes wrong, blow up, hit the ceiling, and look for the guilty party.
7. Encourage active support and participation in corrective measures from those involved.	7. Gossip about and disparage others on the staff when they are not present. Overrespond to casual comments by others about your people.
8. Share credit for successes; assume the bulk of responsibility for criticism of your unit.	8. Take credit for successes. Plan vendettas and other ploys to make other organizations look bad. Draw on subordinates for carrying these out. Always insist on plenty of documentation to protect yourself.

Source: Philip R. Harris and Robert T. Moran, *Managing Cultural Differences*, 2d ed., Gulf Publishing, Houston, 1987, p. 50.

section discusses and analyzes the nature of work and the impact that various cultural dimensions have on motivation.

Do Motivation Theories and Approaches Hold across Cultures?

Chapters 6 and 7 identify the major content and process theories and techniques of motivating human resources. These theories and approaches are almost solely developed in the United States by Americans and about Americans. Nevertheless, there are some research findings indicating that these theories and techniques hold across cultures. For example, one study found that motivational processes such as equity may be found in the United States, Japan, and Korea,[36] and the Russian study cited earlier found that U.S.-based extrinsic reinforcement and behavioral management techniques had a positive impact.[37] However, most cross-cultural researchers emphasize the differences rather than the similarities when discussing the applicability of motivation theories and techniques. For example, after reviewing the cross-cultural motivation literature, Nancy Adler concluded: "American motivation theories, although assumed to be universal, have failed to provide consistently useful explanations outside the United States."[38]

Most of the cross-cultural research on motivation has mainly been limited, to date, to the content theories such as Maslow's hierarchy of needs, Herzberg's two factors, and McClelland's achievement theory (see Chapter 6). The result of this research is that there are definitely variations of these content motivation theories across cultures. For example, since the Chinese stress collective rather than individual needs, it has been suggested that Maslow's hierarchy, from most basic to highest, should be (1) belonging (social); (2) physiological; (3) safety; and (4) self-actualization to society.[39]

The same has been suggested for Herzberg's two factors and McClelland's need for achievement; they need to be recast in light of cultural differences. For example, there is little question that individuals' sense of responsibility and need for achievement differ greatly by culture. Yet, the frameworks of these motivation theories still hold across cultures. That is, the people of all cultures have a hierarchy of needs (Maslow), factors that prevent their dissatisfaction and lead to motivation (Herzberg), and a level of achievement motivation (McClelland). It is not that these theories disappear or are not relevant across cultures, but rather that they have different content and successful application across cultures. In other words, all cultures have a hierarchy of needs, but the ordering of these needs (as in the Chinese example above) may differ by culture.

The same can be said for the process theories of motivation (see Chapter 6). As Adler points out: "Expectancy theories are universal to the extent that they do not specify the types of rewards that motivate a given group of workers."[40] The same could be said for equity, attribution, and reinforcement theories. The motivational process holds across cultures, but the content and successful application will be culture-specific. Thus, the key to the understanding of motivation in the international context is to explore the basic meaning of work and the cultural dimensions that contribute to the possible differences in motivation of people across cultures.

The Meaning of Work

Traditionally in the United States, work has generally been equated with economic rewards. Although Chapter 6 points out that people have diverse needs and individual differences, North Americans can still be generally characterized as working because they want to earn money with which to buy things. Thus, for many North Americans, time on the job is money. This often is reflected in the way they try to get as much done in as little time as possible. North Americans also like to have things spelled out so that they know what is expected of them and by when their tasks are to be accomplished. As Chapter 7 points out, they respond to goals that help improve their performance.

The culturally determined needs help dictate the way those in the United States behave both at home and abroad. Unfortunately, sometimes these behaviors are not regarded in a positive light. Consider some of the following comments made by people from other countries about how people in the United States behave:

India. Americans seem to be in a perpetual hurry. Just watch the way they walk down the street. They never allow themselves the leisure to enjoy life; there are too many things to do.

Colombia. The tendency in the United States to think that life is only work hits you in the face. Work seems to be the one type of motivation.

Ethiopia. The American is very explicit; he wants a "yes" or "no." If someone tries to speak figuratively, the American is confused.

Turkey. Once we were out in a rural area in the middle of nowhere and saw an American come to a stop sign. Though he could see in both directions for miles and no traffic was coming, he still stopped.[41]

Many North Americans still believe in the work ethic. Work is a most dominant and important part of life.[42] Do people in other countries feel the same way? Table 19.7 provides a partial answer to this question. Notice that in all the countries surveyed, work ranked first in terms of its importance in providing income. In Japan and Germany, income was relatively more important than it was to those in the United States. However, in countries such as Israel and the Netherlands, income was of slightly less relative importance but work that was basically interesting and

TABLE 19.7 Average Number of Points Assigned to Working Functions by Country Samples

Country	Working Provides You with an Income That Is Needed	Working Is Basically Interesting and Satisfying to You	Working Permits You to Have Interesting Contacts with Other People	Working Gives You Status and Prestige
Japan	45.4	13.4	14.7	5.6
Germany	40.5	16.7	13.1	10.1
Belgium	35.5	21.3	17.3	6.9
United Kingdom	34.4	17.9	15.3	10.9
United States	33.1	16.8	15.3	11.9
Israel	31.1	26.2	11.1	8.5
Netherlands	26.2	23.5	17.9	4.9
All countries combined	35.0*	19.5	14.3	8.5

* The combined totals weigh each country equally, regardless of sample size.
Source: MOW International Research Team, *The Meaning of Working: An International Perspective*, Academic Press, London and New York, 1985, and reported in Simcha Ronen, *Comparative and Multinational Management*, Wiley, New York, 1986, p. 144.

satisfying was of relatively more importance. In these countries, it would be a mistake to try to motivate employees with financial incentives alone. In other words, while there are some similarities, there are also some motivational differences between employees across cultures.

The role of work in given cultures also changes over time. For example, in recent years because of downsizing and increased competitive pressures facing U.S. firms, the number of hours employees must work has increased. By contrast, the average number of hours Japanese employees work has diminished.[43] In other words, in the early 1990s work became a greater part of the U.S. employees' lives, but a lesser part among Japanese workers.[44] This may change again as Japan tries to bounce back from its economic problems of recent years.

Motivational Differences across Cultures

What contributes to the motivational differences across cultures? The roles of religion, uncertainty avoidance, and power distance provide some insights into this question.

The Role of Religion. One answer to motivational differences across cultures may be found in religions and the accompanying values. For instance, some religious values put emphasis on allowing events to develop in their own way, just letting things happen. An example would be the Hindus in India. Most North Americans, on the other hand, follow religions that teach them to try to control events. Some religions teach that people are reincarnated and will return; most North Americans believe they pass this way only once, so they want to get as much done here and now as they can. Some religions teach the importance of caring for others as much as oneself (collectivism); most North Americans believe that the best way to help others is to ensure one's own success (individualism). These differing religious values may have an indirect and, in some cases, a direct impact on the motivation of the followers.

One international expert recently noted that the old Protestant ethic, which may no longer be dominant in North America and Western European countries, is alive and well in places such as Seoul, Soweto, and Santiago de Chile. He notes that it is operating in these formerly strong Buddhist and Catholic areas of the world much as it did in North America and Western Europe by inculcating religious values and attitudes that are conducive to success in a high-growth, market economy.[45]

The Role of Uncertainty Avoidance. Another contributing factor to motivational differences may revolve around the cultural value of avoiding ambiguity and uncertainty. How willing are people to face uncertainty? How much do they prefer to know what is happening and not take too many risks? If the cultural values of employees make them willing to live with uncertainty, they may be motived quite differently from those who prefer to know what is going on. For example, those who thrive on uncertainty may not have strong job security needs. Or those with a low tolerance for ambiguity and uncertainty may really respond to objective performance feedback. Table 19.8 illustrates a number of specific guidelines that can be followed in dealing with those who can and those who cannot deal with ambiguity and uncertainty.

In light of the present international discussion, this dimension or value of people seems to vary from country to country. Figures 19.2 and 19.3 show that people in Latin countries (both in Europe and South America) generally do not like uncertainty. Neither do those from Mediterranean nations. On the other hand, those from countries such as Denmark, Sweden, Great Britain, Ireland, Canada, and the United States function well under conditions of uncertainty or ambiguity. Asian countries such as Japan and Korea tend to fall between these two extremes.[46]

The Role of Power Distance. Still another contributing factor to motivational differences across cultures may revolve around power distance. Can the people in a particular country accept the fact that others have more power than they, or do they find this difficult to live with? As noted earlier (see Figure 19.3), people in the United States, Britain, Canada, and the Scandinavian countries have trouble accepting that others have more power than they do. On the other hand, people in India, Mexico, Japan, and South Korea do not. Table 19.9 shows some of the ways of managing and organizing both groups.

TABLE 19.8 Ways to Manage People on the Basis of Their Ability to Deal with Uncertainty or Ambiguity

Are Able to Deal with Uncertainty or Ambiguity	Do Not Like to Deal with Uncertainty or Ambiguity
Less structuring of activities	More structuring of activities
Fewer written rules	More written rules
Organizations can take many different forms	Organizations should be as uniform as possible (standardization)
Managers more involved in strategy	Managers more involved in details
Managers more interpersonally oriented and flexible in their style	Managers more task-oriented and consistent in their style
Managers more willing to make individual and risky decisions	Managers less willing to make individual and risky decisions
High labor turnover	Lower labor turnover
More ambitious employees	Less ambitious employees
Lower satisfaction scores	Higher satisfaction scores

Source: Adapted from Geert Hofstede, *Culture's Consequences: International Differences in Work Related Values*, Sage, Beverly Hills, Calif., 1980, p. 187. Copyright © 1980 by Sage Publications, Inc. Used with permission of Sage Publications, Inc.

TABLE 19.9 Ways to Manage People on the Basis of Their Acceptance or Nonacceptance of Power

Are Not Willing to Accept the Fact That Others Have More Power Than They Do	Are Willing to Accept the Fact That Others Have More Power Than They Do
Less centralization	Greater centralization
Flatter organization pyramids	Tall organization pyramids
Smaller proportion of supervisory personnel	Large proportion of supervisory personnel
Manual work same status as clerical work	White-collar jobs valued more than blue-collar jobs

Source: Adapted from Geert Hofstede, *Culture's Consequences: International Differences in Work Related Values*, Sage, Beverly Hills, Calif., 1980, p. 135. Copyright © 1980 by Sage Publications, Inc. Used with permission of Sage Publications Inc.

MANAGERIAL LEADERSHIP ACROSS CULTURES

Like communication and motivation, the important organizational behavior topic of leadership is given earlier detailed attention, in Chapters 13 and 14. Leadership is portrayed as the process of influencing others to direct their efforts toward the pursuit of specific goals.

Because of globalization, leadership takes on added significance. As leadership expert Warren Bennis recently noted: "Given the nature and constancy of change and the transnational challenges facing American business leadership, the key to making the right choices will come from understanding and embodying the leadership qualities necessary to succeed in the volatile and mercurial global economy."[47] In the context of organizational behavior, leadership is mainly concerned with managerial activities and style. Similar to motivation, most of the study of leadership traditionally presented in the field of organizational behavior has come from U.S.-based theories and research samples. Also similar to motivation, the leadership/management activities and styles can be the same across cultures, but the way these approaches to and processes of leadership are used and successfully applied may differ greatly from culture to culture.

Research to date has found both similarities and differences when leadership activities and styles have been examined cross-culturally.[48] For example, the author's (Luthans) Real Managers Study[49] presented in Chapter 14 was replicated in a Russian factory.[50] As shown in Table 19.10, similar to the U.S. managers studied (although the relative frequencies were a little different), the Russian managers in this factory were observed, in order, to perform traditional management, communication, human resources, and networking activities. Also, as was the case with the U.S. manager's studied, the Russian managers' networking activity generally related to their success in the organization. However, the relationship between the Russian managers' various activities and their effectiveness was similar, but less clear.[51]

TABLE 19.10 The Relative Frequencies of Activities of Samples of Managers from a Large Russian Factory and a Cross Section of U.S. Organizations

Managerial Activities	Russian Sample (*N*=66)	U.S. Sample (*N*=248)
Traditional management	42.5%	32%
Communication	34.2%	29%
Human resources management	14.8%	20%
Networking	8.5%	19%

Source: Adapted from Fred Luthans, Dianne H. B. Welsh, and Stuart A. Rosenkrantz, "What Do Russian Managers Really Do? An Observational Study with Comparisons to U.S. Managers," *Journal of International Business Studies*, 4th Quarter, 1993, p. 752. Used with permission.

Although cross-cultural generalizations cannot be made on the basis of one study, the study can serve as a microcosm for beginning to better understand how Russian and U.S. managers are similar and different. On a broader scale, there are a number of possible contributing factors to the differences in effective managerial leadership across cultures. Some of the more important, and those which have been researched, include personal values, the manager's background, interpersonal skills, and decision making.

Personal Values

Managers' personal values help shape their perception of a situation, influence their analysis of alternative solutions to a problem, and have an effect on the ultimate decision. The followers' personal values will also influence their manager. How they accept authority—their power distance—and their loyalty and commitment are examples. Such personal values on the part of both managers and subordinates will differ across cultures. For example, research by George England and his colleagues found that North American and Japanese managers tend to be very pragmatic. Their personal values emphasize productivity, profitability, and achievement. Managers from India, on the other hand, tend to be less pragmatic and more moralistic. Their values emphasize equity, fairness, and the overall good of the work force.[52]

Managers' Background

Managers' background may also influence the way their subordinates are led. Research shows that U.S. managers come from all economic strata: lower, middle, and upper.[53] An increasingly large percentage are college-educated, but because performance is important to promotion, there is no guarantee that attending a certain school will lead to success. Although graduates of Ivy League schools and other prestigious institutions may have an advantage, many U.S. managers from all types and sizes of colleges have made it into the upper ranks. The same pattern may not be as true in other countries. For example, in France managers often are chosen from the graduates of the *grandes écoles*. In Japan, those who gain entrance into the prestigious schools have a much better chance of becoming top managers of the large corporations. In Korea, surprisingly perhaps, many of the newly emerging managerial leaders have been educated in the United States. Traditionally, under the communist-ruled Eastern European countries, career advancement in management was dependent on engineering or technical education and experience. Now, as these countries make the transition to a democratically based market economy, there is a rush toward Western-style management education.[54]

Besides educational background, class and family background also make a difference. In the United States, managers come from all classes. However, in Turkey, many of the top managers come from the upper class. In Poland, most of the business leaders come from the lower middle class. In Argentina and Peru, business leaders come from the middle class. In Chile, the landed aristocracy are the managerial leaders.

At the same time, family upbringing is important. For example, in India, it is common to accept the authority of elders. Thus, in superior-subordinate relations there is generally little delegation of authority. Instead, the head of the enterprise exercises a directive leadership style and everyone follows these orders. In the United States, on the other hand, where managers come from all classes, are relatively well educated, and have a liberal upbringing, there is more of an emphasis on participatory decision making and delegation of authority. This background will influence the way the manager exercises leadership.

Interpersonal Skills

There is research evidence that managers differ across cultures in their interpersonal skills. For example, Bass and Burger conducted a comprehensive study of managers in the United States, Belgium, Britain, France, Germany-Austria, Iberia, India, Japan, Latin America, and Scandinavia. Some of their relevant findings in relation to interpersonal styles and skills include the following:

- Spanish and Portuguese managers were most willing to be aware of others' feelings; to be concerned with their subordinates' welfare; and to accept feedback from others. The Germans, Austrians, and French were less willing to do these things. The other countries fell between these two extremely different groups.
- Managers from India were the most concerned about bureaucratic rules; the Japanese were the least concerned.
- Managers from India saw themselves as most dependent on higher authority. German and Austrian managers viewed themselves as very independent.
- Dutch managers were the most willing to cooperate with others; the French were the least willing.
- Japanese managers had a greater desire to be objective rather than intuitive than did managers from any other country.
- Japanese and Dutch managers were most locked in by group commitments and were less likely to deviate from their initial positions. Managers from the United States and Latin America showed the least commitment to their group positions, were able to reach compromises faster than the other groups, and were deadlocked much less often.
- U.S. and Latin American managers demonstrated much greater interpersonal competence than other managers.[55]

What the above once again demonstrates is that interpersonal approaches differ by culture. A U.S. supervisor on an oil rig in Indonesia learned this the hard way. In a moment of anger, he shouted at his timekeeper to take the next boat to shore. Immediately, a mob of outraged Indonesian coworkers grabbed fire axes and went after the supervisor. He saved himself by barricading himself in his quarters. The cultural lesson this American learned: Never berate an Indonesian in public.[56]

International joint ventures (IJVs) also lead to many interpersonal conflicts between members of the same company from vastly different cultures. For example, local managers of IJVs may become frustrated by the lack of promotion opportunities to key jobs if senior positions are reserved for "outsiders" or those whose loyalty lies not with the current IJV but with the parent company. In such instances, conflicts may arise that prevent full cooperation among the staff.[57]

Decision Making

Besides interpersonal skills, managerial leadership is also often expressed through decision-making skills. Chapter 16 gives specific attention to this function of management. Decision making is simply portrayed as the process of choosing between alternatives. However, how managers make these decisions differs across cultures.

For example, research by Heller and Yukl has found that in Argentina, Chile, and Uruguay authority is equated with rapid decision making and speed is more important than generating information or carefully analyzing the data.[58]

Boards of directors in these Latin countries often hold meetings without pre-circulating the minutes of the last meeting or the agenda of the current one. Other researchers have found that Latin American managers also often fail to plan and rely heavily on intuition or improvisation based on emotional arguments and justifications in making their decisions.[59] Some of them also put off decisions, preferring a "wait and see" attitude that results in eventually having to use stopgap measures to prevent the situation from getting worse.

Other research has found that managers in the United States, Germany, and Sweden tend to emphasize rationality in their decision making.[60] The Japanese, on the other hand, try to balance a concern for rationality and objectivity with the desire for group acceptance and consensus. In the Japanese system, decision making tends to flow from the bottom up. All members of the firm share the responsibility for decisions. After reaching a consensus, the originating group sends its decision to other groups for approval. The more important the decision, the higher it goes for approval within the hierarchy. This is in contrast to the U.S. system in which decisions tend to flow from the top down and individuals, although they may be in a group or committee framework, play a more significant role.

Transnationally Competent Managers

As the new millennium draws nearer, it is becoming increasingly clear that traditionally conceived and practiced international management leadership is no longer sufficient. Adler and her colleagues have identified some of the transnational skills that are needed for the newly emerging global economy. Summarized in Table 19.11, the competencies for the transnational manager go well beyond the traditional approaches used by international managers.

TABLE 19.11 Transnationally Competent Managers

Transnational Skills	Transnationally Competent Managers	Traditional International Managers
Global perspective	Understand worldwide business environment from a global perspective	Focus on a single foreign country and on managing relationships between headquarters and that country
Local responsiveness	Learn about many cultures	Become an expert on one culture
Synergistic learning	Work with and learn from people from many cultures simultaneously	Work with and coach people in each foreign culture separately or sequentially
	Create a culturally synergistic organizational environment.	Integrate foreigners into the headquarters' national organizational culture
Transition and adaptation	Adapt to living in many foreign cultures	Adapt to living in a foreign culture
Cross-cultural interaction	Use cross-cultural interaction skills on a daily basis throughout one's career	Use cross-cultural interaction skills primarily on foreign assignments
Collaboration	Interact with foreign colleagues as equals	Interact within clearly defined hierarchies of structural and cultural dominance
Foreign experience	Transpatriation for career and organization development	Expatriation or inpatriation primarily to get the job done

Source: Nancy J. Adler and Susan Bartholomew, "Managing Globally Competent People," *Academy of Management Executive*, August 1992, p. 54. Used with permission.

The sensitivity to cultural difference and an understanding of the dimensions of communication, motivation, and leadership, as discussed in this chapter, can go a long way toward making a manager transnationally competent. More specifically, Adler and Bartholomew suggest that transnationally competent managers must:

1. Understand the worldwide business environment from a global, rather than a single-country, perspective.
2. Learn about many foreign cultures' perspectives, tastes, trends, technologies, and approaches to conducting business.
3. Be skillful at working with people from many different cultures simultaneously.
4. Be able to adapt to not only living in other cultures but also using cross-cultural skills on regular multicultural business trips and in daily interaction with foreign colleagues and clients worldwide.
5. Interact with foreign colleagues as equals, rather than from within clearly defined hierarchies of structural or cultural dominance and subordination.[61]

This profile of the transnationally competent manager serves as a point of departure for research and guidelines for the successful practice and application of leadership in the international arena now and in the future.

Summary

The international context in which organizational behavior operates is becoming increasingly important as organizations expand beyond their national boundaries. Few would question that there is now a global economy and that cultural differences must be recognized in the study and understanding of organizational behavior.

The chapter starts off by defining culture, which is the acquired knowledge that people use to interpret experience and generate social behavior. Whereas the previous chapter focuses on organizational culture per se, this chapter more directly aims at the culture of overall societies and countries. Although it must be remembered that it is difficult to make generalizations because of the many subcultures operating in societies and countries, there are several dimensions of culture that do pretty well describe societal orientations. These dimensions are identified in the chapter as follows: how people see themselves; people's relationship to their world; individualism versus collectivism; the time dimension; and public and private space. These dimensions lead to organizational behavior differences across cultures. There are many reasons for these differences. The chapter draws heavily from the research of Hofstede, who found that people tend to differ on the basis of individualism/collectivism, power distance, uncertainty avoidance, and masculinity/femininity.

The remainder of the chapter analyzes the major organizational behavior topics of communication, motivation, and managerial leadership across cultures. Communication in an international environment often is influenced by a number of factors such as perception, stereotyping, and ethnocentrism. In helping their managers deal with these communication problems, some companies have developed cultural assimilator training programs.

Another problem in the understanding and application of organizational behavior across cultures is exemplified by the important topic of motivation. What accounts for motivational differences across cultures? A number of factors can be cited, including religion, uncertainty avoidance, and the ways in which the society deals with power acceptance.

Managerial leadership involves influencing others to direct their efforts toward the pursuit of specific goals. There are a number of factors across cultures that influence the way in which managers lead their subordinates. Some of these factors are personal values, the manager's background, interpersonal skills, and decision making. Each of these is discussed in the chapter. When available, research evidence is used to support the conclusions.

The chapter concludes with the profile of the transnationally competent manager. This prototype manager goes beyond the more limited traditional international manager by having a broader, transnational perspective and day-to-day cross-cultural skills. Such an approach to management is, and will continue to be, needed in the global economy.

Questions for Discussion and Review

1. In your own words, what is meant by the term "culture"? How does it differ from "organizational culture"?
2. What are some basic dimensions that describe the cultural orientation of a society? Briefly describe each.
3. In what way do individualism/collectivism, power distance, uncertainty avoidance, and masculinity/femininity help explain cultural differences? Define and give examples of these dimensions.
4. How do perception, stereotyping, and ethnocentrism affect communicating with employees across cultures?
5. How can multinational corporations sensitize their managers to the cultures of host countries before sending them on international assignments?
6. How does work differ in the meaning it takes on in the United States and in other countries? Is the role of work changing?
7. What accounts for some of the motivational differences between employees across cultures?
8. What are some of the major factors that influence the managerial leadership process across cultures?
9. Describe the profile of the transnationally competent manager. How does this profile differ from that of the traditional international manager, and why is this transnational approach now needed?

Footnote References and Supplemental Readings

1. For example, see Christopher A. Bartlett and Sumantra Ghoshal, *Managing Across Borders*, Harvard Business School Press, Boston, 1991; Magoroh Maruyama, "Changing Dimensions in International Business," *Academy of Management Executive*, August 1992, pp. 88–96; and Koh Sera, "Corporate Globalization: A New Trend," *Academy of Management Executive*, February 1992, pp. 89–96.
2. See Nancy J. Adler, *International Dimensions of Organizational Behavior*, 2d ed., PWS-Kent, Boston, 1993.
3. See Peter J. Dowling, Randall S. Schuler, and Denice E. Welch, *International Dimensions of Human Resource Management*, 2d ed., Wadsworth, Belmont, Calif., 1994, and Randall S. Schuler, Peter J. Dowling, and Helen De Cieri, "An Integrative Framework of Strategic International Human Resource Management," *Journal of Management*, vol. 19, 1993, pp. 419–459.
4. Bob Hagerty, "Trainers Help Expatriate Employees Build Bridges to Different Cultures," *The Wall Street Journal*, June 14, 1993, p. B1.

5. Charles J. Cox and Cary L. Cooper, "The Irrelevance of American Organizational Sciences to the UK and Europe," *Journal of General Management*, Winter 1985, pp. 29–30.

6. Dianne H. B. Welsh, Fred Luthans, and Steven M. Sommer, "Managing Russian Factory Workers: The Impact of U.S.-Based Behavioral and Participative Techniques," *Academy of Management Journal*, February 1993, pp. 58–79.

7. Lisa A. Mainiero, "Participation? Nyet: Rewards and Praise? Da!" *Academy of Management Executive*, August 1993, p. 87.

8. David G. Myers, *Social Psychology*, 3d ed., McGraw-Hill, New York, 1990, pp. 226–227.

9. Quoted in Nancy J. Adler, Robert Doktor, and S. Gordon Redding, "From the Atlantic to the Pacific Century: Cross-Cultural Management Reviewed," *Journal of Management*, vol. 12, no. 2, 1986, p. 295.

10. Daniel C. Feldman and Holly B. Thompson, "Entry Shock, Culture Shock: Socializing the New Breed of Global Managers," *Human Resource Management*, Winter 1992, pp. 345–362.

11. Richard G. Linowes, "The Japanese Manager's Traumatic Entry into the United States: Understanding the American-Japanese Cultural Divide," *Academy of Management Executive*, November 1993, p. 21.

12. Adler, op. cit., p. 23.

13. Mark Maremont, "Eastern Europe's Big Cleanup," *Business Week*, Mar. 19, 1990, pp. 114–115.

14. Geert Hofstede, *Cultures and Organizations: Software of the Mind*, McGraw-Hill U.K., London, 1991.

15. Jacquelyn B. Schriber and Barbara A. Gutek, "Some Time Dimensions of Work: Measurement of an Underlying Aspect of Organization Culture," *Journal of Applied Psychology*, vol. 72, 1987, pp. 642–650.

16. Geert Hofstede, *Culture's Consequences: International Differences in Work Related Values*, Sage, Beverly Hills, Calif., 1980. For a recent review and extension of Hofstede's work, see Robert G. Westwood and James E. Everett, "Culture's Consequences: A Methodology for Comparative Management Studies in Southeast Asia?" *Asia Pacific Journal of Management*, May 1987, pp. 187–202, and his more recent book, Geert Hofstede, *Cultures and Organizations: Software of the Mind*, McGraw-Hill U.K., London, 1991.

17. Hofstede, *Cultures and Organizations*, pp. 251–252.

18. Derek S. Pugh and David J. Hickson, *Writers on Organizations*, 4th ed., Sage, Newbury Park, Calif., 1989, p. 94.

19. Adler, op. cit., p. 52.

20. Simcha Ronen, *Comparative and Multinational Management*, Wiley, New York, 1986, pp. 266–267.

21. Jiayuan Yu and Kevin R. Murphy, "Modesty Bias in Self-Ratings of Performance: A Test of the Cultural Relativity Hypothesis," *Personnel Psychology*, Summer 1993, pp. 357–364.

22. David A. Ralston, Priscilla M. Elsass, David J. Gustafson, Fanny Cheung, and Robert H. Terpstra, "Eastern Values: A Comparison of Managers in the United States, Hong Kong, and the People's Republic of China," *Journal of Applied Psychology*, October 1992, pp. 664–671.

23. Bruce D. Kirkcaldy and Cary L. Cooper, "The Relationship Between Work Stress and Leisure Style: British and German Managers," *Human Relations*, May 1993, pp. 669–680.

24. P. Christopher Earley, "East Meets West Meets Mideast: Further Explorations of Collectivistic and Individualistic Work Groups," *Academy of Management Journal*, April 1993, pp. 319–348.

25. Dean M. McFarlin, Paul D. Sweeney, and John L. Cotton, "Attitudes Toward Employee Participation in Decision-Making: A Comparison of European and American Managers in a United States Multinational Company," *Human Resource Management*, Winter 1992, pp. 363–383.

26. Johannes M. Pennings, "Executive Reward Systems: A Cross-National Comparison," *Journal of Management Studies*, March 1993, pp. 261–280, and Richard M. Hodgetts and Fred Luthans, "U.S. Multinationals' Compensation Strategies for Local Management: Cross Cultural Implications," *Compensation & Benefits Review*, March–April 1993, pp. 42–48.

27. Barbara Buell, "Japan's Silent Majority Starts to Mumble," *Business Week*, Apr. 23, 1990, p. 52.

28. Kenichi Ohmae, "Japan's Role in the World Economy," *California Management Review*, Spring 1987, p. 54.

29. Laxmi Nakarmi, "The Korean Tiger Has All But Lost Its Claws," *Business Week*, Apr. 30, 1990, pp. 40–41.

30. Don Hellriegel, John W. Slocum, and Richard W. Woodman, *Organizational Behavior*, 4th ed., West, St. Paul, Minn., 1986, p. 219.

31. Adnan Almaney, "Intercultural Communication and the MNC Executive," *Columbia Journal of World Business*, Winter 1974, p. 27.

32. "Lose That Thick Accent to Gain Career Ground," *The Wall Street Journal*, Jan. 4, 1990, p. B1.

33. P. Christopher Earley, "Intercultural Training for Managers: A Comparison of Documentary and Interpersonal Methods," *Academy of Management Journal*, December 1987, pp. 685–698.

34. J. Stewart Black and Mark Mendenhall, "Cross Cultural Training Effectiveness: A Review and a Theoretical Framework for Future Research," *Academy of Management Review*, January 1990, pp. 113–136.

35. Hagerty, op. cit., p. B6.

36. Ken I. Kim, Hun-Joon Park, Nori Suzuki, "Reward Allocations in the United States, Japan, and Korea: A

Comparison of Individualistic and Collectionistic Cultures," *Academy of Management Journal*, March 1990, pp. 188–198.

37. Welsh et. al., loc. cit.

38. Adler, op. cit., p. 160.

39. Edwin C. Nevis, "Cultural Assumption and Productivity: The United States and China," *Sloan Management Review*, Spring 1983, pp. 17–29.

40. Adler, op. cit., p. 159.

41. Adler, op. cit., pp. 77, 79.

42. Robert A. Baron, *Behavior in Organizations*, 2d ed., Allyn & Bacon, Boston, 1986, p. 150.

43. Tim W. Ferguson, "Japan's Buffeted Banks—and U.S. Opportunity: Long on Jobs," *The Wall Street Journal*, Feb. 25, 1992, p. A15.

44. Christopher J. Chipello, "Japan's Quality of Life," *The Wall Street Journal*, Jan. 28, 1992, p. A9.

45. Professor Peter Berger, quoted in "What Is Culture's Role in Economic Policy?" *The Wall Street Journal*, Dec. 22, 1986, p. 1.

46. Ronen, op. cit., p. 170.

47. Warren G. Bennis, "Managing the Dream: Leadership in the 21st Century," *Journal of Organizational Change Management*, vol. 2, no. 1, 1989, p. 7.

48. For a review of this literature, see Richard M. Hodgetts and Fred Luthans, *International Management*, 2d ed., McGraw-Hill, New York, 1994, Chap. 14.

49. See Fred Luthans, Richard M. Hodgetts, and Stuart A. Rosenkrantz, *Real Managers*, Ballinger, Cambridge, Mass., 1988.

50. Fred Luthans, Dianne H. B. Welsh, and Stuart A. Rosenkrantz, "What Do Russian Managers Really Do? An Observational Study with Comparisons to U.S. Managers," *Journal of International Business Studies*, 4th Quarter, 1993, pp. 741–761.

51. Ibid.

52. George W. England, O. P. Dhingra, and Naresh C. Agarwal, *The Manager and the Man: A Cross-Cultural Study of Personal Values*, Kent State University Press, Kent, Ohio, 1974, p. 30.

53. David C. McClelland, *The Achieving Society*, Van Nostrand, Princeton, N.J., 1961.

54. See Sheila M. Puffer, *The Russian Management Revolution*, M. E. Sharpe, Armonk, N.Y., 1992; Avraham Shama, "Management Under Fire: The Transformation of Managers in the Soviet Union and Eastern Europe," *Academy of Management Executive*, February 1993, pp. 22–35; and Michal Cakrt, "Management Education in Eastern Europe: Toward Mutual Understanding," *Academy of Management Executive*, November 1993, pp. 63–68.

55. B. M. Bass and P. C. Burger, *Assessment of Managers: An International Comparison*, Free Press, New York, 1979.

56. Richard L. Daft, *Management*, 2d ed., Dryden, Chicago, 1991, p. 625.

57. Oded Shenkar and Yoram Zeira, "International Joint Ventures: A Tough Test of HR," *Personnel*, January 1990, pp. 27–28.

58. Frank A. Heller and Gary Yukl, "Participation, Managerial Decision-Making, and Situational Variables," *Organizational Behavior and Human Performance*, vol. 4, 1969, pp. 227–241.

59. E. C. McCann, "An Aspect of Management Philosophy in the United States and Latin America," *Academy of Management Journal*, June 1964, pp. 149–152.

60. See Hodgetts and Luthans, *International Management*, Chap. 8, for a review of this literature.

61. Nancy J. Adler and Susan B. Bartholomew, "Managing Globally Competent People," *Academy of Management Executive*, August 1992, p. 53.

REAL CASE: Everybody's Everywhere

How important is it for managers to understand organizational behavior in the international context? One way to answer this question is by finding out how much companies are doing internationally. The latest data show that industrial corporations, for example, are becoming more and more international and these firms are now making billions of dollars every year through overseas sales. By 1993, the top twenty international industrials were the following:

Company	Home Country	Total Sales (in millions)
General Motors	United States	$132,775
Exxon	United States	103,547
Ford Motor	United States	100,786
Royal Dutch/Shell	Netherlands	97,150
Toyota Motor	Japan	77,374
IBM	United States	65,096
Daimler-Benz	Germany	63,106

(Continued)

General Electric	United States	62,202
Hitachi	Japan	60,418
British Petroleum	United Kingdom	68,792
Mobil	United States	57,389
Matsushita Electric	Japan	56,572
Volkswagen	Germany	54,688
Nissan Motors	Japan	49,680
Siemens Group	Germany	49,646
Fiat Group	Italy	47,960
Unilever	Netherlands	43,544
Philip Morris	United States	40,157
Nestlé	Switzerland	38,756
Elf Aquitane	France	37,893

Of the 500 largest firms, the two largest national groups are the United States, with 161 companies on the list, and Japan, with 128. Other major countries include Great Britain, with 40; Germany, with 32; and France, with 30. Unfortunately, 25 percent of the 500 largest multinationals lost money in 1992 and total sales increased a mere 3.6 percent, just slightly better than inflation in much of the world. Additionally, total employment in this group of 500 fell for the fourth straight year. Even in Japan, which in the past had vigorous overseas growth, the news was not very good. Of the 128 Japanese firms on the list, 21 reported losses, and those that did make money found it was substantially less than the year before. Quite clearly, the international arena offers a great deal of opportunity to business firms, but it also presents a great deal of risk, and this situation is likely to become even more pronounced during the rest of the decade.

1. How important will an understanding of international organizational behavior be to a multinational manager in the years ahead?
2. How can organizations prepare their managers to better understand international organizational behavior?
3. What is the likelihood that by the year 2000 U.S. firms with sales of $100 million or above will be earning at least a portion of this income through international sales? What significance does your answer have for the study of international organizational behavior?

**CASE:
I Want Out**

When the Budder Mining Equipment Company decided to set up a branch office in Peru, top management felt that there were two basic avenues the company could travel. One was to export its machinery and have an agent in that country be responsible for the selling. The other was to set up on an on-site operation and be directly responsible for the sales effort. After giving the matter a great deal of thought, management decided to assign one of their own people to this overseas market. The person who was chosen, Frank Knight, had expressed an interest in the assignment but had no experience in South America. He was selected because of his selling skills and was given a week to clear out his desk and be on location.

When Frank arrived, he was met at the airport by Pablo Gutierrez, the local who was hired to run the office and break Frank in. Pablo had rented an apartment and car for Frank and taken care of all the chores associated with getting him settled. Frank was very impressed. Thanks to Pablo, he could devote all his efforts to the business challenges that lie ahead.

After about six months, the vice president for marketing received a call from Frank. In a tired voice Frank indicated that even though sales were okay, he couldn't take it anymore. He wanted to come home. If nothing could be worked out within the next three months, Frank made it clear that he would resign. When his boss pressed him regarding the problems he was having, here is what Frank reported:

Doing business over here is a nightmare. Everyone comes to work late and leaves early. They also take a two-hour rest period during the afternoon. All the offices close down during this afternoon break. So even if I wanted to conduct some business during this period, there would be no customers around anyway. Also, no one works very hard and they seem to assume no responsibility whatsoever. There seems to be no support for the work ethic among the people. Even Pablo, who looked like he was going to turn out great, has proved to be as lazy as the rest of them. Sales are 5 percent over forecasted but a good 30 percent lower than they could be if everyone here would just work a little harder. If I stay here any longer, I'm afraid I'll start becoming like these people. I want out, while I still can.

1. In Frank's view, how important is the work ethic? How is this view causing him problems?
2. Why do the people not work as hard as Frank does? What is the problem?
3. What mistake is Frank making that is undoubtedly causing him problems in managing the branch office?

CASE:
Getting the Facts

When California-based Dalton & Dalton (D&D) was contacted by a large conglomerate in Taiwan, the president of D&D was quite surprised. For two years D&D had been looking for an overseas conglomerate that would be interested in building and selling its high-tech medical equipment under a licensing agreement. The company had been unsuccessful because the firms with whom it had spoken were not interested in investing any of their own money. They wanted D&D to provide the financial investment while they handled the actual manufacturing and selling.

The Taiwanese conglomerate has proposed to D&D that the two companies enter into a joint venture licensing agreement. The way in which the business deal will work is the following:

- The Taiwanese will set up manufacturing facilities and create a marketing group to sell D&D's high-tech medical equipment.
- D&D will train twenty-five manufacturing and twenty-five salespeople from the conglomerate so that they understand how to make and sell this equipment. This training will take place in the States.
- D&D will have the right to send people to the manufacturing facility to ensure that the equipment is being built according to specifications and will also have the right to travel with the salespeople to ensure that the equipment is being sold properly. (Specifically, D&D would be able to monitor the technical side of the sales presentation to ensure that the equipment is being properly represented and that the capabilities of the machinery are not being exaggerated.)

The arrangement sounds fine to the president of D&D. However, before she agrees to anything, she wants to get more information on how to do business with the Taiwanese. "If we're going to enter into a business venture with a foreign company, I think we owe it to ourselves to know something about their culture and customs. I'd like to know how to interact effectively with these people and to get an idea of the types of problems we might have in communicating with them. The better we understand them, the better the chances that there will be no misunderstandings between us."

1. If you were advising the president, what types of information would you suggest be gathered?
2. What types of culturally related problems are there that could result in misunderstanding between the two parties?
3. Overall, is the president right in suggesting that they learn more about the Taiwanese before doing business with them?

20 Organizational Change and Development

■■■■■■ Learning Objectives

- **Analyze** the changing environment affecting today's and tomorrow's organizations.
- **Discuss** the theoretical background and process of managing change and organization development (OD).
- **Explain** the major techniques used in organization development (OD).
- **Identify** the trends that will affect the study and application of organizational behavior in the future.

Whereas the introductory part of the text identifies and analyzes the dramatic environmental changes facing today's and tomorrow's organizations (globalization, advanced information technology, total quality, and diversity and ethics), depicted as a paradigm shift, this concluding chapter is more concerned with the process of change per se and how to manage it. The term "organization development," or simply OD, is used to represent an applied, macro-level approach to planned change and development of complex organizations. Many of the concepts and techniques (for example, job enrichment, goal setting, and O.B. Mod.) discussed in previous chapters could be considered part of OD. However, this chapter is directly concerned with the general issue of the management of change and with widely recognized OD techniques.

After a general discussion of the impact of change, a theoretical framework for OD is presented. This portion of the chapter is followed by an overview of first the traditional and then the newly emerging OD approaches and techniques. The chapter concludes with a brief look into the future of organizational behavior.

THE CHANGES FACING ORGANIZATIONS

All managers today recognize the inevitability of change, that the only constant is change itself. Organizations have always experienced change—evolutionary, incremental change. But, as Chapter 1 points out, recent years have been characterized by revolutionary change. A cover story of *Fortune* characterized this revolutionary type of change as follows:

> We all sense that the changes surrounding us are not mere trends but the workings of large, unruly forces: the globalization of markets; the spread of information

technology and computer networks; the dismantling of hierarchy, the structure that has essentially organized work since the mid-19th century. Growing up around these is a new, information-age economy, whose fundamental sources of wealth are knowledge and communication rather than natural resources and physical labor.[1]

This revolutionary change is not just talk; it is having practical effects on all organizations. For example, General Electric's appliance factory in Louisville, Kentucky, had a parking lot in 1953 for 25,000 employees' autos; now the total work force at the plant stands at 10,000 and is shrinking. In 1985, IBM, which made profits of $6.6 billion, had a work force of 406,000. Less than ten years later, a third of the people and all of the profits, and then some, are gone. Procter & Gamble, a premier company with rising sales, has recently announced the dismissal of 12 percent of its employees. The same can be said for service sector organizations (Cigna Reinsurance has trimmed its work force by 25 percent) and those outside the United States (Volkswagen has recently announced that it needs only two-thirds of the workers and must drastically cut wages and benefits).[2] Even the federal government is trying to "reinvent" itself. Vice President Gore's proposal will do more than merge a handful of small programs.

> Whole agencies, such as the Energy Department, should be shuttered. The Federal Maritime Commission and the Interstate Commerce Commission can be, too. The Government Printing Office's monopoly should be broken and its work opened to private competition to assure that Uncle Sam gets the best price. Air-traffic control would also be better in private hands.[3]

The accompanying TQM in Action: The Government Teams Up for Efficiency gives some specific examples of how the government is trying to become more efficient.

Globalization simply means that any company can enter any market, at any time. Now, consumers in Santiago, Beijing, Bombay, and Kiev demand Pepsis, Sonys, and Levis. The same goes for expensive industrial products and services, from AT&T's $5 million telephone switches to GE's $100 million large steam turbines. Being number four or five in a given industry, even if still profitable, under the new globalization may be a death warrant.[4] Companies must become world-class.[5] As the head of GE, Jack Welch, warns: "If you can't meet a world standard of quality at the world's best price, you're not even in the game."[6]

Although the premise of this book has been that recognition, strategy, and implementation of globalization, information technology, and total quality are necessary, the key element for competitive advantage is still the people. For example, even though Chrysler is admired as the current world leader in new-car development, the other carmakers will use the Chrysler standards as benchmarks and soon catch up. As one auto expert observed: "That standard is going to be a given for everyone, and I doubt there'll be significant advantage in getting it down 5 percent more. The enduring advantages will come from making better use of people."[7] The head of Chrysler agrees.

> We're not anywhere near world class at a lot of these things. The only way we can beat the competition is with people. That's the only thing anybody has. Your culture and how you motivate and empower and educate your people is what makes the difference.[8]

The people-oriented approach is what the field of organizational behavior and this text are all about. The remainder of this chapter is devoted to some approaches and specific techniques of the human side of the management of change.

TQM in Action

The Government Teams Up for Efficiency

In business organizations, one of the most difficult areas of successfully implementing a TQM program is that of getting everyone to work as a team. Americans have traditionally had individually oriented cultural values and many prefer autonomy over teamwork. In business organizations, such individualism and autonomy have been tried through job enrichment programs and pay-for-performance plans. However, in government organizations, neither the individual/autonomy nor the team-oriented approaches have really been used. Thus, the application of TQM to the government is starting with a clean slate and may have a better chance for success.

Presently, there is a movement toward getting TQM started in government agencies. The initial impetus came at the state level, where legislatures have enacted a wide variety of new programs designed to provide taxpayers with better service at lower costs. For example, a few years ago the Texas comptroller's office conducted a review of state agencies and presented over 950 total quality–based recommendations for action with proposed savings of $5.2 billion. A more recent review proposed 460 recommendations with projected savings of $4.5 billion. So far, the Texas legislature has approved almost 70 percent of these suggestions, thus saving the state billions of dollars and avoiding tax increases.

The federal government is also getting on the total quality bandwagon. One agency in the forefront is the Small Business Administration, which is undergoing a total quality effort to improve customer service. Another is the Internal Revenue Service (IRS), which is using a total quality approach and techniques to improve the entering, processing, reviewing, and correcting of income tax returns. The Ogden, Utah, center of the IRS, which has instituted TQM, handled 26 million returns in 1991 and issued $9 billion in refunds. Most importantly, this center had the lowest error rate that year among the IRS's ten regional centers. For its efforts, the center was awarded the 1992 Presidential Award for Quality, the equivalent of the Malcolm Baldrige National Quality Award, which is given by the government to the highest-quality firms in the private sector.

The current administration in Washington is hoping to spread the TQM message to all agencies and departments. Some of the changes that are being proposed are the following: (1) reform the federal procurement process to allow agencies more freedom to make purchases under $100,000; (2) require all agencies to create customer service programs; and (3) give agencies more leeway in hiring, firing, and promoting federal employees.

TQM supporters welcome this approach to making government more efficient, but point out that more needs to be done. In particular, they would like to see fewer people reporting to the President, so that he can focus attention on a smaller number of issues and deal with them more effectively. Since the White House is often looked at as the example to be followed, this may be good advice. Certainly it will send out a clear message to the federal bureaucracy that the government is teaming up for efficiency. For the moment, however, it will be necessary to see if Washington reality can catch up with its rhetoric.

ORGANIZATIONAL DEVELOPMENT APPROACHES AND TECHNIQUES

The modern approach to the management of change and the development of human resources is called *organization development*. Although there is still not a universally agreed-upon definition, one recent applications view stated that "organization development programs" lead to improved organization performance through an improved decision-making climate. OD practitioners (internal or external consultants) may counsel decision makers on an individual basis; strive to improve working relationships among the members of a work group or team (often including the top management team); work to improve relationships among interacting and interdependent organizational groups; and gather attitudinal data throughout the organization and feed this data back to selected individuals and groups, who use this information as a basis for planning and making needed improvements.[9]

More traditionally, French and Bell offered this comprehensive definition:

> Organization development is a long-range effort to improve an organization's problem-solving and renewal processes, particularly through a more effective and collaborative management of organization culture—with special emphasis on the culture of formal work teams—with the assistance of a change agent, or catalyst, and the use of the theory and technology of applied behavior science, including action research.[10]

Burke has a simple definition:

> Organization development is a planned process of change in an organization's culture through the utilization of behavioral science technology, research, and theory.[11]

Using definitions like these as a point of departure and summarizing what the leaders in the OD movement emphasize, Black and Margulies suggest that the following elements make up the modern OD approach to the management of change:

1. The OD approach to change is planned.
2. It is system-wide or at least takes a systems perspective.
3. It is designed to improve the organization in both the short and long terms.
4. The OD approach to change is aimed primarily at organizational processes rather than substantive content.
5. It is designed to solve problems.
6. It is focused primarily on human and social relationships.[12]

The desired organizational outcomes of OD efforts include increased effectiveness, problem solving, and adaptability for the future. OD attempts to provide opportunities to be "human" and to increase awareness, participation, and influence. An overriding goal is to integrate individual and organizational objectives.

Theoretical Development of OD

As with other behavioral approaches, it is difficult to pinpoint the precise beginning of OD. French and Bell, who have done the most work on the historical development of OD, feel that "organization development has emerged from applied behavioral science and social psychology and from subsequent efforts to apply laboratory training and survey-feedback insights into total systems."[13] Thus, the two major historical roots for OD are laboratory training and survey feedback. The work of the pioneering social psychologist Kurt Lewin was instrumental in both approaches. In recent years, there has been an effort to go beyond these historical beginnings and develop an overall theoretical framework for OD.

Burke and Litwin suggest that the two most important avenues of theorizing for OD are organizational functioning and, especially, organizational change.[14] They depict change in terms of both process and content and give particular emphasis on transformational as compared with transactional factors. More specifically, they note:

Transformational change occurs as a response to the external environment and directly affects organizational mission and strategy, the organization's leadership, and culture. In turn, the transactional factors are affected—structure, systems, management practices, and climate. These transformational and transactional factors together affect motivation, which, in turn, affects performance.[15]

A more precise theoretical framework is shown in Figure 20.1. By using meta-analytic procedures (aggregating results) across fifty-two evaluations of OD interventions, this theoretical model was generally found to be predictive. Specifically, it was found that OD interventions generated positive change in work-setting variables (see Figure 20.1); there was mixed support that work-setting change and individual behavior change are positively related; and there was a positive relationship between individual behavior change and organizational outcome change.[16]

The researchers suggest that their theoretical model and research findings have three key implications for the actual practice of OD:[17]

1. Change agents should focus on systematic change in work settings as the starting point in change and on individual behavior change as a key mediator associated with organizational outcome change.
2. The results for technology interventions indicate that negative behavior change does not necessarily lead to negative organizational outcome change. In some cases, the organization can wait out the negative behavior change until individuals move up the learning curve or successfully adapt to the implemented changes.

FIGURE 20.1

A theoretical model for planned organizational change and development.
(*Source*: Peter J. Robertson, Darryl R. Roberts, and Jerry I. Porras, "Dynamics of Planned Organizational Change: Assessing Empirical Support for a Theoretical Model," *Academy of Management Journal*, June 1993, p. 621. Used with permission.)

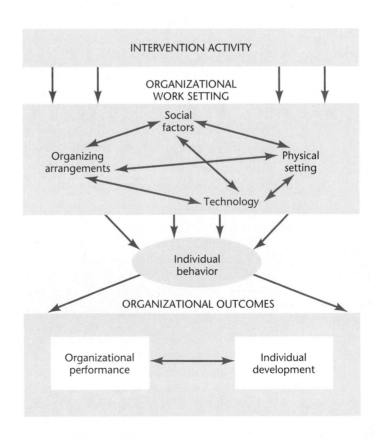

3. Well-developed theories, such as those represented in Figure 20.1, should provide a better basis for choosing interventions than simply the change agent's personal preferences, values, and styles.

There are other recent theoretical contributions to OD besides those discussed above,[18] but the field has been largely technique-driven. A look at the established techniques gives the best indication of what OD is all about.

OD Techniques

Although the beginnings of OD can be traced to laboratory or training group techniques—sometimes called sensitivity training or "T" (for training) groups—the most popular techniques over the years have been grid training, survey feedback, and team building.

Grid Training. Grid training as used in OD is an outgrowth of the managerial grid approach to leadership discussed in Chapter 14. A 9,9 position on Blake and Mouton's leadership grid, shown in Chapter 14, indicating a maximum concern for both people and production, is an implied goal of grid training. A more comprehensive step-by-step approach is taken when grid training is used in OD.

Summarized, the six phases of grid training for OD are the following:

1. *Laboratory-seminar training.* The purpose of this first phase is to introduce the participants to the overall concepts and materials used in grid training. The seminars that are held are not like therapeutic sensitivity training. There is more structure and more concentration on leadership styles than on developing self-insights and group insights.
2. *Team development.* This is an extension of the first phase. Members of the same department are brought together to chart how they are going to attain a 9,9 position on the grid. In this stage, what was learned in the orientation stage is applied to the actual organizational situation.
3. *Intergroup development.* Whereas the first two phases are aimed at managerial development, this phase marks the beginning of overall organization development. There is a shift from the micro level of individual and group development to a macro level of group-to-group organization development. Conflict situations between groups are identified and analyzed.
4. *Organizational goal setting.* In the manner of management by objectives, in this phase the participants contribute to, and agree upon, the important goals for the organization. A sense of commitment and self-control is instilled in the participants.
5. *Goal attainment.* In this phase the participants attempt to accomplish the goals which they set in the fourth phase. As in the first phase, the participants get together, but this time they discuss major organizational issues, and the stakes are real.
6. *Stabilization.* In this final phase, support is marshaled for changes suggested earlier, and an evaluation of the overall program is conducted.[19]

These six phases of grid training may take from three to five years to implement, but in some cases they may be compressed into a shorter period of time.

Most of the support for grid training has come from its founders, Robert R. Blake and Jane S. Mouton. They and their colleagues have maintained over the years that "managerial and team effectiveness *can* be taught by managers with outside assistance. Furthermore, it appears that this type of educational strategy can help to make significant contributions to organizational effectiveness."[20]

In a later work, *The New Managerial Grid*, Blake and Mouton continue to suggest that research indicates that grid training is very effective.[21] A review of the research on OD gives some support to their claims. Although it was found to have the least rigorous research (along with the survey-feedback technique), four studies reviewed found grid training to have a 43 percent substantial positive impact on process variables, and three studies found a 68 percent positive impact on outcome variables.[22] The impact of grid training on outcome variables was higher than that of any of the other OD techniques, but, again, this finding was based on only three studies. Conclusions are still tentative at this point because more and better research is needed before any firm conclusions can be drawn; nevertheless, the use of grid training does seem to be justified. One thing is certain: It has been widely used over the years.

Survey Feedback. Besides grid training, another popular OD technique has been survey research and feedback of the data. Once again Kurt Lewin had the original influence, but over the years the survey-feedback approach has been most closely associated with the University of Michigan's Institute for Social Research (ISR).

As the terminology indicates, this approach to OD surveys the unit of analysis (for example, a work group, a department, or a whole organization) by means of questionnaires and feeds back the data to those who generated them. The data are used in the action research sense of diagnosing problems and developing specific action plans to solve the problems. The questionnaire can be either tailor-made for each situation, or, as has been more common in recent years, a standardized version researched and developed by the ISR. A number of revisions have been made through the years, but the typical ISR questionnaire provides data in the areas of leadership, organizational climate, and employee satisfaction.

Normally an external consultant will accumulate, present, and interpret the data for the group. The consultant will then, usually in a process-consultation or team-building approach (covered in the next section), help the group diagnose and solve its problems.

One review of three rigorous studies on survey feedback indicated it had a 53 percent substantial positive change on outcome variables,[23] and a later review found that three studies yielded an overall 50 percent positive change in productivity. However, the latter analysis found no impact on work-force measures such as turnover, absenteeism, and grievances, and compared with structured laboratory training and team building, survey feedback had the least impact.[24] Used in combination with team building, it had a more positive impact.

Team Building. Both grid training and survey feedback are fairly specialized and associated with a leading advocate (Blake and Mouton in the case of the grid and the Michigan group in the case of survey feedback). Of wider appeal and especially relevant as an increasing number of organizations move toward the team concept (see Chapters 9 and 17) is the OD technique of team building. Although similar to the team approach in general (for example, quality circles, self-managed teams, and interfunctional teams), team building as an OD technique has actually been around longer. Whereas old-time sensitivity training "scared off" many managers because of the controversy surrounding the potentially harmful psychological implications inherent in it, team building is seen as accomplishing some of the same goals as sensitivity training but tends to be more task-oriented. Table 20.1 shows that team-building activities can be applied to either "family" groups or special groups (for example, task forces, committees, or interfunctional groups) within the organization.

In general, it can be said that team building is an organization development effort aimed at improving overall performance. Perhaps with the exception of widely marketed, commercially based grid training, there is little question that team building has become the most popular OD technique in recent years. French and Bell go as far as to say that "probably the most important single group of interventions in OD are the team-building activities, the goals of which are the improvement and increased effectiveness of various teams within the organization."[25]

As an OD technique, team building generally follows the classic change procedure originally formulated by Kurt Lewin:

1. *Unfreezing.* The first task is to make the team aware of the need for change. A climate of openness and trust is developed so that the group is ready for change.
2. *Moving.* Using a survey-feedback technique, the team makes a diagnosis of where it is and develops action plans to get to where it wants to go.
3. *Refreezing.* Once the plans have been carried out and an evaluation has been made, the team starts to stabilize into more effective performance.

The above, of course, represents only a very general idea of what team building is all about and can also apply to the other OD techniques.

A more specific team-building program actually used in a large manufacturing plant is described as follows:

1. *Team skills workshop.* The production team in this plant first went through a two-day workshop that consisted mainly of a series of experience-based exercises. The purpose of this first phase was essentially to unfreeze the various teams and get them ready to accept change.

TABLE 20.1 Various Approaches to Team Building

Family Groups (Members from the Same Organizational Unit)	Special Groups (Start-Up Teams, Task Forces, Committees, and Interfunctional Groups)
1. Task accomplishment (for example, problem solving, decision making, role clarification, and goal setting)	1. Task accomplishment (special problems, role and goal clarification, resource utilization, etc.)
2. Building and maintaining effective interpersonal relationships (for example, boss-subordinate relationships and peer relationships)	2. Relationships (for example, interpersonal or interunit conflict and underutilization of each other as resources)
3. Understanding and managing group processes and culture	3. Processes (for example, communications, decision making, and task allocations)
4. Role analysis technique for role clarification and definition	4. Role analysis technique for role clarification and definition
5. Role negotiation techniques	5. Role negotiation

Source: Wendell L. French and Cecil H. Bell, *Organization Development*, 2d ed., Prentice-Hall, Englewood Cliffs, N.J., 1978, p. 119.

2. *Data collection.* In a questionnaire survey, data were collected on organizational climate, supervisory behavior, and job content from all first-line supervisors in the program.

3. *Data confrontation.* The consultants presented the teams with the data gathered in step 2. The teams, with the consultant present, openly discussed problem areas, established priorities, and made some preliminary recommendations for change.

4. *Action planning.* On the basis of what went on in step 3, the teams developed specific plans for the changes to be actually carried out on the job.

5. *Team building.* The first four phases were preliminary to the actual team building. In this phase, each team met as a whole to identify barriers to effectiveness, developed ways of eliminating the barriers, and agreed upon plans to accomplish the desired changes.

6. *Intergroup building.* In this final phase there were two-day meetings held between various teams that were interdependent in accomplishing goals. The purpose of this phase was to establish collaboration on shared goals and problems and generalize the OD effort to the total organization.[26]

This program took over a year to complete. As an Apple Computer executive experienced in team building recently noted: "Team building is not a fun day away from the office, a strategy for saving a failing manager, a place to go and 'dump' the team's anger, or a group psychotherapy session. Team building is a process for helping a team become more effective."[27]

The advantages of team building are all those which are attributed to old-fashioned teamwork. The process can create a team effort in an open, participatory climate. There can be improved communication and problem solving, and individual team members can experience psychological growth and improve their interpersonal skills. For example, one research study found that four trained teams reported significantly higher levels of group effectiveness, mutual influence, and personal involvement and participation than the eight control groups.[28] Evaluation of the six-step program described above also found that the program produced a positive impact on organizational performance (quality of output and profit but not quantity of output) and favorably affected the attitudes and perceptions of the members of the teams studied.[29]

As the above studies indicate, there is relatively more and better research on team building than on any of the other OD techniques. Porras and Berg found far more acceptable research designs on team building (40 percent of the thirty-five studies met their minimum criteria). Of team-building studies that examined process variables, 45 percent had a substantial positive change, and of the three studies that analyzed the impact on outcome variables, 53 percent were deemed to have a substantial positive change.[30] The later Nicholas review looked at four team-building studies and found that there was a 50 percent overall positive impact on work-force, monetary, and productivity hard measures of performance.[31] Team building came out better than survey feedback, but was behind structured laboratory training. However, a later study conducted with hard-rock miners produced inconclusive results.[32] So, although there is considerable evidence that team building can be beneficial, it is still open to question *how* and, in some cases, *if* team building works.

Besides having demonstrated that it can have a positive impact on its own as an OD intervention strategy, team building has the strength of being able to be used effectively in combination with other OD techniques. For example, as mentioned earlier, Nicholas found that if it was used in combination with survey feedback, there was a much more positive effect on hard performance measures than if survey feedback was used by itself.[33] Also, there have been calls for combining team building with O.B. Mod. approaches. One suggestion along this line was to use a task hierarchy to reinforce the team as it progresses up a behavior skills hierarchy (for example, listening, communicating, monitoring, and feedback skills).[34] There also seem to be successful applications for a team-building approach internationally, but the intervention must be carried out in a culturally sensitive manner.[35] Team building seems to have a bright future.

Emerging OD Approaches and Techniques

Since organizations have been undergoing such revolutionary change in recent years, the traditional approaches and techniques of OD are to an increasing degree giving way to entirely new thinking and new techniques. On the one hand, there are some very practical demands for making OD efforts cost-effective. OD programs may still not be having the intended effects on organizational effectiveness. Very few organizations measure transfer back on the job (one estimate is that only about 15 percent of organizations make such an evaluation),[36] and the cost of failed change efforts is high. It leads to:

1. Diminished competitive position.
2. Lost employee loyalty.
3. A waste of money and resources.
4. Difficulty in reworking the change efforts.[37]

The response to these problems with the management of change are both relatively simplistic and complex. An example of a simplistic approach to overcome the problems associated with traditional change efforts would be that offered by Kirkpatrick. He suggests the following should be used in effectively managing change:

1. *Empathy.* The key is people's attitudes. The feelings and reactions of those who will be affected by change and involved in the implementation of it influence whether a change will be successful. Managers should empathize with subordinates.
2. *Communication.* It's important to communicate an expected change and the reasons for it, as completely and as far in advance as feasible.
3. *Participation.* Managing change through participation can be done in two ways. One way is to receive input from subordinates before the change is made and the other way is to allow participative input into the change itself.[38]

A more complex emerging approach to the management of change stems from the organizational learning concept that is presented in Chapter 2. For example, as the accompanying TQM in Action: Airlines Finally Begin to Listen to Their Customers shows, even the airlines are beginning to learn from their customers. Not only are the notions of double-loop and generative learning (see Chapter 2) from organizational learning applicable to the management of change but also relevant is what has become known as action learning that takes place at the individual and group levels. Current research on learning at the individual and group levels applicable to organizational change includes the following:

TQM in Action

Airlines Finally Begin to Listen to Their Customers

Almost all airlines have been losing money year after year. They have changed, but they have not kept ahead of change, and they have generally failed to really listen to their customers. For example, until recently most airline food met three requirements: indescribability, indestructibility, and tastelessness. However, this situation is finally changing as airlines seek to listen to their customers by offering nutritious, low-calorie meals designed to attract repeat business. In particular, many passengers now want to eat lightly and healthfully. This means cutting down on cholesterol, spices, and desserts, and having more salads and vegetarian and nonmeat offerings. The airlines are also catering to special orders such as kosher meals that, in many cases, are ordered for diet—not religious—reasons. Here are some of the latest offerings from the airlines:

Airline	Types of Special Meals Offered	Most Popular Specialty Meal	Number of Meals Served Daily	% of Specialty Meals Served	Notice Required
American	7	Low cholesterol	170,000	3	6 hours
Continental	12	Kosher	82,000	4	12 hours
Delta	13	Vegetarian	145,000	3	6 hours
Northwest	24	Vegetarian	105,000	4	12 hours
United	12	Vegetarian	183,000	3	6 hours

In addition, the airlines have made some substantial changes in the preparation and selection of their standard coach menus. Beef used to be the most common offering, but no longer. Now most airlines offer it only if there is another choice; it is never the only offering. Other popular dishes include baked chicken—without the fat-retaining skin and sauces—and cold pasta served in olive oil and garlic. Even breakfast menus have been expanded so that the all-too-common cheese omelet now competes with no-yolk Egg Beaters and cold cereal with fruit.

The airlines are learning that customers are interested in more than a reasonable fare to the destination of their choice. They also want the same type of food they would eat at home, which means in-flight meals that help people trim down and shape up. The eating habits of passengers are beginning to influence the quality strategy of airlines.

1. We embed learning in our individual experiences, so we learn best when we direct our own learning.
2. We learn most effectively in context, so learning should be linked directly to work.
3. We learn from each other, so workplaces should enable us to communicate and collaborate freely.
4. We continuously create knowledge, so we need to learn how to capture what we know and share it with others.
5. We learn unconsciously, so we need to learn how to recognize and question our tacit assumptions.[39]

This action learning approach to organizational change and development can be operationalized. For example, Ernst & Young, the big public accounting firm, has their managers help others learn by

1. Establishing an environment conducive to workplace learning.
2. Helping others set and meet learning goals.

3. Helping others identify tools and resources for gaining knowledge.
4. Providing feedback to others on their learning accomplishments so that they can improve their performance and capitalize on successes.
5. Encouraging reflection by asking employees questions to prompt thinking about actions.
6. Recording and transferring learning.[40]

Another way to operationalize the learning approach is through what is called dialogue. Schein feels that dialogue is a central element of any model of organizational change. He feels that dialogue goes beyond old sensitivity training, face-to-face open communication, and active listening. Specifically, he states:

> Dialogue is focused more on the thinking process and how our perceptions and cognitions are performed by our past experiences. The assumption here is that if we become more conscious of how our thought process works, we will think better, collectively, and communicate better. An important goal of dialogue is to enable the group to reach a higher level of consciousness and creativity through the gradual creation of a shared set of meanings and a 'common' thinking process.[41]

In addition to these new action learning and dialogue approaches to the management of change, there is also a recent call for new OD techniques.[42] There is the argument that the relatively simplistic traditional OD techniques cannot handle the dramatic changes currently being experienced by organizations. Again, Schein offers some suggestions of what needs to be done, usually in combination, to produce a new organizational culture that can cope with such change:

1. Leaders may unfreeze the present system by highlighting the threats to the organization if no change occurs, and, at the same time, encourage the organization to believe that change is possible and desirable.
2. Leaders may articulate a new direction and a new set of assumptions, thus providing a clear and new role model.
3. Key positions in the organization may be filled with new incumbents who hold the new assumptions because they are either hybrids or mutants, or are brought in from the outside.
4. Leaders may systematically reward the adoption of new directions and punish adherence to the old direction.
5. Organization members may be seduced or coerced into adopting new behaviors that are more consistent with new assumptions.
6. Visible scandals may be created to discredit sacred cows, to explode myths that preserve dysfunctional traditions, and symbolically destroy the artifacts associated with them.
7. Leaders may create new emotionally charged rituals and develop new symbols and artifacts around the new assumptions to be embraced, using the embedding mechanisms described earlier.[43]

Also, there has been a recent call by some OD experts to develop alternatives to the traditional top-down, single-organization OD interventions which have supported top management's outdated definitions of reality. For example, Bradshaw-Camball suggests a radically new approach to OD involving interventions with the organization's board of directors, taking a bottom-up rather than top-down approach, and focusing the OD effort at an interorganizational level.[44] She points out that this new approach to OD demands different values, skills, techniques, and abilities of change agents and that the actual process of change is fundamentally different.[45]

OD in Perspective

OD has matured but, as the section above points out, with the revolutionary changes taking place, new ways of thinking about and implementing organizational change and development are emerging. The value of OD as an approach to the management of change is not totally supported by the research to date, OD rarely diffuses throughout the entire organization, and it is too limited.[46] Guest makes the point that all the human resource management and behaviorally oriented techniques, not just OD, have also come up short. He notes that "much of the innovation is piecemeal and lacking in the crucial ingredient of strategic integration, and that as a result it is unlikely to have a positive impact on organizational performance."[47]

Besides the need for new approaches, as suggested in the previous section, and strategic integration, as suggested by Guest, there is still a need for commonsense guidelines in order to have successful change efforts. Here is a list of simple things that experience says to avoid in major system changes:

1. Do not promise that all employees undergoing a change effort will be winners.
2. Do not blame those who lose out for their negative attitudes.
3. Do not focus only on the new and forget the old.
4. Avoid symbolic or pseudoparticipation in the change effort.
5. Avoid destroying the old culture without building a new one.
6. Do not launch human resource management programs in the context of a major change without the necessary time and resources to support them.[48]

These practical guidelines are not meant to dampen the excitement and enthusiasm for change efforts but to put realistic expectations into the process.

THE FUTURE OF ORGANIZATIONAL BEHAVIOR

The changes discussed in the introductory part of the text and comments of this chapter dealing with globalization, the information explosion, total quality, and the diverse work force signal the challenges that lie ahead not only for the management of change and organization development but also for the entire field of organizational behavior. Fortunately, some identifiable trends have emerged in organizational behavior. First, it can be said that organizational behavior has truly arrived as an identifiable field of academic study, with definite implications for the effective management of human resources in modern, complex organizations. This recognition of organizational behavior as a legitimate academic and applied field should become even greater in the future.

Second, there is now a clear distinction between organizational behavior and such other areas as general management and human resources management. For example, organizational behavior is concerned with human behavior in organizations, while human resources management is recognized as a function of the organization and is concerned mainly with topics such as selection, compensation, and labor relations. The field of organizational behavior is recognized to be very broad, and as one theorist emphasized: "It is the people behaving in them that make organizations what they are."[49] In addition, the micro-macro split in the topics and conceptual framework for organizational behavior, which was at first thought to be getting wider (even in the past editions of this text), now seems to be lessening. Recognition is given to the important role of macro structural variables and the environment in the social learning theoretical framework. Macro variables play a major role, although still not as proportionately great a role as micro variables, in this edition and in the field in general.

Third, the topical coverage of the field of organizational behavior will continue to move away from the traditional specialized topics in behavioral science and toward topics more identified with organizational behavior per se (organizational culture, job stress, job design, goal setting, job satisfaction, organizational commitment, organizational behavior modification, work teams, job conflict, organizational power and politics, informal organization, managerial roles, interpersonal communication, organizational culture, managerial leadership, organization development, and behavioral decision making). The exceptions here are the mainstays of experimental psychology—attitudes, motivation, and learning. These latter topics continue to be very important areas in organizational behavior.

Finally—and this, of course, most students and practitioners will be happy to hear—the trend toward making the organizational behavior approach more understandable and applications-oriented should continue. Although there is a definite trend away from simple answers to complex organizational behavior problems at all levels of analysis—individual, group, and organizational—in order to be considered useful, it must be both understandable and applicable to the real world.[50] The successive editions of this text have given evidence of this trend. The organizational behavior approach is clearly aimed at the more effective management of people. With emphasis on areas such as coping with organizational culture, international management, job stress, job design, goal setting, organizational behavior modification, negotiation skills, teams, political strategies, leadership styles, organization development, and decision-making techniques, this aim at applications should become clearer and be more likely to hit the target of more effective human resources management in the years to come.

The future of the field of organizational behavior looks very bright and exciting. Although there will be some shifting emphasis in conceptual framework and topical coverage, the "bottom line" is that the study and application of the areas covered in this text will help make better, more effective managers of the most important and underutilized resource in any organization: *people*. The effective management of people (both others and oneself), so that everyone can reach their full potential, is really what organizational behavior is all about.

Summary

Organizations today are faced with tremendous forces for change, stemming mainly from globalization, the information explosion, total quality service, and work-force diversity. A systematic, planned way of managing this change is through the process of organizational development. Although there are some recent theoretical developments, OD has mainly been technique-driven. The traditional techniques of OD are grid training, survey feedback, and team building. Some new approaches, such as action learning and dialogue, are being developed to cope with the revolutionary changes that are taking place. However, like the other techniques and approaches covered in this text, more rigorous research and contingency applications need to be forthcoming. Yet, there is little question that OD has a fairly bright future in helping solve some of the tremendous challenges of change that are facing today's organizations. The last section of the text looks into the crystal ball of the future and identifies some recent trends in the field of organizational behavior and the management of human resources.

Questions for Discussion and Review

1. What are some of the major forces for change that are confronting today's organizations?
2. What are some theoretical frameworks for organization development?
3. In your own words, briefly describe the three traditional techniques of OD. Discuss some of their major advantages and limitations. What are the new approaches of action learning and dialogue about?
4. What is the current perspective of OD?
5. Do you agree with the view that the future of organizational behavior is bright and exciting? Do you have anything to add to this view?

Footnote References and Supplemental Readings

1. Thomas A. Stewart, "Welcome to the Revolution," *Fortune*, Dec. 13, 1993, p. 66.
2. See Stewart, "Welcome to the Revolution," for these and other examples.
3. Howard Gleckman, "Where to Prune and Where to Hack Away," *Business Week*, Sept. 13, 1993, p. 98.
4. Stratford Sherman, "Are You as Good as the Best in the World?" *Fortune*, Dec. 13, 1993, pp. 95–96.
5. See Fred Luthans, Richard M. Hodgetts, and Sang M. Lee, "New Paradigm Organizations: From Total Quality to Learning to World Class," *Organizational Dynamics*, Winter 1994, pp. 5–19.
6. Sherman, op. cit., p. 96.
7. Ibid.
8. Ibid.
9. Gerald D. Klein, "Employee-Centered Productivity and QWL Programs: Findings from an Area Study," *National Productivity Review*, Autumn 1986, p. 350.
10. Wendell L. French and Cecil H. Bell, Jr., *Organization Development*, 2d ed., Prentice-Hall, Englewood Cliffs, N.J., 1978, p. 14.
11. W. Warner Burke, *Organization Development*, Little, Brown, Boston, 1982, p. 10.
12. Stewart Black and Newton Margulies, "An Ideological Perspective on Participation: A Case for Integration," *Journal of Organizational Change Management*, vol. 2, no. 1, 1989, p. 16.
13. French and Bell, op. cit., p. 27.
14. W. Warner Burke and George H. Litwin, "A Causal Model of Organizational Performance and Change," *Journal of Management*, vol. 18, no. 3, 1992, pp. 523–545.
15. Ibid., p. 523.
16. Peter J. Robertson, Darryl R. Roberts, and Jerry I. Porras, "Dynamics of Planned Organizational Change: Assessing Empirical Support for a Theoretical Model," *Academy of Management Journal*, June 1993, pp. 619–634.
17. Ibid., pp. 629–630.
18. For example, see Jan Lowstedt, "Organizing Frameworks in Emerging Organizations: A Cognitive Approach to the Analysis of Change," *Human Relations*, April 1993, pp. 501–526; Gerald E. Ledford, Jr., and Susan Albers Mohrman, "Self-Design for High Involvement: A Large-Scale Organizational Change," *Human Relations*, February 1993, pp. 143–173; Achilles A. Armenakis, Stanley G. Harris, and Kevin W. Mossholder, "Creating Readiness for Organizational Change," *Human Relations*, vol. 46, 1993, p. 681; and Jean M. Bartunek, Catherine A. Lacey, and Diane R. Wood, "Social Cognition in Organizational Change: An Insider-Outsider Approach," *Journal of Applied Behavioral Science*, June 1992, pp. 204–223.
19. Robert R. Blake, Jane S. Mouton, Louis B. Barnes, and Larry E. Greiner, "Breakthrough in Organizational Development," *Harvard Business Review*, November–December 1964, pp. 137–138.
20. Ibid., p. 155.
21. Robert R. Blake and Jane S. Mouton, *The New Management Grid*, Gulf, Houston, 1978.
22. Jerry I. Porras and P. O. Berg, "The Impact of Organization Development," *Academy of Management Review*, April 1978, pp. 259–260.
23. Ibid.
24. John M. Nicholas, "The Comparative Impact of Organization Development Intervention on Hard Criteria Measures," *Academy of Management Review*, October 1982, p. 536.
25. French and Bell, op. cit., p. 119.
26. Warren R. Nielsen and John R. Kimberly, "The Impact of Organizational Development on the Quality of Organizational Output," *Academy of Management Proceedings*, 1973, pp. 528–529.
27. John Boring, quoted in William H. Wagel and Hermine Zagat Levine, "HR '90: Challenges and Opportunities," *Personnel*, June 1990, p. 26.

28. Frank Friedlander, "The Impact of Organizational Training Laboratories Upon Effectiveness and Intervention of Ongoing Work Groups," *Personnel Psychology*, Autumn 1967, pp. 289–308.

29. John R. Kimberly and Warren R. Nielsen, "Organizational Development and Change in Organizational Performance," *Administrative Science Quarterly*, June 1975, pp. 191–206.

30. Porras and Berg, loc. cit.

31. Nicholas, loc. cit.

32. Paul F. Buller and Cecil H. Bell, Jr., "Effects of Team Building and Goal Setting on Productivity: A Field Experiment," *Academy of Management Journal*, June 1986, pp. 305–328.

33. Nicholas, loc. cit.

34. Ray V. Rasmussen, "Team Training: A Behavior Modification Approach," *Group and Organizational Studies*, March 1982, pp. 51–66.

35. Richard B. Polley, "Intervention and Cultural Context: Mediation in the U.S. and Norway," in Frank Hoy (ed.), *Academy of Management Best Papers Proceedings*, 1987, pp. 236–240; Alfred M. Jaeger, "Organization Development and National Culture: Where's the Fit?" *Academy of Management Review*, January 1986, pp. 178–190; and Michal Cakrt, "Team Development Programmes for Top Management Groups in Czechoslovakia," *Journal of Organizational Change Management*, vol. 6, no. 2, 1993, pp. 11–25.

36. Paul L. Garavaglia, "How to Ensure Transfer of Training," *Training and Development*, October 1993, p. 63.

37. John Jacovini, "The Human Side of Organizational Change," *Training and Development*, January 1993, p. 66.

38. Donald L. Kirkpatrick, "Riding the Winds of Change," *Training and Development*, February 1993, p. 38.

39. Erica Gordon Sorohan, "We Do; Therefore, We Learn," *Training and Development*, October 1993, p. 48.

40. Ibid., p. 54.

41. Edgar H. Schein, "On Dialogue, Culture, and Organizational Learning," *Organization Dynamics*, Autumn 1993, p. 43.

42. Michael Beer and Elise Walton, "Developing the Competitive Organization: Interventions and Strategies," *American Psychologist*, February 1990, p. 160.

43. Edgar H. Schein, "Organizational Culture," *American Psychologist*, February 1990, p. 117.

44. Patricia Bradshaw-Camball, "Organizational Development and the Radical Humanist Paradigm: Exploring the Implications," *Academy of Management Best Papers Proceedings*, 1990, p. 256.

45. Ibid.

46. Richard Walton, "The Diffusion of New Work Structures: Explaining Why Success Didn't Take," *Organizational Dynamics*, Winter 1975, pp. 3–22, and George Strauss, "Organizational Development: Credits and Debits," *Organizational Dynamics*, Winter 1973, pp. 2–19.

47. David E. Guest, "Human Resource Management and the American Dream," *Journal of Management Studies*, July 1990, p. 388.

48. Jeffrey K. Liker, David B. Roitman, and Ethel Roskies, "Changing Everything All at Once: Work Life and Technological Change," *Sloan Management Review*, Summer 1987, pp. 43–44.

49. Benjamin Schneider, "The People Make the Place," *Personnel Psychology*, vol. 40, 1987, p. 438.

50. James L. Gibson, John M. Ivancevich, and James H. Donnelly, Jr., *Organizations*, 6th ed., Business Publications, Inc., Plano, Tex., 1988, pp. 755–756.

REAL CASE: Meeting the Challenges of the Next Century

There are many areas where organizational change will affect the management of human resources at all levels in the years ahead. One area is the career ladder, where successful managers are often finding that the road to the top is a lot slower than it used to be. "Hurry up and wait" appears to have replaced "hurry up and succeed." In contrasting the organization manager of the 1970s and 1980s with today's manager, some of the primary differences appear to be these: (1) every career move used to be directed toward promotion up the hierarchy, but now, with flattened structures, lateral moves are becoming more routine and, in some cases, even desirable; (2) promotions often used to come every few years, but now they come more slowly, and while the job title may not change, it is likely that the responsibilities will; (3) success used to mean job security all the way to retirement, but today it often means inner fulfillment and money; and (4) the workweek used to be forty hours, but now it lasts until the job is done—however long that may take.

In addition, there are other changes that warrant mention. One is the trend toward information technology's replacing middle managers, resulting in the reduction of the overall number of managers in industry. A second is the use of small, empowered, self-managed teams that will do more of the work, thus reducing the need for managerial staff. A third is the use of total quality concepts that stimulate managers to work both harder and smarter.

As stated, the cumulative effects of these changes are a slow or now even nonexistent promotion rate. More firms are moving from a bureaucracy with rewards tied to time on the job to a meritocracy where people are rewarded for effective performance. To better measure performance, organizations are leaving people in their jobs for a longer period of time so that they can see how well the person has really done. A pet food marketing manager at Quaker Oats put it this way: "I got to see the effects of changes I made and to work through their implications. It helped me learn to approach every job as a long-term opportunity, to stand back and ask what changes we need to make in this whole picture, even if it has been done one way for the last fifteen years." Others point out that it will become more important to be a generalist than a specialist. An executive search recruiter recently noted: "In the future everybody will have strategic alliances with everybody else, and the executives who thrive will be well-rounded. You can't be a specialist at senior levels anymore."

Does this mean that today's managers are pleased with the new trends and that they are more committed to the organization than ever? Hardly. A recent poll comparing managerial responses in 1959 and thirty years later found that, on average, today's managers rank their companies lower in virtually every category, including advancement opportunity, job security, a place to work, and job satisfaction. The only category that was fairly close was job satisfaction. Of the four categories, it is the only one that is most under the personal control of the manager. Simply put, career opportunities are not as good as they were previously, but managers are learning to live with the situation.

1. In what way will new flatter organization structures affect the career potential of managers?
2. Is the trend toward slower promotions good or bad? Why?
3. How can OD be used to help individuals handle career planning problems? Give some examples.

CASE: The High-Priced OD Consultant

The middle managers of a large firm were told by the corporate human resources office that a group of consultants would be calling on them later in the week. The purpose of the consultants' visit would be to analyze interfunctional relations throughout the firm. The consultants had been very effective in using an OD intervention called *team building*. Their particular approach used six steps. When their approach was explained to the managers, a great deal of tension was relieved. They had initially thought that team building was a lot of hocus-pocus, like sensitivity training, where people attack each other and let out their aggressions by heaping abuse on those they dislike. By the same token, these managers generally felt that perhaps the consultants were not needed. One of them put it this way: "Now that we understand what is involved in team building, we can go ahead and conduct the sessions ourselves. All we have to do is to choose a manager who is liked by everyone and put him in the role of the change agent/consultant. After all, you really don't need a high-priced consultant to do this team-building stuff. You just have to have a good feel for human nature." The other managers generally agreed.

However, the corporate human resources director turned down their suggestion. He hired the OD consultants to do the team building.

1. What is a team-building approach to organization development? Do you think the managers had an accurate view of this OD technique?
2. Do you think the managers had an accurate view of the role of the external consultant? Do you agree or disagree with the corporate human resources director's decision to turn down their suggestion? Why?

INTEGRATIVE CONTEMPORARY CASES/READINGS FOR PART 5

1. Cultural Constraints in Management Theories

Management as the word is presently used is an American invention. In other parts of the world not only the practices but the entire concept of management may differ, and the theories needed to understand it may deviate considerably from what is considered normal and desirable in the USA. The reader is invited on a trip around the world, and both local management practices and theories are explained from the different contexts and histories of the places visited: Germany, Japan, France, Holland, the countries of the overseas Chinese, South-East Asia, Africa, Russia, and finally mainland China.

A model in which worldwide differences in national cultures are categorized according to five independent dimensions helps in explaining the differences in management found; although the situation in each country or region has unique characteristics that no model can account for. One practical application of the model is in demonstrating the relative position of the U.S. versus other parts of the world. In a global perspective, U.S. management theories contain a number of idiosyncrasies not necessarily shared by management elsewhere. Three such idiosyncrasies are mentioned: a stress on market processes, a stress on the individual, and a focus on managers rather than on workers. A plea is made for an internationalization not only of business, but also of management theories, as a way of enriching theories at the national level.

Lewis Carroll's *Alice in Wonderland* contains the famous story of Alice's croquet game with the Queen of Hearts.

> Alice thought she had never seen such a curious croquet-ground in all her life; it was all ridges and furrows; the balls were live hedgehogs, the mallets live flamingoes, and the soldiers had to double themselves up and to stand on their hands and feet, to make the arches.

You probably know how the story goes: Alice's flamingo mallet turns its head whenever she wants to strike with it; her hedgehog ball runs away; and the doubled-up soldier arches walk around all the time. The only rule seems to be that the Queen of Hearts always wins.

Alice's croquet playing problems are good analogies to attempts to build culture-free theories of management. Concepts available for this purpose are themselves alive with culture, having been developed within a particular cultural context. They have a tendency to guide our thinking toward our desired conclusion.

As the same reasoning may also be applied to the arguments in this article, I better tell you my conclusion before I continue—so that the rules of my game are understood. In this article we take a trip around the world to demonstrate that there are no such things as universal management theories.

Diversity in management *practices* as we go around the world has been recognized in U.S. management literature for more than thirty years. The term "comparative management" has been used since the 1960s. However, it has taken much longer for the U.S. academic community to accept that not only practices but also the

Source: Geert Hofstede, "Cultural Constraints in Management Theories," *Academy of Management Executive*, February 1993, pp. 81–93. Used with permission.

validity of *theories* may stop at national borders, and I wonder whether even today everybody would agree with this statement.

An article I published in *Organizational Dynamics* in 1980 entitled "Do American Theories Apply Abroad?" created more controversy than I expected. The article argued, with empirical support, that generally accepted U.S. theories like those of Maslow, Herzberg, McClelland, Vroom, McGregor, Likert, Blake and Mouton may not or only very partly apply outside the borders of their country of origin—assuming they do apply within those borders. Among the requests for reprints, a larger number were from Canada than from the United States.

Management Theorists Are Human. Employees and managers are human. Employees as humans was "discovered" in the 1930s, with the Human Relations school. Managers as humans was introduced in the late 40s by Herbert Simon's "bounded rationality" and elaborated in Richard Cyert and James March's *Behavioral Theory of the Firm* (1963, and recently re-published in a second edition). My argument is that management scientists, theorists, and writers are human too: they grew up in a particular society in a particular period, and their ideas cannot help but reflect the constraints of their environment.

The idea that the validity of a theory is constrained by national borders is more obvious in Europe, with all its borders, than in a huge borderless country like the U.S. Already in the sixteenth century Michel de Montaigne, a Frenchman, wrote a statement which was made famous by Blaise Pascal about a century later: "*Vérite en-deça des Pyrenées, erreur au-delà*"—There are truths on this side of the Pyrenées which are falsehoods on the other.

From Don Armado's Love to Taylor's Science. According to the comprehensive ten-volume Oxford English Dictionary (1971), the words "manage," "management," and "manager" appeared in the English language in the 16th century. The oldest recorded use of the word "manager" is in Shakespeare's "Love's Labour's Lost," dating from 1588, in which Don Adriano de Armado, "a fantastical Spaniard," exclaims (Act I, scene ii, 188):

> "*Adieu, valour! rust, rapier! be still, drum! for your manager is in love; yea, he loveth*".

The linguistic origin of the word is from Latin *manus*, hand, via the Italian *maneggiare*, which is the training of horses in the *manege*; subsequently its meaning was extended to skillful handling in general, like of arms and musical instruments, as Don Armado illustrates. However, the word also became associated with the French *menage*, household, as an equivalent of "husbandry" in its sense of the art of running a household. The theatre of present-day management contains elements of both *manege* and *menage* and different managers and cultures may use different accents.

The founder of the science of economics, the Scot Adam Smith, in his 1776 book *The Wealth of Nations*, used "manage," "management" (even "bad management") and "manager" when dealing with the process and the persons involved in operating joint stock companies (Smith, V.i.e.). British economist John Stuart Mill (1806–1873) followed Smith in this use and clearly expressed his distrust of such hired people who were not driven by ownership. Since the 1880s the word "management" appeared occasionally in writings by American engineers, until it was canonized as a modern science by Frederick W. Taylor in *Shop Management* in 1903 and in *The Principles of Scientific Management* in 1911.

While Smith and Mill used "management" to describe a process and "managers" for the persons involved, "management" in the American sense—which has since been taken back by the British—refers not only to the process but also to the managers as a class of people. This class (1) does not own a business but sells its skills to act on behalf of the owners and (2) does not produce personally but is indispensable for making others produce, through motivation. Members of this class carry a high status and many American boys and girls aspire to the role. In the U.S., the manager is a cultural hero.

Let us now turn to other parts of the world. We will look at management in its context in other successful modern economies: Germany, Japan, France, Holland, and among the overseas Chinese. Then we will examine management in the much larger part of the world that is still poor, especially South-East Asia and Africa, and in the new political configurations of Eastern Europe, and Russia in particular. We will then return to the U.S. via mainland China.

Germany. The manager is not a cultural hero in Germany. If anybody, it is the engineer who fills the hero role. Frederick Taylor's *Scientific Management* was conceived in a society of immigrants—where large number of workers with diverse backgrounds and skills had to work together. In Germany this heterogeneity never existed.

Elements of the mediaeval guild system have survived in historical continuity in Germany until the present day. In particular, a very effective apprenticeship system exists both on the shop floor and in the office, which alternates practical work and classroom courses. At the end of the apprenticeship the worker receives a certificate, the *Facharbeiterbrief*, which is recognized throughout the country. About two thirds of the German worker population holds such a certificate and a corresponding occupational pride. In fact, quite a few German company presidents have worked their way up from the ranks through an apprenticeship. In comparison, two thirds of the worker population in Britain have no occupational qualification at all.

The highly skilled and responsible German workers do not necessarily need a manager, American-style, to "motivate" them. They expect their boss or *Meister* to assign their tasks and to be the expert in resolving technical problems. Comparisons of similar German, British, and French organizations show the Germans as having the highest rate of personnel in productive roles and the lowest both in leadership and staff roles.

Business schools are virtually unknown in Germany. Native German management theories concentrate on formal systems. The inapplicability of American concepts of management was quite apparent in 1973 when the U.S. consulting firm of Booz, Allen and Hamilton, commissioned by the German Ministry of Economic Affairs, wrote a study of German management from an American viewpoint. The report is highly critical and writes among other things that "Germans simply do not have a very strong concept of management." Since 1973, from my personal experience, the situation has not changed much. However, during this period the German economy has performed in a superior fashion to the U.S. in virtually all respects, so a strong concept of management might have been a liability rather than an asset.

Japan. The American type of manager is also missing in Japan. In the United States, the core of the enterprise is the managerial class. The core of the Japanese enterprise is the permanent worker group; workers who for all practical purposes are tenured and who aspire at life-long employment. They are distinct from the non-permanent employees—most women and subcontracted teams led by gang bosses, to be laid off in slack periods. University graduates in Japan first join the permanent worker group and subsequently fill various positions, moving from line to staff as the need occurs while paid according to seniority rather than position. They take part in Japanese-style group consultation sessions for important decisions, which extend the decision-making period but guarantee fast implementation afterwards. Japanese are to a large extent controlled by their peer group rather than by their manager.

Three researchers from the East-West Center of the University of Hawaii, Joseph Tobin, David Wu, and Dana Danielson, did an observation study of typical preschools in three countries: China, Japan, and the United States. Their results have been published both as a book and as a video. In the Japanese preschool, one teacher handled twenty-eight four-year olds. The video shows one particularly obnoxious boy, Hiroki, who fights with other children and throws teaching materials down from the balcony. When a little girl tries to alarm the teacher, the latter answers "what are you calling me for? Do something about it!" In the U.S. preschool, there is one adult for every nine children. This class has its problem child too, Glen, who refuses to clear away his toys. One of the teachers has a long talk with him and isolates him in a corner, until he changes his mind. It doesn't take much imagination to realize that managing Hiroki thirty years later will be a different process from managing Glen.

American theories of leadership are ill-suited for the Japanese group-controlled situation. During the past two decades, the Japanese have developed their own "PM" theory of leadership, in which P stands for performance and M for maintenance. The latter is less a concern for individual employees than for maintaining social stability. In view of the amazing success of the Japanese economy in the past thirty years, many Americans have sought for the secrets of Japanese management, hoping to copy them.

France. The manager, U.S. style, does not exist in France either. In a very enlightening book, unfortunately not yet translated into English, the French researcher Philippe d'Iribarne (1989) describes the results of in-depth observation and interview studies of management methods in three subsidiary plants of the same French multinational: in France, the United States, and Holland. He relates what he finds to information about the three societies in general. Where necessary, he goes back in history to trace the roots of the strikingly different behaviors in the completion of the same tasks. He identifies three kinds of basic principles (*logiques*) of management. In the USA, the principle is the *fair contract* between employer and employee, which gives the manager considerable prerogatives, but within its limits. This is really a labor *market* in which the worker sells his or her labor for a price. In France, the principle is the *honor* of each class in a society which has always been and remains extremely stratified, in which superiors behave as superior beings and subordinates accept and expect this, conscious of their own lower level in the national hierarchy but also of the honor of their own class. The French do not think in terms of managers versus nonmanagers but in terms of *cadres* versus *non-cadres*; one becomes cadre by attending the proper schools and one remains it forever; regardless of their actual task, cadres have the privileges of a higher social class, and it is very rare for a non-cadre to cross the ranks.

The conflict between French and American theories of management became apparent in the beginning of the twentieth century, in a criticism by the great French management pioneer Henri Fayol (1841–1925) on his U.S. colleague and contemporary Frederick W. Taylor (1856–1915). The difference in career paths of the two men is striking. Fayol was a French engineer whose career as a *cadre supérieur* culminated in the position of Président-Directeur-Général of a mining company. After his retirement he formulated his experiences in a pathbreaking text on organization: *Administration industrielle et générale*, in which he focussed on the sources of authority. Taylor was an American engineer who started his career in industry as a worker and attained his academic qualifications through evening studies. From chief engineer in a steel company he became one of the first management consultants. Taylor was not really concerned with the issue of authority at all; his focus was on efficiency. He proposed to split the task of the first-line boss into eight specialisms, each exercised by a different person; an idea which eventually led to the idea of a matrix organization.

Taylor's work appeared in a French translation in 1913, and Fayol read it and showed himself generally impressed but shocked by Taylor's "denial of the principle of the Unity of Command" in the case of the eight-boss-system.

Seventy years later André Laurent, another of Fayol's compatriots, found that French managers in a survey reacted very strongly against a suggestion that one employee could report to two different bosses, while U.S. managers in the same survey showed fewer misgivings. Matrix organization has never become popular in France as it has in the United States.

Holland. In my own country, Holland or as it is officially called, the Netherlands, the study by Philippe d'Iribarne found the management principle to be a need for *consensus* among all parties, neither predetermined by a contractual relationship nor by class distinctions, but based on an open-ended exchange of views and a balancing of interests. In terms of the different origins of the word "manager," the organization in Holland is more *menage* (household) while in the United States it is more *manege* (horse drill).

At my university, the University of Limburg at Maastricht, every semester we receive a class of American business students who take a program in European Studies. We asked both the Americans and a matched group of Dutch students to describe their ideal job after graduation, using a list of twenty-two job characteristics. The Americans attached significantly more importance than the Dutch to earnings, advancement, benefits, a good working relationship with their boss, and security of employment. The Dutch attached more importance to freedom to adopt their own approach to the job, being consulted by their boss in his or her decisions, training opportunities, contributing to the success of their organization, fully using their skills and abilities, and helping others. This list confirms d'Iribarne's findings of a contractual employment relationship in the United States, based on earnings and career opportunities, against a consensual relationship in Holland. The latter has centuries-old roots; the Netherlands were the first republic in Western Europe (1609–1810), and a model for the American republic. The country has been and still is governed by a careful balancing of interests in a multi-party system.

In terms of management theories, both motivation and leadership in Holland are different from what they are in the United States. Leadership in Holland presupposes modesty, as opposed to assertiveness in the United States. No U.S. leadership theory has room for that. Working in Holland is not a constant feast, however. There is a built-in premium on mediocrity and jealousy, as well as time-consuming ritual consultations to maintain the appearance of consensus and the pretense of modesty. There is unfortunately another side to every coin.

The overseas Chinese. Among the champions of economic development in the past thirty years we find three countries mainly populated by Chinese living outside the Chinese mainland: Taiwan, Hong Kong and Singapore. Moreover, overseas Chinese play a very important role in the economies of Indonesia, Malaysia, the Philippines and Thailand, where they form an ethnic minority. If anything, the little dragons—Taiwan, Hong Kong and Singapore—have been more economically successful than Japan, moving from rags to riches and now counted among the world's wealthy industrial countries. Yet very little attention has been paid to the way in which their enterprises have been managed. *The Spirit of Chinese Capitalism* by Gordon Redding (1990), the British dean of the Hong Kong Business School, is an excellent book about Chinese business. He bases his insights on personal acquaintance and in-depth discussions with a large number of overseas Chinese businesspeople.

Overseas Chinese American enterprises lack almost all characteristics of modern management. They tend to be small, cooperating for essential functions with other small organizations through networks based on personal relations. They are family-owned, without the separation between ownership and management typical in the West, or even in Japan and Korea. They normally focus on one product or market, with growth by opportunistic diversification; in this, they are extremely flexible. Decision making is centralized in the hands of one dominant family member, but other family members may be given new ventures to try their skills on. They are low-profile and extremely cost-conscious, applying Confucian virtues of thrift and persistence. Their size is kept small by the assumed lack of loyalty of non-family employees, who, if they are any good, will just wait and save until they can start their own family business.

Overseas Chinese prefer economic activities in which great gains can be made with little manpower, like commodity trading and real estate. They employ few professional managers, except their sons and sometimes daughters who have been sent to prestigious business schools abroad, but who upon return continue to run the family business the Chinese way.

The origin of this system, or—in the Western view—this lack of system, is found in the history of Chinese society, in which there were no formal laws, only formal networks of powerful people guided by general principles of Confucian virtue. The favors of the authorities could change daily, so nobody could be trusted except one's kinfolk—of whom, fortunately, there used to be many, in an extended family structure. The overseas Chinese way of doing business is also very well adapted to their position in the countries in which they form ethnic minorities, often envied and threatened by ethnic violence.

Overseas Chinese businesses following this unprofessional approach command a collective gross national product of some 200 to 300 billion US dollars, exceeding the GNP of Australia. There is no denying that it works.

Management Transfer to Poor Countries. Four-fifths of the world population live in countries that are not rich but poor. After World War II and decolonization, the stated purpose of the United Nations and the World Bank has been to promote the development of all the world's countries in a war on poverty. After forty years it looks very much like we are losing this war. If one thing has become clear, it is that the export of Western—mostly American—management practices *and* theories to poor countries has contributed little to nothing to their development. There has been no lack of effort and money spent for this purpose: students from poor countries have been trained in this country, and teachers and Peace Corps workers have been sent to the poor countries. If nothing else, the general lack of success in economic development of other countries should be sufficient argument to doubt the validity of Western management theories in non-Western environments.

If we examine different parts of the world, the development picture is not equally bleak, and history is often a better predictor than economic factors for what happens today. There is a broad regional pecking order with East Asia leading. The little dragons have passed into the camp of the wealthy; then follow South-East Asia (with its overseas Chinese minorities), Latin America (in spite of the debt crisis), South Asia, and Africa always trails behind. Several African countries have only become poorer since decolonization.

Regions of the world with a history of large-scale political integration and civilization generally have done better than regions in which no large-scale political and cultural infrastructure existed, even if the old civilizations had decayed or been suppressed by colonizers. It has become painfully clear that development cannot be pressure-cooked; it presumes a cultural infrastructure that takes time to grow. Local management is part of this infrastructure; it cannot be imported in package form. Assuming that with so-called modern management techniques and theories outsiders can develop a country has proven a deplorable arrogance. At best, one can hope for a dialogue between equals with the locals, in which the Western partner acts as the expert in Western technology and the local partner as the expert in local culture, habits, and feelings.

Russia and China. The crumbling of the former Eastern bloc has left us with a scattering of states and would-be states of which the political and economic future is extremely uncertain. The best predictions are those based on a knowledge of history, because historical trends have taken revenge on the arrogance of the Soviet rulers who believed they could turn them around by brute power. One obvious fact is that the former bloc is extremely heterogeneous, including countries traditionally closely linked with the West by trade and travel, like Czechia, Hungary, Slovenia, and the Baltic states, as well as others with a Byzantine or Turkish past; some having been prosperous, others always extremely poor.

Let me limit myself to the Russian republic, a huge territory with some 140 million inhabitants, mainly Russians. We know quite a bit about the Russians as their country was a world power for several hundreds of years before communism, and in the nineteenth century it has produced some of the greatest writers in world literature. If I want to understand the Russians—including how they could so long support the Soviet regime—I tend to re-read Lev Nikolayevich Tolstoy. In his most famous novel, *Anna Karenina* (1876), one of the main characters is a landowner, Levin, whom Tolstoy uses to express his own views and convictions about his people. Russian peasants used to be serfs; serfdom had been abolished in 1861, but the peasants, now tenants, remained as passive as before. Levin wanted to break this passivity by dividing the land among his peasants in exchange for a share of the crops; but the peasants only let the land deteriorate further. Here follows a quote:

> (Levin) read political economy and socialistic works . . . but, as he had expected, found nothing in them related to his undertaking. In the political economy books— in (John Stuart) Mill, for instance, whom he studied first and with great ardour, hoping every minute to find an answer to the questions that were engrossing him—he found only certain laws deduced from the state of agriculture in Europe; but he could not for the life of him see why these laws, which did not apply to Russia, should be considered universal. . . . Political economy told him that the laws by

which Europe had developed and was developing her wealth were universal and absolute. Socialist teaching told him that development along those lines leads to ruin. And neither of them offered the smallest enlightenment as to what he, Levin, and all the Russian peasants and landowners were to do with their millions of hands and millions of acres, to make them as productive as possible for the common good.

In the summer of 1991, the Russian lands yielded a record harvest, but a large share of it rotted in the fields because no people were to be found for harvesting. The passivity is still there, and not only among the peasants. And the heirs of John Stuart Mill (whom we met before as one of the early analysts of "management") again present their universal recipes which simply do not apply.

Citing Tolstoy, I implicitly suggest that management theorists cannot neglect the great literature of the countries they want their ideas to apply to. The greatest novel in the Chinese literature is considered Cao Xueqin's *The Story of the Stone*, also known as *The Dream of the Red Chamber*, which appeared around 1760. It describes the rise and fall of two branches of an aristocratic family in Beijing, who live in adjacent plots in the capital. Their plots are joined by a magnificent garden with several pavillions in it, and the young, mostly female members of both families are allowed to live in them. One day the management of the garden is taken over by a young woman, Tan-Chun, who states:

> I think we ought to pick out a few experienced trust-worthy old women from among the ones who work in the Garden—women who know something about gardening already—and put the upkeep of the Garden into their hands. We needn't ask them to pay us rent; all we need ask them for is an annual share of the produce. There would be four advantages in this arrangement. In the first place, if we have people whose sole occupation is to look after trees and flowers and so on, the condition of the Garden will improve gradually year after year and there will be no more of those long periods of neglect followed by bursts of feverish activity when things have been allowed to get out of hand. Secondly there won't be the spoiling and wastage we get at present. Thirdly the women themselves will gain a little extra to add to their incomes which will compensate them for the hard work they put in throughout the year. And fourthly, there's no reason why we shouldn't use the money we should otherwise have spent on nurserymen, rockery specialists, horticultural cleaners and so on for other purposes.

As the story goes on, the capitalist privatization—because that is what it is—of the Garden is carried through, and it works. When in the 1980s Deng Xiaoping allowed privatization in the Chinese villages, it also worked. It worked so well that its effects started to be felt in politics and threatened the existing political order; hence the knockdown at Tiananmen Square of June 1989. But it seems that the forces of privatization are getting the upper hand again in China. If we remember what Chinese entrepreneurs are able to do once they have become overseas Chinese, we shouldn't be too surprised. But what works in China—and worked two centuries ago—does not have to work in Russia, not in Tolstoy's days and not today. I am not offering a solution; I only protest against a naive universalism that knows only one recipe for development, the one supposed to have worked in the United States.

A Theory of Culture in Management. Our trip around the world is over and we are back in the United States. What have we learned? There is something in all countries called "management," but its meaning differs to a larger or smaller extent from one country to the other, and it takes considerable historical and cultural insight into local conditions to understand its processes, philosophies, and problems. If already the word may mean so many different things, how can we expect one country's theories of management to apply abroad? One should be extremely careful in making this assumption, and test it before considering it proven. Management is not a phenomenon that can be isolated from other processes taking place in a society. During our trip around the world we saw that it interacts with what happens in the family, at school, in politics, and government. It is obviously also related to religion and to beliefs about science. Theories of management always had to be interdisciplinary, but if we cross national borders they should become more interdisciplinary than ever.

Cultural differences between nations can be, to some extent, described using first four, and now five, bipolar *dimensions*. The position of a country on these dimensions allows us to make some predictions on the way their society operates, including their management processes and the kind of theories applicable to their management.

As the word culture plays such an important role in my theory, let me give you my definition, which differs from some other very respectable definitions. Culture to me is *the collective programming of the mind which distinguishes one group or category of people from another*. In the part of my work I am referring to now, the category of people is the nation.

Culture is *construct*, that means it is "not directly accessible to observation but inferable from verbal statements and other behaviors and useful in predicting still other observable and measurable verbal and nonverbal behavior." It should not be reified; it is an auxiliary concept that should be used as long as it proves useful but bypassed where we can predict behaviors without it.

The same applies to the *dimensions* I introduced. They are constructs too that should not be reified. They do not "exist"; they are tools for analysis which may or may not clarify a situation. In my statistical analysis of empirical data the first four dimensions together explain forty-nine percent of the variance in the data. The other fifty-one percent remain specific to individual countries.

The first four dimensions were initially detected through a comparison of the values of similar people (employees and managers) in sixty-four national subsidiaries of the IBM Corporation. People working for the same multinational, but in different countries, represent very well-matched samples from the populations of their countries, similar in all respects except nationality.

The first dimension is labelled *Power Distance*, and it can be defined as the degree of inequality among people which the population of a country considers as normal: from relatively equal (that is, small power distance) to extremely unequal (large power distance). All societies are unequal, but some are more unequal than others.

The second dimension is labelled *Individualism*, and it is the degree to which people in a country prefer to act as individuals rather than as members of groups. The opposite of individualism can be called *Collectivism*, so collectivism is low individualism. The way I use the word it has no political connotations. In collectivist societies a child learns to respect the group to which it belongs, usually the family, and to differentiate between in-group members and out-group members (that is, all other people). When children grow up they remain members of their group, and they expect the group to protect them when they are in trouble. In return, they have to remain loyal to their group throughout life. In individualist societies, a child learns very early to think of itself as "I" instead of as part of "we." It expects one day to have to stand on its own feet and not to get protection from its group any more; and therefore it also does not feel a need for strong loyalty.

The third dimension is called *Masculinity* and its opposite pole *Femininity*. It is the degree to which tough values like assertiveness, performance, success and competition, which in nearly all societies are associated with the role of men, prevail over tender values like the quality of life, maintaining warm personal relationships, service, care for the weak, and solidarity, which in nearly all societies are more associated with women's roles. Women's roles differ from men's roles in all countries; but in tough societies, the differences are larger than in tender ones.

The fourth dimension is labelled *Uncertainty Avoidance*, and it can be defined as the degree to which people in a country prefer structured over unstructured situations. Structured situations are those in which there are clear rules as to how one should behave. These rules can be written down, but they can also be unwritten and imposed by tradition. In countries which score high on uncertainty avoidance, people tend to show more nervous energy, while in countries which score low, people are more easy-going. A (national) society with strong uncertainty avoidance can be called rigid; one with weak uncertainty avoidance, flexible. In countries where uncertainty avoidance is strong a feeling prevails of "what is different, is dangerous." In weak uncertainty avoidance societies, the feeling would rather be "what is different, is curious."

The fifth dimension was added on the basis of a study of the values of students in twenty-three countries carried out by Michael Harris Bond, a Canadian working in Hong Kong. He and I had cooperated in another study of students' values which had yielded the same four dimensions as the IBM data. However, we wondered to what extent our common findings in two studies could be the effect of a Western bias introduced by the common Western background of the researchers; remember Alice's croquet game. Michael Bond resolved this dilemma by deliberately introducing an Eastern bias. He used a questionnaire prepared at his request by his Chinese colleagues, the *Chinese Value Survey* (CVS), which was translated from Chinese into different languages and answered by fifty male and fifty female students in each of twenty-three countries in all five continents. Analysis of the CVS data produced three dimensions significantly correlated with the three IBM dimensions of power distance, individualism, and masculinity. There was also a fourth dimension, but it did not resemble uncertainty avoidance. It was composed, both on the positive and on the negative side, from items that had not been included in the IBM studies but were present in the Chinese Value Survey because they were rooted in the teachings of Confucius. I labelled this dimension: *Long-term* versus *Short-term Orientation*. On the long-term side one finds values oriented towards the future, like thrift (saving) and persistence. On the short-term side one finds values rather oriented towards the past and present, like respect for tradition and fulfilling social obligations.

Table 1 lists the scores on all five dimensions for the United States and for the other countries we just discussed. The table shows that each country has its own configuration on the four dimensions. Some of the values in the table have been estimated based on imperfect replications or personal impressions. The different dimension scores do not "explain" all the differences in management I described earlier. To understand management in a country, one should have both knowledge of

TABLE 1 Culture Dimension Scores for Ten Countries

(PD = Power Distance; ID = Individualism; MA = Masculinity;
UA = Uncertainty Avoidance; LT = Long Term Orientation)
H = top third, M = medium third, L = bottom third
(among 53 countries and regions for the first four dimensions; among 23 countries for the fifth)

	PD	ID	MA	UA	LT
USA	40 L	91 H	62 H	46 L	29 L
Germany	35 L	67 H	66 H	65 M	31 M
Japan	54 M	46 M	95 H	92 H	80 H
France	68 H	71 H	43 M	86 H	30*L
Netherlands	38 L	80 H	14 L	53 M	44 M
Hong Kong	68 H	25 L	57 H	29 L	96 H
Indonesia	78 H	14 L	46 M	48 L	25*L
West Africa	77 H	20 L	46 M	54 M	16 L
Russia	95*H	50*M	40*L	90*H	10*L
China	80*H	20*L	50*M	60*M	118 H

*estimated

and empathy with the entire local scene. However, the scores should make us aware that people in other countries may think, feel, and act very differently from us when confronted with basic problems of society.

Idiosyncracies of American Management Theories. In comparison to other countries, the U.S. culture profile presents itself as below average on power distance and uncertainty avoidance, highly individualistic, fairly masculine, and short-term oriented. The Germans show a stronger uncertainty avoidance and less extreme individualism; the Japanese are different on all dimensions, least on power distance; the French show larger power distance and uncertainty avoidance, but are less individualistic and somewhat feminine; the Dutch resemble the Americans on the first three dimensions, but score extremely feminine and relatively long-term oriented; Hong Kong Chinese combine large power distance with weak uncertainty avoidance, collectivism, and are very long-term oriented; and so on.

The American culture profile is reflected in American management theories. I will just mention three elements not necessarily present in other countries: the stress on market processes, the stress on the individual, and the focus on managers rather than on workers.

The stress on market processes. During the 1970s and 80s it has become fashionable in the United States to look at organizations from a "transaction costs" viewpoint. Economist Oliver Williamson has opposed "hierarchies" to "markets." The reasoning is that human social life consists of economic transactions between individuals. We found the same in d'Iribarne's description of the U.S. principle of the contract between employer and employee, the labor market in which the worker sells his or her labor for a price. These individuals will form hierarchical organizations when the cost of the economic transactions (such as getting information, finding out whom to trust, etc.) is lower in a hierarchy than when all transactions would take place on a free market.

From a cultural perspective the important point is that the *"market" is the point of departure or base model*, and the organization is explained from market failure. A culture that produces such a theory is likely to prefer organizations that internally resemble markets to organizations that internally resemble more structured models, like those in Germany or France. The ideal principle of control in organizations in the market philosophy is *competition* between individuals. This philosophy fits a society that combines a not-too-large power distance with a not-too-strong uncertainty avoidance and individualism; besides the USA, it will fit all other Anglo countries.

The stress on the individual. I find this constantly in the design of research projects and hypotheses; also in the fact that in the U.S. psychology is clearly a more respectable discipline in management circles than sociology. Culture however is a collective phenomenon. Although we may get our information about culture from individuals, we have to interpret it at the level of collectivities. There are snags here known as the "ecological fallacy" and the "reverse ecological fallacy." None of the U.S. college textbooks on methodology I know deals sufficiently with the problem of multilevel analysis.

A striking example is found in the otherwise excellent book *Organizational Culture and Leadership* by Edgar H. Schein (1985). On the basis of his consulting experience he compares two large companies, nicknamed "Action" and "Multi." He explains the differences in culture between these companies by the group dynamics in their respective boardrooms. Nowhere in the book are any conclusions drawn from the fact that the first company is an American-based computer firm, and the second a Swiss-based pharmaceutics firm. This information is not even mentioned. A stress on interactions among individuals obviously fits a culture identified as the most individualistic in the world, but it will not be so well understood by the four-fifths of the world population for whom the group prevails over the individual.

One of the conclusions of my own multilevel research has been that culture at the national level and culture at the organizational level—corporate culture—are two very different phenomena and that the use of a common term for both is confusing. If we do use the common term, we should also pay attention to the occupational and the gender level of culture. National cultures differ primarily in the fundamental, invisible values held by a majority of their members, acquired in early childhood, whereas organizational cultures are a much more superficial phenomenon residing mainly in the visible practices of the organization, acquired by socialization of the new members who join as young adults. National cultures change only very slowly if at all; organizational cultures may be consciously changed, although this isn't necessarily easy. This difference between the two types of culture is the secret of the existence of multinational corporations that employ, as I showed in the IBM case, employees with extremely different national cultural values. What keeps them together is a corporate culture based on common practices.

The stress on managers rather than workers. The core element of a work organization around the world is the people who do the work. All the rest is superstructure, and I hope to have demonstrated to you that it may take many different shapes. In the U.S. literature on work organization, however, the core element, if not explicitly then implicitly, is considered the manager. This may well be the result of the combination of extreme individualism with fairly strong masculinity, which has turned the manager into a culture hero of almost mythical proportions. For example, he—not really she—is supposed to make decisions all the time. Those of you who are or have been managers must know that this is a fable. Very few management decisions are just "made" as the myth suggests it. Managers are much more involved in maintaining networks; if anything, it is the rank-and-file worker who can really make decisions on his or her own, albeit on a relatively simple level.

An amusing effect of the U.S. focus on managers is that in at least ten American books and articles on management I have been misquoted as having studied IBM *managers* in my research, whereas the book clearly describes that the answers were from IBM *employees*. My observation may be biased, but I get the impression that compared to twenty or thirty years ago less research in this country is done among employees and more on managers. But managers derive their *raison d'être* from the people managed: culturally, they are the followers of the people they lead, and their effectiveness depends on the latter. In other parts of the world, this exclusive focus on the manager is less strong, with Japan as the supreme example.

Conclusion. This article started with *Alice in Wonderland*. In fact, the management theorist who ventures outside his or her own country into other parts of the world is like Alice in Wonderland. He or she will meet strange beings, customs, ways of organizing or disorganizing and theories that are clearly stupid, old-fashioned or even immoral—yet they may work, or at least they may not fail more frequently than corresponding theories do at home. Then, after the first culture shock, the traveller to Wonderland will feel enlightened, and may be able to take his or her experiences home and use them advantageously. All great ideas in science, politics and management have travelled from one country to another, and been enriched by foreign influences. The roots of American management theories are mainly in Europe: with Adam Smith, John Stuart Mill, Lev Tolstoy, Max Weber, Henri Fayol, Sigmund Freud, Kurt Lewin and many others. These theories were re-planted here and they developed and bore fruit. The same may happen again. The last thing we need is a Monroe doctrine for management ideas.

1. On the basis of what you have read, and your own opinion, do you think that the theories and techniques in the field of organizational behavior are relevant and applicable across borders? Why or why not?
2. Briefly summarize what management means and emphasizes in the highly developed countries (Germany, Japan, France, Holland, and the overseas Chinese), in the lesser developed areas (Southeast Asia and Africa), and in the former communist countries of Eastern Europe and Russia.
3. What aspects of management seem unique to the United States? Do you think this helps or hinders American organizations in their efforts to compete in the global economy?
4. What do you think the future has in store for management approaches around the world? Do you think management in other countries will be more similar or more different than past and present North American management theories and practices?

INTEGRATIVE CONTEMPORARY CASES/READINGS FOR PART 5

2. How We Will Work in the Year 2000

Six Trends That Will Reshape the Workplace

- The average company will become smaller, employing fewer people.
- The traditional hierarchical organization will give way to a variety of organizational forms, the network of specialists foremost among these.
- Technicians, ranging from computer repairmen to radiation therapists, will replace manufacturing operatives as the worker elite.
- The vertical division of labor will be replaced by a horizontal division.
- The paradigm of doing business will shift from making a product to providing a service.
- Work itself will be redefined: constant learning, more high-order thinking, less nine-to-five.

The year 2000 will dawn on a Saturday, perfect for nursing recollections of the Nineties and soberly contemplating the era ahead. Ruminative types among the approximately 133 million people then in the work force will look back on a decade of change all the more head-spinning for its seemingly chaotic, devolutionary quality.

The average size of a U.S. company, measured by the number of individuals it employs, will have decreased. More people will have set up in business for themselves. Many of the industrial colossi, long the pillars of our economy, will have broken up or hollowed out. Taking the place of the hierarchically layered giants will be not just one type of organization but a variety of them, with names such as spider's web.

What Americans do on the job will have changed too, so much so as to cry out for a new definition of work. The old blue-collar elite will have ceded pride of place to an ascendant class, technical workers, who program computers or conduct laboratory tests or fix copiers. Almost everyone, up through the highest ranks of professionals, will feel increased pressure to specialize, or at least to package himself or herself as a marketable portfolio of skills. Executives and what used to be called managers will have undergone probably the most radical rethinking of their role.

And more and more of the population will be caught up in the defining activity of the age: scrambling. Scrambling for footing on a shifting corporate landscape—cynics will call it a freelance economy—where market forces have supplanted older, more comfortable employment arrangements. Scrambling to upgrade their software, their learning, their financial reserves. Scrambling even to carve out moments of tranquility under a banner blazoned FIGHT STRESS, a banner flapping like a Tibetan prayer flag in the gales of change.

Stephen R. Barley, a professor at Cornell's School of Industrial and Labor Relations, builds on the work of others to argue that until recently, "the economies of the advanced industrial nations revolved around electrical power, the electric motor, the internal combustion engine, and the telephone." The development of these "infrastructural technologies" made possible the shift from an agricultural to a manufacturing economy, in the process precipitating "urbanization, the growth of corporations, the rise of professional management, the demise of religion, and the disintegration of the extended family."

Now, Barley writes, the evidence suggests that another shift is taking place, with implications likely to be just as seismic: "Our growing knowledge of how to convert electronic and mechanical impulses into digitally encoded information (and vice versa) and how to transmit such information across vast distances is gradually enabling industry to replace its electromechanical infrastructure with a computational infrastructure."

You already know part of the punch line from this not unfamiliar tale: The computational infrastructure, computers at its heart, takes over progressively more of the work that can be routinized—and ever more can, with the new technology—from guiding machines that make things to transmitting information within the organization or across its boundaries. Bingo, you've got flexible manufacturing, program trading, and point-of-purchase terminals wired into the supplier's factory.

Source: Walter Kiechel, III, "How We Will Work in the Year 2000," *Fortune*, May 17, 1993, pp. 40–42, 46, 48, 52. Copyright 1993, Time Inc. All rights reserved. Reprinted by permission from Time.

Experts on such transformation, people like futurist Tom Mandel at SRI International in Menlo Park, California, correct our impression that new technology drives changes in how we work; rather, it enables them. Posit increased competition through the Eighties, the maturity of existing infrastructural technologies, even a falling rate of profit overall for the postwar U.S. economy. The result of such pressures, argues Mandel, is that "people in business are rethinking, reinventing, reengineering, whatever you want to call it, the structure of work. When they sit down to ask, 'Can we do this a better way?' technology helps provide the answer."

For many companies evolving their way toward 2000, a big part of the answer is to get smaller, or to stay small from the outset. Look at the numbers: IBM now employs 302,000 people, down from 406,000 in 1985; Digital Equipment, 98,000, down from 126,000 in 1989. But then these two old-line computer companies compete against the likes of Apple, with 15,100 employees, Microsoft, with 13,800, and Novell, with 3,500, each of whose market capitalization—the total value of its outstanding stock—exceeds Digital's. AT&T, down to 312,000 people, recently saw the future and sought a piece of it, in the form of a one-third interest in McCaw Cellular, which employs 5,000.

Note that all these companies, the relatively small and the getting-smaller, are in industries central to the new computational infrastructure—what can only be seen as growth industries. If you want to gaze at employment prospects further out on the technology horizon, consider Genentech, the largest biotechnology company. It employs 2,100.

Unfair, the argument might come back: In comparing IBM with an Apple or a Microsoft you're comparing companies at very different stages of corporate development. The younger outfits, as they mature, will surely add lots more employees.

If they do, they will be bucking the trend. Research by professors Erik Brynjolfsson and Thomas W. Malone of MIT's Sloan School indicates that while the average number of employees per company increased until the 1970s, it has been decreasing since then, particularly in manufacturing.

Why should more economic activity be devolving upon small companies? The work done at MIT points again to technology's enabling effects. Brynjolfsson found that even as the typical company in his study eliminated 20% of its employees over ten years, it tripled its investment in information technology. The investment generally preceded the downsizing, but the dynamic was considerably more subtle than a straightforward substitution of computational power for bodies. "Because computers tend to replace more routine workers while augmenting knowledge workers, they change the relative advantages and disadvantages of different types of organization," he explains. "Routine work is organized well in large hierarchical companies. Innovation and knowledge-work type activities"—presumably something like higher-order thinking and analysis—"thrive best under the incentives of small firms." Just ask any of the legion of millionaires at Microsoft.

Malone suggests that the true potential of computers and computer networks, and their effect on organizations, may lie less in their computational power and more in their capacity to take over "coordination activities"—from processing orders to keeping track of inventory to posting accounts. Computerized coordination can be substituted for human effort: Empty out those back offices full of clerks or those plusher spaces inhabited by managers passing information up and down the chain of command. Companies can do more coordination: *Voilà*, elaborate airline reservation systems with fares being constantly adjusted and, because for the first time the airlines can keep track of who goes where, frequent-flier programs.

The biggest effect may be a relatively unexpected one. Malone finds it somewhat surprising, but by now pretty clear, "that the increasing use of information technology appears likely to increase the importance of market mechanisms as a way of coordinating economic activity"—market mechanisms as opposed to a company's internal control systems and procedures. To oversimplify cartoonishly, the benefits of vertical integration melt away. The company discovers that compared with making a product or doing a service in-house, it's cheaper to outsource from one of the many outfits scrambling for the business over the computational infrastructure.

So we all end up working in so-called network organizations, right, hooked in with customers and suppliers via technology and the company itself perhaps structured as a network to mirror its various outside interfaces, pardon the expression? If you've been keeping up on your reading, you will think of the modular or virtual corporation—should the trendies ever agree on a definition for the latter—an outfit pared down to its core competencies and sending out for everything else.

Ah, but it isn't that simple. "There's been a lot of attention, even press attention, to the network organization," sniffs professor James Brian Quinn from Dartmouth's Tuck School of Business. "But when we looked into the way organizations were really developing, the network was only one of about five different new forms. Each of the others was not strictly a network," but each has a distinctive logic behind it.

Quinn's new treatise, *Intelligent Enterprise* (Free Press), the closest approximation we have to a textbook on the emerging economy, describes, for example, the "radically flat organization." Hundreds of separate sites—stores, offices—transmit information to a single headquarters where it's digested, decisions are made, and directions in turn sent back to the sites, which don't need to be in touch with one another. Anyone recognize Wal-Mart here, or Merrill Lynch, with its 12,700 far-flung account executives?

For the Tuck professor, networks are central only to what he calls spider's web organizations, so named for "the lightness yet completeness of their interconnection." Here the examples to bear in mind are an Arthur Andersen Consulting or a McKinsey & Co., an investment banking house or a law firm. The accumulated knowledge in such an organization resides mostly in the heads of its people or in case teams—in network talk, both are at the "nodes"—who don't require, much less want, guidance from a hierarchical superior. What the nodes do require is lots of communication with one another to keep themselves abreast of what each has learned from the latest assignment.

Grant that no single organizational form will take the place of the old multi-layer ziggurat as the new corporate model. Still, if you could pick only one to study for its lessons on how work will be structured and employees accommodated in the year 2000, put your chips on the network, Quinn's spider's web.

This not because more companies will come to resemble consulting firms—though more will—but because the vertical division of labor, based on ranks in a hierarchy, is giving way to a horizontal division, based on individuals' specialties. In the future, the key question for most people will be not "Where do you stand on the corporate ladder?"—sounds of its demolition already ring through the land—but "What do you know how to do?" Pay will be tied less to a person's position or tenure and more to the changing market value of his skills.

Cornell's Barley, who has probably done the most to identify this trend, came at it from study of a remarkably overlooked echelon of the American labor force—

technical workers. These folks don't jibe with our traditional stereotypes of white collar and blue, which may be why we haven't accorded them sufficient notice or respect. As described by Barley, they "often wear white collars, carry briefcases, conduct relatively sophisticated scientific and mathematical analysis, and speak with an educated flair." But many also "use tools and instruments, work with their hands, make objects, repair equipment, and perhaps most important, get dirty." They range from medical technologists to paralegals, from so-called test-and-pay technicians—really—to the person who hooked up the personal computer in your office.

Their ranks are growing. Indeed, if you wonder where the good jobs are going to be in the Nineties, look here. Together with professionals—accountants, scientists, engineers, and the like—whom they increasingly resemble and with whom the Census Bureau lumps them, they already represent about 16% of the work force. If the projections hold, some experts think that by 2000 they could be the biggest segment at 20%, or over 23 million people, substantially exceeding the number of manufacturing operatives and laborers. To the extent that any segment in the employment statistics approximates that much and loosely used term "knowledge workers," these people, along with their professional brethren, are it.

Barley attributes the rise of technical workers to a number of forces. Scientific knowledge has been growing exponentially, by some estimates doubling every six to ten years since the 1960s. Concomitantly, professionals scrambling to keep up with the latest learning have become increasingly specialized, in the process "hiving off" their more routine duties—taking X-rays, for example—to individuals less highly trained. Large professional service organizations—big hospitals, large consultancies, and law firms—can afford to support such increasingly narrow specialization.

But the biggest force behind the ascendance of technicians has been that ol' devil, or angel, technology. Over the past four decades, Barley notes, emerging technologies have created entirely new types of job: air traffic controller, nuclear technician, broadcast engineer, materials scientist. And then, of course, there's the computational infrastructure. Ask Barley what generalizations he can make about technical workers and he shoots back, "The only occupation that we studied where computers aren't integral to the task being done was emergency medical technicians."

What technical workers also have in common, and why they're out front in shifting the division of labor, is that they don't fit well within hierarchical organizations. If you don't believe this, just imagine how effective you would be acting the straw boss to the person who arrives to fix your copying machine.

In Barley's theorization, and more than slightly academic language, "vertical divisions of labor encode expertise in rules, procedures, and positions," meaning that the organization itself is the primary vessel for accumulated learning. A horizontal division, by comparison, "rests on the assumption that knowledge and skills are domain-specific"—reflecting a specialty—"and too complex to be nested" within a hierarchy. Like traditional professionals working within an organization, the technical worker ends up with dual loyalties: some to his employer, but usually more to his specialty.

Which helps explain the attitude of such workers toward their nominal superiors. "When technical people talk about managers they don't discount them," says Barley. "What they do is to impute substantive expertise to managers, saying, 'Well, they know how to make policy' or 'They know about marketing.' So on these issues, they will defer to the managers' wisdom. What they don't defer to is a general, overarching authority based on the hierarchical structure."

What to Call the People We Used to Call Managers

Please, not "facilitator," which suggests someone greasing the skids with the latest lubricant from human resources, someone heavy with process skills but only a slippery grasp of the content at hand. "Coach" and "mentor" still carry too much hierarchical baggage, suggesting a middle-aged male telling others what to do.

The best choice? Probably "coordinator." The double-dome argument for it, as made by MIT's Tom Malone, goes something like this: The old organization chart, which worked perfectly well to explain hierarchies, has become increasingly obsolete as companies become complexly networked, both the people within them and with the outside. As in the fact that your company may now be a supplier to Zorch Corp. in one business, a competitor in another, and a joint-venture partner in a third.

Better to break what you do down into constituent activities and then analyze—and here comes another key word for the Nineties—the dependencies between and among them. Dependencies come in several different forms—from sharing resources to competing for them—and you need an expansive term to cover managing the many varieties. Like coordination.

There's beauty in a well-coordinated group effort. And maybe the clincher—at least for middle-aged males, who might be feeling a little sore by this time—a sports connotation, from football yet: the offensive or defensive coordinator, who reads the shifting plays and patterns of the opposition and then helps his team figure out how to respond.

Barley's concept of a horizontal division of labor clearly has import beyond technical workers. It fits perfectly with the growing importance of smaller, focused organizations. Whom would you expect to find in such outfits if not specialists, those human repositories of core competency? The concept also explains why companies increasingly turn to multifunctional teams to tackle the new.

It sheds light, too, on the growing unwillingness of many in supervisory positions—and just about all baby-boomers—to describe themselves as managers. Ask a woman with 100 people accountable to her what she does for a living, and she will probably say something like, "Oh, I'm in finance." This isn't just boomer egalitarianism. It reflects an intuition that Barley's technical workers are right: If a manager doesn't have substantive expertise—a specialty, if you will—he had better acquire it soon, for by the year 2000 that's what he will be paid for.

Much that nowadays passes for managerial skill probably won't fill the bill then. As Barley points out, a lot of what one learns going up the ranks in a big hierarchical company is "contextual"—the rules and procedures we use here at General Motors, or the Equitable. How useful is such knowledge at another company, especially a smaller one? How much will have been rendered obsolete by computer coordination, anyway?

Not all coordination will be computerized, however, indicating one competence critical to the men and women who will take the place of today's managers. The problem, or opportunity, according to James Brian Quinn: "As more people get more skilled, they also tend to be somewhat more focused, and may not see the whole problem. Getting a team of specialists to come to an answer is a nontrivial event," requiring abilities akin to a diplomat's (see box above).

Indeed, in an economy where market forces increasingly dominate coordination, tomorrow's manager-replacements will have to excel at striking all kinds of deals. (Which may help explain why courses in negotiation have become so popular in recent years.) Deals to put together the best possible team. Deals for partnerships with other companies to jointly develop new products. Deals to obtain resources for less, whether from inside the company or out. Deals to eke out at least a modest profit when more and more product markets act like commodity businesses, what with all that information on features, quality, and price whizzing around the computational infrastructure.

Perhaps paradoxically, a heart, or the ability to feign possession of one, may also be a requisite. Consultant Gifford Pinchot, co-author of the soon-to-be-published *End of Bureaucracy and Rise of the Intelligent Organization*, asserts that for all their Darwinian sharpness, the new masters of coordination will be paid as much "for their ability to make others feel that they care." How do you motivate employees whose specialized skills and ability to operate on their own make them virtually the equivalent of independent contractors? "You make them feel that they're considered meaningful," says Pinchot.

A touch warm-fuzzy-New-Age for your taste? It may seem less so in another context: Pinchot argues that the principle—making others feel you care as a core skill—will apply just as much to salespeople dealing with customers. Then recall the single key piece of learning from the past 20 years on how to manage customer service: An employee treats customers exactly the same way his manager treats him.

If all this—what technical workers do, what organizations and manager-replacements and salespeople will do—begins to sound like an endless daisy chain with one person or organization providing service to another, then you are starting to grasp the future. It's already a truism that America is becoming, or has become, a service economy. Truly understanding this, though, goes beyond knowing the statistics—that service businesses account for three-quarters of U.S. GDP, for example, and a still larger share of employment. Beyond realizing that further decline in manufacturing jobs is inevitable. Beyond figuring out that it's stupid to deride service jobs as mere burger flipping. Who gets paid more, after all, the executives of an average manufacturing company or the partners—service workers all—in an average investment banking house?

Truly understanding the emerging economy takes a change of mind-set or, inevitably, of paradigm: from thinking of business as making things, or churning out product, to realizing that it consists instead of furnishing services, even within what has traditionally been thought of as manufacturing. Much of the quality movement can be understood as building more service into a product. When an Allied-Signal or Eastman Kodak breaks down its operations into the steps by which it adds value, maybe as part of "reengineering its core processes," what is the company doing but identifying a sequence of services performed along the way that eventually leads to the customer?

"Products are a happy way of capturing services," explains Quinn, illustrating the coming view. "A car embodies convenient transportation service and it will until we can either physically move you in some other manner or give you the same experience through, say, electronics. Virtual reality could do the latter." Begin thinking like this and you can fully appreciate the prediction of Lord William Rees-Mogg, former editor of the *Times* of London: "In the future, more business will be based on intangibles than on tangibles."

You can also speculate with greater intelligence on the growth industries of tomorrow. In a sense, 140 years ago Henry David Thoreau posed the fundamental issue for the computational infrastructure, in the process suggesting why, finally, it's so unsatisfying to talk of "the information age" or knowledge workers. Thoreau wrote: "We are in great haste to construct a magnetic telegraph from Maine to Texas; but Maine and Texas, it may be, have nothing important to communicate." Information for what purpose? Knowledge to serve what human aim or itch? Where's the juice?

Many of the best businesses of the year 2000 will deliver not just services, but experiences. According to this line of thought, the flagship companies of corporate America in the 21st century will be not Intel or Microsoft—providers of rolling stock and switches to the computational infrastructure—but Walt Disney Co., or, blush to say, Time Warner, parent of *Fortune*'s publisher. Half the U.S. population east of the Mississippi has visited Disney World in Orlando, Florida, at least once. Today entertainment represents the second-biggest U.S. export, after aerospace. Employment in travel services has been growing 4% a year on average over the past decade.

Other new enterprises will rise up around small ways of making our lives easier that we don't even realize we need now. Just as we didn't understand that we needed to conduct so much business face to face around the globe until jet travel made this possible. Just as teleconferencing may be starting to convince us that electronic face to face is almost as effective, often cheaper, and easier on aging boomer bodies.

Opportunities will abound, too, in services that can't be subsumed by the computational infrastructure because they require a human touch. These aren't merely the janitorial and maid jobs that the Bureau of Labor Statistics projects as among the fastest-growing types of work in the Nineties, measured in the sheer number of positions added. (The total is expected to rise by over 500,000 from the current three million.)

Expect to see a substantial increase in the ranks of what might be termed nurturant service workers. Example: home health care providers, people who tend the sick or recuperating in the patient's home, where convalescents can be treated for much less than in hospitals. How big could the category of nurturant service workers become? Jim Davidson, co-author with Rees-Mogg of a slightly grim predictive work entitled *The Great Reckoning*, notes that about a tenth of the labor force at the start of the 20th century was in domestic service—household help.

Americans won't take that kind of job, the Zoë Bairds of this world might argue. No, probably not if it entailed viewing themselves as servants. "But if they saw themselves as independent professionals," counters Pinchot, "providing their services for a fee." Services like those of a licensed massage therapist, whose numbers have increased fourfold since 1987, or counseling psychologist, or exercise physiologist, the muscular type who oversees your exertions at the fitness center or serves as a high-end personal trainer. These are not just caring professions; they are, even better for their prospects, anti-stress professions.

It will take a major change in our collective social ethic to convince many Americans, particularly men over 40 who worked in giant companies, that jobs like these carry with them anything like the dignity of big-shouldered manufacturing. (But then, how dignified was it really to labor on an assembly line, or to boss those who did?) The proof will come in the answers to three huge questions at the heart of the historic change now under way.

Can technology help make service jobs as productive as manufacturing jobs have been, in ways that are high-paying to the worker and generally enriching to the society? Recent evidence suggests it can. How many Americans have the basic education and the flexibility to become technical workers or new-style service workers? Finally, how many of us are ready for the changes in the very nature of work that the emerging economy will bring with it?

The basic imperative of the computational infrastructure is to push toward the day when, for humans, there is no more business as usual. The decisions kicked to workers by machines will require literacy, numeracy, a capacity for critical thinking and for innovation. Paul Saffo of the Institute for the Future explains what this means, particularly for manufacturing jobs: "Work will become intervention, humans intervening in processes set in motion by us but maintained by our new tools." In his air-conditioned cubicle, the sole remaining human on the factory floor monitors dials and gauges; when they show something awry, his response must be immediate but not automatic, his instincts informed by his intelligence. Scramble.

Work will be learning, too. Ho-hum, another truism—the need for lifelong learning. But attend to Stephen Barley again, this time on how technical workers acquire their skills: "Most of these people will tell you that if they got anything at all out of their formal education it was only a disciplined way of thinking. It's quite possible that practitioners, when it comes to their own technology, know more than what they could get out of a formal course. Take microcomputer support specialists, the people who maintain microcomputers and local area networks. They read trade magazines, they go to trade shows, they collect information produced by vendors, they piece together bits and pieces from the forefront of technology and then try to integrate it with the needs of their organization. What you see them doing is scrambling to stay on top of change." Specialists of all stripes will face this same challenge.

Many of the walls we have traditionally built around work, in part to contain it, will tumble. The computational infrastructure will benefit us by allowing more people to live and work where they want to, probably far from cities, hooked up electronically to their market, their database, or the rest of the organization. The trend will be spearheaded by independent professionals, technicians, and small organizations, particularly those willing to work on a project basis—what used to be called piecework.

Nick Davis moved to Bozeman, Montana, two years ago mostly because it seemed like a great place to raise his children. He found, though, that "electronics are so user-friendly these days" and the data available over various networks so complete that his three-person money management firm, Montana Investment Advisors, can analyze more companies than he could as a Paine Webber broker in New York City and then Denver. Davis devotes the hour a day he used to spend commuting in Colorado to serious study of the piano. Then there's the nearby skiing, of course, and fly-fishing.

But for those who work where they live, it won't all be cozily tapping at the keyboard by the fireplace with the dog curled at their feet. There will be the next project to hustle up, the computer message or fax or phone to be answered forthwith—that's what service is about—the next client visit to drag off to, perhaps somewhat more difficult to launch from Coeur D'Alene, Idaho, than from Los Angeles or Chicago.

"The notion of a workday as we have known it is one of the first casualties of all this," argues Saffo, and not just for the new cottage workers. "Nine-to-five is an artifact of Taylorist thinking," when labor could be measured in the factory or office, and left there when evening came. Harder to leave behind the problem of getting those three specialists to agree when you have no formal authority over them. Or the beeper that signals a glitch in machines back at the plant. Or those sales figures you might go over just one more time on your home PC.

The danger is that we'll be so busy scrambling, so market-driven, that we miss the bigger opportunity presented us by the future—namely, a new freedom. Says MIT's Tom Malone: "Information technology reduces the constraints on information flow and coordination that have limited what we could do in the past. In that sense, we're becoming richer," just as education or wealth give one more options. "To me that raises the importance of what it is we want to do in the first place."

Will we be prepared, for example, to push back from the computer terminal to spend more time with people we love, even if it means missing the next deal and the money to buy the latest gadget? Or willing to walk out into the air and think on what there is to value about ourselves beyond our work?

Good questions for a Saturday.

1. How will we work in the year 2000? Identify some of the major trends.
2. What type of job will be most prevalent in the future? Do you think your education is preparing you for this job market? Why or why not?
3. How does the study of organizational behavior prepare you for your future career?

EXPERIENTIAL EXERCISES FOR PART 5

EXERCISE: Using *Gung Ho* to Understand Cultural Differences
(or Siskel & Ebert Go International)*

"East is east, and west is west. And never the 'twain shall meet.''—Mark Twain

Background:

There is no avoiding the increasing globalization of management. Few, if any, current students of business can expect to pursue a successful career without some encounter of an international nature. Gaining early and realistic exposure to the challenges of cross-cultural dynamics will greatly aid any student of business.

The Pacific Rim will continue to play a dominant role in North American transnational organizations and global markets. The opening doors to China offer an unprecedented market opportunity. Korea, Singapore, and Taiwan continue to be unsung partners in mutually beneficial trading relationships. And, of course, Japan will always be a dominant representative of the Twain quote cited above.

An important aspect of cross-cultural awareness is understanding actual differences in interpersonal style and cultural expectations, and separating this from incorrect assumptions. Many embellished stereotypes have flourished as we extend our focus and attention abroad. Unfortunately, many of these myths have become quite pervasive, in spite of their lack of foundation. Thus, North American managers frequently and confidently err in their cross-cultural interactions. This may be particularly common in our interactions with the Japanese. For example, lifetime employment has long been touted as exemplifying the superior practices of Japanese management. In reality, only one-third of Japanese *male* employees enjoy this benefit, and in 1993, many Japanese firms actually laid off workers for the first time. Also, Japan is promoted as a collectivist culture founded on consensus, teamwork, and employee involvement. Yet, Japan is at the same time one of the most competitive societies, especially when reviewing how students are selected for educational and occupational placement.

Films can provide an entertaining yet potent medium for studying such complex issues. Such experiential learning is most effective when realistic and identifiable with one's own likely experiences. Case studies can be too sterile. Role plays tend to be contrived and void of depth. Both lack a sense of background to help one "buy into" the situation. Films on the other hand can promote a rich and familiar presentation that promotes personal involvement. This exercise seeks to capitalize on this phenomenon to explore cross-cultural demands.

Procedure:

Step I. (110 minutes). Watch the film *Gung Ho*. (This film can be obtained at any video store.)

*Source: Steven M. Sommer, University of Nebraska, Lincoln. Used with permission.

Step II. (30 minutes). Use one of the following four formats to address the discussion topics.

Option A: Address each issue in an open class forum. This option is particularly appropriate for moderate class sizes (forty students), or for sections that do not normally engage in group work.

Option B: Divide the class into groups of four to seven to discuss the assigned topics. A better approach for larger classes (sixty or more students). This approach might also be used to assign the exercise as an extracurricular activity if scheduled class time is too brief.

Option C: Assign one group to adopt the American perspective and another group to take the Japanese perspective. Using a confrontation meeting approach (Walton, 1987), have each side describe its perception and expected difficulties in collaborating with each other. Then, have the two sides break into small mixed groups to discuss methods to bridge the gap (or avoid its extreme escalation as portrayed in the film). Ideas should extend beyond those cited in the movie. Present these separate discussions to the class as a whole.

Option D: Assign students to groups of four to seven to watch the film and write a six-page analysis addressing one or more of the discussion topics.

Discussion topics:

1. In the opening scenes, Hunt observes Kaz being berated in a Japanese "management development center." According to at least one expert, this was a close representation of Japanese disciplinary practices. Would such an approach be possible in an American firm? How does this scene illustrate the different perspectives and approaches to motivation? To reinforcement? To feedback?

2. The concepts of multiculturalism and diversity are emerging issues in modern managerial environments. The importance of recognizing and responding to racial, ethnic, and other demography factors has been widely debated in the popular press. What does *Gung Ho* offer to the discussion (both within and across the two groups)? How does each culture respond to different races, genders, cultures?

3. Individualism and collectivism represent two endpoints on a continuum used to analyze different cultural orientations. Individualism refers to a sense of personal focus, autonomy, and compensation. Collectivism describes a group focus, self-subjugation, obligation, and sharing of rewards. How do you see American and Japanese workers differing on this dimension? You might compare the reactions of the Japanese manager whose wife was about to give birth with those of the American worker who had planned to take his child to a doctor's appointment.

4. How does the softball game illuminate cultural differences (and even similarities)? You might consider this question in reference to topic 3; to approaches to work habits; to having "fun"; to behavioral norms of pride, honor, sportsmanship.

5. On several occasions we see George Wendt's openly antagonistic responses to the exercise of authority by Japanese managers. Discuss the concept of authority as seen in both cultures. Discuss expectations of compliance. How might George's actions be interpreted differently by each culture? Indeed, would they be seen as different by an American manager as compared with a Japanese manager?

6. Throughout the film, one gains an impression of how Americans and the Japanese might differ in their approach to resolving conflict. Separately describe how each culture tends to approach conflict, and how the cultures might be different from each other.

7. Experienced conflict between work and family demands has also gained attention as an important managerial issue. How do both cultures approach the role of work in one's life? The role of family? How does each approach balancing competing demands between the two? Have these expectations changed over time (from twenty years ago, forty years ago, sixty years ago)? How might they change as we enter the twenty-first century?

8. In reality, Japanese managers would be "shamed" if one of their subordinates was seriously injured on the job (the scene where the American worker's hand was caught in the assembly line belt). Taking this into account, what other issues in the film might be used to illustrate differences or similarities between American and Japanese management and work practices?

References

Michael Gordon, L. Allen Slade, and Neal Schmitt, "The 'Science of the Sophomore' Revisited: From Conjecture to Empiricism," *Academy of Management Review*, March 1986, p. 191.

Richard Hodgetts and Fred Luthans, "The Myth of Japanese Management," *Personnel*, April 1989, p. 42.

Leigh Stelzer and Joanna M. Banthin, "A *Gung Ho* Look at the Cultural Clash Between Americans and Japanese," *Journal of Management Inquiry*, September 1992, p. 220.

Richard Walton, *Managing Conflict: Interpersonal Dialogue and Third Party Roles*, Addison-Wesley, Reading, Mass., 1987.

EXERCISE: Organization Development at J. P. Hunt*

Goals: To experience an OD technique—in this case the use of survey feedback—to diagnose strengths and weaknesses and develop an action plan.

Implementation: Set up groups of four to eight members for the one-hour exercise. The groups should be separated from each other and asked to converse only with members of their own group. Each person should read the following:

J. P. Hunt department stores is a large retail merchandising outlet located in Boston. The company sells an entire range of retail goods (appliances, fashions, furniture, and so on) and has a large downtown store plus six branch stores in various suburban areas.

Source: Reprinted with permission from Andrew D. Szilagyi and Marc Wallace, "Survey Feedback," *Organizational Behavior and Performance*, Goodyear, Santa Monica, Calif., 1980, pp. 605–606.

Survey Results for J. P. Hunt Department Store: Credit and Accounts Receivable Department

Variable	Survey Results*			Industry Norms*		
	Managers	Supervisors	Non-supervisors	Managers	Supervisors	Non-supervisors
Satisfaction and rewards:						
Pay	3.30	1.73	2.48	3.31	2.97	2.89
Supervision	3.70	2.42	3.05	3.64	3.58	3.21
Promotion	3.40	2.28	2.76	3.38	3.25	3.23
Coworkers	3.92	3.90	3.72	3.95	3.76	3.43
Work	3.98	2.81	3.15	3.93	3.68	3.52
Performance-to-intrinsic rewards	4.07	3.15	3.20	4.15	3.85	3.81
Performance-to-extrinsic rewards	3.67	2.71	2.70	3.87	3.81	3.76
Supervisory behavior:						
Initiating structure	3.42	3.97	3.90	3.40	3.51	3.48
Consideration	3.63	3.09	3.18	3.77	3.72	3.68
Positive rewards	3.99	2.93	3.02	4.24	3.95	3.91
Punitive rewards	3.01	3.61	3.50	2.81	2.91	3.08
Job characteristics:						
Autonomy	4.13	4.22	3.80	4.20	4.00	3.87
Feedback	3.88	3.81	3.68	3.87	3.70	3.70
Variety	3.67	3.35	3.22	3.62	3.21	2.62
Challenge	4.13	4.03	3.03	4.10	3.64	3.58
Organizational practices:						
Role ambiguity	2.70	2.91	3.34	2.60	2.40	2.20
Role conflict	2.87	3.69	2.94	2.83	3.12	3.02
Job pressure	3.14	4.04	3.23	2.66	2.68	2.72
Performance evaluation process	3.77	3.35	3.19	3.92	3.70	3.62
Worker cooperation	3.67	3.94	3.87	3.65	3.62	3.35
Work-flow planning	3.88	2.62	2.95	4.20	3.80	3.76

*The values are scored from 1, very low, to 5, very high.

As is the case in most retail stores in the area, employee turnover is high (40 to 45 percent annually). In the credit and accounts receivable department, located in the downtown store, turnover is particularly high at both the supervisor and subordinate levels, approaching 75 percent annually. The department employs approximately 150 people, 70 percent of whom are female.

Because of rising hiring and training costs brought on by the high turnover, top department management began a turnover analysis and reduction program. As a first step, a local management consulting firm was contracted to conduct a survey of department employees. Using primarily questionnaires, the consulting firm collected survey data from over 95 percent of the department's employees. The results are shown in the exhibit above, by organizational level, along with industry norms developed by the consulting firm in comparative retail organizations.

Instructions for the exercise:

1. Individually, each group member should analyze the data in the exhibit and attempt to identify and diagnose departmental strengths and problem areas.
2. As a group, the members should repeat step 1 above. In addition, suggestions for resolving the problems and an action plan for feedback to the department should be developed.

REFERENCES FOR BOXES AND REAL CASES

CHAPTER 1

TQM in Action: Going for the Baldy Shari Caudron, "HR Is One Pillar of the Baldrige Award," *Personnel Journal*, August 1993, p. 482; Barbara Ettorre, "Benchmarking: The Next Generation," *Management Review*, June 1993, pp. 10–16; and Richard M. Hodgetts, *Blueprints for Continuous Improvement: Lessons from the Baldrige Winners*, American Management Association, New York, 1993, Chap. 1.

TQM in Action: Reengineering at GTE Michael Hammer and James Champy, *Reengineering the Corporation*, HarperCollins, New York, 1993; Richard J. Schonberger, "Is Strategy Strategic: Impact of Total Quality Management on Strategy," *Academy of Management Executive*, August 1992, pp. 80–87; and Thomas A. Stewart, "Reengineering: The Hot New Managing Tool," *Fortune*, Aug. 23, 1993, pp. 41–48.

Real Case: Going from Fad to Fad Ronald Henkoff, "Companies That Train Best," *Fortune*, Mar. 22, 1993, pp. 62–75; Fred R. Bleakley, "Many Companies Try Management Fads, Only to See Them Flop," *The Wall Street Journal*, July 6, 1993, pp. A1, A8; and Lori Bongiorno, "Corporate America's New Lesson Plan," *Business Week*, Oct. 25, 1993, pp. 102–104.

CHAPTER 2

TQM in Action: Reengineering for Profit Michael Hammer and James Champy, *Reengineering the Corporation*, HarperCollins, New York, 1993, pp. 36–39, 44–47; Thomas H. Davenport, *Process Innovation: Reengineering Work Through Information Technology*, Harvard Business School Press, Cambridge, Mass., 1993, pp. 32–33; and "The Promise of Reengineering," *Fortune*, May 3, 1993, pp. 95–96.

TQM in Action: Just Doing It Richard M. Hodgetts, *Blueprints for Continuous Improvement: Lessons from the Baldrige Winners*, American Management Association, New York, 1993, pp. 89–93; Shari Caudron, "How HR Drives TQM," *Personnel Journal*, August 1993, pp. 175–187; and Rhonda Thomas, "An Employee's View of Empowerment," *Personnel*, July 1993, pp. 14–15.

Real Case: Improving the Quality Richard M. Hodgetts, *Blueprints for Continuous Improvement: Lessons from the Baldrige Winners*, American Management Association, New York, 1993, pp. 58–59; Thomas A. Stewart, "Reengineering: The Hot New Managing Tool," *Fortune*, Aug. 23, 1993, pp. 41–42; and Rhonda Thompson, "An Employee's View of Empowerment," *Personnel*, July 1993, pp. 14–15.

Real Case: Learning How to Learn Brian O'Reilly, "How Execs Learn Now," *Fortune*, Apr. 5, 1993, pp. 52–58; David Kirkpatrick, "Could AT&T Rule the World?" *Fortune*, May 17, 1993, pp. 55–66; and Judith H. Dobrzynski, "Rethinking IBM," *Business Week*, Oct. 4, 1993, pp. 87–97.

CHAPTER 3

Managing Diversity in Action: Nonbiased Testing Brian Brenner and Joseph Weber, "A Spicier Stew in the Melting Pot," *Business Week*, Dec. 21, 1992, pp. 29–30; Aaron Bernstein, "The Young and the Jobless," *Business Week*, Aug. 16, 1993, p. 107; and Charlene Marmer Solomon, "Testing Is Not at Odds with Diversity Efforts," *Personnel Journal*, March 1993, pp. 100–104.

Managing Diversity in Action: Balancing Work and Family Responsibilities Michele Galen, Ann Therese Palmer, Alice Cuneo, and Mark Maremont, "Work and Family," *Business Week*, June 28, 1993, pp. 80–88; Chris Rousch, "Aetna's Family-Friendly Executive," *Business Week*, June 28, 1993, p. 83; and Sam Rivera, "An Easygoing Boss—and a Master Motivator," *Business Week*, June 28, 1993, p. 84.

Real Case: Not Treating Everyone the Same Michele Galen, Ann Therese Palmer, Alice Cuneo, and Mark Maremont, "Work and Family," *Business Week*, June 28, 1993, pp. 80–88; Michelle Carpenter, "Aetna's Family-Friendly Executive," *Business Week*, June 28, 1993, p. 83; Sharon Allred Decker, "We Had to Recognize That People Have Lives," *Business Week*, June 28, 1993, p. 88; and Sue Shellenbarger, "Lessons from the Workplace: How Corporate Policies and Attitudes Lag Behind Workers' Changing Needs," *Human Resource Management*, Fall 1992, pp. 157–169.

Real Case: Putting Harassment in Its Place John J. Keller, "Executive at AT&T's NCR Unit Retires Early, Citing Sex Harassment Charges," *The Wall Street Journal*, Nov. 26, 1993, p. B2; Aaron Epstein, "Sex Harassment Now Easier to Prove," *Miami Herald*, Nov. 10, 1993, pp. A1, A20; Anne B. Fisher, "Sexual Harassment: What to Do," *Fortune*, Aug. 23, 1993, pp. 84–88; and Brigid Moynahan, "Creating Harassment-Free Work Zones," *Training and Development Journal*, May 1993, pp. 67–70.

CHAPTER 4

Application Example: Help from the Public Sector Lois Thierren, "Retooling American Workers," *Business Week*, Sept. 27, 1993, pp. 76, 81; Maria Mallory, "Workers Trained to Order—At State Expense," *Business Week*, Sept. 27, 1993, p. 102; and Jacqueline Graves, "Most Innovative Companies," *Fortune*, Dec. 13, 1993, p. 11.

International Application Example: Sometimes It

Doesn't Translate   Betty Jane Punnett and David A. Ricks, *International Business*, PWS-Kent, Boston, 1992, pp. 340–341; Charles W. L. Hill, *International Business*, Irwin, Homewood, Ill., 1994, pp. 491–492; and Michael R. Czinkota and Ilkka A. Ronkainen, *International Marketing*, 3d ed., Dryden Press, Fort Worth, Tex., 1993, pp. 159–160.

Real Case: Is Patriotism for Sale?   Walter Shapiro, "Is Washington in Japan's Pocket?" *Business Week*, Oct. 1, 1990, pp. 106–107; Steve J. Dryden and Douglas Harbrecht, "When Japan's Lobbyists Talk, Washington Doesn't Just Listen," *Business Week*, July 11, 1989, p. 68; Pat Choate, *Agents of Influence*, Knopf, New York, 1990; and Richard M. Hodgetts and Fred Luthans, *International Management*, 2d ed., McGraw-Hill, New York, 1994, pp. 458–459.

CHAPTER 5

International Application Example: Gift Giving in Western Europe   Roger Axtell, *Do's and Taboos Around the World*, 2d ed., Wiley, New York, 1990; Philip R. Harris and Robert T. Moran, *Managing Cultural Differences*, 3d ed., Gulf Publishing, Houston, 1991, Chap. 16; and Richard M. Hodgetts and Fred Luthans, *International Management*, 2d ed., McGraw-Hill, New York, 1994, pp. 107–108.

Managing Diversity in Action: Flexibility Is the Key   Douglas T. Hall and Victoria Parker, "The Role of Workplace Flexibility in Managing Diversity," *Organizational Dynamics*, Summer 1993, pp. 5–18; Chuck Hawkins, "We Had to Recognize That People Have Lives," *Business Week*, June 28, 1993, p. 88; and Michele Galen, "Work and Family," *Business Week*, June 28, 1993, pp. 81–88.

Real Case: Looking for an Equal Chance   Jaclyn Fierman, "Why Women Still Don't Hit the Top," *Fortune*, July 30, 1990, pp. 40–62; Pamela Kruger, "The Myth of the Mommy Wars," *Working Woman*, March 1993, p. 11; and Maggie Mahar, "The Truth About Women's Pay," *Working Woman*, April 1993, pp. 52–55, 100.

Case: Ken Leaves the Company   Roy J. Blitzer, Colleen Peterson, and Linda Rogers, "How to Build Self-Esteem," *Training and Development*, February 1993, pp. 58–59. Copyright American Society for Training and Development. Reprinted with permission. All rights reserved.

CHAPTER 6

Application Example: High Achievers in Action   "Expert Advice: How to Reduce Your Risk as an Entrepreneur," *Working Woman*, January 1987, p. 62; Duncan Maxwell Anderson, "Inspire Yourself," *Success*, December 1993, pp. 58–59; Richard M. Hodgetts and Fred Luthans, *International Management*, 2d ed., McGraw-Hill, New York, 1994, pp. 401–406; and Richard M. Hodgetts, *Modern Human Relations at Work*, 5th ed., Dryden Press, Fort Worth, Tex., 1993, pp. 47–49.

TQM in Action: Linking Managers' Rewards with Unit Performance   Larry Reibstein, "Firms Trim Annual Pay Increases and Focus on Long Term," *The Wall Street Journal*, Apr. 10, 1987, p. 21; Warren H. Schmidt and Jerome P. Finnigan, *The Race Without a Finish Line*, Jossey-Bass, San Francisco, 1992, Chap. 10; Marshall Sashkin and Kenneth J. Kiser, *Putting Total Quality Management to Work*, Berrett-Koehler, San Francisco, 1993, pp. 87–96; and Richard M. Hodgetts, *Blueprints for Continuous Improvement: Lessons from the Baldrige Winners*, American Management Association, New York, 1993, pp. 94–98.

Real Case: Keeping Them Motivated   Shawn Tully, "Your Paycheck Gets Exciting," *Fortune*, Nov. 1, 1993, pp. 83–98; Anne B. Fischer, "Why Entrepreneurs Are in Demand," *Fortune*, Oct. 18, 1993, pp. 112–113; and Raymond Harrison, "Challenge Should Be Linked to Performance," *HR Focus*, October 1993, p. 9.

CHAPTER 7

TQM in Action: Power to the People   Ronald Henkoff, "Cost Cutting: How to Do It Just Right," *Fortune*, Apr. 9, 1990, p. 48; John H. Dobbs, "The Empowerment Environment," *Training and Development Journal*, February 1993, pp. 55–57; and Richard M. Hodgetts, *Blueprints for Continuous Improvement: Lessons from the Baldrige Winners*, American Management Association, New York, 1993, pp. 89–93.

Application Example: Making Personal Goal Setting Pay Off   "How to Boost Your Career Visibility—for Top Dollar," *Working Woman*, January 1987, p. 55; Scott DeGarmo, "Think Big," *Success*, November 1993, p. 4; and Michael Warshaw, "The Mind-Style of the Entrepreneur," *Success*, April 1993, pp. 28–33.

Real Case: Made by Hand   David Woodruff et al., "A New Era for Auto Quality," *Business Week*, Oct. 22, 1990, pp. 84–96; Richard A. Melcher, "Rolls-Royce Sees the Future—and It's Still Handmade," *Business Week*, Oct. 22, 1990, p. 96; Peter Galuszka, "BMW, Mercedes, Rolls-Royce—Could This Be Russia?" *Business Week*, Aug. 2, 1993, p. 40; and Fred Duterl, Jonathan B. Levine, and Neil Gross, "On the Continent, a New Era Is Also Dawning," *Business Week*, June 14, 1993, p. 61.

CHAPTER 8

Application Example: Monetary Reward Systems in Action   Shari Caudron, "Master the Compensation Maze," *Personnel Journal*, June 1993, pp. 631–644; Michael Markowich, "Does Money Motivate?" *HR Focus*, August 1993, pp. 1, 6–7; and Carolyn Wiley, "Incentive Plan Pushes Production," *Personnel Journal*, August 1993, pp. 86–91.

Real Case: Thanks for the Favor   Carol J. Loomis, "How Drexel Rigged a Stock," *Fortune*, Nov. 19, 1990, pp. 83–91; Kurt Eichenwald, "Milken Gets 10 Years for

Wall Street Crimes," *The New York Times*, Nov. 22, 1990, pp. A1, C5; and "Ethics: A New Profession in American Business," *HR Focus*, May 1993, p. 22.

CHAPTER 9

Application Example: Agreeing to Greater Productivity Doron P. Levin, "Chrysler Wants to Go Nonstop," *The New York Times*, Nov. 20, 1990, pp. C1, C8; Howard Gleckman, "The Technology Payoff," *Business Week*, June 14, 1993, pp. 56–68; Kathleen Kerwin and James B. Treece, "There's Trouble Under Ford's Hood," *Business Week*, Nov. 29, 1993, pp. 66–67; and William J. Cook, "Chrysler's Star Keeps Rising," *U.S. News and World Report*, Feb. 28, 1994, p. 54.

Application Example: Committees May Not Be the Answer Norman B. Sigband, "The Uses of Meetings," *Nation's Business*, February 1987, p. 28; Jane W. Gibson and Richard M. Hodgetts, *Organizational Communication*, 2d ed., HarperCollins, New York, 1992, pp. 399–401; and Arthur G. Bedeian, *Management*, 3d ed., Dryden Press, Fort Worth, Tex., 1993, pp. 515–517.

Real Case: The Grand Experiment at Saturn This case was especially prepared for this text by Richard R. Patrick, University of Nebraska, and used with permission. Sources: "Saturn," *Business Week*, Feb. 8, 1993, pp. 122–124; "Saturn's Grand Experiment," *Training*, June 1992, pp. 69–76; and "Behind the Wheel at Saturn," *Personnel Journal*, June 1991, pp. 72–74.

CHAPTER 10

International Application Example: Cultural Conflict Bill Powell, "Where the Jobs Are," *Newsweek*, Feb. 2, 1987, pp. 42–46; Alan M. Rugman and Richard M. Hodgetts, *International Business*, McGraw-Hill, New York, 1995, Chap. 6; and Richard M. Hodgetts and Fred Luthans, *International Management*, 2d ed., McGraw-Hill, New York, 1994, pp. 455–459

Application Example: Dealing with Crises Mortimer R. Feinberg and Bruce Serlen, "Crash Course in Crisis Management," *Working Woman*, January 1987, pp. 24, 26, 28; Arthur G. Bedeian, *Management*, 3d ed., Dryden Press, Fort Worth, Tex., 1993, pp. 419–421; and James A. F. Stoner and R. Edward Freeman, *Management*, 5th ed., Prentice-Hall, Englewood Cliffs, N.J., 1992, pp. 568–569.

Real Case: Do Just the Opposite Brian Dumaine, "How to Manage in a Recession," *Fortune*, Nov. 5, 1990, pp. 58–72; Andrew S. Serwer, "To Beat the Odds, Stay the Course," *Fortune*, Sept. 6, 1993, pp. 70–71; and Susan Camiti, "A High-Priced Game of Catch-Up," *Fortune*, Sept. 6, 1993, pp. 73–74.

CHAPTER 11

Application Example: Is Being a Type A Dangerous? Joshua Fischman, "Type A on Trial," *Psychology Today*, February 1987, pp. 42–50; Don Hellriegel and John W. Slocum, Jr., *Management*, 6th ed., Addison-Wesley, Reading, Mass., 1992, pp. 601–603; and Richard M. Hodgetts, *Modern Human Relations at Work*, 5th ed., Dryden, Fort Worth, Tex., 1993, pp. 511–514.

Application Example: Taking Time to Manage Time "Ten Tricks to Keep Time Eaters Away!" *Working Woman*, August 1986, p. 71; Richard M. Hodgetts, "Set Limits to Reduce Time Spent with Drop-in Visitors," *Fort Lauderdale Sun Sentinel*, Weekly Business, Nov. 29, 1993, p. 12; and Lawrence L. Steinmetz and H. Ralph Todd, Jr., *Supervision: First Line Management*, 5th ed., Irwin, Homewood, Ill., 1992, pp. 244–253.

Real Case: Getting Along Without the Boss Everett T. Suters, "Overdoing It," *Inc.*, November 1986, pp. 115–116; Donald C. Mosley, Leon C. Megginson, and Paul H. Pietri, Jr., *Supervisory Management: The Art of Empowering and Developing People*, Southwestern, Cincinnati, Ohio, 1993, pp. 571–574; and Julia Kagan, "Success: Not What It Used to Be," *Working Woman*, November 1993, pp. 54–55, 100.

CHAPTER 12

International Application Example: Keeping the Inside Track Allen R. Myerson, "Suddenly, the Specter of Capitalism Is Haunting Intourist," *The New York Times*, Nov. 18, 1990, p. 4F; Steven Erlanger, "New Yeltsin Steps on Economy Hint Easing of Reforms," *The New York Times*, Dec. 18, 1993, pp. 1, 5; and Steven Erlanger, "A 'New' Russia: Yeltsin Needs Consensus and Cash," *The New York Times*, Dec. 23, 1993, p. A6.

Real Case: Fighting Back Donald M. Spero, "Patent Protection or Piracy—a CEO Views Japan," *Harvard Business Review*, September–October 1990, pp. 58–67; Fred Luthans and Richard M. Hodgetts, *Business*, 2d ed., Dryden, Fort Worth, Tex., 1993, pp. 640–641; and Donald F. Kuratko and Richard M. Hodgetts, *Entrepreneurship*, 2d ed., Dryden, Fort Worth, Tex., 1992, pp. 357–361.

CHAPTER 13

International Application Example: Yeltsin Speaks Paul Hofheinz, "The New Russian Revolution," *Fortune*, Nov. 19, 1990, pp. 127–134; Bruce W. Nelan, "The Last Best Chance for Yeltsin," *Time*, Oct. 18, 1993, pp. 69–70; Claudia Rosett, "Russia's Reformers Can't Agree on Course After Election Defeat," *The Wall Street Journal*, Dec. 15, 1993, p. A10; and Carla Anne Robbins and Barbara Rosewicz, "U.S. Hopes to Move Moscow into the West Through Deeper Ties," *The Wall Street Journal*, Dec. 13, 1993, pp. A1, A6.

Managing Diversity in Action: Breaking the Glass Ceiling with Charisma "More Businesses Look at Diversity as an Obligation, Not a Choice," *HR Focus*, October 1993, p. 14; Alan Farnham, "Mary Kay's Lessons in Leadership," *Fortune*, Sept. 20, 1993, pp. 68–77; and Clint

Willis, "The 10 Most Admired Women Managers in America," *Working Woman*, December 1993, pp. 44–55.
Real Case: The Teflon Leader Ann Reilly Dowd, "What Managers Can Learn from Manager Reagan," *Fortune*, Sept. 15, 1986, pp. 33–41; Paul Magnusson and Owen Ullmann, "The Second Year: Clinton Weaves a Security Blanket for America," *Business Week*, Jan. 24, 1994, pp. 69–74; Mike McNamee, Bill Javetski, and Owen Ullmann, "The Slippery Slopes of Clinton's 'Jobs Summit,' " *Business Week*, July 19, 1993, p. 35; and Richard S. Dunham, "Clinton's Stealth Spending Bills Are Slipping Through Congress," *Business Week*, July 26, 1993, p. 43.

CHAPTER 14

TQM in Action: First Japan, Now Korea Laurie Baum, "Korea's Newest Export: Management Style," *Business Week*, Jan. 19, 1987, p. 66; Sangjin Yoo and Sang M. Lee, "Management Style and Practice of Korean Chaebols," *California Management Review*, Summer 1987, pp. 95–110; and George S. Easton, "The 1993 State of U.S. Total Quality Management: A Baldrige Examiner's Perspective," *California Management Review*, Spring 1993, pp. 32–54.
International Application Example: Balancing People and Profits James B. Hayes, "Wanna Make a Deal in Moscow?" *Fortune*, Oct. 22, 1990, pp. 113–118; "Such Good Friends with IBM," *Fortune*, Oct. 4, 1993, p. 118; and Tim Smart, Pete Engardio, and Geri Smith, "GE's Brave New World," *Business Week*, Nov. 8, 1993, pp. 64–70.
Real Case: A New Breed of Business Leaders Tim Smart and Judith H. Dobrzynski, "Jack Welch on the Art of Thinking Small," *Business Week/Enterprise 1993*, pp. 212–216; Brian Dumaine, "The New Non-Manager Managers," *Fortune*, Feb. 22, 1993, pp. 80–84; and "A Master Class in Radical Change," *Fortune*, Dec. 13, 1993, pp. 82–90.

CHAPTER 15

International Application Example: Nonverbal and Verbal Communication Philip R. Harris and Robert T. Moran, *Managing Cultural Differences*, 3d ed., Gulf Publishing, Houston, 1991, Chap. 16; Dara Khambata and Riad Ajami, *International Business: Theory and Practice*, Macmillan, New York, 1992, Chap. 13; Alan M. Rugman and Richard M. Hodgetts, *International Business*, McGraw-Hill, New York, 1995, Chap. 16; Karen Matthes, "Mind Your Manners When Doing Business in Europe," *Personnel*, January 1992, p. 19; and Roger E. Axtell, *Do's and Taboos Around the World*, Wiley, New York, 1990.
International Application Example: Different Cultures, Different Meanings Jane Whitney Gibson, Richard M. Hodgetts, and Charles W. Blackwell, "Cultural Variations in Nonverbal Communication," Paper presented at the 55th Annual Business Communication meetings, San An-

tonio, Tex., Nov. 9, 1990; Philip R. Harris and Robert T. Moran, *Managing Cultural Differences*, 3d ed., Gulf Publishing, Houston, 1991, Chap. 2; and Betty Jane Punnett and David A. Ricks, *International Business*, PWS-Kent, Boston, 1992, Chap. 6.
Real Case: 800 to the Rescue Faye Rice, "How to Deal with Tougher Customers," *Fortune*, Dec. 3, 1990, pp. 38–48; Richard Hodgetts, "Do Homework, Get Feedback to Improve Customer Service," *Fort Lauderdale Sun Sentinel*, Dec. 6, 1993, p. 12; and Richard Hodgetts, "Great Customer Service Is Doing Little Things Right," *Fort Lauderdale Sun Sentinel*, Dec. 6, 1993, p. 12.

CHAPTER 16

Application Example: Management Decisions Alex Taylor, III, "Shaking Up Jaguar," *Fortune*, Sept. 6, 1993, pp. 65–68; William Stern, "A Lesson Learned Early," *Forbes*, Nov. 8, 1993, pp. 220–221; and Bill Saporito, "David Glass Won't Crack Under Fire," *Fortune*, Feb. 9, 1993, pp. 75–80.
International Application Example: Some Basic Rules of Protocol Philip R. Harris and Robert T. Moran, *Managing Cultural Differences*, 3d ed., Gulf Publishing, Houston, 1991; Letitia Baldrige, "Global Manners and the Manager," *Management Review*, October 1993, pp. 18–19; Nancy J. Adler, *International Dimensions of Organizational Behavior*, 2d ed., PWS-Kent, Boston, 1991, Chap. 3; and Roger E. Axtell, *Do's and Taboos Around the World*, Wiley, New York, 1990.
Real Case: Getting Additional Information Anne R. Field and Catherine L. Harris, "The Information Business," *Business Week*, Aug. 25, 1986, pp. 82–90; Elizabeth Corcoran, "Why Kids Love Computer Nets," *Fortune*, Sept. 20, 1993, pp. 103–108; and Tony Horowitz, "Gee-Whiz Gadgetry Lets Many Americans Go It Alone," *The Wall Street Journal*, Dec. 14, 1993, pp. B1, B10.

CHAPTER 17

International Application Example: Organization Epigrams by Country Simcha Ronen, *Comparative and Multinational Management*, Wiley, New York, 1986, pp. 318–319. The epigrams in turn were derived from a variety of sources, including Robert M. Worcester of the UK-based Market and Opinion Research International (MORI), Ole Jacob Road of Norway's PM Systems, and anonymous managers. Also see Richard M. Hodgetts and Fred Luthans, *International Management*, 2d ed., McGraw-Hill, New York, 1994, pp. 364–365, and John A. Byrne, "Congratulations: You're Moving to a New Pepperoni," *Business Week*, Dec. 20, 1993, p. 81.
Application Example: Managing Across Rather Than Up and Down John A. Byrne, "The Horizontal Corporation," *Business Week*, Dec. 20, 1993, pp. 76–81; Craig J. Contini, "Eliminating Bureaucracy—Roots and All," *Management Review*, December 1993, pp. 30–33; and

"Government Would Follow Big Business," *Omaha World-Herald*, Sept. 8, 1993, p. 5.

Real Case: Two Out of Three "Bite the Dust" Noel M. Tichy, "Revolutionize Your Company," *Fortune*, Dec. 13, 1993, pp. 114–118; Kathleen Kerwin, "Can Jack Smith Fix GM?" *Business Week*, Nov. 1, 1993, pp. 126–131; and Judith H. Dobrzynski, "Rethinking IBM," *Business Week*, Oct. 4, 1993, pp. 86–97.

CHAPTER 18

Application Example: Strong Managers, Strong Cultures Brian Dumaine, "The New Turnaround Champs," *Fortune*, July 16, 1990, pp. 36–44; David Kirkpatrick, "Could AT&T Rule the World?" *Fortune*, May 17, 1993, pp. 55–56; and John Huey, "The World's Best Brand," *Fortune*, May 31, 1993, pp. 44–54.

International Application Example: Theory Z in Action William G. Ouchi, *Theory Z: How American Business Can Meet the Japanese Challenge*, Addison-Wesley, Reading, Mass., 1981; Richard M. Hodgetts, *Modern Human Relations at Work*, 5th ed., Dryden Press, Fort Worth, Tex., 1993, pp. 233–236; and Richard M. Hodgetts and Fred Luthans, *International Management*, 2d ed., McGraw-Hill, New York, 1994, pp. 430–432.

Real Case: Yo-yo Impacts on Organizational Culture Kenneth Labich, "American Takes on the World," *Fortune*, Sept. 24, 1990, pp. 40–48; Wendy Zellner, "Continental: In for the Short Haul," *Business Week*, Dec. 6, 1993, pp. 120, 122; and Wendy Zellner, Mike McNamee, and Seth Payne, "Did Clinton Scramble American's Profit Picture?" *Business Week*, Dec. 6, 1993, p. 44.

CHAPTER 19

International Application Example: New Rules in Japan Are on the Way Douglas Harbrecht, "In Japan They Call It 'Clinton Shock,'" *Business Week*, May 3, 1993, p. 46; Larry Holyoke and Stanley Reed, "Why the Soaring Yen Won't Shrink Japan's Trade Surplus," *Business Week*, May 3, 1993, p. 47; and Robert Neff, "Well, It's a Start," *Business Week*, Sept. 13, 1993, pp. 48–49.

International Application Example: Reaching a Win-Win Solution in China Emily Slate, "Success Depends on an Understanding of Cultural Differences," *HR Focus*,

October 1993, pp. 16–17; Joyce Barnathan and Matt Forney, "Between Reform and a Hard Line," *Business Week*, Sept. 6, 1993, pp. 38–39; and Amy Borrus, Pete Engardio, and Russell Mitchell, "Getting Tough with China Could Be Tough on the U.S.," *Business Week*, Sept. 6, 1993, p. 39.

Real Case: Everybody's Everywhere "The World's Largest Industrial Corporations: Another Year of Pain," *Fortune*, July 26, 1993, pp. 188–190; "The Forbes Foreign Rankings," *Forbes*, July 19, 1993, pp. 126–158; and Tom Martin and Deborah Greenwood, "The World Economy in Charts," *Fortune*, July 26, 1993, pp. 88–96.

CHAPTER 20

TQM in Action: The Government Teams Up for Efficiency David Warner, "Bureaucracy, Heal Thyself," *Nation's Business*, October 1993, pp. 66–67; Noel M. Tichy and Stratford Sherman, "Walking the Talk at GE," *Training and Development Journal*, June 1993, pp. 26–35; "Autonomy Is In!" *HR Focus*, October 1993, p. 10; Ellen F. Glanz and Lee K. Dailey, "Benchmarking," *Human Resource Management*, Spring–Summer 1992, pp. 9–20; Howard Gleckman, "Where to Prune and Where to Hack Away," *Business Week*, Sept. 13, 1993, pp. 98–99; and Howard Gleckman and Susan B. Garland, "Al Gore: What Business Can Teach the Feds," *Business Week*, Sept. 13, 1993, p. 102.

TQM in Action: Airlines Finally Begin to Listen to Their Customers Jean Seligman, "A Lighter Than Airline Load," *Newsweek*, Nov. 26, 1990, pp. 70–72; "Implementing Change Programs for a Better Quality Service," *Catalyst*, August 1993, p. 1; and David E. Bowen and Edward E. Lawler, III, "The Empowerment of Service Workers: What, Why, How, and When," *Sloan Management Review*, Spring 1992, pp. 31–39.

Real Case: Meeting the Challenges of the Next Century David Kirkpatrick, "Is Your Career on Track?" *Fortune*, July 2, 1990, pp. 38–48; Erich Schine, "Out at the Skunk Works, the Sweet Smell of Success," *Business Week*, Apr. 26, 1993, p. 101; Rahul Jacob, "TQM: More Than a Dying Fad?" *Fortune*, Oct. 18, 1993, pp. 66–72; and Stratford Sherman, "How Will We Live with the Tumult?" *Fortune*, Dec. 13, 1993, pp. 123–125.

Name Index

Subject Index